MOON HANDBOOKS

BRITISH COLUMBIA

W9-BKE-904

© ANDREW HEMPSTEAD

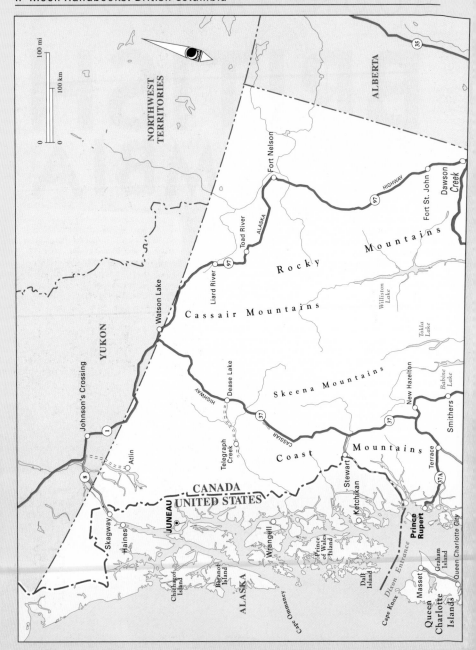

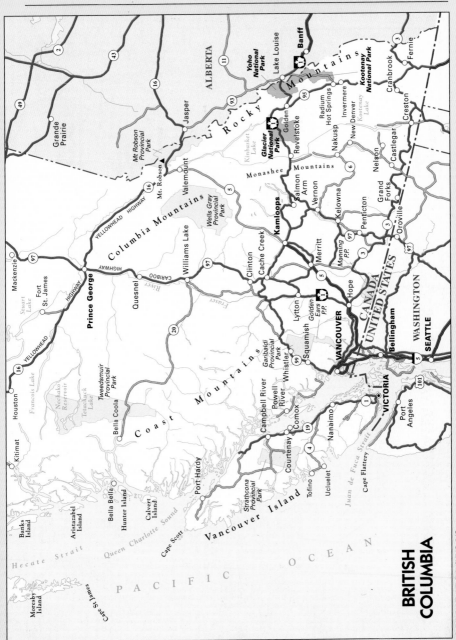

BRITISH COLUMBIA

© AVALON TRAVEL PUBLISHING, INC.

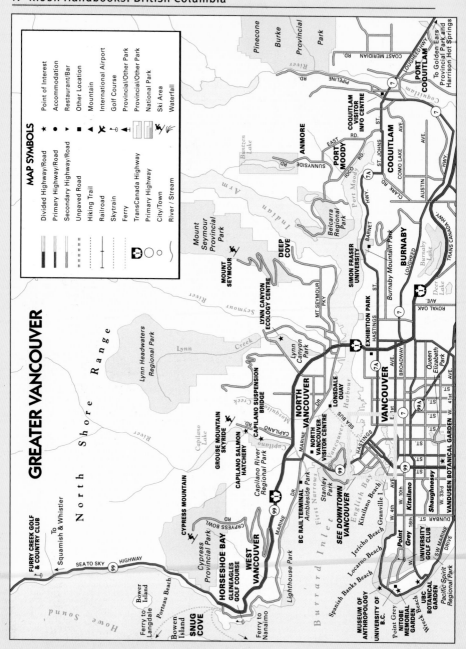

GREATER VANCOUVER

MAP SYMBOLS

★	Point of Interest	
●	Accommodation	
▼	Restaurant/Bar	
■	Other Location	
◀	Mountain	
✈	International Airport	
⛳	Golf Course	
	Provincial/Other Park	
	Provincial/Other Park	
	National Park	
	Ski Area	
	Waterfall	

Divided Highway/Road
Primary Highway/Road
Secondary Highway/Road
Unpaved Road
Hiking Trail
Railroad
Skytrain
Ferry
TransCanada Highway
Primary Highway
City/Town
River / Stream

North Shore Range

Pinecone Burke Provincial Park

To Golden Ears Provincial Park and Harrison Hot Springs

COAST MERIDIAN RD.

LOUGHEED HWY

PORT COQUITLAM

PIPELINE RD.

Coquitlam River

COQUITLAM VISITOR INFO CENTRE

ANMORE

PORT MOODY

Bantzen Lake

SUNNYSIDE RD.

EAST RD.

ST. JOHNS ST.

COQUITLAM

COMO LAKE AVE.

CLARKE RD.

AUSTIN AVE.

Belcarra Regional Park

Port Moody Arm

Indian Arm

Mount Seymour Provincial Park

MOUNT SEYMOUR

DEEP COVE

LYNN CANYON ECOLOGY CENTRE

SIMON FRASER UNIVERSITY

Burnaby Mountain Park

BURNABY

Burnaby Lake

TRANS CANADA HWY

Deer Lake

ROYAL OAK AVE.

EXHIBITION PARK

HASTINGS

Lynn Headwaters Regional Park

Lynn Creek

Lynn Canyon Park

Seymour River

MT. SEYMOUR PKY

LONSDALE QUAY

NORTH VANCOUVER

NORTH VANCOUVER VISITOR CENTRE

SEA BUS

Harbour

BROADWAY

Queen Elizabeth Park

VANCOUVER

Capilano Lake

GROUSE MOUNTAIN SKYRIDE

CAPILANO SUSPENSION BRIDGE

CAPILANO RD.

Mosquito Creek

Capilano River Regional Park

CAPILANO SALMON HATCHERY

MARINE DR.

Ambleside Park

Stanley Park

First Narrows

Vancouver Harbour

SEE DOWNTOWN VANCOUVER

HASTINGS

W. 1st

W. 4th

W. 10th

Kitsilano

Shaughnessy

W. 33rd

W. 41st AVE.

VANDUSEN BOTANICAL GARDEN

CYPRESS MOUNTAIN

Cypress Provincial Park

CYPRESS BOWL RD.

WEST VANCOUVER

Lighthouse Park

BC RAIL TERMINAL

MARINE DR.

English Bay

Kitsilano Beach

Point Grey

W. 10th

16th

DUNBAR ST.

SW MARINE DRIVE

FURRY CREEK GOLF & COUNTRY CLUB

To Squamish & Whistler

SEA TO SKY HIGHWAY

HORSESHOE BAY

GLENEAGLES GOLF COURSE

Ferry to Nanaimo

Burrard Inlet

Jericho Beach

Locarno Beach

Spanish Banks Beach

Point Grey

Wreck Beach

MUSEUM OF ANTHROPOLOGY

UNIVERSITY OF B.C.

NITOBE MEMORIAL GARDEN

UBC BOTANICAL GARDEN

UNIVERSITY GOLF CLUB

Pacific Spirit Regional Park

Howe Sound

Bower Island

Bowen Island

Ferry to Langdale

Porteau Beach

SNUG COVE

Ferry to Langdale

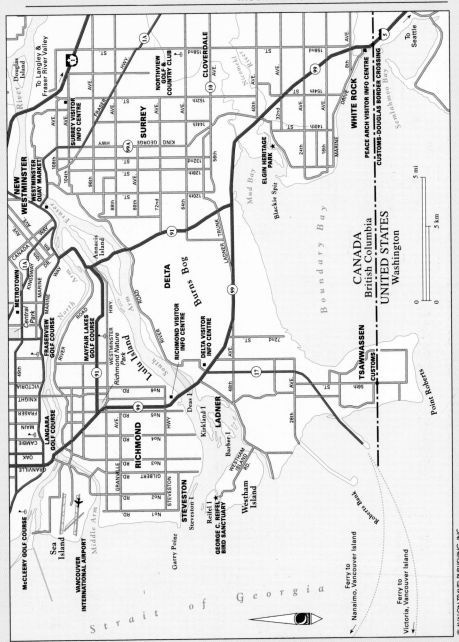

© AVALON TRAVEL PUBLISHING, INC.

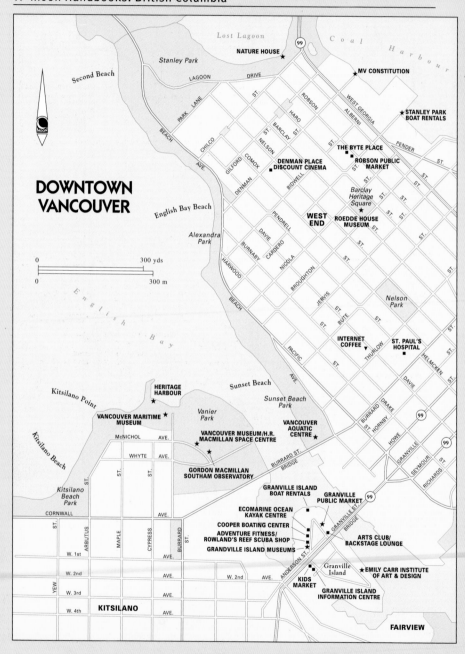

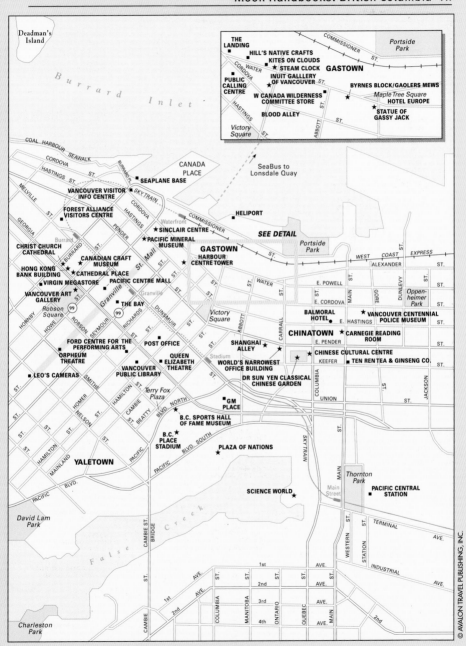

Deadman's
Island

B u r r a r d   I n l e t

Detail (Gastown inset):
THE LANDING
HILL'S NATIVE CRAFTS
KITES ON CLOUDS
STEAM CLOCK
INUIT GALLLERY OF VANCOUVER
PUBLIC CALLING CENTRE
W CANADA WILDERNESS COMMITTEE STORE
BLOOD ALLEY
GASTOWN
BYRNES BLOCK/GAOLERS MEWS
Maple Tree Square
HOTEL EUROPE
STATUE OF GASSY JACK
Victory Square
COMMISSIONER ST.
Portside Park
WATER ST.
CORDOVA ST.
HASTINGS ST.
ABBOTT ST.
ST.

COAL HARBOUR SEAWALK
CORDOVA ST.
HASTINGS ST.
MELVILLE ST.
GEORGIA ST.
BURRARD ST.

CANADA PLACE
SEAPLANE BASE
VANCOUVER VISITOR INFO CENTRE
SKY-TRAIN
FOREST ALLIANCE VISITORS CENTRE
SINCLAIR CENTRE
PACIFIC MINERAL MUSEUM
CHRIST CHURCH CATHEDRAL
CANADIAN CRAFT MUSEUM
CATHEDRAL PLACE
HONG KONG BANK BUILDING
VIRGIN MEGASTORE
PACIFIC CENTRE MALL
VANCOUVER ART GALLERY
Robson Square
THE BAY
Granville
FORD CENTRE FOR THE PERFORMING ARTS
ORPHEUM THEATRE
POST OFFICE
QUEEN ELIZABETH THEATRE
VANCOUVER PUBLIC LIBRARY
LEO'S CAMERAS
Terry Fox Plaza
GM PLACE
B.C. SPORTS HALL OF FAME MUSEUM
B.C. PLACE STADIUM
YALETOWN
PLAZA OF NATIONS
SCIENCE WORLD

SeaBus to Lonsdale Quay
HELIPORT
SEE DETAIL
Waterfront
COMMISSIONER
Portside Park
WEST COAST EXPRESS
ALEXANDER ST.
GASTOWN
HARBOUR CENTRE TOWER
WATER ST.
E. POWELL ST.
E. CORDOVA ST.
DUNLEVY
GORE
MAIN
Oppenheimer Park
Victory Square
BALMORAL HOTEL
E. HASTINGS ST.
VANCOUVER CENTENNIAL POLICE MUSEUM
CHINATOWN
E. PENDER
CARNEGIE READING ROOM
SHANGHAI ALLEY
WORLD'S NARROWEST OFFICE BUILDING
KEEFER
CHINESE CULTURAL CENTRE
TEN REN TEA & GINSENG CO.
DR SUN YEN CLASSICAL CHINESE GARDEN
COLUMBIA ST.
UNION
JACKSON
CARRALL
Stadium
MAIN ST.
SKY TRAIN
Thornton Park
Main Street
PACIFIC CENTRAL STATION
David Lam Park
Creek
WESTERN ST.
STATION ST.
TERMINAL AVE.
INDUSTRIAL AVE.
CAMBIE ST.
BRIDGE ST.
F a l s e   C r e e k
Charleston Park
1st AVE.
2nd AVE.
COLUMBIA ST.
MANITOBA ST.
ONTARIO ST.
QUEBEC ST.
MAIN ST.
3rd AVE.
4th AVE.
2nd

99

© AVALON TRAVEL PUBLISHING, INC.

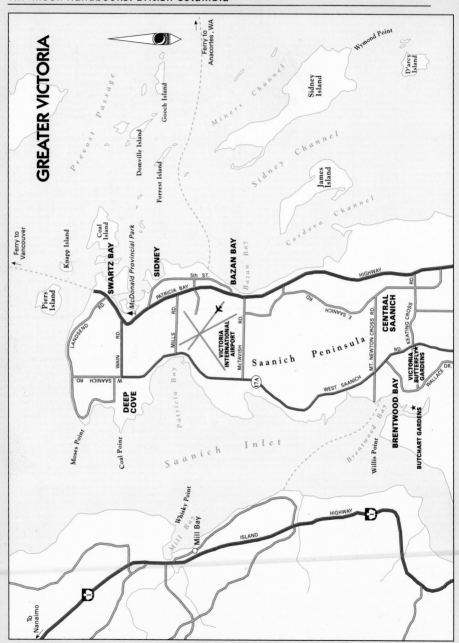

GREATER VICTORIA

3 mi

3 km

0

0

Cordova Bay

CORDOVA BAY

CADBORO BAY

Gordon Head

Cattle Point

OAK BAY

Gonzales Point

Trial
Islands

Clover Point

Juan de Fuca Strait

UNIVERSITY
OF VICTORIA

HILL CROSS

SINCLAIR

SHELBOURNE ST.

LANSDOWNE RD.

FOUL BAY RD.

VICTORIA

ROSS BAY
CEMETERY

ASH

BAY RD.

CORDOVA

QUADRA

Highway

McKENZIE AVE.

ST.

DOUGLAS ST.

17

SAANICH

SEE "DOWNTOWN
VICTORIA" MAP

Ferry to
Seattle, WA

PATRICIA BAY

17

ROYAL
OAK

*Elk
Lake*

OLDFIELD   RD.

PROSPECT LAKE   DR.

THE HERITAGE
HOUSE

ROYAL VICTORIA
HOSPITAL

1A

West Bay

ESQUIMALT

Point Ellice House and Garden

CFB ESQUIMALT NAVAL
& MILITARY MUSEUM

ANNE HATHAWAY'S
THATCHED COTTAGE

Macaulay Point

Ferry to
Port Angeles, WA

17A

*Thetis
Lake*

VIEW
ROYAL

LANGFORD

FORT RODD HILL
NATIONAL HISTORIC
SITE

COLWOOD

Esquimalt
Lagoon

ROYAL ROADS
UNIVERSITY

METCHOSIN RD.

Albert Head

Finlayson Arm

Malahat

ISLAND   HIGHWAY

*Goldstream
Provincial
Park*

ROAD

14

Luxton

SOOKE

To
Sooke

© AVALON TRAVEL PUBLISHING, INC.

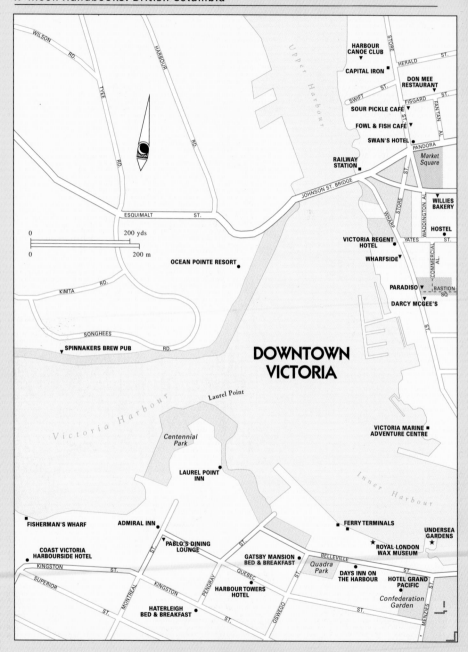

WILSON RD.
HARBOUR RD.
TYEE RD.
RD.

HARBOUR CANOE CLUB ▼
CAPITAL IRON ■

DON MEE RESTAURANT

STORE ST.
HERALD ST.

SWIFT ST.
FISGARD ST.
FANTAN AL.

SOUR PICKLE CAFE ▼

FOWL & FISH CAFE ▼

SWAN'S HOTEL ■
PANDORA

Market Square

Upper Harbour

RAILWAY STATION ■

JOHNSON ST. BRIDGE

ESQUIMALT ST.

0   200 yds
0   200 m

OCEAN POINTE RESORT ■

STORE ST.

WADDINGTON AL.
WILLIES BAKERY

WHARF ST.
HOSTEL
YATES ST.

VICTORIA REGENT HOTEL ■

WHARFSIDE ■

COMMERCIAL AL.

PARADISO ▼
BASTION SQ.

DARCY MCGEE'S ▼

KIMTA RD.

SONGHEES

SPINNAKERS BREW PUB ▼
RD.

DOWNTOWN VICTORIA

Victoria Harbour

Laurel Point

Centennial Park

VICTORIA MARINE ADVENTURE CENTRE ■

LAUREL POINT INN ■

Inner Harbour

FISHERMAN'S WHARF ■

ADMIRAL INN ■

PABLO'S DINING LOUNGE ▼

ST.

FERRY TERMINALS ■

ROYAL LONDON WAX MUSEUM ★

UNDERSEA GARDENS ★

COAST VICTORIA HARBOURSIDE HOTEL ■

KINGSTON ST.
SUPERIOR ST.

MONTREAL ST.
KINGSTON ST.

PENDRAY ST.

GATSBY MANSION BED & BREAKFAST ●
QUEBEC ST.

HARBOUR TOWERS HOTEL ●

BELLEVILLE
Quadra Park

DAYS INN ON THE HARBOUR ●

HOTEL GRAND PACIFIC ●

Confederation Garden

HATERLEIGH BED & BREAKFAST ●

OSWEGO ST.
ST.
MENZIES ST.

HERALD STREET CAFFE
TRAVELLER'S INN DOWNTOWN
HERALD ST.
DOUGLAS ST.
GOVERNMENT ST.
WAH LAI YUEN
QV CAFÉ & BAKERY
FISGARD ST.
HUNAN VILLAGE CUISINE
Centennial Square
CORMORANT ST.
MCPHERSON PLAYHOUSE
PANDORA ST.
OLD VIC FISH & CHIPS
HOTEL DOUGLAS
JOHN'S PLACE
SNOWDON'S BOOK STORE
BOSUN'S LOCKER
JOHNSON
COWICHAN TRADING
LOTUS LAND
BLENZ
DOWNTOWN PHOTO CENTRE
YATES ST.

AREA OF DETAIL
ESQUIMALT
Victoria Harbour
SUPERIOR
SIMCOE
OSWEGO
DALLAS
Ogden Point Breakwall
Holland Point
Juan de Fuca Strait
Finlayson Point
Clover Point
TURTLE REFUGE
MAYTAG HOMESTYLE LAUNDRY
JOHNSON
YATES
ART GALLERY OF GREATER VICTORIA
CRAIGDARROCH CASTLE
CRAIGMYLE GUEST HOUSE
MOSS
GOVERNMENT HOUSE
EMILY CARR HOUSE
SURF MOTEL
JAMES BAY INN
HOLLAND HOUSE INN
COOK
FAIRFIELD
AMBLESIDE BED & BREAKFAST
Beacon Hill Park
RD.
DASHWOOD MANOR
GOVERNMENT
DOUGLAS
BLANSHARD

PERIKLIS
ELECTRIC JUICE CAFE
POST OFFICE
DOMINION HOTEL
BOOK ENDS
MARITIME MUSEUM OF B.C.
PAGLIACCI'S
TROUNCE AL.
CHAPTERS
BROAD
VIEW
LANGLEY
ELEPHANT & CASTLE
BEDFORD REGENCY
MURCHIES
MUNRO'S BOOKSTORE
COMPANY'S COMING
HERMANN'S JAZZ CLUB
WELLS BOOKS
FORT
CROWN PUBLICATIONS
JAMES BAY TRADING CO.
HILL'S NATIVE ART
BROUGHTON
GOVERNMENT
BROAD
DOUGLAS
BLANSHARD
QUADRA
MEARES AVE.
Pioneer Square
ROGERS CHOCOLATE
BROUGHTON
GREATER VICTORIA PUBLIC LIBRARY
ROYAL THEATRE
COURTNEY
STRATHCONA HOTEL
ROCKLAND AVE.
HARBOUR RENTALS
HUMBOLDT
SAM'S DELI
MAGNOLIA HOTEL & SPA
GORDON
BUDGET CYCLE-TIME
CHRIST CHURCH CATHEDRAL
VICTORIA VISITOR INFO CENTRE
CALFOREX
MILLOS
BURDETT
CHERRY BANK HOTEL
AVE.
FAIRFIELD
RUPERT TERR.
McCLURE AVE.
FAIRMONT EMPRESS
HUMBOLDT
CRYSTAL GARDEN
QUADRA
CONVENT
BELLEVILLE
BUS DEPOT
PARLIAMENT BUILDINGS
ROYAL BRITISH COLUMBIA MUSEUM
DOUGLAS
CRYSTAL COURT MOTEL
BLANSHARD
Beacon Hill Park
Thunderbird Park
HELMCKEN HOUSE
GOVERNMENT

© AVALON TRAVEL PUBLISHING, INC.

Stanley Park

© ANDREW HEMPSTEAD

MOON HANDBOOKS

BRITISH COLUMBIA

SIXTH EDITION

ANDREW HEMPSTEAD

AVALON
TRAVEL

Moon Handbooks: British Columbia
Sixth Edition

Andrew Hempstead

Published by
Avalon Travel Publishing
5855 Beaudry St.
Emeryville, CA 94608, USA

Please send all comments, corrections,
additions, amendments, and critiques to:

Moon Handbooks: British Columbia
AVALON TRAVEL PUBLISHING
5855 BEAUDRY ST.
EMERYVILLE, CA 94608, USA
email: atpfeedback@avalonpub.com
website: www.moon.com

Text © 2002 by Andrew Hempstead.
Illustrations and maps © 2002 by Avalon Travel Publishing, Inc.
All rights reserved.
Photos and some illustrations are used by permission
and are the property of their original copyright owners.

Printing History
1st edition—1989
6th edition—April 2002
5 4 3 2 1

ISBN: 1-56691-384-5
ISSN: 1538-1196

Lead Editor: Angelique S. Clarke
Assisting Editor: Deana Shields
Series Manager: Erin Van Rheenen
Graphics Coordinator: Melissa Sherowski
Production: Darren Alessi, Karen Heithecker
Map Editor: Naomi Adler Dancis
Cartographers: Mike Morgenfeld, Suzanne Service, Chris Folks,
    Mark Stroud/Moon Street Cartography
Proofreader and Indexer: Deana Shields

Front cover photo: © 1988 Joel W. Rogers

Distributed by Publishers Group West

Printed in China through Colorcraft Ltd., Hong Kong

All rights reserved. No part of this book may be translated or reproduced in any form, except
brief extracts by a reviewer for the purpose of a review, without written permission of the copyright
owner.

Although every effort was made to ensure that the information was correct at the time of going to
press, the author and publisher do not assume and hereby disclaim any liability to any party for any
loss or damage caused by errors, omissions, or any potential travel disruption due to labor or financial
difficulty, whether such errors or omissions result from negligence, accident, or any other cause.

ABOUT THE AUTHOR
Andrew Hempstead

Although Andrew Hempstead lives across the mountains from British Columbia in neighboring Alberta, he spends a large portion of his time in Canada's western-most province. In fact, he put this edition on hold to honeymoon at a ranch in central British Columbia and wound up the summer with a vacation in the Kootenays. Rather than having an itinerary laid out for him by local tourism offices or relying on the Internet and the telephone to update his books, Andrew spends as much time as possible out on the road, experiencing the many delights of British Columbia the same way his readers do.

Andrew began travel writing in 1989, when, after leaving a well-established career in advertising, he took off for Alaska, linking up with veteran travel writer Deke Castleman to help research and update the fourth edition of *Moon Handbooks: Alaska-Yukon*. Andrew is now the author of books on British Columbia, Alberta, the Canadian Rockies, the Northwest Territories, and Nunavut, and has been a regular contributor to *Road Trip USA* and other guides. He recently traveled to eastern Canada to help research and write for the third edition of *Moon Handbooks: Atlantic Canada*. His writing and photographs have also appeared in a wide variety of magazines, including *National Geographic Traveler, Interval World,* and *Travesias*.

Farther afield, Andrew is coauthor of *Moon Handbooks: Australia* and has traveled to New Zealand multiple times on assignment to write and photograph for *Moon Handbooks: New Zealand*. He has also traveled purely for pleasure throughout most of the United States, Europe, the South Pacific, and India.

When not working on his books, Andrew enjoys hiking, fishing, golfing, camping, and the simple pleasures in life, such as skimming stones down on the river. He lives in Canmore, Alberta, with his wife, Dianne, and their two dogs.

The website **www.westerncanadatravel.com** showcases Andrew's work.

Contents

INTRODUCTION **1**

THE LAND **2**
  Climate
FLORA AND FAUNA **4**
  Flora; Mammals; Reptiles; Birds; Fish
HISTORY **11**
  The Earliest Inhabitants; European Exploration and Colonization; Law, Order,
  and Gold; The People
ECONOMY AND GOVERNMENT **17**

SPECIAL TOPICS

Wildlife and You ....*6*   *Totem Poles* *12*
Whales of British Columbia *9*

ON THE ROAD **21**

RECREATION **21**
  Hiking; Cycling and Mountain Biking; On the Water; Fishing; Golfing; Skiing
  and Snowboarding; Entertainment; Shopping for Native Arts and Crafts; Festivals
  and Events
ACCOMMODATIONS AND FOOD **30**
  Hotels and Motels; Bed and Breakfasts; Backpacker Accommodations; Camping;
  Food and Drink
GETTING THERE **35**
  Air; Rail; Bus; Ferry
GETTING AROUND **39**
  Air; Rail; Bus; Ferry; Driving
OTHER PRACTICALITIES **43**
  Visas and Officialdom; Money; Health; Services, Communications, and
  Measurements; Maps and Information

SPECIAL TOPICS

National Park Passes ....*23*   *Alaska Marine Highway* *39*
Parks and Protected Areas ....*24*   *Currency Exchange* *44*
Departure Taxes ....*35*   *Tourism Offices* *47*
Cutting Flight Costs ....*36*   *Heading Farther Afield?* *48*

VANCOUVER 49
History
SIGHTS 51
Getting Oriented; Downtown; False Creek; West End; Stanley Park; South of
Downtown; Richmond; Delta; Surrey; North Shore; East from Downtown
RECREATION 71
Walking and Hiking; Bicycling; Golf; Water Sports; Skiing and Snowboarding;
Spectator Sports; Arts and Entertainment; Shopping; Festivals and Events
ACCOMMODATIONS 85
Downtown Hotels and Motels; Hotels and Motels along Robson Street; Hotels and
Motels in the West End; Hotels and Motels on the North Shore; Hotels and Motels
South of Downtown; Hotels and Motels in Richmond (Vancouver Airport); Hotels
and Motels in Delta; Hotels and Motels in Burnaby; Hotels and Motels in
Abbotsford; Bed and Breakfasts; Budget Accommodations; Camping
FOOD 100
Downtown; Gastown Gourmet; Chinatown; Granville Island; Robson Street;
West End; Kitsilano; West Broadway; North Shore
TRANSPORTATION 112
Getting There; Getting Around; Tours
SERVICES AND INFORMATION 118
Books, Magazines, and Newspapers; Information

SPECIAL TOPICS

Vancouver Views 52		Dining in Stanley Park 109
Kitsilano 62		Airlines Serving Vancouver 113
Bowen Island 68		Royal Hudson 115
Downtown Dining Classics 101		Rental Car Agencies 116

VANCOUVER ISLAND 123

VICTORIA 127
History; Inner Harbour Sights; Old Town; South of the Inner Harbour;
Rockland and Oak Bay; West of Downtown; Saanich Peninsula; Recreation;
Arts and Entertainment; Shopping; Festivals and Events; Downtown Hotels and
Motels; Hotels and Motels West of Downtown; Hotels and Motels on the
Saanich Peninsula; Malahat Accommodations; Bed and Breakfasts; Budget
Accommodations; Camping; Food; Getting There; Getting Around;
Services and Information
VICINITY OF VICTORIA 155
Sooke; Continuing along Highway 14 to Port Renfrew; The West Coast Trail;
Duncan; Lake Cowichan and Vicinity; North toward Nanaimo
SOUTHERN GULF ISLANDS 162
Salt Spring Island; North Pender Island; Galiano Island; Mayne Island;
Saturna Island

NANAIMO AND VICINITY 168
Sights; Recreation; Accommodations and Camping; Food; Transportation; Services and Information; Gabriola Island

HIGHWAY 4 TO THE WEST COAST 178
Highway 4 toward Port Alberni; Port Alberni and Vicinity; Bamfield; West from Port Alberni; Ucluelet; Pacific Rim National Park

TOFINO 186
Sights and Recreation; Accommodations and Camping; Other Practicalities

NORTH FROM NANAIMO 191
Parksville toward Courtenay; Comox Valley; North toward Campbell River

NORTHERN VANCOUVER ISLAND 197
Campbell River; Quadra Island; Cortes Island; Highway 28; North to Port McNeill; Alert Bay (Cormorant Island); Port Hardy; Cape Scott Provincial Park

SPECIAL TOPICS

Touring Victoria ....*136*   *The Broken Group Islands* *185*
Heading up the Island from Victoria ....*153*   *Forbidden Plateau* *194*
Nanaimo's World Championship Bathtub Race ..*173*   *Whale-watching in Johnstone Strait* *203*

SOUTHWESTERN BRITISH COLUMBIA 209

THE SUNSHINE COAST 211
Langdale to Saltery Bay; Powell River; Vicinity of Powell River

SEA TO SKY HIGHWAY 221
Horseshoe Bay toward Squamish; Squamish; North toward Whistler

WHISTLER 225
Summer Recreation; Skiing and Snowboarding; Wet Weather Recreation; Entertainment and Events; Accommodations and Camping; Food; Transportation; Services and Information

THE GOLD NUGGET ROUTE 237

EAST FROM VANCOUVER 238
Fraser Valley; Hope and Vicinity; Fraser River Canyon; Coquihalla Highway; Manning Provincial Park; Continuing toward the Okanagan Valley

SPECIAL TOPICS

Circlepac ....*211*   *Summer Skiing* *231*
Powell Forest Canoe Route ....*217*   *Hollywood Comes to Hope* *241*
The Eagles of Brackendale ....*223*   *White-water Rafting* *243*

OKANAGAN VALLEY 250
Osoyoos

PENTICTON 253
Sights and Recreation; Accommodations and Camping; Other Practicalities; North of Penticton

KELOWNA 258

Sights; Recreation; Accommodations and Camping; Food; Services and
Information

VERNON AND VICINITY 271

Sights and Recreation; Accommodations and Camping; Other Practicalities;
Silver Star Mountain Resort

SPECIAL TOPICS

Okanagan Wines ....*256*   *Ogopogo* *263*

THE KOOTENAYS 277

WEST KOOTENAYS 279

Grand Forks and Vicinity; Rossland; Trail and Vicinity; Castlegar; The Slocan
Valley; Nakusp; West to the Okanagan

NELSON 289

Sights; Parks and Recreation; Accommodations and Camping; Food and Drink;
Services and Information

KOOTENAY LAKE AND CRESTON 294

Ainsworth Hot Springs; Kaslo and Vicinity; Across Kootenay Lake to Creston;
Creston

EAST KOOTENAYS 299

East from Creston; Cranbrook; Fernie and Vicinity; Fort Steele and Vicinity;
Kimberley; Continuing North toward Invermere; Invermere and Vicinity

SPECIAL TOPICS

Olaus Jeldness ....*281*   *Valhalla Wilderness Society* *286*

CANADIAN ROCKIES 315

The Land; Flora; Fauna

RADIUM HOT SPRINGS AND VICINITY 321

Sights and Recreation; Accommodations and Camping; Food; Information;
North from Radium along Highway 95; Mount Assiniboine Provincial Park

KOOTENAY NATIONAL PARK 326

The Land; History; Driving Highway 93; Hiking; Practicalities

YOHO NATIONAL PARK 334

The Land; History; Road-Accessible Sights; Lake O'Hara; Yoho Valley Hiking;
Emerald Lake Hiking; Hikes in Other Areas of the Park; Accommodations and
Camping; Food; Services and Information

GOLDEN 343

Sights and Recreation; Accommodations and Camping; Other Practicalities

SPECIAL TOPICS

National Park Passes ....*318*   *Takakkaw Falls* *337*
Burgess Shale *335*

CENTRAL BRITISH COLUMBIA 347

GLACIER NATIONAL PARK 348
The Land; History; Hiking; Accommodations and Camping; Information

REVELSTOKE 354
Sights; Mount Revelstoke National Park; Recreation; Accommodations and
Camping; Food; Services and Information

WEST TOWARD KAMLOOPS 359
Salmon Arm; Continuing West

KAMLOOPS 362
Sights; Recreation; Accommodations and Camping; Food; Services and
Information

NORTH TO MOUNT ROBSON 368
Wells Gray Provincial Park; Continuing toward Mount Robson; Mount Robson
Provincial Park

CARIBOO COUNTRY 376
Cache Creek; Lillooet; Clinton to 100 Mile House; Williams Lake; Highway 20;
Bella Coola; Discovery Coast Passage; Quesnel; East from Quesnel

SPECIAL TOPICS

Time Travel 353   Echo Valley Guest Ranch Resort 378
Terry Fox 370

NORTHERN BRITISH COLUMBIA 389

PRINCE GEORGE 391
Sights; Recreation; Entertainment; Festivals and Events; Accommodations and
Camping; Food; Transportation; Services and Information

WEST FROM PRINCE GEORGE 399
Vanderhoof; Fort St. James; Fort Fraser to Fraser Lake; Burns Lake and Vicinity;
Tweedsmuir Provincial Park (North); Topley to Telkwa; Smithers and Vicinity;
New Hazelton and Vicinity; Terrace and Vicinity; Kitimat; West toward
Prince Rupert

PRINCE RUPERT 414
Sights; Recreation; Accommodations and Camping; Food; Transportation;
Services and Information

QUEEN CHARLOTTE ISLANDS 425
Transportation; Queen Charlotte City; North to Port Clements; Masset and
Vicinity; Naikoon Provincial Park; Sandspit and Vicinity; Gwaii Haanas National
Park Reserve

THE STEWART-CASSIAR HIGHWAY 437
From Yellowhead Highway to Meziadin Junction; Stewart; Hyder and Vicinity;
North of Meziadin Junction

NORTH FROM PRINCE GEORGE 444
Along the Crooked River; Chetwynd and Vicinity; Hudson's Hope

THE ALASKA HIGHWAY 448

Dawson Creek; Fort St. John; Wonowon to Prophet River; Fort Nelson;
Continuing to Watson Lake; Atlin

SPECIAL TOPICS

The Elusive Kermode 410	*Beachcombing on the Charlottes* 431
Port Essington 414	*Stewart and Hyder: Some Quick Facts* 439
The Khutzeymateen 418	*Dinosaurs in the Peace River Valley* 447
King Pacific Lodge 419	

RESOURCES 459

Suggested Reading 460

Internet Resources 464

Index 466

MAP SYMBOLS

═══ Divided Road	★ Point of Interest	▲ Park
═══ Primary Road	• Accommodation	⌂ Campground
─── Secondary Road	▾ Restaurant/Bar	ℳ Waterfall
------- Unpaved Road	▪ Other Location	▲ Mountain
------ Hiking Trail	◉ Provincial Capital	⚑ Golf Course
┼─┼─┼ Railroad	○ City	P.P. = Provincial Park
············ Ferry	○ Town	N.P. = National Park
⊞ TransCanada Highway	⚐ Ski Area	P.R.A. = Provincial
◯ Highway Route	✗ Airfield/Airstrip	Recreation Area

© AVALON TRAVEL PUBLISHING, INC.

Abbreviations

C$—Canadian dollars
CBD—central business district
CPR—Canadian Pacific Railway
d—double
4WD—four-wheel drive
Hwy.—Highway
kg—kilograms
km—kilometer
kph—kilometers per hour
mm—millimeter

no.—number
NWMP—North West Mounted Police
P.O.—post office
RCMP—Royal Canadian Mounted Police
RV—recreational vehicle
s—single
t—triple
UBC—University of British Columbia
UNESCO—United Nations Educational, Scientific, and Cultural Organization

Keeping Current

Although we have strived to produce the most up-to-date guidebook humanly possible, things change—restaurants and accommodations open and close, attractions come and go, and prices go up. If you come across a great out-of-the-way place, a new restaurant or lodging, or you think a particular hike warrants a mention, please write to us. Letters from tour operators and British Columbians in the tourism and hospitality industries are also appreciated. When writing, be as accurate as possible; write notes on the road or even send brochures. Write to:

Moon Handbooks: British Columbia
Avalon Travel Publishing
5855 Beaudry St.
Emeryville, CA 94608 USA
email: atpfeedback@avalonpub.com
(please put "British Columbia" in
the subject line of your email)

Maps

COLOR SUPPLEMENT

British Columbia . . . . ii–iii
Greater Vancouver . . . . iv–v
Downtown Vancouver . . . . vi–vii
Greater Victoria . . . . viii–ix
Downtown Victoria . . . . x–xi

VANCOUVER

Stanley Park 58–59
Downtown Vancouver Entertainment . . 77
Downtown Vancouver
    Accommodations 86–87
Downtown Vancouver Dining . . 102–103
Downtown Vancouver Bookstores . . . 119

VANCOUVER ISLAND

Vancouver Island 124–125
West Coast Trail 157
Southern Gulf Islands 163
Nanaimo 169
Downtown Nanaimo 171
Pacific Rim National Park (Long Beach
    Unit) and Vicinity 182–183
Campbell River 197
Port Hardy 205

SOUTHWESTERN BRITISH COLUMBIA

Southwestern British Columbia 210
Sunshine Coast 212–213
Powell River 216
Whistler 226–227
Vicinity of Hope 240

OKANAGAN VALLEY

Okanagan Valley 251
Penticton 254

Kelowna 260–261
Downtown Kelowna 262
Vernon and Vicinity 272

THE KOOTENAYS

The Kootenays 278
Castlegar 283
Nelson 289
Cranbrook 301
Kimberley 307

CANADIAN ROCKIES

Canadian Rockies 316–317
Radium Hot Springs 323
Yoho and Kootenay
    National Parks 328–329
Golden 344

CENTRAL BRITISH COLUMBIA

Central British Columbia 348–349
Revelstoke 355
Kamloops 363
Mount Robson Provincial Park . . 372–373
Williams Lake 380
Quesnel 386

NORTHERN BRITISH COLUMBIA

Northern British Columbia 390
Prince George 392
Downtown Prince George 394–395
Smithers 406
Terrace 409
Prince Rupert 415
Downtown Prince Rupert 417
Queen Charlotte Islands 426
The Alaska Highway 449
Dawson Creek 450

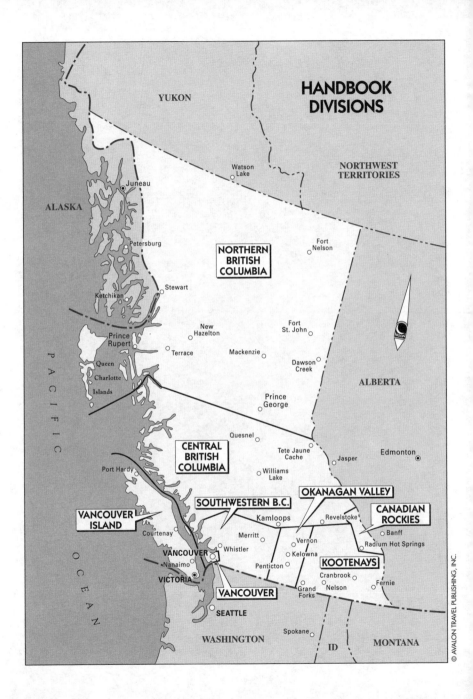

HANDBOOK
DIVISIONS

YUKON

NORTHWEST
TERRITORIES

ALASKA

Juneau

Petersburg

Watson
Lake

Fort
Nelson

NORTHERN
BRITISH
COLUMBIA

Stewart

Ketchikan

Prince
Rupert

New
Hazelton

Fort
St. John

Terrace

Mackenzie

Dawson
Creek

Queen
Charlotte
Islands

Prince
George

ALBERTA

Quesnel

Tete Jaune
Cache

Jasper

Edmonton

CENTRAL
BRITISH
COLUMBIA

Port Hardy

Williams
Lake

OKANAGAN VALLEY

SOUTHWESTERN B.C.

Kamloops

Revelstoke

CANADIAN
ROCKIES

VANCOUVER
ISLAND

Courtenay

Merritt

Vernon

Banff

Radium Hot Springs

Whistler

Kelowna

VANCOUVER

Nanaimo

Penticton

KOOTENAYS

VICTORIA

VANCOUVER

Cranbrook

Grand
Forks

Nelson

Fernie

SEATTLE

WASHINGTON

Spokane

ID

MONTANA

PACIFIC

OCEAN

© AVALON TRAVEL PUBLISHING, INC.

Introduction

British Columbia, the westernmost province of Canada, stretches from the Pacific Ocean to the towering heights of the Rocky Mountains. Sandwiched in between is some of this planet's most magnificent scenery—an enormous variety of terrain including spectacular mountain ranges, glaciers, rivers, lakes, rugged coastline, and hundreds of islands.

The province's largest city is **Vancouver,** a splendid conglomeration of old and new architectural marvels, parks and gardens, and sheltered beaches on the coast in the southwestern corner of the province. The provincial capital is old-world **Victoria,** perched at the southeastern tip of **Vancouver Island,** just across the Strait of Georgia from Vancouver. Victoria boasts an intriguing mixture of old English architecture, customs, and traditions, along with modern attractions, cosmopolitan restaurants, and an infectious joie de vivre.

But most of British Columbia lies away from the cities, in the surrounding vastness. The protected coastal waterways, the rugged west coast of Vancouver Island, the famous Canadian Rockies and many other mountain ranges, the remote northern wilderness, and the intriguing Queen Charlotte Islands provide experiences you'll never forget, along with enough ooh-and-aah scenery to keep even the most jaded jet-setter in awe. In these wild areas, you'll find endless opportunities for hiking or climbing, viewing the abundant wildlife, fishing in the hundreds of lakes and rivers, skiing and boarding any of the dozens of resorts, or immersing yourself in native culture.

© CANADIAN MOUNTAIN HOLIDAYS

experiencing the high points of British Columbia

The Land

British Columbia is Canada's third-largest province in area, behind Ontario and Quebec. Covering 948,596 square kilometers, it's four times larger than Great Britain, two and a half times as large as Japan, larger than all U.S. states except Alaska, and larger than California, Oregon, and Washington combined. The province is long north to south, relatively narrow east to west, and lies between the 49th and 60th parallels. Its largest city, Vancouver, is on the same latitude as Paris and the same longitude as San Francisco. To the south are the U.S. states of Washington, Idaho, and Montana; to the west the Pacific Ocean and the narrow panhandle of southeastern Alaska. To the north are Canada's Yukon Territory and Northwest Territories; to the east, across the Continental Divide, lies the Canadian province of Alberta. The land within those borders is dominated by mountain ranges, which trend northwest-southeast and are highest in the south.

Mountains

Mountains dominate British Columbia; half of the land area lies more than 1,000 meters above sea level. The province occupies part of the mountainous terrain that runs down the entire western margin of the Americas. It lies mainly in the Cordilleran Region, which is composed of Precambrian to Cenozoic rock formed into mountain ranges, deep intermountain troughs, and wide plateaus.

The landscape is defined by parallel north-south mountain ranges and a series of parallel valleys. The steep **Coast Mountains,** an unbroken chain extending for 1,500 km, rise abruptly from the Pacific Ocean. Their high point, and the highest peak completely in British Columbia, is 4,016-meter-high **Mount Waddington.** The province's highest point is shared with Alaska; 4,663-meter **Mount Fairweather** (sixth highest in Canada) is part of the **St. Elias Range,** a northern extension of the Coast Mountains that straddles the B.C.–Alaska border in the extreme northwest corner of the province. The province's

eastern border is defined by the **Continental Divide** of the **Rocky Mountains,** which reach a high point north of the 49th parallel at 3,954-meter **Mount Robson.** In the south of the province between the Coast Mountains and the Rockies lie the **Columbia Mountains,** the collective name for the **Cariboo, Monashee, Selkirk,** and **Purcell Ranges.** These ranges rise to peak elevations of just over 3,000 meters and are separated by deep valleys and long, narrow lake systems. Only the highest of the Columbia Mountains—including some glaciated peaks in the Selkirks and Purcells—are snow-covered year-round. In the northern half of the province, the ranges are lower, wider, and less well defined, rising to vast plateaus that extend hundreds of kilometers in all directions. The least obvious of the province's mountain ranges lies mostly underwater, off the west coast. The range rises above

Mount Robson (3,954 meters) is the highest peak in the Canadian Rockies.

© ANDREW HEMPSTEAD

sea level at thousands of points, forming a string of islands, including Vancouver Island, whose high point is 2,200-meter **Mount Golden Hinde.**

Waterways

The province enjoys more than its share of waterways. Some 24,000 lakes, rivers, and streams contribute to British Columbia's two million hectares of freshwater surface area (approximately 2 percent of the province's landmass). The largest watershed is drained by the **Fraser River.** With its headwaters around Mt. Robson, this mighty river drains 233,000 square kilometers, almost 25 percent of the province, on its 1,368-km journey to the Pacific Ocean at Vancouver. The Fraser is not the province's longest river, though. That title belongs to the 2,000-km-long **Columbia River,** which follows a convoluted course through southeastern B.C. before crossing the U.S. border and draining into the Pacific Ocean in Oregon.

The northern half of British Columbia comprises three major drainage basins: the 580-km-long **Skeena River** flows westward through the heart of the province to the Pacific Ocean at Prince Rupert; the 1,900-km-long **Peace River,** the only river system to cut across the Rocky Mountains, flows in a northeasterly direction into the Mackenzie River System, whose waters eventually flow into the Arctic Ocean; and in the far north, the **Liard River** drains a vast area of remote wilderness to also join the Mackenzie River.

Islands

British Columbia's deeply indented coastline comprises 6,500 islands. While most of these are uninhabited and many unexplored, the largest, 31,284-square-km **Vancouver Island,** is home to over 500,000 people and holds the provincial capital (this island confusingly shares its name with the province's largest city, which lies on the mainland 50 km to the east). Between the mainland and Vancouver Island, 200 islands dot the Strait of Georgia, some of which are populated and all of which are protected from the wind- and wave-battering action of the Pacific Ocean by Vancouver Island. The other major island group

is the **Queen Charlottes,** a remote archipelago linked geologically to Vancouver Island but with its own unique natural and human history.

CLIMATE

British Columbia's varied topography makes for radically varying **temperatures,** which rise or fall with changes in elevation, latitude, slope aspect, and distance from the ocean. The coastal region boasts the mildest climate of all Canada, but this comes with one drawback—it rains a lot. The two main cities, Vancouver and Victoria, lie within this zone. Most of the interior is influenced by both continental and maritime air, resulting in colder, relatively dry winters and hot, dry summers. And the northern latitudes are influenced by polar continental and arctic air masses, making for extremely cold, snowy winters and short, cool, wet summers.

Precipitation in British Columbia is strongly influenced by the lay of the land and the waft of the wind, resulting in an astonishing variation in rainfall from place to place. For example, Lillooet, in the sheltered Fraser River Valley, is Canada's driest community, whereas Port Renfrew on Vancouver Island's west coast averages 4,000 mm of precipitation annually. The amount of precipitation any given area receives is greatly determined by its location on the windward or lee side of the major mountain ranges—the windward side usually cops most of the downpour. Hence, the western side of the Coast Range is wet, the Interior Plateau on the east side of the Coast Range is relatively dry, and the western, windward side of the Rockies along the Alberta border is once again wet.

Travel Seasons

Summer is by far the most popular time to visit British Columbia. Daytime temperatures in Vancouver average a pleasant 23° C (73° F), while the provincial hot spot, the Okanagan Valley, experiences temperatures in the 30s (86–102° F) on many days. Summer in the province sees the parks come alive with campers, the lakes and streams with anglers, the mountains with hikers, the woods with wildlife, and the roadsides with stalls selling fresh produce. Wherever you travel in summer, try to make accommodation reservations in advance.

Temperatures through spring and fall are, naturally, cooler than summer, but in many ways these are prime travel periods. June and September are especially pleasant, as crowds are minimal and wildlife is most active.

The main attractions of winter are skiing and boarding. Most resorts open well before Christmas, with Whistler/Blackcomb open from early November. Winter temperatures along the coast remain relatively mild (on only a few occasions each year does snow fall in downtown Vancouver); Vancouver Island is a particularly popular winter destination for those from the eastern provinces. The interior and northern latitudes of the province are a different story: The average daily winter temperature is well below freezing, with temperatures of 40 below (C and F) not uncommon.

Environment Canada maintains the website www.weatheroffice.ec.gc.ca, with links to all provinces, where you'll find local weather reports, live weather cams, marine forecasts, and road reports.

Flora and Fauna

FLORA

Two colors invariably jump to mind when you say "British Columbia": green and blue. Just about everywhere you travel in B.C. you see trees, trees, and more trees—around two-thirds of the province is forested. But the types of trees differ in each geographic and climatic region. Coastal regions are dominated by temperate rainforest, which requires at least 1,000 millimeters of rain annually and is predominantly evergreens. This biome is extremely rare: at the end of the last ice age it is estimated that 0.2 percent of the world's land area was temperate rainforest. Only 10 percent of these forests remain, 25 percent in British Columbia. This forest is mostly hemlock, western red cedar, and Sitka spruce. A unique species in southern coastal areas is the arbutus (known as Pacific madrone in the United States), an evergreen hardwood with distinctive red bark and shiny leaves. Forests of Douglas fir thrive in drier areas of the coast. Engelmann spruce is common throughout the interior at subalpine elevations. The interior also supports a mixture of Douglas fir and ponderosa pine in the south; interior western hemlock in the southeast; aspen and lodgepole pine in the central reaches; subboreal spruce, birch, and willow in the north, with Sitka spruce in the west; and white spruce and black spruce in the northeast. The Queen Charlottes' rainforest is thickly covered in spongy pale green moss, which grows alongside coastal Douglas fir. In the region's subalpine areas you'll find mountain hemlock.

The official provincial floral emblem is the **Pacific dogwood,** a small tree sporting huge clusters of cream-colored flowers in spring and bright foliage and red berries in autumn. The tree is a protected plant in British Columbia; it's a punishable offense to pick from it or destroy it.

In summer, British Columbia turns on a really magnificent floral display. Wildflowers every color of the rainbow pop up on the roadsides—white and yellow daisies, purple lupines, pale pink and dark pink wild roses, bloodred Indian paintbrush, orange and black lilies, red and white clover, yellow buttercups, to name but a handful. And if you venture off the beaten track and up into the alpine meadows, the floral beauty is hard to believe. You can pick up a wildflower guide at most any local bookshop, and most of the national park visitor centers stock brochures on wildflower identification.

MAMMALS

British Columbia is one of the best provinces in Canada for wildlife-watching. Thanks to a diverse topography that provides a wide variety of habitat, more species of mammals are found here than in any other province or territory in the country.

Bears

Two species of bears—black bears and grizzlies—are present in British Columbia. Both species are widespread and abundant across the province. The two can be differentiated by size and shape. Grizzlies are larger than black bears and have a flatter, dish-shaped face and a distinctive hump of muscle behind the neck. Color is not a reliable way to tell them apart. Black bears are not always black. They can be brown or cinnamon, causing them to be confused with the brown grizzly.

If you spot a bear feeding beside the road, chances are it's a **black bear.** These are the most common of all large mammals in British Columbia, estimated to number around 120,000, with the highest concentrations on Vancouver Island and the Queen Charlotte Islands. Their weight varies considerably (the larger ones are found in coastal areas), but males average 150 kg, females 100 kg. Their diet is omnivorous, consisting primarily of grasses and berries but supplemented by small mammals. They are not true hibernators, but in winter they can sleep for up to a month at a time before changing position. Young are born in late winter, while the mother is still asleep.

British Columbia's estimated 10,000 **grizzlies** are widespread in all mainland areas of the province but are only occasionally seen by casual observers. Most sightings occur along coastal areas (where they are generally called **brown bears**) during salmon runs (the Khutzeymateen, near Prince Rupert, is world-renowned as a grizzly viewing spot) and in spring and fall in alpine and subalpine zones. The bears' color ranges from light brown to almost black, with dark tan being the most common. On average, males weigh 250–350 kg. The bears eat small and medium-sized mammals, and salmon and berries in fall. Like black bears, they sleep through most of the winter. When they emerge in early spring, the bears scavenge carcasses of animals that succumbed to the winter until the new spring vegetation becomes sufficiently plentiful.

© ANDREW HEMPSTEAD

Along the coast, grizzly bears spend much of the fall months fishing for salmon.

WILDLIFE AND YOU

British Columbia's abundance of wildlife is one of its biggest drawcards. To help preserve this unique resource, obey fishing and hunting regulations and use common sense.

- **Do not feed the animals.** Many animals may seem tame, but feeding them endangers yourself, the animal, and other visitors. Animals become aggressive when looking for handouts.
- **Store food safely.** When camping, keep food in your vehicle or out of reach of animals. Just leaving it in a cooler isn't good enough.
- **Keep your distance.** Although it's tempting to get close to animals for a better look or a photograph, it disturbs the animal and, in many cases, can be dangerous.
- **Drive carefully.** The most common cause of premature death for larger mammals is being hit by cars.

Bears

Bears are dangerous, and while bear-human encounters happen regularly, their infamous reputation far exceeds the actual number of attacks that occur (in the last 20 years black bears have accounted for 12 fatalities and grizzly bears for five within British Columbia). That said, common sense is your best weapon against an attack. First and foremost, *keep a safe distance,* particularly if cubs are present—the protective mother will not be far away. *Never harass or attempt to feed a bear,* and resist the temptation to move in for an award-winning close-up photo; they are wild animals and are totally unpredictable.

Before heading out on a hike, *ask local park or forest-service staff about the likelihood of encountering bears in the area,* and heed their advice. *Travel in groups,* never by yourself. Out on the trail, *watch for signs of recent bear activity,* such as fresh footprints or scat. *Make noise* when traveling through dense woods (take a noisemaker—a few rocks in a soft-drink can or a bell—or let out a loud yell every now and again to let wildlife know you're coming). *Bear spray* has become popular in recent years, but don't trust your life to it by taking unnecessary risks.

Bears will usually avoid you; however, you may come across the odd bruin. Bear talk is a favorite topic in the north, and everyone who has ever spent time in the wilderness has his or her own theory about the best course of action in the event of an encounter or an unlikely attack. On a few things, everyone agrees: *Stay in a group and back away slowly,* talking firmly the whole time; *do not run*—a bear can easily outrun a human. Black bears can climb trees but grizzlies can't. If an attack seems imminent and it's a black bear, the general consensus is to try to fight the animal off; if it's a grizzly, drop to the ground in a hunched-up position, covering your neck, and play dead.

Park staff can supply you with bear-aware literature, and many books have been written on the subject. One of the best is *Bear Attacks: Their Causes and Avoidance,* by Canadian bear expert Stephen Herrero.

The Deer Family

Mule deer and **white-tailed deer** are similar in size and appearance. Their color varies with the season but is generally light brown in summer, turning dirty gray in winter. While both species are considerably smaller than elk, the mule deer is a little stockier than the white-tailed deer. The mule deer has a white rump, a white tail with a dark tip, and large mule-like ears. It inhabits open forests along valley floors. The white-tailed deer's tail is dark on top. But when the animal runs, it holds its tail erect, revealing an all-white underside. White-tailed are common along valleys throughout British Columbia, but especially prevalent on Vancouver Island. **Sitka** deer, a subspecies, inhabit the Queen Charlotte Islands.

The giant of the deer family, the **moose,** is an awkward-looking mammal that appears to have been designed by a cartoonist. It has the largest antlers of any animal in the world, stands up to 1.8 meters at the shoulder, and weighs up to 500 kg. Its body is dark brown, and it has a prominent nose, long spindly legs, small eyes, big ears, and an odd flap of skin called a "bell" dangling beneath its chin. Apart from all that, it's good-looking. Each spring the bull begins to grow palm-shaped antlers that by August will be fully grown. Moose are solitary animals, preferring marshy areas and weedy lakes, but they are known to wander to higher elevations searching out open spaces in summer. They forage in and around ponds on willows, aspen, birch, grasses, and all aquatic vegetation. They are most common in northern British Columbia.

The **elk** (also known as wapiti) has a tan body with a dark-brown neck, dark-brown legs, and a white rump. This second-largest member of the deer family weighs 250–450 kg and stands 1.5 meters at the shoulder. Pockets of elk inhabit valleys in the east of the province, but the animals are not particularly common.

Small populations of **woodland caribou** are restricted to the far north of the province. You may see them feeding in open areas at higher elevations along the Alaska Highway. Native people named the animal "caribou" ("hoof scraper") for the way in which they feed in winter, scraping away snow with their hooves. Caribou are smaller than elk and have a dark brown coat with creamy patches on the neck and rump.

Wild Dogs and Cats

Once inhabiting the region from Mexico to Alaska, the **wolf** was perceived as a threat by early European settlers and was target of a relentless campaign to exterminate the species. Numbers have rebounded across the continent, including in British Columbia, where the vast wilderness is home to a widespread and stable population that numbers around 8,000 and is distributed across the province everywhere except the lower mainland and coastal islands. Wolves weigh up to 65 kg, stand a meter high at the shoulder, and resemble large huskies or German shepherds. Their color ranges from snow white to brown or black; those in British Columbia are most often shades of gray or brown. Unlike other predators they are not solitary but are intriguing animals that adhere to a complex social order, living in packs of 5–10 animals and roaming over hundreds of kilometers in search of prey.

The **coyote** is often confused for a wolf, when in fact it is much smaller, weighing up to only 15 kg. It has a pointed nose and long bushy tail. Its coloring is a mottled mix of brown and gray, with lighter-colored legs and belly. The coyote is a skillful and crafty hunter preying mainly on rodents. Coyotes have the remarkable ability to hear the movement of small mammals under the snow, allowing them to hunt these animals without actually seeing them. They are common and widespread at lower elevations throughout British Columbia (often patrolling the edges of highways and crossing open meadows in low-lying valleys).

Cougars (also called mountain lions, Mexican lions, pumas, and catamounts) are relatively plentiful in British Columbia, especially on Vancouver Island, where it is estimated the population numbers around 500. Adult males can grow to over two meters in length and weigh up to 90 kg. The fur generally ranges in color from light brown to a reddish-tinged gray, but occasionally black cougars are reported. Their athletic prowess puts Olympians to shame. They can spring forward more than eight meters from a standstill, leap four meters into the air, and safely jump from a height of 20 meters. These solitary animals are versatile hunters whose acute vision takes in a peripheral span in excess of 200 degrees. They typically kill a large mammal such as a deer every two to three weeks, eating part of it and caching the rest. Their diet also includes coyotes, grouse, chipmunks, ground squirrels, and snowshoe hares.

The elusive **lynx** is identifiable by its pointy black ear tufts and an oversized "tabby cat" appearance. The animal has broad, padded paws that distribute its weight, allowing it to "float" on the surface of snow. It weighs up to 10 kg but appears much larger because of its coat of long, thick fur. The lynx, uncommon but widespread throughout the interior, is a solitary creature that prefers the cover of subalpine forests, feeding mostly at night on snowshoe hares and other small mammals.

Sheep and Goats

Dall's sheep (also known as Rocky Mountain or bighorn sheep) are one of the most distinctive mammals of Canada. Easily recognized by their impressive horns, they are often seen grazing on grassy mountain slopes or at salt licks beside the road. The color of their coat varies with the season; in summer it's a brownish gray with a cream-colored belly and rump, turning lighter in winter. Bighorn sheep are particularly tolerant of humans and often approach parked vehicles; although they are not especially dangerous, as with all mammals, you should not approach or feed them.

The remarkable rock-climbing ability of nimble **mountain goats** allows them to live high in the mountains, retreating to rocky ledges or near-vertical slopes when threatened by predators.

Small Mammals

One of the animal kingdom's most industrious mammals is the **beaver.** Growing to a length of 50 centimeters and tipping the scales at around 20 kg, it has a flat, rudderlike tail and webbed back feet that enable it to swim at speeds up to 10 kph. The exploration of western Canada can be directly attributed to the beaver, whose pelt was in high demand in fashion-conscious Europe in the early 1800s. The beaver was never entirely wiped out from the mountains, and today the animals inhabit almost any forested valley with flowing water. Beavers build their dam walls and lodges of twigs, branches, sticks of felled trees, and mud. They eat the bark and smaller twigs of deciduous plants and store branches underwater, near the lodge, as a winter food supply.

Several species of **squirrel** are common in British Columbia, including the golden-mantled ground, Columbian, and red squirrel. **Marmots** are common and widespread, with various species living in different habitats. They are stocky creatures, weighing 4–9 kg. The **porcupine,** a small, squat animal, is easily recognized by its thick coat of quills. It eats roots and leaves but is also known for being destructive around wooden buildings and vehicle tires.

REPTILES

Reptiles don't like cold climates, and therefore they don't like Canada. British Columbia is home to just 17 of the world's 10,000-odd reptile species. All 17 inhabit dry, hot valleys of grassland, such as the Okanagan Valley. The breakdown includes nine species of snakes, five turtles, two lizards, and one species of skink. The province's only poisonous snake is the extremely rare **western rattlesnake,** which lives in the southern interior. Like other rattlers, it waits for prey rather than actively hunting and won't bite unless provoked.

BIRDS

Of the 454 bird species recorded in British Columbia, 300 breed within the province (the most of any province or territory), and of these, 35 species nest nowhere else in Canada. The lower mainland is a migration stop for the million-odd birds that travel the Pacific flyway each year. Huge populations of waterfowl winter at Boundary Bay near Vancouver, and large concentrations can also be seen around Fort St. James, Cranbrook, Prince George, and Lac La Hache. The province is home to half of the world's populations of both trumpeter swans and blue grouse, as well as a quarter of the world's bald eagles. You'll see beautiful Canada and snow geese, trumpeter and whistling swans, and all kinds of ducks.

British Columbia's official bird is the often-cheeky, vibrant blue-and-black **Steller's jay,** found throughout the province.

FISH

Of the 72 species of fish in British Columbia, 22 are considered sport fish. The two varieties most sought-after by anglers are salmon, found in tidal waters along the coast, and trout, inhabiting the freshwater lakes and rivers of interior British Columbia. (For more information on fishing, please see Recreation in the On the Road chapter.)

Salmon

Five species of salmon are native to the tidal waters of British Columbia. All are *anadromous;* that is, they spend their time in both freshwater and saltwater. The life cycle of these creatures is truly amazing. Hatching from small red eggs often hundreds of miles upriver from the ocean, the fry find their way to the ocean, undergoing massive internal changes along the way that allow them to survive in saltwater. Depending on the species, they then spend between two and six years in the open water, traveling as far as the Bering Sea. After reaching maturity, they begin the epic journey back to their birthplace, to the exact patch of gravel on the same river from where they emerged. Their navigation system has evolved over a million years, using, it is believed, a sensory system that uses measurements of sunlight, the earth's magnetic field, and atmospheric pressure to find their home river. Once the salmon are in range of their home river, scent takes over, returning them to the exact spot where they were born. Once the salmon reach freshwater they stop eating. Unlike other species of fish (including Atlantic salmon), Pacific salmon die immediately after spawning; hence the importance of returning to their birthplace, a spot the salmon instinctively know gives them the best opportunity for their one chance to reproduce successfully.

Largest of the five salmon species is the **chinook,** which grows to 30 kg in B.C. waters.

Known as king salmon in the United States, chinooks are a prized sportfish most recognizable by their size but also by black gums and silverspotted tails.

Averaging 2–3 kg, **sockeye** (red salmon) are the most streamlined of the Pacific salmon. They are distinguished from other species by a silvery-blue skin and prominent eyes. While other species swim into the ocean after hatching, the sockeye remain inland, in freshwater lakes and rivers, for at least a year before migrating into the Pacific. When ready to spawn, the body of the sockeye turns bright red and the head a dark green.

Chum (dog) salmon are very similar in appearance to sockeye, and the bodies also change dramatically when spawning; a white tip on the anal fin is the best form of identification. Bright, silver-colored **coho** (silver) average 1.5–3 kg. This species can be recognized by white gums and spots on the upper portion of the tail.

Smallest of the Pacific salmon are the **pinks,** which rarely weigh over four kg and usually average around two. Their most dominant feature is a tail covered in large oval spots. They are most abundant in northern waters in even-

WHALES OF BRITISH COLUMBIA

Whale-watching has gained great popularity off the B.C. coast in recent years. Most towns along the Vancouver Island coast offer trips out in various watercraft, many staying in sheltered waters where the whales are resting on migratory routes between Mexico and Alaska.

Once nearly extinct, today an estimated 20,000 **gray whales** swim the length of the British Columbia coast twice annually between Baja Mexico and the Bering Sea. The spring migration (March–April) is close to the shore, with whales stopping to rest and feed in places such as Clayoquot Sound and the Queen Charlotte Islands.

Orcas, best known as **killer whales,** are the largest member of the dolphin family. Adult males can reach 10 meters in length and up to 10 tons in weight, but their most distinctive feature is a dorsal fin that protrudes more than 1.5 meters from

the back. Orcas are widespread in oceans around the world, but especially common along the B.C. coast, including Robson Bight, the world's only sanctuary established specially for the protection of the species. Three distinct populations live in B.C. waters: *resident* orcas feed primarily on salmon and travel in pods of up to 50; *transients* travel by themselves or in very small groups, feeding on marine mammals such as seals and whales; and, finally, *offshore* orcas live in the open ocean, traveling in pods and feeding only on fish. In total, they number around 500, with around 300 residents living in 15 pods.

Local waters are home to an abundance of other marine mammals. Porpoises, dolphins, and humpback whales frolic in coastal waters, and colonies of seals and sea lions can be viewed by boat or kayak.

numbered years and in southern waters in odd-numbered years.

Freshwater Fish

Trout are part of the same fish family as salmon, but, with one or two exceptions, they live in freshwater their entire lives. Interestingly, the trout of British Columbia are more closely related to Atlantic salmon than to any of the species of Pacific salmon detailed above. The predominant species is the **rainbow trout,** common in lakes and rivers throughout the province. It has an olive-green back and a red strip running along the center of its body. Many subspecies exist, such as the large Gerrard rainbow trout of the southern interior; the steelhead, an ocean-going rainbow, inhabits rivers flowing into the Pacific Ocean.

Other trout species present include the **bull trout,** which struggles to survive through high levels of fishing and a low reproductive cycle. **Cutthroat trout,** found in high elevation lakes, are named for a bright red dash of color that runs from below the mouth almost to the gills.

Colorful **brook trout** can be identified by their dark green backs with pale splotches and purple-sheened sides. **Brown trout** are the only trout with both black and red spots.

The **lake trout,** which grows to 20 kg, is native to large, deep lakes throughout the province, but it is technically a member of the char family. **Kokanee** are a freshwater salmon native to major lakes and rivers of the southern interior. They are directly related to sockeye salmon and look similar in all aspects but size (kokanee rarely grow to over 30 cm in length), spawning in the same freshwater range as sockeye.

The **whitefish,** a light gray fish, is native to lower elevation lakes and rivers across the province. Inhabiting northern waters are **arctic grayling** and **Dolly Varden trout** (named for a colorful character in a Charles Dickens story). **Walleye** (also called pickerel) grow to 4.5 kg and are common in sandy-bottomed areas of lakes in northeastern British Columbia. The monster freshwater fish of British Columbia is the **sturgeon,** growing to over 100 kg in size and living for upwards of 100 years.

History

THE EARLIEST INHABITANTS

Human habitation of what is now British Columbia began around 15,000 years ago, when *Homo sapiens* migrated from northeast Asia across a land bridge spanning the Bering Strait. During this time, the northern latitudes of North America were covered by an ice cap, forcing these people to travel south down the west coast before fanning out across the ice-free southern latitudes. As the ice cap receded northward, the people drifted north also, perhaps only a few kilometers in an entire generation, and began crossing the 49th parallel about 12,000 years ago. By the time the ice cap had receded from all but the far north and the highest mountain peaks, two distinct cultures had formed—one along the coast and one in the interior. Within these two broad groups, many tribes formed, developing distinct cultures and languages.

The Northwest Coast

Around 12,000 years ago, Canada's west coast had become ice-free, and humans had begun settling along its entire length. Over time they had broken into distinct linguistic groups, including the **Coast Salish, Kwagiulth, Tsimshian, Gitksan, Nisga'a, Haida,** and **Tlingit,** but all had two things in common: their reliance on cedar and on salmon. They lived a very different lifestyle to the stereotypical "Indian"—they had no bison to depend on, they didn't ride horses, nor did they live in tepees, but instead developed a unique and intriguing culture that remains in place in small pockets along the west coast. These coastal bands lived comfortably off the land and the sea, hunting deer, beaver, bear, and sea otters; fishing for salmon, cod, and halibut; and harvesting edible kelp. They built huge 90-meter-long cedar houses and 20-meter-long dugout cedar canoes, and developed a distinctive and highly decorative arts style featuring animals, mythical creatures, and oddly shaped human forms believed to be supernatural ancestors.

West coast native society emphasized the material wealth of each chief and his tribe, displayed to others during special events called potlatches. The potlatch ceremonies marked important moments in tribal society, such as marriages, puberty celebrations, deaths, or totem-pole raisings. The wealth of a tribe became obvious when the chief gave away enormous quantities of gifts to his guests—the nobler the guest, the better the gift. The potlatch exchange was accompanied by much feasting, speech-making, dancing, and entertainment, all of which could last many days. Stories performed by hosts garbed in elaborate costumes and masks educated, entertained, and affirmed each clan's historical continuity.

The Interior Salish

Moving north with the receding ice cap around 10,000 years ago, the Salish fanned out across most of southwestern and interior British Columbia. After spending summers in the mountains hunting and gathering, they would move to lower elevations to harvest their most precious natural resource—salmon. At narrow canyons along the Fraser River and its tributaries, the Salish put their fishing skills to the test, netting, trapping, and spearing salmon as the fish traveled upstream to spawn. Much of the catch was preserved by drying or roasting, then pounded into a powder known as "pemmican" for later use or to be traded. The Salish wintered in earth-covered log structures known as pit houses. Depressions left by these ancient structures can still be seen in places such as Keatley Creek, alongside the Fraser River. Within the Salish Nation, four distinct tribes have been identified: the Lillooet, the Thompson (Nlaka'pamux), the Okanagan, and the Shuswap. The Shuswap occupied the largest area, with a territory that extended from the Fraser River to the Rocky Mountains; they were the only Salish who crossed the Rockies to hunt buffalo on the plains.

The Kootenay

The Kootenay (other common spellings include Kootenai, Kootenae, and Kutenai) were once hunters of buffalo on the great American plains,

INTRODUCTION

TOTEM POLES

Traveling through British Columbia you can't help but notice all the totem poles decorating the landscape. Totem poles are made of red (or occasionally yellow) cedar painted black, red, blue, yellow, and white, with colored pigment derived from minerals, plants, and salmon roe. They are erected as validation of a public record or documentation of an important event. Six types of poles are believed to have evolved in the following order: house post (an integral part of the house structure), mortuary (erected as a chief's or shaman's grave post, often with the bones or ashes in a box at the top of the pole), memorial (commemorating special events), frontal (a memorial or heraldic pole), welcome, and shame poles. None is an object of worship; each tells a story or history of a person's clan or family. The figures on the pole represent family lineage, animals, or a mythical character.

Since 1951, when a government ban on potlatch ceremonies (of which the raising of totem poles is an integral part) was lifted, the art form has been revived. Over the years, many totem poles have been moved from their original locations. Both historic and more modern poles can be viewed in British Columbia. The Haida, of the Queen Charlotte Islands, were renowned for their totem poles; many "totem villages," long since abandoned, remain on the remote southern tip of the archipelago. Of these, **Ninstints** is regarded as the world's best example of an ancient Haida totem village. More modern totems can be found at **Stanley Park,** Vancouver; **Thunderbird Park,** Victoria; **Alert Bay,** Cormorant Island; and **Kitwancool,** at the south end of the Stewart-Cassiar Highway. The **Museum of Anthropology** in Vancouver also has an excellent collection.

© ANDREW HEMPSTEAD

Totem poles can be found all over the place in British Columbia, like this one in Vancouver's Stanley Park.

but were pushed westward by fierce enemies. Like the Salish did farther west, they then moved north with the receding ice cap. They crossed the 49th parallel around 10,000 years ago, settling in the Columbia River Valley, along the western edge of the Canadian Rockies. Like the Salish, they were hunters and gathers and came to rely on salmon. The Kootenay were generally friendly, mixing freely with the Salish and treating the earliest explorers, such as David Thompson, with respect. They regularly traveled east over the Rockies to hunt—to the wildlife-rich Kootenay Plains or farther south to

the Great Plains in search of bison.

The Athabascans

Athabascan (often spelled Athapaskan) is the most widely spread of all North American linguistic groups, extending from the Rio Grande to Alaska. In 1793, when Alexander Mackenzie made his historic journey across the continent, he spent the last summer before reaching the west coast in Athabascan territory, which at that time included most of what is now northern British Columbia. The largest division of the Athabascans within this area was the **Carrier** group, so named for their custom requiring a woman to carry the ashes of her husband with her for a least a year. Aside from the fact that they cremated their dead, the Carrier had similar traits to those found throughout the Athabascan peoples—they lived simply and were generally friendly toward each other and neighboring tribes. They lived throughout the northern reaches of the Fraser River basin and along the Skeena River watershed. The Carrier, along with Athabascan tribes that lived farther north (including the Chilcotin, Tahltan, and Inland Tlingit) adopted many traits of their coastal neighbors, such as potlatch ceremonies and raising totem poles. Another Athabascan group inhabiting British Columbia was the **Beaver,** who were forced westward, up the Peace River watershed, by the warlike Cree (the name Peace River originated after the two groups eventually made peace). With no access to salmon-rich waters west of the Rocky Mountains, the Beaver hunted bison, moose, and caribou and were strongly influenced by the fur trade. Over the subcontinental divide to the north is the upper watershed of the mighty Mackenzie River; extending into the northeast corner of the province, this was the traditional home of the **Slavey,** one of seven groups of the Dene (DEN-ay) people. Like the Beaver, they were nomadic hunters and gatherers but also relied heavily on fishing.

EUROPEAN EXPLORATION AND COLONIZATION

It was only a little more than 200 years ago that the first European explorers began to chart the northwest corner of North America. The area's geography presented formidable natural barriers to the east (the lofty Rocky Mountains) and the west (long stretches of ocean away from other landmasses).

By Sea

In the second half of the 18th century, curiosity about a western approach to the fabled Northwest Passage and a common desire to discover rich natural resources lured Russian, Spanish, British, and American explorers and fur traders along the coastline that is now British Columbia. In 1774, the ship of Mexican **Juan Perez** was the first vessel to explore the coastline and trade with the natives. He was quickly followed by Spaniard **Don Juan Francisco de la Bodega y Quadra,** who took possession of the coast of Alaska for Spain. England's **Captain James Cook** arrived in 1778 to spend some time at Nootka, becoming the first nonnative to actually come ashore, trading with the natives while he overhauled his ship. Cook received a number of luxuriantly soft sea otter furs, which he later sold at a huge profit in China. This news spawned a fur-trading rush that began in 1785 and continued for 25 years. Ship after loaded ship called in along the coast, trading iron, brass, copper, muskets, cloth, jewelry, and rum to the natives in exchange for furs. The indigenous people were eager to obtain the foreign goods, but they were also known for driving a hard bargain. The traders took the furs directly to China to trade for silk, tea, spices, ginger, and other luxuries. In 1789, Bodega y Quadra established a settlement at Nootka, but after ongoing problems with the British (who also claimed the area), he gave it up. In 1792, **Captain George Vancouver,** who had been the navigator on Cook's 1778 expedition, returned to the area and sailed into Burrard Inlet, claiming the land for Great Britain.

By Land

In the meantime, adventurous North West Company fur traders were crossing the Rockies in search of waterways to the coast. The first European to reach the coast was **Alexander Mackenzie,** who traveled via the Peace, Fraser, and West Road Rivers—you can still see the rock in the Dean Channel (off Bella Coola) where he inscribed "Alexander Mackenzie from Canada by land 22nd July 1793." Not far behind came other explorers, including **Simon Fraser,** who followed the Fraser River to the sea in 1808, and **David Thompson,** who followed the Columbia River to its mouth in 1811. Today the names of these men grace everything from rivers to motels. In the early 19th century, the North West Company established trading posts in **New Caledonia** (the name Simon Fraser gave to the northern interior). These posts were taken over by Hudson's Bay

Company after amalgamation of the two companies in 1821.

The Native Response

The fur trade brought prosperity to the indigenous society, which was organized around wealth, possessions, and potlatches. The Hudson's Bay Company had no interest in interfering with the natives and, in general, treated them fairly. This early contact with Europeans resulted in expanded trade patterns and increased commerce between coastal and interior tribes. It also spurred the production of indigenous arts and crafts to new heights, as chiefs required more carved headgear, masks, costumes, feast dishes, and the like for the increasingly frequent ceremonial occasions that came with increased wealth.

However, commerce between the Europeans and locals also caused the indigenous tribes to abandon their traditional homesites and instead to cluster around the forts for trading and protection. In addition, the Europeans introduced muskets, alcohol, and disease (most significantly smallpox), all of which took their toll on the native population, which stood at around 60,000 in 1850. Christian missionaries soon arrived and tried to ban the natives' traditional potlatches. But not until land-grabbing white colonists showed up did major conflicts arise between native peoples and whites. Those land-ownership conflicts proved tenacious, continuing to this day.

The first European to reach the west coast by land was Alexander Mackenzie, who traveled via the Peace, Fraser, and West Road Rivers—you can still see the rock in the Dean Channel (off Bella Coola) where he inscribed "Alexander Mackenzie from Canada by land 22nd July 1793."

Vancouver Island

The British government decided in 1849 that Vancouver Island should be colonized to confirm British sovereignty in the area and forestall any American expansion. Though mostly content to leave the island in the hands of the Hudson's Bay Company, the Brits nevertheless sent **Richard Blanshard** out from England to become the island colony's first governor. Blan-

shard soon resigned and was replaced in 1851 by **James Douglas,** chief factor of the Hudson's Bay Company. Douglas had long been in control of the island, and his main concerns were to maintain law and order and to purchase land from the natives. He made treaties with the tribes in which the land became the "entire property of the white people forever." In return, tribes retained use of their village sites and enclosed fields, and could hunt and fish on unoccupied lands. Each indigenous family was paid a pitiful compensation.

In 1852, coal was discovered near Nanaimo, and English miners were imported to develop the deposits. Around the same time, loggers began felling the enormous timber stands along the Alberni Canal, and the Puget Sound Agricultural Association (a subsidiary of Hudson's Bay Company) developed several large farms in the Victoria region. By the 1850s, the town of Victoria, with its moderate climate and fertile soil, had developed into an agreeable settlement.

LAW, ORDER, AND GOLD

Firsts

In 1856 the first parliament west of the Great Lakes was elected, and Dr. J. S. Helmcken became Speaker. (Today you can still see his house in Victoria.) Only two years later this still relatively unexplored and quiet part of the world was turned upside down with the first whispers of "gold" on the mainland, along the banks of the Fraser River. As the news spread, miners—mostly Americans—arrived by the shipload at Victoria, increasing the town's population from several hundred to more than 5,000. Fur trading faded as gold mining jumped to the forefront. Realizing that enormous wealth could be buried on the mainland, the British government quickly responded by creating a mainland colony that at first was named New Caledonia. Because

France possessed a colony of the same name in the South Pacific, Queen Victoria was asked to change the name, which she did, using "Columbia," which appeared on local maps, and adding "British," making the name distinct from the Columbia River district across the border. In 1858, Governor James Douglas of Vancouver Island also became governor of B.C., giving up his Hudson's Bay Company position to serve both colonies. In 1866 the two colonies were combined into one.

Cariboo Gold

The lucrative Cariboo gold rush resulted in construction of the Cariboo Wagon Road (also called the Gold Rush Trail), an amazing engineering feat that opened up British Columbia's interior. Completed in 1865, the road connected Yale with Barkerville, one of the richest and wildest gold towns in North America. Mule trains and stagecoaches plied the route, and roadhouses and boomtowns dotted its entire length. Among the colorful characters of this era was Judge Matthew Baillie Begbie, an effective chief of law and order during a time when law and order might as easily have been nonexistent.

In addition to the gold miners, groups of settlers soon began arriving in the Cariboo. One such group, a horde known as the **Overlanders**, left Ontario and Quebec with carts, horses, and oxen in summer 1862, intent on crossing the vast plains and the Rockies to British Columbia. One detachment rafted down the Fraser River, the other down the North Thompson. Both arrived in Kamloops in autumn that same year. Some continued north up the Cariboo Gold Rush Trail, but others headed for the coast, having had more than their fill of adventure on the trip across.

Rapid Development

In addition to the Cariboo Wagon Road, other trails opened up more of the province in the early 1860s. The Hope-Princeton and Dewdney Trails into the Kootenays led to settlement in B.C.'s eastern regions. Salmon canning was also developed in the 1860s, and several canneries on both the lower Fraser and Skeena Rivers had

the world market in their pockets. (You can still see one of the old canneries near Prince Rupert today.)

It wasn't until 1862 that Burrard Inlet—site of today's city of Vancouver—sprang onto the map with the building of a small lumber mill on the north shore. The region's tall, straight trees became much in demand. More lumber mills started up, and a healthy export market developed in only a few years. Farmers began to move into the area, and by the end of the 1860s a small town had been established. "Gassy Jack" Deighton started a very popular saloon on the south shore of Burrard Inlet near a lumber camp, and for some time the settlement was locally called Gastown. After the townsite was surveyed in 1870, the name was changed to Granville. Then in 1886, the town was officially renamed Vancouver, in honor of Captain George Vancouver. At this time, New Westminster was the official capital of the colony of British Columbia, much to the concern and disbelief of Vancouver Islanders, who strongly believed Victoria should have retained the position. Two years later, with the mainland gold rushes over, the capital reverted to Victoria, where it has remained ever since.

Confederation and Beyond

The next big issue to concern British Columbia was confederation. The eastern colonies had become one large dominion, and B.C. residents were invited to join. London and Ottawa both wanted B.C. to join to assist in counterbalancing the mighty U.S. power to the south. After much public debate, the southwesternmost colony entered the Confederation as the Province of British Columbia in July 1871—on the condition that the west coast be connected to the east by railway. Many roads were built during the 1870s, but it was the completion of the transcontinental railway in 1885 that really opened up B.C. to the rest of the country. Other railways followed, steamships plied the lakes and rivers, more roads were built, and industries—including logging, mining, farming, fishing, and tourism—started to develop.

During the 20th century, B.C. moved from

roads to major multilane highways, from horses to ferries, and from gold mining to sportfishing. Yet it still attracts explorers—backcountry hikers and mountain climbers in search of untrammeled wilderness, plenty of which remains.

THE PEOPLE

When British Columbia joined the confederation to become a Canadian province in 1871, its population was only 36,000, and 27,000 of the residents were natives. With the completion of the Canadian Pacific Railway in 1885, immigration during the early 20th century, and the rapid industrial development after World War II, the provincial population burgeoned. Between 1951 and 1971 it doubled. Today 3.7 million people live in British Columbia (12 percent of Canada's total). The population is concentrated in the southwest, namely in Vancouver, on the south end of Vancouver Island, and in the Okanagan Valley. These three areas make up less than 1 percent of the province but account for 80 percent of the population. The overall population density is just 3.5 people per square kilometer.

British Columbia is second only to Alberta as Canada's fastest growing province. Annual population growth through the 1990s averaged 2.5 percent, against a national average of 1.1 percent. Around 60 percent of this population growth can be attributed to westward migration across the country. Retirees make up a large percentage of these new arrivals, as to a lesser extent do young professionals.

Around 40 percent of British Columbians are of British origin, followed by 30 percent of other European lineage, mostly French and German. To really get the British feeling, just spend some time in Victoria—a city that has retained its original English customs and traditions from days gone by. While the native peoples of British Columbia have adopted the technology and the ways of the European, they still remain a distinct group, contributing to and enriching the culture of the province. Asians have made up a significant percentage of the population since the mid-1800s, when they came in search of gold. More recently, the province saw an influx of settlers from Hong Kong prior to the 1997 transfer of control of that city from Britain to China. First Nations make up 3.7 percent of the population.

Language

The main language spoken throughout the province is English, though almost 6 percent of the population also speaks French, Canada's second official language. All government information is written in both English and French throughout Canada.

The natives of British Columbia fall into 10 major ethnic groups by language: Nootka (west Vancouver Island), Coast Salish (southwest B.C.), Interior Salish (southern interior), Kootenay (in the Kootenay region), Athabascan (in the central and northeastern regions), Bella Coola and Northern Kwakiutl (along the central west coast), Tsimshian (in the northwest), Haida (on the Queen Charlotte Islands), and Inland Tlingit (in the far northwest corner of the province). However, most natives still speak English more than their mother tongue.

Economy and Government

ECONOMY

British Columbia's economy has always relied on resource-based activities. The first indigenous people hunted the region's abundant wildlife and fished in its trout- and salmon-filled rivers. Then Europeans arrived on the scene, reaping a bounty by cutting down forests for timber and slaughtering the wildlife for its fur. Luckily, the province is blessed with a wealth of natural resources. In addition to timber and wildlife, B.C. holds rich reserves of minerals, petroleum, natural gas, and coal, and water for hydroelectric power is plentiful.

As rising population numbers have put ever-increasing demands on these resources, conservation measures have become necessary. The province has imposed fishing and hunting seasons and limits, a freeze on rezoning agricultural land, and mandatory reforestation regulations, and has restrained hydroelectric development to protect salmon runs. By preserving its superb physical environment, the province will continue to attract outdoor enthusiasts and visitors from around the world, ensuring a steady stream of tourism revenues. But the ongoing battle between concerned conservationists and profit-motivated developers continues.

Forestry

Almost two-thirds of British Columbia—some 60 million hectares—is forested, primarily in coniferous softwood (fir, hemlock, spruce, and pine). These forests provide about half the country's marketable wood and about 25 percent of the North American inventory. Along the coast the hemlock species is dominant; in the interior are forests of spruce and lodgepole pine. Douglas fir, balsam, and western red cedar

Almost two-thirds of British Columbia is forested, primarily in coniferous softwood. These forests provide about half the country's marketable wood and about 25 percent of the North American inventory. Around 75 million cubic meters of lumber are harvested annually. The forestry industry generates $10 billion annually in exports, more than all other industries combined.

are the other most valuable commercial trees. The provincial government owns 94 percent of the forestland, private companies own 5 percent, and the national government owns the remaining 1 percent. Private companies log much of the provincially owned forest under license from the government. Around 75 million cubic meters of lumber are harvested annually, directly employing 85,000 workers. The forestry industry generates $10 billion annually in exports, more than all other industries combined.

Forestry has been the mainstay of the economy in this century. But pressures on the industry are steadily increasing as the demand grows to preserve the forests for wildlife, recreation, and as a resource for following generations.

Tourism

Tourism has rapidly ascended in economic importance; it's now the second-largest industry and the province's largest employer (more than 100,000 are directly employed in the industry). This segment continues to grow, as more and more people become aware of B.C.'s outstanding scenery, its numerous national, provincial, historic, and regional parks, and the bountiful outdoor recreation activities available year-round. **Tourism BC** promotes British Columbia to the world; latest figures record 25.5 million annual "visitor nights" (the number of visitors multiplied by the number of nights they stayed within British Columbia). Official visitor numbers are broken down to show that four million visitors were Canadians from outside British Columbia, four million were from the United States, while one million visitors originated from outside North America (Japan, Great Britain, and Germany provided most of these).

Mining

British Columbia is a mineral-rich province, and historically mining has been an important part of the economy. Since the first Cariboo gold rush in the late 1850s, the face of the industry has changed dramatically. Until the mid-1900s, most mining was underground, but today open-pit mining is the preferred method of mineral extraction. The province is home to 26 major mines and three mineral processing plants that produce $3.6 billion worth of exports. Coal is the most valuable sector of the mining industry, accounting for $800 million of exports (most to Japan and other Asian markets). Other mining is for metals (such as copper, gold, zinc, silver, molybdenum, and lead), industrial minerals (sulfur, asbestos, limestone, gypsum, and others), and structural materials (sand, gravel, dimension stone, and cement). In northeastern B.C., drilling for petroleum and natural gas also helps fuel the economy.

Agriculture

Cultivated land is sparse in mountainous B.C.— only 4 percent of the province is arable, with just 25 percent of this land regarded as prime for agriculture. Nevertheless, agriculture is an important part of the provincial economy; 19,000 farms growing 200 different crops contribute $1.4 billion annually. The most valuable sector of the industry is dairy farming, which is worth $260 million (that works out to an output of 510 million liters of milk a year). The best land for dairy cattle is found in the lower Fraser Valley, on southeast Vancouver Island, and in the north Okanagan-Shuswap areas. Almost all of British Columbia's fruit crops are grown in the Okanagan Valley; apples are the best known produce, but a burgeoning viticulture industry relies on grapes from 44 vineyards. The province holds around 600,000 beef cattle, with these farms mainly found in the Cariboo, Chilcotin, Kamloops, Okanagan, and Kootenay regions. Although neighboring Alberta is renowned for its beef, Canada's largest ranch is operated by the Douglas Lake Cattle Co. near Merritt; 20,000 cattle are run on 200,000 hectares. Poultry farms, vegetables, bulbs, and ornamental shrubs are found mostly in the Fraser River Valley and the southern end of Vancouver Island, while the northern Peace River region is the provincial grain basket, supporting a mixture of cereal crops. Agriculture provides an estimated 55–60 percent of the food required for British Columbia's needs.

Fishing

Commercial fishing, one of B.C.'s principal industries, is worth $1 billion annually and comes

commercial halibut fishermen at work

© ANDREW HEMPSTEAD

INTRODUCTION

almost entirely from species that inhabit tidal waters. The province has 6,000 registered fishing boats and 600 fish farms. The industry concentrates on salmon (60 percent of total fishing revenues come from six species of salmon), with boats harvesting the five species indigenous to the Pacific Ocean and the aquaculture industry revolving around Atlantic salmon, which is more suited to farming. Other species harvested include herring, halibut, cod, sole, and a variety of shellfish, such as crabs. Canned and fresh fish are exported to markets all over the world—the province is considered the most productive fishing region in Canada. Japan is the largest export market, followed by Europe and the United States.

Recreational salt- and freshwater sportfishing for salmon, steelhead, and trout is also very popular. More than 600 licensed fishing guides, sportfishing lodges, and charter operators scattered throughout the province eagerly offer their services and expertise to both resident and nonresident fishing enthusiasts.

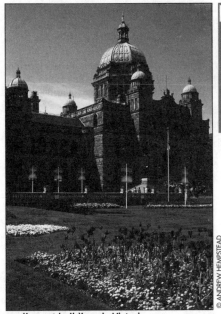

© ANDREW HEMPSTEAD

parliament buildings in Victoria

Film Industry

The film industry is the fastest-growing sector of the provincial economic pie; its value has quadrupled since 1997 to be worth $1.2 billion annually and to directly employ 35,000 locals. The province is ideal both as a location for shooting and as a production center (Vancouver ranks third behind only Los Angeles and New York as a production center, with 70 post-production facilities). Since the late 1970s more and more Hollywood production companies have discovered the beauty of B.C., its studio facilities, on-site production crews, and support services, as well as more recently a favorable exchange rate. The industry is overseen by the **BC Film Commission,** a government agency that can be contacted at 604/660-3569 or on the Internet at website www.bcfilmcommission.com.

Shipping and Maritime Commerce

The province boasts year-round ports, deep-sea international shipping lanes, log-towing vessels, specialized freight and passenger steamers, and all the requisite marine facilities. The United States

and Japan are B.C.'s main export and import trading partners.

GOVERNMENT

Canada is a constitutional monarchy. Its system of government is based on England's, and the British monarch is also king or queen of Canada. However, because it's an independent nation, the British monarchy and government have no control over the political affairs of Canada. An appointed **governor general** based in Ottawa represents the Crown, as does a **lieutenant governor** in each province. Both roles are mainly ceremonial, but their "royal assent" is required to make any bill passed by Cabinet into law.

Elected representatives debate and enact laws affecting their constituents. The head of the federal government is the **prime minister,** and the head of each provincial government is its **premier.** The **speaker** is elected at the first session of each parliament to make sure parliamentary rules are followed. A bill goes through three grueling sessions in the legislature—a reading, a debate, and a second reading. When all the fine print has been given the royal nod, the bill then becomes a law.

In the B.C. legislature, the lieutenant governor is at the top of the ladder. Under him are the members of the **Legislative Assembly** (MLAs). Assembly members are elected for a period of up to five years, though an election for a new assembly can be called at any time by the lieutenant governor or on the advice of the premier. In the Legislative Assembly are the premier, the cabinet ministers and backbenchers, the leader of the official opposition, other parties, and independent members. All Canadian citizens and B.C. residents 19 years old and over can vote, providing they've lived in the province for at least six months.

The current ruling party is Gordon Campbell's **Liberal Party,** which swept to power in April 2001. Provincial politics in British Columbia have traditionally been a two-party strug-gle. In the most recent election, the Liberals defeated the New Democrats (NDP), who came to be reviled by the business community for tax burdens that stalled the local economy. The NDP first came to prominence in the late 1960s as the official opposition to the **Social Credit Party** (Socreds), advocating free enterprise and government restraint, who had ruled the province for two decades. After a 1972 NDP election win, the support of these two parties seesawed back and forth until 1991, when the Social Credit Party was almost totally destroyed by a string of scandals that went as high as the premier, Bill Vander Zalm.

The laws of B.C. are administered by the cabinet, premier, and lieutenant governor; they are interpreted by a **judiciary** made up of the Supreme Court of B.C., Court of Appeal, and County or Provincial Courts.

For information on the provincial government, its ministries, and current issues, surf the web to www.gov.bc.ca.

On the Road

Recreation

The great outdoors: British Columbia certainly has plenty of it. The province encompasses some 948,600 square kilometers of land area and a convoluted coastline totaling 25,000 kilometers. With spectacular scenery around every bend, millions of hectares of parkland, and an abundance of wildlife, the province is an outdoorsperson's fantasy come true. Hiking, mountain climbing, fishing, hunting, boating, canoeing, white-water rafting, scuba diving, downhill and cross-country skiing—it's all here. For specific recreation information, contact **Tourism British Columbia**, P.O. Box 9830, Station Provincial Government, Victoria, BC V8W 9W5, 250/387-1642 or 800/435-5622, website www.hellobc.com.

HIKING

Just about everywhere you go in British Columbia you'll find good hiking opportunities, from short, easy walks in city and regional parks to long, strenuous hikes in wilderness parks.

The mountains are great places to hike. Short trails lead to waterfalls, lakes, rock formations, and viewpoints, and longer trails wander high into alpine meadows tangled with wildflowers, past turquoise lakes, and up to snow-dusted peaks providing breathtaking views. Rustic huts are provided at regular intervals along wilderness trails. Perhaps the best known of British Columbia's hikes lies not in the Rockies but along

© ANDREW HEMPSTEAD

Pacific Central Station, Vancouver's transportation hub

the wild and remote west shore of Vancouver Island; backpackers return time and again to the **West Coast Trail,** an unforgettable 77-km trek through Pacific Rim National Park.

To get the most out of a hiking trip, peruse the hiking section of any major bookstore—many books have been written on British Columbian hiking trails. Before setting off on a longer hike, study the trail guides and a topographical map of the area. Leave details of your intended route and itinerary with a relative or friend. And try to travel in groups of at least two in the backcountry.

CYCLING AND MOUNTAIN BIKING

Cycling is a great way to explore British Columbia. The casual pace allows riders time to stop and appreciate the scenery, wildlife, and flowers that can easily be overlooked at high speeds. Some of the most popular areas for cycling trips are the **Southern Gulf Islands** between Vancouver Island and the mainland (quiet, laid-back, loads of sunshine, rural scenery, and lots of artists), the **east coast of Vancouver Island** (following the Strait of Georgia past lazy beaches and bustling towns), the **Kootenays** (forest-clad mountains, deep lakes, curious old gold- and silver-mining communities, and ghost towns—good mountain-bike country), and the **Rockies** (outstanding mountain scenery second to none, abundant wildlife often right beside the highways, hot springs, and hiking trails). Rocky Mountain routes suit the intermediate to advanced cyclist.

For information on touring, racing, books, bicycle routes, or clubs, contact **Cycling B.C.,** 1367 W. Broadway, Suite 332, Vancouver, BC V6H 4A9, 604/737-3034, or the **Outdoor Recreation Council of B.C.,** Suite 334, 1367 W. Broadway, Vancouver, BC V6H 4A9, 604/737-3058. The Outdoor Recreation Council also publishes a series of maps covering much of

The mountains are great places to hike. Short trails lead to waterfalls, lakes, rock formations, and viewpoints, and longer trails wander high into alpine meadows tangled with wildflowers, past turquoise lakes, and up to snow-dusted peaks providing breathtaking views.

British Columbia. These maps can be purchased directly from the council or at many sporting goods stores and bookstores.

Cycling Tours

Several companies offer cycling tours, among them: **Benno's Adventure Tours,** 604/738-5105, which offers eight-day trips through B.C. and the Canadian Rockies; **Whistler Backroads,** 604/923-3111, website www.whistlermountainbiking.com, through the Whistler Valley and beyond; **Okanagan Mountain Bike Tours,** 250/766-5124 or 800/683-1223, website www.okbiketours.com, through the orchards and wineries of the Okanagan Valley; **Backroads,** 510/527-1555 or 800/462-2848, website www.backroads.com, in the Canadian Rockies and island-hopping through the Southern Gulf Islands; and **Vermont Bike Tours,** 800/245-3868, website www.vbt.com, which offers luxury overnight accommodations on its tours through Yoho and Kootenay National Parks.

ON THE WATER
Canoeing and Kayaking

Canoes are a traditional form of transportation along British Columbia's numerous lakes and rivers. You can rent one at many of the more popular lakes, but if you bring your own you can slip into any body of water whenever you please, taking in the scenery and viewing wildlife from water level. One of the most popular canoe routes is in **Bowron Lake Provincial Park,** where a 117-km-long circuit leads through a chain of lakes in the Cariboo Mountains. Shorter but no less challenging is the **Powell Forest Canoe Route,** on the Sunshine Coast. Other, less-traveled destinations include **Slocan Lake, Wells Gray Provincial Park,** and the **Stikine River.** For information on canoe routes, courses, and clubs, contact the **Outdoor Recreation**

Council of B.C., Suite 334, 1367 W. Broadway, Vancouver, BC V6H 4A9, 604/737-3058.

Anywhere suitable for canoeing is also prime kayaking territory, although most keen kayakers look for white-water excitement. The best wilderness kayaking experiences are in the north, where access can be difficult but crowds are minimal. The **Stikine River** is challenging, with one stretch—the Grand Canyon of the Stikine—successfully run only a handful of times.

The province's long coastline is great for sea kayaking, and rentals are available in most coastal communities. The **Gulf Islands** are ideal for kayakers of all experience levels, while destinations such as **Desolation Sound**, the **Broken Group Islands**, and the **Queen Charlotte Islands** are the domain of experienced paddlers. Most outfits offering kayak rentals also provide lessons and often tours. One such Vancouver operation is the **Ecomarine Ocean Kayak Centre**, 604/689-7575, based on Granville Island. Tofino, on Vancouver Island's west coast, is a mecca for sea kayakers. Here, **Tofino Sea Kayaking Company**, 250/725-4222 or 800/863-4664, website www.tofino-kayaking.com, rents kayaks and leads tours through local waterways. **Northern Lights**

NATIONAL PARK PASSES

Permits are required for entry into all Canadian national parks. A **National Parks Day Pass** is adult $5, senior $4, child $2 to a maximum of $10 per vehicle. The day pass is valid until 4 P.M. the day following its purchase. The **Western Canada Annual Pass,** good for entry to British Columbia national parks as well as those in Alberta, Saskatchewan, and Manitoba, is adult $35, senior $27 to a maximum of $70 per vehicle ($54 for two or more seniors). Both types of passes are available at park gates, at all park information centers, and at campground fee stations. Day passes are also available from automated ticket machines at popular stopping points in Pacific Rim National Park. Annual passes can also be bought by calling 800/748-7275 or online at the Parks Canada website, www.parkscanada.gc.ca.

Expeditions, 360/734-6334 or 800/754-7402, website www.seakayaking.com, specializes in overnight expeditions along the B.C. coast. Each Northern Lights trip features three knowledgeable guides, all necessary equipment, and an emphasis on gourmet meals, such as shoreline salmon bakes, complete with wine and freshly baked breads. The six-day trip through the Strait of Georgia is US$1,295, but Northern Lights also offers other trips, including the luxury of a yacht-based trip for US$1,320.

White-Water Rafting

The best and easiest way to experience a white-water rafting trip is on a half- or full-day trip with a qualified guide. Close to Vancouver, the **Green, Fraser, Nahatlatch,** and **Thompson Rivers** are run commercially. In the Rockies, the **Kicking Horse River** provides the thrills. Expect to pay $90–100 for a full day's excitement, transfers, and lunch.

No experience is needed for most extended river trips. Close to Vancouver, the classic of these runs the Chilko, Chilcotin, then Fraser Rivers and lasts up to two weeks. In the far north of the province, the Tatshenshini and Alsek Rivers are a popular destination. **Canadian River Expeditions,** 604/938-6651 or 800/898-7238, website www.canriver.com, Canada's oldest rafting company, offers trips to both destinations from $1,300 and $2,900 respectively.

Boating

British Columbia's 25,000 km of coastline, in particular the sheltered, island-dotted Strait of Georgia between Vancouver Island and the mainland, is a boater's paradise. Along it are sheltered coves, sandy beaches, beautiful marine parks, and facilities specifically designed for boaters—many accessible only by water. One of the most beautiful marine parks is **Desolation Sound,** north of Powell River; locals claim it's one of the world's best cruising grounds. Many of the enormous freshwater lakes inland are also excellent places for boating.

For the entire rundown on facilities for boaters, pick up a copy of the invaluable *Pacific Yachting Cruising Services Directory,* put out by *Pacific*

for a one-year license, or $25 for a six-day license. Separate licenses are required for steelhead and Kootenay Lake rainbow trout. For more information contact the Ministry of Agriculture, Food, and Fisheries, 250/387-4573, and request the *Freshwater Fishing Regulations Synopsis*. These regulations are also online at website www.gov.bc.ca/wgf.

Tidal

The tidal waters of British Columbia hold some of the world's best fishing, which can be accessed on a day trip from remote lodges scattered along the coast catering to all budgets. The five species of Pacific salmon are most highly prized by anglers. The chinook (king) salmon in particular is the trophy fish of choice. They commonly weigh over 10 kg and are occasionally caught at over 20 kg (those weighing over 12 kg are often known as "tyee"). Other salmon present are coho (silver), pink (humpback), sockeye (red), and chum (dog). Other species sought by local recreational anglers include halibut, ling cod, rockfish, cod, perch, and snapper.

A resident tidal-water sportfishing license, good for one year from 31 March, costs $22.47 ($11.77 for those 65 and over); for nonresidents of British Columbia, the same license costs $108.07, or pay $7.49 for a single-day license, $20.33 for three days, or $34.17 for five days. A **salmon conservation stamp** is an additional $6.42. Licenses are available from sporting stores, gas stations, marinas, and charter operators. When fish-tagging programs are on, you may be required to make a note of the date, location, and method of capture, or to record on the back of your license statistical information on the fish you catch. Read the current rules and regulations. For further information contact **Fisheries and Oceans Canada,** 604/666-0561, website www.pac.dfo-mpo.gc.ca.

The **Sport Fishing Institute of British Columbia,** 604/689-3438, website www.sportfishing.bc.ca, produces an annual magazine (free), *Sport Fishing,* that lists charter operators and fishing lodges and details license requirements.

GOLFING

Relative to the rest of Canada, British Columbia's climate is ideal for golfing, especially on Vancouver Island, where the sport can be enjoyed year-round. Many of the province's 280 courses are in spectacular mountain, ocean, or lake settings. Municipal courses offer the lowest greens fees, generally $10–25, but the semiprivate, private, and resort courses usually boast the most spectacular locations. At these courses, greens fees can be as high as $175. At all but the smallest municipal courses, club rentals, power carts, and lessons are available, and at all but the most exclusive city courses, nonmembers are welcomed with open arms. The mild climate and abundance of water create ideal conditions for the upkeep of golf courses in the south of the province—you'll be surprised at how immaculately manicured most are. (In the north, many courses have oil-soaked or artificial grass greens to make upkeep easier.) The best place to check out the province's golf offerings is at the excellent website www.golfbc.com.

> *Relative to the rest of Canada, British Columbia's climate is ideal for golfing, especially on Vancouver Island, where the sport can be enjoyed year-round. Many of the province's 280 courses are in spectacular mountain, ocean, or lake settings.*

SKIING AND SNOWBOARDING

Most of the developed winter recreation areas are in the southern third of the province. Whether you're a total beginner or an advanced daredevil, British Columbian resorts have a slope to suit you. The price of lift tickets is generally reasonable, and at the smaller, lesser-known resorts, you don't have to spend half your day lining up for the lifts.

The best known of all Canadian winter resorts is **Whistler/Blackcomb,** north of Vancouver, but others scattered through the southern interior provide world-class skiing and boarding

British Columbia holds some of North America's finest ski slopes.

© ANDREW HEMPSTEAD

on just-as-challenging slopes. The best of these include: **Big White Ski Resort** and **Silver Star Mountain Resort** in the Okanagan Valley; **Red Mountain** and **Whitewater** near Nelson; **Fernie Alpine Resort** near Fernie; **Panorama Resort** near Invermere; and **Sun Peaks Resort** north of Kamloops. In the north of the province, **Powder King Mountain Resort,** north of Prince George, lives up to its name with an average annual snowfall around 12 meters (among the highest of any North American resort). You can even go skiing and boarding out on Vancouver Island at **Mount Washington** or **Forbidden Plateau.**

Heli- and Sno-Cat Skiing and Boarding

Alternatives to resorts are also available. If you're an intermediate or advanced skier or snowboarder, you can go heli-skiing and heli-boarding in the mind-boggling scenery and deep, untracked powder of the Coast and Chilcotin Ranges, the central Cariboo Mountains, the Bugaboos, and the Canadian Rockies. The world's largest heli-ski operation is **CMH Heli-skiing,** 403/762-7100 or 800/661-0252, website www.cmhski.com, founded by Austrian mountain guide Hans Gmoser in the Bugaboos in 1965. Today the operation has grown to include almost limitless terrain over five mountain ranges accessed from 11 lodges. **Mike Wiegele Helicopter Skiing,** 250/673-8381 or 800/661-9170, offers heli-skiing and heli-boarding in the Monashee and Cariboo Mountains from a luxurious lodge at Blue River. From Panorama Resort, near Invermere, **R.K. Heli-ski,** 250/342-3889 or 800/661-6060, website www.rkheliski .com, offers heli-skiing day trips, one of the only operators to do so.

Another, less-expensive alternative is to hook up with one of the many Sno-Cat operations in the province. Sno-Cats are tracked, all-terrain vehicles that can transport skiers and boarders up through the snow to virgin slopes in high-country wilderness (similar to snow groomers but capable of carrying passengers). British Columbia has been a world leader in this type of skiing, and many operators are scattered through the province. Revelstoke is the Sno-Cat capital of the province. In this central B.C. town, **CAT Powder Skiing,** 250/837-5151 or 877/422-8754, website www.catpowder.com, offers day trips or overnight packages from its Revelstoke base. Through its location amid some of the continent's most consistent powder snow and because of high-profile part owners (Scott Schmidt and Craig Kelly), **Island Lake Lodge,** near Fernie, 250/423-3700 or 888/422-8754, website www.islandlakelodge.com, has gained a reputation for both its Sno-Cat skiing and its luxurious lodgings.

ENTERTAINMENT
Museums
The best way to gain an appreciation of British Columbia's unique and colorful history is by visiting its museums. Almost every town has a small museum showcasing the surrounding area, but the larger facilities attract the most attention. In the capital, Victoria, don't miss the **Royal British**

ON THE ROAD

Columbia Museum, a magnificent facility that catalogs the province's entire natural and human history. In Vancouver, the **Museum of Anthropology** boasts a fantastic collection of totem poles and other native artifacts. Outside of the major cities, museums generally reflect local heritage; pick of the bunch are the **Historic O'Keefe Ranch** outside Vernon, the **Museum of Northern British Columbia** in Prince Rupert, and the **Haida Gwaii Museum** out on the Queen Charlotte Islands.

Performing Arts

British Columbia's largest city boasts a lively performing-arts community; more than 30 theater groups call Vancouver home, and the city also supports an opera, an orchestra, and Ballet British Columbia. Vancouver's magnificent **Ford Centre** hosts world-class productions. Victoria, Kamloops, and Prince George also have noteworthy performing-arts communities.

SHOPPING FOR NATIVE ARTS AND CRAFTS

Indigenous artistry tends to fall into one of two categories: "arts" such as woodcarving and painting, argillite carving, jade- and silverwork, and totem restoration (all generally attended to by the men), and "handicrafts" such as basketry, weaving, beadwork, skinwork, sewing, and knitting (generally created by the women). Today, all of these arts and crafts contribute significant income to First Nations communities.

Painting and woodcarving are probably the most recognized art forms of the northern west coast tribes. Throughout B.C.—in museums and people's homes, outdoors, and of course in all the shops—you can see brightly colored carved totems, canoes, paddles, fantastic masks, and ceremonial rattles, feast dishes, bowls, and spoons. Fabulous designs, many featuring animals or mythical legends, are also painstakingly painted in bright primary colors on paper. You can buy limited-edition, high-quality prints of these paintings at many Indian craft outlets. They are more reasonable in cost than carvings, yet just as stunning when effectively framed.

Basketry comes in a variety of styles and materials. Watch for decorative cedar-root (fairly rare) and cedar-bark baskets, still made on the west coast of Vancouver Island; spruce-root baskets from the Queen Charlotte Islands; and beautiful, functional, birch-bark baskets from the Hazelton area, between Prince George and Prince Rupert.

Beaded and fringed moccasins, jackets, vests, and gloves are available at most craft outlets. And all outdoorspersons should consider forking out for a heavy, water-resistant, raw sheep-wool sweater; they're generally white or gray with a black design, and much in demand because they're warm, good in the rain, rugged, and last longer than one lifetime. One of the best places to get your hands on one is the Cowichan Valley on Vancouver Island, although you can also find them in the Fraser Valley from Vancouver to Lytton and in native craft outlets. Expect to pay around $90–160 for the real thing, more in tourist shops.

Carved argillite (black slate) miniature totem poles, brooches, ashtrays, and other small items, highly decorated with geometric and animal designs, are created exclusively by the Haida on the Queen Charlotte Islands; the argillite comes from a quarry near Skidegate and can only be used by the Skidegate band. You can find argillite carvings in Skidegate and in craft shops in Prince Rupert, Victoria, and Vancouver. Silverwork is also popular, and some of the best is created by the Haida. Particularly notable is the work of Bill Reid, a Haida artist living in Vancouver. Jade jewelry can be seen in the Lillooet and Lytton areas.

FESTIVALS AND EVENTS

British Columbia seems to have at least one festival or event going on somewhere in the province every day of the year. To make sure you don't miss anything, stop by one of the province's many Visitor Info Centres at the beginning of your trip and pick up a current copy of *Arts and Entertainment,* a brochure produced by Tourism BC.

Many of the most popular festivals are held

during summer, the peak visitor season, but special events and artistic performances take place year-round. Many towns hold winter events featuring zany happenings such as snow golf, bed races on ice, and anything they can come up with that's good for a laugh. The following section lists some provincial event highlights; see the Festivals and Events sections of the particular town listings in this book for more.

Vancouver and Vicinity

Raise a toast to the beginning of a packed festival season at the **Vancouver Playhouse International Wine Festival,** in early April. Later in the month, the world's best freestylers gather at Whistler for the **World Ski & Snowboard Festival.** Kids of all ages will love the late May **Vancouver International Children's Festival** at Vanier Park. Around the last week of June, check out the **Vancouver International Jazz Festival,** held at venues all across town. July is a festival-filled month, starting on the first with a **Canada Day** salmon barbecue at seaside Steveston. Two weeks later the **Vancouver Folk Music Festival** comes to town. One of Vancouver's best attended events is the **Festival of Light,** a magnificent musical fireworks display over four nights in early August. In mid-August, Abbotsford hosts the **Abbotsford International Airshow.** The following month Harrison Hot Springs hosts the **Harrisand World Championship Sand Sculpture Competition.**

Vancouver Island

Many of Victoria's most popular events are music-related, including the **TerrifVic Jazz Party** the third weekend of April, the **FolkFest** in late June, and the **Rootsfest** one month later. North of Victoria, the fishing town of Port Alberni hosts a **salmon derby** the first weekend of September. In late March, Tofino's **Pacific Rim Whale Festival** coincides with the spring migration of whales along the B.C. coast. In July, crowds gather along the Nanaimo foreshore for the annual **World Championship Bathtub Race,** with competitors racing around local waters in motorized bathtubs. In early August,

attend the artistic **Filberg Festival,** a juried craft show at Comox.

Okanagan and the Kootenays

Many of the Okanagan's biggest festivals relate to the harvest of local crops. The first of these is the **Spring Wine Festival** throughout the valley's wineries in late April. Following closely is the **Apple Blossom Festival** in Penticton every May. The **Spring Wine Festival** is hosted by venues along the valley through May, but the year's biggest vino gathering is for the **Fall Wine Festival,** which showcases local wines to the world through early October. Some celebrations are on a smaller scale, such as the October Pumpkin Festival at Davison Orchards, on the outskirts of Vernon.

In the Kootenays, big events include Cranbrook's **Sam Steele Days** in the latter half of June. Kimberley's **International Old Time Accordion Championship** attracts a mass of accordion players to the Bavarian city each July. The **Nelson Artwalk** is set up each summer, with art displays across the city.

Central and Northern British Columbia

If you're spending a summer's night in Revelstoke, grab a chair and make your way downtown for free evening concerts in the local bandshell. Another summer-long musical event is **Two River Junction,** a nightly musical revue in Kamloops. Rodeos take place throughout the province in summer, but the biggest is the **Williams Lake Stampede** on the first weekend of July. (For a full rodeo schedule, contact the Canadian Professional Rodeo Association, 403/250-7440, website www.rodeocanada .com.) Quesnel celebrates the historical importance of the gold rush the third weekend of July during **Billy Barker Days.**

Two **winter carnivals** help Prince George locals get through the long winter, but the city's largest get-together is the **Forest Expo;** held in May on even-numbered years, it's North America's biggest forestry exposition. The following month, Prince Rupert celebrates **Seafest** with a multitude of zany water-based events. Dawson

Creek's biggest annual event is **Mile Zero Celebrations** in May. The **Dawson Creek Rodeo,** the second weekend of August, is one of the province's biggest.

Holidays

British Columbia celebrates 10 statutory holidays, on which most businesses are closed. But you can always find open some restaurants, pubs, and a few stores selling basic necessities.

The officially recognized holidays are: **New Year's Day,** 1 January; **Good Friday,** March or April; **Victoria Day,** closest Monday to 24 May; **Canada Day,** 1 July; **B.C. Day,** first Monday in August; **Labour Day,** first Monday in September; **Thanksgiving,** second Monday in October; **Remembrance Day,** 11 November (only banks and government offices are closed); **Christmas Day,** 25 December; and **Boxing Day,** 26 December.

Accommodations and Food

HOTELS AND MOTELS

The best guide to hotels and motels is the free *Accommodations* book put out annually by Tourism BC. It's available at all information centers, from the website www.hellobc.com, or by calling 250/387-1642 or 800/435-5622. The book lists hotels, motels, lodges, resorts, bed and breakfasts, and campgrounds. It contains no ratings, simply listings with facilities and rates.

All rates quoted in this book are for a double room in the high season (summer, except in winter resort towns). Expect to pay less for downtown accommodations on weekends, and less outside of the busy July–Aug. period. To all rates quoted, you must add the following taxes: an 8 percent provincial hotel tax, a 7 percent goods and services tax, and in many cases a 2 percent local tourism/hotel tax. The GST is refundable to non-Canadian visitors.

Prices for a basic motel room in a small town start at $40 s, $45 d. In Vancouver and Victoria expect to pay at least double this amount for the least expensive rooms. The most luxurious lodgings in the province—Vancouver's Pan Pacific Hotel Vancouver, Victoria's grand old Fairmont Empress, or any one of Whistler's resort hotels, for example—charge over $250 per night for a basic room. Room rates outside the two major cities fluctuate greatly. For example, few lodgings on Vancouver Island charge less than $70, but along the TransCanada Highway, in places like Kamloops and Revelstoke, you can pay as little as $45 for a room. Try to plan ahead for summer travel and book as far in advance as possible, especially for accommodations in Vancouver and Prince Rupert, on Vancouver Island, and on the Queen Charlotte Islands.

Making Reservations

Rates quoted in this book are for a standard double room through the high season, which generally extends from June to early September (except in alpine resort towns such as Whistler). Almost all accommodations are less expensive outside of these busy months, some cutting their rates by as much as 50 percent. You'll enjoy the biggest seasonal discounts at properties that rely on summer tourists, such as those in Vancouver, on Vancouver Island, and the Okanagan Valley. The same applies in Vancouver and to a lesser extent Victoria on weekends—many of big downtown hotels rely on business and convention travelers to fill a bulk of their rooms; when the end of the week rolls down, the hotels are left with rooms to fill at discounted rates Friday, Saturday, and Sunday nights.

While you have no influence over the seasonal and weekday/weekend pricing differences detailed above, *how* you reserve a room *can* make a difference in how much you pay. First and foremost, when it comes to searching out actual rates, the Internet is an invaluable tool. Tourism British Columbia offers discounted rates through its toll-free number (800/435-5622) and the website www.hellobc.com. All hotel websites listed in *Moon Handbooks: British Columbia* show rates and have online reservation forms. Use these websites to search out specials, many of which are available only on the Internet.

Most hotels offer auto association members an automatic 10 percent discount, and whereas senior discounts apply only to those over 60 or 65 on public transportation and at attractions, most hotels offer discounts to those aged over 50, with chains such as Best Western also allowing senior travelers a late checkout. "Corporate Rates" are a lot more flexible than in years gone past; some hotels require nothing more than the flash of a business card for a 10–20 percent discount.

When it comes to frequent flyer programs, you really do need to be a frequent flyer to achieve free flights, but the various loyalty programs offered by hotels often provide benefits simply for signing up.

BED AND BREAKFASTS

Bed-and-breakfast accommodations are found throughout British Columbia. Staying at this type of accommodation is great way to meet British Columbians. They are usually private residences, with up to four guest rooms, and as the name suggests breakfast is included. Rates fluctuate enormously. In Vancouver and Victoria they range $60–180 s, $70–210 d. Guests can expect hearty home cooking, a peaceful atmosphere, personal service, knowledgeable hosts, and conversation with fellow travelers. On the downside, facilities and the amount of privacy afforded can vary greatly. This uncertainty as to what to expect upon arrival can be off-putting for many people, especially sharing a bathroom with other guests—which is both a common and accepted practice in European bed and breakfasts. If having a bathroom to yourself is important to you, clarify with the bed and breakfast operator when reserving. To ease confusion in terms used, the Western Canadian Bed and Breakfast Innkeepers Association offers the following descriptions:

Ensuite: Refers to a bathroom that is private, inside, and attached to the sleeping unit (literally "in suite").

Private: A bathroom that is for the sole use of a sleeping unit but may be outside of the room.

Shared or **Semi-Private:** Bathrooms that are used in common by more than one room. No more than two guest rooms should share a single bathroom.

Western Canadian Bed and Breakfast Innkeepers Association

This association, at P.O. Box 74534, 2803 W. 4th Ave., Vancouver, BC V6K 4P4, 604/255-9199, website www.wcbbia.com, represents more than 140 bed and breakfasts across the province. The association produces an informative brochure with simple descriptions and a color photo of each property, but it doesn't take bookings. Many bed and breakfasts are listed in the *Accommodations* guide, and local information centers provide information and often make bookings.

Reservation Agencies

Bed-and-breakfast agencies maintain lists of offerings, including city homes, rural homes, homes with sea views, or farms where you can join in the activities. Call and tell them what you're looking for and the price you're prepared to pay, and they'll find the right place for you. Get details from the following associations: **AB&C B&B of Vancouver,** 4390 Frances St., Vancouver, BC V5C 2R3, 604/298-8815 or 800/488-1941, website www.vancouverbandb.bc.ca.; **Beachside B&B Registry,** 4208 Evergreen Ave., West Vancouver, BC V7V 1H1, 604/922-7773 or 800/563-3311, website www.beach.bc.ca; and **Old English B&B Registry,** 1226 Silverwood Crescent, North Vancouver, BC V7P 1J3, 604/986-5069, website www.oldenglish bandb.com. Beachside B&B Registry promotes the excellent bed and breakfast of the same name but also provides links to others on its website.

In the world of the Internet, **Bed and Breakfast Online,** website www.bbcanada.com, is an old-timer, having been online since 1995. You can't make bookings through this company, but links are provided and an ingenious search engine helps you find the accommodation that best fits your needs.

BACKPACKER ACCOMMODATIONS

Budget travelers are enjoying more and more options in British Columbia, ranging from a converted downtown Vancouver hotel to a treehouse on Salt Spring Island, all for around $20 per person per night. Hostelling International (formerly the Youth Hostel Association) has undergone a radical change in direction and now appeals to all ages, and privately run "hostels" within the province fill the gaps. Either way, staying in what have universally become known as "backpackers" hostels is an enjoyable and inexpensive way to travel through the province. Generally, you need to provide your own sleeping bag or linen, but most hostels supply extra bedding (if needed) at no charge. Accommodations are in dormitories (2–10 beds) or double rooms. Each also offers a communal kitchen, lounge area, and laundry facilities, while some have Internet access, bike rentals, and organized tours.

Hostelling International

The curfews and chores are long gone in this worldwide nonprofit organization of 4,200 hostels in 60 countries. Hostelling International Canada operates 18 hostels in British Columbia, including two in Vancouver and one in each of the following locations: Victoria, Salt Spring Island, Pender Island, Tofino, Whistler, Penticton, Kelowna, Vernon, Nelson, Rossland, Cranbrook, Fernie, Yoho National Park, Squilax, Revelstoke, and Kamloops. For a dorm bed, members of Hostelling International pay $14–22 per night, nonmembers pay $20–32; single and double rooms are often available but are more expensive.

You don't *have* to be a member to stay in an affiliated hostel of Hostelling International, but membership pays for itself after only a few nights of discounted lodging. Aside from discounted rates, benefits of membership vary from country to country but often include discounted air, rail, and bus travel; discounts on car rental; and discounts on some attractions and commercial activities. For Canadians, the membership charge is $35 annually, or $175 for a lifetime membership. For more information write Hostelling In-

ternational, 402-134 Abbott St., Vancouver, BC V6B 2K4, call 604/684-7101 or 800/661-0020, or surf the Internet to www.hihostels.com. The Canadian head office is at 400-205 Catherine St., Ottawa, ON K2P 1C3, 613/237-7884, website www.hihostels.ca. Another handy website is www.hostels.bc.ca, which highlights the Revelstoke hostel but provides links to others across the province.

Joining the Hostelling International affiliate of your home country entitles you to reciprocal rights in Canada, as well around the world. In the United States the contact address is **Hostelling International—American Youth Hostels,** Suite 840, 733 15th St. NW, Washington, DC 20005, 202/783-6161, website www.hiayh.org; annual membership is adult US$25 and senior US$15, or become a lifetime member for US$250.

Other contact addresses include: **YHA England and Wales,** Trevelyan House, St. Stephen's Hill, St. Albans, Herts. AL1 2DY, England, (0170) 870-8808, website www.yha.org.uk; **YHA Australia,** based in all capital cities, including at 422 Kent St., Sydney, NSW 2000, Australia, (02) 9261-1111, website www.yha.com; and **YHA New Zealand,** P.O. Box 436, Christchurch, (03) 379-9970, website www.yha.org.nz. For other countries, click through the links on the International Youth Hostel Federation website, www.iyhf.com, to your country of choice.

Other Backpacker Accommodations

In recent years, many privately run backpacker accommodations have come under the wing of Hostelling International, and they must meet a certain standard to do so. The locations are listed above. Standards of those that stand alone vary considerably, but are generally excellent, ranging from old motels to purposely built additions to existing lodges. They can be found in Vancouver, along the east coast of Vancouver Island, Whistler, Kelowna, and on the Queen Charlotte Islands.

CAMPING

Almost every town in British Columbia has at least one campground, often with showers and water, electricity, and sewer hookups. Prices range $8–17.50 in smaller towns, and up to $30 in the cities and more popular tourist destinations. If you're planning a summer trip to Vancouver, Vancouver Island, the Sunshine Coast, Whistler, or the Okanagan Valley, you should try to book in advance. At other times and places, advance reservations aren't usually necessary.

National parks provide some of the nicest campgrounds in B.C. All have picnic tables, fire grates, toilets, and fresh drinking water, although only some provide showers. Prices range $7–17 depending on facilities and services. They are all open through summer, with each park having one area designated for winter camping. Parks Canada now charges $6 per person per night for backcountry camping in national parks.

You'll find 13,800 campsites scattered through 344 campgrounds in 275 provincial parks. Rates range $9–18.50 a night depending on facilities, most of which are basic. The fee is collected in different ways at different parks, but it's always *cash only*. Reserve a spot at the 60 most popular provincial parks by calling BC Parks' Discover Camping hotline at 604/689-9025 or 800/689-9025, website www .discovercamping.ca. Reservations are taken between 15 March and 15 September for dates up to three months in advance. The reservation fee is $6.42 per night, to a maximum of $19.26, and is in addition to applicable camping fees.

Until recently campers enjoyed the use of over 1,400 **Forest Service Campgrounds** scattered throughout British Columbia for free. In April 1999, the Ministry of Forests began charging a fee of $8–10 per site per night, which is collected on-site. A better option is the annual camping pass, which is a bargain at $27. Few of the campgrounds are signposted, and facilities comprise nothing more than pit toilets and a few picnic tables. For a list of site locations, pick up a Forest District recreation map

from local information centers or surf the Internet to www.gov.bc.ca/for.

Commercial and provincial park campgrounds are listed in Tourism BC's invaluable *Accommodations* guide, available at all information centers, online at website www.hellobc.com, or by calling 250/387-1642 or 800/435-5622.

FOOD AND DRINK

British Columbia is not world-renowned for its culinary delights, but the province does offer excellent **West Coast** cuisine (also called fusion cooking), meaning an abundance of seafood and fresh produce prepared with an Asian influence. Otherwise, Canadian food is similar to American food—in general, bland and not very interesting. Burgers, hot dogs, chicken-in-a-box, and ready-made sandwiches are available across the province. In the large cities, you'll also find fine-dining restaurants and gourmet continental cuisine. Vancouver is the best place to eat; the city's 3,000-odd eateries serve a wide variety of ethnic foods and standard Canadiana at a complete range of prices. Victoria also enjoys its share of good restaurants, but it has the reputation of serving predominantly British food in as British an atmosphere as you could imagine outside of Britain.

Drink

British Columbian **wine** is highly regarded, having won awards throughout the world. The province is one of the few places in the world capable of producing **ice wines,** made by a process in which the grapes aren't harvested until *after* the first frost; the frost splits the skins and the fermentation process begins with the grapes still on the vine. These concentrated juices from classic varietals such as Riesling and Gewürztraminer create a super-sweet wine. Ice wine is generally marketed in a distinctively narrow 375-ml bottle and promoted as a dessert wine. The province holds four wine-growing

> *British Columbia produces ice wines, made by a process in which the grapes aren't harvested until after the first frost; the frost splits the skins and the fermentation process begins with the grapes still on the vine. These concentrated juices create a super-sweet dessert wine.*

ON THE ROAD

© ANDREW HEMPSTEAD

Kokanee, British Columbia's best-loved beer, is brewed in Creston.

regions. The largest concentration of B.C.'s 46 vineyards is in the Okanagan Valley, with more than 35 wineries ranging from large-scale commercial operations to small plots of grapes grown on hobby farms. Vancouver Island, the Fraser Valley, and the Similkameen Valley are also home to a number of wineries. Expect to pay $15–24 for a bottle of locally produced wine. For more information on the province's wine industry contact the **B.C. Wine Information Centre,** 250/490-2006.

All the popular Canadian and American beers are available at bars and liquor stores. **Kokanee,** brewed in Creston and widely available throughout British Columbia, is a fine-tasting beer that should be taken on all camping trips.

The legal drinking age varies throughout Canada. In British Columbia it is 19.

Getting There

AIR

Vancouver International Airport (YVR) is British Columbia's main gateway and Canada's second-busiest airport. Regularly scheduled service to and from Vancouver is offered by major airlines throughout the world. Victoria may be the capital, but it comes in a distant second when it comes to international flights; the only destinations served from its international airport are major Canadian cities and Seattle.

Air Canada

After merging with Canadian Airlines in 2000, Air Canada, 604/688-5515 or 888/247-2262, website www.aircanada.ca, became one of the world's largest airlines, serving five continents. It offers direct flights to Vancouver from the following North American cities: Whitehorse, Calgary, Edmonton, Winnipeg, Toronto, Ottawa, Montreal, Halifax, Boston, Chicago, Dallas, Denver, Honolulu, Los Angeles, New York (JFK), Portland, San Francisco, Seattle, Spokane, and Washington, D.C. From Europe, Air Canada flies direct from London to Vancouver, and from other major cities via Toronto. From the South Pacific, Air Canada

operates flights via Honolulu from Sydney and in alliance with Air New Zealand from Auckland and other South Pacific islands to Honolulu, where passengers change to an Air Canada plane for the flight to Vancouver. Asian cities, served by direct Air Canada flights from Vancouver, include Beijing, Hong Kong, Nagoya, Osaka, Seoul, Shanghai, Taipei, and Tokyo. Air Canada's flights originating in the South American cities of Santiago, Buenos Aires, Sao Paulo, and Rio de Janeiro are routed through Toronto.

Other Canadian Airlines

WestJet, 604/606-5525 or 800/538-5696, website www.westjet.com, is a budget-priced airline, with specials advertised year-round. Based in Calgary, its western hub is the airport at Abbotsford, 72 km east of downtown. As well as to major regional centers across the province, flights to Vancouver originate in Calgary, Edmonton, Saskatoon, Regina, Thunder Bay, Hamilton, Ottawa, and as far east as St. Johns.

U.S. Airlines

Air Canada (see above) offers the most flights into Vancouver from the United States, but the city is also served by the following U.S. carriers: **Alaska Airlines,** 800/252-7522, website www.alaskaair.com, from Las Vegas, Los Angeles, Palm Springs, Phoenix, and San Francisco; **American Airlines,** 800/433-7300, website www.aa.com, from Dallas and St. Louis; **Continental Airlines,** 800/231-0856, website www.continental.com, from its Houston hub and New York; **Horizon Air,** 800/547-9308, website www.horizonair.com, from nearby Portland and Seattle; **Northwest Airlines,** 800/225-2525, website www.nwa.com, from Detroit and Minneapolis; **Skywest,** 800/221-1212, website www.skywest.com, from throughout the western states with connections through Seattle; and finally **United Airlines,** 800/241-6522, website www.ual.com,

DEPARTURE TAXES

The federal government imposes a tax of 7 percent of the ticket price plus $6 to a maximum of $55 on all flights departing Canada for the United States. For all other international destinations, the departure tax is set at $55. These taxes are generally included in the ticket purchase price, but it pays to ask when booking.

Additionally, all passengers departing Vancouver must pay an **Airport Improvement Fee.** The "fee" on flights destined for all points within British Columbia and the Yukon is $5, elsewhere in North America it's $10, and for all other international flights it's $15. Pay the fee at the vending machines or at the desk beside the security check.

ON THE ROAD

CUTTING FLIGHT COSTS

In today's topsy-turvy world of air travel, finding the cheapest fare and best-suited route can be a challenge. The Internet has changed the way many people shop for tickets, but even if you use this invaluable tool for preliminary research, having a travel agent that you are comfortable dealing with—who takes the time to call around, does some research to get you the best fare, and helps you take advantage of any available special offers or promotional deals—is an invaluable asset in starting your travels off on the right foot.

In the first instance, though, to get an idea of what your agent should be able to come up with, call the airlines or check their websites and compare fares. Also look in the travel sections of major newspapers, particularly in weekend editions, where budget fares and package deals are frequently advertised.

Within Canada, **Travel Cuts,** website www.travelcuts.com, and **Flight Centre,** website www.flightcentre.ca, both with offices in all major cities, consistently offer the lowest airfares available, with the latter guaranteeing the lowest. Flight Centre offers a similar guarantee from its U.S. offices (877/967-5347, website www.flightcenter.com), as well as those in Great Britain (08705-66-66-77, website www.flightcentre.co.uk), Australia (13-16-00, website www.flightcentre.com.au), and New Zealand (09-275-5423, website www.flightcentre.co.nz). In London, **Trailfinders,** 215 Kensington High St., Kensington, (020) 7937-5400, website www.trailfinders.com, always has good deals to Canada and other North American destinations. Reservations can be made directly through airline or travel agency websites, or use the services of an Internet-only company such as **Travelocity** (website www.travelocity.com).

Many cheaper tickets have strict restrictions regarding changes of flight dates, lengths of stay, and cancellations. A general rule: The cheaper the ticket, the more restrictions. Most travelers today fly on APEX (advance-purchase excursion) fares. These are usually the best value, though some (and, occasionally, many) restrictions apply. These might include minimum and maximum stays, and nonchangeable itineraries (or hefty penalties for changes); tickets may also be nonrefundable once purchased.

When you have found the best fare, open a **frequent flyer** membership with the airline—**Air Canada,** part of the Star Alliance, has a popular program that makes rewards very obtainable.

from Chicago, Denver, Los Angeles, San Francisco, and Seattle.

International Airlines

In addition to Air Canada's daily London-Vancouver flight, **British Airlines,** 800/247-9297, website www.britishairlines.com, also flies this route daily. Air Canada flights between Vancouver and continental Europe are routed through Toronto, but **KLM,** 604/278-3485, website www.klm.nl, flies nonstop to Vancouver from Amsterdam, and **Lufthansa,** 800/563-5954, website www.Lufthansa.de, from Frankfurt.

Since the demise of Canadian Airlines, **Qantas,** 800/227-4500, website www.qantas.com.au, has begun flying between Sydney, Melbourne, and Brisbane to Vancouver via Honolulu. **Air New Zealand,** 800/663-5494, website www.nzair.com, operates in alliance with Air Canada, with a change of airline in Honolulu or Los Angeles. This airline makes stops throughout the South Pacific, including Nandi (Fiji). **Air Pacific,** 800/227-4446, website www.airpacific.com, flies from points throughout the Pacific to Honolulu and then on to Vancouver.

As a major west coast gateway, British Columbia is well-served by Asian airlines. In addition to Air Canada's eight Asian destinations (see above), Vancouver is served by: **Air China,** 800/685-0921, website www.airchina.com, from Beijing, Shanghai, and Taipei; **All Nippon Airways,** 888/422-7533, website www.ana.co.jp, from Osaka in affiliation with Air Canada; **Eva Air,** 800/695-1188, website www.evaair.com.tw, also from Taipei; **Japan Airlines,** 800/525-3663, website www.jal.co.jp, from Tokyo; **Korean Air,** 800/438-5000, website www.koreanair.com, from Seoul; **Philippine Air-**

lines, website www.philippineair.com, from Manila; and **Singapore Airlines,** 604/689-1223, website www.singaporeair.com, from Singapore via Seoul.

Japan Airlines flies twice weekly between Mexico City and Vancouver.

RAIL

Rail travel opened up the province to the rest of the country in 1885, but it had lost much of its appeal by the beginning of the 1990s thanks to drastically reduced airfares. Today, however, improved service, a refitting of carriages, a competitive pricing structure, and the luxurious privately operated Rocky Mountaineer have helped trains regain popularity in western Canada.

VIA Rail

Government-run VIA Rail provides passenger-train service right across Canada. The **Canadian** is a thrice-weekly service between Toronto and Vancouver via Winnipeg, Saskatoon, Edmonton, Jasper, and Kamloops. Service is provided in two classes of travel: **Economy** features lots of legroom, reading lights, pillows and blankets, and a Skyline Car complete with bar service, while **Silver and Blue** is more luxurious, featuring sleeping rooms, daytime seating, all meals, a lounge and dining car, and shower kits for all passengers. At Jasper (Alberta) the westbound transcontinental line divides, with one set of tracks continuing slightly north to Prince Rupert. Along this route, the **Skeena** makes three trips a week. It is a daytime-only service, with passengers transferred to Prince George accommodations for an overnight stay. It also offers first-class travel, in **Totem Class.**

If you're traveling to British Columbia from any eastern province, the least expensive way to travel is on a **Canrailpass,** which allows unlimited travel anywhere on the VIA Rail system for 12 days within any given 30-day period. During high season (1 June–15 Oct.) the pass is adult $658, senior (over 60) and child $592, with extra days (up to three are allowed) $56 and $49 respectively. The rest of the year adult passes cost $411, senior and student passes $370, with extra days $36 and $33 respectively. (Even if you plan limited train travel the pass is an excellent deal; the regular Toronto-Vancouver one-way fare alone is $592). VIA Rail has cooperated with Amtrak to offer a North American Rail Pass, with all the same seasonal dates and discounts as the Canrailpass. The cost is adult $1,004, senior and child $892; $702 and $632 respectively through the low season. For Amtrak information call 800/872-7245.

On regular fares, discounts of 25–40 percent apply to travel in all classes Oct.–June. Those over 60 and under 25 receive a 10 percent discount that can be combined with other seasonal fares. Check for advance-purchase restrictions on all discount tickets.

The VIA Rail website, www.viarail.ca, provides route, schedule, and fare information, takes reservations, and offers links to towns and sights en route. Or pick up a train schedule at any VIA Rail station or call 800/561-8630 within western Canada; in other North American locations call 888/842-7245.

Rocky Mountaineer

Rocky Mountaineer Railtours, 604/606-7245 or 800/665-7245, website www.rockymountaineer.com, runs a luxurious rail trip to Vancouver from Banff or Calgary and Jasper, through the spectacular interior mountain ranges of British Columbia. Travel is during daylight hours only so you don't miss anything. Trains depart in either direction in the morning (every second or third day), overnighting at Kamloops. One-way travel in RedLeaf Service, which includes light meals, nonalcoholic drinks, and Kamloops accommodations, costs $660 pp d, $715 s from either Banff or Jasper and $720 and $775 respectively from Calgary. GoldLeaf Service is the ultimate in luxury. Passengers ride in a two-story glass-domed car, eat in a separate dining area, and stay in Kamloops' most luxurious accommodations. GoldLeaf costs $1,245 pp d, $1,300 s from Banff or Jasper to Vancouver and $1,345 and $1,400 respectively from Calgary. Outside of high season (mid-April to May and the first two weeks of October), fares are reduced around $150 pp in RedLeaf and $200 pp in GoldLeaf Services.

BUS

Greyhound

Bus travel throughout Canada is easy with **Greyhound,** 604/482-8747 or 800/661-8747, website www.greyhound.ca. The company offers Trans-Canada Highway service from Toronto, Winnipeg, Regina, and Calgary (Alberta), through Kamloops to Vancouver, as well as a more southerly route from Calgary through Cranbrook and the Kootenays to Vancouver. Among the northern routes: Edmonton and Jasper (Alberta) southwest to Vancouver or west to Prince Rupert; and Grande Prairie (Alberta) northwest through Dawson Creek to Whitehorse (Yukon). From the thousands of depots throughout North America, you can go just about anywhere you desire. Reservations are not necessary—just turn up when you want to go, buy your ticket, and kick back. As long as you use your ticket within 30 days, you can stop over wherever the bus stops and stay as long as you want.

When calling for information, ask about any special deals—sometimes excursion fares offered to certain destinations save you money if you buy a round-trip ticket; other times Greyhound offers good prices if you buy your ticket a month in advance. Other standard discounts apply to regular-fare tickets bought seven or 14 days in advance; to travelers 65 and over; and for two people traveling together. At last report, Greyhound was offering a Go Anywhere Fare, on which you can travel between any two points in North America for one low fare; $129 one-way and $199 round-trip if bought 14 days in advance.

Greyhound's **Discovery Pass** comes in many forms, including passes valid only in Canada, in the western states and provinces, and in all of North America. The Canada Pass is sold in periods of seven days ($249), 10 days ($319), 15 days ($379), 21 days ($419), 30 days ($449), 45 days ($535), and 60 days ($599) and allows unlimited travel west of Montreal. The Canada Pass Plus, which allows unlimited travel on all of Greyhound's Canadian routes, is sold in the same increments and ranges from $279 for seven days to $685 for 60 days. Passes can be bought 14 or more days in advance online, seven or more days in advance from any Canadian bus depot, or up to the day of departure from U.S. depots. The Domestic North America CanAm Pass, valid for Greyhound travel through North America, ranges from US$399 for a 15-day pass to US$639 for a 60-day pass. Outside of North America, the passes are the same, but they're sold as International Discovery Passes, with significant discounts; purchase them online more than seven days in advance or at the Vancouver bus depot with proof of foreign residency.

Backpacker Buses

Bigfoot Adventure Tours, 604/278-8224 or 888/244-6673, website www.backpackertours .com, and **Moose Travel Network,** 604/944-3007 or 888/388-4881, website www.moose run.com, operate along a variety of routes between Alberta and British Columbia. For details see Bus under Getting Around, below.

FERRY

One of the most pleasurable ways to get your first view of British Columbia is from sea level. Many scheduled ferry services cross from Washington State to Victoria, on Vancouver Island, but no ferries run to Vancouver from south of the border.

From Washington State

The *Victoria Clipper,* 206/448-5000, 250/382-8100, or 800/888-2535, website www.victoria clipper.com, is a fast passenger-only service connecting Seattle's Pier 69 with Victoria. From farther north, at Anacortes, **Washington State Ferries,** 206/464-6400 or 250/381-1551, website www.wsdot.wa.gov/ferries, runs a once-daily passenger and vehicle service to Sidney, 30 km north of Victoria. If you're traveling up the east coast of Washington State to Vancouver Island and want to bypass the built-up corridor between Tacoma and the international border, consider heading out to Port Angeles on the Olympic Peninsula, from where the **MV *Coho,*** 360/457-4491 or 250/386-2202, website www.northolympic.com/coho, makes a twice

ALASKA MARINE HIGHWAY

The Alaska Marine Highway System is an extensive network of government-run ferries through Alaska's Inside Passage and along the British Columbia coast. Due to international border regulations, the only Canadian port of entry used by the ferry system is Prince Rupert in northern British Columbia. The system's southern terminus, though, is Bellingham, 70 km south of Vancouver in Washington State. (If you're Alaska-bound and would like to include British Columbia in your itinerary, consider driving to Port Hardy, at the northern tip of Vancouver Island, and catching a B.C. Ferries vessel to Prince Rupert to link up with the Alaska Marine Highway). For Alaska Marine Highway schedules and reserva-tions, call 907/465-3941 or 800/642-0066, website www.dot.state.ak.us/external/amhs. Make all reservations as far in advance as possible.

The **Alaska Pass** combines travel on the Alaska Marine Highway with a number of other northern operators, including the White Pass & Yukon Railroad, Alaska Railroad, and Alaskon Express. Eight days' travel within any given 12-day period costs US$549, 12 days' travel within 21 days is US$699, or a straight 22-day pass is US$749. In previous years, travel on Canadian carriers was included in the Alaska Pass. Now it's available as an add-on—US$299 with B.C. Ferries or US$349 with BC Rail. For details call 206/463-6550 or 800/248-7598, website www.alaskapass.com.

daily crossing to Victoria. Another option from Port Angeles is the passenger-only **Victoria Express,** 250/361-9144, 360/452-8088, or 800/663-1589, website www.victoriaexpress.com. For details on all of the above options see the Getting There section of the Victoria chapter.

Getting Around

The best way to get around British Columbia is via your own vehicle—be it a car, RV, motorbike, or bicycle. It's easy to get around by bus and train, but you can't get off the beaten track and, let's face it, that's exactly where most of British Columbia is. It's also easy to get around by air—all the larger airports are served by scheduled intraprovincial flights, and charter services fly out of many of the smaller ones.

AIR

Air BC, a connector airline for **Air Canada,** 604/688-5515 or 888/247-2262, website www.aircanada.ca, serves major cities around the province. The other major regional carrier is **WestJet,** based at Abbotsford, 604/606-5525 or 800/538-5696, website www.westjet.com, with scheduled flights to and from Vancouver, Victoria, Comox, Kelowna, and Prince George.

Pacific Coastal, 604/273-8666 or 800/663-2872, website www.pacific-coastal.com, flies daily from Vancouver International Airport's South Terminal to Nanaimo, Comox, Campbell River, Port Hardy, Powell River, and many remote coastal towns along the B.C. coast. **Hawk Air,** 250/635-4295, website www.hawkair.net, offers scheduled flights between Vancouver's South Terminal and Terrace and Prince Rupert. Also from the South Terminal, **KD Air,** 604/688-9957 or 800/665-4244, website www.kdair.com, flies daily to Qualicum (Vancouver Island), with a connecting ground shuttle to Port Alberni. **North Vancouver Air,** 604/278-1608 or 800/228-6608, website www.northvanair.com, flies from its base near the South Terminal to Tofino/Ucluelet and has recently extended its schedule inland to Nelson and Creston.

Seaplanes not only provide access to remote locations, but also fly between downtown

Vancouver and downtown Victoria. From Coal Harbour, on Burrard Inlet, **Harbour Air,** 604/688-1277 or 800/663-4267, website www.harbour-air.com, and **West Coast Air,** 604/606-6888 or 800/347-2222, website www.westcoast air.com, have scheduled floatplane flights to Victoria's Inner Harbour, with the former and **Baxter Aviation,** 604/683-6525 or 800/661-5599, website www.baxterair.com, offering a similar service to Nanaimo.

RAIL

As well as the **VIA Rail** service between Jasper and Vancouver and Jasper and Prince Rupert (see Getting There, above), other passenger services run within British Columbia, most operated by **BC Rail,** 604/984-5246 or 800/663-8238, website www.bcrail.com, from Vancouver to points north. The rail line between Vancouver and the northern city of Prince George took 40 years to complete, finally opening in 1952. The regular passenger service, the **Cariboo Prospector,** is unique in that it uses self-propelled passenger cars (with no visible engine). The trip between the two cities costs from $212 one way. The **Whistler Northwind** traverses the same route, but it is a luxurious, tourist-oriented service, complete with glass-domed observation cars. The northbound trip takes three days, with passengers overnighting in Whistler and 100 Mile House (Panorama $1,375, Summit $1,050). Southbound, it's a two-day trip that terminates at Whistler, with the night spent at 100 Mile House (Panorama $750, Summit $1,100). All rates are inclusive of accommodations and meals and are discounted in May, June, and September (no service Oct.–April). A number of other BC Rail services run along the line from Vancouver, including the **Pacific Starlight Dinner Train** and the **Royal Hudson Steam Train.**

VIA Rail's **E&N Railiner,** 450 Pandora Ave., Victoria, 250/383-4324 or 800/561-8630, runs daily up the east coast of Vancouver Island between Victoria and Courtenay, making a pleasant day trip from the capital or a good alternative to scheduled buses.

BUS

British Columbia by bus is a snap. Just about all the cities have local bus companies providing transportation in town and, in many cases, throughout their local region—check the transportation sections of each individual chapter for more details. **Greyhound** operates daily bus service to just about anywhere in the province. You don't need to make reservations—just buy your ticket and go. All scheduled services are non-smoking. The bus depot in Vancouver is Pacific Central Station at 1150 Station St., 604/482-8747 or 800/661-8747.

The one part of the province where Greyhound doesn't operate is Vancouver Island. There, **Laidlaw** (also known as Island Coach Lines), 250/388-5248 or 800/663-8390, website www.victoriatours.com, serves all of the island, running up the east coast to Port Hardy and out to the west coast at Tofino. Getting to the island itself is easy with **Pacific Coach Lines,** 604/662-8074, which provides bus service between Victoria and both Vancouver city center and Vancouver International Airport.

Backpacker Buses

Bigfoot Adventure Tours, 604/278-8224 or 888/244-6673, website www.backpacker tours.com, offers a leisurely bus trip between Vancouver and Calgary via Banff. A different route is taken in each direction, and the pace is leisurely, with time spent at major natural attractions en route and one night spent in dormitory accommodations near Salmon Arm. Specifically designed for budget travelers, the trip leaves three times a week throughout summer and costs just $99 one-way. Various other combinations are offered, including a three-day trip through the Okanagan for $149.

Moose Travel Network, 604/944-3007 or 888/388-4881, website www.mooserun.com, is a similar setup; through summer buses make a continuous 10-day loop between Vancouver, Whistler, Kamloops, Jasper, Banff, Revelstoke, and Kelowna. You can get on and off wherever you please (and jump aboard the next bus as it passes through) or bond with the crowd and spend the 10 days together. Either way, it's $399 for the loop (transportation only).

FERRY

B.C. Ferries

Chances are, at some stage of your British Columbia adventure, you'll use the services of **B.C. Ferries,** 1112 Fort St., Victoria, BC V8V 4V2, 250/386-3431 or, toll-free in B.C., 888/223-3779, website www.bcferries.com, which serves 46 ports with a fleet of 40 vessels. All fares listed for "vehicles" in this book cover cars and trucks up to 20 feet long and under seven feet high (or under six feet eight inches high on a few routes). Larger vehicles such as RVs pay more. Also note that prices listed for all types of vehicles are in addition to the passenger price; the vehicle's driver/rider/porter is not included in the vehicle fare.

Vancouver has two major ferry terminals. From **Tsawwassen,** south of downtown, ferries run regularly across the Strait of Georgia to the Vancouver Island centers of Swartz Bay (32 km north of Victoria) and Nanaimo. From **Horseshoe Bay,** west of downtown Vancouver, ferries ply the strait to Nanaimo. On weekends and holidays, the one-way fare on all routes between the mainland and Vancouver Island is adult $9.50, vehicle $33.50, motorcycle $16.75, bicycle $2.50, canoe or kayak $4; rates for all motor vehicles are slightly lower on weekdays.

Also from Horseshoe Bay, ferries run across Howe Sound to **Langdale,** gateway to the Sunshine Coast; round-trip fare is adult $8, vehicle $27.75, motorcycle $14, bicycle $2.50, canoe or kayak $4.

From **Powell River,** at the north end of the Sunshine Coast, ferries depart for **Comox** (Vancouver Island), making it possible to visit both the island and the Sunshine Coast without returning to Vancouver.

B.C. Ferries also provides regular services from both Vancouver Island and the mainland to the **Southern Gulf Islands** of Salt Spring, North Pender, Mayne, Galiano, and Saturna. Other islands in the Strait of Georgia linked to Vancouver Island by ferry include: Thetis and Kuper (from Chemainus), Gabriola (from Nanaimo),

Lasqueti (from Parksville), Denman and Hornby (from Buckley Bay), Quadra and Cortes (from Campbell River), Malcolm and Cormorant (from Port McNeil), and Texada (from Powell River). Fares for travel to these islands range adults $4.50–6.50, vehicles $11.50–21.50.

Prepaid vehicle reservations are required on all sailings to the Southern Gulf Islands from Tsawwassen (Vancouver). Limited reservations are available for the routes between the mainland and Vancouver Island; call 604/444-2890 or 888/724-5223. No reservations are taken for the other routes listed above, so you can expect a wait in summer.

From **Port Hardy** at the northern tip of Vancouver Island, a ferry runs north up the coast to **Prince Rupert.** From the end of May through September the ferry goes every other day, from October through April once a week, and during May twice a week. Peak one-way fare is adult $106, child 5–11 $53, vehicle $218, kayak or canoe $19, bicycle $8. Reservable cabins are available, as are discounts for B.C. seniors. The trip takes 15 hours and links up with the **Alaska Marine Highway** (see the special topic). Also from Prince Rupert, ferries run out to the **Queen Charlotte Islands;** one-way fare is adult $25, child 5–11 $12.50, vehicle $93, kayak or canoe $7, bicycle $6; discounts for B.C. seniors. These longer sailings require reservations, which should be made as far in advance as possible.

Inland Ferries

Many interior lakes and rivers are crossed by ferries owned and operated by the government. Of course, no service is available between freeze-up and breakup, but the rest of year, expect daily service from 6 A.M. until at least 10 P.M. Some of the ferries are small, capable of carrying just two vehicles, while others can transport up to 50. Passage is free on all these ferries, including the 45-minute sailing across Kootenay Lake between Balfour and Kootenay Bay—the world's longest free ferry trip.

DRIVING

United States and international driver's licenses are valid in Canada. All highway signs in British

© ANDREW HEMPSTEAD

B.C. Ferries has connected the mainland and islands for more than 40 years.

Columbia give distances in kilometers and speeds in kilometers per hour. Unless otherwise posted, the maximum speed limit on the highways is 100 kph (62 mph).

Use of safety belts is mandatory, and motorcyclists must wear helmets. Infants and toddlers weighing up to nine kg (20 pounds) must be strapped into an appropriate children's car seat. Use of a child car seat for larger children weighing 9–18 kg (20–40 pounds) is required of B.C. residents and recommended to nonresidents. Before venturing off into the wilds, U.S. residents should ask their vehicle insurance company for a Canadian Non-resident Inter-provincial Motor Vehicle Liability Insurance Card. You may also be asked to prove vehicle ownership, so carry your vehicle registration form. If you're involved in an accident with a B.C. vehicle, contact the nearest Insurance Corporation of British Columbia (ICBC) office, 800/663-3051.

If you're a member in good standing of an automobile association, take your membership card—the Canadian AA provides members of related associations full services, including free maps, itineraries, excellent tour books, road- and weather-condition information, accommoda-

tions reservations, travel agency services, and emergency road services. For more information write British Columbia Automobile Association, 999 W. Broadway Ave., Vancouver, BC V5Z 1K5, 604/268-5600.

Note: Drinking and driving (with a blood-alcohol level of .08 percent or higher) in B.C. can get you imprisoned for up to five years on a first offense and will cost you your license for at least 12 months.

Car Rental

All major car rental companies have outlets at Vancouver International Airport, in downtown Vancouver, and in Victoria. Many companies also have cars available in towns and cities throughout the province. Try to book in advance, especially in summer. Expect to pay from $50 a day and $250 a week for a small economy car with unlimited kilometers.

Major rental companies include: **Alamo,** 604/684-1401 or 800/327-9633, website www.alamo.com; **Avis,** 604/606-2869 or 800/879-2847, website www.avis.com; **Budget,** 604/668-7000 or 800/268-8900, website www.budget.com; **Discount,** 604/310-2277 or

800/263-2355, website www.discountcar.com; **Dollar,** 604/689-5303 or 800/800-4000, website www.dollar.com; **Enterprise,** 604/688-5500 or 800/325-8007, website www.enterprise.com; **Hertz,** 604/606-3700 or 800/263-0600, website hertz.com; **National,** 604/609-7150 or 800/227-7368, website www.nationalcar.com; **Rent-a-wreck,** 604/688-0001 or 800/327-0116, website www.rentawreck.ca; and **Thrifty,** 604/647-4599 or 800/847-4389, website www.thrifty.com. You may also get a good deal in Vancouver from **Lo-Cost,** 604/689-9664 or 800/986-1266, website www.locost.com, or in Victoria from **Ada Rent a Used Car,** 250/474-3455.

RV and Camper Rental

You might want to consider renting a camper-van or other recreational vehicle for your trip. With one of these apartments-on-wheels, you won't need to worry about finding accommodations each night. Even the smallest units aren't cheap,

but they can be a good deal for longer-term travel or for families or two couples traveling together. **Cruise Canada,** 604/946-5775 or 800/327-7799, is the northern affiliate of Cruise America (website www.cruiseamerica.com), which has over 100 rental agencies across North America, including in Vancouver. Two local companies are **C.C. Canada Camper RV Rentals,** 604/270-1833 or 877/327-3003, website www.canada-camper.com; and **Go West,** 604/987-5288 or 800/661-8813, website www.go-west.com. Rates for all three companies are generally similar. Go West, for example, charges $140 per day with 100 km or $185 with 250 km for a camper-van. A 10-meter motor home costs $212 and $255 per day respectively. Additional charges include extra kilometers, insurance, a bedding/cutlery charge ($60 per person per rental), drop-off charges outside of Vancouver, and those hefty local taxes (14 percent of the total cost).

Other Practicalities

VISAS AND OFFICIALDOM

Entry for U.S. Citizens

United States citizens and permanent residents need only present some form of identification that proves citizenship and/or residency, such as a birth certificate, voter registration card, driver's license with photo, or alien card (essential for nonresident aliens to reenter the United States). It never hurts to carry your passport as well.

Other Foreign Visitors

All other foreign visitors must have a valid passport and may need a visa or visitor permit depending on their country of residence and the vagaries of international politics. At present, visas are not required for citizens of the United States, British Commonwealth, or Western Europe. The standard entry permit is for six months, and you may be asked to show onward tickets or proof of sufficient funds to last you through your intended stay. Extensions ($60 per person) are available from the **Citizenship and Immigra-**

tion Canada offices in Vancouver and Victoria, website www.cic.gc.ca.

Employment and Study

Anyone wishing to work or study in Canada must obtain authorization *before* entering Canada. Authorization to work will only be granted if no qualified Canadians are available for the work in question. Applications for work and study are available from all Canadian embassies and must be submitted with a nonrefundable processing fee. The Canadian government has a reciprocal agreement with Australia for a limited number of **holiday work visas** to be issued each year. Australian citizens under the age of 30 are eligible; contact your nearest Canadian embassy or consulate. For general information on immigrating to Canada call **Citizenship and Immigration Canada,** 604/666-2171, website www.cic.gc.ca.

Entry by Private Aircraft or Boat

If you're going to be entering Canada by private plane or boat, contact Customs in advance for a

ON THE ROAD

list of official ports of entry and their hours of operation. Write Revenue Canada, Customs Border Services, Regional Information Unit, 333 Dunsmuir St., Vancouver, BC V6B 5R4, or call 604/666-0545, website www.ccra-adrc.gc.ca.

Customs

You can take the following into Canada duty-free: reasonable quantities of clothes and personal effects, 50 cigars and 200 cigarettes, 200 grams of tobacco, 1.14 liters of spirits or wine, food for personal use, and gas (normal tank capacity). Pets from the United States can generally be brought into Canada, with certain caveats. Dogs and cats must be over three months old and have a rabies certificate showing date of vaccination. Birds can be brought in only if they have not been mixing with other birds, and parrots need an export permit because they're on the endangered species list.

Handguns, automatic and semiautomatic weapons, and sawn-off rifles and shotguns are not allowed entry into Canada. Visitors with firearms must declare them at the border; restricted weapons will be held by Customs and can be picked up on exit from the country. Those not declared will be seized and charges may be laid. It is illegal to possess any firearm in a national park unless it is dismantled or carried in an enclosed case. Up to 5,000 rounds of ammunition may be imported but should be declared on entry.

On reentering the United States, if you've been in Canada more than 48 hours you can bring back up to US$400 worth of household and personal items, excluding alcohol and tobacco, duty-free. If you've been in Canada less than 48 hours, you may bring in only up to $200 worth of such items duty-free.

For further information on all customs regulations write Revenue Canada, Customs and Excise, Public Inquires Unit, 333 Dunsmuir St., Vancouver, BC V6B 5R4, 604/666-0545, website www.ccra-adrc.gc.ca.

MONEY

Canadian currency is based on dollars and cents, with 100 cents equal to one dollar. **All prices** quoted in this handbook are in Canadian dollars and cents unless otherwise noted. The exchange rate is roughly US$1 = C$1.50. American dollars are accepted at many tourist areas, but don't expect a favorable exchange rate.

Coins come in denominations of one, five, 10, and 25 cents, and one and two dollars. The 11-sided, gold-colored, one-dollar coin is known as a "loonie" for the bird featured on it. The unique two-dollar coin is silver with a gold-colored insert. The most common notes are $5, $10, $20, and $50. A $100 bill does exist but is uncommon.

The safest way to carry money is in the form of traveler's checks from a reputable and well-known U.S. company such as American Express, Visa, or Bank of America; those are also the easiest checks to cash. Cash only the amount you need when you need it. Banks offer the best exchange rates, but other foreign-currency exchange outlets are available. It's also a good idea to start off with a couple of traveler's checks in Canadian dollars so you're never caught without *some* money if you don't make it to a bank on time.

Visa and MasterCard credit cards are also readily accepted throughout British Columbia. Cred-

CURRENCY EXCHANGE

The Canadian dollar lost value against the greenback through the second half of the 1990s, steadied through 2000, and then dipped slightly again to reach almost record lows through 2001 and into 2002. It currently trades at roughly **US$1 per CDN$1.60.**

At press time exchange rates (into C$) for other major currencies were:

AUS$1 =	80 cents
DM1 =	72 cents
EURO1 =	$1.40
HK$10 =	$2.03
NZ$1 =	66 cents
UK£1 =	$2.38
¥100 =	$1.22

On the Internet, check current exchange rates at www.rubicon.com/passport/currency/currency.html.

it cards eliminate the necessity of thinking about the exchange rate—the transaction and rate of exchange on the day of the transaction will automatically be reflected in the bill from your credit card company.

Costs

The cost of living in British Columbia is similar to all other Canadian provinces, but higher than in the United States. By planning ahead, having a tent or joining Hostelling International, and being prepared to cook your own meals it is possible to get by on well under $50 per person per day. If you will be staying in hotels or motels, accommodations will be your biggest expense. Gasoline is sold in liters (3.78 liters equals one U.S. gallon) and is generally 65–75 cents a liter for regular unleaded; surprisingly, Vancouver is one of the most expensive places to fill your gas tank.

Tipping charges are not usually added to your bill. You are expected to add a tip of 15 percent to the total amount for waiters and waitresses, barbers and hairdressers, taxi drivers, and other such service providers. Bellhops, doormen, and porters generally receive $1 per item of baggage.

Taxes

Canada imposes a 7 percent **goods and services tax (GST)** on most consumer purchases. The provincial government imposes its own 7 percent tax (PST) onto everything except groceries and books. So when you are looking at the price of anything, remember that the final cost you pay will include an additional 14 percent in taxes. Instead of a provincial sales tax, accommodations are subject to an 8 percent provincial hotel room tax.

Nonresident visitors can get a rebate for the GST they pay on short-term accommodations and on most consumer goods bought in the country and taken home. Items not included in the Visitor Rebate Program include: gifts left in Canada, meals and restaurant charges, campground fees, services such as dry cleaning and shoe repair, alcoholic beverages, tobacco, automotive fuels, groceries, agricultural and fish products, prescription drugs and medical devices, and used goods that tend to increase in value, such as paintings, jewelry, rare books, and coins.

The rebate is available on services and retail purchases of at least $50 each, that total at least $200, and that were paid for within 60 days prior to your exit from the country. Rebates can be claimed any time within one year from the date of purchase. You'll need to include with your claim all receipts or vouchers that prove the GST was paid. Most visitors apply for the rebate at duty-free shops (also called Visitor Rebate Centres) when exiting the country. The duty-free shops can rebate up to $500 on the spot. For rebates over $500, you'll need to mail your completed GST rebate form directly to Visitor Rebate Program, Summerside Tax Centre, Canada Customs and Revenue Agency, 275 Pope Rd., Suite 104, Summerside, PE C1N 6C6, Canada. You can also submit rebate forms for amounts less than $500 directly to Revenue Canada. If you've claimed by mail before, be aware that the rules have changed. Claims for goods (not accommodations) must be accompanied by a Proof of Export stamp, which you'll get at the border upon presentation of both the goods and corresponding receipts. Rebate checks from the government are issued in Canadian funds. For more info, call toll-free from anywhere in Canada 800/668-4748; from outside Canada phone 902/432-5608; on the Internet, the website is www.ccra-adrc.gc.ca/visitors.

HEALTH

British Columbia is a healthy place. To visit, you don't need to get any vaccinations or booster shots. And when you arrive you can drink the water from the faucet and eat the food without worry.

Backcountry travelers should take a few extra precautions. It's always wise to boil or filter water from streams and lakes, just to be on the safe side. Be aware of poison oak, which causes itchy open blisters and sores a short time after contact, and keep your eyes peeled for rattlesnakes. If you bathe in hot springs, keep your head above water and *do not* let the water enter your nose, ears, or mouth—a variety of parasites thrive in the hot water.

AIDS and other venereal and needle-communicated diseases are as much of a concern here as anywhere in the world today. Take exactly the same precautions you would at home—use condoms, and don't share needles.

It's a good idea to get health insurance or some form of coverage before heading to Canada if you're going to be there for a while, but check that your plan covers foreign services. Hospital charges vary from place to place but can start at around $1,000 a day, and some facilities impose a surcharge for nonresidents. Some Canadian companies offer coverage specifically aimed at visitors.

If you're on medication take adequate supplies with you, and get a prescription from your doctor to cover the time you will be away. You may not be able to get a prescription filled at Canadian pharmacies without visiting a Canadian doctor, so don't wait till you've almost run out. If you wear glasses or contact lenses, ask your optometrist for a spare prescription in case you break or lose your lenses, and stock up on your usual cleaning supplies.

If you need an ambulance, call the number listed on the inside front cover of the local telephone directory, and if you're unsure of your whereabouts ask the operator for assistance. All the cities and most of the large towns have local hospitals—look in each chapter of this book for locations and telephone numbers.

Be aware that some of B.C.'s highways snake for many kilometers through high mountain areas. In the Rockies particularly, roads can climb into the thin-air heights, reaching elevations of up to 1,774 meters. If you or your passengers can't handle high elevations well, read a good topographical map before you set off and try to find a low-lying route to your destination.

Visitors with Disabilities

For information on travel considerations in British Columbia for the physically handicapped, contact the Canadian Paraplegic Association, 780 Southwest Marine Dr., Vancouver, BC V6P 5Y7, 604/324-3611.

Winter Travel Considerations

Travel through the province during winter months should not be undertaken lightly. Before setting out in a vehicle, check antifreeze lev-els, and always carry a spare tire and blankets or sleeping bags.

Frostbite occurs in varying degrees. Most often it leaves a numbing, bruised sensation and the skin turns white. Exposed areas of skin such as the nose and ears are most susceptible, particularly when cold temperatures are accompanied by high winds.

Hypothermia occurs when the body fails to produce heat as fast as it loses it. Cold weather combined with hunger, fatigue, and dampness creates a recipe for disaster. Symptoms are not always apparent to the victim. The early signs are numbness, shivering, slurring of words, dizzy spells, and, in extreme cases, violent behavior, unconsciousness, and even death. The best treatment is to get the patient out of the cold, replace wet clothing with dry, slowly give hot liquids and sugary foods, and place the victim in a sleeping bag. Prevention is a better strategy; dress for cold in layers, including a waterproof outer layer, and wear a warm wool cap or other headgear.

SERVICES, COMMUNICATIONS, AND MEASUREMENTS

Postal Services

Canada Post issues postage stamps that must be used on all mail posted in Canada. First-class letters and postcards within Canada are 48 cents, to the U.S. 65 cents, to foreign destinations $1.25. Prices increase along with the weight of the mailing. You can buy stamps at post offices, automatic vending machines, most hotel lobbies, railway stations, airports, bus terminals, and at many retail outlets and some newsstands. Visitors can have their mail sent to them c/o General Delivery, Main Post Office, in the city or town you request, British Columbia, Canada. The post office will hold the mail for 15 days, then return it to the sender.

Telephones

The **area code** for Vancouver and the lower mainland, including the Sunshine Coast, as far north as Whistler, and east to Hope, is **604**. The rest of the province, including all of Vancouver Island, is **250**. These prefixes must be dialed for all long-distance calls, including those made within the province. The country code for Canada is 1, the same as the United States. Public phones accept 5-, 10-, and 25-cent coins; local calls are 35 cents, and most long-distance calls cost at least $2.50 for the first minute.

Internet

If your Internet provider doesn't allow you to access your email away from your home computer, open an email account with a web-based email host such as **Hotmail** (website www.hotmail.com) or **Yahoo** (website www.yahoo.com). Although there are restrictions to the size and number of emails you can store, and junk mail can be a problem, these services are handy for traveling and, best of all, free.

Public Internet access is available throughout British Columbia. Many hotels in larger cities have high-speed access from guest rooms. Those that don't—usually mid- and lower-priced properties—often have an Internet booth in the lobby. All backpacker lodges and even campgrounds now provide public Internet access. You'll also find Internet booths in many cafés, in some McDonald's restaurants, and in public areas such as bus depots. Aside from a lack of privacy, the downside to these public access points is the lack of a mouse at most terminals—instead you must move around the screen using a touch pad.

Time and Measurements

British Columbia is mostly in the **Pacific time zone,** one hour before mountain time and three hours before eastern time. The East Kootenays and the Dawson Creek area are in the mountain time zone.

The province is officially on the **metric system,** though you still hear everyone talking in pounds and ounces, miles, and miles per hour (see the metric conversion chart in the back of this book).

Electricity

Electrical voltage in British Columbia is 120 volts AC.

Business Hours

Shops throughout British Columbia are generally open Mon.–Fri. 9 A.M.–5 P.M. and Saturday 9 A.M.–1 P.M. Major malls stay open all weekend. If you're in a city or large town, you can always find a store open for essentials, as well as restaurants and fast-food outlets. Most **banks** are open Mon.–Fri. 10 A.M.–3:30 P.M.

MAPS AND INFORMATION
Maps

Specialty bookstores are the best places to search out or order maps. In Vancouver, try **International Travel Maps and Books,** 552 Seymour St., 604/687-3320, website www.itmb.com, or **Wanderlust,** 1929 W. 4th Ave., Kitsilano, 604/739-2182; in Victoria, check out **Crown Publications,** 521 Fort St., 250/386-4636. These

ON THE ROAD

TOURISM OFFICES

In addition to **Tourism BC,** 250/387-1642 or 800/435-5622, website www.hellobc.com, and the Canadian Tourism Commission, website www.canadatourism.com, the following regional offices will assist in planning your trip to British Columbia:

- **Tourism Association of Vancouver Island,** #203 335 Wesley St., Nanaimo, BC V9R 2T5, 250/754-3500, website www.islands.bc.ca

- **Tourism Victoria,** 812 Wharf St., Victoria, BC V8W 1T3, 250/953-2033, website www.tourismvictoria.com

- **Thompson/Okanagan Tourism Association,** 1332 Water St., Kelowna, BC V1Y 9P4, 250/860-5999 or 800/567-2275, website www.thompsonokanagan.com

- **Tourism Rockies,** P.O. Box 10, Kimberley, BC V1A 2Y5, 250/427-4838, website www.bcrockies.com

- **Cariboo Tourism Association** (Central British Columbia), 266 Oliver St., Williams Lake, BC V2G 1M1, 250/392-2838 or 800/663-5885, website www.landwithoutlimits.com

- **Northern BC Tourism Association,** P.O. Box 2373, Prince George, BC V2N 2S6, 250/561-0432 or 800/663-8843, website www.northernbctravel.com

stores stock many topographical maps and can order specific maps and marine charts for you.

Information

General information on just about everything in the province can be obtained from **Tourism British Columbia,** P.O. Box 9830, Station Provincial Government, Victoria, BC V8W 9W5, 250/387-1642 or 800/435-5622, website www.hellobc.com. As well as being a great source of tourist information, the agency produces the invaluable *Accommodations* guide and a road map. Another couple of handy web addresses are www.canadatourism.com, the official site of the Canadian Tourism Commission, and www.tbc.gov.bc.ca, the site of the Ministry of Small Business, Tourism, and Culture.

Each town of any size in B.C. has a **Visitor Info Centre;** hours vary, but most are open June–August. When these are closed, head to the local chamber of commerce for information. Most chamber offices are open Mon.–Fri. year-round.

HEADING FARTHER AFIELD?

- **Yukon Department of Tourism,** 867/667-5036 or 800/789-8566, website www.touryukon.com
- **Alaska Division of Tourism,** 907/465-2010, website www.dced.state.ak.us/tourism
- **Alberta Tourism,** 780/427-4321 or 800/661-8888, website www.travelalberta.com
- **Northwest Territories Arctic Tourism:** 403/873-7200 or 800/661-0788, website www.nwttravel.nt.ca
- **Nunavut Tourism:** 819/979-6551 or 800/491-7910, website www.nunatour.nt.ca
- **Tourism Saskatchewan:** 306/787-2300 or 800/667-7191, website www.sasktourism.com
- **Travel Manitoba:** 204/945-3777 or 800/665-0040, website www.gov.travelmanitoba.com

Vancouver

Let your mind fill with images of dramatic, snow-capped mountains rising vertically from a city's backyard. Century-old inner-city buildings and steel-and-glass skyscrapers facing the sheltered shores of a large wide inlet. Manicured suburbs perching along the edge of the sea, fringed by golden sandy beaches. Lush tree-filled parks and brilliant flower gardens overflowing with color. Flocks of Canada geese overhead, noisily honking to one another as they fly toward the setting sun. These are the magnificent images of Vancouver.

If you view this gleaming mountain- and sea-dominated city for the first time on a beautiful sunny day, you're bound to fall for it in a big way. See it on a dull, dreary day when the clouds are low and Vancouver's backyard mountains are hidden and you may come away with a slightly less enthusiastic picture—you'll have experienced the "permagray," as residents are quick to call it with a laugh.

But even gray skies can't dampen the city's vibrant, outdoorsy atmosphere. By day, the active visitor can enjoy boating right from downtown, or perhaps venture out to one of the nearby provincial parks for hiking in summer and skiing and snowboarding in winter. More urban-oriented visitors can savor the aromas of just-brewed coffee and freshly baked bread wafting from cosmopolitan sidewalk cafés, join in the bustle at seaside markets, bake on a local beach, or simply relax and do some people-watching in one of the city's tree-shaded squares. By night, Vancouver's myriad fine restaurants, nightclubs, and performing-arts venues beckon visitors to continue enjoying themselves on into the wee hours.

Rain or shine, night or day, Vancouver is an alluring and unforgettable city.

HISTORY

The first Europeans to set eyes on the land encompassing today's city of Vancouver were gold-seeking Spanish traders who sailed through the Strait of Georgia in 1790. Although the forested wilderness they encountered seemed impenetrable, it had been inhabited by humans since becoming ice-free

© ANDREW HEMPSTEAD

Vancouver as seen from Coal Harbour

some 10,000 years earlier.

Not to be outdone, the Brits sent Captain George Vancouver to the area in 1792. Vancouver cruised through the Strait of Georgia in search of a northwest passage to the Orient, charting Burrard Inlet and claiming the land for Great Britain in the process. As stories of an abundance of fur-bearing mammals filtered east, the fur companies went into action. The North West Company sent fur trader/explorer Simon Fraser overland to establish a coastal trading post. In 1808 he reached the Pacific Ocean via the river that was later named for him, and he built a fur fort on the riverbank east of today's Vancouver. In 1827, the Hudson's Bay Company established its own fur fort on the Fraser River, 48 km east of present-day Vancouver. Neither of these two outposts spawned a permanent settlement.

Vancouver Is Born

It wasn't until the discovery of gold up the Fraser River in the late 1850s that settlement really took hold in the area. The town of New Westminster,

just southeast of present-day Vancouver, was declared British Columbia's first capital in 1866.

The settlement of Vancouver began with the establishment of a brickworks ("Bricks? Why on earth make bricks when we've got all these trees?" said the Woodcutters' Union spokesman) on the south side of Burrard Inlet. Sawmills and related logging and lumber industries followed, and soon several boomtowns were carved out of the wilderness. The first was Granville (now downtown Vancouver), which the original settlers called Gastown after one of its earliest residents, notorious saloon owner "Gassy Jack" Deighton. In 1886 Granville, pop. 1,000, became the City of Vancouver. Not long thereafter, fire roared through the timber city. Just about everything burned to the ground, but with true pioneering spirit Vancouver was rebuilt at lightning speed.

A Growing City

In 1887, the struggling city got a boost with the arrival of the first transcontinental railroad. Selected as the western terminus for the Canadian

the distinct Vancouver skyline

© ANDREW HEMPSTEAD

Pacific Railway, Vancouver suddenly became Canada's transportation gateway to the Orient and an important player in the development of international commerce around the Pacific Rim. Additionally, the opening of the Panama Canal in 1915 created the perfect outlet for transporting the province's abundant renewable resources to North America's east coast and Europe, resulting in further development of the port facilities and a population boom. Granville Island and the far reaches of Burrard Inlet sprawled with industry,

the West End developed as a residential area, the University of British Columbia grew in stature, and the opening of the Lions Gate Bridge encouraged settlement on the north side of Burrard Inlet.

Today, Vancouver is Canada's third-largest city, holding a multicultural population of 1.82 million in its greater metropolitan area. It's also the largest port on North America's west coast, boasting 27 specialized terminals that handle more tonnage than any other port in Canada.

Sights

GETTING ORIENTED

Vancouver isn't a particularly easy city to find your way around, although an excellent transit system helps immensely. **Downtown** lies on a spit of land bordered to the north and east by Burrard Inlet, to the west by English Bay, and to the south by False Creek, which almost cuts the city center off from the rest of the city. Due to the foresight of city founders, almost half of the downtown peninsula has been set aside as parkland.

The **City of Vancouver** officially extends south and west from downtown, between Burrard Inlet and the Fraser River. Here lie the trendy beachside suburb of **Kitsilano** (known as "Kits" to the locals) and **Point Grey,** home of the University of British Columbia. To the east, the residential sprawl continues, through the suburbs of **Burnaby, New Westminster,** and **Coquitlam,** which have a combined population of well over 250,000.

Farther south, the low-lying Fraser River delta extends all the way south to the border. Between the north and south arms of the river is **Richmond,** home of Vancouver International Airport. South of the south arm is the mostly industrial area of **Delta,** as well as **Tsawwassen,** departure point for ferries to Vancouver Island.

Southeast of the Fraser River lies **Surrey,** another of those never-ending suburbs, this one with a population of 349,000. The sprawl continues east from Surrey. With Vancouver growing

at an incredible rate, and as development to the south and north are restricted—by the international border and the Coast Mountains—there's nowhere to go but east. From Surrey, the Trans-Canada Highway passes through the Fraser River Valley and towns such as **Langley** (pop. 85,000), **Abbotsford** (pop. 110,000), and **Chilliwack** (pop. 65,000)—all now part of the city sprawl.

Across Burrard Inlet to the north of downtown, **North Vancouver** is a narrow developed strip backed up to the mountains and connected to the rest of the city by the Lions Gate Bridge. To its west are **Horseshoe Bay,** departure point for Sunshine Coast and Vancouver Island ferries, and **West Vancouver,** an upscale suburb.

DOWNTOWN

Granville Street was Vancouver's first commercial corridor, and if today you stand at its junction with West Georgia Street, you're as close to the "center" of the city as it's possible to be. From this busy intersection Granville Street extends north toward Burrard Inlet as a pedestrian mall, leading through the central business district (CBD) to Canada Place and the main tourist information center. Also within a three-block radius of this intersection are Vancouver Art Gallery, all major banking institutions, shopping centers, and the city's best hotels. To the south, between Dunsmuir and Robson Streets, is the **theater district** and Library Square. **Yaletown,** the hot spot for tech companies, is farther south, bordered by

VANCOUVER VIEWS

Commercial

For immediate orientation from downtown, catch the high-speed, stomach-sinking glass elevator up the outside of 40-story Harbour Centre Tower, 555 W. Hastings St., 604/689-0421. The ride takes less than a minute and ends at **The Lookout!** an enclosed room 167 meters above street level, from where views extend as far away as Mt. Baker, 140 km to the south. Walk around the circular room for 360-degree views and interpretive panels describing interesting facts about the panorama below and beyond. In summer, the elevator runs daily 8:30 A.M.–10:30 P.M., the rest of the year daily 9:30 A.M.–9 P.M. The trip to the top costs adult $9, senior $8, student $6; keep the receipt and you can return any time during the same day (the top of the tower is a great place to watch the sun setting over the Strait of Georgia).

On the north side of the city, take the **Grouse Mountain Skyride,** Nancy Greene Way, 604/984-0661, up the slopes of Grouse Mountain. The panorama extends back across the inlet to downtown and beyond to Mt. Baker, in Washington State, and west to Vancouver Island. In summer, the gondola departs the base station every 10 minutes 10 A.M.–10 P.M.; adult $17.95, senior $15.95, child $6.95.

Taking to the air offers the opportunity to get a bird's-eye view of the city. **Harbour Air,** 604/688-1277, offers a 20-minute flightseeing trip from a seaplane base on the west side of Canada Place for $72 pp, and **Helijet** flights, 604/270-1484, take off from the heliport on the east side of Canada Place (enter through Waterfront Station) for a 30-minute trip over the heart of downtown, Stanley Park, and the North Shore for $225 pp.

Free

You certainly don't need to pay money for a view of the city. Downtown, wander around the **Canada Place** promenade for neck-straining views of the city close up, as well as North Vancouver and the rugged mountains beyond. For a look at the skyline and sparkling Canada Place from sea level, take the SeaBus from the adjacent Waterfront Station across Burrard Inlet to **Lonsdale Quay** ($2.50). In Stanley Park, stroll or bike the 10-km-long **Seawall Promenade** to appreciate the skyline to the east, the busy shipping lanes of First Narrows to the

north, and the sandy beaches of English Bay to the west. Sunsets from **English Bay Beach,** in the West End, are delightful.

While Grouse Mountain Skyride accesses the best-known viewpoint north of Burrard Inlet, the panorama from **Cypress Provincial Park,** up Cypress Bowl Rd., is no less spectacular. On the way back down, take Marine Dr. west to **Lighthouse Park,** from where English Bay, Stanley Park, and Kitsilano Beach are laid out in all their glory. **Seymour Provincial Park,** east of the gondola, provides views across the city from afar, but from a wilderness area with plenty of hiking opportunities.

South of downtown, the **Kitsilano** foreshore provides that well-known view of the city skyline backed by the Coast Mountains. The south side of the city is relatively flat. The high point is 152-meter-high **Little Mountain,** in Queen Elizabeth Park, where the city skyline and abruptly rising mountains starkly contrast with the residential sprawl of Central Vancouver all around.

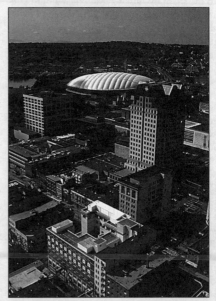

© ANDREW HEMPSTEAD

The view across the city from The Lookout! atop the Harbour Centre Tower is spectacular.

VANCOUVER

Homer, Drake, and Nelson Streets. East along the waterfront from Canada Place, and still within easy walking distance of the Granville and Georgia Streets intersection, is the oldest part of the city, **Gastown.** Beyond Gastown, North America's third largest **Chinatown** is a hive of activity day and night. On the opposite side of the CBD is the **West End** and enormous **Stanley Park,** reached by walking along **Robson Street,** a two-km-long strip of boutiques and restaurants.

Canada Place

The stunning architectural curiosity with the billowing 27-meter-high Teflon-coated fiberglass "sails" on Burrard Inlet—the one that looks as if it might weigh anchor and cruise off into the sunset at any moment—is Canada Place, a symbol of Vancouver and a city icon. Built as the Canada Pavilion for Expo86, this integrated waterfront complex is primarily a convention center and cruise-ship dock. The Vancouver Trade and Convention Centre, which makes up the bulk of the complex, is currently being expanded to triple its size at adjacent Burrard Landing, in a half-billion-dollar expansion project that will change the face of the downtown waterfront. The existing complex at the foot of Burrard Street also houses the luxurious 405-room Pan Pacific Hotel (the glass marvel with domed top), restaurants, shops, and an IMAX theater. Start your self-guided tour at the information booth near the main entrance, then allow at least an hour to wander through the complex. Don't miss walking the exterior promenade—three and a half city blocks long—for splendid views of the harbor, the North Shore, the Coast Mountains, and docked Alaska-bound cruise ships.

Vancouver Art Gallery

Francis Rattenbury, architect of Victoria's Empress Hotel and many other masterpieces, designed Vancouver's imposing neoclassical-revival courthouse, which now houses Vancouver Art Gallery, 750 Hornby St., 604/662-4700. The gallery maintains a large collection of works by Canada's preeminent female artist, Emily Carr, who was born on Vancouver Island in 1871 and traveled the world honing her painting and drawing skills

before settling in Vancouver in 1906. Her style reflects the time she spent with the natives of the Pacific Northwest coast, but she was also influenced by techniques acquired during periods she lived in London and Paris. Carr combined these influences to create unique works, and the gallery is well worth visiting for these alone. The Carr collection is on the third floor, along with the works of many other local artists. The gallery also holds pieces by other contemporary artists, from both North America and Europe, as well as an impressive collection of historical art.

Summer hours are daily 10 A.M.–5:30 P.M. (until 9 P.M. on Thursday). Between October and May, the gallery is closed Monday and Tuesday. Admission is adult $10, senior $8, children 12 and under free.

In the Vicinity

The late 1960s saw a renaissance of civic buildings in major cities across the country, and Vancouver was no exception. An entire block was designated for a new courthouse complex, replacing the original across Robson Street. Architect Arthur Erickson's unique design incorporates street level public spaces adorned with sculptures and the **Law Courts,** a magnificent glass structure signifying an open and accessible court system.

On the other side of the art gallery and behind Cathedral Place is the **Canadian Craft Museum,** 639 Hornby St., 604/687-8266, which catalogs the history of arts and crafts throughout the ages; open Mon.–Sat. 10 A.M.–5 P.M. (Thursday until 9 P.M.), Sunday noon–5 P.M. Admission to the museum is adult $5, senior $3. **Cathedral Place** itself is worth visiting for an intriguing sculpture, *Navigational Device,* located in the lobby. Nearby, on the corner of West Georgia and Burrard Streets, is **Christ Church Cathedral.** When built in 1895, it is was in the heart of a residential area. Over the ensuing century, it has been engulfed by modern developments and is today Vancouver's oldest church. Across West Georgia Street from these buildings is the **Hotel Vancouver.** Built in 1887, the original hotel on this site featured 200 rooms, half of which had private bathrooms—unheard of in that day. It burnt to the ground in 1932 and was replaced by the hotel that stands today, which reflects the heritage of CPR-built hotels across the country with its distinctive château-style design topped by a copper roof.

Mining and Forestry Displays

The **Pacific Mineral Museum** is a small exhibit in the historic neo-Georgian B.C. and Yukon Chamber of Mines Building at 848 W. Hastings St., 604/689-8700. A large three-dimensional map of British Columbia shows mineral deposits and current mining operations, while other exhibits point out the importance of the industry to the province. Gemstones, fossils, and even meteorites are also displayed. It's open Tues.–Fri. 10 A.M.–5 P.M. and on weekends 10 A.M.–6 P.M.

Three blocks west, the **Forest Alliance Visitors Centre,** 1055 Dunsmuir St., 604/685-7507, is a good place to learn about the provincial forestry industry through interactive displays, computer programs, and information boards. It's open Mon.–Fri. 8 A.M.–5 P.M.

Gastown

Named for the owner of the city's first saloon, Gastown is a marvelous place to spend a few hours. "Gassy Jack" Deighton, an English boat pilot, offered locals all the whiskey they could drink in return for helping him build a saloon beside Burrard Inlet in 1867. The town that grew around the saloon was officially named Granville in 1869, but it has always been known as Gastown. The district's tree-lined cobblestone streets and old gas lamps front brightly painted restored buildings housing galleries, restaurants, and an abundance of gift and souvenir shops.

Most of the action centers along **Water Street,** which branches east off Cordova Street, an easy five-minute walk from Canada Place. As you first enter Water Street, you're greeted by **The Landing,** a heritage building that has had its exterior restored to its former glory and its interior transformed to an upmarket shopping arcade. It also holds eateries and the Steamworks Brewing Co., a pub/restaurant boasting harbor views.

On the corner of Water and Cambie Streets is a **steam clock,** one of only two in the world (the other is a replica of this, the original one). Built by a local clock maker in the mid-1970s, it is powered by a steam system originally put in place to heat buildings along a 10-km-long underground pipeline that snakes through downtown. Watch for the burst of steam every 15 minutes, which sets off steam whistles to the tune of Westminster chimes.

Continue east along Water Street to the 1899 **Dominion Hotel,** then half a block south down Abbott Street to **Blood Alley,** the hangout of many infamous turn-of-the-century rogues. Most buildings still standing along Water Street were built immediately after the Great Fire of 1886, but the **Byrnes Block,** at 2 Water St., is generally regarded as the oldest; it stands on the site of Deighton House, Gassy Jack's second and more permanent saloon. Behind this building is **Gaolers Mews,** the site of Vancouver's first jail.

Water Street ends just around the corner at cobbled **Maple Tree Square,** the intersection of Water, Carrall, Powell, and Alexander Streets. Here stands a bronze **statue of Gassy Jack** watching over the square and the site of his original saloon from the top of a whiskey barrel. The **Alhambra Hotel,** which occupies the actual saloon site, was built in 1886 from bricks used as ballast in ships that sailed into Burrard Inlet. Across from the statue is the **Hotel Europe,** a narrow triangular building. After its 1892 opening, the hotel quickly became recognized as the city's finest hostelry.

Chinatown

With the second-largest Chinese community in North America and one of the largest outside Asia, Vancouver's Chinatown is an exciting place any time of year. But it's especially lively during a Chinese festival or holiday, when thronging masses follow the ferocious dancing dragon, avoid exploding firecrackers, sample tasty tidbits from outside stalls, and pound their feet to the beat of the drums.

Chinatown lies several blocks southeast of Gastown, along East Pender Street between Carrall and Gore Streets. Its commercial center is the block bordered by Main, East Pender, Gore, and Keefer Streets. Stroll through the neighborhood to admire the architecture—right down to the pagoda-roofed telephone booths—or to seek out one of the multitude of restaurants. You'll find genuine Cantonese-style cuisine at the east end and tamer Chinese-Canadian dishes at the west.

The district's intriguing stores sell a mind-boggling array of Chinese goods: wind chimes, soy sauce, teapots, dried mushrooms, delicate paper fans, and much, much more. Along Main Street a number of shops sell ginseng, sold by the Chinese ounce (38 grams). Cultivated ginseng costs from $10 an ounce, while wild ginseng goes for up to $400 an ounce. In addition to selling the herb, the staff at **Ten Ren Tea and Ginseng Co.,** 550 Main St., 604/684-1566, explains ginseng preparation methods to buyers and offers tea tastings as well.

> *Chinatown's intriguing stores sell a mind-boggling array of Chinese goods: wind chimes, soy sauce, teapots, dried mushrooms, delicate paper fans, and much, much more.*

The **Chinese Cultural Centre,** 50 E. Pender St., 604/687-0729, is the epicenter of community programs for the local Chinese population; even so, it holds interest for outsiders. The distinctive museum and archives building is a recent extension to the center cataloging the history of Chinese-Canadians in Vancouver. It's at 555 Columbia St., 604/687-0282, and is open to the public Tues.–Sun. 11 A.M.–5 P.M. Admission is adult $4, senior $2.50.

Gardening enthusiasts won't want to miss **Dr. Sun Yat-Sen Classical Chinese Garden,** at 578 Carrall St. (behind the Cultural Centre), 604/662-3207. Designed by artisans from Suzhou, China—a city famous for its green-thumbed residents—the garden features limestone rockeries, a waterfall and tranquil pools, and beautiful trees and plants hidden away behind tall walls. It's open daily from 10 A.M.; admission is adults $7, seniors and students $5.50. Tours are conducted four to six times daily. Adjacent to the gardens is **Dr. Sun Yat-Sen Park,** where admission is free.

Opposite the entrance to Dr. Sun Yat-Sen Classical Chinese Garden, at 8 W. Pender St. (corner of Carrall St.), is the **Sam Kee Building,** best known as the world's narrowest office building. When city developers widened surrounding streets in 1912, the Chinese consortium that owned the lot decided to proceed with its planned building, just making it narrower than at first planned. The result is a building 1.8 meters wide, noted in the *Guinness Book of Records* as the "narrowest building in the world."

To get to Chinatown from downtown catch bus no. 19 or 22 east along Pender Street. Try to avoid East Hastings Street at all times; it's Vancouver's skid row, inhabited by unsavory characters day and night.

Vancouver Centennial Police Museum

Vancouver's Eastside neighborhood lies between touristy Gastown and bustling Chinatown. Its only official "sight" is this museum, one block north of the Hastings and Main intersection at 240 E. Cordova St., 604/665-3346. It catalogs the history of Vancouver's police and the notorious criminals they chased. Formerly the city morgue, the museum houses historic police equipment, some intriguing seized items, and re-creations of the city's most famous crime scenes. Summer hours are Mon.–Sat. 10 A.M.–3 P.M., the rest of the year Mon.–Fri. 9 A.M.–3 P.M. Admission is adults $5, seniors and children $3. To get there from downtown, avoid walking the length of East Hastings Street and instead take bus no. 3, 4, 7, or 8 north along Granville Mall.

FALSE CREEK

False Creek, the narrow tidal inlet that almost cuts downtown off from the rest of the city, has undergone enormous changes over the last 25 years and is now a bona fide tourist attraction. The head of False Creek was transformed for Expo86 with the construction of the Plaza of Nations and Expo headquarters, now Science World. The expo spurred further changes, including a waterfront path that made it possible to walk or cycle between downtown and Granville Island. In the time since, much of the land has been rezoned, allowing the construction of modern inner city apartment complexes.

B.C. Place Stadium

On the central business district side of False Creek, this complex at 777 Pacific Blvd., 604/669-2300, is the world's largest air-supported domed stadium. It is the home of the B.C. Lions, one of the Canadian Football League teams, and is the venue for major trade shows, concerts, and other big events. Stadium tours depart from Gate H every Tuesday and Friday through summer at 11 A.M. and 1 P.M. Tours cost adult $6, senior $5, child $4; for bookings call 604/661-7362. At Gate A is the **B.C. Sports Hall of Fame and Museum,** 604/687-5520, open Tues.–Sun. 10 A.M.–5 P.M.; admission is adults $6, seniors and children $4 (admission is half price if you've taken a stadium tour). The easiest way to get there is to take the SkyTrain to Stadium Station.

Science World

This impressive, 17-story-high geodesic silver dome (it's best known locally as "the golf ball") sits over the waters of False Creek on the southeast side of city center, at 1455 Quebec St., 604/443-7440. It was built as the Expo Preview Centre for Expo86. For a time it housed restaurants, shops, and the world's largest Omnimax theater. Today the Vancouver landmark is home to Science World, a museum providing exhibitions that "introduce the world of science to the young and the young at heart." The three main galleries explore the basics of physics, natural history, and music through hands-on displays, while the Science Theatre shows the feature *Over Canada,* a high definition aerial tour over Canada accompanied by the sounds of Canadian musicians. The Omnimax theater, with one of the world's largest such screens (27 meters wide), is still here, featuring science-oriented documentaries. Admission to Science World is adult

© ANDREW HEMPSTEAD

Science World is locally known as "the golf ball."

$19.25, senior or child $14.25; in combination with a ticket to one Omnimax film admission is $24.75 and $17.25 respectively. The complex is open daily 10 A.M.–5 P.M.

The most enjoyable way to get to Science World is aboard a False Creek Ferry from Granville Island or the Vancouver Aquatic Centre. You can also drive to the west end of Terminal Avenue (plenty of parking is available) or take the SkyTrain to Main Street Station then walk across the street.

Granville Island

Follow Granville Street southwest through downtown and cross False Creek by bridge or ferry to reach Granville Island, regarded as one of North America's most successful inner-city industrial site redevelopments. The jazzed-up island is *the* place to go on a bright sunny day—allow at least several hours or an entire afternoon for this hive of activity.

Start your island exploration at **Granville Island Information Centre,** 1398 Cartwright St., 604/666-5784, website www.granvilleisland.com; open daily 9 A.M.–6 P.M., closed Monday in winter. The center offers a ton of local information, as well as displays and an audiovisual presentation detailing the island's colorful history.

After a preliminary stop at the information center, you can spend the better part of a day just walking around the island looking at the marina, the many specialty businesses reflecting the island's maritime heritage, fresh food markets, gift shops, restaurants, and theaters. The highlight is colorful **Granville Island Public Market,** open daily 9 A.M.–6 P.M., a hub of activity from dawn to dusk and a lot more than a tourist attraction. The market sells all kinds of things to eat—fresh fruit and vegetables, seafood from local waters, a wide variety of meats, specialty ingredients, and prepared ready-to-go meals—as well as unique jewelry and crafts, potted plants, and cut flowers.

At the opposite end of the island is the **Emily Carr Institute of Art and Design,** 1399 Johnston St., 604/844-3800. Named for one of Canada's best known artists, the facility attracts students from across the country to study fine

arts, applied arts, and media arts. Two galleries are open to the public. Near the island's vehicular access point, **Granville Island Museums,** 1502 Duranleau St., 604/683-1939, combines three museums under one roof. If you're into fishing, the **Sport Fishing Museum** is worth a visit alone for the collection of historic rods, reels, flies, and gaffs, as well as fishing-related artwork and the photographic history of fishing in British Columbia. In keeping with the island's heritage, the **Model Ships Museum** displays models of vessels similar to those built on the island, such as tugs, steamers, and fishing boats, as well as the signature exhibit, a four-meter-long replica of a warship. The **Model Trains Museum** claims to hold the world's largest collection of model trains on permanent public display, all running on operational layouts. Museum admission is $3.50, and hours are daily 10 A.M.–5:30 P.M.

To get to the island by boat, jump aboard one of the small **False Creek Ferries.** The boats run regularly between the island, Vancouver Aquatic Centre at Sunset Beach ($2), and Vanier Park ($3.50). To get to the island by land, take a no. 50 (False Creek) bus from Howe Street to the stop under Granville Street Bridge at the entrance to the island, or take a Granville Island bus from downtown. Parking on the island is almost impossible, at best, especially on weekends when locals do their fresh-produce shopping. If you do find a spot, it'll have a three-hour maximum time limit.

WEST END

The West End (not to be confused with the West Side, south of downtown, or West Vancouver, on the north side of the harbor) lies west of the central business district between Burrard Street and **English Bay Beach,** the gateway to Stanley Park. On foot, walk along Robson Street, then south on Denman Street, to reach pretty, park-fringed English Bay Beach. The golden sands, tree-shaded grassy roadsides, and sidewalks at the west end of the West End are popular with walkers, joggers, cyclists, and sun worshippers year-round.

VANCOUVER

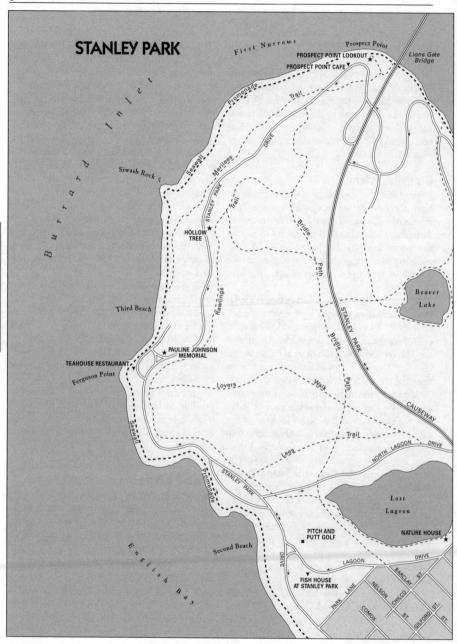

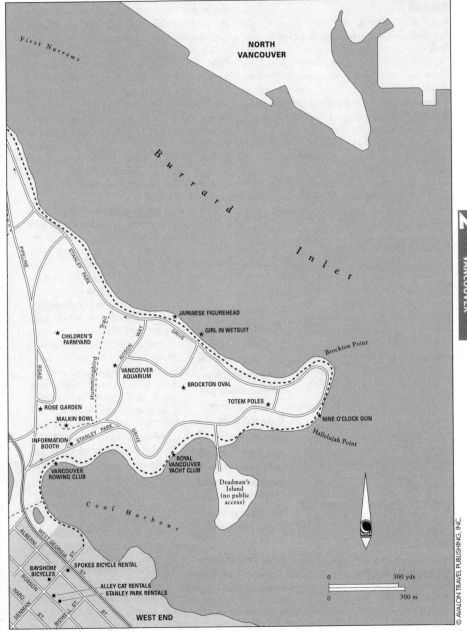

First Narrows

NORTH
VANCOUVER

Burrard Inlet

VANCOUVER

Brockton Point

JAPANESE FIGUREHEAD

GIRL IN WETSUIT

CHILDREN'S
FARMYARD

VANCOUVER
AQUARIUM

BROCKTON OVAL

TOTEM POLES

ROSE GARDEN

NINE O'CLOCK GUN

MALKIN BOWL

Hallelujah Point

INFORMATION
BOOTH

STANLEY PARK DRIVE

ROYAL
VANCOUVER
YACHT CLUB

VANCOUVER
ROWING CLUB

Deadman's
Island
(no public
access)

Coal Harbour

WEST GEORGIA ST.

ALBERNI ST.

SPOKES BICYCLE RENTAL

BAYSHORE
BICYCLES

ROBSON ST.

ALLEY CAT RENTALS

STANLEY PARK RENTALS

HARO ST.

DENMAN ST.

BIDWELL ST.

CHILCO ST.

WEST END

0   300 yds
0   300 m

PIPELINE ROAD

STANLEY PARK

Hummingbird Trail

AVISON WAY

DRIVE

© AVALON TRAVEL PUBLISHING, INC.

Robson Street

If you like to shop in trendy boutiques, sample European delicacies, and sip cappuccinos at sidewalk cafés, saunter along this colorful and exciting street linking downtown to the West End. Once the center of a predominantly German neighborhood, Robson Street is also known as **Robsonstrasse.** At 1610 Robson (the west end), **Robson Public Market** occupies an impressive atrium-topped building filled with meat, seafood, dairy products, fruits and veggies, nuts, flowers, craft vendors, fresh juice and salad bars, and an international food fair. To get there catch bus no. 3, which runs west along Robson Street from Granville Mall. Between the market and Burrard Street is the trendy Robsonstrasse shopping area.

Roedde House Museum

Most of the West End's turn-of-the-century buildings are long gone, but a precinct of nine homes built between 1890 and 1908 has been saved and is preserved as **Barclay Heritage Square.** Each building looks much as it would have when first built, right down to the style of surrounding gardens. The only one of the nine open to the public is Roedde House, at 1415 Barclay St. (take Broughton St. off Robson St.), 604/684-7040. Built in 1893, this Queen Anne Revival–style home is a classic example of Vancouver's early residential architecture. It was restored using historical records to ensure accuracy—right down to the color of the walls and interior furnishings. Costing adult $4, senior $3, tours of the house are conducted Tues.–Fri. at 11 A.M. (call to reserve a spot).

STANLEY PARK

Beautiful Stanley Park, a lush 405-hectare tree- and garden-carpeted peninsula jutting out into Burrard Inlet, is a sight for sore eyes in any weather—an enormous peaceful oasis

Beautiful Stanley Park, a lush 405-hectare tree-and garden-carpeted peninsula jutting out into Burrard Inlet, is a sight for sore eyes in any weather—an enormous peaceful oasis sandwiched between the city center's skyscrapers and the North Shore at the other end of Lions Gate Bridge.

sandwiched between the city center's skyscrapers and the North Shore at the other end of Lions Gate Bridge. Unlike other famous parks, such as New York's Central Park and London's Royal Park, Stanley Park is a permanent preserve of wilderness in the heart of the city, complete with dense coastal forests and abundant wildlife. It was Alexander Hamilton, land commissioner for the Canadian Pacific Railway, whose proposal to preserve the end of Burrard Peninsula led to the creation of the park, which was later named for Lord Stanley, Canada's governor-general from 1888 to 1893. It is dedicated for "the use and enjoyment of all peoples of all colors, creeds, and customs for all time."

Walk or cycle the 10-km **Seawall Promenade** or drive the perimeter via **Stanley Park Drive** to take in beautiful water and city views. Travel along both is one-way in a counterclockwise direction (those on foot can go either way, but if you travel clockwise you'll be going against the flow). For vehicle traffic, the main entrance to Stanley Park is the beginning of Stanley Park Drive, which veers right from the end of Georgia Street; on foot, follow Denman Street to its north end to find a pathway leading around Coal Harbour into the park. Either way, you'll pass a small information booth where park maps are available. Just before the booth, take Pipeline Road to access **Malkin Bowl,** home to outdoor theater productions; a **rose garden;** a **children's farmyard,** and forest-encircled **Beaver Lake.** Pipeline Road rejoins Stanley Park Drive near the Lions Gate Bridge, but by not returning to the park entrance you'll miss most of the following sights.

Vancouver Aquarium

In the forest behind the information booth is Canada's largest aquarium, the third largest in North America. Guarding the entrance is a five-meter-long killer whale sculpture by preeminent native artist Bill

Reid. More than 8,000 aquatic animals and 600 species are on display, representing all corners of the planet, from the oceans of the Arctic to the rainforests of the Amazon. A number of exhibits highlight regional marinelife, including the Wild Coast pool and Pacific Canada Pavilion. In the Amazon Gallery, there's a computer-generated hourly tropical rainstorm and creatures such as crocodiles and piranhas as well as fascinating misfits such as a four-eyed fish. The Tropical Gallery re-creates an Indonesian marine park, complete with colorful sealife and coral, and small reef sharks. At the far end of the aquarium, a large pool holds beluga whales—distinctive pure white marine mammals—and sea lions, representing Arctic Canada. They can be viewed from above or below ground. The aquarium is open in summer daily 9:30 A.M.–7 P.M., the rest of the year daily 10 A.M.–5:30 P.M. Admission is adult $14, senior $11.70, child $9. For information call 604/659-3474.

Seawall Sights

The following sights are listed from the information booth, which overlooks Coal Harbour, in a counterclockwise direction. From this point, Stanley Park Drive and the Seawall Promenade pass the Royal Vancouver Yacht Club and **Deadman's Island.** Now a naval reserve, the island has a dark history, having seen many battles between native tribes, been the burial place of the last of the Coast Salish people, and been used as a quarantine station during an early smallpox epidemic.

The first worthwhile stop at **Brockton Point** (which refers to the entire eastern tip of the park) is a collection of authentic totem poles from the Kwagiulth people, who lived along the coast north of present-day Vancouver. Before rounding the actual point itself, you'll pass the **Nine O'Clock Gun,** which is fired each evening at, you guessed it, 9 P.M. Around the point, the road and the seawall continue to hug the shoreline, passing the famous *Girl in Wetsuit* bronze sculpture and a figurehead commemorating Vancouver's links to Japan.

The Lions Gate Bridge marks the halfway point of the seawall and a change in scenery.

From this point to Second Beach the views are westward toward the Strait of Georgia and across English Bay to Central Vancouver. The next stretch of pleasant pathway, about two kilometers long, is sandwiched between the water and steep cliffs, with **Siwash Rock** the only distinctive landmark. Continuing south, the seawall and Stanley Park Drive converge at the south end of **Third Beach,** a popular swimming and sunbathing spot (and a great place to watch the setting sun). From Second Beach it's only a short distance to busy Denman Street and English Bay Beach, or you can cut across the park past **Lost Lagoon** and back to Coal Harbour. Even at a casual pace, it's possible to walk the seawall in three hours.

Horse-drawn trams leave regularly from the information booth, 604/681-5115, on a one-hour tour in a 20-person carriage; adult $16.80, senior $15.85, child $10.95. Riding around the Seawall is also popular. Rent a bike (under $20 a day) from one of the many bike shops around the corner of Robson and Denman Streets. The least expensive is **Alley Cat Rentals,** 1779 Robson St., 604/684-5117.

SOUTH OF DOWNTOWN

Officially divided into 23 neighborhoods, the City of Vancouver encompasses the entire peninsula south of downtown, a largely residential area of the city extending west to Point Grey and the University of British Columbia. Vancouver's three largest museums and a number of public gardens lie south of downtown.

Vancouver Museum

Regional history from Precambrian times to the present comes to life at Vancouver Museum, 1100 Chestnut St. in Vanier Park, 604/736-4431. The West Coast Archaeology and Culture galleries hold ravishing masks, highly patterned woven blankets, and fine baskets. The Discovery and Settlement Gallery details European exploration of British Columbia—both by land and by sea. After browsing through the forestry and milltown displays and the metropolis of Vancouver exhibit, you end up in the gallery of changing

KITSILANO

Named for a Squamish chief and known simply as "Kits" to locals, Kitsilano is a trendy beachside suburb southwest of downtown boasting a young, active population. Extending south to West 16th Avenue and west to Alma Street from Burrard Street, its main attractions are two not-to-be-missed museums in **Vanier Park.** This park extends from Burrard Street Bridge to Maple Street and is a popular spot for walkers, joggers, and cyclists. It's home to the famous Bard on the Beach summertime theater. Greenspace continues beyond Vanier Park to **Kitsilano Beach,** facing English Bay. Vancouver's most popular beach, this spot attracts hordes of bronzed (and not so bronzed) bodies for its long sandy beach, warm shallow waters, spectacular mountain views, the city's largest outdoor pool, beach volleyball, and surrounding cafés and restaurants.

Away from the Kitsilano waterfront are two main shopping and dining precincts: West 4th Avenue between Burrard and Balsam Streets and Broadway between Larch and Collingwood Streets.

exhibitions, where you never know what you'll find. The complex also holds a gift shop and a self-serve restaurant overlooking Vanier Park. It's open year-round daily 10 A.M.–5 P.M., and Thursday until 9 P.M. Admission is a worthwhile adult $8, child $5.50. To reach the museum catch bus no. 22 on Burrard Street and get off after Burrard Street Bridge at the Cornwall and Chestnut Street stop, or catch a ferry to Vanier Park from Granville Island or the Aquatic Centre at Sunset Beach. There's also plenty of free parking.

In the same building as the museum is the **H.R. MacMillan Space Centre,** 604/738-7827, which features displays related to planet Earth, the surrounding universe, and space exploration. Many of these exhibits are hands-on and enjoyable for all ages. The Ground Station Canada theater shows 20-minute audiovisual presentations on the universe throughout the day. The center is open in summer daily 10 A.M.–5 P.M., closed Monday the rest of the year. Admission is adult $12.75, senior $9.75, child $8.75. Com-

bined tickets for the Space Centre and Vancouver Museum are $15, $10, and $9, respectively.

Adjacent to the museum complex is the **Gordon MacMillan Southam Observatory,** 604/738-2855, which is open for public stargazing Fri.–Sat. 7–11 P.M. when the skies are clear; admission is free.

Vancouver Maritime Museum

Just a five-minute stroll from Vancouver Museum is Vancouver Maritime Museum, 1905 Ogden Ave. (the end of Cypress Ave.) in Vanier Park, 604/257-8300. British Columbia's seafaring legacy is the focus here. Exhibits chronicle everything from the province's first sea explorers and their vessels to today's oceangoing adventurers, modern fishing boats, and fancy ships. Kids will love the Children's Maritime Discovery Centre and its model ships, computer terminals, underwater robot, and telescopes for viewing ships out in the harbor. The historic RCMP vessel *St. Roch* is dry-docked within the building, and admission includes a tour. Now a National Historic Site, the *St. Roch* was the first patrol vessel to successfully negotiate the infamous Northwest Passage. The museum is open in summer daily 10 A.M.–5 P.M., the rest of the year Tues.–Sat. 10 A.M.–5 P.M. and Sunday noon–5 P.M. Admission is adult $7, senior and child $4. From downtown, take bus no. 22 south on Burrard Street or walk down Burrard Street to the Aquatic Centre and hop aboard a False Creek Ferry.

When you're through inside the museum, you can wander down to the water to view the small fleet of historic vessels docked in the manmade harbor.

Museum of Anthropology

Containing the world's largest collection of arts and crafts of the Pacific Northwest native peoples, this excellent museum at the University of British Columbia, 6393 Northwest Marine Dr., 604/822-5087, should not be missed. Designed by innovative Canadian architect Arthur Erickson, the ultramodern concrete-and-glass building perches on a high cliff overlooking the Pacific Ocean and mimics the post-and-beam structures favored by the Coast Salish.

The entrance is flanked by panels that create the shape of a Bent-box, which the Salish believed contained the meaning of life. Inside, a ramp lined with impressive sculptures by renowned modern-day carvers leads to the Great Hall, a cavernous 18-meter-high room dominated by towering totem poles collected from along the coast and interspersed with other ancient works. A museum highlight is the collection of works by Haida artist Bill Reid, which includes *The Raven* and the *First Men,* a sculpture carved from a four-ton chunk of cedar. Other displays include intricate carvings, baskets, and ceremonial masks, fabulous jewelry, and European ceramics. The museum holds over 200,000 artifacts, most of which are stored in uniquely accessible research collections. Instead of being stored in musty boxes out back and available only to crusty old anthropologists, the collections are stored in the main museum—in row upon row of glass-enclosed cabinets and in drawers that visitors are encouraged to open. Details of each piece are noted in handy catalogs.

Outside, a deliciously scented woodland path on the left side of the museum leads to a reconstructed Haida village and a number of contemporary totem poles with descriptive plaques.

In summer, the museum is open daily 10 A.M.–5 P.M., and till 9 P.M. on Tuesday nights. The rest of the year the museum is open Tues.–Sun. 11 A.M.–5 P.M., and till 9 P.M. Tuesdays. Admission is adult $7, senior and child $5, everyone free on Tuesday after 5 P.M. If you have your own vehicle, make sure you have a fistful of change in order to park in the lot beside the museum.

Other Sights on the University Campus

About 300 meters south of the Museum of Anthropology is the serene **Nitobe Memorial Garden,** 604/822-9666. This traditional Japanese garden of shrubs and miniatures has two distinct sections: the Stroll Garden, laid out in a form that symbolizes the journey through life, and the Tea Garden, the place to contemplate life from a ceremonial teahouse. In summer it's open daily 10 A.M.–6 P.M. and admission is adult $2.75,

senior and child $1.75; the rest of the year it's open weekdays only 11 A.M.–2:30 P.M., but admission is free.

Also on campus is the **UBC Botanical Garden,** 6804 Marine Dr. (at 16th Ave. 2.4 km south of the Museum of Anthropology), 604/822-4208. Set among coastal forest, the 44-hectare garden features eight separate sections representing specific regions or environments. Highlights include Canada's largest collection of rhododendrons in the Asian Garden; a B.C. Native Garden alive with the plants, flowers, and shrubs found along the Pacific Northwest coast; and a display of mountain plants from the world's continents in the Alpine Garden. It's open in summer 10 A.M.–6 P.M., the rest of the year 10 A.M.–2:30 P.M. Admission is adult $4.75, senior $2.50, or combine a visit with the Nitobe Memorial garden for $6 and $3.75 respectively.

On the east side of campus is the **B.C. Golf Museum,** 2545 Blanca St., 604/222-4653, housed in a Tudor-style building that was originally a clubhouse. The museum holds a collection of British Columbia golfing memorabilia, extensive archives, and a library. It's open year-round Tues.–Sun. noon–4 P.M.; admission is by donation.

VanDusen Botanical Garden

In the mid-1960s, Shaughnessy residents lost their golf course to encroaching residential development, but they managed to save a plot of land that was later redeveloped as a public garden. VanDusen Botanical Garden is home to more than 7,500 species from every continent except Antarctica. It's the place to feast your eyes on more than 1,000 varieties of rhododendrons, as well as roses, all kinds of botanical rarities, winter blossoms, an Elizabethan hedge maze, and a children's topiary garden featuring animal shapes. At popular **Sprinklers Restaurant,** 604/261-0011, the light and airy decor, picture windows, and garden view bring the outside inside. Sprinklers is open daily 11:30 A.M.–3 P.M. for a reasonably priced lunch and 5:30–9 P.M. for a more expensive, dressier dinner; reservations recommended. The garden itself is open in summer daily 10 A.M.–8 P.M., April and October daily

10 A.M.–6 P.M., and the rest of the year daily 10 A.M.–4 P.M. Admission April–Oct. is adult $6, senior $4, child $3.25; the rest of the year it's adult $3.50, senior $2, child $1.75. The garden is at 5251 Oak St. (at 37th Ave.), 604/878-9274. To get there by bus, take no. 17 south along Burrard Street. Oak Street runs parallel to Granville Street; access to the garden is on the corner of East 33rd Avenue.

Queen Elizabeth Park

Less than two km from the VanDusen Botanical Garden, this 53-hectare park sits atop 152-meter-high **Little Mountain,** the city's highest point, with magnificent views of Vancouver and the Coast Mountains. It's a paradise of sweeping lawns, trees, flowering shrubs, masses of rhododendrons—a vivid spectacle in May and June—formal flower gardens including a rose garden in the park's southwest corner, sunken gardens in the old quarry pits, and mature plantings of native trees from across Canada.

The highlight of the park is the magnificent **Bloedel Floral Conservatory,** 604/257-8584, a glass-domed structure rising 40 meters and enclosing a temperature-controlled, humid tropical jungle. Inside you'll find a profusion of exotic flowering plants and a resident avian population including multihued parrots. The conservatory is open in summer Mon.–Fri. 9 A.M.–8 P.M. and Sat.–Sun. 10 A.M.–9 P.M., the rest of the year daily 10 A.M.–5 P.M. Visitors are free to wander around the park, but an admission is charged to the conservatory: adult $3.75, senior and child $2.25. The main entrance is by the junction of 33rd Avenue West and Cambie Street; to get there from downtown take bus no. 15 south on Burrard Street.

RICHMOND

The incorporated city of Richmond (pop. 170,000) sprawls across 12,240-hectare **Lulu Island** at the mouth of the Fraser River. Most visitors to Vancouver cross the island on their way north from the United States on Highway 99, or to or from the airport or Tsawwassen Ferry Terminal.

Steveston

On Lulu Island's southwestern extremity, the historic fishing village of Steveston is a lively spot worth a visit. In the 1880s it had more than 50 canneries and was the world's largest fishing port. The harbor still holds Canada's largest fleet of commercial fishing boats. To get to Steveston, take Highway 99 to the Steveston Highway exit, then head west, passing by a magnificent Buddhist temple. Town center is south from the Steveston Highway along the No. 1 Road. By bus from downtown, take no. 401, 406, or 407 south on Howe Street.

On the harborfront sits the **Gulf of Georgia Cannery National Historic Site,** 12138 4th Ave., 604/664-9009, a cannery that operated between 1894 and 1979. Much of the original cannery has been restored. In addition to canning line exhibits and demonstrations of the various machinery, an audiovisual presentation is offered in the Boiler House Theatre, and the Discovery area is set aside for children. It's open in summer daily 10 A.M.–5 P.M. and in spring and fall Thurs.–Mon. 10 A.M.–5 P.M. Admission is adult $6.50, senior $5, child $3.25. Another historic site, the **Britannia Heritage Shipyards,** is reached by following the signs east along Moncton Street to 5180 Westwater Dr., 604/718-8050. The site and a visitor center are open in summer Tues.–Sat. 10 A.M.–4 P.M. and Sunday noon–4 P.M. Another interesting Steveston attraction is **Steveston Museum,** in the old Royal Bank building at 3811 Moncton St., 604/271-6868. It's open Mon.–Sat. 9:30 A.M.–5 P.M. (closed for lunch 1–1:30 P.M.).

One block south of Moncton Street and a short walk from the old cannery is a touristy area known as **Steveston Landing.** This waterfront complex is lined with fishing-supply outlets, shops selling packaged seafood products, boutiques, and restaurants, and it bustles with activity in summer. Below the landing, fishing boats sell the day's catch, which could be halibut, salmon, crab, or shrimp. The latter are particularly good value (avoid the headless ones) at around $8 per pound. To watch all the action, grab a seat on the deck of **Shady Island Seafood,** 3800 Bayview Rd., 604/275-6587, where daily specials are around $8–10, a bowl of incredibly good clam chowder costs $5, and burgers with fries start at $6.

DELTA

Pass under the south arm of the Fraser River via Highway 99 and the George Massey Tunnel and you'll emerge in the sprawling industrial and residential district of Delta (pop. 100,000). The first township in the Delta area was Ladner's Landing, which was developed as a port facility for local farmers. Take Highway 17 (Exit 28) south from Highway 99 and turn right on Ladner Trunk Road to access the modern-day **Ladner Village.** River Road, west from the village, passes through a typical suburban scene of modern houses and well-tended gardens before entering a time warp of intriguing fishing shacks, maritime-related businesses, and floating houses.

George C. Reifel Bird Sanctuary

Two km from Ladner Village along River Rd., cross Canoe Passage on the old wooden bridge to access this great attraction missed by most visitors. The 350-hectare sanctuary protects the northern corner of low-lying Westham Island, a stopover for thousands of migratory birds in spring and fall. In the middle of a wide delta at the mouth of the Fraser River, the island is a world away from surrounding city life. The best time for a visit is during the spectacular snow goose migration, which runs from early November to mid-December. Otherwise, you'll see abundant migratory birdlife anytime between October and April. The island also serves as a permanent home for many bird species, including bald eagles, peregrine falcons, herons, swans, and owls, and a parking lot is filled with ducks. Within the sanctuary are many kilometers of trails, an observation tower, free birdseed, and a couple of picnic areas. It's open year-round daily 9 A.M.–4 P.M. Admission is adults $4, seniors and children $2.

Point Roberts

In 1846, when it was agreed that the international boundary would run along the 49th parallel, an exception was made for Vancouver Island, which was retained as a Canadian possession, even though its southern extremity dips well below this latitude. No such exception was made for Point Roberts, south of Tsawwassen and accessible by road only through Canada (take 56th Street south from Highway 17). Although most basic services are provided by British Columbia, the 12-square-km chunk of land is officially part of Washington State, and a 24-hour border crossing controls entry. The point's main attractions are the beaches, which face the Strait of Georgia to the west and the warm, shallow waters of Boundary Bay to the east. At the end of the road is a park with picnic tables and a campground overlooking the water. Most visitors are Vancouver locals, who take advantage of not only the point's natural attractions but also cheap liquor at the two huge taverns (until provincial liquor laws in British Columbia were relaxed, these bars were *especially* popular on Sunday).

Blue herons are one of many species at the George C. Reifel Bird Sanctuary.

SURREY

The City of Surrey is well within the Greater Vancouver Regional District (GVRD), but it's officially its own incorporated city. With a population of 349,000, it's British Columbia's third-largest city, after Vancouver and Victoria. It sprawls from the Fraser River in the north to White Rock and the international boundary in the south and from Delta in the west to Langley in the east. Surrey's first settlers were the Stewarts, who built a homestead beside the Nicomekl River in 1894. The original homestead is now the centerpiece of **Elgin Heritage Park,** 13723 Crescent Rd., 250/543-3456. The farm's original workers' accommodations have been transformed into a weaving center, where textiles are created on antique looms and spinning wheels. Also on the property is a barn full of antique farm machinery. The park is open Tues.–Fri. 10 A.M.–4 P.M., Sat.–Sun. noon–4 P.M. To get there, take the King George Highway Exit off Highway 99, then turn onto Elgin Road, which becomes Crescent Road.

The Nicomekl River drains into Boundary Bay just north of **Crescent Beach.** Most of the surrounding foreshore is protected as parkland, including a narrow finger of land that protrudes northward around the mouth of the river. A surrounding buildup of silt has created tidal flats that attract a wide variety of birdlife; almost 200 species have been recorded on the spit.

South of Crescent Beach is **White Rock,** a seaside residential area named for a 400-ton glacial erratic that sits by the shoreline. Follow 8th Avenue west from Highway 99 to reach seaside **Semiahoo Park** and the beginning of a five-km promenade that extends around the Semiahoo Bay foreshore, passing dozens of cafés and restaurants, modern condos, and historic seaside cottages. Immediately south of White Rock is the international boundary and **Douglas Border Crossing.** This is the main border crossing for Vancouver-bound travelers heading north on Highway 5 from Seattle (Highway 99 north of the border). At the 24-hour checkpoint are duty-free shops and a 22-meter-high archway symbolizing the friendly relationship enjoyed between Canada and the United States.

NORTH SHORE

North of downtown lie the incorporated cities of **North Vancouver** (pop. 48,000) and **West Vancouver** (pop. 43,000), both of which are dramatically sandwiched between the North Shore Range of the Coast Mountains and Burrard Inlet. Road access from downtown is via the **Lions Gate Bridge,** but more enjoyable than getting caught up in bridge traffic is taking the SeaBus from Waterfront Station to **Lonsdale Quay** (adults $2.50 each way). At the lively quay, a small information center (to the right as you come out of the SeaBus terminal) dispenses valuable information, and transit buses depart regularly for all the sights listed below.

Capilano Suspension Bridge

The first bridge across the Capilano River opened in 1899. That remarkable wood-and-hemp structure stretched 137 meters across the deep canyon. Today, several bridges later, the canyon is spanned by a wood-and-wire suspension bridge a fearsome 70 meters above the Capilano River. Allow 30 minutes to walk the bridge and the nature trails on the far side, view the totem-pole carvers in the Big House, and browse the requisite gift shop. Admission is a bit steep—adult $11.95, senior $9.75, child $3.50, reduced to $8.95, $7.50, and $3 respectively outside summer—but it's one of Vancouver's most popular sights. (If you don't want to spend the money, you can get much the same thrill by crossing the free bridge in Lynn Canyon Park; see below.) The Capilano Suspension Bridge is open in summer daily 8 A.M.–dusk, the rest of the year daily 9 A.M.–5 P.M. For more information call 604/985-7474. To get there by car, cross Lions Gate Bridge, turn east onto Marine Drive, then immediately north onto Capilano Road, continuing to 3735 Capilano, on your left. By bus, take no. 246 north on Georgia Street or jump aboard the SeaBus and take bus no. 236 from Lonsdale Quay.

Capilano Salmon Hatchery and Regional Park

If you've always wanted to know more about the miraculous life cycle of salmon, or want some facts to back up your fish stories, visit this hatchery on the Capilano River, two km upstream from the suspension bridge (turn onto Capilano Park Rd. from Capilano Rd.), 604/666-1790. Along with educational displays and nature exhibits you can see what the fish see from an underwater point of view. From July through October, magnificent adult coho and chinook salmon fight their way upriver to the hatchery. It's open daily 8 A.M.–4 P.M., until 6 P.M. the rest of the year. Admission is free.

The hatchery is within **Capilano River Regional Park,** which extends north to **Cleveland Dam.** The dam was built in 1954 to form Capilano Lake—Vancouver's main drinking-water supply. Within the park wind many kilometers of hiking trails, including one that leads all the way down to where the Capilano River drains into Burrard Inlet; seven km (two hours) each way.

Grouse Mountain

Continuing north, Capilano Road becomes Nancy Greene Way and ends at the base of the **Grouse Mountain Skyride,** 604/984-0661, North America's largest aerial tramway. For an excellent view of downtown Vancouver, Stanley Park, the Pacific Ocean, and as far south as Mount Baker (Washington), take the almost-vertical eight-minute ride on the gondola to the upper slopes of 1,250-meter Grouse Mountain. Tickets are adult $17.95, senior $15.95, child $6.95. The gondola runs year-round, departing every 15 minutes 10 A.M.–10 P.M. in summer.

The trip to the top is a lot more than a gondola ride—and it's easy to spend the better part of a day exploring the surrounding area and taking advantage of the attractions included in the price of the ride up. Theatre in the Sky is a bird's eye, wide-screen presentation of the outdoor wonders of British Columbia. In addition, the Peak Chair continues higher up the mountain, and paved paths and nature trails skirt mountain meadows. Of the many possible hikes, the one-km **Blue Grouse Interpretive Trail** is the easiest and most enjoyable, winding around a lake and through a rainforest. More ambitious hikers will have ready access to the rugged West Coast Range. Other activities include a logging show, a

First Nations longhouse with dancing and storytelling, and helicopter rides with **Helijet** ($65 per person for an eight-minute Crown Mountain Tour; $95 for a 15-minute flight through the famous Lion Peaks).

Mountaintop dining facilities include a café, the casual **Bar 98 Bistro,** where you can drink in some high-elevation sunshine along with the view (open daily 11 A.M.–10 P.M.); the fancy **Grouse Nest Restaurant,** which provides free Skyride tickets with dinner reservations (open daily 5:30 P.M.–9:30 P.M.); and a picnic area.

To get to the gondola cross the Lions Gate Bridge from downtown, take the North Vancouver exit, then follow Capilano Road for five km up the valley. By public transport, take the SeaBus to Lonsdale Quay, then take bus no. 236 to the end of the road.

Lynn Canyon Park

On its way to Burrard Inlet, Lynn Creek flows through a deep canyon straddled by this 240-hectare park. Spanning the canyon is the "other" suspension bridge. The one here, built in 1912, is half as wide as its more famous counterpart over the Capilano River, but it's a few meters higher and, best of all, it's free. An ancient forest of Douglas fir surrounds the impressive canyon and harbors a number of hiking trails. Also visit **Lynn Canyon Ecology Centre,** 604/981-3103, where displays, models, and free slide shows and films explore plant and animal ecology. The center is open daily 10 A.M.–5 P.M.; admission is free.

Lynn Canyon Park is seven km east of the Capilano River. To get there by car, take the Lynn Valley Road Exit off Highway 1, east of the Lions Gate Bridge. By public transport, take the SeaBus to Lonsdale Quay, then bus no. 228 or 229.

Farther upstream is **Lynn Headwaters Regional Park,** a remote tract of wilderness on the edge of the city. Contact the Ecology Centre for more information.

Mount Seymour Provincial Park and Vicinity

Hikers and skiers flock to this 3,508-hectare park 20 km northeast of downtown. The park lies off Mt. Seymour Parkway, which spurs east off the

BOWEN ISLAND

From Vancouver, this is the most accessible of hundreds of islands dotting the Strait of Georgia. The island is only a short ferry trip from Horseshoe Bay, but seems a world away from the city. The first European settlers were loggers, but the island has also been home to fishing and whaling industries. Vancouverites began holidaying on the island as early as 1900, and soon a hotel, complete with tennis courts, lawn bowling, and grove of fruit trees, had opened. By the 1920s, the island was catering to tens of thousands of summer visitors annually and grand plans were put in place to open North America's most luxurious resort. But the development never eventuated, and today the island is home to a permanent population of 2,800, many of whom work in Vancouver, commuting daily across the water.

The ferry docks at the island's main settlement, aptly named **Snug Cove,** where you'll find all the services of a small town, including bed and breakfasts and cafés. There's good swimming at Mannion Bay, near Snug Cove, and **Bowen Island Sea Kayaking,** 604/947-9266, rents kayaks and offers tours, but the rest of island is also good to explore. A two-km trail leads from Snug Cove to Killarney Lake, where birdlife is prolific and roads lead across to the island's west coast.

B.C. Ferries, 604/669-1211, operates a 20-minute service between Horseshoe Bay and the island daily 6 A.M.–9:45 P.M. approximately once an hour. The fare is adult $5.75, child $3. The ferries also take vehicles ($18.25), but these aren't necessary as most visitors set out on foot. **Harbour Air,** 604/688-1277, offers an interesting evening tour to Bowen Island. For $142 you'll be whisked from downtown to the island by floatplane, enjoy dinner at an island restaurant, and return to your hotel by ferry and limousine. General information (including on island accommodations) is available on the website www.bowenisland.org.

TransCanada Highway just north of Burrard Inlet. The long and winding access road to the park climbs steadily through an ancient forest of western hemlock, cedar, and Douglas fir to a small facility area at an elevation of 1,000 meters. From the parking lot, trails lead to the summit of 1,453-meter Mt. Seymour; allow one hour for the two km (one-way) trek.

If you continue along Mount Seymour Parkway instead of turning north toward the park, you end up in the scenic little village of **Deep Cove** on the west shore of Indian Arm (off the northeast end of Burrard Inlet)—an excellent spot for a picnic. Take your sack lunch to the waterfront park and watch the fishing and pleasure boats coming and going in the bay. More adventurous visitors can swim, kayak, or scuba dive.

Cypress Provincial Park

This 3,012-hectare park northwest of downtown encompasses a high alpine area in the North Shore Mountains. To get to the park, take the TransCanada Highway 12 km west of Lions Gate Bridge and turn north onto Cypress Bowl Road (Exit 8). Even the park access road up from the TransCanada Highway is worthwhile for the views. The Highview Lookout provides a stunning panorama of the city. While at the fourth major switchback, pull into the turnout to see an old growth yellow cedar tree. Estimated to be over 1,000 years old, this ancient giant stands 40 meters tall and has a base circumference of 10 meters. At the 15-km mark, the road dead-ends at a parking lot.

Cypress is best known for its wintertime skiing and boarding, but there's plenty of hiking in the vicinity. From the main day lodge, well-marked hiking trails radiate out like spokes, through alpine meadows, to a subalpine lake, and to low peaks with views across Howe Sound. With a vivid imagination, maybe you'll spot Say-noth-kai, the two-headed sea serpent of native Salish legend, believed to inhabit the sound. On a clear day you can also make out the cone of Mt. Baker, one of a row of Pacific Coast volcanoes to the southeast, in Washington State. (For information on winter activities within the park, see Skiing and Snowboarding in the Recreation section.)

Lighthouse Park

On a headland jutting into Howe Sound, 70-hectare Lighthouse Park lies eight km west of the Lions Gate Bridge. Trails lead through the park to coastal cliffs and a lighthouse that guides shipping into narrow Burrard Inlet. Views from the lighthouse grounds are spectacular, extending west over the Strait of Georgia and east to Stanley Park and the Vancouver skyline. Get there along Marine Drive or aboard bus no. 250 from Georgia Street.

Horseshoe Bay

The pretty little residential area of Horseshoe Bay offers plenty to see and do while you wait for the Vancouver Island or Sunshine Coast ferry. If you and your trusty vehicle are catching one of the ferries, buy your ticket at the car booth, move your automobile into the lineup, then explore the town. Several restaurants, a bakery, a supermarket, a pub, and a couple of good delis cater to the hungry and thirsty. A stroll along the beautiful waterfront marina is a good way to cool your heels and dawdle away some waiting time.

EAST FROM DOWNTOWN

When you leave Vancouver and head due east, you travel through the most built-up and heavily populated area of British Columbia, skirting modern commercial centers, residential suburbs, and zones of heavy industry. Greater Vancouver extends almost 100 km along the Fraser Valley, through mostly residential areas. The main route east is the TransCanada Highway, which parallels the Fraser River to the south, passing through Burnaby, Langley, and Abbotsford. The original path taken by this highway crosses the Fraser River at New Westminster, the capital of British Columbia for a short period in the 1860s.

Burnaby

Immediately east of downtown, Burnaby was incorporated as a city in 1992 (its population of 195,000 makes it British Columbia's fourth largest city), but in reality it's part of Vancouver's suburban sprawl. It extends east from Boundary Road to Coquitlam, while Burrard Inlet lies to the north and riverside New Westminster to the southeast. The TransCanada Highway bisects Burnaby, but access is easiest via the SkyTrain, which makes four stops within the city, including at **Metrotown,** which is Vancouver's largest shopping mall.

Burnaby Village Museum lies in Deer Lake Park, on the south side of the TransCanada Hwy., 604/293-6500. It's a reconstruction of how a B.C. town would have looked in the first 20 years of the 1900s, complete with more than 30 shops and houses, heritage-style gardens, a miniature railway, and costumed staff. But the highlight is a historic carousel with more than 30 restored wooden horses. It's open May–early Sept. and in December 11 A.M.–4:30 P.M. Admission is adult $7.50, senior and child $5.35.

On the north side of the TransCanada Hwy. is **Burnaby Mountain Park,** home to **Simon Fraser University,** the province's second largest campus with a student population of 20,000. Centennial Way (off Burnaby Mountain Parkway) leads to the park's high point, where views extend down Burrard Inlet to North Vancouver and its stunning mountain backdrop. Also at the summit is a collection of totem poles, Japanese sculptures, a rose garden, and a restaurant. The university itself is worthy of inspection. Its unique design of "quadrants" linked by a massive fountain-filled courtyard is typical of architect Arthur Erickson, who was partly responsible for its design.

Vicinity of Coquitlam

Coquitlam (pop. 115,000) is a residential area north and east of Burnaby. It lies at the head of Burrard Inlet, near Port Moody, which was once slated as the terminus of the transcontinental railway. There's nothing of real interest in Coquitlam itself, but Loco Road leads around Burrard Inlet to **Belcarra Regional Park,** which is lapped by the waters of Indian Arm.

North of Coquitlam is the 38,000-hectare **Pinecone Burke Provincial Park,** which extends along the west shoreline of Pitt Lake (opposite Golden Ears Provincial Park) and as far west as the Boise Valley, scene of a short-lived gold rush in the late 1800s. Much of the park was logged over 100 years ago, but a few sections of old growth forest remain, including a 1,000-year-old stand of cedar in the Cedar Spirit Grove. To get to the park from Highway 7 take Coast Meridian Road north to Harper Road, which leads to Munro and Bennett Lakes.

Golden Ears Provincial Park

Encompassing 55,590 hectares of the Coast Mountains east of downtown Vancouver, this park extends from the Alouette River, near the suburb of Maple Ridge, north to Garibaldi Provincial Park. To get to the main facility areas, follow Highway 7 east from Coquitlam to Maple Ridge, then follow signs north along 232nd Street and 132nd Avenue. The park access road follows the Alouette River into the park, ending at Alouette Lake. The river and lake provide fair fishing, but the park's most popular activity is hiking. **Lower Falls Trail** begins at the end of the road and leads 2.7 km (one-way) along Gold Creek to a 10-meter-high waterfall; allow one hour each way. Across Gold Creek, **West Canyon Trail** climbs 200 meters over 1.5 km (allow 40 minutes each way) to a viewpoint of Alouette Lake. This trail begins from the West Canyon parking lot, where you'll also find a 12-km trail along the west bank of Gold Creek to Panorama Ridge and to the summit of the park's namesake, the **Golden Ears.** The name comes from the way the setting sun reflects off the twin peaks of Mt. Blanchard. This trail gains 1,500 meters, making it an extremely strenuous hike best undertaken as an overnight trip.

A number of riverside and lakeside picnic areas line the park access road, and at road's end are two large campgrounds ($18.50 per night).

New Westminster

"New West," as it's best known, is a densely populated residential area 15 km southeast of downtown. Its strategic location, where the Fraser River divides, caused it to become a hub of river transportation and a thriving economic center. It was declared the capital of the mainland colony in 1859, then the provincial capital in the years 1866–68. Only a few historic buildings remain, and the old port area has been totally overtaken by modern developments. Although still a busy inland port, the north side of the river, along Columbia Street, was redeveloped in the late 1980s, with a riverside promenade linking attractive stretches of green space to the Westminster Quay development and other modern shopping areas.

The center of the action is **Westminster Quay Market,** which holds markets of fresh produce, takeout food stalls, and specialty shops. Immediately to the south of the market is the *Samson V,* built in 1937 and the last remaining paddle-wheeler left on the river when it was retired in 1980. It's now open for public inspection through summer Wed.–Sun. noon–5 P.M. Call the local museum at 604/527-4640 for details. **Irving House Historic Centre,** 302 Royal Ave., 604/527-4640, once the home of riverboat captain William Irving and his family, is one of western Canada's oldest standing residential buildings. The adjacent **New Westminster Museum** catalogs the history of the area. Both are open in summer Tues.–Sun. 11 A.M.–5 P.M., weekends 1–5 P.M. the rest of the year.

The easiest way to reach New West from downtown is by SkyTrain. By vehicle, take the Kingsway out of the city. This stretch of road becomes 10th Avenue, winding around the north side of New West's downtown commercial district before crossing the Fraser River as McBride Boulevard. Turn right at the last intersection (Columbia Street) on the north side of the river to reach the riverfront and the heart of the action. Alternatively, take the SkyTrain from any downtown station.

Recreation

WALKING AND HIKING

Stanley Park

Vancouver is not a particularly good city to explore on foot, but it does have one redeeming factor for foot travelers—Stanley Park, an urban oasis crisscrossed with hiking trails and encircled by a 10-km promenade that hugs the shoreline. Along the way are many points of interest (see Sights, above), benches, and interpretive plaques pointing out historical events. Allow three hours for the entire circuit. The promenade can be walked in either direction, but those on bikes and skates must travel counterclockwise. It is *always* busy, especially in late afternoon and on weekends.

Away from the Seawall Promenade, you'll find most trails a lot less used. A good alternative to one long section of the promenade is to ascend the steps immediately north of Lions Gate Bridge to Prospect Point (and maybe stop for a snack at the café), then continue west along the Merilees Trail, which follows the top of the cliff band to Third Beach. Along the way, an old lookout point affords excellent views of Siwash Rock and the Strait of Georgia.

The isthmus of land linking the park to the rest of the downtown peninsula is less than one kilometer wide, but it's mostly taken up by Lost Lagoon. A 1.5-km trail (30-minute round-trip) encircles this bird-filled body of water. In the heart of the park is Beaver Lake, a smaller body of water, but still alive with birds throughout summer. Trails lead into this lake from all directions, and it can easily be walked around in 20 minutes.

False Creek

From English Bay Beach, a promenade continues along English Bay to Sunset Beach and Vancouver Aquatic Centre. The small ferries that operate

VANCOUVER

© ANDREW HEMPSTEAD

The Seawall Promenade around Stanley Park is the city's most popular walk.

on False Creek, extending service as far west as the aquatic center, open up a number of walking combinations around False Creek. Granville Island is a good starting point. No official trails go around the island, but if you walk east from the market, you pass a flotilla of floating houses and go through a grassy area to Lookout Hill. Continue around the island and you'll come across a small footbridge leading to the mainland. From this point, it's seven km (allow two hours) around the head of False Creek, passing Science World and the Plaza of Nations, then closely following the water to the foot of Hornby Street for the short ferry trip back across to Granville Island.

Pacific Spirit Regional Park and Vicinity

This 762-hectare park out near the university offers 35 km of hiking trails through a forested environment similar to that which greeted the first European settlers over 200 years ago. A good starting point is the Park Centre, 604/224-5739, which has a supply of trail maps. The entire park is crisscrossed with trails, so although getting seriously lost is impossible, taking the wrong trail and ending up away from your intended destination is easy. One good trailhead is in the southeast of the park, at the junction of King Edward and 29th Avenues. From this point, the Imperial Trail heads west through a forest of red cedar and fir, crosses Salish Creek, then emerges on Southwest Marine Drive, at a monument commemorating the journey of Simon Fraser. From this lofty viewpoint, the view extends across the Strait of Georgia. This trail is 2.8 km (allow one hour) one-way. In the same vicinity as the trailhead detailed above, at the west end of 19th Avenue, a short boardwalk trail leads to Camosun Bog, home to a great variety of unique plant- and birdlife.

In the north of the park, north of Chancellor Boulevard, trails lead through deep ravines and across Marine Drive to Arcadia and Spanish Banks Beaches. Walk along these beaches, then up any ravine, across Marine Drive, and along Admiral Trail, following the bluffs for a circuit that can be as short or as long as you wish.

For the more ambitious, it is possible to use the trails of Pacific Spirit Park and around Point Grey to circumnavigate the University of British Columbia campus; 14 km round-trip (allow 4–5 hours).

North Shore

The provincial parks along the North Shore contain outstanding scenery and wildlife, crystal-clear lakes and rivers, and established hiking trails that are generally well maintained and easy to follow. (These trails are covered under North Shore in the Sights section.)

BICYCLING

Stanley Park is a mecca for cyclists; among its network of bike paths is the popular Seawall Promenade, which hugs the coast for 10 km (bike travel is in a counterclockwise direction). On the south side of English Bay, a cycle path runs from Vanier Park to Point Grey and the university, passing some of the city's best beaches on the way. On the north side of Burrard Inlet, hard-core mountain-bike enthusiasts tackle the rough trails of Cypress Provincial Park and Grouse Mountain.

Near the entrance to Stanley Park, where Robson and Denman Streets meet, is a profusion of bike-rental shops. These include **Alley Cat Rentals,** 1779 Robson St., 604/684-5117; **Bayshore Bicycles,** 745 Denman St., 604/688-2453; **Spokes Bicycle Rental,** 1798 W. Georgia St., 604/688-5141; and **Stanley Park Rentals,** 1741 Robson St., 604/608-1908. With this many outlets crowded around one block competition is fierce. Alley Cat Rentals offers the best deals, $6 per hour or $18 per day for a basic mountain bike and $12 per hour or $36 per day for a suspension bike.

GOLF

Golf in Vancouver has come a long way since 1892, when a few holes were laid out across the sand dunes of Jericho Beach. Today, the city is blessed with over 50 courses, most of which are open to the public. It is often quoted that in

Vancouver it is possible to ski in the morning and golf in the afternoon, and because most courses are open year-round this really is true.

The Courses

There's a pitch-and-putt golf course in Stanley Park ($9) and another in Queen Elizabeth Park (also $9), but for serious golfers, the following courses provide a truer test of the game.

One the best courses open to the public is the **University Golf Course,** 5185 University Blvd., Point Grey, 604/224-1818. The course has no affiliation with its namesake, but does have a strong teaching program. The course itself features fairways lined with mature trees and plays to 6,584 yards. The clubhouse exudes old-world charm and features an adjacent golf museum. Greens fees are a reasonable $40; reservations can be made up to a week in advance.

Vancouver Parks and Recreation operates three 18-hole courses on the south side of the city. **McCleery Golf Course,** 7188 McDonald St., Southlands, 604/257-8191, is a flat, relatively easy layout with wide fairways. Rebuilt in the late 1990s, **Fraserview Golf Course,** 7800 Vivian Dr., Fraserview, 604/257-6923, winds through a well-established forest. **Langara Golf Course,** 6706 Alberta St. (off Cambie St.), South Cambie, 604/713-1816, is the most challenging of the three. Each course offers club rentals, carts, and lessons, and all but Langara have driving ranges. Greens fees at all three courses are $41 during the week and $44 on weekends. Mon.–Thurs. seniors play for a discounted rate of $24.50. Make bookings up to five days in advance by calling 604/280-1818, or call the courses direct on the day you want to play.

Water comes into play on 13 holes of the **Mayfair Lakes & Country Club,** 5460 No. 7 Rd., Richmond, 604/276-0505, but its most unique feature is the salmon, which spawn in its waterways. It plays to a par of 71 and 6,641 yards from the back markers. Greens fees Mon.–Thurs. are $65, $75 Friday and weekends, with discounted twilight and off-season rates.

Formerly a private club, **Gleneagles Golf Course,** on the North Shore, is a sloping nine-hole layout with ocean views. Operating on a first-come, first-served basis, greens fees for nine holes are just $18. It's at 6190 Marine Dr., West Vancouver, 604/921-7353.

Of the many golf courses spread out along the Fraser River Valley, **Meadow Gardens Golf Course,** on the north side of the river at 19675 Meadow Gardens Way (off Hwy. 7), Pitt Meadows, 604/465-5474 or 800/667-6758, stands out. Water comes into play on 13 holes, including the signature 18th hole, a par 5 that comprises island-only landing areas for the drive and the second shot, and then the approach is played on an island green. Adding to the fun is a course length of a scary 7,041 yards from the back markers. Facilities include a huge clubhouse featuring a restaurant with views, hot tubs, and a sauna, plus a driving range. Greens fees start at $48 for 18 holes.

West Coast Golf Shuttle

The West Coast Golf Shuttle, 604/730-1032 or 888/599-6800, website www.golf-shuttle.com, transports golfers to a "course of the day" and includes hotel pick-ups, a booked tee time, greens fees, club, a power cart, and even umbrellas and sunscreen for a fee of $79–154 per person, depending on the course and day of the week. Club rentals are an additional $25. This company also organizes overnight Vancouver and Whistler golf packages.

WATER SPORTS
Swimming and Sunbathing

All of Vancouver's best beaches are along the shoreline of English Bay; 10 have lifeguards on duty through the summer months 11:30 A.M.–8:45 P.M. Closest to downtown is **English Bay Beach,** at the end of Denman Street. Flanked by a narrow strip of parkland and a wide array of cafés and restaurants, this is *the* beach for people-watching. From English Bay Beach the Seawall Promenade leads north to **Second** and **Third Beaches,** both short, secluded stretches of sand. To the south is **Sunset Beach,** most popular with families.

Swimmers take note: Even at the peak of summer, the water here only warms up to about

17° C (63° F), tops. If that doesn't sound very enticing, continue to the south end of Sunset Beach to **Vancouver Aquatic Centre,** 1050 Beach Ave., 604/665-3424. Inside is a 50-meter heated pool, saunas, whirlpools, and a small weight room. Admission is adult $4, senior $2.40, child $2.

On the south side of English Bay, **Kitsilano Beach** offers spectacular views back across the bay to downtown and the mountains beyond. Take a dip in the adjacent public pool, which is 137 meters long and was built in 1931. The beach and pool are an easy walk from both Vanier Park and a False Creek Ferries dock.

Canoeing and Kayaking

Granville Island is the center of action for paddlers, and the calm waters of adjacent False Creek make the perfect place to practice your skills. For the widest choice of equipment, head to **Adventure Fitness,** 1510 Duranleau St., 604/687-1528, or **Ecomarine Ocean Kayak Centre,** 1668 Duranleau St., 604/689-7575. Both rent single sea kayaks from $14 for two hours or $25 for 24 hours, and double sea kayaks and canoes from $19 for two hours, $30 for 24 hours. Both companies also teach kayaking.

The **Indian Arm** of Burrard Inlet allows for a real wilderness experience, right on the city's back doorstep. This 22-km-long fjord cuts deeply into the North Shore Range; the only development is at its southern end, where the suburb of Deep Cove provides a takeoff point for the waterway. **Deep Cove Canoe and Kayak Centre,** 2156 Banbury Rd., Deeo Cove, 604/929-2268, rents canoes and kayaks from $40 per day for a single kayak. For a tour, contact **Lotus Land Tours,** 604/684-4922 or 800/528-3531, which charges $135 pp for a full-day tour including downtown hotel pickups, a salmon barbecue on an uninhabited island, and instruction.

Fishing, Boating, and Yachting

Most keen anglers will want to head farther afield for the best fishing opportunities, but a few runs of salmon occur within city limits, and rainbow trout, kokanee, and Dolly Varden inhabit the larger mountain lakes north of the city.

The calm waters of False Creek and Burrard Inlet are perfect for boating and are always busy with pleasure craft. For puttering around the inner-city waterways, rent a boat from **Stanley Park Boat Rentals,** Coal Harbour Marina, 566 Cardero St., 604/682-6257, or **Granville Island Boat Rentals,** 1696 Duranleau St., 604/682-6287. Both companies will suggest a trip to suit your boating ability and time schedule, while also providing bait and tackle and directing you to the fishing hot spots.

Yachties and yachties-to-be should head for **Cooper Boating Center,** 1620 Duranleau St., Granville Island, 604/687-4110, website www.cooperboating.com, which boasts Canada's largest sailing school and also holds the country's biggest fleet for charters. For those with experience, Cooper's rents yachts (from $140 per day for a Catalina 22) for a day's local sailing, or take to the waters of the Strait of Georgia on a bareboat charter (from $1,154 per week for a Catalina 27).

Scuba Diving

A quick flip through the Vancouver Yellow Pages tells you that scuba diving is alive and well north of the 49th parallel. The city's many scuba shops have everything you need, and they're excellent sources of information on all the best local spots. They can also usually tell you who is chartering what, and when. Coming highly recommended is **Rowand's Reef Scuba Shop,** 1512 Duranleau St., Granville Island, 604/669-3483, a full-service dive shop offering rentals, sales, organized diving trips, and PADI dive-certification courses throughout the year. Available here and in most local bookstores are the diver's bibles *101 Dives from the Mainland of Washington and British Columbia* and *99 Dives from the San Juan Islands in Washington to the Gulf Islands,* both by Betty Pratt-Johnson. The local *Diver* magazine is another good source of information; its scuba directory lists retail stores, resorts, charter boats, and other services.

SKIING AND SNOWBOARDING

While Vancouver is the gateway to world-renowned Whistler/Blackcomb (see Whistler in the Southwestern British Columbia chapter), the city boasts three other alpine resorts on its back doorstep. They don't offer the terrain or facilities of Whistler, and their low elevations can create unreliable conditions, but a day's skiing or riding at any one of the three sure beats being stuck in the hustle and bustle of the city on a cold winter's day.

Grouse Mountain

Towering above North Vancouver, the cut slopes of this resort can be seen from many parts of the city, but as you'd expect, on a clear day views from *up there* are much more spectacular. To get there, take Capilano Road north from the TransCanada, following it onto Nancy Greene Way, from where a gondola lifts you up 1,000 vertical meters to the slopes. Four chairlifts and a couple of T-bars serve 24 runs and a vertical rise of 365 meters. Advanced skiers and boarders shouldn't get too excited about a day on the slopes here—even the runs with names like Purgatory and Devil's Advocate are pretty tame. But schussing down the slopes of Grouse Mountain after dark is an experience you won't soon forget. Most runs are lighted and overlook the city of Vancouver, laid out in all its brilliance far below. Facilities at the resort include a snowboard park, a rental shop, ski and snowboard school, and a couple of dining choices. Lift tickets are adult $32, youth $24, senior and child $17. Night skiing (after 4 P.M.) costs adult $24, youth $18, senior and child $13 until closing at 10 P.M. For Grouse Mountain information call 604/986-0661; for a snow report call 604/986-6262; website www.grousemountain.com.

Cypress Mountain

In Cypress Provincial Park, this small resort offers about 25 runs on a vertical rise of 534 meters. Its four double chairs open a wide variety of terrain on two mountain faces, most suited to beginners and intermediates. Spectacular views take in Howe Sound and Vancouver Island. Another highlight of Cypress is the night skiing; many

Schussing down the slopes of Grouse Mountain after dark is an experience you won't soon forget. Most runs are lighted and overlook the city of Vancouver, laid out in all its brilliance far below.

runs are lighted until 11 P.M. Other facilities include a rental shop, ski and snowboard school, café, and lounge. Lift tickets are adult $36, senior $18, child $17. Cypress also caters to cross-country skiers; 16 km of groomed and track-set trails lead from the historic Hollyburn Lodge and five km are lighted for night skiing.

To get to the resort, take the TransCanada Highway 12 km west from Lions Gate Bridge and turn north on Cypress Bowl Road. If you don't feel like driving up the mountain, catch the shuttle bus that departs hourly from Lonsdale Quay and Cypress Mountain Sports in Park Royal Mall, West Vancouver; $10 round-trip. For resort and shuttle bus information, call 604/926-5612; for a snow report call 604/419-7669; website www.cypressmountain.com.

Mount Seymour

With the highest base elevation of Vancouver's three alpine resorts, Seymour's snow is somewhat reliable, but the area's relatively gentle terrain will be of interest only to beginning and intermediate skiers and boarders. Four chairlifts serve 20 runs and a vertical rise of 365 meters. On-hill facilities include a snowboard park, toboggan run, and massive day lodge with rental shop. Weekend lift passes are adult $29, senior $19, child $14, while through the week rates are discounted to $22, $14, and $11 respectively.

The resort is in Mt. Seymour Provincial Park. To get there, head north off the TransCanada Highway 15 km east of the Lions Gate Bridge, following the Mt. Seymour Parkway to Mt. Seymour Road. Call the resort for a shuttle schedule from the North Shore; $7 per person round-trip. For resort information call 604/986-2261; for a snow report call 604/718-7771; website www.mountseymour.com.

SPECTATOR SPORTS

Vancouverites love their sports—not just being involved themselves, but supporting local teams.

With a long season and outside activities curtailed by the winter weather, ice hockey—known in Canada simply as "hockey"—draws the biggest crowds.

Ice Hockey

In 1911 the world's second (and largest) artificial ice rink opened at the north end of Denman Street, complete with seating for 10,000 hockey fans. The local team, then known as the Vancouver Millionaires, played in a small professional league, and in 1915 Vancouver won its first and only **Stanley Cup,** the holy grail of professional ice hockey. Today, the **Vancouver Canucks** struggle to get the best players in a U.S.-dollar-oriented market, but the team is still competitive, and it came closest to reclaiming the Cup in 1994, when it lost in the finals. The team plays out of General Motors Place (across from B.C. Place Stadium on Griffith Way), built for the now defunct Vancouver Grizzlies NBA franchise. The season runs from October to April; ticket prices range $24–68. For more information call 604/899-4625 or 604/280-4400, or check out website www.canucks.com.

Football

The **B.C. Lions,** 604/589-7627 or 604/280-4400, website www.bclions.com, are Vancouver's Canadian Football League franchise. (American football fans might be surprised by some of the plays—the rules are slightly different than those of the NFL. And no, you're not imagining things, the playing field is larger than those used in the game's American version.) CFL teams have been competing for the Grey Cup, named for Earl Grey, a former governor-general of Canada, since 1909. Vancouver joined the competition in 1954, first winning the Cup a decade later in 1964. In recent years, the Lions have struggled to gain a large support base, but they continue to perform well, last winning the Grey Cup in 2000 and before that in 1994. Home games are played at B.C. Place Stadium, on the south side of downtown at the corner of Robson and Beatty Streets, 604/669-2300, website www.bclions.com. The season runs June–Nov., with most games played in the evening; tickets range $15–48.

Soccer

Vancouver is a soccer stronghold, with two professional teams and dozens of intracity leagues. The **Whitecaps,** Vancouver's professional men's soccer team, play in the A-League of the United Soccer League, competing against 20 other teams across North America through the months of summer. Home games are played at Swangard Stadium, in Burnaby's Central Park. To get there, take the Kingsway out of the city to Boundary Road (Patterson SkyTrain station). For information and tickets call 604/899-9283. The team's website is www.whitecapssoccer.com.

Local women players are represented in the United Soccer League by the **Vancouver Breakers** (formerly the Vancouver Angels). This team also plays at Burnaby's Swangard Stadium. Team contacts are 604/899-9283 or the website www.breakerssoccer.com.

Horse Racing

Thoroughbred racing takes place in **Hastings Park Racecourse** in the Pacific National Exhibition grounds, six km east of downtown, 604/254-1631, website www.hastingspark.com. Full betting and a variety of dining facilities are offered. The season runs April–Oct., with the first race starting at 1:23 P.M. on weekends and 5:53 P.M. on Wednesday and Friday. The biggest races fall near the end of the season, including the BC Derby on the last Saturday in September. Even for nonbetters, a day at the races can be exciting—and admission is cheap, just $3.50 for adults and $1.50 for seniors.

ARTS AND ENTERTAINMENT

There's never a dull moment in Vancouver when it comes to nightlife. The city's unofficial entertainment district extends southwest along Granville Street from Granville St. Mall, and south from this strip to False Creek. Cinemas line Granville St. Mall, while beyond the mall is a smattering of nightclubs, with the main concentration in Yaletown. Performing arts and concert venues are scattered through the city, but the three largest—Ford Centre for the Performing Arts, Queen Elizabeth Centre, and B.C. Place

VANCOUVER

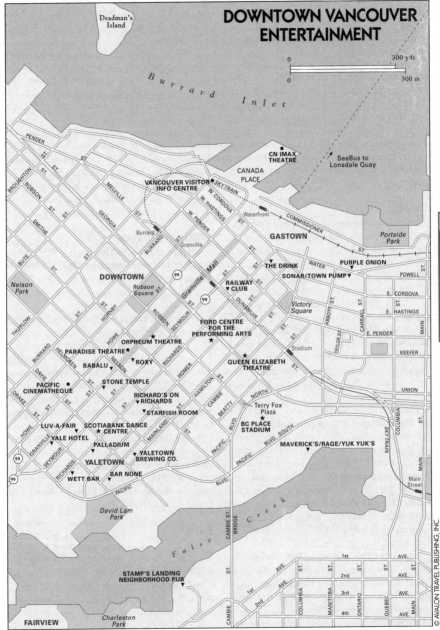

DOWNTOWN VANCOUVER ENTERTAINMENT

VANCOUVER

Stadium—are south of Granville Street along Georgia Street.

For complete listings of all that's happening around the city, pick up the free *Georgia Strait* (weekly), the offspring of an entertainment rag started by the flower children of the late 1960s. Friday and weekend editions of Vancouver's two daily newspapers, the *Province* or the *Vancouver Sun*, offer comprehensive entertainment listings.

As in all other major cities across Canada, **Ticketmaster,** 604/280-3311, website www .ticketmaster.ca, has a monopoly on ticket sales to major entertainment events; have your credit card ready.

Theater

Vancouver has theaters all over the city—for professional plays, amateur plays, comedy, and "instant" theater. In total, the city boasts 30 professional theater companies and more than 20 regular venues. One of the great joys of summer in the city is sitting around Malkin Bowl in Stanley Park watching **Theatre under the Stars.** The show goes Mon.–Sat. at 7 P.M.; $18 per person. For details call 604/687-0174. Another summer production is **Bard on the Beach,** 604/739-0559, a celebration of the work of Shakespeare that takes place in huge, open-ended tents in Vanier Park. Tickets are well priced at just $15–25.

Designed by renowned architect Moshe Safdie, the **Ford Centre for the Performing Arts,** 777 Homer St., 604/602-0616, hosts the biggest musical hits. Matinees cost from $50 while evening shows range $55–90. One-hour tours of the complex depart from the lobby Mon.–Sat. at 10 A.M.; $4 per person. A similar facility is the **Chan Centre for the Performing Arts,** comprising three stages including the 1,400-seat Chan Shun Concert Hall. It's on the UBC campus at 6265 Crescent Rd., Point Grey, 604/822-2697.

The **Arts Club,** 604/687-1644, always offers excellent theater productions at two Granville Island locations—the **New Revue Stage** and adjacent **Mainstage.** Productions range from drama to comedy to improv. Tickets run $21–35; book in advance and pick up your tickets at the door 30 minutes prior to showtime. Another venue

for the Arts Club is the restored **Stanley Theatre,** on Granville Street, south of the island at 12th Avenue.

Since its inception in 1964, the **Playhouse Theatre Company** has grown to become the city's largest theater company. Seven productions are performed each year, ranging from classical to contemporary, with 8 P.M. start times and tickets ranging $31–42. Matinees (2 P.M.) cost around half the price of evening performances. The company is based at the **Playhouse Theatre,** 160 W. 1st St., 604/873-3311. In the same vicinity, **Vancouver Little Theatre,** 3102 Main St., 604/876-4165, features productions by national and international companies, as well as works by up-and-coming local artists. Expect to pay $8–15.

Music and Dance

The **Queen Elizabeth Theatre,** at 630 Hamilton St., is the home of **Vancouver Opera,** 604/683-0222; tickets begin at $35, rising to $90 for the best seats. The theater also hosts various music recitals and stage performances.

The historic **Orpheum Theatre,** on the corner of Smithe and Seymour Streets, dates to 1927 and houses its original Wurlitzer organ. Now fully restored, the theater provides excellent acoustics for the resident **Vancouver Symphony,** 604/684-9100, as well as for concerts by the professional **Vancouver Chamber Choir,** 604/738-6822, the amateur **Vancouver Bach Choir,** 604/921-8012, and other musical groups.

Ballet British Columbia, 604/732-5003, performs in the Queen Elizabeth Theatre at 630 Hamilton St., throughout a winter season. Tickets range $18–45. Vancouver's newest dance venue is the **Scotiabank Dance Centre,** 677 Davie St., 604/606-6400.

Bars

In the historic building The Landing, at 375 Water St., Gastown, **Steamworks Brewing Co.,** 604/689-2739, is the perfect place to relax with a beer from the in-house brewery. The atmosphere is casual yet stylish, and you'll have great views across Burrard Inlet. Hours are 11:30 A.M.–10 P.M. daily.

Yaletown Brewing Co., 1111 Mainland St.,

604/688-0039, is the premier drinking hole for the dot-commers of Yaletown. The in-house brewery produces a variety of excellent beers, there's a great patio, and the food meets a high standard for a pub. Up the hill, the old **Yale Hotel**, 1300 Granville St., 604/681-9253, is primarily a blues venue, but is a pleasant place for a quiet drink even without the music. Toward the head of False Creek from Yaletown, **Maverick's**, 770 Pacific Blvd. S, 604/683-4436, is the quintessential bar for college-age drinkers. Always lively, the Maverick's patio (Vancouver's largest) overlooks the water and is always crowded and noisy.

Toward the West End, **Joe Fortes Seafood and Chophouse**, 777 Thurlow St., 604/669-1940, boasts a great bar, complete with a wide range of beers and a condensed menu from the adjacent restaurant.

The small but always lively **Stamp's Landing Neighbourhood Pub** overlooks False Creek at 610 Stamp's Landing (just east of Granville Island), 604/879-0821. Aside from beer and liquor, Stamp's offers delicious tasty snacks to keep you going, live music on weekends, and great sunset views overlooking the harbor. On Granville Island itself, the **Backstage Lounge**, 1585 Johnston St., has a few outdoor tables with water views.

Farther south, near where the Arthur Laing Bridge crosses to Richmond, the atmosphere at **Wild Coyote**, 1312 Southwest Marine Dr., 604/264-7625, is reflected in its slogan, "Where animals come to play." Spring break seemingly never ends for the college crowd at the "Yote." Thursdays are legendary, with lots of drinking, boisterous inhouse promotions, and impromptu strip shows. Friday and Saturday nights are officially Ladies Nights, which attract hordes of young single women, attracting in turn hordes of single men.

Across Burrard Inlet from downtown, the **Rusty Gull Neighbourhood Pub**, 175 E. 1st St. in North Vancouver, 604/988-5585, features more than a dozen locally brewed beers. Another favorite north of Burrard Inlet, **Queens Cross Neighbourhood Pub** on Upper Lonsdale at the corner of Queens Rd., 604/980-7715, is a favorite local hangout for lunch, after-work drinks, conversation, and evening meals.

Nightclubs

Nightclubs change names and reputations with regularity, so check with the free entertainment newspapers or the website www.clubvibes.com for the latest hot spots. Naturally, weekends are busiest, with the most popular clubs having cover charges up to $10 and long lineups after 9 P.M. The rest of the week, cover charges are reduced and many places hold promotions with giveaways or discounted drinks.

Downtown, nightclubs are concentrated along and immediately south of Granville Street. Best known as Dick's on Dicks, **Richard's on Richards**, 1036 Richards St., 604/687-6794, has been a staple of the Vancouver nightclub scene for over 20 years. It's most popular with the late 20s and over 30s. Best known as "the Fair," **Luv-A-Fair**, around the corner at 1275 Seymour St., 604/685-3288, is a longtime favorite with serious dancers. One of the hottest local nightclubs in recent years has been **Wett Bar**, 1320 Richards St., 604/662-7077. The centerpiece is a massive dance floor featuring a hanging light system that produces incredible effects. Above this a moving re-creation of the Milky Way is projected onto the high ceiling, and below the dance floor is imbedded with thousands of lights. Music varies from hip hop to progressive. Expect a lineup at the **Palladium**, 1250 Richards St., 604/688-2648, which is the home of Vancouver's underground music scene. Inside, you'll find a large dance floor, a laid-back atmosphere, and local and imported DJs. Saturday night attracts a more pretentious crowd. In the immediate vicinity, **Bar None**, 1222 Hamilton St., 604/689-7000, attracts a young single crowd throughout the week.

Back up the hill from all of the above, at **Stone Temple**, 1082 Granville St., 604/488-1333, a DJ spins hip hop, retro, and top 40 discs nightly until 4 A.M. Across the road and appealing to a slightly older age group than most other Vancouver nightclubs, **Babalu**, 654 Nelson St. (at Granville), 604/605-4343, is an upmarket spot, with drink prices to match.

Away from the main entertainment district, Gastown holds three nightclubs. At popular **Sonar,** 66 Water St., 604/683-6695, most nights feature the latest techno, hip-hop, and house music, occasionally giving a nod to soul and jazz. The **Purple Onion,** 15 Water St., 604/602-9442, combines the Lounge, an intimate live music (usually jazz) venue, and the Club, a crowded, hot, and sweaty dance floor. Head to **Drink,** 398 Richards St., 604/687-1307, for music ranging from house to Latin.

Rock

The world's biggest rock, pop, and country acts usually include Vancouver on their world tours, and the city's thriving local music industry supports live bands at a variety of venues. Most big-name acts play B.C. Place Stadium, the Orpheum, or Queen Elizabeth Theatre. Attracting a huge crowd every night of the week, at the classic **Roxy,** 932 Granville St., 604/331-7999, two house bands play rock 'n' roll music from all eras to a packed house during the week, with imported bands on weekends. The young hip crowd, good music, and performance bartenders make this the city's most popular live music venue, so expect a lineup, especially after 9 P.M. weekends; cover charges range $5–10. A similar venue is the **Starfish Room,** 1055 Homer St., 604/682-4171, although the acts have been more diverse in recent years, ranging from alternative to country. "Pulse," a longtime Friday night favorite at the Palladium, moved to the Starfish Room in 2001. On the downside, the cover here is as high as $10, drinks are also expensive, and the doormen are renowned for their attitude. For bands, dancing, video, and a piano lounge head for the **Town Pump,** 66 Water St. in Gastown, 604/683-6695. Acoustically, it isn't the best of venues, but it attracts occasional big-name acts. The **Railway Club,** 579 Dunsmuir St., 604/681-1625, is a private club where non-members are welcome (at a higher cover charge) to listen to acts ranging from rock to country.

Jazz, Blues, and Comedy

The **Hot Jazz Society,** 2120 Main St., 604/873-4131, presents live jazz on a regular basis; cover charge is $6–9. The **Coastal Jazz and Blues Society,** 604/872-5200, website www.jazzvancouver.com, maintains a listing of all the city's jazz and blues events.

Serious blues lovers head for the historic **Yale Hotel,** 1300 Granville St., 604/681-9253, which has hosted some of the greatest names in the business, including Junior Wells and Stevie Ray Vaughan. Sunday is the only night without live performances, although a jam session starts up about 3 P.M. on Saturday and Sunday afternoons. Drinks are expensive and a $5–15 cover charge is collected Thurs.–Sat. nights. The **Purple Onion,** next to the Old Spaghetti Factory at 15 Water St. in Gastown, 604/602-9442, features live jazz and blues some nights. Admission is free before 9 P.M. Also downtown, the **Wedgewood Hotel,** 845 Hornby St., 604/689-7777, features a resident blues guitarist performing nightly in the hotel's stylish lounge. No cover, but the drinks aren't cheap.

Yuk Yuk's, 750 Pacific Blvd. S (Plaza of Nations), 604/687-5233, offers comedy nights Wed.–Sat.; admission costs $4 on Wednesday (amateur night), $7.50 on Thursday, $15 on Friday and Saturday nights. **Lafflines,** 26 4th St., New Westminster, 604/525-2262, offers a similar program and attracts acts from throughout Canada. Wednesday through Sunday, the Arts Club, 604/687-1644, hosts a **TheatreSports League** of improvised comedy on its New Revue Stage, Granville Island.

Cinemas

Cinemas are in all the major shopping malls and elsewhere throughout the city. Combined, **Cineplex Odeon,** 604/434-2463, and **Famous Players,** 604/272-7280, operate 20 cinemas in Vancouver. Call the respective numbers or check the two daily papers for locations and screenings. Admission to first-run screenings is about $8.

The **Paradise Theatre,** 919 Granville St., 604/681-1732, features commercial hits for the bargain-basement price of $5. If you're staying at a Robson Street or West End accommodation, head over to **Denman Place Discount Cinema,** corner of Denman and Comox Streets,

© ANDREW HEMPSTEAD

VANCOUVER

The Yale Hotel is a classic blues venue.

604/683-2201, for first- and second-run hits for $2.50–5. For foreign and fringe films, check out **Pacific Cinematheque,** 1131 Howe St., 604/688-8202.

At the far end of Canada Place, the **CN IMAX Theatre,** 604/682-4629, provides spectacular movie entertainment and special effects on a five-story-high screen with wraparound surround sound. Films are generally on the world's natural wonders and last around 45 minutes, with two or three features showing each day, beginning around noon. Ticket prices range $8–11.50 per screening, or catch a double feature for a few bucks extra.

SHOPPING

Vancouver has shopping centers, malls, and specialty stores everywhere. Head to Gastown for native arts and crafts, Robson Street for boutique clothing, Granville St. Mall for department stores, Granville Island for everything from ships' chandlery to kids' clothing, Yaletown for the trendy clothes of local designers, the Eastside for army-surplus stores and pawnbrokers, Chinatown for Eastern foods, and the junction of Main Street and East 49th Avenue for Indian goods.

Before you set out, drop in at Vancouver Visitor Info Centre, 200 Burrard St., and ask for the free *Shopping Guide.* In addition to listing all the department stores and specialty shops you're likely to want to visit, the guide contains handy fold-out maps of downtown Vancouver and Greater Vancouver, with all the shops and malls marked. If you're serious about your shopping, search out a copy of Anne Gerber's book *Vancouver's Best Bargains* (Vancouver: Serious Publishing, 1995).

Gastown

Sandwiched between the many cafés, restaurants, and tacky souvenir stores along Water Street are other stores selling Vancouver's best selection of native arts and crafts. One of the largest outlets, **Hill's Native Crafts,** 165 Water St., 604/685-4249, sells $10 T-shirts, towering $12,000 totem poles, and everything in between, including genuine Cowichan sweaters and carved ceremonial masks. Also featuring traditional native art is **Images for a Canadian Heritage,** 164 Water St., 604/685-7046. The **Inuit Gallery of Vancouver,** 206 Cambie St., 604/688-7323, exhibits the work of Inuit and northwest coast native artists and sculptors. Among the highlights are many soapstone pieces by carvers from Cape Dorset, a remote Inuit village in Canada's territory of Nunavut.

Down the street from Hill's Native Crafts, **Kites on Clouds,** 131 Water St., 604/669-5677, sells hundreds of different kites, from the simplest designs to elaborate constructions priced at over $200. The **Western Canada Wilderness Committee Store,** 227 Abbott St., 604/683-2567, features environmentally friendly souvenirs, including shirts, posters, and calendars. A couple of blocks from Water Street in the Sinclair Centre is **Dorothy Grant,** 757 W. Hastings St., 604/681-0201, a clothing store named for its owner. Dorothy and her husband are renowned for their contemporary Haida-inspired designs. The **Sinclair Centre** itself is a local landmark; its four historic buildings now hold galleries, boutiques, and food outlets.

Granville Island

Arts and crafts galleries on Granville Island include **Wickaninnish Gallery,** 1666 Johnston St., 604/681-1057, selling stunning native art, jewelry, carvings, weavings, and original paintings; **Gallery of B.C. Ceramics,** 1359 Cartwright St., 604/669-5645, showcasing the work of the province's leading potters and sculptors; and **Forge & Form,** 1334 Cartwright St., 604/684-6298, which creates and sells gold and silver jewelry.

Duranleau Street is home to many maritime-based businesses, adventure-tour operators, and charter operators. The **Quarterdeck,** 1660 Duranleau St., 604/683-8232, stocks everything from marine charts to brass shipping bells. The **Ocean Floor,** 1522 Duranleau St., 604/681-

5014, sells a similar range of treasures, including seashells and model ships. To buy a sea kayak or canoe (from $1,100 secondhand), head to **Adventure Fitness,** 1528 Duranleau St., 604/687-1528, or **Ecomarine Ocean Kayak Centre,** 1668 Duranleau St., 604/689-7575. Both shops also carry related equipment, books, and nautical charts. Before heading over to Vancouver Island, divers pick up gear at **Rowand's Reef Scuba Shop,** 1512 Duranleau St., 604/669-3483.

Department Stores, Plazas, and Malls

Despite looking pretty dowdy these days, **Granville St. Mall** nevertheless forms the heart of the downtown shopping precinct; the two-block stretch of Granville Street is closed to private vehicles, though buses and taxis still pass through. Here you'll find the city's largest department store, **The Bay,** 674 Granville St., 604/681-6211, a Canadian chain that evolved from the historic Hudson's Bay Company. Today the store emphasizes Canadian goods, from souvenirs to household appliances. Also on the mall, the **Pacific Centre** features 165 shops, a massive food court, and a three-story-high waterfall. In the center's southwest corner, you'll find **Oh Yes!, Vancouver,** a great place to shop for colorful city souvenirs.

Across Lions Gate Bridge in West Vancouver are a couple of shopping centers worth a mention. In a scenic location at Marine Drive and Taylor Way, **Park Royal Shopping Centre** holds almost 200 shops and three department stores. Also on the north side of Burrard Inlet is **Lonsdale Quay Market,** the terminus of the SeaBus from downtown. This bustling center features a great fresh food market on the first floor and a range of boutiques and galleries on the second.

British Columbia's largest shopping complex, **Metrotown,** houses more than 200 shops. It's on the Kingsway in Burnaby; get there from downtown on the SkyTrain.

Outdoor and Camping Gear

A small stretch of West Broadway, between Main and Cambie Streets, holds Vancouver's largest concentration of outdoor equipment stores. The

VANCOUVER

largest of these, and the largest in British Columbia, is **Mountain Equipment Co-op,** 130 W. Broadway, 604/872-7858. Like the American R.E.I stores, it is a cooperative owned by its members; to make a purchase, you must be a member (a once-only charge of $5). The store holds a massive selection of clothing, climbing and mountaineering equipment, tents, backpacks, sleeping bags, books, and other accessories. It's open Mon.–Wed. 10 A.M.–7 P.M., Thurs.–Fri. 10 A.M.–9 P.M., Saturday 9 A.M.–6 P.M. To order a copy of the mail-order catalog, call 800/663-2667. One block west, **Great Outdoors Equipment Co.,** 222 W. Broadway, 604/872-8872, sells a similar range of gear and has a particularly wide choice of footwear. Next door, **Helly Hansen,** 202 W. Broadway, 604/872-7858, specializes in high-quality outdoor clothing.

FESTIVALS AND EVENTS

Festivals of some description take place in Vancouver just about every month of the year. Whether it's a celebration of local or international culture, the arts, sporting events, or just a wacky long-time tradition, there's always a reason to party in Vancouver. Most of the popular festivals are held during summer, the peak visitor season, but the rest of the year is the main season for performances by the city's dance, theater, and music companies, and not-to-be-missed events such as the Christmas Carol Ship Parade. For details and exact dates of the events listed below contact the numbers or visit the websites given, or visit any local tourist information center.

Tickets for most major events can be booked through **Ticketmaster;** for the arts call 604/280-3311, for sporting events call 604/280-4400; website www.ticketmaster.ca.

Spring

The spring event schedule kicks off in a big way with the **Vancouver Playhouse International Wine Festival,** 604/873-3311, website www.winefest.bc.ca, in early April. Hosted by various downtown venues, it is one of North America's largest, bringing together representatives

from more than 150 wineries and 14 countries. Other public events include a variety of nighttime gatherings, such as Bacchanalia, a gala dinner hosted by the Fairmont Vancouver.

The **Vancouver Sun Run,** 604/689-9441, website www.sunrun.com, is a 10-km run (or walk) through the streets of downtown on the fourth Sunday in April. Attracting over 45,000 participants, it is Canada's largest (and the world's third largest) such run. For more serious runners, the **Vancouver International Marathon,** 604/872-2928, website www.vanmarathon.bc.ca, takes place the following Sunday.

The streets of New Westminster come alive in late May for **Hyack Festival,** 604/522-6894, website www.hyack.bc.ca, in celebration of spring and the history of British Columbia's one-time capital. Farther east, the country comes to the city for one of British Columbia's biggest rodeos, the **Cloverdale Rodeo and Exhibition** on the third weekend of May; 604/576-9461, website www.cloverdalerodeo.com.

The last week of May is the **Vancouver International Children's Festival,** 604/708-5655, website www.vancouverchildrensfestival.com, at Vanier Park; it's a kid's paradise, with face painting, costumes, plays, puppetry, mime, sing-alongs, storytelling, and fancy-hat competitions.

Summer

Two of summer's most popular cultural events take place from mid-June through to late in the season, meaning you can enjoy them at any time through the warmer months. **Bard on the Beach,** 604/739-0559, website www.bardonthebeach.org, comprises three favorite Shakespeare plays performed in open-ended tents in Vanier Park, allowing a spectacular backdrop of English Bay, the city skyline, and the mountains beyond. Tickets are well priced at just $15–21.50 for 1 P.M. and 4 P.M. matinees and from $25 for 7:30 P.M. evening performances. The other event, the **Kitsilano Showboat,** 604/734-7332, takes place at nearby Kitsilano Beach. Amateur variety acts have been taking to this stage since 1935. Performances are Monday, Wednesday, and Friday nights over a 10-week summer season.

The **Alcan Dragon Boat Festival,** 604/688-2382, website www.canadadragonboat.com, comes to False Creek over two weekends in mid-June. In addition to the races, a blessing ceremony and a variety of cultural activities take place in and around the Plaza of Nations.

The last week of June, Vancouver taps its feet to the beat of the annual **Vancouver International Jazz Festival,** 604/872-5200, website www.jazzvancouver.com, when more than 1,500 musicians from countries around the world gather to perform traditional and contemporary jazz at 40 venues around the city.

Canada Day is 1 July. The main celebrations—music, dancing, and fireworks—are held at Canada Place, but if you head out to the **Steveston Salmon Festival,** 604/277-6812, you'll come across a massive salmon barbecue and be granted free admission to the Gulf of Georgia Cannery.

The middle weekend of July, Jericho Beach Park draws lots of folks to the **Vancouver Folk Music Festival,** 604/602-9798, website www.thefestival.bc.ca. In addition to the wonderful music, the festival features storytelling, dance performances, live theater, and a food fair. Hosted at the Crofton House School (corner of Blenheim St. and W. 41st Ave., Kerrisdale), the **Vancouver Chamber Music Festival,** 604/602-0363, website www.vanrecital.com, presents six evenings of performances over two weeks by chamber musicians, such as piano, cello, and violin players. This is performing arts at its most casual—while the actual concerts are inside, the school's gardens come alive before each performance with hundreds of concert-goers enjoying catered dinners or a pre-ordered picnic basket

Year after year, Vancouverites await with much anticipation the early August **Celebration of Light** (formerly the Symphony of Fire), 604/641-1193, website www.celebration-of-light.com, the world's largest musical fire-

The last week of June, Vancouver taps its feet to the beat of the annual Vancouver International Jazz Festival, when more than 1,500 musicians from countries around the world gather to perform traditional and contemporary jazz at 40 venues around the city.

works competition. Each year, three countries compete; each has a night to itself (the last Saturday in July, then the following Wednesday and Saturday), putting on a display that lasts up to an hour from 10:15 P.M.; then on the final night (second Wednesday in August), the three competing countries come together for a grand finale. The fireworks are let off from a barge moored in English Bay, allowing viewing from Stanley Park, Kitsilano, Jericho Beach, and as far away as West Vancouver. Music that accompanies the displays can be heard around the shoreline; if you're away from the action tune your radio to 101.1 FM for a simulcast.

Abbotsford International Airshow, 604/852-8511, website www.abbotsfordairshow.com, featuring Canada's famous Snowbirds, is held at Vancouver's "other" airport, east of the city in Abbotsford, on the second weekend of August.

Summer's busy event schedule winds up at the Pacific National Exhibition Grounds with **The Fair (Pacific National Exhibition)** in late August. For details of this agricultural exposition, including the twice-daily RCMP musical ride, a precision drill performed by Canada's famous Mounties, call 604/253-2311, website www.pne.bc.ca.

Fall

Beginning the second week of September, **The Fringe Festival,** 604/257-0350, website www.vancouverfringe.com, schedules around 500 performances by 100 artists from around the world at indoor and outdoor stages throughout Granville Island.

The **Vancouver International Film Festival,** 604/685-0260, website www.viff.org, is held late in September and features more than 300 of the very best movies from around 60 countries at theaters across downtown. One month later, literary types congregate on Granville Island for the **Vancouver International Writers Festival,** 604/681-6330, website www.writersfest.bc.ca.

Winter

Through the month of December, VanDusen Botanical Garden is transformed each evening by over 80,000 lights and seasonal displays such as a nativity scene during the **Festival of Lights,** 604/878-9274. Another popular pre-Christmas event is the **Carol Ships Parade of Lights,** 604/878-9988, website www.carol ships.org. For three weeks leading up to Christmas Eve, the waterways of Vancouver come alive with the sounds of the festive season as each night a flotilla of up to 80 boats, each decorated with colorful lights, sails around Burrard Inlet, Port Moody, Deep Cove, and around English Bay to False Creek, while on-board carolers sing the songs of Christmas through sound systems that can clearly be heard from along the shoreline.

While most normal folk spend New Year's Day recovering from the previous night's celebrations, up to 2,000 brave souls head down to English Bay Beach and go *swimming.* The information hotline for the **Polar Bear Swim** is 604/732-2304, but all you really need to know is that the water will be *very* cold.

Accommodations

Whether you're looking for a campsite, hostel, bed-and-breakfast inn, motel, or luxury hotel, Vancouver has accommodations to suit your whim and budget. **Vancouver Visitor Info Centre,** 200 Burrard St., 604/683-2000, is the best place to get all the accommodations information in one shot. The center maintains accommodation listings for Vancouver and the entire province and stocks a good selection of brochures provided by the lodgings. The staff will make bookings, too.

Before arriving in Vancouver, wise travelers will obtain a copy of Tourism BC's free guide, *Accommodations,* using it to make advance reservations at their lodgings of choice. If you show up in late spring or summer without reservations, you may find all the best places, and definitely all the most reasonable, booked for the season. To request a copy of the guide, contact **Tourism British Columbia,** P.O. Box 9830, Station Provincial Government, Victoria, BC V8W 9W5, 250/387-1642 or 800/435-5622, website www.hellobc.com. You can also make reservations through those numbers and on the website.

All rates quoted below are for high season (summer). Expect to pay less on weekends, especially for downtown accommodations, and outside of the busy July–Aug. period. The 8 percent provincial hotel and motel tax, a 2 percent tourism tax, and, like the rest of Canada, the 7 percent goods and services tax must be added; the latter is refundable to visitors from outside the country.

DOWNTOWN HOTELS AND MOTELS

Under $100

A few inexpensively priced accommodations lie in the downtown area, but only the following can be recommended.

The **Dominion Hotel,** 210 Abbott St., 604/681-6666 or 877/681-1666, website www.dominionhotel.bc.ca, is in the heart of Gastown, a five-minute walk from Canada Place along Water Street. Dating to 1910, it has a bar and restaurant downstairs, and is popular with international travelers. All rooms have a telephone, but TV viewing is in a communal lounge. In summer, rooms with a sink and mirror that share a bathroom are $50–60 s, $60–70 d, while those with a private bathroom range $100–115 s, $110–125 d. Summer rates include a light breakfast of toast and tea or coffee.

The location of the **Budget Inn—Patricia Hotel,** at 403 E. Hastings St., 604/255-4301, website www.budgetpathotel.bc.ca, isn't the best—it's separated from downtown by infamous East Hastings Street—but the price is

Lost Lagoon

Coal Harbour

99

Stanley Park

LAGOON DRIVE

Second Beach

ROSELLEN SUITES

PARK LANE

ROBSON ST.

WEST GEORGIA

1st ALBERNI

BUCHAN HOTEL

WESTIN BAYSHORE

BEACH

CHILCO

NELSON

GILFORD

BARCLAY

HARO

ENGLISH BAY INN

COMOX

PENDER ST.

ST.

ST.

AVE.

BIDWELL

SYLVIA HOTEL

RIVIERA MOTEL
GREENBRIAR HOTEL

English Bay Beach

DENMAN

PENDRELL

BARCLAY HOTEL

Barclay Heritage Square

PACIFIC PALISADES HOTEL

LISTEL VANCOUVER

WEST END

ST. ST.

BLUE HORIZON HOTEL

DAVIE

CARDERO

NICOLA

Alexandra Park

BURNABY

ST. ST.

ST.

HARWOOD

BROUGHTON

Nelson Park

First Beach

BEACH

JERVIS

BUTE

YMCA

English Bay

PARKHILL HOTEL

CENTURY PLAZA HOTEL

PACIFIC

SHERATON VANCOUVER WALL CENTRE

MELMCKEN

Sunset Beach

HOSTELLING INTERNATIONAL VANCOUVER DOWNTOWN

BURRARD MOTOR INN

THURLOW

BURRARD

DAVIE

Kitsilano Point

Vanier Park

Sunset Beach Park

AVE.

QUALITY HOTEL DOWNTOWN

DRAKE

HOWARD JOHNSON HOTEL DOWNTOWN

Kitsilano Beach

MCNICHOL AVE.

VANCOUVER CENTRE TRAVELODGE

HORNBY

WHYTE AVE.

HOWE

BEST WESTERN DOWNTOWN VANCOUVER

BURRARD ST. BRIDGE

SEYMOUR

Kitsilano Beach Park

ST.

ST.

ST.

GRANVILLE

RICHARDS

CORNWALL

AVE.

99

GRANVILLE ST.

BRIDGE

ST.

ST.

ABBUTUS

MAPLE

CYPRESS

BURRARD

ANDERSON ST.

W. 1st

AVE.

Granville Island

GRANVILLE ISLAND HOTEL

YEW

W. 2nd

W. 2nd AVE.

W. 3rd

AVE.

W. 4th

KITSILANO

AVE.

FAIRVIEW

VANCOUVER

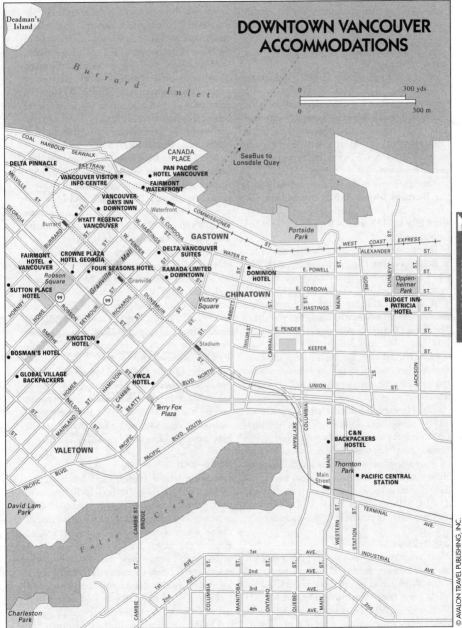

DOWNTOWN VANCOUVER ACCOMMODATIONS

Deadman's Island

Burrard Inlet

0 — 300 yds
0 — 300 m

CANADA PLACE

SeaBus to Lonsdale Quay

COAL HARBOUR SEAWALK

SKYTRAIN

DELTA PINNACLE

MELVILLE ST.

VANCOUVER VISITOR INFO CENTRE

PAN PACIFIC HOTEL VANCOUVER

FAIRMONT WATERFRONT

GEORGIA ST.

VANCOUVER-DAYS INN DOWNTOWN

Burrard

HYATT REGENCY VANCOUVER

W. HASTINGS

Waterfront

W. CORDOVA

COMMISSIONER

ST.

GASTOWN

Portside Park

WEST COAST EXPRESS

ALEXANDER ST.

FAIRMONT HOTEL VANCOUVER

CROWNE PLAZA HOTEL GEORGIA

FOUR SEASONS HOTEL

DELTA VANCOUVER SUITES

W. PENDER

WATER ST.

GORE

DUNLEVY

Oppenheimer Park

Robson Square

Granville Mall

Granville

RAMADA LIMITED DOWNTOWN

DOMINION HOTEL

E. POWELL

ST.

ST.

SUTTON PLACE HOTEL

HORNBY

HOWE

ROBSON

SEYMOUR

RICHARDS

DUNSMUIR

CHINATOWN

E. CORDOVA

E. HASTINGS

MAIN

ST.

ST.

BUDGET INN-PATRICIA HOTEL

ST.

99

99

Victory Square

ABBOTT ST.

CARRALL ST.

E. PENDER

SMITHE

KINGSTON HOTEL

TAYLOR ST.

KEEFER

ST.

BOSMAN'S HOTEL

Stadium

ST.

JACKSON

GLOBAL VILLAGE BACKPACKERS

HOMER

NELSON ST.

HAMILTON ST.

CAMBIE ST.

BEATTY

YWCA HOTEL

BLVD. NORTH

UNION

ST.

ST.

Terry Fox Plaza

COLUMBIA ST.

MAIN ST.

YALETOWN

MAINLAND ST.

PACIFIC

BLVD. SOUTH

PACIFIC

SKYTRAIN

C&N BACKPACKERS HOSTEL

BLVD.

Thornton Park

PACIFIC

PACIFIC CENTRAL STATION

David Lam Park

CAMBIE ST.

BRIDGE

False Creek

Main Street

WESTERN ST.

STATION ST.

TERMINAL AVE.

INDUSTRIAL AVE.

Charleston Park

CAMBIE ST.

1st AVE.

2nd AVE.

COLUMBIA ST.

MANITOBA ST.

ONTARIO ST.

1st AVE.

2nd

3rd

4th

QUEBEC ST.

MAIN ST.

AVE.

AVE.

AVE.

2nd

© AVALON TRAVEL PUBLISHING, INC.

VANCOUVER

right, parking is free, and downstairs is popular Pat's Pub with daily food and drink specials; from $49 s, $64 d.

$100–150

The three-story **Kingston Hotel,** 757 Richards St., 604/684-9024 or 888/713-3304, website www.kingstonhotelvancouver.com, dates to the early 1900s but has been extensively renovated. Amenities include a sauna, laundry, TV rental, and guest parking. Most rooms share a bathroom; from $85 s, $105 d, including a continental breakfast.

Least expensive of the old downtown motels is the **Burrard Motor Inn,** 1100 Burrard St., 604/681-2331 or 800/663-0366, which charges from $99 s, $115 d for a large but simply furnished room.

Immediately to the east of Burrard Motor Inn is **Bosman's Hotel,** 1060 Howe St., 604/682-3171 or 888/267-6267, website www.bosmans hotel.com, which offers rooms from $139 s or d.

A few blocks farther south, and just a five-minute walk to a Granville Island Ferry wharf, is **Vancouver Centre Travelodge,** 1304 Howe St., 604/682-2767 or 800/578-7878, website www.travelodge.com. Rooms are clean and comfortable, but this accommodation has seen better days, making the summer rates of $129 s, $139 d a little steep.

The **Howard Johnson Hotel Downtown,** 1176 Granville St., 604/688-8701 or 888/654-6336, website www.hojovancouver.com, is in a historic hotel that was totally renovated in 1998, creating a good-value, centrally located property. Rooms are air-conditioned and guests have use of a small fitness room. Rooms with one bed are $149 s, with two beds $179 d, discounted to $99 and $109 respectively in the off-season.

$150–200

Most accommodations in this price range are scattered between the central business district and Granville Island. Least expensive of the CBD hotels is **Days Inn—Vancouver Downtown,** 921 W. Pender St., 604/681-4335 or 800/329-7466, website www.daysinnvancouver.com. The 85 rooms are small, and surrounding high-rises block

any views. But each room is decorated in bright and breezy pastel colors, and tea- and coffee-makers are provided; in summer rooms start at $195 s or d, discounted to $125 in the low season.

While guest facilities at **Ramada Limited Downtown** are limited compared to other properties in this price category, like the Days Inn, the location is very central. As an old hotel the 80 rooms are small, but they are well appointed and come with everything from hair dryers to Nintendo. The summer rate is $199 s or d.

The 12-story **Best Western Downtown Vancouver,** 718 Drake St., 604/669-9888 or 888/669-9888, website www.bestwesterndown town.com, lies at the southern end of downtown. Rooms with one and two queen-size beds are $189 and $209 respectively; kitchenettes are $234. All rates include a light breakfast.

Century Plaza Hotel, 1015 Burrard St., 604/687-0575 or 800/663-1818, website www.century-plaza.com, offers 236 rooms, each with a kitchen. The biggest attraction is Spa at the Century, a full-service day spa facility. Studio rooms are $159–189 s or d, one-bedroom suites, each with a balcony, are $209, and the 30th-floor penthouse suites are a relatively reasonable $350.

At the **Quality Hotel Downtown,** 1335 Howe St., 604/682-0229 or 800/663-8474, website www.qualityhotelvancouver.com, a few rooms can be had for $179 s, $199 d, but the one-bedroom suites, each with a full kitchen, are the best value at $229 s or d.

$200–250

Granville Island Hotel, 1253 Johnston St., 604/683-7373 or 800/663-1840, website www.granvilleislandhotel.com, enjoys a fabulous location on the island of the same name immediately south of downtown. Contemporary and elegant, the rooms are very spacious and furnished with Persian rugs, marble-floored bathrooms, and modern necessities such as high-speed Internet access. Most also have water views. Summer rates range $200–220 s or d, discounted to as low as $150 the rest of the year.

On the western edge of the downtown district, where office buildings blend with the residential apartments of the West End, is the **Parkhill Hotel,** 1160 Davie St., 604/685-1311 or 800/663-1525, website www.parkhillhotel.com. Parkhill offers views over a residential area to English Bay. Rooms are spacious and have private balconies, and guests have use of a heated outdoor pool, fitness room, sauna, and restaurant. Rooms on the lower levels start at $220 s or d.

$250–300

Delta Vancouver Suites, in the heart of downtown at 550 W. Hastings St., 604/689-8188 or 800/268-1133, website www.deltahotels.com, holds 226 spacious units, each with a separate bedroom and comfortable lounge area. In-room business facilities include a work desk stocked with supplies, two phone lines, high-speed Internet access, and personalized voice mail. Other guest facilities include a health club, indoor pool, saunas and a whirlpool, and a street level New York–style restaurant open for breakfast, lunch, and dinner. Rack rates are $279 s or d, but check the website for deals.

The **Hyatt Regency Vancouver** towers above the Royal Centre Mall at 655 Burrard St., 604/683-1234 or 800/233-1234, website www.vancouver.hyatt.com. Needless to say, most of the 600-plus rooms have views. Rooms start at $290 s or d.

The centrally located **Delta Pinnacle,** 1128 W. Hastings St., 604/684-1128 or 800/268-1133, website www.deltahotels.com, opened in 2000. This full service property features 434 spacious rooms, each with stylish furniture, elegant bathrooms, a writing desk full of office supplies, two telephones (including a cordless) with voice mail and Internet access, a coffeemaker, ironing facilities, and also an umbrella for Vancouver's occasional rainy days. Guests also enjoy complimentary use of the hotel's health club, which features a 17-meter-long indoor pool, a hot tub, a sauna, and a large outdoor patio area. Advertised rates are from $309, discounted to $199 and $219 outside of summer. Weekend rates and special packages (check the Delta Hotels website) are offered year-round.

Fairmont Hotels and Resorts, best known for landmark accommodations like the Fairmont Empress in Victoria and the Fairmont Banff Springs in Banff, operate two properties in the downtown area. The copper-roofed **Fairmont Hotel Vancouver,** 900 W. Georgia St., 604/684-3131 or 800/866-5577, website www.fairmont.com, is the company's Vancouver flagship and a downtown landmark—you can't help but notice the distinctive green copper roof, the gargoyles, and the classic Gothic château-style architecture of this grand old lady. Today, with its former glory restored, the Hotel Vancouver is one of Canada's grandest accommodations, from the cavernous marble-lined lobby to the high ceilings and 556 elegantly furnished rooms. Facilities include restaurants, a comfortable lounge, an indoor pool, saunas, a weight room, health facilities, 24-hour room service, ample parking, and a large staff to attend to your every whim. The smallish standard rooms start at $350 s or d, but upgrading to a larger "Fairmont Room" is only a few dollars extra, and a number of good-value packages are offered year-round, such as bed and breakfast for $259 high season, $199 low season.

The other Fairmont property is the 23-story **Fairmont Waterfront,** 900 Canada Place Way, 604/691-1991 or 800/866-5577, website www.fairmont.com, linked by a concourse to Canada Place. The 489 rooms are all spacious, and over half of them enjoy stunning harbor views. Summer rates are from $359 s or d.

The historic **Crowne Plaza Hotel Georgia** is at 801 Georgia St., 604/682-5566 or 800/663-1111, website www.hotelgeorgia.bc.ca. Built in 1927 in a Georgian-revival style, this 313-room grande dame was restored to her former glory through the second half of the 1990s. Original oak furnishings, the oak-paneled lobby, and the brass elevator have been restored and all facilities upgraded, including a fitness center and various eating establishments. Summer rates start at $369 s or d but drop to $169 in winter.

One block from the city end of Robson Street is the super-luxurious, European-style **Sutton Place Hotel,** 845 Burrard St., 604/682-5511 or 800/961-7555, website www.suttonplace.com, which gets a precious five-diamond rating from the American AA. This, Vancouver's most elegant accommodation, features original European art-works in public areas and reproductions in the 397 rooms. Rooms are furnished with king-size beds, plush bathrobes, and two phone lines, and guests enjoy a twice-daily maid service, complete with fresh flowers; from $385 per night.

Over $400

No expense was spared in the construction of the stylish **Sheraton Vancouver Wall Centre,** 1088 Burrard St., 604/331-1000 or 800/663-9255, website www.sheratonvancouver.com. Many of the furnishings were specially commissioned. Facilities include two restaurants, a fitness center, indoor pool, a business center, and a half-hectare garden planted with specially imported Japanese maples. Rates for a standard room start at $400 s or d.

The Vancouver **Four Seasons Hotel,** above the Pacific Centre at 791 W. Georgia St., 604/689-9333 or 800/268-6282, website www.fourseasons.com, is generally regarded as one of the world's great hotels, garnering a five-diamond rating from the AAA. The spacious rooms are luxuriously appointed, with guests enjoying fresh flowers, a wide range of in-room amenities, and twice-daily housekeeping. Summer rates start at $425 s, $455 d, discounted as low as $200 at other times of the year.

For all the modern conveniences along with unbeatable city and harbor views, head for the sparkling **Pan Pacific Hotel Vancouver,** Canada Place, 604/662-8111 or 800/937-1515 from the U.S., 800/663-1515 from Canada, website www.panpacific-hotel.com. It's part of the landmark Canada Place, whose Teflon sails fly over busy, bustling sidewalks and a constant flow of cruise ships. Each of the 504 spacious rooms boasts stunning views, contemporary furnishings, a luxurious marble bathroom, and in-room video checkout. Rooms start at $540 s or d, while weekend rates outside of summer are $250.

© ANDREW HEMPSTEAD

Pan Pacific Hotel provides breathtaking harbor views.

HOTELS AND MOTELS ALONG ROBSON STREET

Robson Street—with its sidewalk cafés, restaurants open till the wee hours, and fashionable boutiques—provides a great alternative to staying right downtown.

$100–150

Built in the 1920s, the European-style **Barclay Hotel**, 1348 Robson St., 604/688-8850, website www.barclayhotel.com, holds 80 medium-size rooms, a small lounge, and an intimate restaurant. The rooms are stylish in an unpretentious way; each holds a comfortable bed, writing desk, couch, and older television. Summer rates of $95 s, $115 d include a continental buffet breakfast, making the Barclay good value during the busy season. Outside of summer rooms start at $80.

The **Greenbrier Hotel**, 1393 Robson St., 604/683-4558 or 888/355-5888, looks a bit rough on the outside, but all of the 32 units were refurbished in the mid-1990s, and each has a large living area, full kitchen, and separate bedroom. Rates are $129–169 s or d.

One block farther toward Stanley Park the **Riviera Hotel**, 1431 Robson St., 604/685-1301 or 888/699-5222, offers similar facilities, as well as harbor or city views from the upper floors. All rooms are large and comfortably furnished; from $108 s, $128 d and with larger one-bedroom suites for $168.

$150–200

A few blocks closer to downtown and a step up in quality from the above three accommodations is the 214-room **Blue Horizon Hotel**, 1225 Robson St., 604/688-1411 or 800/663-1333, website www.bluehorizonhotel.com. Facilities include an indoor lap pool, a fitness room, a sauna, and a variety of services for business travelers. Rooms are large, brightly lit, and have a private balcony, work desk, and coffee-making facilities. Rates range $159–199 s or d depending on the view.

$200–250

The **Pacific Palisades Hotel**, 1277 Robson St., 604/688-0461 or 800/663-1815, website www.pacificpalisadeshotel.com, is touted as being a cross between "South Beach (Miami) and Stanley Park," a fairly apt description of this chic Robson Street accommodation. Interior designers have given the entire hotel a "beachy," ultra contemporary feel—each of the 233 spacious rooms is decorated with sleek furnishings in a dynamic color scheme. Rates are a reasonable $200–225 s or d.

Diagonally opposite Pacific Palisades, **Listel Vancouver**, 1300 Robson St., 604/684-8461 or 800/663-5491, website www.listel-vancouver.com, is an elegant full-service lodging best known for its innovative use of original and limited-edition artwork through many rooms. Summer rates for a regular room are $240 s or d while those on the two Gallery Floors, which in addition to artworks feature separate bedrooms and bay windows, are $300.

Over $250

The 510-room **Westin Bayshore**, 1601 W. Georgia St., 604/682-3377 or 800/837-8461, website www.westinbayshore.com, is unique within the downtown peninsula in that it offers a distinctive resort-style atmosphere. Lying right on Coal Harbour and linked to Stanley Park by a waterfront promenade, it features a large outdoor pool surrounded by outdoor furniture settings and a poolside lounge, a health club, and a yacht charter operation down on the marina; $329–399 s or d.

HOTELS AND MOTELS IN THE WEST END

The few accommodations at the west end of downtown are near some fine restaurants, close to Stanley Park and English Bay, and a 25-minute walk along bustling Robson Street from downtown proper.

$50–100

Overlooking English Bay and the closest beach to downtown, the **Sylvia Hotel**, 1154 Gilford St., 604/681-9321, website www.sylviahotel.com, is a local landmark sporting a brick and terra-cotta exterior covered with Virginia creeper. Built in

VANCOUVER

1912 as an apartment building, today it provides excellent value as rates range $85–205 s or d (the less expensive rooms are fairly small), with more expensive rooms featuring fantastic views and full kitchens. The Sylvia also has a restaurant and lounge.

Another less expensive choice is the three-story **Buchan Hotel,** in a quiet residential area at 1906 Haro St., 604/685-5354 or 800/668-6654, website www.buchanhotel.com. Rooms are small, but the atmosphere is friendly and Stanley Park is only one block away; from $69 s, $75 d with shared bathroom facilities.

Over $100

Right by Stanley Park is **Rosellen Suites,** 2030 Barclay St., 604/689-4807 or 888/317-6648, website www.rosellensuites.com, where each of the 30 spacious units features modern furnishings, a separate living and dining area, a full kitchen, and modern conveniences such as stereos and voice mail. Rates are $189 for a one-bedroom unit, $219 for a two-bedroom unit, and $269–399 for larger units with fireplaces and private patios. Through summer, a three-night minimum stay policy is in effect.

HOTELS AND MOTELS ON THE NORTH SHORE

The best reason to stay on the North Shore is to enjoy the local hospitality of one of the many bed and breakfasts (see below), but a number of hotels and motels are also scattered through this part of the city.

$50–100

One of the least expensive north of Burrard Inlet is the **Horseshoe Bay Motel,** 6588 Royal Ave., 604/921-7454, 12 km west of the Lions Gate Bridge, tucked below the highway in Horseshoe Bay and right by the B.C. Ferries terminal (from where ferries depart for the Sunshine Coast and Nanaimo). It's within easy walking distance of numerous cafés and restaurants, and the nearby Horseshoe Bay Marina is a pleasant place for an evening stroll. Rooms are $90 s or d.

$100–150

Without a doubt, the pick of accommodations on the north side of Burrard Inlet is the **Park Royal Hotel,** 540 Clyde Ave., West Vancouver, 604/926-5511 or 877/926-5511, website www.parkroyalhotel.com. The Tudor-style accommodation sits on the banks of the Capilano River—you can fish for salmon and steelhead right on the property—and is surrounded by well-maintained gardens. Inside you'll find an English-style pub with a congenial atmosphere, elegant dining in the Tudor Room, and an inviting lounge area with fireplace. The 30 rooms are small, but each has a brass bed. Rates start at $140 s or d, with rooms that have garden views ranging $180–240 depending on their size.

In the same vicinity, close to the north end of the Lions Gate Bridge, the **Holiday Inn Express Vancouver North Shore,** 1800 Capilano Rd., 604/987-4461 or 800/663-4055, website www.holiday-inn.com, charges from $139 s or d.

Over $150

If you don't have transportation but don't want to stay right downtown, **Lonsdale Quay Hotel,** 123 Carrie Cates Court, North Vancouver, 604/986-6111 or 800/836-6111, website www.lonsdalequayhotel.com, is a good choice. It enjoys an absolute waterfront location above lively Lonsdale Quay Market and the SeaBus Terminal, making it just 12 minutes to downtown by water. Each of the 70 rooms is equipped with modern furnishings and amenities that come with a more expensive downtown room, such as Internet access, a daily newspaper, and a water cooler. One and two-bedroom suites start at $205 and $265 respectively.

HOTELS AND MOTELS SOUTH OF DOWNTOWN

If you have your own transportation, the lodgings south of downtown are worth consideration. They're generally less expensive than the downtown hotels, and you won't have to worry about parking (or paying for parking). Nearby is a cluster of inexpensive restaurants, the perfect place for a budget-conscious traveler to end the day with a good meal.

$50–100
The least expensive choices lie along the Kingsway, the main route between downtown and New Westminster. At the bottom of the price spectrum is the **2400 Motel,** 2400 Kingsway (near Nanaimo St. and within walking distance of the 29th Ave. SkyTrain station), 604/434-2464 or 888/833-2400, an old roadside-style place with basic rooms, cable TV, and coffee and newspapers offered in the office each morning. Rates start at $75 s or d, with kitchenettes for $105. Check in here during winter and you'll find rooms for $50.

Back toward downtown—and the closest of the Kingsway accommodations to the city center—is the **Biltmore Hotel,** 395 Kingsway, 604/872-5252 or 800/663-5713, website www.biltmorehotelvancouver.com. The rooms are on the small side, but many have city views and there's an outdoor pool for guest use. Rates are from $89 s, $99 d.

$100–150
Within walking distance of a SkyTrain station is **Days Inn—Vancouver Metro,** 2075 Kingsway, 604/876-5531 or 800/546-4792, website www.daysinn.com. The renovated rooms are typical of other Days Inn properties with a simple, contemporary feel. Each room has amenities such as hair dryers and alarm clocks. Summer rates are $109–129 s or d, dropping as low as $69 the rest of the year.

HOTELS AND MOTELS IN RICHMOND (VANCOUVER INTERNATIONAL AIRPORT)
The following Richmond accommodations are good choices for those visitors who arrive late at or have an early departure from the international airport. Also, if you arrive in Vancouver and want to head straight over to Vancouver Island, staying in this vicinity saves an unnecessary trip into downtown. All accommodations detailed in this section offer complimentary airport shuttles.

$100–150
The **Delta Pacific Resort & Conference Centre,** five km from the airport at 10251 St. Edwards Dr. (across Hwy. 99), 604/278-9611 or 800/268-1133, website www.deltahotels.com, offers a wide range of facilities, including a fitness center, large water slide, one indoor and two outdoor pools, tennis and squash courts, a business center, and bike rentals. Packages are offered year-round, such as one night's accommodation, breakfast, and two weeks' free parking for $119 s or d.

Farther from the airport, the **Coast Vancouver Airport Hotel,** 1041 Southwest Marine Dr., 604/263-1555 or 800/663-1144, website www.coasthotels.com, offers 134 modern rooms, a fitness center, sports bar, and family restaurant. Instead of paying the rack rate ($119 s or d), inquire about the Coast's many packages suited to arriving and departing air passengers.

Also on the downtown side of the Fraser River is **Quality Inn Airport,** 725 Southeast Marine Dr., 604/321-6611 or 800/663-6715, website www.airmetro.com, charging from $105 s or d (discounted 10 percent for travelers aged 50 and over) including a continental breakfast. The hotel is part of a large complex that includes a casino, bowling center, sports bar, and restaurant.

$150–200
Centrally located three km from the main airport terminals, the **Radisson President Hotel and Suites,** 8181 Cambie Rd., 604/276-8181 or 800/333-3333, website www.radissonvancouver.com, is a sprawling complex of 184 guest rooms, a fitness center, indoor pool, and several restaurants. The rooms are spacious and well appointed, making the rates of $179 s or d including breakfast reasonable. Travelers 55 and older get a better deal—they pay from $129 s or d.

Right at the international airport, the **Fairmont Vancouver Airport,** 3111 Grant McConachie Way, 604/207-5200 or 800/866-5577, website www.fairmont.com, is one of the world's most modern hotels. Opened in late 1999, it is a technological wonder. Rooms are equipped with remote controlled everything, right down to the drapes, fog-free bathroom mirrors, and floor-to-ceiling soundproofed windows. Standard rooms are $189 s or d. As a Fairmont guest, you can check into the hotel at the arrivals level of the international terminal, and if you're departing on an Air Canada flight, have your bags exchanged for a boarding pass right from the comfort of your room.

HOTELS AND MOTELS IN DELTA

Separated from Richmond by the South Arm of the Fraser River, Delta is a continuation of Vancouver's sprawl. It's an ideal place to stay if you're planning to get an early morning jump on the crowds for the ferry trip over to Vancouver Island, or if you're arriving from the United States and don't feel like tackling city traffic after a long day's drive.

$50–100

The **Delta Town and Country Inn,** 6005 Hwy. 17, 604/946-4404 or 888/777-1266, website www.deltainn.com, is both ideally situated and excellent value. It's at the junction of Highway 99 and Highway 17, halfway between the airport and ferry terminal, but the setting is parklike and quiet, with most of the 50 rooms enjoying views over extensive gardens and a landscaped pool area. Rates through summer are $99 s or d including breakfast, dropping to $75 the rest of the year.

$100–150

The closest accommodation to the southern departure point for ferries to Vancouver Island is the **Best Western Tsawwassen Inn,** four km northeast of the ferry terminal back toward the city along Highway 17 at 1665 56th St., 604/943-8221 or 800/943-8221, website www.tsawwasseninn.com. The hotel comprises two separate sections, one containing 50 newly decorated guest rooms, an indoor and outdoor pool, a fitness center, two restaurants, and a lounge. The other part of the complex holds 89 much larger suites, each with a kitchen and private patio. Regular rooms are $119 s or d and the suites $149; both these rates include a light breakfast and a shuttle service that runs to both the ferry and airport terminals and to a local shopping mall.

HOTELS AND MOTELS IN BURNABY

$50–100

The least expensive motel in this sprawling suburban area immediately east of downtown is the **401 Motor Inn,** 2950 Boundary Rd., 604/438-3451 or 877/438-3451, charging $70 s, $75 d. From the TransCanada Highway eastbound take Exit 28A south onto Boundary Rd. or westbound Exit 28B onto the Grandview Highway and take Boundary Rd. to the south; either way it's less than 200 meters from the highway and on the left.

Falling in the same price range, the **Happy Day Inn,** 7330 6th St., 604/524-8501 or 800/665-9733, website www.happydayinn.com, is farther east (almost in New Westminster) but offers more modern guest rooms, a small fitness facility, and a sauna. Standard rooms are $74 s, $79 d; kitchenettes $79 s, $83 d.

$100–150

Within walking distance of the huge Metrotown shopping complex, **Quality Inn & Suites Metrotown,** 3484 Kingsway, 604/433-8255, website www.qualityinnvancouver.com, has a pool, café, restaurant, and lounge. Each of the 123 spacious rooms has two TVs and a coffeemaker. Rates start at $109 s, $129 d, while larger rooms that sleep four are $139.

If you're coming into the city on the TransCanada Highway, you'll find a cluster of motels just west of where the highway crosses the Fraser River, including **Best Western Chelsea Inn,** 725 Brunette Ave. (take Exit 40B northbound), 604/525-7777 or 800/528-1234, website www.bestwestern.com. This motel features 61 well-appointed rooms, each with a lounge and coffeemaker. Rates range $114–138 s or d, including breakfast.

$150–200

Holiday Inn Metrotown, 4405 Central Blvd., 604/438-1881 or 877/323-1177, website www.holiday-inn.com, is part of the province's biggest shopping complex and is connected to downtown by the SkyTrain. More than 100 rooms are spread over six stories of this contemporary hotel, each spacious and well appointed. Guests enjoy an evening turndown service. Other facilities include a wide range of recreational facilities including an outdoor swimming pool, a tennis court, and a fitness center. Rack rates are $169 s, $179 d, but Holiday Inn Great Rates ($129 s or d) apply year-round, and weekend rates ($139) include a breakfast voucher.

HOTELS AND MOTELS IN ABBOTSFORD

$100–150

If you are using Vancouver's second airport, at Abbotsford, **Holiday Inn Express,** three km away at 2073 Clearbrook Rd., Clearbrook, 604/859-6211 or 800/665-7252, website www.holiday-inn.com, is a convenient accommodation. It features large rooms and an indoor pool. Summer rates are $109 s or d, discounted to under $70 in winter. Like all Holiday Inn Express hotels a light breakfast is included in the rates, but there's also an adjacent family-style restaurant.

BED AND BREAKFASTS

If you want to meet locals and prefer the idea of staying in someone's home rather than in an impersonal hotel room, stay in a bed and breakfast. B&Bs sprouted all over Vancouver just before Expo86 and today can be found all across the greater metropolitan area. Styles run the gamut—heritage homes, modern townhouses, renovated boutique hotels. Some have ensuite bathrooms, others shared facilities; some have swimming pools and saunas, others are on the beach or close to city attractions. Most often, bed and breakfasts also function as private residences, so book in advance—don't just turn up. Also, check payment methods when booking; not all establishments take credit or debit cards.

Most bed and breakfasts belong to an association or are listed with an agency. The **Western Canadian Bed and Breakfast Innkeepers Association** represents many Vancouver bed and breakfasts; call 604/255-9199 or go to website www.wcbbia.com. The following agencies

take actual bookings: **AB&C B&B of Vancouver,** 4390 Frances St., Vancouver, BC V5C 2R3, 604/298-8815 or 800/488-1941, website www.vancouverbandb.bc.ca.; **Old English B&B Registry,** 1226 Silverwood Crescent, North Vancouver, BC V7P 1J3, 604/986-5069, website www.oldenglishbandb.com; **Beachside B&B Registry,** 4208 Evergreen Ave., West Vancouver, BC V7V 1H1, 604/922-7773 or 800/563-3311. Beachside promotes the excellent bed and breakfast of the same name but also provides links to others at the website www.beach.bc.ca.

West End

In the heart of downtown Vancouver, only one block from Robson Street is **West End Guest House,** 1362 Haro St., 604/681-2889, website www.westendguesthouse.com. Built at the turn of the century, this accommodation has been lovingly refurbished in Victorian-era colors and furnished with stylish antiques to retain its original charm. Each of the seven guest rooms has a brass bed complete with cotton linen and a goosedown duvet, an ensuite bathroom, a television, and a telephone. Rates start at $120 s, $135 d, which includes a full breakfast.

Toward Stanley Park and nestled among towering apartment blocks is **English Bay Inn,** 1968 Comox St., 604/683-8002, a quiet retreat from the pace of the city. The decor is stylish, in an old-fashioned way. Highlights include a lounge area with log fireplace, and a small garden out the back. Rates start at $175 s or d, and the luxurious two-room suite goes for $295.

Uptown

South of False Creek you'll find a profusion of bed and breakfasts. Many lie in quiet residential areas, yet are close to public transportation.

Behind City Hall between Cambie and Yukon Streets, **Cambie Lodge,** 446 W. 13th Ave., Mt. Pleasant, 604/872-3060 or 888/872-3060, website www.cambielodge.com, has the reputation of being a friendly, clean, and comfortable place to stay for international travelers. Each room has a TV and heritage-style furnishings, while communal facilities include a TV lounge and a small garden. Rates for the six rooms range $95–105 s or d, which includes a cooked breakfast.

Pillow 'n Porridge Guest Suites is a unique lodging three bocks south of Broadway and a few hundred meters east of City Hall at 2859 Manitoba St., Mt. Pleasant, 604/879-8977, website www.pillow.net. The seven suites are spread through three adjacent colorfully painted heritage houses. Each unit is fully self-contained with a kitchen, ensuite bathroom, telephone, cable TV, fireplace, and private entrance. Rates range from $135 for a small suite to $255 for a complete three-bedroom house.

On the southern edge of Shaughnessy, **Beautiful B&B**, 428 W. 40th Ave. (just off Cambie St.), 604/327-1102, website www.beautifulbandb.com, is a Colonial-style two-story home on a high point of land where views extend across the city to the North Shore Range. Both Queen Elizabeth Park and VanDusen Botanical Garden are within walking distance. The house is decorated with antiques and fresh flowers from the surrounding garden. Two rooms share a bathroom ($125–160 s or d) while the Honeymoon Suite features a fireplace, panoramic views, and a huge ensuite bathroom complete with soaker tub ($235 s or d).

Arbutus Garden House, 4470 Maple Cres., Shaughnessy, 604/738-6432, website www.arbutushouse.com, is a magnificent 1922 three-story home surrounded by similar grandiose homes that make up one of Vancouver's most prestigious suburbs. The four guest rooms are spacious, and each features fresh flowers picked daily, a small writing desk, robes, slippers, and tea- and coffee-making facilities. Guests also enjoy use of separate TV and sitting rooms, decks, and the surrounding gardens and outdoor furniture. Summer rates range $100–165 s or d (closed the rest of the year).

Farther west, in the suburb of Kitsilano, is **Penny Farthing Inn**, 2855 W. 6th Ave., 604/739-9002, www.pennyfarthinginn.com, another heritage house, this one with four antique-filled rooms. The least expensive room is $105 s, $115 d, while the suite, complete with mountain views, a brass bed, and separate lounge area with a television, video player, and compact disc player, is $170 s or d.

North Shore

Adjoining Deep Cove's Myrtle Park, **Queen Anne Manor B&B**, 4606 Wickenden Rd., 604/929-3239, website www.n-vancouver.com, is a modern home with a Victorian-era look, furnished with period antiques. Each of the three guest rooms has its own distinct look; the grandest is the Chelsea Suite, featuring a huge canopied bed, private balcony, hot tub, and a sitting room in a turret. This room is $175 s or d, while the other two range $95–145 s or d.

Deep Cove B&B, 2590 Shelley Rd., 604/929-3932, is in North Vancouver, not in Deep Cove as the name suggests. Set on a large property and surrounded by gardens adjoining a residential area, the atmosphere is informal and relaxing. Amenities include an outdoor hot tub, lounge, and billiard table. The two guest rooms, each with ensuite bathroom, rent for $95 s or d.

Close to Grouse Mountain Gondola, **Mountainside Manor,** 5909 Nancy Greene Way, North Vancouver, 604/990-9772, is a great place to unwind—especially in the outdoor hot tub. This modern home high above the city also features four comfortable rooms of different configurations, each with an ensuite bathroom and television. The least expensive of the rooms is $110 s or d.

Thistledown House, 3910 Capilano Rd., North Vancouver, 604/986-7173 or 888/633-7173, website www.thistle-down.com, has been restored to resemble a country-style inn. Each room features its own character and has a balcony. The Under the Apple Tree room contains a king-sized bed, split-level sitting room, and a large bathroom complete with a Jacuzzi tub. Rates of $125–220 s or d include a gourmet breakfast.

If you're prepared to spend a bit more money (and to book well ahead), **Beachside B&B**, 4208 Evergreen Ave., West Vancouver, 604/922-7773 or 800/563-3311, website www.beach.bc.ca, is an excellent choice, with views extending across Burrard Inlet to Stanley Park to downtown. The two larger suites have water views, semi-private patios, and Jacuzzi tubs; $250 s or d. The smallest of the three rooms, which opens to a private patio, is $150 s or d.

M
VANCOUVER

BUDGET ACCOMMODATIONS

Hostelling International

Opened in summer 1996, **HI Vancouver Downtown,** 1114 Burnaby St., 604/684-4565 or 888/203-4302, website www.hihostels.com, is part of the new wave of facilities run by the world's largest and longest running network of backpacker accommodations. The complex offers a large kitchen, library, game room, public Internet access, a travel agency, bike rentals, bag storage, and a laundry. The dormitories hold a maximum of four beds but are small. For these beds members of Hostelling International pay $20, nonmembers $24; private rooms range $48–56 s or d. A daily shuttle runs between this hostel and the one out at Jericho Beach.

If you don't need to stay right downtown, **HI Vancouver Jericho Beach,** 1515 Discovery St. (near the intersection of Northwest. Marine Dr. and W. 4th Ave.), Point Grey, 604/224-3208, website www.hihostels.com, is a good alternative choice. The location is fantastic—in scenic parkland and linked to downtown by extensive biking and walking trails. Amenities include separate dorms for men and women, rooms for couples and families, a communal kitchen, a café, public Internet access, a handy information board, left-luggage service ($5 a bag per week), and a shuttle to the downtown hostel and rail/bus station. Members pay $18 per night, nonmembers $22 for a dorm bed, or $45 and $53 respectively for double room.

Other Backpacker Lodges

Privately owned backpacker lodges in Vancouver come and go with predictable regularity. Many should be avoided, but the newest addition to the backpacker scene, **Global Village Backpackers,** 1018 Granville St., 604/682-8226 or 888/844-7875, website www.globalbackpackers .com, is excellent in all respects. Each of the smallish rooms has been tastefully decorated, and the communal lounge and kitchen areas serve guests well. Other facilities include a separate TV room, public Internet access, and a rooftop patio. Rates are $21.40 pp in a dorm or $58.50–65.50 d with discounted winter rates.

In addition to offering some of the city's best-value hotel rooms (see above), the **Dominion Hotel,** 210 Abbott St., Gastown, 604/681-6666 or 877/681-1666, website www.dominion hotel.bc.ca, offers backpacker rooms, with shared bathrooms and kitchen, a laundry, communal lounge, public Internet access, and bag/bike storage; $20 per person.

C&N Backpackers Hostel, 927 Main St., 604/682-2441 or 888/434-6060, has undergone some improvements since new owners took over, but the rooms and kitchen are still sparse and the lounge area leaves a lot to be desired. There's a sink in every dorm room and other bathroom facilities on every floor. Other amenities include a laundry and public Internet access. The location is central to Pacific Central Station, but the neighborhood is among the worst in the city after dark. Dorm beds are $12, singles $25, and doubles $30.

YWCA Hotel

This lodging for female travelers, couples, and families at 733 Beatty St., 604/895-5830 or 800/663-1424, website www.ywcahotel.com, is very central to downtown and offers basic but modern facilities in more than 150 rooms spread over 11 floors. Each room has a telephone, and the private rooms have televisions. Communal facilities include two kitchens, three lounges, and two laundries. Guests also have use of the nearby YWCA Health and Wellness Centre, which houses a pool and gym. Single rooms share a bathroom and cost $56–72, and double rooms range $69–111.

YMCA

Though not as modern as the YWCA, the 113-room YMCA, 955 Burrard St., 604/681-0221 or 888/595-9622, website www.vanymca.org, enjoys a good downtown location, only two blocks from busy Robson Street and all the restaurants and nightlife. Guests are also afforded privileges at the YMCA fitness facility. No cooking facilities are available, but the in-house café is open daily except Sunday for breakfast and lunch. Parking up the alley beside the building costs $5 for 24 hours; it's supervised during the day. Rooms, none with private bathroom, are available for men, women, and couples. Rates are $42 s, $51 d, $60 twin ($2 extra per night for a television).

Vanier Hostel

The UBC Conference Centre provides basic accommodations on the grounds of the University of British Columbia, out at Point Grey, 16 km west of city center. Summer options include single rooms with shared bathrooms, and one- or two-bedroom suites or studio suites with private bathrooms and kitchenettes. Some suites are available year-round. A restaurant is close by, and UBC recreational facilities, including a swimming pool, sauna, whirlpool, and tennis and fitness center, are available to guests; $24–48 s, $90–110 d. For further information and reservations, contact UBC Conference Centre, 5961 Student Union Blvd., 604/822-1000.

Simon Fraser University

Although it's about 20 km east of downtown Vancouver, Simon Fraser University offers inexpensive dorm rooms to travelers in summer. The hilltop campus is known for its modern architecture and excellent city views. Single or twin fully furnished townhouse units with shared bathrooms are available May–Aug.; from $27 s, $45 d. The university is between Highways 7 and 7A in Burnaby. To get there by bus, catch no. 10 or 14 on Granville Mall (get a transfer ticket and ask the driver to tell you where to get off), then transfer to bus no. 135. Contact Housing and Conference Services, Room 212, McTaggart-Cowan Hall, Burnaby, Vancouver, BC V5A 1S6, 604/291-4503.

CAMPING

You won't find any campgrounds in the city center area, but a limited number dot the suburbs along the major approach routes. Before trekking out to any of them, ring ahead to check for vacancies. Commercial and provincial park campgrounds are listed in Tourism BC's invaluable *Accommodations* guide, available at all information centers or by calling 250/387-1642 or 800/435-5622, or online at website www.hellobc.com.

North

The closest campground to downtown is **Capilano RV Park,** 295 Tomahawk Ave., North Vancouver, 604/987-4722, website www.capilanorvpark.com. To get there from downtown, cross Lions Gate Bridge, turn right on Marine Dr., right on Capilano Rd., and right again on Welch Street. From Highway 1/99 in West Vancouver, exit south on Taylor Way toward the shopping center and turn left over the Capilano River. It's about an hour walk to downtown from the campground, over Lions Gate Bridge and through Stanley Park. Amenities include a 13-meter pool, a hot tub, a TV and games room, and a laundry. Sites are equipped with 15- and 30-amp power as well as sewer, water, cable, and telephone hookups. These sites range $35–45 per night. It gets crowded in summer; even though there are more than 200 sites, book well ahead to be assured of a site through summer. The park is really intended for vehicle camping and RVs, but limited spots are available for tents ($25); however, no bookings are taken, so call ahead and ask if they have any grassy areas left.

South

Large **Richmond RV Park,** 15 km (20 minutes) south of downtown at 6200 River Rd., 604/270-7878 or 800/755-4905, website www.richmondrvpark.com, is just off the final flight path for Vancouver International Airport. Aside from noise from the airport, the riverside location is excellent. Facilities include free showers, a coin-op laundry, and a game room. Tent sites are $17, while serviced sites range $23–28. Open April–October. To get there, take Exit 36 from Highway 99, head west along Westminster Highway, then take No. 2 Road north to River Road and turn right.

Parkcanada, beside Hwy. 17 (take the 52nd St. exit north then the first left), 604/943-5811, website www.parkcanada.com, is very convenient to the B.C. Ferries terminal at Tsawwassen, a 30-minute drive south of city center. The campground has a small outdoor pool, but next door is a much larger waterpark—perfect for the kids. Other amenities include a store with groceries and some RV supplies, laundromat, lounge, and free showers. Unserviced sites, suitable for tents, are $18; serviced sites range $21–34 depending on the size of the RV or trailer and the amp required. It's open year-round.

Open year-round, **Peace Arch RV Park,** 14601 40th Ave., 604/594-7009, website www .peacearchrvpark.com, sprawls over four hectares between the suburbs of White Rock and Delta, 10 km from Douglas Border Crossing; take Exit 10 (King George Highway) north from Highway 99, then the first right, 40th Avenue. The well-tended facilities include a heated pool, playground and mini-golf, game room, coin-operated showers, and a laundry. Sites in the tenting area are $18.50 while hookups go for $24.50.

East

Adjacent to Burnaby Lake Regional Park, **Burnaby Cariboo RV Park (BCRV)**, 8765 Cariboo Place, Burnaby, 604/420-1722, website www.bcrvpark.com, offers luxurious facilities including a large indoor heated pool, fitness room, hot tub, sundeck, playground, lounge, barbecue area, grocery store, and laundry facility. The campground offers 217 paved sites, each with full hookups, including 30-amp power, cable TV, telephone, and Internet access; $32–38 per night. Sites in the private, walk-in tenting area cost $23 per night. The park is 17 km east of downtown. To get there, take Exit 37 (Gaglardi) from the TransCanada Highway, turn right at the first traffic light, then take the first left, then the first right into Cariboo Place. Open year-round.

Farther east, **Dogwood Campgrounds of B.C.,** 15151 112th Ave., Surrey, 604/583-5585, is 35 km from downtown and close to the end of the SkyTrain railway. It's right beside the Trans-Canada Highway, but to get there take Exit 50 north along 160th St., then head west on 112th Avenue. Facilities are adequate and modern, but basic, and include a pool and laundry. Hookups are $22–33.

Anmore Camp & RV Park is tucked away on Buntzen Lake, near the head of Burrard Inlet, north of Coquitlam and the TransCanada Highway, at 3230 Sunnyside Rd., Anmore, 604/469-

2311. To get there, head north along Highway 7 from Exit 44 of the TransCanada Highway; take Highway 7A west, back toward the city, then Ioco Road north, and follow the signs. It's the forested setting that makes this campground worth the drive, but other facilities include a small heated pool, canoe and bike rentals, a barbecue area, a laundry, and a small general store. Tent sites are $24 per night, hookups $28–30.

Provincial Parks

Most provincial parks that surround Vancouver offer camping, but none offer hookups and all are seasonal. They also fill up very fast, especially on weekends. Reserve a spot by calling BC Parks' Discover Camping hotline at 604/689-9025 or 800/689-9025, or online at www.discover-camping.ca. Reservations are taken between 15 March and 15 September, for dates up to three months in advance. The reservation fee is $6.42 per night, to a maximum of $19.26, and is in addition to applicable camping fees.

Of the provincial parks immediately north of the city, the only one with a campground is **Golden Ears,** 40 km northeast from downtown near the suburb of Maple Ridge. To get there, take Highway 7 from downtown through Coquitlam and Pitt Meadows to Maple Ridge and follow the signs north on 232nd Street. The park holds almost 400 sites in two campgrounds near Alouette Lake. The campgrounds are linked by hiking trails. Facilities include hot showers, flush toilets, and a picnic table and fire ring at each site; $18.50 per night.

Traveling north on Highway 99 toward Whistler, **Porteau Cove Provincial Park,** 20 km north of Horseshoe Bay, offers 60 sites in a pleasant treed setting with mountain views. Through summer sites are $18.50, discounted to $12 the rest of the year.

If you're traveling the TransCanada Highway, the closest provincial park campground is at **Cultus Lake,** 100 km east of downtown and seven km south of downtown Chilliwack (Exit 119). All sites are $18.50, which includes the use of hot showers.

Food

With an estimated 2,000 restaurants and hundreds of cafés and coffeehouses, Vancouver is a gastronomical delight. The city is home to more than 60 different cultures, so you won't be surprised to find a smorgasbord of ethnic restaurants. The local specialty is West Coast or "fusion" cuisine, which combines fresh Canadian produce, such as local seafood and seasonal game, with Asian flavors and ingredients, usually in a healthy, low-fat way. Vancouver has no tourist-oriented, San Francisco-style Fisherman's Wharf, but however and wherever it's prepared, seafood will always dominate local menus. Pacific salmon, halibut, snapper, shrimp, oysters, clams, crab, and squid are all harvested locally, while mussels, lobster, tiger prawns, and Atlantic salmon are imported from Canada's Atlantic provinces or from farther afield. Restaurants throughout the city specialize in seafood; for the freshest, straight from the trawlers, along with a lively atmosphere, head to Steveston on the city's southern outskirts. Granville Island and Chinatown are also good bets to find fresh seafood.

One thing that will soon become apparent to first-time visitors is the amount of coffee consumed by the locals; specialty coffeehouses are *everywhere.* Seattle-based Starbucks Coffee Co. alone has more than 85 Vancouver outlets, including two sitting kitty-corner to each other on Robson Street.

DOWNTOWN

Cafés and Cheap Eats

Downtown Vancouver has so many good dining options that it is a shame to eat in a food court, but like in cities around the Western world, they are good places for a fast, reliable, and inexpensive meal. The southwest corner of the Pacific Centre (at Howe and Georgia Streets, diagonally opposite the art gallery) holds a glass-domed food court with many inexpensive food bars and seating indoors or outdoors. A good place for food on the run is one of the many takeout pizza joints scattered throughout the city. While in the trendy West End a slice of pizza can cost up to $3, downtown many places charge just 99 cents a slice, and for an extra 50 cents you get a can of pop. Three of these cheapies lie along West Pender between Granville and Richards Streets. Two blocks up from Canada Place **Scoozis,** 808 W. Hastings St., 604/684-1009, offers dimly lit surroundings but good breakfasts for under $7. The rest of the day, it's pitas, pizzas, and main meals such as lamb chops for $14. Next door (up the hill) is **Richard and Co.,** 451 Howe St., 604/681-9885, a sparsely but stylishly furnished café where a coffee and muffin is just $2.50, soups start at $3 a bowl, and focaccia bread sandwiches are all around $5. It's open daily 7 A.M.–2 P.M.

West Coast

With its prime waterfront location between Canada Place and Gastown, **Aqua Riva,** 200 Granville St., 604/683-5599, features stunning views across Burrard Inlet. The least expensive way to enjoy the dramatic view is with a pizza baked in a wood-fired oven ($13–16). Other mains, mostly seafood and including a delicious alderwood-grilled salmon, are all under $30 (pastas average $20). Mains, including a wide variety of gourmet sandwiches, range $9–20. Vancouver's licensing regulations say that alcohol served in a restaurant can't be consumed without food, so although it's okay to stop here and soak up the views over a locally brewed beer or one of the many martinis on the drink list, you'll probably be offered a menu.

Typifying the new wave in Vancouver's hotel dining scene is **Show Case,** at street level of the Delta Pinnacle Hotel at 1128 W. Hastings St., 604/639-4040. Floor-to-ceiling windows and contemporary styling create an environment very different from the elegant old-world feel of Vancouver's other top-end hotel restaurants. Exotic dishes prepared using local seafood and game are simply and stylishly presented; the Tasting menu gives diners the opportunity to experience a variety of dishes, accompanied by matching wines. Mains range $18–32.

As you'd expect, views are stunning from the **Top of Vancouver Revolving Restaurant** atop the Harbour Centre Tower at 555 W. Hastings St., 604/689-7304. The menu features contemporary North American dishes prepared with a local slant; diners get a free ride to the top and then can expect to pay under $20 for most mains at lunch and over $20 (up to $45 for Alaskan king crab) at dinner.

Seafood

One of Vancouver's finest seafood restaurants is **A Kettle of Fish,** near the Burrard Street Bridge

at 900 Pacific St., 604/682-6853. The casual decor features café-style seating and abundant greenery, while the menu swims with schools of piscatory pleasures. New England clam chowder ($6) is one of over 20 appetizers, while traditionally prepared entrées such as grilled snapper ($19) or a seafood platter for two ($41.50) make up the main menu.

A throwback to the overindulgences of the 1980s, **C,** 1600 Howe St., 604/681-1164, employs one of Canada's brightest young chefs to deliver immaculately presented seafood in a chic-industrial setting. Main meals offered change with the seasons, with halibut, salmon, and Alaskan crab regular staples. Lunch mains range

DOWNTOWN DINING CLASSICS

While the best known of Vancouver's restaurants are judged by their food, the service, the decor, and the crowd they attract, none of that matters to the following places. At the places listed below, though, you can expect hearty portions, inexpensive prices, and, at all except the infamous Elbow Room, friendly service.

The **Elbow Room,** downtown at 560 Davie St., 604/685-3628, is a good place to start this culinary tour on the wrong side of the tracks. At this Vancouver institution portions are huge and the prices reasonable ($8 for the Lumberjack breakfast), but it's the service, or lack of it, that you'll remember long after the meal. The waiters take no nonsense, and the constant banter from the open kitchen, if not memorable, is in the least very unique. But it's all in good fun, and if you get abused you'll join a long list of celebrities whose photos adorn the walls. If you don't finish your meal, you must make a donation to a local charity; if it's a pancake you can't finish, you're advised to "just rub it on your thighs, because that's where it's going anyway!" The Elbow Room is open Mon.–Fri. 7:30 A.M.–3:30 P.M., Sat.–Sun. 8:30 A.M.–4 P.M., but breakfast is most popular and is served all day; Sunday morning is when the kitchen and wait staff are at their wittiest.

Along Granville Street, between the Elbow Room and the business district, are other greasy spoons, including **The Templeton,** 1087 Granville

St., 604/685-4612, which offers adventurous dishes such as veggie burgers and jambalaya, and the **Grade A Café,** 1175 Granville St., 604/669-7495, which keeps the locals happy with a classic Canadian and Chinese menu. In the same vicinity, Davie Street north of Granville holds a couple of classic diners, including **Hamburger Mary's,** 1202 Davie St., 604/687-1293, complete with chrome chairs, mirrored walls, and an old jukebox. Delicious hamburgers attract the crowds to Mary's; starting at $5.50, they aren't particularly cheap, but they come with fries, and extras such as salad are just $1. Breakfast ($5 for eggs, bacon, hash browns, and toast) begins daily at 7 A.M., and the last burgers are flipped in the early hours of the morning. Wash down your meal with one of Mary's famous milkshakes.

Vancouver's oldest restaurant, the **Only Cafe,** between downtown and Chinatown at 20 E. Hastings St., 604/681-6546, has been serving bargainbasement seafood for over 80 years. The decor is very 1950s, with two U-shaped counters, two ducttaped booths, and no bathrooms, but the food is always fresh and cooked to perfection. It's open daily 11 A.M.–8 P.M. Up the hill from the Only Cafe, beyond Main Street, is the **Ovaltine Café,** 251 E. Hastings St., 604/685-7021, easily spotted by the classic neon sign hanging out front. This classic diner has been serving up cheap chow for over 50 years. It's open 6 A.M.–midnight.

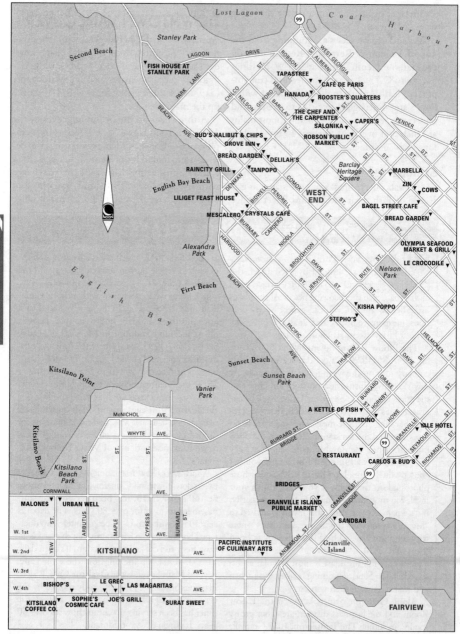

Lost Lagoon

Coal Harbour

99

Stanley Park

Second Beach

LAGOON   DRIVE

FISH HOUSE AT
STANLEY PARK

WEST GEORGIA

ST. ALBERNI

ROBSON

ST.

TAPASTREE

CAFÉ DE PARIS

PARK   LANE

HANADA

ROOSTER'S QUARTERS

BEACH

CHILCO

NELSON

GILFORD

HARO

BARCLAY

THE CHEF AND
THE CARPENTER

CAPER'S

PENDER

AVE.

BUD'S HALIBUT & CHIPS

SALONIKA

GROVE INN

ROBSON PUBLIC
MARKET

ST.

ST.

ST.

ST.

BREAD GARDEN

DELILAH'S

Barclay
Heritage
Square

MARBELLA

English Bay Beach

RAINCITY GRILL

TANPOPO

DENMAN

COMOX

ST.

ST.

ZIN

COWS

LILIGET FEAST HOUSE

BIDWELL

PENDRELL

WEST
END

BAGEL STREET CAFE

MESCALERO

CRYSTALS CAFÉ

BURNABY

CARDERO

ST.

BREAD GARDEN

NICOLA

ST.

OLYMPIA SEAFOOD
MARKET & GRILL

Alexandra
Park

HARWOOD

BROUGHTON

DAVIE

BUTE

Nelson
Park

LE CROCODILE

English   Bay

First Beach

BEACH

JERVIS

ST.

ST.

ST.

ST.

KISHA POPPO

STEPHO'S

PACIFIC

ST.

THURLOW

HELMCKEN

Kitsilano Point

Sunset Beach

AVE.

DAVIE   ST.

Kitsilano Beach

Vanier
Park

Sunset Beach
Park

BURRARD

DRAKE

HORNBY

HOWE

A KETTLE OF FISH

Kitsilano
Beach
Park

McNICHOL   AVE.

IL GIARDINO

GRANVILLE

SEYMOUR

RICHARDS

YALE HOTEL

ST.

WHYTE   AVE.

ST.

ST.

BURRARD ST.
BRIDGE

99

C RESTAURANT

CARLOS & BUD'S

ST.

99

CORNWALL

AVE.

BRIDGES

GRANVILLE ST.
BRIDGE

MALONES

URBAN WELL

GRANVILLE ISLAND
PUBLIC MARKET

SANDBAR

W. 1st

ARBUTUS
ST.

MAPLE

CYPRESS

BURRARD
ST.

ANDERSON   ST.

W. 2nd

YEW
ST.

KITSILANO

AVE.

PACIFIC INSTITUTE
OF CULINARY ARTS

Granville
Island

W. 3rd

AVE.

W. 4th

BISHOP'S

LE GREC

LAS MAGARITAS

AVE.

FAIRVIEW

KITSILANO
COFFEE CO.

SOPHIE'S
COSMIC CAFÉ

JOE'S GRILL

SURAT SWEET

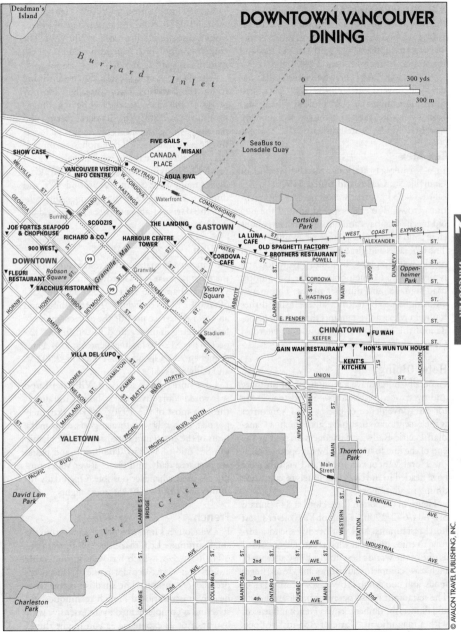

DOWNTOWN VANCOUVER DINING

Deadman's Island

Burrard Inlet

SeaBus to Lonsdale Quay

0   300 yds
0   300 m

SHOW CASE

FIVE SAILS

MISAKI

CANADA PLACE

SKY TRAIN

VANCOUVER VISITOR INFO CENTRE

AQUA RIVA

W. CORDOVA

W. HASTINGS

W. PENDER

MELVILLE ST.

GEORGIA

Burrard

BURRARD

Waterfront

COMMISSIONER

THE LANDING

GASTOWN

Portside Park

JOE FORTES SEAFOOD & CHOPHOUSE

SCOOZIS

RICHARD & CO.

HARBOUR CENTRE TOWER

LA LUNA CAFE

OLD SPAGHETTI FACTORY

BROTHERS RESTAURANT

WEST COAST EXPRESS

ALEXANDER ST.

900 WEST

DOWNTOWN

FLEURI RESTAURANT

Robson Square

BACCHUS RISTORANTE

99

Granville Mall

Granville

WATER ST.

CORDOVA CAFE

POWELL ST.

E. CORDOVA ST.

GORE

DUNLEVY

Oppenheimer Park

HORNBY

HOWE

ROBSON

SEYMOUR

RICHARDS

DUNSMUIR

ST.

ST.

Victory Square

ABBOTT

CARRALL

E. HASTINGS

MAIN ST.

99

SMITHE

Stadium

E. PENDER ST.

CHINATOWN

FU WAH

KEEFER

VILLA DEL LUPO

HOMER

HAMILTON

CAMBIE

BEATTY

GAIN WAH RESTAURANT

HON'S WUN TUN HOUSE

KENT'S KITCHEN

JACKSON ST.

NELSON ST.

MAINLAND

BLVD. NORTH

UNION ST.

COLUMBIA ST.

PACIFIC

BLVD. SOUTH

SKY TRAIN

MAIN ST.

YALETOWN

PACIFIC BLVD.

Thornton Park

PACIFIC BLVD.

David Lam Park

False Creek

CAMBIE ST.

BRIDGE ST.

Main Street

WESTERN ST.

STATION ST.

TERMINAL AVE.

INDUSTRIAL AVE.

Charleston Park

CAMBIE

1st AVE.

2nd AVE.

COLUMBIA

MANITOBA

ONTARIO

QUEBEC

MAIN

1st AVE.

2nd AVE.

3rd AVE.

4th AVE.

2nd

© AVALON TRAVEL PUBLISHING, INC.

N

VANCOUVER

$12–20, dinner mains $24–35. An addition to the lunchtime menu is a dim sum–style three-course seafood deal for $18.50. C is open daily 11:30 A.M.–2:30 P.M. and 5:30 A.M.–11 P.M. and for Sunday brunch 11 A.M.–2 P.M.

At Canada Place is **Five Sails,** in the Pan Pacific Vancouver Hotel, 604/891-2892. It's open for dinner only, and the fabulous setting and harbor views are reflected in the prices of modern, mostly seafood-oriented dishes.

Tex-Mex

In a former gas station near the far end of Granville St., **Carlos and Bud's,** 555 Pacific St., 604/684-5335, attracts a young and unpretentious crowd. Tables are spread around the two old mechanics' bays and outside, on a large concrete patio where vehicles once sat awaiting repair. The tool racks and girlie posters have been ripped off the walls, replaced by a funky paint job and typical Route 66 memorabilia like gas pumps, road signage, and number plates. The menu, amusing in itself, features all the usual dishes found in Mexican restaurants throughout Canada and the States, but portions are generous. Open daily for lunch and dinner.

Hotel Dining

Generally, hotels have a reputation for ordinary and overpriced restaurants—in existence only for the convenience of guests—but Vancouver is the exception to that rule. Since the first Canadian Pacific Railway passengers arrived at the end of the line to be spoiled by European chefs at the Hotel Vancouver, locals and visitors alike have headed to the city's best hotels to enjoy fine dining in all its glory.

Fleuri, in the Sutton Place Hotel at 845 Burrard St., 604/642-2900, is one of Vancouver's best hotel restaurants, and you needn't spend a fortune to enjoy dining in what is generally regarded as one of the world's best hotels. Every afternoon, high tea—complete with scones and cream, finger foods, and nonalcoholic beverages—costs $17.50. The restaurant is also open for breakfast, lunch, and dinner; the dinner menu is French influenced, with a magnificent "Taste of Atlantis" seafood buffet offered on Friday and Saturday nights.

At the Hotel Vancouver, 900 W. Georgia St., 604/669-9378, enjoy the atmosphere of a luxurious cruise ship dining room at **900 West.** The contemporary North American menu is varied, with mains starting at $26.

The Wedgewood Hotel's signature dining room, the **Bacchus Ristorante,** 845 Hornby St., 604/608-5319, has the feeling of a romantic European bistro with its dark cherrywood paneling, stone fireplace, and elegant table settings over white linen. The emphasis is on Italian cuisine, but the menu relies heavily on local produce, changing with the seasons. Breakfast dishes range $6–16, lunch is around $15, and dinner mains range $18–35. It's open throughout the day, and afternoon tea is served daily 2–4 P.M.

Italian

Of Vancouver's many Italian restaurants, one of the most popular is **Il Giardino,** in a distinctive yellow Italian-style villa at 1382 Hornby St., 604/669-2422. The light, bright furnishings and an enclosed terrace provide the perfect ambience for indulging in the featured Tuscan cuisine. Expect to pay $12–16 for lunch entrées, $14–33 for dinner entrées. Open Mon.–Fri. noon–2:30 P.M. and daily 5:30–11 P.M.

Of a similar high standard, **Villa del Lupo** was voted Vancouver's best Italian restaurant through most of the 1990s. It's still extremely popular, especially with theater-goers, as it's in the heart of the entertainment district at 869 Hamilton St., 604/688-7436. The breads and pastas are prepared daily, and Fraser River Valley produce is used whenever possible. Open daily for dinner and until 11:30 P.M. most nights.

French

For Vancouver's finest French cuisine, go to the small, intimate **Le Crocodile,** 909 Burrard St., 604/669-4298, which has won innumerable awards over its two decades as one of Vancouver's premier restaurants. The smallish menu relies heavily on traditional French techniques and style and is complemented by an extensive wine list. It's not as expensive as you might think; mains range $14–22. Open for lunch Mon.–Fri.

and for dinner Mon.–Sat.; make reservations for weekend dining.

Greek

Expect to wait for a table at **Stepho's,** 1124 Davie St., 604/683-2555, one of Vancouver's best-value restaurants. Locals line up here to enjoy the atmosphere of a typical Greek taverna—complete with a terra-cotta floor, white stucco walls, arched doorways, blue and white tablecloths, travel posters, and lots of colorful flowering plants. All the favorite Greek dishes are offered, such as souvlakis or a steak and Greek salad combination for under $10, and portions are generous. Start with freshly prepared tzatziki ($3.50) and finish off with a delicious baklava, which costs just $3, and coffee for a buck. Stepho's is open daily noon–11:30 P.M.

Japanese

Southwest from the central business district, **Kisha Poppo,** 1143 Davie St., 604/681-0488, serves up westernized Japanese food in a sterile diner-style atmosphere. But the price is right. All-you-can-eat soup, starters, sushi, hot mains such as teriyaki, and dessert is offered through lunch (11:30 A.M.–3 P.M.; $7.95 per person) and dinner (5–11:30 P.M.; $11.95). The regular menu is also well priced, with, for example, a sushi/teriyaki combo dinner for $14.95.

At the opposite end of the Japanese-dining-experience-spectrum, **Misaki,** in Canada Place, 604/891-2893, offers the peace and tranquility of an upmarket Tokyo restaurant. The cuisine combines traditional Japanese and contemporary fusion cooking, with most dishes making use of produce available locally. It's not particularly cheap (expect to pay $80 for two), but Misaki is among the best in the city and is half the price you would expect to pay in Tokyo.

GASTOWN GOURMET

Gastown is the most tourist-oriented part of Vancouver, yet it has many fine eating establishments that attract locals as well as visitors. At 375 Water St., adjacent to the SeaBus terminal, is The Landing, a restored warehouse now

housing elegant boutiques and a couple of good-value eateries.

Some of Gastown's best coffee is ground and brewed at **La Luna Cafe,** 131 Water St., 604/687-5862. The café's striking yellow-and-black decor, daily papers, great coffee, and inexpensive light snacks make this a pleasant escape from busy Water Street.

Simple surroundings show off innovative artworks at **Cordova Cafe,** 307 W. Cordova St., 604/688-3440. Light meals are good value—a bowl of chili is $4, a Greek salad is $5, and the daily soup-and-sandwich special is $6.

Family-Style

At the bottom end of Gastown, the unique decor at **Brothers Restaurant,** 1 Water St., 604/683-9124, features monastery-like surroundings of wood, brick, stained glass, chandeliers, and monkish murals. Enjoy delicious soups (try the Boston clam chowder), salads, sandwiches, and a variety of entrées ($9.50–17), all served by waiters appropriately dressed in monk attire and accompanied by congregational sing-alongs and laser light shows. The daily lunch specials are good value, as are the early dinner deals available Mon.–Thurs. before 6 P.M.

The **Old Spaghetti Factory,** 53 Water St., 604/684-1288, is a family-style favorite offering lunch entrées from $6 and dinner entrées from $10, including salad, bread, dessert, and coffee. This place is worth a visit for the eclectic array of furnishings, from old lamps to a 1904 trolley car.

West Coast

The designers of **Raintree,** 375 Water St., 604/688-5570, have taken advantage of a historic building, The Landing, to create an elegant setting without taking away the views extending across Burrard Inlet. Exposed beams, red-brick walls, and a slate floor all give class to what was originally a warehouse. The least expensive lunch items are the pastas, which cost under $15, while seafood dishes are only a couple of dollars more. Dinner mains, ranging $20–30, take advantage of local produce, such as salmon, which is served with goat cream cheese from the

Southern Gulf Islands. Vegetarians and vegans are catered to at Raintree. It's open daily 11:30 A.M.–2:30 P.M. and 5:30–10 P.M.

CHINATOWN

For Chinese food, you can't go wrong in Chinatown, a few blocks east of the city center. Chinatown encompasses six blocks, but restaurants and fresh-produce stalls are concentrated within the two blocks bordered by Main, Keefer, Gore, and East Hastings Streets. Within this area, look for stalls selling fish, fruit, vegetables, and other exotic goodies up Pender Street and one block either side of Pender along Gore Street. These markets are especially busy early in the morning when local restaurateurs are stocking up for the day's trade.

Dining in Chinatown offers two distinct options—traditional eateries where you'll find the locals and the larger, westernized restaurants that attract non-Chinese and a younger Chinese crowd. A perfect combination of the two is **Kent's Kitchen,** 232 Keefer St., 604/669-2237, a modern café-style restaurant where the service is fast and efficient, the food freshly prepared, and the prices incredibly low. Two specialty dishes, rice, and a can of pop make a meal that costs just $5. Next door to Kent's, **Hon's Wun Tun House,** 230 Keefer St., 604/688-0871, is a large, bright, and modern restaurant that attracts a younger Chinese crowd for mostly westernized Chinese under $10 for a main. Tiny **Gain Wah Restaurant,** 218 Keefer St., 604/684-1740, is a westernized noodle house where congee—a simple soup of water extracted from boiling rice—is $1.50 (flavorings an additional 25 cents to $2) and no meal containing seafood is over $10.

Around the corner from Keefer Street, Gore Street is less westernized; beyond the large fish market you'll find **Fu Wah,** 555 Gore St., 604/688-8722, which has a ridiculously inexpensive lunchtime dim sum menu.

GRANVILLE ISLAND

The **Granville Island Public Market,** on Johnston Street, bustles with locals and tourists alike throughout the day. In the tradition of similar European markets, shopping here is an unpretentious and practical affair, with lots of talking, poking, and enquiring at stalls selling fresh meats, seafood, fruit and vegetables, and cheeses and at specialty stalls stocked with pre-packaged goodies to go. At the Burrard Inlet end of the market nestle takeout stalls, and while there's a large expanse of indoor tables, most people head outside to enjoy their meal among the sights and sounds of False Creek. It is difficult to go past the **Stock Market** when recommending a stall from which to grab lunch. Starting at $3.50, the soups are absolutely mouthwatering, but it's worth the extra for a huge serving of red snapper chowder for $6 (or go for the small serving for $4.50). Around the corner from the Stock Market is a stall selling good fish and chips.

Waterfront Dining

On Granville Island's northern tip is **Bridges,** a distinctive yellow building at 1696 Duranleau St., 604/687-4400, with stunning water views. Diners have the choice of four dining areas, but the most popular spot is the Dock, an outside, absolute-waterfront eating area that entails waiting for a table whenever the sun is shining. The menu features typical wide-ranging bistro-style fare of hamburgers, salads, and pastas, as well as basic seafood dishes such as a platter to share for $34.

Under the Granville Street Bridge, **SandBar,** 1535 Johnston St., 604/669-9030, features a private deck complete with its own elevated waterfront bar. Downstairs features an open kitchen and more water views, a world away from the hustle and bustle of the nearby marketplace. The menu, mostly seafood, ranges $10–18. It's open daily 11:30 A.M. to 11 P.M.

Pacific Institute of Culinary Arts

Students from around the world are attracted to this Vancouver-based private cooking school for its state-of-the-art facilities and world-class teachers led by chef Walter Messiah. Cuisine prepared by these budding chefs is served up to the public in the institute's 50-seat dining room. While the quality of the food is impossible to fault, its presentation is also impeccable. Lunch is offered weekdays 11:30 A.M.–2 P.M. and dinner Mon.–Sat. 6–9 P.M. The set menus are a bargain at $20 and $30 respectively (dinner Saturday is $34). Desserts and pastries produced by the institute's bakery classes must also be consumed—and weekdays 3–5 P.M. they are offered in the form of afternoon tea for just $4 including tea and coffee. The institute is at 1505 W. 2nd Ave., 604/734-4488.

ROBSON STREET

Linking downtown to the West End, Robson Street holds the city's largest concentration of eateries, including dozens of cafés sprinkling the sidewalks with outdoor tables—perfect for people-watching.

Coffee and Cafés

This street harbors multiple outlets of the main coffeehouse chains, including **Starbucks** at 788, 1099, 1100, and 1702 Robson, and **Blenz** at 345, 605, and 1201 Robson.

One of the best spots in all of Vancouver for coffee and a light snack is at one of the 20-odd **Bread Garden** cafés scattered throughout the metropolitan area. In this part of the city, the Bread Garden is half a block off busy Robson Street at 812 Bute St., 604/688-3213. It's open 24 hours a day and is always busy—so much so that patrons often need to take a number and wait for service. The coffee is great, as are the freshly baked muffins and pastries. Salads and healthy sandwiches are also available.

At the west end of Robson Street, **Caper's,** 1675 Robson St., 604/687-5288, is a cavernous store selling groceries and pre-made meals for the health-conscious. Caper's also has an in-house bakery, deli, and juice bar.

Seafood

Joe Fortes Seafood and Chophouse, 777 Thurlow St. (half a block off Robson St.), 604/669-1940, is a city institution. The comfortable interior offers elegant furnishings, bleached-linen tablecloths, a rooftop patio, and an oyster bar where you can relax while waiting for your table. At lunch, the specialty grilled fish goes for

$14–18. The dinner menu is slightly more expensive. Open daily 11:30 A.M.–10:30 P.M.

While the oysters at Joe's are hard to beat, those at the **Olympia Seafood Market and Grill,** just off Robson at 820 Thurlow, 604/685-0716, come pretty close. Eat in or take out a variety of fresh and cooked seafood daily 11 A.M.–8 P.M.

Global

At street level of the trendy Pacific Palisades Hotel, **Zin,** 1277 Robson St., 604/408-1700, steers away from fusion cooking, instead offering cuisine from around the world that sticks to its country of origin in all respects. The origin of dishes is truly global—from southern-style fried chicken accompanied with macaroni and cheese to Brazilian-style beef tenderloin served with traditional fritas and chimichurri. Dinner mains range $17–28. The drinks menu is equally diverse, with countries from around the world represented on the wine list, but the local favorite is the unusual combination of Chai tea infused with a shot of sambuca. Zin is open daily for lunch and dinner.

European

Salonika is a modern Greek restaurant with a rooftop patio at 1642 Robson St., 604/681-8141. Some main dishes are under $10, but the typical Greek platters for two provide the best value.

Continuing toward Stanley Park, **The Chef and the Carpenter,** 1745 Robson St., 604/687-2700, serves up great country-French cuisine in an intimate yet relaxed atmosphere. Main meals range $18–22. Open weekdays for lunch and daily for dinner (reservations required).

Diners at **Marbella,** 1368 Robson St., 604/681-1175, eat from stylish tiled tables, listen to traditional music, and generally immerse themselves in the culture of Spain. The 20 tapas range $2.50–5 each, while the rest of the menu features entrées from $14.50. Try the Spanish-style soup at lunch. Open Tues.–Sat. for lunch, Tues.–Sun. for dinner.

CinCin, 1154 Robson St., 604/688-7338, is a Mediterranean-style restaurant with a loyal local following. The specialty is pizza cooked in a wood-fired oven (from $14), but the oven is also used to cook dishes such as halibut roasted in a lightly flavored mint broth and accompanied by fresh mussels ($35). This restaurant has been honored by dozens of awards, including for its wine list, featuring over 300 well-priced choices. It's open for lunch Mon.–Sat. and daily for dinner.

WEST END

Denman Street is the center of the dining action in this trendy part of downtown, with a definite seaside atmosphere toward the English Bay, where many restaurants have water views.

Cheap Eats

For a quick bite to eat before heading back to the beach, search out your favorite flavors from the strip of sidewalk eateries along the south end of Denman Street. The **Bread Garden,** 1040 Denman St., 604/685-2996, is a busy café open 24 hours. Raised a few steps from street level, the long row of outdoor tables is great for people-watching.

One block from Denman, **Crystals Café,** 1702 Davie St., 604/682-5775, is away from the crowds and offers diners a few outdoor tables on quiet Bidwell Street.

Away from the beach, near the crest of Denman Street, a couple of older-style places have survived, offering old-fashioned service and good value. The best of these for breakfast is the **Grove Inn,** 1047 Denman St., 604/687-0557, where the breakfast special is $4 before 10 A.M.

On the same block as the Grove Inn, **Bud's Halibut and Chips,** 1007 Denman St., 604/683-0661, has been serving up battered fish and crispy fries for over 20 years. The portions are generous, and all fish comes with a massive dollop of creamy tartar sauce. One piece of halibut and chips is just $5. If you want to eat down on the beach, the staff will happily wrap your meal in paper for you.

For chicken cooked to perfection, head over the hill to **Rooster's Quarters,** 836 Denman St., 604/689-8023, a casual eatery chock-full of

chicken memorabilia. A full chicken with accompanying vegetables and fries (for two) is a reasonable $17.

West Coast

Head for the West End to find the city's finest traditional First Nations cuisine at the native-owned and -operated **Liliget Feast House,** 1724 Davie St., 604/681-7044. From street level, a narrow stairway leads down to the restaurant, a cavernous room styled on a traditional longhouse. Peeled cedar columns rise from the hardwood floor, native artwork adorns the walls, and traditional music plays softly in the background. Menu items include oolichan in lemon butter, bannock bread, seaweed and wild rice, watercress salad, a traditional salmon soup, seafood or caribou barbecued over an alderwood fire, and steamed fern shoots. The food is cooked using traditional techniques and recipes. Dining here isn't particularly cheap; most people opt for either the Potlatch Platter (seafood) or Liliget Feast Platter (game such as caribou and buffalo), which let you sample a variety of delicacies ($48.50 for two). But it's an experience you won't forget in a hurry. Open daily 5–10 P.M.

A few blocks away, contemporary West Coast cuisine is served at **Delilah's,** 1789 Comox St., 604/687-3424. One of Vancouver's favorite restaurants, Delilah's features well-prepared dishes that take advantage of seasonal produce and locally harvested seafood served in an elegant European-style setting. The fixed-price two-course dinner costs from $21, depending on the season; a five-course feast ($34) is also offered. Start your evening meal with one of Delilah's delicious martinis. Open daily for dinner from 5:30 P.M.

The innovative menu and extensive by-the-glass wine list at nearby **Raincity Grill,** 1193 Denman St., 604/685-7337, have gained this restaurant numerous awards. The interior is stylish and table settings more than adequate, but it's the views across English Bay through high windows that are most impressive. Lunch entrées are $10–17, dinner ranges $18–34. Open daily 11:30 A.M.–2:30 P.M. and 5–10:30 P.M.; make reservations for dinner.

Mexican and Cajun

In a sprawling converted residence just off Denman Street, **Mescalero,** 1215 Bidwell St., 604/669-4155, is a good choice for a reasonably priced Mexican meal in a fun atmosphere. Tapas ($6–10) are the most popular menu items, but Mexican grills are also featured. It's open weekdays for lunch from 11:30 A.M., on weekends for brunch from 10:30 A.M., and daily for dinner from 5:30 P.M.

European

The atmosphere at **Tapastree Restaurant,** 1829 Robson St. (one block off Denman St.), 604/606-4680, is inviting and cozy, and the service faultless. But it's the food that really shines; the tapas-only menu features a wide variety of meats, seafood, and even some vegetarian choices, all for under $10. Tapastree is open daily for dinner.

Around the corner, **Café de Paris,** 745 Denman St., 604/687-1418, is an intimate yet casual city-style French bistro. Classic French main courses (don't dare call them entrées at this very French restaurant) range $18–26, but the daily three-course table d'hôte is best value at around $25. Wines offered are almost exclusively French. It's open daily for dinner and also Mon.–Fri. for lunch and on Sunday for brunch.

Japanese

For inexpensive, no-frills Japanese food head to **Hanada House,** 823 Denman St., 604/685-1136. The atmosphere is nothing special, but the service is efficient, and all the traditional Japanese dishes are offered at reasonable cost, with no entrées over $15.

The contemporary **Tanpopo,** upstairs at 1122 Denman St., 604/681-7777, features a wide range of Japanese dishes, including a very popu-

---

DINING IN STANLEY PARK

Stanley Park is home to three restaurants, each offering a very different atmosphere, but each reasonably priced considering the location.

Prospect Point Café

The perfect halfway-point stop on a walk around the promenade is this popular café near the Lions Gate Bridge (it's a short but steep uphill detour from the main walking path). Featuring a large cantilevered deck from where views extend across busy Burrard Inlet to the North Shore and beyond to the mountains, it's the least expensive place to eat in the park. The menu is extensive, but salmon is the specialty, with dishes starting at $15. It's open daily for lunch and dinner.

Teahouse Restaurant

Overlooking English Bay, between Second and Third Beaches, is the Teahouse Restaurant, 7501 Stanley Park Rd., 604/669-3281. Originally built as an officers' mess within army barracks, the building of today contains an intimate restaurant of connected rooms with bright, elegant surroundings set among towering trees. Every afternoon between

2:30 P.M. and 5 P.M. an English tea is served—this is the place to come for the real thing, complete with cucumber sandwiches, scones and fresh cream, and not a tea bag in sight. Light lunches are also served, while after 5:30 P.M. a game and seafood menu makes use of all the best local ingredients. Expect to pay from $12 for lunch and from $17 for dinner. Reservations aren't generally necessary through the day, but reserve a table on the deck to enjoy watching the evening sunset.

Fish House at Stanley Park

This fine restaurant lies in park-like surroundings on a rise in the southwest corner of the park, away from the crowded promenade, surrounded by a bowling green and tennis courts at 8901 Stanley Park Dr., 604/681-7275. Seating is in one of three rooms or out on a deck, the service efficient, and the food well prepared. All the usual seafood dishes are offered, as well as a few unique dishes, such as a personal favorite, Alaskan scallops grilled in a sweet chili glaze. Dinner mains range $18–30, and the Fish House is open daily for lunch and dinner.

lar sushi lunch buffet for $12 and a dinner buffet for $18. This restaurant is open daily 11:30 A.M.–9:30 P.M.

KITSILANO

Biceps and butts are the order of the day along trendy Kitsilano Beach, and when the beautiful people have finished sunning themselves they head across the road to **Malone's Bar and Grill,** at 2202 Cornwall Ave. (at Yew St.), 604/737-7777. Pub grub is the order of the day, with all the usual burgers and salads for $8–12, but the real reason to stop by is to soak up the beachside atmosphere and take in the view. Across the road, the **Urban Well,** 1516 Yew St., 604/737-7770, has a few outdoor tables with a healthy menu of wraps, salads, and vegetarian burgers.

Cool and Casual

Away from the beach, cafés line West 4th Avenue between Burrard and Vine Streets. This part of the city was the heart of hippiedom 30 years ago, and while most restaurants from that era are long gone, a few remain, and other, newer additions to the local dining scene reflect that period of the city's history. **Sophie's Cosmic Café,** 2095 W. 4th Ave. (at Arbutus St.), 604/732-6810, typifies the scene, with a definite "cosmic" look, but also providing good value (daily specials under $10). Expect a wait for Sunday breakfast. It's open daily 8 A.M.–9:30 P.M. **Joe's Grill,** on the next block to the east at 2061 W. 4th Ave., 604/736-6588, has survived from the 1960s serving up typical greasy spoon fare at good prices. A cooked breakfast of eggs, bacon, and hash browns is just $4, the daily soup-and-sandwich special is just $6, the milkshakes are to die for, and coffee refills are free. In diner tradition, seating is at tables or booths. Joe's is open daily 8 A.M.–9 P.M.

One block west, **Kitsilano Coffee Co.,** 2198 W. 4th Ave., is a quintessential Vancouver coffeehouse, complete with a terraced area surrounded by flowering plants along one side.

West Coast

At the **Livingroom,** 2958 W. 4th Ave., 604/737-7529, the menu may reflect modern tastes, but as a throwback to days gone by in Kitsilano, the atmosphere is typically bohemian. The owners have cleverly created a classy restaurant using retro-style furnishings, right down to mismatched plates. Mains, such as grilled salmon, average $16 and are accompanied by an extensive wine list. The Livingroom is open daily from 6 P.M. for dinner.

Vegetarian

A throwback to the hippie era of the 1960s is **Naam,** 2724 W. 4th Ave. (at Stephens St.; look for the wagon wheel out front), 604/738-7151, a particularly good natural-food restaurant in a renovated two-story private residence. Boasting large servings, excellent service, and an easygoing atmosphere that has become legendary, it's open 24 hours a day, every day of the week. Veggie burgers start at $5, while full meals range $8–11.

Surat Sweet, 1938 W. 4th Ave. (between Cypress and Maple Streets), 604/733-7363, needs a coat of paint, but the decor plays second fiddle to the food, which is remarkably inexpensive. The menu is entirely vegetarian and vegan—even eggs aren't used. Apart from the curries, most diners will be unfamiliar with many of the dishes, such as *bhajia,* a deep-fried potato dish covered in a coconut chutney ($6.50). Surat Sweet is open Tues.–Sat. for lunch and dinner.

European

The much-lauded **Bishop's,** 2183 W. 4th Ave., 604/738-2025, is very French in all aspects. Owner and longtime Vancouver restaurateur John Bishop makes all diners feel special, personally greeting them at the door, escorting them to their table, and then describing the menu and wine list as required. Elegant surroundings, starched white linen, and soft jazz background music complete the picture. The menu features French classics but changes as seasonal produce such as salmon and halibut becomes available. Expect to pay around $100 for three courses for two. Bishop's is open only for dinner, nightly 5:30–10 P.M., and reservations are required.

Continuing west, **Quattro on Fourth,** 2611 W. 4th Ave., 604/734-4444, exudes an elegant yet casual atmosphere, and walls lined with cabinets are filled with wines from around the world. An outdoor deck features table settings amid flowers and shrubbery. The menu emphasizes traditional country-style Italian cooking, including pastas ($16–20) and specialty dishes ($22–30) such as a delicious prawn-and-scallop ravioli ($24.50). Open daily for dinner.

African

One of Vancouver's few African eateries, **Nyala Ethiopian Restaurant,** 2930 W. 4th Ave. (at McDonald St.), 604/731-7899, provides the opportunity to try some unique dishes without spending a fortune. *Pakora,* a dish of battered vegetables, is an Ethiopian staple, and it can be combined with a variety of stir-fries for around $18 per person. Vegetarians are well catered to with all meat-free dishes under $10. On Wednesday and Sunday nights a vegetarian buffet is offered for $11. Nyala is open daily 11:30 A.M.–2 P.M. and 5–11 P.M. (until 2 A.M. Thurs.–Sat.).

WEST BROADWAY

Broadway runs parallel to 4th Avenue five blocks farther south. The restaurants listed below are farther east than those along West 4th Avenue and are generally less "trendy," appealing to those looking for value.

Asian

In the small mall at the intersection of Broadway and Oak Street (behind 7-Eleven), **Sami's,** 986 W. Broadway, 604/736-8330, offers westernized East Indian cooking, including a mouthwatering lamb vindaloo. Considering its unpretentious location and low prices (all mains $9–14), the food here is remarkably good. Wine by the glass or bottle is also among the cheapest in the city. It's open daily for lunch and dinner.

One block north of West Broadway at Granville Street is **Vij's,** 1480 11th Ave., 604/736-6664, one of Vancouver's most acclaimed Asian restaurants. Presentation and service are of the highest standard, but the food really shines. No reservations are taken, and get-

ting a table often involves a wait. Vij's is open for dinner daily from 5:30 P.M.

Nakornthai, 401 W. Broadway (at Yukon St.), 604/874-8923, is a small, inexpensive restaurant specializing in the cuisine of Thailand. Open daily for lunch and dinner.

Russian

Vancouver's only Russian restaurant is **Rasputin's,** 457 W. Broadway (near Cambie St.), 604/879-6675, with a welcoming atmosphere and waitpersons who understand that most diners aren't going to be familiar with many items on the menu. Borsch, a hearty beet-based soup, is the best-known Russian dish, and Rasputin's does it well. A big steaming bowl, almost a meal in itself, is $5, but the best way to sample everything (including a shot of vodka) is with The Feast, which is $26.50 pp.

NORTH SHORE

If you've crossed Burrard Inlet on the SeaBus, visit **Lonsdale Market** for local produce, including a couple of market stalls selling seafood fresh from the trawlers. Between the market and the SeaBus terminal (near the bus interchange) is the **Lonsdale Café,** 147 Chadwick Court, 604/988-2761, with a few outdoor tables. Service is fast, and the daily lunch soup-and-sandwich special is just $5.

Lonsdale Avenue, which climbs from the waterfront to the residential heart of North Vancouver, holds many eateries on its lower end. The antithesis of the city's many bars dressed up as restaurants is **Cheers,** 125 E. 2nd St., 604/985-9192, a family-style restaurant named for the TV show bar. At this inexpensive eatery, fish and chips with unlimited trips to the salad bar costs just $8.50. Open daily for lunch and dinner. (If you snag one of the two tables in the far left-hand corner, you'll enjoy filtered harbor views).

Seafood

On the north side of Burrard Inlet, **Salmon House on the Hill,** 2229 Folkstone Way, West Vancouver, 604/926-3212, offers a relaxed atmosphere while providing panoramic views across

Burrard Inlet to Stanley Park and the city center from its elevated mountainside location. The intriguing interior is full of northwest coast native arts and crafts—including a dugout canoe suspended over the main dining area. Out front, a rhododendron garden blooms in stark contrast to the surrounding forest of Douglas fir.

For an appetizer, the seafood chowder is my recommendation. It's not a huge serving, but it's thick and delicious. The house specialty of salmon barbecued over an open-flame, alderwood-fired grill is also hard to go past. And the price for this signature dish is right, just $20. A North Shore local wrote me recommending the sea bass, smothered in a balsamic vinaigrette, for $25. Starters run $6–9, other dinner entrées range $17–30, and desserts are around $6. Lunch ranges a reasonable $10–15. Sunday brunch is a popular affair. Choose an omelet and your own fillings or try the smoked salmon eggs Benedict, both of which are $12. The wine list features plenty of local B.C. choices. It's open for lunch Mon.–Sat. 11:30 A.M.–2:30 P.M., for dinner daily from 5 P.M., and for Sunday brunch 11 A.M.–2:30 P.M. Make dinner reservations unless you plan on eating at 5 P.M. or after 9 P.M. To get there, take the 21st Street exit off Upper Levels Highway to Folkstone Way, then follow the signs.

Transportation

GETTING THERE

Air

Vancouver International Airport is on Sea Island, 15 km south of Vancouver city center. Over 16 million passengers pass through the terminal annually. A new International Terminal opened in May 1996; it's linked to the Domestic Terminal by a concourse. The three-level complex holds coffee shops and restaurants, car-rental agencies, a post office, currency exchanges, newsstands, gift shops, and duty-free shops. Numerous information boards provide a quick airport orientation, and an **information booth** on Level 3 offers tourist brochures, bus schedules, and taxi information. The original terminal underwent a $100 million expansion and renovation through late 2001 and early 2002, and it now handles domestic arrivals and departures. The South Terminal is a terminus for local airlines, such as Pacific Coastal.

The **Vancouver Airporter,** 604/946-8866 or 800/668-3141, leaves the Arrivals level of both terminals every 15–30 minutes between 6:30 A.M. and 11:30 P.M. daily, shuttling passengers along three routes between the airport and more than 40 downtown accommodations and Pacific Central Station. The one-way fare is adult $12, senior $8, child $5, with a slight discount offered for a round-trip purchase. Buy tickets from the driver or from the ticket offices on the Arrivals levels of both terminals. To get to downtown by public transport, jump aboard bus no. 100 (Midway Connector) on Level 3 (basic fare $2.25) and get off at 70th Street and Granville, then take bus no. 20 (Vancouver) to downtown. A cab from the airport to downtown takes from 25 minutes and runs around $30. Cabs line up curbside on the Arrivals level of both the international and domestic terminals 24 hours daily.

Short-term parking at the airport at the lot closest to the terminals is $2.75 for every 30 minutes for a maximum of four hours. Beyond this section of the parkade is the economy parking lot, where leaving your vehicle for 30 minutes costs $2.25 to a maximum of $11 per day, $66 per week, and $170 per month. The airport authority also manages a long-term parking lot on Sea Island ($8.55 per day, $55.58 per week, $162.58 per month) and provides shuttles to the terminals, 604/276-6104. Many other companies offer long-term parking, including **Park 'N Fly,** 6380 Miller Rd., 604/270-9476; $52 per week, $138 per month, with a complimentary shuttle to either terminal.

Canada's national airline, **Air Canada,** 604/688-5515 or 888/247-2262, website www.aircanada.ca, has the most flights to Vancouver from international destinations. Another Canadian airline serving Vancouver International Airport is **WestJet,**

AIRLINES SERVING VANCOUVER

U.S.

Alaska Airlines	800/252-7522	www.alaskaair.com
American Airlines	800/433-7300	www.aa.com
Continental Airlines	800/231-0856	www.continental.com
Horizon Air	800/547-9308	www.horizonair.com
Northwest Airlines	800/225-2525	www.nwa.com
Skywest	800/221-1212	www.skywest.com
United Airlines	800/241-6522	www.ual.com

International

Air China	800/685-0921	www.airchina.com
Air New Zealand	800/663-5494	www.nzair.com
Air Pacific	800/227-4446	www.airpacific.com
All Nippon Airways	888/422-7533	www.ana.co.jp
British Airlines	800/247-9297	www.britishairlines.com
Eva Air	800/695-1188	www.evaair.com.tw
Japan Airlines	800/525-3663	www.jal.co.jp
KLM	604/278-3485	www.klm.nl
Korean Air	800/438-5000	www.koreanair.com
Lufthansa	800/563-5954	www.Lufthansa.de
Philippine Airlines		www.philippineair.com
Qantas	800/227-4500	www.qantas.com.au
Singapore Airlines	604/689-1223	www.singaporeair.com

604/606-5525 or 800/538-5696, website www.westjet.com. WestJet is based at Abbotsford, 72 km east of downtown, but flies to and from both destinations. Air Canada offers the most flights into Vancouver from the United States, but the city is also served by the U.S. carriers listed in the accompanying chart. The chart also lists other international airlines with flights to Vancouver.

Rail

The **VIA Rail** terminus is **Pacific Central Station,** two km southeast of downtown at 1150 Station St., a $7 cab ride or just a few minutes on the SkyTrain from any of the four downtown stations. Inside the station you'll find a currency exchange, cash machines, lockers, a newsstand, information boards, and a McDonald's restaurant. Pacific Central Station is also the long-distance bus depot. Pick up a schedule in the station or call 800/561-8630 within western Canada (888/842-7245 elsewhere in North America), website www.viarail.ca.

The **Rocky Mountaineer,** 604/606-7245 or 800/665-7245, website www.rockymoun taineer.com, is the only rail service to Banff ($660 pp d, $715 s). It's a luxurious summer-only rail trip through the spectacular interior of British Columbia.

See Rail under Getting There in the On the Road chapter for details of the above two services as well as those operated by BC Rail.

Bus

The **Greyhound** bus depot is in the Pacific Central Station, two km southeast of downtown at 1150 Station St. (see Rail, above), 604/482-8747 or 800/661-8747, website www.greyhound.ca. Buses run daily between Vancouver and Nanaimo, Kamloops, Kelowna, Cranbrook, Banff, Jasper, Prince George, Prince Rupert, and Whitehorse. Always check out special deals this company may be offering, or buy a pass (see Getting Around in the On the Road chapter for details).

Pacific Central Station is the Vancouver terminus of all long-distance rail and bus services.

Also from Pacific Central Station, **Pacific Coach Lines,** 604/662-8074, website www.pacificcoach.com, runs bus service to Victoria.

Ferry

From **Tsawwassen Ferry Terminal,** 30 km south of Vancouver, ferries run to the Southern Gulf Islands and Swartz Bay, 32 km north of Victoria, and to Nanaimo on Vancouver Island. For information, call **B.C. Ferries** at 250/386-3431 or, toll-free in B.C., 888/223-3779, website www.bcferries.com.

To get to the terminal from downtown by car, follow Highway 17 south—in summer this road gets crazy with traffic. Buses also link the ferry terminal with downtown; catch no. 601 from downtown or no. 640 from the ferry terminal, transferring from one to the other at Ladner Exchange (ask the driver for a transfer ticket); $2–3.50 depending on the time of day. To get to

Vancouver International Airport from the ferry terminal, catch a no. 640 bus to Ladner Exchange, then a no. 601 to Massey Exchange, then a no. 404 to the airport.

In high season (June–Sept.), the ferries run about once an hour, 7 A.M.–10 P.M. The rest of the year they run a little less frequently. The crossing takes around 90 minutes. Expect a wait in summer, particularly if you have an oversized vehicle (each ferry can accommodate far fewer large vehicles than standard-size cars and trucks). Limited reservations are accepted; 604/444-2890 or 888/724-5223.

The other ferry route linking the mainland to Vancouver Island runs between **Horseshoe Bay** and Nanaimo. Horseshoe Bay is on the north side of Burrard Inlet, a 20-minute drive northwest of downtown. You don't save any money on this route—the fares are the same as above—and the wait is often longer. This is also

© ANDREW HEMPSTEAD

VANCOUVER

the departure point for ferries to the Sunshine Coast.

GETTING AROUND

Translink

Translink, 604/953-3333, website www.trans link.bc.ca, operates an extensive network of buses, trains, and ferries that can get you just about anywhere you want to go within Vancouver. The free brochure *Discover Vancouver on Transit* is available from all city information centers and is an invaluable source of information. The brochure includes details of many attractions and how to reach them by public transportation.

ROYAL HUDSON

The only steam train in North America that runs a scheduled service along a main line track is the Royal Hudson, which departs daily from Vancouver for a day tour up to Squamish. The trip is spectacular. Squamish lies at the head of Howe Sound, and along the way the train is always in sight of the water and snowcapped peaks (sit on the left-hand side of the train on the outward journey for the best views), while on the other side the Coast Mountains rise precipitously, densely forested and with numerous waterfalls cascading down their slopes. The trip takes two hours each way, with two hours allotted in Squamish to visit the local heritage park and for lunch. It departs daily mid-May to the end of September from the BC Rail terminal, 1311 W. 1st St., North Vancouver, 604/984-5246 or 800/663-8238. Round-trip fare is adult $49.95, senior $42.95, child $12.95. Travel in the more luxurious Parlour Class Car is $82.95, $77.95, $57.95, respectively, and includes either brunch or high tea. A train/boat package is also offered, allowing visitors to take the Royal Hudson in one direction and the **MV Britannia** (which cruises Howe Sound between Squamish and downtown Vancouver) in the other. The fare for the combination trip is adult $69.50, senior $64.15, child $21.40.

Buses run to all corners of the city between 5 A.M. and 2 A.M. every day of the year. Transfers are valid for 90 minutes of travel in one direction.

SkyTrain is a computer-operated (no drivers) light-rail transit system that runs along 28 km of elevated track from downtown Vancouver through New Westminster and over the Fraser River to Surrey. It stops at 20 stations along its 39-minute route. The four city-center stations are underground but are clearly marked at each street entrance.

The double-ended, 400-passenger **SeaBus** scoots across Burrard Inlet every 15–30 minutes, linking downtown Vancouver to North Vancouver in just 12 minutes. The downtown terminus is Waterfront Station, beside Canada Place and a five-minute walk from the Vancouver Visitor Info Centre. The terminal in North Vancouver is at Lonsdale Quay, from where you can catch Translink buses to most North Shore sights.

On weekdays between 5:30 A.M. and 6:30 P.M. the city is divided into three zones, and fares vary adult $1.75–3.50, senior $1.25–2.50, for each sector (Zone 1 encompasses all over downtown and Greater Vancouver; Zone 2 covers all the North Shore, Burnaby, New Westminster, and Richmond; and Zone 3 extends to the limits of the Translink system). At other times (including all weekend), travel anywhere in the city costs $1.75 one-way. Pay the driver (exact change only) for bus travel or purchase tickets from machines at any SkyTrain station or SeaBus terminal. A **DayPass** costs adult $7, senior $5 and allows unlimited travel for one day anywhere on the Translink system. They are available at all SeaBus and SkyTrain stations and FareDealers (convenience stores such as 7-Eleven and Mac's) throughout the city).

Vancouver Trolley Company

From the main pick-up point, a trolley-shaped booth at the top end of Water Street, this company operates an old-fashioned trolley through the streets of downtown Vancouver. The two-hour loop stops at 16 tourist attractions, from Stanley Park in the north to Science World in the south. Trolleys run April–Oct. daily 9 A.M.–4 P.M., coming by each stop every half hour.

Tickets are adult $19, child $11. In July and August an extra loop is made, starting at 7 P.M. in Gastown, with hotel pick-ups until 7:40 P.M., then it's off on a two-hour tour through downtown, to Stanley Park, and as far away as Queen Elizabeth Gardens; adult $24, child $12. Reservations aren't necessary, but for more information call 604/801-5515 or 888/451-5581.

West Coast Express

Primarily a commuter service for residents living along the Fraser Valley, this relatively new rail service is extremely comfortable, with passengers enjoying the use of work desks, power outlets for computers, and speeds of up to 120 kph. Terminating at Waterfront Station, this service originates at Mission ($15.75 to downtown round-trip). Other stops are made at Port Moody, Coquitlam, Port Coquitlam, Pitt Meadows, and Maple Ridge. For further information contact TransLink at 604/953-3333.

Boat

Apart from the SeaBus (see Translink, above), the only other scheduled ferry services within the city are on False Creek. Two private companies, **Granville Island Ferries,** 604/684-7781, and **Aquabus,** 604/689-5858, operate on this narrow waterway. From the main hub of Granville Island, ferries run every 15 minutes to the foot of Hornby Street, and under the Burrard Street Bridge to the Aquatic Center (at the south end of Thurlow Street) and Vanier Park (Vancouver Museum). Every 30–60 minutes both companies also run down the head of False Creek

to Stamps Landing, the Plaza of Nations, and Science World. Fares range $2.50–5 each way, with discounts for seniors and kids; schedules are posted at all docking points.

Taxi

Cabs are easiest to catch outside major hotels or transportation hubs. Fares in Vancouver are a uniform $2.30 flag charge plus $1.25 per kilometer (plus 30 cents per minute when stopped). Trips within downtown usually run under $10. The trip between the airport and downtown is $30. A 10–15 percent tip to the driver is expected. Major companies include: **Black Top,** 800/494-1111; **Vancouver Taxi,** 888/871-8294; and **Yellow Cab,** 604/681-1111 or 800/898-8294.

A number of wheelchair-accommodating taxicabs are available from Vancouver Taxi. The fares are the same as regular taxis.

Car Rental

Vancouver is full of car-rental agencies offering a wide range of vehicles, prices, and deals. Some throw in extras such as coupon books giving you discounts at attractions and certain restaurants.

Recognized low-cost agencies in Vancouver are **Rent-a-wreck,** 604/688-0001 or 800/327-0116, website www.rentawreck.ca, and **Lo-cost,** 604/689-9664 or 800/986-1266, website www.locost.com. See the accompanying chart for other major rental companies represented in Vancouver.

Bicycle

Downtown Vancouver is not particularly bicycle friendly, but nearby areas such as Stanley

RENTAL CAR AGENCIES

Alamo	604/684-1401 or 800/327-9633	www.alamo.com
Avis	604/606-2869 or 800/879-2847	www.avis.com
Budget	604/668-7000 or 800/268-8900	www.budget.com
Discount	604/310-2277 or 800/263-2355	www.discountcar.com
Dollar	604/689-5303 or 800/800-4000	www.dollar.com
Enterprise	604/688-5500 or 800/325-8007	www.enterprise.com
Hertz	604/606-3700 or 800/263-0600	www.hertz.com
National	604/609-7150 or 800/227-7368	www.nationalcar.com
Thrifty	604/647-4599 or 800/847-4389	www.thrifty.com

Park and the coastline west of Kitsilano are perfect places for pedal power. The main concentration of rental shops surrounds the corner of Robson and Denman Streets, two blocks from Stanley Park. Expect to pay from $5 per hour or $15 per day for the most basic mountain bike and $12 per hour or $36 per day for a suspension mountain bike. Most of the shops also rent in-line skates and tandem bikes. **Alley Cat Rentals,** 1779 Robson St., 604/684-5117, is by far the least expensive place to rent, but you can also try: **Bayshore Bicycles,** 745 Denman St., 604/688-2453; **Bikes and Blades,** 718 Denman St., 604/602-9899; **Spokes Bicycle Rental,** 1798 W. Georgia St., 604/688-5141; or **Stanley Park Rentals,** 1741 Robson St., 604/608-1908.

TOURS

If you don't have a lot of time to explore Vancouver on your own, or just want an introduction to the city, consider one of the many tours available—they'll maximize your time and get you to the highlights with minimum stress.

Bus Tours

Gray Line, 604/879-3363 or 800/667-0882, offers a large variety of tours. The 3.5-hour Deluxe Grand City Tour, which includes Stanley Park, Grouse Mountain, Chinatown, Gastown, Robson Street, and English Bay, costs $42 per person. Another option with Gray Line is a downtown loop tour aboard an old English double-decker bus. You can get on and off as you please at 22 stops made on the two-hour loop. Tickets cost adult $24.50, senior $23.50, child $13 and are valid for two consecutive days. Farther afield, Gray Line has daily tours from Vancouver to Whistler, $67, and a 12-hour tour to Vancouver Island, $109. All ticket prices include pick-ups at major downtown hotels.

More personalized tours are run by **Rockwood Adventures,** 604/926-7705. On its two-hour Stanley Park tour, guides describe local natural and human history and take you to all the best viewpoints; $26 per person. The company also offers a guided walk along the Capilano River with a visit to a fish hatchery; four hours, $42 per person.

Harbor Cruises

From June to September, **Harbour Cruises,** 604/688-7246 or 800/663-1500, offers a 70-minute tour of bustling Burrard Inlet on the paddlewheeler MV *Constitution.* Tours depart from the north foot of Denman Street, Coal Harbour, three times daily; adult $18, senior and student $15. In the evening (7 P.M. departure), the paddlewheeler heads out onto the harbor for a three-hour Sunset Dinner Cruise. The cruise costs $69, which includes dinner and, if booked through Gray Line (604/879-3363), hotel transfers. This same company operates the MV *Britannia,* which departs daily at 9:30 A.M. for a cruise up Howe Sound to Squamish. This trip is best taken in conjunction with the **Royal Hudson** steam train (see special topic) for adult $69.50, senior $64.15, child $21.40, which includes transfers between the train station and Coal Harbour.

While puttering around False Creek on a small ferry is an inexpensive way to see this part of the city from water level, **Granville Island Ferries,** 604/684-7781, also offers a 30-minute guided tour of the historic waterway for just $6 per person. Departures are daily 10 A.M.–5 P.M. from below Bridges Restaurant on Granville Island.

Flightseeing

Flightseeing tours of the city are offered by **Harbour Air** from its seaplane base on the west side of Canada Place, 604/688-1277. A 20-minute flight is $76 pp, or include the Southern Gulf Islands on a 90-minute flight for $188 pp. **Helijet,** based at a heliport on the east side of Canada Place (enter through Waterfront Station), 604/270-1484, offers a short flight for $75 pp, or take a 20-minute flight over the heart of downtown, Stanley Park, and across to the North Shore and Capilano Valley for $180 pp. This company also offers helicopter flights from the top of Grouse Mountain.

Services and Information

M

VANCOUVER

Emergency Services

For emergencies call 911. For medical emergencies contact **St. Paul's Hospital,** downtown at 1081 Burrard St., 604/682-2344, which has an emergency ward open 24 hours a day, seven days a week. Other major hospitals are: **Vancouver General Hospital,** 899 W. 12th Ave., 604/875-4111, and **Lions Gate Hospital,** 231 E. 15th St., 604/988-3131. **Seymour Medical Clinic,** 1530 W. 7th Ave., 604/738-2151, is open 24 hours. For emergency dental help, call the **AARM Dental Group,** 604/681-8530 or 604/683-5530. For the **RCMP** call 911 or 604/264-3111.

Visitors with Disabilities

For information on travel considerations for the physically handicapped, contact the British Columbia chapter of the **Canadian Paraplegic Association** at 780 Southwest Marine Dr., Vancouver, BC V6P5Y7, 604/324-3611 or 877/324-3611, website www.canparaplegic.org. In general, disabled visitors are well cared for, with most major hotels taking disabilities into consideration. Vancouver's public transit system, Translink, has HandyDART buses that provide door-to-door wheelchair-accessible service for about the same price you'd pay on regular buses (call 604/453-4634 for bookings), and the SkyTrain and SeaBus are wheelchair accessible. **Vancouver Taxi,** 604/871-1111, has wheelchair-accommodating cabs.

Post Offices

Vancouver's **main post office** is at 349 W. Georgia St., 604/662-5722. It's open Mon.–Saturday. **Postal Station A,** 757 W. Hastings St., and the branch at **Bentall Centre,** 595 Burrard St., are also open on Saturdays.

Money Exchange

Custom House Currency Exchange is in The Landing at 375 Water St., 604/482-6000. Also downtown is **Calforex,** 1016 W. Georgia St., 604/608-0381. **Thomas Cook Foreign Exchange** operates a small money-changing facility

in the lobby of the Pan Pacific Vancouver Hotel, Canada Place, 604/641-1229, as well as in the Pacific Centre and in Burnaby's Metrotown. Another option for currency exchange is the banks, which can deal with most common transactions.

Telephone and Internet

Local calls from public phones cost 35 cents; long-distance calls are much more expensive. The area code for Vancouver and the southwest mainland is 604, while the rest of the province, including Vancouver Island, is 250. The **Public Calling Centre,** 470 W. Cordova St., 604/687-2040, is designed especially for visitors. From its private booths you can call anywhere in North America for 50 cents a minute or anywhere in the world at posted, discounted rates; pay by cash or credit card. The center can also be used for sending and receiving faxes.

Digital U, out of downtown at 1595 W. Broadway (corner Fir St.; walk up the hill from Granville Island), 604/731-1011, is the city's best and longest running Internet café. It features high-speed connections, 21-inch monitors, booth stations (for two people), computers for regular work and loaded with games. Rates range $8–11 per hour. It's open Mon.–Fri. 9 A.M.–midnight, Sat.–Sun. 10 A.M.–midnight. Other downtown Internet cafés include **Internet Coffee,** 1104 Davie St., 604/682-6668, and **The Byte Place,** 1636 Robson St., 604/683-2688. Both charge around $2.50 for 15 minutes.

Film and Processing

One-hour film processing is offered by dozens of outlets throughout Vancouver. Two of the most reliable are **London Drugs,** with branches throughout Greater Vancouver (call 604/872-8114 for the location nearest to you), and **Lens and Shutter,** which has an outlet in the lower level of the Pacific Centre and another at 2912 W. Broadway, 604/736-3461. For high-quality color-print film processing and overnight slide developing, take your precious films to **Totemcolor,** 119 E. 1st St., North Vancouver, 604/986-2271.

Don't be put off by the dowdy exterior of **Leo's Cameras,** on Granville Mall at 1055 Granville St., 604/685-5331; it holds a massive selection of new and used cameras and photographic equipment.

BOOKS, MAGAZINES, AND NEWSPAPERS

Vancouver Public Library

In November 1995, after two years of construction and $100 million, Vancouver Public Library, 350 W. Georgia St., 604/331-3600, opened its doors to the public. The magnifi-

cent nine-story facility is a far cry from the city's first library, which opened with a grant of £250 back in 1887. Its elliptical facade contains a glass-walled promenade rising six stories above a row of stylish indoor shops and cafés. Once inside, you'll soon discover that the city also found enough money to stock the shelves; the library holds over one million books. To help you find that one book you're searching for, use the self-guided tour brochure available at the information desk. The library is open year-round Mon.–Wed. 10 A.M.–9 P.M., Thurs.–Sat. 10 A.M.–6 P.M., and also Sunday 1–5 P.M. from October to April.

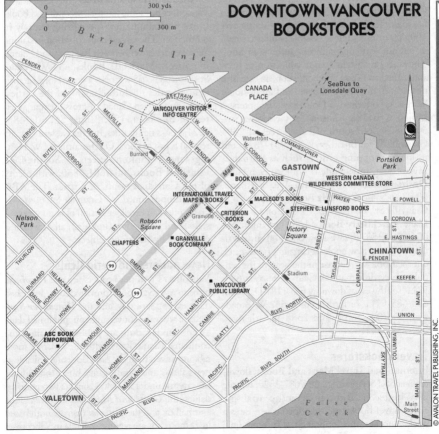

© AVALON TRAVEL PUBLISHING, INC.

VANCOUVER

More than 20 other affiliated libraries are spread across the city. Call 604/331-3600 or go to www.vpl.Vancouver.bc.ca for addresses and opening hours. One branch library of particular interest is the **Carnegie Reading Room,** on the corner of East Hastings and Main Streets. It is named for its benefactor, U.S. philanthropist Andrew Carnegie, whose $50,000 donation went a long way toward its 1902 completion as Vancouver's first permanent library.

General Bookstores

Per capita, residents of Vancouver buy more books than the residents of any other North American city. And they buy them from a huge number of bookstores scattered throughout the city. The Canadian bookstore giant **Chapters—Indigo** has multiple Vancouver stores, each stocking over 100,000 titles. Public-accessible computers help search out particular subjects, authors, or titles. The stores maintain a large collection of local and Canadian fiction and nonfiction, an extensive newsstand, discounted books, and an in-house Starbucks coffeehouse. Downtown, Chapters—Indigo is at 788 Robson St. (at Howe St.), 604/682-4066; south of False Creek at 2505 Granville St. (at Broadway), 604/731-7822; and in major shopping centers such as Burnaby's Metrotown. Independent bookstores include **Duthie Books,** 2339 W. 4th Ave., Kitsilano, 604/732-5344; **Granville Book Company,** 850 Granville St., 604/687-2213; and on Granville Island, **Blackberry Books,** 1663 Duranleau St., 604/685-6188. To save a few bucks on current titles or pick up new books at bargain prices, search out the **Book Warehouse** in the heart of the central business district at 550 Granville St., 604/683-5711, southwest of downtown at 1181 Davie St., 604/685-5711, or farther out at 632 W. Broadway, 604/872-5711, and 2388 W. 4th Ave., 604/734-5711.

Travel Bookstores

International Travel Maps and Books, downtown at 552 Seymour St., 604/687-3320, website www.itmb.com, is the city's most central specialty travel bookstore. It's open seven days a week. Another, smaller branch of International Travel Maps and Books is at 530 W. Broadway, 604/879-3621. With over 10,000 titles, Canada's largest travel bookstore is **Wanderlust,** just west of Cypress St. at 1929 W. 4th Ave., Kitsilano, 604/739-2182. As well as general travel guides, Wanderlust stocks maps, atlases, and a range of travel accessories. It's open Mon.–Fri. 10 A.M.–7 P.M., Saturday 10 A.M.–5 P.M., Sunday noon–5 P.M. Also in Kits is the **Travel Bug,** 2667 W. Broadway, Kitsilano, 604/737-1122. For environmentally aware literature head for the **Western Canada Wilderness Committee Store,** 227 Abbott St., Gastown, 604/687-2567.

Secondhand and Antiquarian Bookstores

Vancouver has some fantastic secondhand bookstores, including a few specializing entirely in nonfiction. The largest concentration lies along West Pender Street between Richards and Hamilton Streets. **Macleod's Books,** 455 W. Pender St., 604/681-7654, stocks a wide range of antiquarian titles, including many of the earliest works on western Canada. Across the road, **Criterion Books,** 434 W. Pender St., 604/685-2224, stocks newer titles, but the western Canada section is just as good. On the corner of W. Hastings and Hamilton Streets is **Stephen C. Lunsford Books,** 604/681-6830, with plenty of old Canadian nonfiction titles. The **ABC Book Emporium,** 1247 Granville St., 604/682-3019, offers an excellent section of fiction (downstairs) and nonfiction (upstairs), all of which is organized by author or subject.

Newspapers and Periodicals

Vancouver's two newspapers are the *Province,* website www.vancouverprovince.com, published daily except Saturday, and the *Vancouver Sun,* website www.vancouversun.com, published daily except Sunday. Both are published by the same company, Pacific Press, with the *Province* more tabloid-driven than the *Sun.* Both are available at newsstands and vending machines throughout the city for under a buck. Canada's two national dailies, the *Globe and Mail,* website www.globeandmail.ca, and the *National Post,* are both based in Toronto but are readily available in Vancouver.

Many free publications are distributed throughout the city. The weekly *Georgia Strait* features articles on local issues, as well as a full entertainment rundown for the city. The *Westender,* also a weekly, spotlights downtown issues and has good restaurant reviews. The fortnightly *Terminal City* and, for the hip set, *Loop* both have offbeat articles and music and entertainment diaries. *Coast* is a lifestyle magazine focusing on outdoor recreation in the region, while the quarterly *Common Ground* is dedicated to health and personal development.

INFORMATION

Many organizations make planning a trip to Vancouver easy. **Tourism Vancouver,** Suite 210, 200 Burrard St., Vancouver, BC V6C 3L6, 604/682-2222, promotes the city throughout the world. The official Tourism Vancouver website, www.tourismvancouver.com, is an excellent source of information for pre-trip planning. It contains a wealth of information on everything there is to do and see in the city, an online booking form for accommodations, and a currency converter. It is updated almost daily, with news on new attractions, festivals and events, and other elements that may affect your travel plans, such as transit strikes or street closures. The next best website is www.foundlocally.com/vancouver, which has been around since the beginning of the Internet phenomenon; this site features all of the above as well as a distance calculator, a search engine, and locally oriented information such as TV listings.

Downtown

The city's main information center is **Vancouver Visitor Info Centre,** right downtown in the heart of the waterfront district one block from Canada Place, 200 Burrard St., 604/683-2000. Brochures line the lower level while on the upper level specially trained staff members provide free maps, brochures, and public transportation schedules; book sightseeing tours; and make accommodations reservations. Look for public transportation information and timetables to the right as you enter the center. It's open May–Sept.

daily 8 A.M.–6 P.M., the rest of the year Mon.–Sat. 8:30 A.M.–5:30 P.M.

In summer, information booths also operate in Stanley Park and downtown on the corner of Granville and Georgia Streets.

On Granville Island, **Granville Island Information Centre,** 1398 Cartwright St., 604/666-5784, website www.granvilleisland.com, is open year-round, daily 9 A.M.–6 P.M.

South

If you approach Vancouver from the south on Highway 5 (Highway 99 in Canada), the first official information center you'll come to is the **Peace Arch Visitor Centre,** immediately north of the border and right beside the highway. A currency exchange is on-site. The center is open in summer 8 A.M.–8 P.M., the rest of the year 9 A.M.–5 P.M.

In the same vicinity, **White Rock Visitor Info Centre** is in the local chamber of commerce building at 15150 Russell Ave., 604/536-6844; to get there take Exit 2 west along 8th Avenue, then north on Stayte Road, then west on Russell Avenue. Open year-round Mon.–Fri. 9 A.M.–4:30 P.M.

While the detour through White Rock and along Marine Drive is a great introduction to Vancouver, those heading into the city may want to continue to the **Delta Visitor Info Centre,** which is handier to the main highway. Take Exit 28 north beyond the Delta Town & Country Inn to 6201 60th Ave. (it's signposted and impossible to miss), 604/946-4232, website www.deltachamber.com; open daily in summer, weekdays only the rest of the year.

Continuing north along Highway 99, **Richmond Visitor Info Centre** is right by the highway, to the right as you emerge on the north side of the George Massey Tunnel under the Fraser River. Operated by Tourism Richmond, 604/271-8280 or 877/247-0777, website www.tourismrichmond.com, it's open through summer daily 9 A.M.–7 P.M., spring and fall daily 9 A.M.–5 P.M., winter daily 10 A.M.–4 P.M.

Vancouver International Airport has information booths on the Arrivals levels of the International and Domestic Terminals; both are open every day of the year 8 A.M.–11:30 P.M.

North

North Vancouver Visitor Info Centre, along Marine Drive between the Lions Gate Bridge and Lonsdale Quay at 131 E. 2nd St., 604/987-4488, website www.nvchamber.bc.ca, is open Mon.–Fri. 9 A.M.–5 P.M. A more handy source of information north of the harbor is the small information center in the historic building beside Lonsdale Quay, which is open in summer daily 9 A.M.–6 P.M.

East

If you're approaching the city from the east along Highway 1, **Chilliwack Visitor Info Centre** is a good place to stop, stretch your legs, and gather some brochures. It's at 44150 Luckakuck Way, 604/858-8121 or 800/567-9535, website www.tourismchilliwack.com.

A further 40 km west toward the city, take Exit 92 to reach the **Abbotsford Visitor Info Centre.** It's in the local chamber of commerce building at 2462 McCallum Rd., 604/859-9651, website www.abbotsfordchamber.com.

Continuing west, take Highway 10 south from Exit 66 and follow Glover Road into downtown Langley for the **Langley Visitor Info Centre,** 5761 Glover Rd., 604/530-6656, website www.langleychamber.com. Glover Road also leads north of the TransCanada Highway (take Exit 66 and head north along 232nd St.) to Fort Langley, a delightful riverside community, and the **Fort Langley Visitor Info Centre,** on the west side of the main street just before the river at 23325 Mavis Ave., 604/513-8787, website www.fortlangley.com.

At Exit 50 of the TransCanada Highway, cross back over the highway and continue west along 104th Avenue to the **Surrey Visitor Info Centre,** 14439 104th Ave., 604/581-7130, website www.surreychamber.org, which is closed weekends outside of the busy summer season.

Across the Fraser River from Surrey, Tourism New Westminster operates **New Westminster Visitor Info Centre,** at 810 Quayside Dr., 604/526-1905, www.tourismnewwestminster.org. This location is out of the way for highway travelers, but if you do make the detour, take Brunette Avenue south from Exit 40 of the TransCanada Highway.

Approaching Vancouver from the east along Highway 7, **Mission Visitor Info Centre,** in the town of the same name, has a wealth of Vancouver information. It's on the north side of the road at 34033 Lougheed Hwy., 604/826-6914, website www.missionchamber.bc.ca.

Continuing toward the city along Highway 7, **Maple Ridge Visitor Info Centre** is 40 km from downtown and also right beside the highway; at 22238 Lougheed Hwy. (look for it on the south side of the highway between 222nd and 223rd Streets), 604/463-3366, website www.mapleridge-chamber.bc.ca.

Operated by the local chamber of commerce, **Coquitlam Visitor Info Centre,** 1180 Pinetree Way, 604/464-2716, website www.chamberof commerce.bc.ca, is also by Hwy. 7, at the north side of its intersection of Hwy. 7A. As well as Coquitlam and Port Coquitlam, the center represents Port Moody and the wilderness areas to the north.

Vancouver Island

Vancouver Island, the largest isle in North America's Pacific, stretches for more than 450 superb kilometers off the west coast of mainland British Columbia. A magnificent chain of rugged snow-capped mountains, sprinkled with lakes and rivers and pierced by deep inlets, effectively divides the island into two distinct sides: dense, rain-drenched forest and remote surf- and wind-battered shores on the west, and well-populated, sheltered, beach-fringed lowlands on the east. At the northern and southern tips lie large regions of low, rolling hills.

Much of the lush, green island is covered with dense forests of Douglas fir, western red cedar, and hemlock. The climate, stabilized by the Pacific Ocean and warmed by the Japanese current, never really gets too hot or too cold, but be prepared for cloudbursts, especially in winter.

Victoria, the provincial capital, lies at the southern tip of the island and is connected to the much larger city of Vancouver by regular ferry services. Its deeply entrenched British traditions make Victoria unique among North American cities. The rest of the island draws scenery buffs, outdoor adventurers, wildlife watchers, and students of northwest Native American art and culture.

Backpackers head west from Victoria to Port Renfrew, the starting point of the **West Coast Trail.** Island-hoppers take Highway 17 north up the Saanich Peninsula to Swartz Bay, jump on

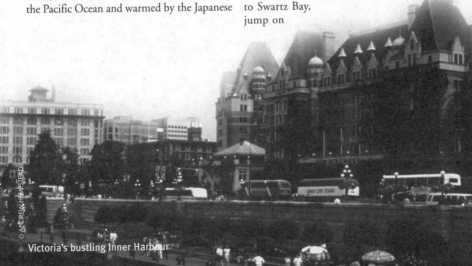

© ANDREW HEMPSTEAD

Victoria's bustling Inner Harbour

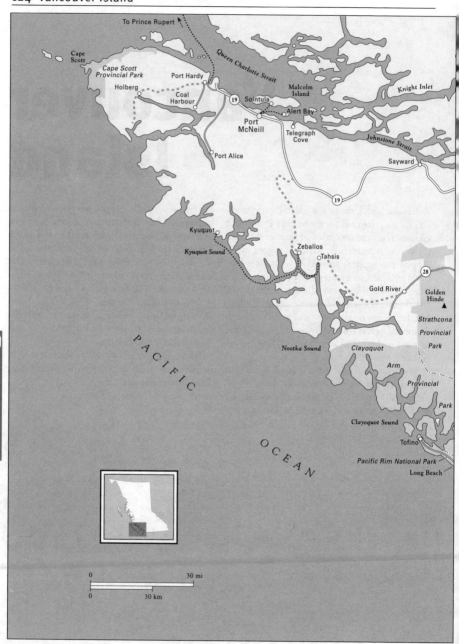

VANCOUVER ISLAND

Quadra Island
Cortes Island
Campbell River
28
19
Powell River
Buttle Lake
Courtenay
Comox
Forbidden Plateau
Denman Island
Cumberland
Texada Island
Hornby Island
Lasqueti Island
Qualicum Beach
Parksville
Strait of Georgia
Coombs
4
Port Alberni
Nanaimo
Gabriola Island

Whistler
99
Squamish
Sechelt
Gibsons
Horseshoe Bay
VANCOUVER
1
Tsawwassen

Albernis Inlet
Ucluelet
Thetis Island
Ladysmith
Chemainus
Duncan
Galiano Island
Mayne Island
North Pender Island
Saltspring Island
Saturna Island

Barkley Sound
Bamfield
Cowichan Lake
Lake Cowichan
Cowichan River Provincial Park
Sidney

Broken Group Islands
West Coast Trail
Carmanah Walbran Provincial Park
Pacific Rim National Park
Port Renfrew
17
1
VICTORIA
San Juan Islands

CANADA
UNITED STATES
14
Jordan River
Sooke
14
Juan de Fuca Strait
Olympic Peninsula

© AVALON TRAVEL PUBLISHING, INC.

a ferry, and cruise the scenic **Southern Gulf Islands.** Other explorers head north up the Island Highway, Highway 1/19, which follows the Strait of Georgia all the way to the island's northern tip. The old highway has mostly been replaced by the Inland Island Highway, but to take in the best the island has to offer, stick to the old route. Along the way you'll pass sandy beaches, resorts, and old logging, mining, and fishing towns that now base their existence to a large degree on tourism.

At Parksville, Highway 4 turns off west and leads through "oooh" and "aaah" mountain scenery to the relatively untamed west coast. There you'll find picture-perfect fishing villages, driftwood-littered sand for as far as you can see, and **Pacific Rim National Park,** the only national park on the island. Also on the west coast is **Tofino,** a base for sea kayaking and whale-watching on Clayoquot Sound. Farther north up Highway 19, at Campbell River, Highway 28 cuts west to Gold River, passing through enormous **Strathcona Provincial Park.**

A magnificent chain of rugged snowcapped mountains, sprinkled with lakes and rivers and pierced by deep inlets, effectively divides the island into two distinct sides: dense, rain-drenched forest and remote surf- and wind-battered shores on the west, and well-populated, sheltered, beach-fringed lowlands on the east.

North of Campbell River lies a surprisingly large area mostly untouched by civilization—in fact, today you can still find maps of the island that fizzle out above Campbell River. Does life exist farther north? Anything to see or do? Can birds fly? Travel kilometer after kilometer along Highway 19 through impressive mountain scenery where the road itself, rest areas at all the very best views, and some unfortunate stretches of clear-cutting are the only human signatures on the landscape. Avail yourself of excellent camping spots, hiking trails, lakes perfect for canoeing and fishing, and more than a smattering of indigenous art and culture along the way. Unique **Telegraph Cove,** a boardwalk village known for its fishing and whale-watching activities, and intriguing **Alert Bay** on Cormorant Island are definitely worthwhile side trips on your way north. Finally, the road ends at **Port Hardy,** the largest community north of Campbell River and the terminus for ferries to Prince Rupert.

Victoria

Victoria, the elegant capital of British Columbia, boasts a mild climate, friendly people, and a distinct holiday atmosphere somewhat unusual for a capital city. Standing proudly at the southern tip of Vancouver Island, the fashionable city of 350,000 projects an intriguing mixture of images, old and new. Well-preserved century-old buildings line inner-city streets; ancient totem poles sprout from shady parks; restored historic areas house trendy shops, offices, and exotic restaurants; double-decker buses and horse-drawn carriages compete for summer trade; and the residents keep alive the original traditions and atmosphere of Merry Olde England.

Many people view the city for the first time from the Inner Harbour, coming in by boat the way people have for almost 150 years; on rounding Laurel Point, Victoria sparkles into view. Ferries, fishing boats, and seaplanes bob in the harbor, backdropped by manicured lawns and flower gardens, quiet residential suburbs, and striking inner-city architecture. Despite the pressures that go with city life, easygoing Victorians still find time for a stroll along the waterfront, a round of golf, or a typically English high tea.

Victoria has so many attractions, both free and commercial, that if you want to see *everything* you'd better give yourself a few extra days. The best way to get to know this beautiful city is on foot. All the downtown attractions are within a short walk of each other, and the more remote sights are easily reached by bus. In summer various tours are offered, giving you the choice of seeing Victoria by horse-drawn carriage, bus, boat, bicycle, limo—you name it! But if you still feel the need to have a car readily available, note that parking is plentiful just a few blocks from the Inner Harbour.

The city relies on tourism as its economic mainstay. High season is May through October, and low season falls in winter when the weather can be less appealing, although it's still the mildest in all of Canada. In spring, the city jumps to life and shakes out the welcome mat; enormous baskets of daffodils and other blooming bulbs are hung from all the lampposts, turning downtown into one big flower garden. Summer is the busiest time—time to enjoy the hustle and bustle of a city full of visitors, and to join in the plethora of warm-weather activities the city offers. If you prefer a more laid-back atmosphere, don't mind the possibility of rain and nippy sea breezes, and like meeting relaxed locals enjoying their few months of peace and quiet, take advantage of the lower prices, grab your windbreaker and brolly, and discover Victoria in the off season.

HISTORY

In 1792, Captain George Vancouver sailed through the Strait of Georgia, noting and naming Vancouver Island. But this had little effect on the many indigenous communities living along the shoreline. Europeans didn't see and exploit the island's potential for another 50 years, when the Hudson's Bay Company established control over the entire island and the mainland territory of "Columbia."

Fort Victoria

Needing to firmly establish British presence on the continent's northwest coast, the Hudson's Bay Company built Fort Victoria—named after Queen Victoria—on the southern tip of Vancouver Island in 1843. Three years later, the Oregon Treaty fixed the U.S./Canada boundary at the 49th parallel, with the proviso that the section of Vancouver Island lying south of that line would be retained by Canada. To forestall any claims that the United States may have had on the area, the British government went about settling the island. In 1849, the island was gazetted as a Crown colony and leased back to the Hudson's Bay Company. Gradually land around Fort Victoria was opened up by groups of British settlers brought to the island by the company's subsidiary, Puget Sound Agricultural Company. Several large company farms were developed, and Esquimalt Harbour became a major port for British ships.

The Growth of Victoria

In the late 1850s gold strikes on the mainland's Thompson and Fraser Rivers brought thousands of gold miners into Victoria, the region's only port and source of supplies. Overnight, Victoria became a classic boomtown, but with a distinctly British flavor; most of the company men, early settlers, and military personnel firmly maintained their homeland traditions and celebrations. Even after the gold rush ended, Victoria remained an energetic bastion of military, economic, and political activity, and was officially incorporated as a city in 1862. In 1868, two years after the colonies of Vancouver Island and British Columbia were united, Victoria was made capital. Through the two world wars, Victoria continued to grow. The commencement of ferry service between Tsawwassen and Sidney in 1903 created a small population boom, but Victoria has always lagged well behind Vancouver in the population stakes.

INNER HARBOUR SIGHTS

Initially, Victoria's Inner Harbour extended farther inland; prior to the construction of the massive stone causeway that now forms the marina, the area on which the impressive Empress Hotel now stands was a deep, oozing mudflat. Walk along the lower level, then up the steps in the middle to come face-to-face with an unamused Captain James Cook; the bronze statue commemorates the first recorded British landing, in 1778, on the territory that would later become British Columbia. Above the northeast corner of the harbor is the **Victoria Visitor Info Centre,** 812 Wharf St., 250/953-2033, the perfect place to start your city exploration. Be sure to return to the Inner Harbour after dark, when the parliament buildings are outlined in lights and the Empress Hotel is floodlit.

Empress Hotel

Overlooking the Inner Harbour, the pompous, ivy-covered 1908 Empress Hotel is Victoria's most recognizable landmark. Its architect was the well-known Francis Rattenbury, who also designed the parliament buildings, the CPR steamship ter-

minal (now housing the wax museum), and Crystal Garden. It's worthwhile walking through the hotel lobby to gaze—head back, mouth agape—at the interior razzle-dazzle, and to watch people-watching people partake in traditional afternoon tea (see Food section). Browse through the conservatory and gift shops, drool over the menus of the various restaurants, see what tours are available, and exchange currency if you're desperate (banks give a better exchange rate). Get a feeling for the hotel's history by joining a tour. Taking in public areas and the gardens, the tours depart from the Tea Lobby daily at 10 A.M.; $7 pp. Call 250/389-2727 for details.

Royal British Columbia Museum

Canada's most visited museum and easily one of North America's best, the Royal British Columbia Museum, 675 Belleville St., 250/356-7226, is a must-see attraction for even the most jaded museum-goer.

Its fine Natural History Gallery displays are extraordinarily true to life, complete with appro-

Fairmont Empress Hotel

© ANDREW HEMPSTEAD

VANCOUVER ISLAND

priate sounds and smells. Come face-to-face with an ice-age woolly mammoth, stroll through a coastal forest full of deer and tweeting birds, meander along a seashore or tidal marsh, then descend into the Open Ocean Exhibit via submarine—a very real trip not recommended for claustrophobes. The First Peoples Gallery holds a fine collection of artifacts from the island's first human inhabitants, the Nuu-chah-nulth (Nootka). Many of the pieces were collected by Charles Newcombe, who paid the Nuu-chah-nulth for them on collection sorties in the early 1900s. More modern human history is also explored here in creative ways. Take a tour through time via the time capsules; walk along a turn-of-the-20th-century street; and experience hands-on exhibits on industrialization, the gold rush, and the exploration of B.C. by land and sea in the Modern History and 20th Century Galleries.

The main gift shop stocks an excellent collection of books on Canadiana, wildlife, history, and native Indian art and culture, along with postcards and tourist paraphernalia, while the Out of the Mist gift shop sells native arts and crafts. Next door, the tearoom is always crowded. A new addition to the museum is the **National Geographic Theatre,** showing nature-oriented IMAX films daily 9 A.M.–8 P.M. (additional charge).

The museum is open in summer daily 9 A.M.–7:30 P.M., the rest of the year daily 9 A.M.–5 P.M. Admission is a very worthwhile adult $9, senior and youth $6; $16.75 and $14 respectively with admission to one IMAX feature.

Surrounding the Museum

In front of the museum, the 27-meter-high **Netherlands Centennial Carillon** was a gift to the city from British Columbia's Dutch community. The tower's 62 bells range in weight from eight to 1,500 kilograms and toll at 15-minute intervals daily 7 A.M.–10 P.M.

On the museum's eastern corner, at Belleville and Douglas Streets, lies **Thunderbird Park,** a small green spot chockablock with authentic totem poles intricately carved by northwest coast First Nations.

Beside Thunderbird Park is **Helmcken House,** 10 Elliot St., 250/361-0021, the oldest house in the province still standing on its original site. It was built by Dr. J. S. Helmcken, pioneer surgeon and legislator, who arrived in Victoria in 1850 and aided negotiating the union of British Columbia with Canada in 1870. Inside this 1852 residence you'll find restored rooms decorated with Victorian period furniture, as well as a collection of the good doctor's gruesome surgical equipment (which will help you appreciate modern medical technology). The house is open in summer daily 10 A.M.–5 P.M., the rest of the year daily noon–4 P.M. (closed January). Admission is adult $5, senior $4, child $3.

Parliament Buildings

Satisfy your lust for governmental, historic, and architectural knowledge all in one go by taking a free tour of the harborside Provincial Legislative Buildings, a.k.a. the parliament buildings. These prominent buildings were designed by Francis Rattenbury and completed in 1897. The exterior is British Columbia Haddington Island stone, and if you walk around the buildings you'll no doubt spot many a stern or gruesome face staring down from the stonework.

On either side of the main entrance stand statues of Sir James Douglas, who chose the location of Victoria, and Sir Matthew Baillie Begbie, who was in charge of law and order during the gold-rush period. Atop the copper-covered dome stands a gilded statue of Captain George Vancouver, the first mariner to circumnavigate Vancouver Island. Walk through the main entrance and into the memorial rotunda, look skyward for a dramatic view of the central dome, then continue upstairs to peer into the legislative chamber, the home of the democratic government of British Columbia. Free guided tours are offered every 20 minutes 9 A.M.–noon and 1–5 P.M. in summer, less frequently (Mon.–Fri. only) in winter. Tour times differ according to the goings-on inside; for current times, call the tour office at 250/387-3046.

Laurel Point

For an enjoyable short walk from downtown, continue along Belleville Street from the parliament buildings, passing a conglomeration of modern hotels, ferry terminals, and some intriguing architecture dating back to the late 19th century. A path leads down through a shady park to Laurel Point, hugging the waterfront and providing good views of Inner Harbour en route. If you're feeling really energetic, continue to **Fisherman's Wharf Park** and the crowded marina.

Crystal Garden

Designed by Francis Rattenbury and built by Percy James, the Crystal Garden, 713 Douglas St., 250/381-1213, opened in 1925 as the largest saltwater pool in the British Empire. It held tearooms, ballrooms, and a promenade, and was the venue for flower shows, craft shows, and big-band dancing, along with swimming, of course. In 1971, rising maintenance costs forced its closure. The provincial government then bought it and turned it into a two-story conservatory.

Today's visitors will find themselves surrounded by lush greenery, tropical plants, a waterfall, and the cacophony of an enormous variety of exotic birds from South America, New Guinea, and Australia. Woodcarvings from the remote corners of Asia peek out of the lush undergrowth, coral-colored flamingos strut their stuff at a series of placid pools, and iguanas, monkeys, squirrels, lemurs, wallabies, and marmosets cavort nearby. Sip afternoon tea on the humid upper floor, close your eyes, and you'll swear you're in the tropics. The garden is open daily 9 A.M.–6 P.M., till 8 P.M. in summer. Admission is adult $8, senior $7, and child $4. An English tea, served 2:15–4:15 P.M., costs extra.

Commercial Attractions

Oodles of ways to trim bulging wallets confront you in Victoria, some excellent, some routine. Along the waterfront on Belleville Street, across the road from the parliament buildings, is the former CPR steamship terminal, now

the **Royal London Wax Museum,** 470 Belleville St., 250/388-4461. This building, completed in 1924, was also designed by Francis Rattenbury. The museum features around 300 wax figures direct from London. It's open daily 9:30 A.M.–5 P.M., until 7:30 P.M. in summer; adult $8.50, senior $7.50, child $4.

On the water beside the wax museum, **Pacific Undersea Gardens,** 490 Belleville St., 250/382-5717, boasts more than 5,000 marine specimens in their "natural" habitat, as well as performing scuba divers and Armstrong the giant octopus. It's open in summer daily 10 A.M.–7 P.M., the rest of the year daily 10 A.M.–5 P.M. Admission is adult $8, child $6.

Behind the Empress Hotel is **Miniature World,** 649 Humboldt St., 250/385-9731, a longtime favorite among Victoria's many commercial attractions. Featuring 80 settings—from the historic Canadian Pacific Railway to a futuristic space—admission is adult $8.50, child $5.50.

OLD TOWN

The oldest section of Victoria lies immediately north of the Inner Harbour between Wharf and Government Streets. Start by walking north from the Inner Harbour along historic Wharf Street, where Hudson's Bay Company furs were loaded onto ships bound for England, gold seekers arrived in search of fortune, and shopkeepers first established businesses. Cross the road to cobblestoned **Bastion Square,** lined with old gas lamps and decorative architecture dating from the 1860s to 1890s. This was the original site chosen by James Douglas in 1843 for Fort Victoria, the Hudson's Bay Company trading post. At one time the square held a courthouse, jail, and gallows. Today restored buildings house trendy restaurants, cafés, nightclubs, and fashionable offices.

Cobblestoned Bastion Square, lined with old gas lamps and decorative architecture dating from the 1860s to 1890s, was the original site chosen by James Douglas in 1843 for Fort Victoria, the Hudson's Bay Company trading post.

Maritime Museum of British Columbia

At the top (east) end of Bastion Square, the Maritime Museum of British Columbia, 250/385-4222, is housed in the old provincial courthouse building. It traces the history of seafaring exploration, adventure, commercial ventures, and passenger travel through displays of dugout canoes, model ships, Royal Navy charts, figureheads, photographs, naval uniforms, and bells. One room is devoted to exhibits chronicling the circumnavigation of the world, and another holds a theater. The museum is open daily 9:30 A.M.–4:30 P.M., until 6 P.M. in summer. Admission is adult $6, senior $5, child $2 (check the museum's website, www.mmbc.bc.ca, for a two-for-one entry coupon). The museum also has a nautically oriented gift shop.

Other Old Town Sights

Centennial Square, bounded by Government Street, Douglas Street, Pandora Avenue, and Fisgard Street, is lined with many buildings dating from the 1880s and '90s, refurbished in recent times for all to appreciate. Don't miss the 1878 **City Hall** (fronting Douglas Street) and the imposing Greek-style building of the Hudson's Bay Company. Continue down Fisgard Street into colorful **Chinatown,** one of Canada's oldest Chinese enclaves. It's a delicious place to breathe in the aroma of authentic Asian food wafting from the many restaurants. Chinese prospectors and laborers first brought exotic spices, plants, and a love of intricate architecture and bright colors to Victoria in the 19th century. Poke through the dark little shops along Fisgard Street, where you can find everything from fragile paper lanterns and embroidered silks to gingerroot and exotic canned fruits and veggies, then cruise Fan Tan Alley, the center of the opium trade in the 1800s. Walk south along Store Street and Wharf Street back to Bastion Square.

SOUTH OF THE INNER HARBOUR

Emily Carr House

In 1871, artist Emily Carr was born in this typical upper-class 1864 Victorian-era home at 207 Government St., 250/383-5843. Carr moved to the mainland at an early age, escaping the confines of the capital to draw and write about the British Columbian natives and the wilderness in which she lived. She is best remembered today for her painting, a medium she took up in later years. The house is open mid-May to mid-October daily 9 A.M.–5 P.M. Admission is adult $5.50, senior and student $4.50, child $3.25.

Beacon Hill Park

This large, hilly city park—a lush, sea-edged oasis of grass and flowers—extends from the back of the museum along Douglas Street out to cliffs that offer spectacular views of Juan de Fuca Strait and, on a clear day, the distant Olympic Mountains. Add a handful of rocky points to scramble on and many protected pebble-and-sand beaches and you've found yourself a perfect spot to indulge your senses. Catch a sea breeze (along with numerous hang gliders, windsurfers, and kite-fliers) and gaze at all the strolling, cycling, dog-walking, and pram-pushing Victorians passing by. On a bright sunny day you'll swear that most of Victoria is here, too. The park is within easy walking distance from downtown and can also be reached by bus no. 5. For a tidbit of history, walk through the park to rocky Finlayson Point, once the site of an ancient fortified native village. Between 1878 and 1892 two enormous guns protected the point against an expected but unrealized Russian invasion.

A Scenic Coastal Drive

This route starts south of the Inner Harbour and follows the coastline all the way to the University of Victoria. If you have your own transportation, this is a "must-do" in Victoria; if you don't, most city tours take in the sights detailed below. You'll not be missing anything by taking Douglas Street south alongside Beacon Hill Park (see above) to access the coast, but it's possible to continue east along the Inner Harbour to the mouth of Victoria Harbour proper, passing the Canadian Coast Guard Base and the vehicular ferry terminals to Dallas Road, the official start of the Scenic Drive (marked by blue signs). For the first few kilometers, the Olympic Mountains in Washington State are clearly visible across the Strait of Georgia, and many lookouts allow you to stop and take in the panorama, including **Clover Point.** A few hundred meters beyond Clover Point, **Ross Bay Cemetery** is the final resting place of many of early Victoria's most prominent residents. Volunteer hosts are on hand through summer to point out the graves of Emily Carr; British Columbia's first governor, Sir James Douglas; members of the coal-baron Dunsmuir family; and Billy Barker, of gold rush fame. The gates are open weekdays through the hours of daylight.

Continuing east, Dallas Road takes you through quiet residential areas, past small pebble beaches covered in driftwood, and into the ritzy mansion district east of downtown, where the residents have grand houses, manicured gardens, and stunning water views.

Continue through the well-manicured fairways of Victoria Golf Club on Gonzales Point to **Oak Bay Marina,** where you'll find a casual café and the **Marina Restaurant** (250/598-8555), a favorite hangout for Sunday brunch. From the marina, the coastal road continues north to Cadboro Bay, home to the **Royal Victoria Yacht Club.** The **University of Victoria** lies on a ridge above Cadboro Bay; from here head southwest along Cadboro Bay Road then Yates Street to get back downtown, or north take Sinclair Road then Mackenzie Avenue to reach Highway 17, the main route north up the Saanich Peninsula toward famous Butchart Gardens.

ROCKLAND AND OAK BAY

This historic part of downtown lies behind the Inner Harbour, east of Douglas Street, and is easily accessible on foot.

Christ Church Cathedral

On the corner of Quadra and Courtney Streets, Christ Church Cathedral, 250/383-2714, is the seat of the Bishop of the Diocese of British Columbia. Built in 1896, in 13th-century Gothic style, it's one of Canada's largest churches. Self-guided tours are possible Mon.–Fri. 8:30 A.M.–5

P.M. and Sunday 7:30 A.M.–8:30 P.M. In summer, the cathedral sponsors free choral recitals each Saturday at 4 P.M. The park next to the cathedral is a shady haven to rest weary feet, and the gravestones make fascinating reading.

Art Gallery of Greater Victoria

From Christ Church Cathedral, walk up Rockland Avenue through the historic Rockland district, passing stately mansions and colorful gardens on tree-lined streets. Turn left on Moss Street and you'll come to the 1889 Spencer Mansion and its modern wing, which together make up the Art Gallery of Greater Victoria, 1040 Moss St., 250/384-4101. The gallery contains Canada's finest collection of Japanese art, a range of contemporary art, Emily Carr pieces, and traveling exhibits, as well as a Japanese garden with a Shinto shrine. The Gallery Shop sells art books, reproductions, and handcrafted jewelry, pottery, and glass. Hours are Mon.–Sat. 10 A.M.–5 P.M., Thursday 10 A.M.–9 P.M., and Sunday 1–5 P.M. Admission is adult $5, senior and child $3 (under 12 free); pay what you can on Monday.

Government House

Continue up Rockland Avenue from the art gallery to reach Government House, the official residence of the lieutenant governor, the queen's representative in British Columbia. The surrounding gardens, including an English-style garden, rose garden, and rhododendron garden, along with green velvet lawns and picture-perfect flower beds, are open to the public throughout the year.

Craigdarroch Castle

A short walk up (east) from the art gallery along Rockland Avenue and left on Joan Crescent brings you to the baronial four-story mansion known as Craigdarroch Castle, 1050 Joan Crescent, 250/592-5323. From downtown take bus no. 11 (Uplands) or no. 14 (University) to Joan Crescent, then walk 100 meters up the hill. The architectural masterpiece was built in 1890 for Robert Dunsmuir, a wealthy industrialist and politician who died just before the building was completed. For all the nitty-gritties, tour the mansion with volunteer guides who really know their Dunsmuir, then admire at your leisure all the polished wood, stained-glass windows, Victorian-era furnishings, and the great city views from upstairs. Admission and tour costs adult $10 ($8 outside summer), child $2.50. Open in summer daily 9 A.M.–7 P.M., the rest of the year daily 10 A.M.–4:30 P.M.

WEST OF DOWNTOWN

Point Ellice House and Garden

Built in 1861, this restored mansion sits amid beautiful gardens on Point Ellice, less than two km from the Inner Harbour. The house's second owner, Peter O'Reilly, a successful entrepreneur and politician, bought the house in 1868 and entertained many distinguished guests there. Original Victorian-era artifacts clutter every nook and cranny of the interior. Admission is adult $5, senior $4, child $3, but the best reason to visit is to enjoy a traditional English afternoon tea served noon–4 P.M. ($16.95 includes admission). The house itself, 250/380-6506, is open mid-May to mid-September, daily 10 A.M.–5 P.M. To get there from the Inner Harbour, jump aboard a **Victoria Harbour Ferry**, 250/708-0201 (10 minutes and $3 each way), or by road take Government or Douglas Street north from downtown, turn left on Bay Street, and turn left again on Pleasant Street.

Anne Hathaway's Thatched Cottage

The Stratford-upon-Avon cottage of Anne Hathaway, William Shakespeare's wife, has been recreated at 429 Lampson St., 250/388-4353; catch bus no. 24 (Munro) from downtown and return on no. 24 (Colville). The cottage is authentically furnished with 16th-century antiques. It's open for tours in summer daily 9 A.M.–7 P.M., the rest of the year daily 10 A.M.–4 P.M. Admission is adult $8.50, senior and child $5.

Next to the cottage is the **Olde England Inn** (see the Accommodations section, below) and a series of Tudor-style buildings that make up an English village. The food at the inn is excellent and oh so English. For a splurge, stay in one of the inn's antique-furnished rooms. Each one has a fireplace and a draped four-poster bed so high you need a stool to clamber up.

CFB Esquimalt Naval & Military Museum

This small museum lies within the confines of **CFB Esquimalt,** on Esquimalt Harbour west of downtown. A couple of buildings have been opened to the public, displaying naval, military, and general maritime memorabilia. Admission is $2, and the museum, 250/363-4312, is open Mon.–Fri. 8 A.M.–4 P.M. To get there from downtown, take the Johnson Street Bridge and follow Esquimalt Road to Admirals Road, turn north, then take Naden Way and you're on the base; follow the museum signs.

A free one-hour bus tour of the base, taking in the oldest operating dry dock on North America's west coast, departs from the museum in summer daily at 10 A.M.

Fort Rodd Hill National Historic Site

Clinging to a headland across the harbor entrance from CFB Esquimalt, this picturesque site at 603 Fort Rodd Hill Rd., Colwood, 250/478-5849, comprises **Fort Rodd,** built in 1898 to protect the fleets of ships in the harbor, and **Fisgard Lighthouse,** which dates to 1873. It's an interesting place to explore; audio stations bring the sounds of the past alive, workrooms are furnished as they were at the turn of the century, and the lighthouse has been fully restored and is open to visitors. The grounds are open daily 10 A.M.–5:30 P.M. Admission is adult $3, senior $2.25, child $1.50. To get there from downtown, take the Old Island Highway (Gorge Road) and turn left on Belmont Road, then left onto Ocean Boulevard. By bus, take no. 50 from downtown then transfer to no. 52.

While you're in the vicinity, continue down the forested road beyond the historic site turnoff to **Esquimalt Lagoon,** a haven for a great variety of birdlife. The lagoon is separated from the open water by a narrow 1.5-km-long causeway. An unpaved road leads along its length, providing access to a driftwood-strewn beach that is a popular swimming and sunbathing spot in summer.

© ANDREW HEMPSTEAD

VANCOUVER ISLAND

Beyond the Fort Rodd turnoff you'll descend to Esquimalt Lagoon, a delightful stretch of water that seems a world away from the city.

Goldstream Provincial Park

Lying just 20 km from the heart of Victoria, this 390-hectare park straddles Highway 1 northwest of downtown. The park's main natural feature is the Goldstream River, which flows north into the Finlayson Arm of Saanich Inlet. Forests of ancient Douglas fir and western red cedar flank the river, orchids flourish in forested glades, and at higher elevations forests of lodgepole pine, western hemlock, and maple thrive.

The park's highlight event occurs in November and December, when chum, coho, and chinook salmon fight their way upriver to spawn themselves out on the same shallow gravel bars where they were born four years previously. From the picnic area parking lot two km north of the campground turnoff, a trail leads 400 meters (10 minutes) along the Goldstream River to Freeman King Visitor Centre, 250/478-9414, where the life cycle of salmon is described. The center is open daily 9 A.M.–5 P.M.

Beyond the visitor center, the **Marsh Trail** leads 200 meters (five minutes) to the mouth of the Goldstream River and the head of Finlayson Arm, a great bird-watching spot. One of the park's longer hikes is the **Goldmine Trail,** which begins from a parking lot on the west side of Highway 1 halfway between the campground and picnic area. This trail winds two km (45 minutes) each way through a mixed forest of lodgepole pine, maple, and western hemlock, passing the site of a short-lived gold rush and coming to **Niagara Falls,** a poor relation of its eastern namesake but still a picturesque flow of water. Of a similar length, but more strenuous, is the trail to the summit of 419-meter-high **Mount Finlayson,** which takes around one hour each way and rewards successful summiteers with views back across the city and north along Saanich Inlet. The trail is accessed from Finlayson Arm Road. (For details about camping in Goldstream Provincial Park, see Campgrounds in the Accommodations section.)

SAANICH PENINSULA

The Saanich Peninsula is the finger of land that extends north from downtown. It holds Victoria's most famous attraction, Butchart Gardens, as well as Victoria International Airport and the main arrival point for ferries from Tsawwassen. If you've caught the ferry over to Vancouver Island from Tsawwassen, you'll have arrived at **Swartz Bay,** on the northern tip of the Saanich Peninsula; from here it's a clear run down Highway 17 to downtown Victoria. If you've been in Goldstream Provincial Park (see above) or are traveling down the island from Nanaimo on Highway 1, head north and south, respectively, to **Mill Bay,** where a ferry departs regularly for **Brentwood Bay** on the Saanich Peninsula. (Brentwood Bay is home to Butchart Gardens.) Ferries run in both directions nine times daily between 7:30 A.M. and 6 P.M. Peak one-way fares for the 25-minute crossing are adult $4, child $2.25, vehicle $11. For exact times call **B.C. Ferries** at 250/386-3431.

Butchart Gardens

These delightful gardens on Tod Inlet are Victoria's best-known attraction. They're approximately

20 km north of downtown at 800 Benvenuto Dr., Brentwood Bay, 250/652-4422.

A Canadian cement pioneer, R.P. Butchart, built a mansion near his quarries. He and his wife, Jennie, traveled extensively, collecting rare and exotic shrubs, trees, and plants from around the world. By 1904, the quarries had been abandoned, and the couple began to beautify them by transplanting their collection into a number of formal gardens interspersed with concrete footpaths, small bridges, waterfalls, ponds, and fountains. The gardens now contain more than 5,000 varieties of flowers, and the extensive nurseries test-grow some 35,000 new bulbs and more than 100 new roses every year. Go there in spring, summer, or early autumn to treat your eyes and nose to a marvelous sensual experience (many a gardener would give both hands to be able to work in these gardens). In winter, when little is blooming and the entire landscape is green, the basic design of the gardens can best be appreciated. Summer visitors are in for a special treat on Saturday nights (July and August only), when a spectacular fireworks display lights up the garden.

Also on the premises are two restaurants, a café, and a gift shop specializing in—you guessed it—floral items. The gardens are open every day of the year from 9 A.M., closing in summer at 10 P.M. and in winter at 4 P.M. Admission in summer is adult $18, student $9.25, child $2; admission is much lower in winter.

To get there from downtown take Highway 17 north to the Brentwood–Butchart Gardens turnoff, turn left on Keating Crossroad, and follow the signs. **Laidlaw,** 250/388-6534, runs a regular shuttle out to the gardens from its downtown depot at 700 Douglas St. for $4 each way, or join one of the many guided tours of Victoria that include this famous attraction. Buses no. 74 and 75 from downtown go to Brentwood Bay.

Victoria Butterfly Gardens

In the same vicinity as Butchart Gardens, Victoria Butterfly Gardens, corner of Benvenuto and W. Saanich Roads, 250/652-3822, offers you the opportunity to view and photograph some of the world's most spectacular butterflies at close range. Thousands of these beautiful creatures—species from around the world—live here, flying freely around the enclosed gardens and feeding on the nectar provided by colorful tropical plants. The gardens are open in summer daily 9 A.M.–5 P.M., March to mid-May and October daily 9:30 A.M.–4:30 P.M., closed the rest of the year; admission is adult $8, senior 55 and over $7, child $4.50.

Sidney

The small town of Sidney lies on the east side of the Saanich Peninsula, overlooking the Strait of Georgia. As well as being the departure point for ferries to the San Juan Islands (Washington), it's a pleasant spot to spend a sunny day exploring the colorful marina and the many outdoor cafés. From the marina, the **Sidney Harbour Cruise,** 250/655-5211, runs four tours daily around the harbor and to a couple of the inner Gulf Islands; $15 per person. The only official attraction is **Sidney Museum,** next to the marina at 9801 Seaport Place (off the end of Beacon Ave.), 250/656-2140, open in summer daily 10 A.M.–5 P.M., the rest of the year weekends only 10 A.M.–4 P.M. The highlight is a display pertaining to whales, which includes skeletons.

RECREATION

All of Vancouver Island is a recreational paradise, but Victorians find plenty to do around their own city. Walking and biking are especially popular, and from the Inner Harbour, it's possible to travel on foot or by pedal power all the way along the waterfront to Oak Bay. Commercial activities are detailed below, but the best place to get information on a wide variety of operators is the **Victoria Marine Adventure Centre,** based on a floating dock just around the corner from the information center along Wharf St., 250/995-2211 or 800/575-6700.

Pacific Wilderness Railway

The Esquimalt & Nanaimo (E&N) Railroad was built in the 1880s, connecting the coal mines of Nanaimo to Victoria docks. Today, in addition to VIA Rail's scheduled service (see Getting Around section), the Pacific Wilderness Railway,

TOURING VICTORIA

The classic way to see Victoria is from the comfort of a horse-drawn carriage. Throughout the day and into the evening **Victoria Carriage Tours,** 250/383-2207, has horse carriages lined up along Menzies Street at Belleville Street awaiting passengers. A 30-minute tour costs $60, a 45-minute tour costs $65, or take a 60-minute Royal Tour for $105. These prices are per carriage (up to four passengers). Tours run 9 A.M.–midnight and bookings aren't necessary, although there's often a line.

Big red double-decker buses are as much a part of the Victoria tour scene as horse-drawn carriages. These are operated by **Gray Line,** 250/388-6539 or 800/663-8390, from beside the Inner Harbour. There are many tours to choose from, but to get yourself oriented while also learning some city history, take the 90-minute Grand City Drive Tour. It departs from the harborfront every half hour 9:30 A.M.–4 P.M.; adult $17.50, child $8.75. The most popular of Gray Line's other tours is the one to Butchart Gardens ($38.50, including admission price).

Take to the Water
Victoria Harbour Ferry, 250/708-0201, offers boat tours of the harbor and Gorge Waterway. The company's funny-looking boats each seat around 20 passengers and depart regularly 10 A.M.–10 P.M. from below the Empress Hotel. The 45-minute loop tour allows passengers to get on and off at will; adult $14, senior $12, child $5, or travel just pieces of the entire loop for $3 per sector. You can also take to the waters of the Inner Harbour and beyond in a motorized replica of a Nuu-chah-nulth cedar canoe. The 90-minute trip costs adult $25, child $10, while the three-hour trip is adult $35, child $15. For all the details call **Blackfish Wilderness Expeditions** at 250/216-2389.

250/381-8600 or 800/267-0610, operates a trip along a section of the historic line in restored railcars. Departing from the downtown railway station at 11 A.M., the train passes through Esquimalt and Victoria's outer suburbs, crossing two 100-meter-high trestle bridges en route to the Malahat Summit. This is the turnaround point for the 2.5-hour round-trip (adult $29–79, depending on the class of travel), but many passengers combine the rail journey with a guided hike in Goldstream Provincial Park (from $49 pp) or lunch at the Aerie ($99 pp).

Whale-watching

Heading out from Victoria in search of whales is something that can be enjoyed by everyone. Both resident and transient whales are sighted, along with sea lions, porpoises, and seals. Trips last two to three hours, are generally made in sturdy inflatable boats with an onboard naturalist, and cost $65–85 pp. Recommended operators departing from the Inner Harbour include **Cuda Marine,** 250/812-6003; **Prince of Whales,** 250/383-4884 or 888/383-4884; **Spy Hopper,** 250/388-6222 or 877/388-6111; and **Seacoast** (based across the harbor at the Ocean Pointe Resort), 250/383-2254 or 800/386-1525. **Sea Quest Adventures,** 250/655-4256, is based in Sidney, on the Saanich Peninsula, and offers whale-watching cruises on the Strait of Georgia. The waters here are calmer than those experienced from trips departing the Inner Harbour. The local whale-watching season runs from mid-April to October.

Kayaking

Ocean River Sports, Market Square, 1437 Store St., 250/381-4233 or 800/909-4233, website www.oceanriver.com, organizes guided three-hour paddles in the Inner Harbour (Wednesday and Friday; $60 pp). Ocean River also offers kayaking courses (full day on Thetis Lake costs $179), sells and rents kayaks and other equipment, and offers overnight tours as far away as the Queen Charlotte Islands. **Sports Rent,** 611 Discovery St., 250/385-7368, rents canoes, kayaks, and a wide range of other outdoor equipment. Expect to pay about $35 per day and from $135 per week for a canoe or single kayak.

Scuba Diving

Close to downtown Victoria lie a number of good dive sites, notably the Ogden Point breakwall. At the breakwall, **Ogden Point Dive Centre,** 199 Dallas Rd., 250/380-9119, offers rentals, instruction, and daily guided dives from its base, which features showers, lockers, and a café. A recommended Victoria dive shop for sales, service, and rentals is **Ocean Sports,** 800 Cloverdale Ave., 250/475-2202.

To access the great diving in the Straits of Georgia and Juan de Fuca you'll need to charter a boat. One particularly interesting site lies in the shallow waters off Sidney, just north of Victoria, where a 110-meter destroyer escort was scuttled especially for divers.

Swimming and Sunbathing

The best beaches are east of downtown. At **Willows Beach,** Oak Bay, most of the summer crowds spend the day sunbathing, although a few hardy individuals brave a swim; water temperature here tops out at around 17° C (63° F). Closer to downtown, at the foot of Douglas Street, the foreshore is mostly rocky, but you can find a couple of short sandy stretches here and there. **Elk Lake,** toward the Saanich Peninsula, and **Thetis Lake,** west of downtown along Highway 1, are also popular swimming and sunbathing spots. **Crystal Pool,** one km north of downtown at 2275 Quadra St., 250/361-0732, has an Olympic-size pool as well as diving facilities, a kids' pool, sauna, and whirlpool.

Biking

For those keen on getting around by bike, it doesn't get much better than the bike path following the coastline of the peninsula on which Victoria lies. From downtown, ride down Government Street to Dallas Road, where you'll pick up the separate bike path running east along the coast to the charming seaside suburb of Oak Bay. From there, Oak Bay Road takes you back into the heart of the city for a round-trip of 20 km. You can rent bikes at **Sports Rent,** just north of downtown at 611 Discovery St., 250/385-7368; from $6–8 per hour, $25–35 per day.

ARTS AND ENTERTAINMENT

Victoria has a vibrant performing arts community, with unique events designed especially for the crowds of summer. The city lacks the wild nightlife scene of neighboring Vancouver, but a large influx of summer workers keeps the bars crowded and a few nightclubs jumping during the busy season. The city does have more than its fair share of British-style pubs, and you can usually get a good meal along with your pint of lager. The magazine *Monday,* website www.monday .com, offers a comprehensive arts and entertainment section.

Bars

The **Strathcona Hotel,** 919 Douglas St., 250/383-7137, is Victoria's largest entertainment venue, featuring four bars, including one on a magnificent rooftop patio and the Sticky Wicket, an English bar complete with mahogany paneling.

Closer to the Inner Harbour and converted from an old grain warehouse is **Swans Hotel,** 506 Pandora St., 250/361-3310, which brews its own beer. Unlike many other smaller brewing operations, this one uses traditional ingredients and methods, such as allowing the brew to settle naturally rather than be filtered. The beer is available at the hotel's bar, in its restaurants, and in the attached liquor store. The main bar, a popular hangout for local businesspeople, gets busy weeknights 5–8 P.M. Open daily from 11 A.M.

A few blocks farther north and right on the water is the **Harbour Canoe Club,** 450 Swift St., 250/361-1940, housed in an 1894 building that was at one time home to generators that powered Victoria's street lights. This place is also popular with the downtown crowd and has a great deck.

Also offering magnificent water views is **Spinnakers Brew Pub,** across the Inner Harbour from downtown at 308 Catherine St., 250/384-6613. Opened in 1984 as Canada's first brew pub, Spinnakers continues to produce its own European-style ales, including the popular Spinnakers Ale. A casual atmosphere, large waterfront deck, and great food make this place well worth the diversion. It's open daily 11 A.M.–2 P.M.

Victoria's many English-style pubs usually feature a wide variety of beers, congenial atmosphere, and inexpensive meals. Closest of these to downtown is the **James Bay Inn,** 270 Government St., 250/384-7151. Farther out, **Six Mile House,** 494 Island Hwy. (head west out of the city along Highway 1 and take the Colwood exit), 250/478-3121, is a classic Tudor-style English pub that was extensively restored in 1980.

Nightclubs and Live Music Venues

Most of Victoria's nightclubs double as live music venues attracting a great variety of acts. **Legends,** in the Strathcona Hotel, 919 Douglas St., 250/383-7137, comes alive with live rock 'n' roll some nights and a DJ spinning the latest dance discs on other nights. In the same hotel, **Big Bad John's** is the city's main country music venue. Known locally as the "Ingy," the **Ingraham Hotel,** north of downtown at 2915 Douglas St., 250/385-6731, has cover bands playing Wed.–Sat. and a country jam on Sunday afternoon. At the bottom of Bastion Square, **D'Arcy McGee's,** 1127 Wharf St., 250/380-1322, offers live music Friday and Saturday nights—Celtic sounds draw the biggest crowds. Below street level of the Wharfside complex, the **Boom Boom Room,** 1208 Wharf St., 250/381-2331, with bright lights and a large dance floor, is the city's most popular dance-only club.

Victoria boasts several good jazz venues. The best of these is **Hermann's Jazz Club,** 753 View St., 250/388-9166. **Steamers,** 570 Yates St., 250/381-4340, draws diverse acts but generally features jazz and blues on Tuesday and Wednesday nights.

Theater

Dating to 1914 and originally called the Pantages Theatre, the grand old **McPherson Playhouse** (known lovingly as the "Mac" by local theater-goers) went through hard times during the 1990s but has seen a recent revival of fortunes and now hosts a variety of performing arts. It's in Centennial Square, at the corner of Pandora Avenue and Government Street. The Mac's sister theater, the **Royal Theatre,** across downtown at

805 Broughton St., began life as a roadhouse and was used as a movie theater for many years. Today it hosts stage productions and musical recitals. For schedule information and tickets at both theaters call the Royal & McPherson Theatre Society at 250/386-6121 or 888/717-6121.

Performing arts on a smaller scale can be appreciated at the **Belfry Theatre,** in a historic church at 1291 Gladstone St., 250/385-6815, which offers live theater Oct.–April; tickets cost $22 per person.

Music and Dance

Pacific Opera Victoria, 250/385-0222, performs three productions each year (usually through the winter months) in the McPherson Playhouse. Tickets run $20–65. The **Victoria Operatic Society,** 250/381-1021, presents opera year-round; call for current schedule.

At the **Symphony Splash** on the first Sunday of August, the **Victoria Symphony Orchestra** performs on a barge moored at the Inner Harbour. This kicks off the performing-arts season, with regular performances through to May at the Royal Theatre and other city venues. Tickets range $16–32. For details call 250/385-9771 or the box office at 888/717-6121.

SHOPPING

Victoria is a shopper's delight. Most shops and all major department stores are generally open Mon.–Sat. 9:30 A.M.–5:30 P.M. and stay open for late-night shopping Thursday and Friday nights until 9 P.M. The touristy shops around the Inner Harbour and along Government Street are all open Sunday. Government Street is the main strip of tourist and gift shops. The bottom end, behind the Empress Hotel, is where you'll pick up all those tacky T-shirts and such. Farther up the street are more stylish shops, such as **James Bay Trading Co.,** 1102 Government St., 250/388-5477, which specializes in native arts from coastal communities; **Hill's Native Art,** 1008 Government St., 250/385-3911, selling a wide range of authentic native souvenirs; and **Cowichan Trading,** 1328 Government St., 250/383-0321, featuring Cowichan sweaters.

Traditions continue at **Rogers Chocolates,** 913 Government St., 250/384-7021, which is set up like a candy store of the early 1900s, when Charles Rogers first began selling his homemade chocolates to the local kids.

In Old Town, the colorful, two-story **Market Square** courtyard complex was once the haunt of sailors, sealers, and whalers, who came ashore looking for booze and brothels. It's been jazzed up, and today shops here specialize in everything from kayaks to condoms. Walk out of Market Square on Johnson Street to find camping-supply stores and the interesting **Bosun's Locker,** 580 Johnson St., 250/386-1308, filled to the brim with nautical knickknacks. Follow Store Street north from Market Square to find a concentration of arts and crafts shops along Herald Street. In the vicinity, **Capital Iron** is the real thing. Housed in a building that dates to 1863, this business began in the 1930s by offering the public goods salvaged from ships. Since then, it's evolved into a department store stocking an eclectic variety of hardware and homeware products.

Malls line all routes into the city. Victoria's largest downtown department store is **The Bay,** 1701 Douglas Street.

FESTIVALS AND EVENTS

The first of Victoria's many music-related festivals is the **TerrifVic Jazz Party,** the third week of April, when performers from around the world come together at downtown venues. Contact 250/953-2011, website www.terrifvic.com, for ticket information and a schedule. The second half of May has always been a busy time for festivals in Victoria, and in recent years these events have come to be known collectively as the **Victoria Harbour Festival,** website www.victoria harbourfestival.com. The "festival" incorporates the rodeo and yacht race detailed below, as well as a writing festival, special events at Fort Rodd Hill National Historic Site, bicycle races, and a parade of bands in front of the parliament buildings. Check the festival website for links to all of the above. The third weekend in May, the **Luxton Pro Rodeo,** 250/478-4250, website

www.rodeocanada.com, comes to the Luxton Rodeo Grounds west of downtown. The following weekend of May, the harbor comes alive as the finishing point for the historic **Swiftsure International Yacht Race,** website www.swift sure.org, through local waterways.

For eight days from the last Sunday in June, the **FolkFest** features contemporary and traditional jazz along waterfront Wharf Street. The best part of this festival is that entry to most performances is free. Call 250/388-4728 or surf the Internet to website www.icavictoria.org for details. Hosted by the local symphony orchestra, the **Summer Cathedral Festival** takes in soloist and orchestra performances over 10 evenings in the historic surroundings of Victoria's best-known church. Contact the organizers at 250/386-6121, website www.victoriasymphony.bc.ca. A new but popular addition to the local music scene is **Rootsfest,** held the last weekend of July on the grounds of Royal Roads University, west of downtown. It features traditional music on four outdoor stages. The first Sunday in August brings the unique **Symphony Splash,** when the local symphony orchestra performs from a barge moored in the Inner Harbour to masses crowded around the shore. Running the last week of August, the **Victoria Fringe Festival** is a celebration of fringe theater with more than 350 acts performing at venues throughout the city, including the harbor foreshore. All tickets are under $10. For dates and venues call Intrepid Theatre at 250/383-2663, website www.victoriafringe.com.

DOWNTOWN HOTELS AND MOTELS

Finding a room in Victoria can be difficult during the summer months, when gaggles of tourists compete for a relative paucity of motel rooms. All the best lodgings are in smaller boutique hotels offering only a few dozen rooms. Most of the major worldwide hotel chains are not represented downtown—the city has no Four Seasons, Hilton, Hotel Inter-Continental, Hyatt, Marriott, Radisson, or Regent. In the off season, nightly rates are discounted up to 50 percent, but again, occupancy rates are high as Canadians flock to the country's

VANCOUVER ISLAND

winter hot spot. All things considered, you'd be wise to make reservations as far ahead as possible, no matter what time of year you plan to visit. Bookings can be made direct or through the **Victoria Tourist Info Centre** at 250/953-2022 or 800/663-3883, website www.victoriatourism.com.

$50–100

The centrally located **Hotel Douglas,** 1450 Douglas St., 250/383-4157 or 800/332-9981, website www.hoteldouglas.com, is one of Victoria's many old hotels, this one five stories tall and with 75 refurbished rooms. Guests have use of a coin laundry, and downstairs is a 24-hour café and quiet bar. Rooms with shared bathroom (but with a wash basin) are $55 s, $65 d, while larger rooms with their own bathroom facilities are $95–125 s or d.

Just one block from the Inner Harbour and kitty-corner to the bus depot is the old **Crystal Court Motel,** 701 Belleville St., 250/384-0551, with 60 park-at-the-door-style motel rooms, half with kitchenettes. As you'd expect with any accommodation falling into this price category in such a prime position, the rooms are fairly basic; $77–90 s or d.

Farther from the harbor but still within walking distance is the 1897 **Cherry Bank Hotel,** across Douglas St. in a quiet location at 825 Burdett Ave., 250/385-5380 or 800/998-6688. Aside from a choice of rooms in either the original or new wing, the hotel offers a bar and lounge, and a restaurant known for excellent ribs. The rooms have no TV or phone. High-season rates are from $70 s, $78 d, including a cooked breakfast.

In the heart of the city center, the six-story 1913 **Strathcona Hotel,** 919 Douglas St., 250/383-7137 or 800/663-7476, website www.strathconahotel.com, holds a variety of bars—including a couple of the city's most popular—as well as 86 guest rooms. They are sparsely furnished but clean and comfortable. In summer, rates are $89 s, $99 d, but the rest of the year they are reduced considerably.

$100–150

Traveller's Inn, website www.travellersinn.com, is a local chain of eight properties strung out along the main highways into downtown. The company advertises *everywhere* with an eye-catching $29.95 room rate. That's what you'll pay for a single room in the middle of winter, midweek, and with the company brochure's $10 discount coupon. Rates at other times of year are competitive and good value—but still a little less enticing than at first impression. The two best choices are **Traveller's Inn Downtown,** 1850 Douglas St., 250/381-1000 or 888/254-6476, and **Traveller's Inn on Douglas,** 710 Queens St., 250/370-1000 or 888/753-3774, a few blocks farther north. Rates at both are $99.95 s, $109.95 d in July and August, discounted at other times of the year and through the week outside of summer. These rates include a light breakfast.

Every time I visit Victoria I expect to see that the old **Surf Motel** has been demolished. But it's still there, offering priceless ocean and mountain views for a reasonable $115 s or d. It's south of the Inner Harbour at 290 Dallas Rd. (take Oswego Rd. from Belleville St.), 250/386-3305.

Away from the water, but still just one block from Douglas St., is the 1876 **Dominion Hotel,** 759 Yates St., 250/384-4136 or 800/663-6101, website www.dominion-hotel.com, Victoria's oldest hotel. Millions of dollars have been spent restoring the property with stylish wooden beams, brass trim and lamps, ceiling fans, and marble floors reliving the Victorian era. Yet staying at the Dominion is still reasonable. Advertised rates are $119–139 s, $129–149 d, but off-season deals here are especially attractive, such as one night's accommodation and a three-course dinner for $99 d.

On a quiet residential street behind the parliament buildings is **Holland House Inn,** 595 Michigan St., 250/384-6644 or 800/335-3466, website www.hollandhouse.victoria.bc.ca, a boutique hotel dating to 1934 that has been restored in a casual yet elegant style. Each of the 17 antique-filled rooms has a four-poster bed and luxurious linens. Rooms range from $100 for a smallish room with a private bathroom across the hall to $295 for an Italian-style suite complete with a fireplace and hot tub. Rates include a delicious cooked breakfast served in a glass-roofed breakfast room filled with greenery.

Dating to 1911 and once home to artist Emily Carr, **James Bay Inn,** 270 Government St., 250/384-7151 or 800/836-2649, website www.jamesbayinn.bc.ca, is five blocks from the harbor and within easy walking distance of all city sights and Beacon Hill Park. The place has an old-fashioned look but a bright and breezy decor and new beds in the simply furnished rooms. Rates start at $121 s or d; outside of summer, pay for five nights and receive two nights free. All guests enjoy discounted meals at the in-house restaurant and pub.

$150–200

Centrally located **Swans Suite Hotel,** 506 Pandora Ave., 250/361-3310 or 800/668-7926, website www.swanshotel.com, is part of a restaurant/pub complex that was built in the 1880s as grain storehouse. Each of the 30 split-level suites holds a loft, full kitchen, dining area, and bedroom. The furnishings are casual yet elegantly rustic, with west coast artwork adorning the walls and fresh flowers in every room. The rates of $159 for a studio, $179 for a one-bedroom suite, and $249 for a two-bedroom suite are great value. In the off-season all rooms are discounted up to 50 percent.

Right at harborside is the four-story **Days Inn on the Harbour,** 427 Belleville St., 250/386-3451 or 800/665-3024, website www.days innvictoria.com. Befitting the location, rooms have a subtle nautical feel, and like all Days Inns, practical yet comfortable furnishings. Standard rooms are $151 s or d while suites offer a small kitchen and balcony for $171.

In the oldest section of downtown, surrounded by the city's best dining and shopping opportunities, is the **Bedford Regency,** 1140 Government St., 250/384-6835 or 800/665-6500, featuring 40 luxuriously appointed rooms restored to their original 1930s' art deco glory. Rates start at $165 s, $195 d, while the most luxurious suites feature fireplaces and Jacuzzi tubs for $250 s or d.

Around the southern end of the Inner Harbour (close to the ferry terminals), the **Admiral Inn,** 257 Belleville St., 250/388-6267, website www.admiral.bc.ca, has clean and comfortable rooms, each with a balcony or patio. Other extras include free parking, a light breakfast, kitchens in many rooms, and discount coupons for local attractions. Throw in friendly owner-operators, and you have good value at $199–215 s or d ($99–109 in winter).

$200–250

Coast Harbourside Hotel, 146 Kingston St., 250/360-1211 or 800/663-1144, website www.coasthotels.com, is the last of the string of accommodations along the south side of the harbor, but is still within easy walking distance of downtown. This hotel dates to the mid-1990s, so furnishings are new and modern. Rates here fluctuate greatly. The rack rate for a harbor-view room (with an ultra-small balcony) is $205 s or d, but use the Internet to book and you'll get the same room with breakfast included for $180.

In the same vicinity and sitting on a point of land jutting into the Inner Harbour, the **Laurel Point Inn,** 680 Montreal St., 250/386-8721 or 800/663-7667, website www.laurelpoint.com, offers a distinct resort atmosphere within walking distance of downtown. Two wings hold around 200 rooms (those in the south wing are newer); each has a water view and private balcony, and even the standard rooms have a king bed. Amenities include an indoor pool, beautifully landscaped Japanese-style gardens, a sauna, a small fitness facility, two restaurants, and a lounge. Rates range $225–275 s or d with the more expensive suites not larger but with better furnishings. Outside of summer, rates range $110–170.

Enjoyng an absolute waterfront location right downtown is the **Victoria Regent Hotel,** 1234 Wharf St., 250/386-2211 or 800/663-7472, website www.victoria-regent-hotel.com. The exterior of this renovated building is nothing special, but inside, the rooms are spacious and comfortable. The best value rooms at the Regent are the suites, which include a separate living area, full kitchen, balcony, and a daily newspaper; $239 s or d, or $269 with a water view. Regular rooms are $179 s or d.

If it's modern luxury you prefer over old-world excellence, consider the **Harbour Towers Hotel,**

VANCOUVER ISLAND

345 Quebec St., 250/385-2405 or 800/663-5896, website www.harbourtowers.com, one block from the harbor. Moat of the 193 rooms have a private balcony, and each is designed with sleek lines and a stylish red and brown color scheme. Most also have water views. Guests have use of an indoor pool and fitness room. Rack rates are $239 s or d or $259 s or d for a one-bedroom suite, but a percentage of rooms are sold in advance as low as $159 and $179 respectively, even in summer.

The **Magnolia Hotel & Spa,** 623 Courtney St., 250/381-0999 or 877/624-6654, website www.magnoliahotel.com, is a European-style boutique hotel just up the hill from the harbor. It features an elegant interior with mahogany-paneled walls, Persian rugs, chandeliers, a gold-leafed ceiling, and fresh flowers throughout public areas. The rooms themselves are each elegantly furnished and feature floor-to-ceiling windows, heritage-style furniture in a contemporary room layout, down duvets, a work desk with cordless phone, and coffee-making facilities. Many also feature a gas fireplace. The bathrooms are huge, with each having marble trim, a soaker tub, and separate shower stall. The Magnolia is also home to a day spa, two restaurants, and a small inhouse brewery. Rates of a reasonable $249–289 s or d include a light breakfast, daily newspaper, passes to a nearby fitness facility, and, unlike most other downtown hotels, free parking. Off-season rates range $169–209 s or d.

Across the Inner Harbour from downtown, offering stunning city views, is the luxurious **Delta Victoria Ocean Pointe Resort**, 45 Songhees Rd., 250/360-2999 or 800/268-1133, website www.deltahotels.com. Opened in 1992, this hotel offers all the services of a European-style spa resort with the convenience of downtown just a short ferry trip away. The rooms are simply yet stylishly furnished, with huge windows taking advantage of the views. Each comes with a work desk and high-speed Internet access, two phone lines, and plush robes. Facilities include a large health club, indoor glass-enclosed pool, spa and massage services, tennis, lounge, seasonal outdoor terrace, and two

restaurants. Rates for the 250-odd rooms are advertised at $338, $398, and $458, with views of the courtyard, Outer Harbour, and Inner Harbour respectively, but book in advance and courtyard rooms are a more reasonable $179 and harbor views are from $199.

$250–300

Holding a prime waterfront position next to the parliament buildings is the **Hotel Grand Pacific,** 463 Bellleville St., 250/386-0450 or 800/228-5151, website www.hotelgrandpacific.com. Opened in 1989, the Grand Pacific has been an ongoing construction project. Most recently, an extra 160 rooms were added where a Quality Inn used to stand nearby. Aside from more than 300 rooms, this property is also home to Spa at the Grand, a health club, restaurants and lounges, and a currency exchange. Standard rooms, with a king or twin beds, cost $259 s or d (check the Internet for these same rooms sold for under $200), or pay $329 for water views. All rooms are well-appointed, spacious, and have a private balcony.

Over $300

Completely restored in 1996, the grand old **Fairmont Empress,** 721 Government St., 250/384-8111 or 800/441-1414, website www.fairmont. com, is Victoria's best-loved accommodation. Covered in ivy and with only magnificent gardens separating it from the Inner Harbour, it's also in the city's best location. Designed by Francis Rattenbury in 1908, the Empress is one of the original Canadian Pacific Railway hotels. Rooms are offered in 90 different configurations; like other hotels of the era, most are small, but each is filled with Victorian period furnishings and antiques. The least expensive Fairmont Rooms start at $299, but if you really want to stay in this Canadian landmark, consider upgrading to an Entrée Gold room. All though not necessarily larger, these rooms have views, a private check-in, nightly turndown service, and a private lounge where hors d'oeuvres are served in the evening; $429–499 includes a light breakfast. All rates are reduced considerably outside of summer.

HOTELS AND MOTELS WEST OF DOWNTOWN

$50–100

The alternative to taking Highway 1 out of the city is to travel along Gorge Road (Highway 1A), where you'll find a string of well-priced motels. The least expensive is the **Fountain Inn,** 356 Gorge Rd. E, 250/385-1361, which charges $60 s, $70 d for the simply decorated rooms.

The **Olde England Inn,** 429 Lampson St., 250/388-4353 or 877/688-4353, website www.oldeenglandinn.com, is across the Johnson Street Bridge from downtown in the suburb of Esquimalt. It's within the grounds of the Anne Hathaway's Cottage tourist attraction, a re-creation of a Shakespearean village. The surrounding two-hectare gardens and smattering of Tudor-style buildings are delightful, but can get crowded in the height of summer. Rooms are furnished in period style but aren't particularly large; from $99 s or d for a basic room, $149 with a four-poster canopy bed.

$100–150

Back along Gorge Road, and more comfortable than the Fountain Inn, **Days Inn Victoria Waterway,** 123 Gorge Rd. E, 250/386-1422, website www.victoriadaysinn.com, has 95 large rooms, each with a kitchen. Other facilities include an outdoor pool, restaurant, and lounge. Rates start at $109 s, $119 d.

In the same vicinity (upgraded in 2000) is the **Howard Johnson,** 310 Gorge Rd. E, 250/382-2151 or 800/952-2151, website www.howardjohnson-victoria.com, featuring an indoor pool, restaurant, and rates from $139 s or d, $189 with a kitchen.

HOTELS AND MOTELS ON THE SAANICH PENINSULA

Highway 17, the main route between downtown Victoria and the B.C. Ferries terminal at Swartz Bay, holds many motels suited to travelers arriving at or departing from the airport or ferry terminal.

$50–100

Western 66 Motel, flanking the highway at 2401 Mt. Newton Cross Rd., 250/652-4464 or 800/463-4464, website www.western66travel.bc.ca, has a large variety of affordable rooms, English-style gardens, complimentary coffee in the lobby each morning, and a family restaurant on the premises; from $70 s, $93 d.

At the same intersection is **Quality Inn Waddling Dog,** 2476 Mt. Newton Cross Rd., 250/652-1146 or 800/567-8466, styled as an old English guesthouse complete with an English pub; one bed $99, two beds $129. If you're planning a visit to Butchart Gardens, the Waddling Dog offers good accommodations/admission packages.

$100–150

Off the main highway between the ferry terminal and downtown, on the road into downtown Sidney, is **Cedarwood Inn & Suites,** 9522 Lochside Dr., 250/656-5551 or 877/656-5551. The rooms are fairly standard, but the setting is glorious, highlighted by a colorful garden with outdoor seating overlooking the Strait of Georgia. Rates start at $100 s or d for a regular motel room, with the self-contained suites ranging $109–175—an excellent deal.

MALAHAT ACCOMMODATIONS

This small community is strung out along the main route up the island 25 km from downtown Victoria, making it a good place to spend the night for those who want to get an early start on northward travel.

$50–100

If you just need somewhere to spend the night, it's hard to go past the eight-room **Malahat Oceanview Motel,** Hwy. 1, 250/478-9231 or 877/478-8181. It offers views from private and semi-private balconies but is fairly basic; $65–85 s or d.

Over $250

For a splurge, consider **The Aerie,** 600 Ebedora Lane, 250/743-7115, website www.aerie.bc.ca, a

VANCOUVER ISLAND

sprawling complex of Mediterranean-style villas high above the waters of Saanich Inlet and surrounded by well-manicured gardens. No expense has been spared fitting out the 23 units. Each features a king-size bed, private balcony, lounge with fireplace, and luxurious bathroom complete with soaker tub. Upon arrival guests receive fresh flowers and gourmet chocolates. The resort also has an indoor pool, outdoor hot tub, hiking trails leading through the forested hillside, tennis courts, and a restaurant considered one of the province's best. Rates start at $285 s or d, which includes a small hamper of breakfast treats delivered to the room followed by a full breakfast in the dining room. To get there take the Spectacle Lake Provincial Park turnoff from Highway 1, then take the first right and follow the winding road up to the resort.

BED AND BREAKFASTS

Victoria's bed and breakfasts are even more abundant than tour operators in the height of the season—over 300 at last count. Prices range from reasonable to outrageous. Check the brochures at the Visitor Info Centre, but if you're looking for something specific you may want to contact the **Western Canadian Bed and Breakfast Innkeepers Association,** P.O. Box 74534, 2803 W. 4th Ave., Vancouver, BC V6K 4P4, 604/255-9199, website www.wcbbia.com, and request a brochure. This association doesn't take bookings, though. For these call **Canada West Victoria Reservation Service,** 250/652-8685 or 800/561-3223, website www.b-b.com. Alternatively, you can't go wrong staying at one of the personally selected places below.

$50–100

In a quiet residential area immediately east of downtown, **Craigmyle Guest House,** 1037 Craigdarroch Rd., Rockland, 250/595-5411 or 888/595-5411, has been converted from part of the original Craigdarroch Estate (it stands directly in front of the famous castle). This rambling old home is full of character, comfortable furnishings, and lots of original stained-glass windows. Rooms include singles, doubles, and

family suites, all with private or ensuite bathrooms. An inviting living room with a TV, a bright sunny dining area, and friendly longtime owners make this a real home-away-from-home. Rates are $70 s, $85–95 d.

Another excellent choice at the lower end of the price spectrum is **Selkirk Guest House,** on the Gorge Waterway three km from the Inner Harbour at 934 Selkirk Ave., Esquimalt, 250/389-1213 or 800/974-6638, website www.selkirk guesthouse.com. While the house has been extensively renovated and offers comfortable accommodations, it's the location that sets this place apart from similarly priced choices. The only thing separating the house from the water is the manicured garden, complete with a hot tub that sits under an old willow tree. Three of the guest rooms share bathrooms and a kitchen ($65–75 s or d), while the more spacious Rose Room has an ensuite bathroom, patio, fireplace, and its own kitchen ($85 s or d). Breakfast is an additional $5 pp.

$100–150

One of the best choices in this price category is **Ambleside Bed and Breakfast,** southeast of downtown at 1121 Faithful St., 250/383-9948 or 800/916-9948, website www.amblesidebb.com, a 1920s Craftsman-style home restored in heritage colors and decorated with stylish antiques. The two comfortable guest rooms are extremely spacious, and each has an ensuite bathroom. Rates range $140–210.

East of downtown in the suburb of Oak Bay, the Tudor-style **Oak Bay Guest House,** one block from the waterfront at 1052 Newport Ave., 250/598-3812 or 800/575-3812, website www.oakbayguesthouse.com, has been taking in guests since 1922. It offers 11 antique-filled rooms, each with a private balcony and a bathroom. The Sun Lounge holds a small library and tea- and coffee-making facilities while the Foyer Lounge features plush chairs set around an open fireplace. Rates of $135–180 s or d include a delicious four-course breakfast.

Heritage House, 3808 Heritage Lane, 250/479-0892, a beautiful 1910 mansion surrounded by trees and gardens, sits in a quiet residential area near Portage Inlet, five km northwest of city center. Friendly owners Larry and Sandra Gray have lovingly restored the house to its former glory. Guests choose from several outstanding rooms, one with a view of Portage Inlet from a private veranda. The three bathrooms are shared. Enjoy the large communal living room and a cooked breakfast in the elegant dining room. It's very busy in summer but quieter Nov.–April. Reservations are necessary year-round. Rooms vary in size and furnishings; from $135 s or d. Heritage Lane is not shown on any Victoria maps; from city center, take Douglas Street north to Burnside Road East (bear left off of Douglas). Just across the TransCanada Highway, Burnside makes a hard left (if you continue straight instead you'll be on Interurban Road). Make the left turn and continue down Burnside to just past Grange Road. The next lane on the right is Heritage Lane.

$150–200

Separated from downtown by Beacon Hill Park, **Dashwood Manor,** 1 Cook St., 250/385-5517 or 800/667-5517, website www.dashwood manor.com, a 1912 Tudor-style heritage house on a bluff overlooking Juan de Fuca Strait, enjoys a panoramic view of the entire Olympic mountain range. The 14 rooms are elegantly furnished, and host Derek Dashwood will happily recount the historic details of each room. Rates range from $165 s or d up to $285 for the Oxford Grand, which holds a chandelier, stone fireplace, and antiques. Off-season rates range $75–145.

A few blocks back from the Inner Harbour is **Andersen House Bed and Breakfast,** 301 Kingston St., 250/388-4565, website www .andersenhouse.com. Built late last century for a retired sea captain, the house features large high-ceilinged rooms all overlooking gardens that supply the kitchen with berries and herbs. Each has an ensuite bathroom, private entrance, and CD player (complete with CDs). In the traditions of its original owner, the house is decorated with furnishings from around the world, including contemporary paintings. Summer rates for the four guest rooms range $195–225 s or d while in the cooler months these same rooms are offered for $95–145.

© ANDREW HEMPSTEAD

Gatsby Mansion B&B is a great accommodation in an even better location.

Over $200

Right on the Inner Harbour, **Gatsby Mansion B&B,** 309 Belleville St., 250/388-9191 or 800/563-9656, website www.bellevillepark.com, has the best and most central position of any local bed and breakfast. Dating to 1897, this magnificent 20-room bed and breakfast has been elegantly restored, with stained-glass windows, a magnificent fireplace, lots of exposed wood, crystal chandeliers under a gabled roof, and antiques decorating every corner. Afternoon tea is served in a comfortable lounge area off the lobby, and the restaurant has a nice veranda. Through summer rooms start at $235 s, $245 d; the biggest and best of these, with a king bed and harbor view, is $309 s, $319 d. Packages offered make staying at the Gatsby Mansion more reasonable, or visit in winter for as little as $129 s, $139 d.

A few blocks back from the Inner Harbour, but still within pleasant walking distance, **Haterleigh Heritage Inn,** 243 Kingston St., 250/384-9995, website www.haterleigh.com, has been

VANCOUVER ISLAND

beautifully restored to its early 1900s' glory, complete with period furnishings and stained glass windows. Each of the six spacious rooms features a luxurious ensuite bathroom; from $210 s or d.

BUDGET ACCOMMODATIONS

Budget travelers are well catered to in Victoria, and while the accommodation choices in the capital are more varied than in Vancouver, there is no one backpacker lodge that stands out above the rest.

Hostelling International

In the heart of downtown Victoria's oldest section is **Hostelling International Victoria,** 516 Yates St., 250/385-4511 or 888/883-0099, website www.hihostels.com. The totally renovated hostel enjoys a great location only a stone's throw from the harbor. Separate dorms and bathroom facilities for men and women are complemented by two fully equipped kitchens, a large meeting room, lounge, library, game room, travel services, public Internet terminals, and an informative bulletin board. Members of Hostelling International pay $18 per night, nonmembers $22; private rooms range $45–54 s or d.

Other Backpacker Lodges

Housed in the upper stories of an old commercial building, **Ocean Island Backpackers Inn** lies just a couple of blocks from downtown at 791 Pandora Ave., 250/385-1788 or 888/888-4180, website www.oceanisland.com. Guests have use of kitchen facilities, a laundry, and a computer for Internet access. There's also plenty of space to relax, such as a reading room, music room, and television room. Dorm beds (up to six in a room) are $19.50 pp while private rooms are $40 s or d. Parking is an additional $3 per day, or the owners will make pick-ups from the bus depot.

In the same general direction but farther out (a 20-minute walk from the harbor) is the **Turtle Refuge,** 1608 Quadra St., 250/386-4471, which provides cooking and laundry facilities, free coffee, luggage storage, and parking. A dorm bed is $14–15 and doubles go for $45.

If you have your own transportation, **Selkirk Guest House,** 934 Selkirk Ave., 250/389-1213 or 800/974-6638, website www.selkirkguesthouse.com, is a good choice. This family-run accommodation is in an attractive historic home on the south side of the Gorge Waterway just under three km from downtown (cross the Johnson Street Bridge from downtown and take Craigflower Road). It has all the usual facilities, as well as a private dock, waterfront hot tub, and pleasant gardens. Cost is $20 for a dorm bed, with breakfast offered for an additional $5.

YWCA

A few blocks east of the harbor, the **YM-YWCA of Victoria,** 880 Courtney St., 250/386-7511, website www.ymywca.victoria.bc.ca, offers exercise facilities for both sexes, but the accommodations are for women only. The small, clean rooms share bathrooms. No cooking facilities are available, but the ground-floor café is good (it's usually crowded at lunchtime). Rates are $37 s, $49 twin.

University of Victoria

When University of Victoria students leave on summer vacation, their campus dormitory rooms become available to travelers. The rooms are sparse, and each has one or two single beds with shared bathroom and kitchen facilities. Rates are $38 s, $50 d or twin, which includes linen and a full breakfast. The rooms are at the corner of Sinclair and Finnerty Roads; for details call Housing and Conference Services at 250/721-8395. Also ask about summer accommodations in university-owned townhouses; from $146 for up to four people.

CAMPING
West

Closest camping to downtown is at **Westbay Marine Village,** across Victoria Harbour from downtown at 453 Head St., Esquimalt, 250/385-1831, website www.westbay.bc.ca. Facilities at this RV-only campground include full hookups and a laundromat. It is part of a new marina complex comprising floating residences and commercial businesses such as fishing charter operators and restaurants. Water taxis connect the "village" to downtown. Rates are $32 per night.

Fort Victoria RV Park, 340 Island Hwy., 250/479-8112, is six km northwest of city center on Highway 1A. This campground provides hookups (no official tent sites), free showers, laundry facilities, and opportunities to join charter salmon-fishing trips. During the summer, sites are $28.

Continuing west along Highway 1, take Exit 10, stay in the Colwood Lane, and then take Six Mile Road back under the highway to reach **Thetis Lake Campground,** West Park Lane, 250/478-3845, featuring pleasant shaded sites, coin-operated showers, and laundry facilities. It adjoins Thetis Lake Park, which is crisscrossed by hiking trails and holds one of the city's favorite swimming and sunbathing spots. Unserviced sites are $20, hookups $22–26.

North along Highway 1

Continuing west from the two campgrounds detailed above, Highway 1 curves north through **Goldstream Provincial Park** (19 km from downtown) and begins its up-island journey north. The southern end of the park holds 161 campsites scattered around an old-growth forest—it's one of the most beautiful settings you could imagine close to a capital city. The campground offers free hot showers but no hookups. Sites are $18.50 per night. Good hiking trails and many other recreational opportunities are available in the area.

In Malahat, seven km farther north along Highway 1, is **KOA Victoria West,** 250/478-3332 or 800/562-1732, website www.koa.com. Facilities include free showers, an outdoor pool, laundry, store, and game room. Unserviced sites are $24, hookups $28–32, and Kamping Kabins from $54.

Saanich Peninsula

If you're coming from or heading for the ferry terminal, consider staying at **McDonald Provincial Park,** near the tip of the Saanich Peninsula 31 km north of the city center. Facilities are limited (no

showers or hookups); campsites are $11.50 per night.

Also on the peninsula, halfway between downtown Victoria and Sidney, is **Island View Beach RV Park,** Homathko Dr., 250/652-0548, right on the beach three km east of Hwy. 17. Sites are $20–25 and you'll need quarters for the showers.

FOOD
Coffeehouses and Cafés

Murchies, 1110 Government St., 250/381-5451, is a large coffeehouse on Victoria's busiest downtown street. It has all the usual choices of coffee concoctions as well as light snacks. Continuing away from the harbor, and across the road, is the **Electric Juice Café,** 1223 Government St., 250/380-0009. Here you'll find a huge selection of fruit and vegetable juices mixed to your liking and with the option of adding extras such as ginseng and bee pollen. At the foot of Bastion Square, a cobbled pedestrian mall, quiet **Paradiso,** 10 Bastion Square, 250/920-7266, serves a range of coffees, pastries, and muffins. In Old Town, **Willies Bakery,** 537 Johnson St., 250/381-8414, is an old-style café offering cakes, pastries, and sodas, with a quiet cobbled courtyard in which to enjoy them. Across the road, on the second story of Market Square, 560 Johnson St., the **Bavarian Bakery,** 250/388-5506, also sells a wide range of bakery delights. Farther north along the waterfront is the "arty" part of downtown; in the **Capital Iron** store is a small concession stand and a few tables offering water views.

While tourists flock to the cafés and restaurants of the Inner Harbour and Government Street, Douglas Street remains the haunt of lunching locals. Reminiscent of days gone by, **John's Place,** just off Douglas St. at 723 Pandora Ave., 250/389-0711, serves up excellent value for those in the know. The walls are decorated with movie posters, old advertisements, and photos of sports stars, but this place is a lot more than just another greasy-spoon restaurant. The food is good, the atmosphere casual, and the waitresses actually seem to enjoy working here. It's breakfast, burgers, salads, and sandwiches through the week, but weekend brunch is busiest, when there's nearly always a line spilling onto the street. This part of town is home to all the more modern coffeehouses also, including **Blenz** at 1328 Douglas St., **Company's Coming** at 670 Fort St., and at 801 Fort St. one of Victoria's dozen **Starbucks.**

Casual Dining

Right across from the information center, and drawing tourists like a magnet, is **Sam's Deli,** 805 Government St., 250/382-8424. Many places nearby have better food, but Sam's boasts a superb location and cheerful atmosphere. The ploughman's lunch, a staple of English pub dining, costs $8.50, while sandwiches range $5.50–9 and salads are all around $6–9. Open daily 7:30 A.M.–10 P.M.

Wharfside Eatery, 1208 Wharf St., 250/360-1808, is a bustling waterfront complex with a maritime theme and family atmosphere. Behind a small café section and a bar is the main dining room and a two-story deck, where almost every table has a stunning water view. The menu features mostly local seafood, as well as soups, salads, pizza from a wood-fired oven, and meat dishes. The seafood-oriented tapas menu is a good choice for sharing a variety of dishes between two or more. Sunday brunch, $10–14, is very popular. In the same complex, **Nasty Jacks,** 1208 Wharf St., 250/360-1808, is named for a South Seas pirate who spent the 1860s in Victoria. It's open all day, every day; breakfasts start at $5, but the café is best known for Nasty Stacked Sandwiches from $6.50.

In Old Town, the small **Sour Pickle Cafe,** 1623 Store St., 250/384-9390, comes alive with funky music and an enthusiastic staff. The menu offers bagels from $1.60, full cooked breakfasts from $5.50, soup of the day $3, healthy sandwiches $5–6.50, and delicious single-serve pizza for around $7.50. Open Mon.–Fri. 7:30 A.M.–4:30 P.M.

Away from the tourist-clogged streets of the Inner Harbour, right at sea level, is **Barb's Place,** on Fisherman's Wharf at the end of St. Lawrence St., 250/384-6515. The specialty is fish and chips to go, but the seafood chowder is also good. Open daily from 8 A.M.

Empress Dining

Afternoon tea is served just about everywhere in Victoria—it's a local tradition—but the most popular place to indulge is the **Fairmont Empress,** 721 Government St.; it's also the most over-commercialized, but try to keep in mind that you're taking part in one of the oldest Victorian rituals. Sample English honey crumpets, homemade scones with cream and jam, finger sandwiches, pastries, and an Empress blend tea while enjoying the soft music of a pianist for $42 per person ($32 outside summer). It is served in three different areas of the hotel, including the most traditional location, tableside in the Tea Lobby; still, it's so popular that reservations are necessary up to two weeks in advance; sittings are at 12:30 P.M., 2 P.M., and 3:30 P.M.; dress is smart casual.

The **Empress Room** is the hotel's most formal restaurant (and the most expensive; mains *start* at $30), dishing up West Coast cuisine in an elegant setting accompanied by the soft tones of a harpist. Dress is smart casual, with no jeans allowed.

You needn't spend a fortune to dine at the Empress, although a buffet is a far cry from the two options detailed above. Head to the hotel's **Bengal Lounge** for a curry lunch buffet 11:30 A.M.–3 P.M. or a curry dinner buffet Sun.–Thurs. 6–9 P.M. Friday and Saturday evenings an à la carte East Indian menu is offered, with live background jazz. Prices range from $6.50 for soup to a reasonable $14–23 for main courses. The Empress's even less formal **Kipling's** serves up buffets for breakfast, lunch, and dinner in a casual atmosphere.

Reservations are necessary only for afternoon tea and dining in the Empress Room; for these call 250/384-8111.

Seafood

Victoria's many seafood restaurants come in all forms. Fish and chips is a British tradition and is sold as such at **Old Vic Fish & Chips,** in a heritage-listed building at 1316 Broad St., 250/383-4536; open Mon.–Thurs. 11 A.M.–7 P.M., Fri.–Sat. 11 A.M.–8 P.M. **Chandlers** is on the main strip of tourist-catching restaurants along the waterfront at 1250 Wharf St., 250/385-3474, but is generally regarded as Victoria's finest seafood restaurant. It's open daily for lunch and dinner, with mains at dinner ranging $16–28. North beyond the Johnson Street Bridge (just past Market Square) at street level of Swan's Hotel is the **Fowl & Fish Café,** 1605 Store St., 250/361-3150. The red-brick and exposed beam interior reflects its past use as a grain warehouse. The cuisine can best be described as "fusion"—local seafood and game prepared using Asian techniques. Starters include a creamy oyster chowder and seafood tapas for $5–8, while most main dishes, including salmon and halibut, are around $20–25. It's open for dinner only from 5 P.M. daily.

Pub Meals

Right in the heart of downtown is the **Elephant and Castle,** corner Government and View Streets, 250/383-5858. This English-style pub features exposed beams, oak paneling, and traditional pub decor. A few umbrella-shaded tables line the sidewalk out front. All the favorites, such as steak and kidney pie and fish and chips, range $8–14.50. Open daily for lunch and dinner.

As well as the Fowl & Fish Café detailed above, **Swan's Hotel,** 506 Pandora St., 250/361-3310, is home to an English-style pub with matching food, such as bangers and mash (sausages and mashed potatoes) and shepherd's pie, all around $10–12. As well as the typical pub pews, the hotel has covered a section of the sidewalk with a glass-enclosed atrium.

The **James Bay Inn,** 270 Government St., 250/384-7151, also serves up typical English pub food at reasonable prices. Look for traditional dishes such as kippers and poached eggs for breakfast, ploughman's lunches, and roast beef with Yorkshire pudding or steak and kidney pie in the evening; dinner entrées start at $9.50.

While all the above pubs exude the English traditions for which Victoria is famous, **Spinnakers Brew Pub,** 308 Catherine St., Esquimalt, 250/386-2739, is in a class by itself. It was Canada's first in-house brew pub, and it's as popular today as when it opened in 1985. The crowds come for the beer, but also for great food served up in a casual, modern atmosphere. British-style pub fare such as a ploughman's lunch is served in the bar, while West Coast and seafood dishes such as sea bass basted in an ale sauce are offered in the downstairs restaurant. Spinnakers is open daily from 11 A.M.

Ribs

Bowman's Rib House is in the original dining room of the old Cherry Bank Hotel at 825 Burdett Ave., 250/385-5380. It's been serving up its specialty baby back loin ribs for over 50 years, with a lively atmosphere as the piano player starts pounding out one old-fashioned tune after another. Local seafood and steak are also on offer, and kids are catered to with their own inexpensive menu. Main courses run $12–24 and come with salad, potato, vegetable, and garlic bread. Open Sun.–Thurs. 5–9 P.M. and Fri.–Sat. 5–10 P.M.

Vegetarian

Green Cuisine, in Market Square at 560 Johnson St., 250/385-1809, takes the vegetarian theme to the fullest, with a vegan menu that uses no oils, sugars, or refined flours. A small buffet is offered, but the regular menu provides many choices, from chili to fruit juices. Open daily.

Mexican

On the waterfront side of Market Square is **Cafe Mexico,** 1425 Store St., 250/386-1425. The atmosphere is very casual, with Mexican paraphernalia hanging everywhere and loud music playing. A large buffet lunch is served Mon.–Fri. from 11:30 A.M. The regular menu is extensive, ranging from $3 salsa dips to $12–18 gourmet dishes.

Italian

One of the most popular restaurants in town is **Pagliacci's,** 1011 Broad St., 250/386-1662, known for hearty Italian food, homemade bread, great desserts, and loads of atmosphere. Small and always busy, the restaurant attracts a lively local crowd; you'll inevitably have to wait for a table during the busiest times. Pastas range $10–14. This is also one of the few late-night restaurants in Victoria; open daily 11:30 A.M.–midnight. A jazz trio plays Wed.–Sun. nights.

Housed in a heritage building in Old Town, the **Herald Street Caffe,** 546 Herald St., 250/381-1441, is also good, with a menu comparable to Pagliacci's but more extensive. The atmosphere is casual, with artworks adorning the walls and flowering plants everywhere. Open Wed.–Sat. for lunch and daily for dinner.

Other European Restaurants

A good place to go for traditional Greek food, and live entertainment on weekends, is **Periklis,** 531 Yates St., 250/386-3313. Main courses range $12–25, and almost anything can be happening on the floor—from exotic belly dancers to crazy Greek dancing.

For a more subdued atmosphere, head to **Millos,** 716 Burdett Ave., 250/382-4422, which also presents belly dancing some nights.

Beyond the west end of Belleville St. is **Pablo's Dining Lounge,** 225 Quebec St., 250/388-4255, a longtime Victorian favorite serving a variety of European cuisines. Atmosphere in the Edwardian house is relaxed yet intimate, and the dishes are all well-prepared and well-presented. Entrées range $15–26. Open daily from 5 P.M.

The **Garlic Rose Café,** 1205 Wharf St., 250/384-1931, offers a Mediterranean-inspired menu (lots of herbs are used) with seating out front, inside, and upstairs. Dinner mains start at $15, but the daily specials include a starter for around the same price.

Med Grill, 1010 Yates St., 250/360-1660, features West Coast produce cooked with southern European techniques. The menu is short, with one dish of each meat offered, including a delicious steamed salmon dish ($21) hard for seafood lovers to pass up.

Chinese

Victoria's small Chinatown surrounds a short, colorful strip of Fisgard Street between Store and Government Streets. Near the top (east) end of Fisgard is **QV Cafe and Bakery,** 1701 Govern-

VANCOUVER ISLAND

© ANDREW HEMPSTEAD

Victoria's Chinatown is small, but it boasts a variety of inexpensive restaurants.

ment St., 250/384-8831, offering inexpensive Western-style breakfasts in the morning and Chinese delicacies the rest of the day. One of the least expensive places in the area is **Wah Lai Yuen,** 560 Fisgard St., 250/381-5355, a large, simply decorated, well-lighted restaurant with fast and efficient service. The wonton soups (from $3) are particularly good, or try the hearty chicken hot pot ($8.50) or scallops and broccoli ($14.50). Open daily 10 A.M.–9 P.M.

Named for the Chinese province renowned for hot and spicy food, **Hunan Village Cuisine,** 546 Fisgard St., 250/382-0661, offers entrées ranging $8–15. It's open Mon.–Sat. for lunch and daily for dinner. Down the hill a little is **Don Mee Restaurant,** 538 Fisgard St., 250/383-1032, specializing in the cuisine of Canton. Entrées run about $7 each, while four-course dinners for two or more diners are a good deal at under $15 per person. Open Mon.–Fri. for lunch, daily for dinner.

A few blocks from Chinatown and just off Douglas St. is **Lotus Pond,** 617 Johnson St., 250/380-9293, a no-frills vegetarian Chinese restaurant. It's open Mon.–Sat. 11 A.M.–8 P.M.

GETTING THERE
Air
Vancouver Island's main airport is on the Saanich Peninsula 20 km north of Victoria's city center. The terminal building houses a cocktail lounge, café, and various rental car agencies. The **AKAL Airporter,** 250/386-2525 or 877/386-2525, operates buses between the airport and major downtown hotels every 30 minutes; $13 per person each way. A taxi costs approximately $45 to downtown.

Scheduled flights link the international airports of Vancouver and Victoria, but it's such a short flight (25 minutes from terminal to terminal) that unless you are on a connecting flight, the alternatives are more practical. **Air Canada,** 888/247-2262, website www.aircanada.ca, and its main regional connector, **Air BC,** fly the route multiple times daily. Air Canada also flies to Victoria from most western Canadian cities and Seattle. **Horizon Air,** 800/547-9308, also flies

daily into Victoria International Airport from Seattle.

Also from Seattle, **Kenmore Air,** 206/486-1257 or 800/543-9595, offers scheduled floatplane flights between the north end of Lake Washington and Victoria's Inner Harbour (terminating at the Victoria Marine Adventure Centre), with a pick-up point at Lake Union.

Smaller airlines, including those with floatplanes and helicopter services, provide a direct link between Victoria and Vancouver, departing from the downtown Vancouver waterfront and landing on or beside the Inner Harbour. These include **Harbour Air,** 250/384-2215 or 800/665-0212, website www.harbour-air.com; **West Coast Air,** 250/388-4521 or 800/347-2222, website www.westcoastair.com; and **Helijet International,** 250/382-6222 or 800/665-4354, website www.helijet.com. All three have terminals in the vicinity of Wharf Street.

Bus
The main Victoria **bus depot** is behind the Empress Hotel at 710 Douglas Street. **Pacific Coach Lines,** 604/662-8074 or 250/385-4411, website www.pacificcoach.com, operates bus service between Vancouver's Pacific Central Station and downtown Victoria, via the Tsawwassen–Swartz Bay ferry. In summer the coaches run hourly 6 A.M.–9 P.M.; $28 one-way, $54 round-trip, which includes the ferry fare. The trip takes 3.5 hours. This same company also runs three daily buses from Vancouver International Airport directly to Victoria; $32.50 one-way, $63 round-trip. If you take the ferry over independently, you can catch the **Victoria Regional Transit System** bus no. 70, 250/385-2551, from the Swartz Bay ferry terminal to downtown for $2.50.

Ferry
From Tsawwassen (Vancouver): Ferries run regularly across the Strait of Georgia from Tsawwassen, 30 km south of Vancouver, to the **Swartz Bay Ferry Terminal,** 32 km north of Victoria. Through summer, ferries run hourly 7 A.M.–10 P.M., the rest of the year slightly less frequently. The crossing takes 90 minutes. You can expect a wait in summer; limited vehicle

VANCOUVER ISLAND

reservations are accepted at 604/444-2890 or 888/724-5223; $15 per booking. Peak fares are adult $9.50, child 5–11 $4.75, vehicle $33.50, motorcycle $16.75, bicycle $2.50, canoe or kayak $4. For information, call **B.C. Ferries** at 250/386-3431 or 888/223-3779 (within B.C.), website www.bcferries.com.

From Seattle: Clipper Navigation offers a fleet of foot-passengers-only ferries connecting Seattle's Pier 69 with Victoria's Inner Harbour. Its turbojet catamaran, the *Victoria Clipper IV,* is North America's fastest passenger ferry, traveling at speeds of up to 45 knots (over 80 kph). This speedy vessel makes the crossing in two hours and costs adult US$75 one-way, US$125 round-trip. The company's other vessels make the trip in 2.5 hours and cost adults US$66 one-way, US$109 round-trip. The service runs year-round. In summer, up to five sailings a day are offered, with some stopping off at Friday Harbor in the San Juan Islands (US$58 one-way, through to Victoria). All vessels feature spacious seating arrangements, writing tables, complimentary tea and coffee, and light snacks. Discounts apply outside of the busy summer months and to tickets purchased 14 or more days in advance. Seniors also get a break, and children travel for half price. Clipper Navigation also offers a plethora of reasonably priced accommodations and tour packages in Victoria (from US$145 including transportation from Seattle; high season). For schedules and tour information, call 800/888-2535, or drop by one of its offices: Pier 69, Seattle, 206/448-5000, or at the Inner Harbour terminal on Belleville St., 250/382-8100. The company's website is www.victoriaclipper.com.

From Anacortes: Washington State Ferries, 206/464-6400 or 250/381-1551, website www.wsdof.wa.gov/ferries, runs a regular ferry schedule between Anacortes and the San Juan Islands, with the 7:50 A.M. sailing continuing to Sidney, on the Saanich Peninsula 32 km north of Victoria. The return sailing departs Sidney at 11.45 A.M. The one-way fare is adult US$11, senior $5.50, vehicle and driver US$41. Reservations must be made at least 24 hours in advance.

From Port Angeles: The **MV** *Coho* crosses Juan de Fuca Strait in just over 90 minutes, arriving in Victoria's Inner Harbour. It makes four crossings daily in each direction from mid-May to mid-October, two crossings daily the rest of the year. Advance reservations are not accepted—phone a day or so before your planned departure for estimated waiting times. The one-way fare is adult US$7.75, child US$3.90, vehicle US$29.75. For details call Black Ball Transport Inc. at 250/386-2202 in Victoria, or 360/457-4491 in Port Angeles, website www.northolympic.com/coho. The other option from Port Angeles is the passenger-only **Victoria Express,** 250/361-9144, 360/452-8088, or 800/663-1589, website www.victoriaexpress.com. This company operates 2–3 sailings daily in each direction between June and September; US$25 each way.

GETTING AROUND

Bus

Most of the inner-city attractions can be reached on foot. However, the **Victoria Regional Transit System** is an excellent bus network, and it's easy to jump on and off and get everywhere you want to go. Pick up an *Explore Victoria* brochure at the information center for details of all the major sights, parks, beaches, and shopping areas, and the buses needed to reach them. Bus fare for travel within Zone 1, which covers most of the city, is adult $1.75, senior or child $1.10. Zone 2 covers outlying areas such as the airport and Swartz Bay ferry terminal; adult $2.50, senior or child $1.75. Transfers are good for travel in one direction within 90 minutes of purchase. A DayPass, valid for one day's unlimited bus travel, costs adult $5.50, senior or child $4. For general bus information call 250/385-2551 or surf the Internet to www.transitbc.com.

Water Taxi

Take to the water with **Victoria Harbour Ferry,** 250/708-0201. The company's distinctive 12-passenger boats ply two routes departing from the Inner Harbour. One takes in harborside docks,

HEADING UP THE ISLAND FROM VICTORIA

Once you've finished exploring the delights of Victoria, there's only one way to head, and that's north. Vancouver Island is blessed with an excellent public transport system, including buses that travel to all corners and a rail service that closely follows the Strait of Georgia as far north as Courtenay. If you're driving, the road ends at Port Hardy, from where B.C. Ferries provides service to Prince Rupert, the gateway to northern British Columbia and a stop on the long route north to Alaska.

By Road

From downtown Victoria, take Douglas Street north for three km to Highway 1, which jogs westward through Victoria's residential suburbs before turning north and running up the east side of the island to Nanaimo (113 km), Courtenay (220 km), Campbell River (260 km), and Port Hardy (495 km). It's not necessary to return to Victoria to get back to the mainland; ferries operate between Nanaimo and Vancouver, Comox and the Sunshine Coast, and Port Hardy and Prince Rupert.

By Rail

VIA Rail's **E&N Railiner** (also known as the **Malahat**) is the only scheduled train service on Vancouver Island. It departs Victoria for Courtenay Mon.–Sat. at 8:15 A.M. and Sunday at noon, and departs Courtenay for Victoria Mon.–Sat. at 1:15 P.M. and Sunday at 5:15 P.M. Several stops are made along the way. This route is so scenic that many make the train trip a one-day excursion, going as far as Nanaimo and spending a few hours in the city before returning; it's a cheap day out at under $40 for the round-trip. Make reservations as far ahead as possible in summer, and buy your ticket the day before departure. For more information, stop in at the station, 450 Pandora Ave., 250/383-4324 or 800/561-8630, website www.viarail.ca.

By Bus

Laidlaw, 250/385-4411 or 800/318-0818, website www.victoriatours.com, serves all of Vancouver Island from the main bus depot centrally located in downtown Victoria at 710 Douglas St. (corner of Belleville Street). The depot is small, and it gets extremely busy during summer; schedules are posted, as are fares. No bookings are taken, so just roll up, pay the fare, and jump aboard. Seven buses daily depart Victoria for Nanaimo, with one continuing to Tofino, three to Campbell River, and one or two to Port Hardy (depending on ferry departures from Port Hardy to Prince Rupert). Fares are calculated on "sectors" rather than exact destinations, but the fare to Nanaimo is under $25, to Tofino $55; to Campbell River $54; and to Port Hardy $96.

including Fisherman's Wharf, Ocean Pointe Resort, and Westbay Marine Village, while the other heads up the Gorge Waterway; $3 per sector, or make the round-trip as a tour for $14.

Taxi

Taxis operate on a meter system, charging $2.75 at the initial flag drop plus around $2 per kilometer. Call **Blue Bird Cabs** at 250/382-3611 or 800/665-7055; **Empress Taxi** at 250/381-2222; or **Victoria Taxi** at 250/383-7111.

Car Rental

Victoria is home to all the major car rental agencies. Demand is high through summer, so book well in advance. If you don't want to return the car to Victoria, you'll probably have to pay a drop charge; usually the farther up the island you go, the higher the fee. For a used car in the low season, rates start around $30 a day, plus 15 cents per kilometer, plus gas. As with accommodations and many attractions, prices are higher in peak tourist periods. Rental car agencies in Victoria include: **Ada Rent a Used Car,** 250/474-3455; **Avis,** 250/386-8468 or 800/879-2847; **Budget,** 250/953-5300 or 800/668-9833; **Enterprise,** 250/475-6900 or 800/736-8222; **Hertz,** 250/656-2312 or 800/263-0600; **Island Auto Rentals,** 250/384-4881; **National,** 250/386-1213 or 800/387-4747; **Rent-a-wreck,** 250/384-5343; and **Thrifty,** 250/383-3659 or 800/847-4389.

Bikes and Such

Victoria doesn't have the great network of bicycle paths that Vancouver boasts, but bike-rental shops are nevertheless plentiful. Try: **Sports Rent,** 611 Discovery St., 250/385-7368; **James Bay Bicycle Works,** 131 Menzies St., 250/380-1664; or **Oak Bay Bicycle,** 1968 Oak Bay Ave., 250/598-4111. Expect to pay from around $8 an hour, $25 per day. As well as renting bikes, **Harbour Rentals,** directly opposite the information center at 811 Wharf St., 250/995-1661, rents strollers, scooters, and a variety of watercraft.

SERVICES AND INFORMATION

Emergency Services

In a medical emergency call 911 or contact **Royal Jubilee Hospital,** 1900 Fort St., 250/370-8000, or **Victoria General Hospital,** 1 Hospital Way, 250/727-4212. For non-urgent cases, a handy facility is **James Bay Medical Treatment Centre,** 230 Menzies St., 250/388-9934. The **Cresta Dental Centre** is at 3170 Tillicum Rd. (at Burnside St.), 250/384-7711. **Shopper's Drug Mart,** at 1222 Douglas St., 250/381-4321, is open daily 7 A.M.–7 P.M.

Other Services

The main **post office** is on the corner of Yates and Douglas Streets.

To change your money to the colorful Canadian variety, head to any of the major banks or to **Calforex,** in the Victoria Conference Centre at 724 Douglas St., 250/384-6631.

Lens & Shutter, right downtown at 615 Fort St., 250/383-7443, offers full photographic services, including one-hour photofinishing, sales, and repairs.

Maytag Homestyle Laundry is at 1309 Cook St., 250/386-1799.

Books and Bookstores

Greater Victoria Public Library is at 735 Broughton St., at the corner of Courtney St.,
250/382-7241. It's open Mon.–Fri. 9 A.M.–6 P.M., Saturday 9 A.M.–1 P.M. **Crown Publications,** 521 Fort St., 250/386-4636, is a specialty bookstore with a great selection of western Canadiana and maps. Right downtown, **Munro's Bookstore,** 1108 Government St., 250/382-2464 or 888/243-2464, is in a magnificent neoclassical building that originally opened as the Royal Bank in 1909. Munro's may be the grandest bookstore in town, but it's not the largest. That distinction goes to **Chapters,** at 1212 Douglas St., 250/380-9009, open Mon.–Sat. 8 A.M.–11 P.M., Sunday 9 A.M.–11 P.M. For new books at discounted prices, head to **Book Ends,** 907 Yates St., 250/380-0740. For secondhand and rare west coast and nautical titles, search out **Wells Books,** 824 Fort St., 250/360-2929. Also, **Snowdon's Book Store,** 619 Johnson St., 250/383-8131, holds a good selection of secondhand titles.

Tourist Information

Tourism Victoria runs the bright, modern **Victoria Visitor Info Centre,** 812 Wharf St. on the Inner Harbour, 250/953-2033 or 800/663-3883 (accommodations reservations), website www.tourismvictoria.com. The friendly staff can answer most of your questions. They also book accommodations, tours and charters, restaurants, entertainment, and transportation, all at no extra cost; sell local bus passes and map books with detailed area-by-area maps; and stock an enormous selection of tourist brochures. Also collect the free *Accommodations* publication and the free local news and entertainment papers—the best way to find out what's happening in Victoria while you're in town. The center is open year-round daily 9 A.M.–5 P.M. Coming off the ferry from Vancouver, stop in at **Saanich Peninsula Visitor Info Centre,** three km south of the terminal, 250/656-0525, website www.spcoc.org; open daily 9 A.M.–5 P.M. For **weather forecasts** call 250/656-3978, or for **marine weather** forecasts call 250/656-7515.

Vicinity of Victoria

Two highways lead out of Victoria: Highway 14 heads west and Highway 1 heads north. Highway 14 is a spectacular coastal route that ends in **Port Renfrew,** 104 km from Victoria. Along this ocean-hugging stretch of road are provincial parks, delightful oceanfront lodgings, and a panorama that extends across Juan de Fuca Strait to the snowcapped peaks of the Olympic Mountains in Washington State. Port Renfrew is the southern terminus of the rugged and remote 77-km **West Coast Trail,** which challenges hikers from around the world each summer. Highway 1 leads north from Victoria to **Duncan, Chemainus,** and **Ladysmith,** each with its own particular charm. West of Duncan are massive **Cowichan Lake,** an inland paradise for anglers and boaters, and **Carmanah Walbran Provincial Park,** protecting a remote watershed full of ancient Sitka spruce that miraculously escaped logging.

SOOKE

About 34 km from Victoria, Sooke (pop. 4,500) is a logging, fishing, and farming center best known for a lodge that combines luxurious accommodations with one of Canada's most renowned restaurants. As far as actual local sights go, **Sooke Regional Museum** lies just beyond Sooke River Bridge on the corner of Sooke and Phillips Roads, 250/642-6351. When you've finished admiring the historic artifacts, relax on the grassy area in front or wander around the back to count all 478 growth rings on the cross-section of a giant spruce tree. The museum is open daily 9 A.M.–6 P.M., and it also houses the **Sooke Visitor Info Centre.**

Sooke Harbour House

Combining the elegance of an upmarket country-style inn with the atmosphere of an exclusive oceanfront resort, Sooke Harbour House, 1528 Whiffen Spit Rd., 250/642-3421 or 800/889-9688, website www.sookeharbourhouse.com, is one of British Columbia's finest accommodations

as well as one of its most renowned restaurants. It sits high above the ocean on a bluff that affords panoramic views across the ocean. Each of the 28 well-appointed rooms has views, with the more expensive ones featuring a hot tub and fireplace. Rates range $270–465 s or d. On the grounds, three rooms of what was originally a private residence have been converted to a restaurant. The decor is country-style simple, not that anything could possibly take away from the food and views. The menu changes daily, but most dishes feature local seafood, prepared to perfection with vegetables and herbs picked straight from the surrounding garden. Many diners disregard the cost and choose the eight-course table d'hôte menu ($99 pp), which represents a wide variety of seafood, including wild sea asparagus harvested from tidal pools below the restaurant. Otherwise, dinner entrées range $26.50–38. The cellar is almost renowned as the food—it holds upward of 10,000 bottles. The restaurant is open daily from 5 P.M.; make reservations well in advance.

CONTINUING ALONG HIGHWAY 14 TO PORT RENFREW

The road west from Sooke takes you past gray pebbly beaches scattered with shells and driftwood, past **Gordon's Beach** to 59-hectare **French Beach Provincial Park** (about 20 km from Sooke). Here you can wander down through a lush forest of Douglas fir and Sitka spruce to watch Pacific breakers crashing up on the beach—and keep an eye open for orcas and gray whales. It's a great place for a windswept walk, a picnic, or camping ($12 per night, pit toilets provided). An information board at the park entrance posts fairly detailed maps and articles on area beaches, points of interest, plants, and wildlife.

Continuing west, the highway winds up and down forested hills for another 12 km or so, passing evidence of regular logging as well as signposted forest trails to sandy beaches. Along this stretch of coast are two great accommodations. The first, three km beyond French Beach, is **Point No Point Lodge,** 250/646-2020, website www.pointnopointresort.com, which features 26 beautiful log cabins, each with views, a full kitchen, and fireplace. Explore the shore out front, relax on the nearby beach, or scan the horizon for migrating whales, with the Olympic Mountains as a backdrop. Rates range $130–220 s or d, with the least expensive cabins older and smaller (you're really paying for the position). Meals are available in the lodge restaurant. Two km farther west, high upon oceanfront cliffs, **Fossil Bay Resort,** 250/646-2073, website www.fossilbay.com, offers six modern cottages, each with a hot tub, private balcony, fireplace, king-size bed, and full kitchen; $240 s or d, discounted for more than two nights. These two places are understandably popular, so make reservations well in advance, especially for weekends.

Jordan River

When you emerge at the small logging town of Jordan River, take time to take in the smells of the ocean and the surrounding windswept landscape. The town comprises only a few houses, a local logging operation, and a small recreation area. The recreation area lies on a point at the mouth of the Jordan River. It's not the best camping spot you'll ever come across, but no signs prohibit overnight stays; surfers often spend the night here, waiting for the swells to rise and the long right-handed waves known as Jordans to crank up. Note: **Sports Rent,** 611 Discovery St., Victoria, 250/385-7368, rents surfboards and wetsuits for $18 per day.

Across the road from the ocean is **Shakies,** a popular burger stand, and a little farther along is **Breakers,** a small café with great ocean views.

China Beach

Three km west of Jordan River, a 700-meter (15 minutes) one-way trail leads through Sitka spruce to pebbly China Beach, which is strewn with

driftwood and backed by a couple of protected picnic sites. Camping (back up by the highway) is $12 per night. The beach and campground have recently been incorporated within 1,277-hectare **Juan de Fuca Provincial Park,** which protects a narrow coastal strip between Jordan River and Botanical Beach near Port Renfrew. China Beach is also the beginning of the 47-km **Juan de Fuca Trail,** a coastal hiking route that ends at Port Renfrew.

Port Renfrew

This small seaside community clings to the rugged shoreline of Port San Juan, 104 km from Victoria. An eclectic array of houses leads down the hill to the waterfront. Follow the signs to **Botanical Beach,** a fascinating intertidal pool area where low tide exposes all sorts of marine creatures at the foot of scoured-out sandstone cliffs. The road to the beach is rough and can be impassable in winter.

Accommodations are available at the **Trailhead Resort,** in the heart of town, 250/647-5468, website www.trailhead-resort.com. The motel rooms are relatively new, basic but practical, with a balcony out front; $75 s or d. Campers enjoy a pleasant wooded setting beyond the main lodge and pay just $5 pp per night. On site a store sells camping and fishing gear. Right on the water, **Arbutus Beach Lodge,** 5 Queesto Dr., 250/647-5458, offers basic accommodations but a great communal lounge and deck area overlooking the ocean. Rates of $65–95 s or d include a light breakfast. Beyond town, at the mouth of the San Juan River, **Port Renfrew Marina and RV Park,** 250/647-5430, offers open tent sites but no showers; $15–17. Boat charters and fishing gear are available.

San Juan Valley

If you don't want to return to Victoria along Highway 14, and you're eventually heading north up the island, consider taking the gravel road

butter clam

© LOUISE FOOTE

from Port Renfrew through the San Juan Valley to **Lake Cowichan.** The road's usually in good condition, but find out from locals the present conditions and whether logging is active in the area—logging trucks don't give way, *you* do. Make sure you have enough gas, and drive with your headlights on so the trucks see you from a good distance. You'll find campgrounds at **Fairy Lake,** six km from Port Renfrew, and **Lizard Lake,** 12 km farther along the road; both offer limited facilities. Camping is $6 per night.

THE WEST COAST TRAIL

The magnificent West Coast Trail meanders 77 km along Vancouver Island's untamed western shoreline, through the West Coast Trail unit of **Pacific Rim National Park.** It's one of the world's great hikes, exhilaratingly challenging, incredibly beautiful, and very satisfying—many hikers come back to do it again. The very quickest hikers can complete the trail in four days, but by allowing six, seven, or eight days you'll have time to fully enjoy the adventure. The trail extends from the mouth of the Gordon River near Port Renfrew to Pachena Bay, near the remote fishing village of Bamfield on Barkley Sound. Along the way you'll wander along beaches, steep clifftops, and slippery banks; ford rivers by rope, suspension bridge, or ferry; climb down sandstone cliffs by ladder; cross slippery boardwalks, muddy slopes, bogs, and deep gullies; and balance on fallen logs. But for all your efforts you're rewarded with panoramic views of sand and sea, dense lush rainforest, waterfalls cascading into deep pools, all kinds of wildlife—gray whales, eagles, sea lions, seals, and seabirds—and the constant roar and hiss of the Pacific surf pummeling the sand.

History

This stretch of the coast, the southernmost section of Pacific Rim National Park, was nicknamed "Graveyard of the Pacific" due to the great number of shipwrecks that occurred along here. After the SS *Valencia* ran aground in 1906 and most of the passengers and crew drowned or died from exposure, the Canadian government constructed a lifesaving trail to help future survivors penetrate the dense coastal forest. The trail followed a rugged telegraph route toward Victoria that connected lighthouses and towns and was kept open by telegraph linesmen and lighthouse keepers. Since the trail was incorporated into Pacific Rim National Park in the mid-1960s,

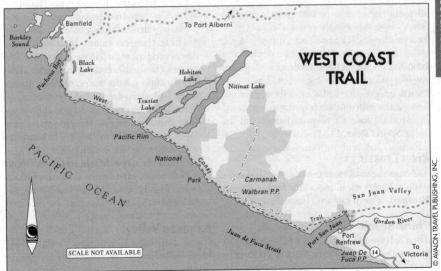

it has gained enormous popularity. A quota system is now in use to prevent degradation of the fragile coastal environment.

Hiking Conditions

The trail can be hiked in either direction, so take your choice. The first two days out from Gordon River traverse difficult terrain, meaning more enjoyable hiking for the remaining days. The first two days out from Pachena Bay are relatively easy, meaning a lighter pack for the more-difficult section. West Coast Trail Express offers transportation between trailheads, but if you leave your vehicle at Port Renfrew and return by bus, you won't have to shuttle a vehicle out to remote Bamfield. Pachena Bay lies 11 km from Bamfield, and taxis operate between the two points.

Hikers must be totally self-sufficient, as no facilities exist along the route. Go with at least two other people, and travel as light as possible. Wear comfortable hiking boots, and take a stove, at least 15 meters of strong light rope, head-to-toe waterproof gear (keep your spare clothes and sleeping bag in a plastic bag), a small amount of fire starter for an emergency, suntan lotion, insect repellent, a first-aid kit (for cuts, burns, sprains, and blisters), and waterproof matches. Also take enough cash to pay for boat crossings (allow $15) and transportation at the end of the trail (reservations required). Rainfall is least likely in the summer; July is generally the driest month, but be prepared for rain, strong winds, thick fog, and muddy trail conditions even then. The trail is closed 1 Oct.–15 April. Not only is traveling through this period treacherous due to guaranteed bad weather and no trail maintenance, but the rivers can't be crossed.

River Crossings

Two major water crossings along the trail necessitate ferry service. One is at the Gordon River outside of Port Renfrew. The other, midway along the trail, crosses Nitinat Narrows, the treacherous mouth of tidal Nitinat Lake. Ferries run 15 April–30 Sept. daily 9 A.M.–5 P.M.; $5 per person. These crossings cannot be made without the ferry services. Crossing fees totaling $25

pp are collected on behalf of private operators in conjunction with the trail user fee (see below).

Trail User Fee

A quota system is in effect on the trail to reduce the environmental impact caused by overuse. Between 15 April and 30 September only 52 hikers a day are issued permits to start down the trail (26 from each end). Reservations for 40 of the 52 slots are accepted starting 1 March for the following season; call Tourism BC at 250/387-1642 or 800/435-5622 7 A.M.–6 P.M. (Pacific time) daily. The nonrefundable reservation fee is $25 per person, which includes a waterproof trail map. The remaining 12 spots a day are allocated on a first-come, first-served basis (six from each end; no reservation fee), but expect a wait of up to three days in summer. Once at Port Renfrew or Bamfield, all hikers must head for the registration office to obtain a trail-use permit, which costs an additional $70 per person. These permits are compulsory and checked regularly, and you'll need to show one to board the two ferries along the trail.

Transportation

Getting to and from either end of the trail is made easier by **West Coast Trail Express,** 250/477-8700, website www.trailbus.com, which departs Victoria daily in the morning to both ends of the trail. The fare between Victoria and Port Renfrew is $30 one-way, while between Victoria and Pachena Bay it's $50. Pick-ups are made along the way, including from the Swartz Bay ferry terminal ($5 extra), Nanaimo, and Port Alberni.

With your own transportation, leave your vehicle at either end of the trail and pay $15 for transportation between trailheads. The company also rents camping and hiking gear.

To get to the northern end of the trail from Port Alberni, catch the delightful **MV** *Lady Rose,* 250/723-8313 or 800/663-7192, departing Alberni Harbour Quay on Tuesday, Thursday, and Saturday at 8 A.M. and arriving Bamfield at 12:30 P.M. the same day. The fare is $23 each way.

Information

The first step in planning to hike the West Coast

Trail is to request the free *West Coast Trail Hiker Preparation Guide* from park headquarters; write Superintendent, Pacific Rim National Park, P.O. Box 280, Ucluelet, BC V0R 3A0, 250/726-7721. The invaluable guide covers everything you need to know, including an overview of what to expect, instructions on trail user fees, a list of equipment you should take, a list of relevant literature, tide tables, and advertisements for companies offering trailhead transportation. A condensed version of this package is available on the website www.parkscanada.gc.ca/pacrim.

Seasonal park information/registration centers are in Port Renfrew, 250/647-5434, and Pachena Bay, 250/728-3234. The recommended topographic map *West Coast Trail, Pacific Rim National Park—Port Renfrew to Bamfield* is available at most specialty map stores, as well as at the information centers (registration offices) at each end of the trail. The cost of a trail-use permit includes this map. The best reference book for trail preparation is the *Official Guidebook to Pacific Rim National Park Preserve,* available through official park outlets.

DUNCAN

Duncan, self-proclaimed "City of Totems," lies at the junction of Highways 1 and 18, about 60 km north of Victoria. The small city of 5,500 serves the surrounding farming and forestry communities of the Cowichan Valley. Native carvers, many from the local Cowichan band, have created some 80 intricate and colorful totem poles here. Look for the poles along the main highway near the information center, beside the railway station in the old section of town, by City Hall, and inside local businesses.

Sights
Follow the signs off the main highway to the city center for a quick wander around the renovated **Old Town.** (Free two-hour parking is available by the old railway station on Canada Avenue.) Start your totem-pole hunt here or just wander down the streets opposite the railway station to appreciate some of the pleasing older architecture, such as City Hall on the corner of

Kenneth and Craig Streets. Two distinctly different native carvings stand side by side behind City Hall—a Native American carving and a New Zealand Maori carving donated by Duncan's sister city, Kaikohe.

Apart from the famous totem poles, Duncan's main attraction is the excellent **Quw'utsun' Cultural Centre,** on the south side of downtown at 200 Cowichan Way, 250/746-8119. Representing the arts, crafts, legends, and traditions of a 3,500-strong Quw'utsun' population spread through the Cowichan Valley, this facility features a long house, a carving shed, dance performances, and a café with native cuisine. It's open daily 9 A.M.–6 P.M. (until 5 P.M. outside summer) and admission is adult $10, senior $8, child $6.

Another local attraction is the 40-hectare **BC Forest Discovery Centre,** one km north of town, 250/715-1113. You can catch a ride on an old steam train and puff back in time, through the forest and past a farmstead, a logging camp, and Somenos Lake. Then check out the working sawmill, restored planer mill, blacksmith's shop, and forestry and lumber displays. The main museum building holds modern displays pertaining to the industry, including hands-on and interactive computer displays and an interesting audiovisual. The grounds are a pleasant place to wander—through shady glades of trees (most identified) or over to the pond where you'll find a gaggle of friendly geese awaiting a tasty morsel. It's open May–Sept. daily 10 A.M.–6 P.M.; admission is adult $8, senior and child $7.

Practicalities
Motels line the highway through town. Best of the bunch is the **Days Inn,** south of the river at 5325 Hwy. 1, 250/748-0331, website www.daysinn.com. The 35 renovated rooms go for $69–99 s or d. Also south of the river is the turnoff to **Duncan RV Park and Campground,** 2950 Boys Rd., 250/748-8511, which is one block west of the highway, right beside the river. Sites are $16–20; full hookups available.

Always crowded with locals, **Arbutus Cafe,** on the corner of Kenneth and Jubilee Streets, 250/746-5443, concocts a great shrimp salad for

$7, sandwiches and hamburgers for $5–9, and specialty pies from $4.

Stop at **Duncan Visitor Info Centre,** on the west side of the highway in Overwaitea Plaza, 250/746-4636, website www.duncancc.bc.ca, for the complete rundown on the area. The center staff provides information on local hiking and fishing, and on traveling the logging roads beyond Lake Cowichan. They also offer a map showing the location of all Duncan's totem poles. Hours are Mon.–Sat. 9 A.M.–5 P.M.

LAKE COWICHAN AND VICINITY

Cowichan River

This famous salmon and steelhead fishing river has its source at Lake Cowichan, draining into the Strait of Georgia beyond Duncan. Much of its length is protected by **Cowichan River Provincial Park,** which extends over 750 hectares and 20 km. There are three access points to the park, including Skutz Falls, where salmon spawn each fall. Camping is $12. **Sahtlam Lodge and Cabins,** 5720 Riverbottom Rd. W, 250/748-7738 or 877/748-7738, website www.sahtlamlodge.com, is right on the river, closer to Duncan than Lake Cowichan. Three cabins are spread across the property, and each is equipped with an old-style fireplace, woodstove, and full kitchen. Rates of $150 s, $180 d include a breakfast basket delivered daily to your cabin. Overlooking the river, the original 1920s lodge now houses an intimate restaurant open Thurs.–Sun. for dinner.

Lake Cowichan

Don a good pair of walking shoes, grab your swimsuit, sleeping bag, fishing pole, and frying pan, and head west from Duncan to Lake Cowichan, Vancouver Island's second-largest lake. The massive, 32-km-long inland waterway, called Kaatza ("Land Warmed by Sun") by local Coast Salish, is a popular spot for canoeing, water-skiing, swimming, and especially fishing—the lake and river are well stocked with kokanee and trout (steelhead, rainbow, brown, and cut-throat). Boat-launching facilities and excellent campsites are found at regular intervals along the lakeshore. Numerous logging roads, some paved, encircle the lake (75 km round-trip) and provide hikers access into the adjacent wilderness, which includes the legendary **Carmanah Valley** (see Carmanah Walbran Provincial Park, below).

The sleepy lakeside village of **Lake Cowichan** (pop. 3,200) lies on the eastern arm of Cowichan Lake, 30 km from Duncan. Campers have the choice of staying at the local municipal campground, **Lakeview Park,** three km west of Lake Cowichan, 250/749-6244, $17 per night, or **Gordon Bay Provincial Park,** on the south side of the lake 23 km farther west, $18.50 per night. Both campgrounds have hot showers. **Rail's End Pub,** 109 Southshore Rd., 250/749-4001, has a good family-style restaurant overlooking the outlet of Cowichan Lake; open daily from 11 A.M.

On the waterfront is **Cowichan Lake Visitor Info Centre,** 125 Southshore Rd., 250/749-3244, open daily in summer Mon.–Sat. 9 A.M.–4 P.M., Sunday 1–4 P.M. The center is a good source of information on fishing conditions and on the logging roads leading to the Carmanah Valley and Port Renfrew. Next door is the **Kaatza Station Museum,** at the end of a rail line that once linked the lake to the main line up Vancouver Island's east coast.

Carmanah Walbran Provincial Park

Eyed by logging companies for many years, the remote **Carmanah Valley** was first protected with provincial park status in 1990. The Upper Carmanah Valley and adjacent Walbran Valley were added in 1995, providing complete protection of the 16,450-hectare watershed. For environmentalists, creation of the park was a major victory—this mist-shrouded valley extending all the way to the rugged west coast holds an old-growth forest of absolute wonder. Man's impact in the valley has been almost nonexistent. Many 800-year-old Sitka spruce and 1,000-year-old cedar trees—some of the world's oldest—rise up to 95 meters off the damp valley floor here. Others lie where they've fallen, their slowly decaying moss- and fern-cloaked hulks providing homes for thousands of small mammals and insects.

It's possible to reach the park via logging roads from Port Renfrew in the south and Port Alberni in the north, but the easiest access is gained by following the south shore of Cowichan Lake to Nitinat Main, a logging road that leads south to Nitinat Junction (no services). There the road is joined by a logging road from Port Alberni. From this point Nitinat Main continues south to a bridge across the Caycuse River. Take the first right after crossing the river. This is Rosander Main, a rough road that dead-ends at the park boundary. The park is signposted from Nitinat Junction, but the signs are small and easy to miss.

From the road's-end parking lot, a rough 1.3-km hiking trail (30 minutes each way) descends to the valley floor and Carmanah Creek. From the creek, trails lead upstream to the Three Sisters (2.5 km; 40 minutes), through Grunt's Grove to August Creek (7.5 km; two hours), and downstream through a grove of Sitka spruce named for Randy Stoltmann, a legendary environmentalist who first brought the valley's giants to the world's attention (2.4 km; 40 minutes).

Facilities in the park are limited to a primitive camping area at the end of the access road; $5 pp per night. For park information call the South Vancouver Island District office of BC Parks, 250/391-2300.

NORTH TOWARD NANAIMO

Chemainus

Continuing north from Duncan, the next place well worth a visit is the small town of Chemainus (pop. 600), which bills itself as "The Little Town that Did." Did what, you ask? Well, Chemainus has always been a sleepy little mill town; its first sawmill dates back to 1862. In 1982, MacMillan Bloedel shut down the town's antiquated mill, which employed 400 people, replacing it a year later with a modern mill em-

ploying only 155 people. Chemainiacs did not want their town to die. Needing tourists, they hired local artists to cover many of the town's plain walls with larger-than-life murals depicting the town's history and culture. The result was outstanding. In 1983, the town received a First Place award at a downtown revitalization competition held in New York.

Follow the signs to Chemainus from Highway 1 and park at **Chemainus Visitor Info Centre,** 9758 Chemainus Rd., 250/246-3944 (open May–Sept. daily 9 A.M.–5 P.M.), where you'll see the first enormous mural—a street scene. From there you can explore the rest of Chemainus on foot, following the yellow footprints into town. Walk down to shady, waterfront **Heritage Park,** passing a mural information booth (where there's a small replica of the waterwheel that powered the original 1862 sawmill) and a detailed map of the town. Then wander through the park to the small museum on Maple Street.

Chemainus Tours, 250/246-5055, operates horse-drawn carriage rides around town, passing all the murals along the route. The rides depart from Waterwheel Park every half hour; adult $6, senior $5, child $3.50.

Ladysmith

Ladysmith's main claim to fame is its location straddling the 49th parallel, the invisible boundary line separating Canada from the United States. After much bargaining for the 1846 Oregon Treaty, Canada got to keep all of Vancouver Island despite the 49th parallel chopping the island in two. Ladysmith was originally designed as a dormitory and recreation town for Nanaimo coal miners. Today the pretty little waterfront village 25 km north of Duncan is home to loggers and commercial fishermen. If you appreciate old-style architecture, wander through town to see many of the original buildings still in use.

Ladysmith's main claim to fame is its location straddling the 49th parallel, the invisible boundary line separating Canada from the United States. After much bargaining for the 1846 Oregon Treaty, Canada got to keep all of Vancouver Island despite the 49th parallel chopping the island in two.

VANCOUVER ISLAND

Southern Gulf Islands

This group of islands lies in the Strait of Georgia, off the southeastern coast of Vancouver Island and just north of Washington's San Juan Islands, which are part of the same archipelago. Five of the islands—Salt Spring, North Pender, Galiano, Mayne, and Saturna—are populated. The largest of the islands, Salt Spring, is home to more than triple the population of the other four combined.

The islands' mild, almost Mediterranean climate, beautiful pastoral scenery, driftwood-strewn beaches, and prolific marinelife (sea lions, bald eagles, harbor seals, killer whales, blue herons, cormorants, and diving ducks, among other species) are a haven from the hectic urban life of nearby Vancouver and Victoria. These appealing qualities have attracted creative people in search of life in the slow lane, as well as swarms of hikers, campers, cyclists, canoeists, fishermen, beachcombers, island-hoppers, and art lovers.

Getting There and Around
B.C. Ferries, 250/386-3431 or 888/223-3779, website www.bcferries.com, operates scheduled services among the Southern Gulf Islands and out to the islands from both the B.C. mainland and Vancouver Island. See the Transportation sections for the individual islands listed below for specific ferry information. If you're catching the ferry between Tsawwassen and the Southern Gulf Islands you need to make reservations. From Swartz Bay, Crofton, and Chemainus, no reservations are necessary.

All ferries take cars, motorcycles, bicycles, canoes, and kayaks. Keep in mind that some of the islands are large, and if you don't have your own transportation you'll see only the ferry terminal area or have to fork out for a taxi (available on some islands) to see the rest. Traveling the islands by bicycle or sea kayak is both feasible and rewarding.

Other Practicalities
Accommodations are abundant throughout the islands. Make reservations as far in advance as possible, especially for weekends. Call direct or book through the **Canadian Gulf Islands B&B Reservation Service,** 250/539-3089, website www.gulfislandreservations.com. This agency books not only bed and breakfasts but also motels and resorts, and can organize tours. You'll also find plenty of campsites in the provincial parks on the islands. In summer, grab a campsite by midafternoon.

Before you head for the islands, get the latest rundown from the Information Centre in downtown Victoria, from the Saanich Peninsula Info Centre on Highway 17 near the Swartz Bay Ferry Terminal, or from Tourism Association of Vancouver Island, 250/754-3500, website www.islands.bc.ca. You might also want to pick up a copy of *The Gulf Islands Explorer,* published by Whitecap Books and available in most local bookstores.

SALT SPRING ISLAND
Largest of the Southern Gulf Islands, Salt Spring (pop. 9,500) lies close to the coast of Vancouver Island, immediately north of Saanich Inlet. Ferries link the south and north ends of the island to Vancouver Island, and myriad roads converge on the service town of **Ganges.** The laid-back island is home to a large number of artisans, along with hobby farmers, retirees, and those attracted by island life.

Salt Spring Island Visitor Info Centre is on the north side of the island in Ganges, at 121 Lower Ganges Rd., 250/537-5252, website www.saltspringisland.bc.ca. It's open in summer daily 8 A.M.–6 P.M., the rest of the year Mon.–Fri. 8:30 A.M.–4:30 P.M.

Sights and Recreation
From the Fulford Harbour ferry terminal, take Beaver Point Road east to 486-hectare **Ruckle Provincial Park.** The access road ends at the rocky headland of Beaver Point, from where trails

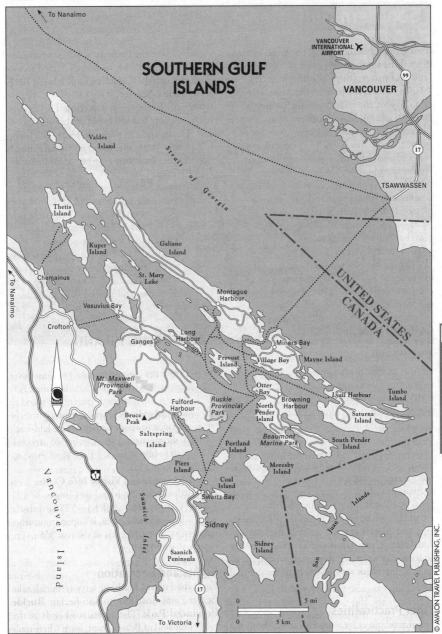

To Nanaimo

VANCOUVER INTERNATIONAL AIRPORT

VANCOUVER

99

17

TSAWWASSEN

SOUTHERN GULF ISLANDS

Valdes Island

Strait of Georgia

Thetis Island

Kuper Island

Galiano Island

UNITED STATES
CANADA

Chemainus

To Nanaimo

St. Mary Lake

Vesuvius Bay

Montague Harbour

Crofton

Long Harbour

Ganges

Miners Bay

Prevost Island

Village Bay

Mayne Island

Mt. Maxwell Provincial Park

Otter Bay

Lyall Harbour

Tumbo Island

Fulford Harbour

Ruckle Provincial Park

North Pender Island

Browning Harbour

Saturna Island

Bruce Peak

Saltspring Island

Portland Island

Beaumont Marine Park

South Pender Island

Piers Island

Moresby Island

Coal Island

Swartz Bay

Sidney

Vancouver Island

Saanich Inlet

Sidney Island

Juan Islands

Saanich Peninsula

San

17

To Victoria

0   5 mi

0   5 km

© AVALON TRAVEL PUBLISHING, INC.

VANCOUVER ISLAND

© ANDREW HEMPSTEAD

Vesuvius Bay

lead north along the coastline, providing great views across to North Pender Island.

Along the road north to Ganges, small **Mt. Maxwell Provincial Park** protects the slopes of its namesake mountain. From the 588-meter summit, views extend south across the island to Vancouver Island and east to the other Gulf Islands. South of Mt. Maxwell is 704-meter **Mount Bruce,** the island's highest peak. A rough unsealed road off Musgrave Road leads to the summit.

Although the island offers good hiking opportunities, it's better known for water-oriented activities such as kayaking, boating, and fishing. Based at Fulford Harbour, **Saltspring Kayaking,** 250/653-4222, offers guided trips, including a two-hour sunset paddle for $35 pp. The company also rents kayaks for a reasonable $25 per day (additional days just $10) and will deliver anywhere on the island for $10. **Salt Spring Marine Rentals,** Salt Spring Marina,

250/537-9100 or 800/334-6629, rents boats and offers fishing charters.

Accommodations and Camping

The island's least expensive accommodation is the **Salt Spring Island Hostel,** on the east side of the island at 640 Cusheon Lake Rd., 250/537-4149. As well as regular dorms, three tepees and two tree houses are spread through the four-hectare property. One of the tree houses is accessed via a ladder and hatch. The interior features a tree through the middle, a skylight over the bed, and wicker furniture. All regular beds are $17 pp; $60 s or d for the tree house. **Maple Ridge Cottages,** on St. Mary Lake at 301 Tripp Rd., 250/537-5977, is a lakefront property with canoes and kayaks available for guest use. Each of the nine cottages has a kitchen, private deck, and fireplace. Rates range $100–150 s or d. In the south is one of the island's premier accommodations, **A Perfect Perch Bed and**

Breakfast, 225 Armand Way, 250/653-2030 or 888/663-2030, a magnificent modern home set on two hectares high above sea level, with views extending west to Vancouver Island. Each of the three rooms has a large hot tub, balcony, and private entrance. The rates of $135–175 s or d include a full breakfast. **Salt Springs Spa Resort,** 1460 North Beach Rd., 250/537-4111 or 800/665-0039, website www.saltspringsresort .com, is a waterfront spa resort offering Quonset-shaped cabins, each casually yet elegantly furnished and containing a kitchen and fireplace. As well as full spa services, guests have use of rowboats, mountain bikes, a game room, and a barbecue area. Standard summer rates are $239 s or d, but these are discounted as low as $100 in winter.

The campground in **Ruckle Provincial Park** holds 78 sites in a forest of Douglas fir overlooking Swanson Channel. All sites are a short walk from the parking lot, making this place unsuitable for RVs; $12 per night. On the north side of the island on St. Mary Lake **Lakeside Gardens Resort,** 250/537-5773, offers sites with full hookups for $18–22 and self-contained cottages for $50–100, along with showers and a beach with boat rentals.

Transportation

Closest of the Southern Gulf Islands to Vancouver Island, Salt Spring is served by **B.C. Ferries,** 250/386-3431. Ferries run 10–12 times daily between Swartz Bay and Fulford Harbour, and even more frequently between Vesuvius Bay, at the island's north end, and Crofton. Fares for travel on either route are the same, and as all prices are for the round-trip you can leave the island from either end at no extra charge. Peak round-trip fares are adult $6.25, child $3.25, vehicle $21.55.

From the B.C. mainland, at least two sailings a day leave the Tsawwassen terminal (south of downtown Vancouver), 604/669-1211, bound for Long Harbour on the east side of Salt Spring Island. The night sailings are nonstop (or stop just once), while all others make multiple stops, extending the 80-minute trip to three hours. The peak one-way fare from Tsawwassen to Salt

Spring Island is adult $9, child $4.50, vehicle $35.50.

Long Harbour is also the departure point for interisland travel. Sailings to North Pender Island are direct; to all other islands at least one stop is required. Peak fares for all interisland travel are the same: adult $3, child $1.50, vehicle $7, bicycle 75 cents, canoe or kayak $1.75.

NORTH PENDER ISLAND

A short ferry ride from Salt Spring Island's Long Harbour ferry terminal, this 24-square-km island (pop. 2,000) has many great little beaches and provides ocean access at over 20 points. One of the nicest spots is **Hamilton Beach** on Browning Harbour. This is also the main service area, from where roads radiate out to all points of the island. One road leads across a rickety old wooden bridge to **South Pender Island,** site of **Beaumont Provincial Marine Park.**

Pender Island Visitor Info Centre is east of the ferry terminal, up the hill, 250/629-6541. The small booth is open through summer daily 9 A.M.–6 P.M.

Accommodations and Camping

The least expensive way to enjoy an overnight stay on North Pender Island is to camp at **Prior Centennial Provincial Park,** six km south of the Otter Bay ferry terminal. Sites are primitive, with no showers or hookups, but the location is excellent; $12 per night. The island's premier accommodation is the **Oceanside Inn,** on Armadale Rd. five km from the ferry terminal, 250/629-6691, website www.penderisland.com. Each room is elegantly furnished, and a wide balcony takes advantage of the waterfront location. Off-season rates start at $129 s or d, rising to $175–225 in summer. Rates include breakfast, and the small luxurious include fluffy bathrobes.

Transportation

Up to seven times a day ferries depart the Swartz Bay terminal, 250/656-5571, for North Pender Island. Most sailings are direct (40 minutes), although a couple of the early-morning trips go via Galiano and Mayne Islands (over two hours), so check the timetable carefully before boarding. The peak round-trip fare is adult $6.25, child $3.25, vehicle $20.50. Sailings from the Tsawwassen ferry terminal, 604/669-1211, depart twice daily; adult $9, child $4.50, vehicle $35.50. The peak one-way fare between North Pender Island and any of Salt Spring, Mayne, Galiano, and Saturna Islands is adult $3, child $1.50, vehicle $7.

GALIANO ISLAND

Named for a Spanish explorer who sailed through the Strait of Georgia over 200 years ago, this long, narrow island, 27 km from north to south but only a few km wide, lies north of Salt Spring Island. Most of the population lives in the south, around the ferry terminal at Sturdies Bay. Right at the terminal is **Galiano Island Visitor Info Centre,** 250/539-2233, website www.galiano island.com; open in July and August only, daily 9 A.M.–5 P.M.

Sights and Recreation

One of the best ways to explore local waterways is with **Galiano Island Kayaking,** based at the marina in Montague Harbour, 250/539-2442. Three-hour guided tours, either early in the morning or at sunset, are $40. Another tour takes in the local marinelife on a six-hour paddle for $60. Those with previous experience can rent a kayak; $33 per day for a single or $55 for a double.

Climbing out of Sturdies Bay, Porlier Pass Road crosses through **Montague Harbour Provincial Park,** which protects 89 coastal hectares. The park offers a variety of short hikes through bird-filled forests of Douglas fir and along the shoreline—or follow a trail of your own along beaches strewn with broken seashells. Manmade piles of shells lie at the park's north end. Known as middens, they accumulated over centuries of native use.

Accommodations and Camping

Within walking distance of the ferry terminal and set right on the water is **Bellhouse Inn,** 29 Farmhouse Rd., 250/539-5667 or 800/970-

7464, website www.bellhouseinn.com. With rates ranging $135–195, the three rooms are large. The more expensive features a hot tub, private balcony, and fireplace. Rates include a full breakfast and personal touches such as tea or coffee delivered to the room before breakfast.

The only campground on Galiano Island is at **Montague Harbour Provincial Park,** 10 km from the ferry. As with all provincial park campgrounds through the Southern Gulf Islands, the location is superb and the facilities are limited to picnic tables, pit toilets, and drinking water; $12 per night.

Transportation

B.C. Ferries, 250/539-2622, schedules four sailings daily between Swartz Bay and Galiano Island; peak round-trip fare is adult $6.25, child $3.25, vehicle $21.50. From the B.C. mainland, Galiano Island is the first stop for the Gulf Islands ferries, which depart at least twice daily from the Tsawwassen terminal, 604/669-1211. Peak one-

Sea kayaking is a great way to experience Southern Gulf Islands.

way fare is adult $9, child $4.50, vehicle $35.50. Galiano Island is linked to Mayne Island by four sailings daily, with a couple of those continuing to the other islands. Interisland travel is adult $3, child $1.50, vehicle $7.

MAYNE ISLAND

Separated from Galiano Island by a narrow channel, Mayne Island is just 21 square kilometers in area. Roads lead from the ferry dock at Village Bay to all corners of the island. "Village" Bay has no village; all commercial facilities are at nearby **Miners Bay,** which got its name during the Cariboo gold rush when miners used the island as a stopping point. Island beaches are limited to those at Oyster Bay, but visitors can enjoy interesting shoreline walks or take the road to the low summit of Mount Park for panoramic views.

Accommodations

Overlooking Miners Bay, two km east of the ferry terminal, is **Tinkerers' Bed and Breakfast,** 417 Georgina Point Rd., 250/539-2280. This delightful old house sits right on the bay, a great base for exploring the area on foot or bike (bike rentals available). Rooms are smallish and simply furnished, but guests have use of a communal lounge and the relaxing gardens. Rates are $80–105 s or d; the least expensive rooms share bathroom facilities. Open April to October.

Set on four hectares overlooking a protected waterway, less than two km south of the ferry terminal, is **Oceanwood Country Inn,** 630 Dinner Bay Rd., 250/539-5074, website www.oceanwood.com. Paths lead through the very private property, past herb and rose gardens and down to the water's edge. Within the lodge itself are four communal areas, including a well-stocked library and comfortable lounge. Each of the 12 rooms has its own character; some have a private balcony, others a deck or hot tub, and the largest features a split-level living area, luxurious bathroom, and private deck with hot tub.

Rates start at $159 s or d; rooms with ocean views range $230–329. A cooked breakfast and

tea and coffee throughout the day are included, and a four-course table d'hôte dinner is available in the restaurant.

Mayne Island has no designated camping areas.

Transportation

From Swartz Bay, **B.C. Ferries,** 250/539-2321, schedules four sailings daily to Mayne Island; peak round-trip fare is adult $6.25, child $3.25, vehicle $21.50. Sailings from the Tsawwassen ferry terminal, 604/669-1211, depart at least once daily, with a stop at Galiano Island en route; the peak one-way fare is adult $9, child $4.50, vehicle $35.50. Regular interisland sailings are offered from Saturna, North Pender, and Galiano Islands. The peak fare for all interisland travel is adult $3, child $1.50, vehicle $7.

SATURNA ISLAND

Most remote of the populated Southern Gulf Islands, Saturna protrudes into the heart of Georgia Strait and features a long, rugged northern coastline. From the ferry dock at **Lyall Harbour,** the island's main road follows this stretch of coast for 14 km, ending at East Point.

Accommodations

Most accommodations on Saturna Island are in private home bed and breakfasts. The island has no campgrounds. Right where the ferry docks is **Lyall Harbour B&B,** 121 E. Point Rd., 250/539-5577 or 877/473-9343. Each of the three guest rooms is spacious and features modern furnishings, a fireplace, and a deck with ocean views; $85 s, $95 d. Also within walking distance of Lyall Harbour is **Saturna Lodge,** overlooking Boot Cove at 130 Payne Rd., 250/539-2254 or 888/539-8800, website www.saturna-island.bc.ca. Right on the water, this modern accommodation offers seven guest rooms, a hot tub, and extensive gardens. Rates range $135–175 including breakfast. Within the lodge a small restaurant has a big reputation for seafood and local game and produce. The owners are involved in various projects around the island, including a successful vineyard and winery.

Transportation

Although Saturna is the most difficult of the main islands to reach by ferry, fares are no higher than on other routes. Direct ferries are available, but you might want to take one of the other ferries and explore one or more of the other islands on the way out to Saturna. Peak one-way fare on any interisland route is adult $3, child $1.50, vehicle $7. Two to three sailings daily come direct from the Swartz Bay ferry terminal, 250/539-2321; peak round-trip fare is adult $6.25, child $3.25, vehicle $21.50. Sailings to Saturna from the Tsawwassen ferry terminal, 604/539-5105, depart twice daily but require a transfer at Mayne Island. The peak one-way fare is adult $9, child $4.50, vehicle $35.50.

Nanaimo and Vicinity

Nanaimo (pronounced na-NYE-mo) sprawls lazily up and down the hilly coastal terrain between sparkling Nanaimo Harbour and Mt. Benson, on the east coast of Vancouver Island. With a population of 75,000, it's the island's second-largest city and one of the 10 largest cities in British Columbia. It's also a vibrant city enjoying a rich history, mild climate, wide range of visitor services, and a direct ferry link to both of Vancouver's ferry terminals.

The **Nanaimo Parkway** bypasses the city to the west along a 21-km route that branches off the original highway five km south of downtown, rejoining it 18 km north of downtown.

History

Five native bands lived here (the name Nanaimo is a derivative from the Salish word Sney-Ny-Mous, or "Meeting Place"), and it was they who innocently showed dull, black rocks to Hudson's Bay Company employees in 1851. For most of the next century, mines in the area exported huge quantities of coal. Eventually, oil-fueled ships replaced the coal burners, and by 1949 most of the mines had closed. Surprisingly, no visible traces of the mining boom remain in Nanaimo, aside from a museum (built on top of the most productive mine) accurately depicting those times and a sturdy fort (now a museum) built in 1853 in case of a native attack.

Nanaimo was officially incorporated in 1874, which makes it the province's third-oldest town. When the coal mines closed, forestry and fishing became mainstays of the city. Today Nanaimo is also a major deep-sea shipping port.

SIGHTS

Downtown Nanaimo lies in a wide bowl sloping down to the waterfront, where forward thinking by early town planners has left wide expanses of parkland. Down near the water, the Civic Arena building makes a good place to park your car and go exploring on foot. Right in front of the Civic Arena is **Swy-A-Lana Lagoon,** a unique man-made tidal lagoon full of interesting marinelife. A promenade leads south from the lagoon to a bustling downtown marina filled with commercial fishing boats and leisure craft. Beside the marina is a distinctive mast-like sculpture that provides foot access to a tiered development with various viewpoints. Up in downtown proper, many historic buildings still stand, most around the corner of Front and Church Streets and along Commercial Street. Look for hotels dating to last century, the Francis Rattenbury–designed courthouse, and various old commercial buildings. Up Fitzwilliam Street are the 1893 St. Andrew's Church and the 1883 railway station.

The Bastion

Overlooking the harbor at the junction of Bastion and Front Streets stands the Bastion, a well-protected fort built in 1853 by the Hudson's Bay Company to protect employees and their families against an attack by natives. Originally used as a company office, arsenal, and supply house, today the fort houses the **Bastion Museum,** open in summer daily except Tuesday 10 A.M.–4 P.M.; admission is $1. For the benefit of tourists, a group of local university students dressed in

To Piper's Lagoon Park

To Horseshoe Bay (Vancouver)

DEPARTURE BAY RD.

HAMMOND BAY RD.

To Long Lake and Parksville

★ PACIFIC BIOLOGICAL STATION

Departure Bay Beach

Departure Bay

To Tsawwassen (Vancouver)

ISLAND HWY

Beban Park

■ NORTHFIELD RD.

Newcastle Island

Gabriola

19

BRECHIN RD.

VISITOR INFO CENTRE

To Bailey Theatre

NANAIMO REGIONAL GENERAL HOSPITAL ■

■ OCEAN EXPLORERS DIVING

BUCCANEER INN ■

TOWNSITE RD.

BLUEBIRD MOTEL ■

COLONIAL MOTEL ■

■ MOBY DICK OCEANFRONT LODGE

Protection Island

WESTWOOD RD.

Millstone River

BOWEN RD.

STEWART AVE.

CASTAWAY MOTEL ■

JINGLE POT RD.

SEE "DOWNTOWN NANAIMO" MAP

CAMPBELL ST.

2ND ST.

WENTWORTH ST.

Island

TERMINAL AVE.

WAKESIAH AVE.

3RD ST.

FITZWILLIAM ST.

To Westwood Lake RV Camping and Cabins

ALBERT ST.

Duke Point

Westwood Lake

4TH ST.

MALASPINA ■ COLLEGE

VICTORIA RD.

Northumberland Channel

NANAIMO LAKES RD.

■ NICOL STREET HOSTEL

6TH ST.

■ DAYS INN HARBOURVIEW

7TH ST.

Nanaimo Harbour

Nanaimo River

10TH ST.

NANAIMO PKWY.

Petroglyph P.P. ▲

DUKE POINT HWY.

NANAIMO

MOON

SCALE NOT AVAILABLE

LIVING FOREST OCEANSIDE CAMPGROUND AND RV PARK

1

To Bungy Zone and Victoria

Z VANCOUVER ISLAND

© AVALON TRAVEL PUBLISHING, INC.

the Bastion, a fort built in 1853

© ANDREW HEMPSTEAD

VANCOUVER ISLAND

appropriate gunnery uniforms and led by a piper parades down Bastion Street daily at noon in summer. The parade ends at the Bastion, where the three cannons are fired out over the water. It's the only ceremonial cannon firing west of Ontario. For a good vantage point, be there early.

Nanaimo District Museum

In Piper Park, just across Front Street from the Bastion and up the stairs, is Nanaimo Museum, 100 Cameron St., 250/753-1821. Walk around the outside to appreciate harbor, city, and mountain views, as well as replica petroglyphs of animals, humans, and spiritual creatures. Then allow at least an hour for wandering through the two floors of displays inside, which focus on life in early Nanaimo and include topics such as local geology, native peoples, and pioneers. An exhibit on the coal-mining days features a realistic coal mine from the 1850s. Don't miss the impressive native carvings by James Dick. Displays are changed regularly, so something's always new, and the summer interpretive program includes

walks, talks, and shows. Admission is adult $2, senior $1.75, child 75 cents. The museum is open in summer daily 9 A.M.–6 P.M., the rest of the year Tues.–Sat. 9 A.M.–4 P.M.

Newcastle Island Provincial Marine Park

Newcastle Island is a magnificent chunk of wilderness separated from downtown Nanaimo by a narrow channel. It's mostly forested, ringed by sandstone cliffs and a few short stretches of pebbly beach. Wildlife inhabitants include deer, raccoons, beavers, and more than 50 species of birds.

When Europeans arrived and began mining coal, they displaced natives who had lived on the island for centuries. Coal was mined until 1883, and sandstone—featured on many of Nanaimo's historic buildings—was quarried here until 1932. The pavilion and facilities near the ferry dock date to the 1940s. Back then, the island was a popular holiday spot, at one point even boasting a floating hotel.

A 7.5-km trail (allow 2–3 hours) encircles the island, leading to picturesque Kanaka Bay, Mallard Lake, and a lookout offering views east to the snowcapped Coast Mountains.

Camping on the island costs $12, and meals are available in the **Pavilion Restaurant;** open 9 A.M.–7:15 P.M. (until 9:15 P.M. Fri.–Sat. nights). Ferries depart for the island from Maffeo-Sutton Park in summer daily 10 A.M.–7 P.M. on the hour, with extra sailings at 8 P.M. and 9 P.M. on Friday and Saturday. The round-trip fare is adult $4.75, senior or child $3.75, bicycle $1.50. For details call **Scenic Ferries** at 250/753-5141.

Other Parks

Along the Millstone River and linked by a trail to the waterfront promenade, 36-hectare **Bowen Park** remains mostly in its natural state, with stands of Douglas fir, hemlock, cedar, and maple. It's home to beavers and birds, and even deer are occasionally sighted within its boundaries. Street access is from Bowen Road.

On the road into downtown Nanaimo from the south, two km north of the new Nanaimo Parkway intersection, **Petroglyph Provincial**

Park features a short trail leading to ancient petroglyphs (rock carvings). Petroglyphs, found throughout the province and common along the coastal waterways, were made with stone tools, and they recorded important ceremonies and events. The designs at this park were carved thousands of years ago and are believed to represent human beings, animals (real and supernatural), bottom fish, and the rarely depicted sea wolf, a mythical creature part wolf and part killer whale.

West of downtown (take Wentworth Street then Jingle Pot Road across the Nanaimo Park-

way), 106-hectare **Westwood Lake Park** surrounds the crystal-clear waters of its namesake lake. Resident flocks of Canada geese and ducks, tame enough to snatch food from your fingers, inhabit the park. The lake's healthy population of cutthroat trout attracts anglers year-round.

Along Hammond Bay Road, north of downtown and beyond Departure Bay, is **Piper's Lagoon Park,** encompassing an isthmus and a rocky headland that shelter a shallow lagoon. A trail from the parking lot leads to the headland, with views of the mainland across the Strait of

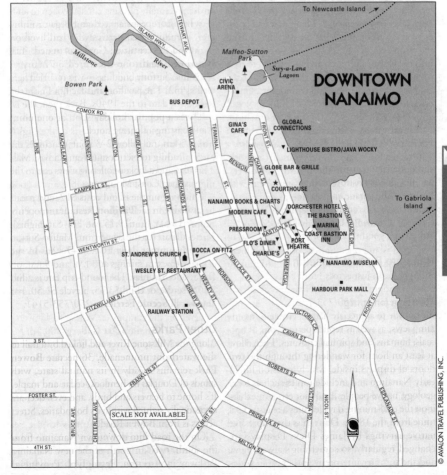

VANCOUVER ISLAND

© AVALON TRAVEL PUBLISHING, INC.

Georgia. Continuing north, more trails lead through **Neck Point Park** to rocky beaches and oceanside picnic areas.

RECREATION

On and Under the Water

The obvious way to appreciate the harbor aspect of Nanaimo is by boat. To arrange a cruise, wander down to the marina below the Bastion and inquire among the fishing and sightseeing charter boats, or stop by the Nanaimo Visitor Info Centre and ask for a list of local guides and charters, plus current prices. One vessel, the **Bastion City,** takes passengers on 2.5-hour narrated cruises of the harbor and adjacent islands. During the cruise, you might spot sea lions—who come into the harbor in March and early April to feed on abundant schools of herring—seals, orcas, bald eagles, blue herons, and cormorants. Cruises cost adult $28, senior $23, child $15; call 250/753-2852 for reservations and information.

A great variety of dives can be accessed from Nanaimo, including the HMAS *Saskatchewan,* a 120-meter-long navy destroyer escort recently sunk off the city for the pleasure of divers. Marinelife is also varied, with divers mixing with harbor seals, anemones, sponges, salmon, and "tame" wolf eels. Near the Departure Bay ferry terminal, **Ocean Explorers Diving,** 1956 Zorkin Rd., 250/753-2055 or 800/233-4145, is a well-respected island operation, offering equipment rentals, charters, guided tours (including night diving), and lessons.

Bungee Jumping

Nanaimo is home to North America's only bridge-based commercial bungee jump. People flock here from afar to have their ankles tied and connected to "Bungee Bridge" by a long elastic rope. Next they dive head first 42 meters down almost to the surface of Nanaimo River, rebounding until momentum dissipates. To receive this thrill of a lifetime you have to part with $95, and if you have any cash left over, you'll find must-have T-shirts, hats, posters, videos, stickers, and other souvenirs to prove to the world that you really did it. At the same facility, other adren-

aline rushes can be had by taking the Ultimate Swing ($50 per person) or the Flying Fox ($50). All of the above are thoroughly entertaining to watch, with good viewing areas and plenty of parking provided. The site is 13 km south of downtown. For details and reservations call **Bungy Zone** at 250/716-7874.

Arts and Entertainment

Lovers of the arts will find Nanaimo to be quite the cultural center, especially since the opening of the **Port Theatre,** 125 Front St., 250/754-8550, in 1998. This magnificent 800-seat theater in an architecturally pleasing circular concrete-and-glass building opposite the harbor showcases theater productions, musicals, and music performances by a wide range of artists. The **Nanaimo Theatre Group,** 250/758-7246, presents live performances at the Port Theatre as well as in the Bailey Theatre at 2373 Rosstown Road.

The best place in Nanaimo for a quiet drink in a relaxing atmosphere is upstairs in the **Lighthouse Pub,** 50 Anchor Way, 250/754-3212, built out over the water in front of downtown. This casual pub gets very busy in summer, with nightly drink specials, a pool table, and a good selection of pub food. For nautical atmosphere, head over to the **Dinghy Dock Marine Pub,** moored at Protection Island, 250/753-2373; ferries depart regularly from Nanaimo Boat Basin. Bands play nightly at the **Queens Hotel,** 34 Victoria St., 250/754-6751, while night owls head to the **Pressroom,** 150 Skinner St., 250/716-0030, for DJ-spun dance music until the wee hours.

Over on the campus of Malaspina University-College, **Nanaimo Art Gallery,** 900 5th St., 250/755-8790, displays works of art, primarily of Canadian origin. At the gift shop you can buy arts and crafts by island artists. The center is open Mon.–Sat. 10 A.M.–5 P.M., Sunday noon–5 P.M.

Events

The year kicks off in early April with the **Sea Lion Festival,** which coincides with the end of the Dec.–April herring run through the Strait of Georgia. Attracted by the fish, hundreds of

NANAIMO'S WORLD CHAMPIONSHIP BATHTUB RACE

On the last Sunday of every July the waters off Nanaimo come alive for the World Championship Bathtub Race, the grand finale of the annual Nanaimo Marine Festival. The idea for the race was conceived back in 1967, when the chairman of the city's Canada Centennial Committee, Frank Ney, was asked to come up with a special event for the occasion. Bathtub racing was born over a cup of coffee, and Ney went on to be elected mayor of Nanaimo.

Originally, competitors raced across the Strait of Georgia between Nanaimo and Kitsilano Beach, Vancouver. Today, they leave from downtown, racing around Entrance and Winchelsea Islands to the finish line at Departure Bay in a modified bathtub fitted with a 7.5-horsepower outboard motor. The racers are escorted by hundreds of boats of the more regular variety, loaded with people just waiting for the competitors to sink! Every bathtubber wins a prize—a golden plug for entering, a small trophy for making it to the other side of the strait, and a silver plunger for the first tub to sink! These days, the sport and the festivities around it have grown enormously, attracting tens of thousands of visitors to Nanaimo. And "tubbing," as the locals call it, has spread to other provincial communities, where preliminary races qualify entrants for the big one.

---

sea lions congregate on log booms for a quick and easy feed. Festivities include boat trips out on the water, onshore entertainment, and educational displays. The **Heritage Days** festival in late June celebrates the city's past with concerts and historical displays. **Canada Day** celebrations center on Maffeo-Sutton Park and end with an evening concert in nearby Bowen Park. July's **Nanaimo Marine Festival** is best known for the World Championship Bathtub Race (see the special topic), but also includes a silly boat race on Swy-A-Lana Lagoon, a parade of boats on wheels, street fair, and fireworks. The year's most colorful event is the **Festival of Banners,** organized by the local art gallery. Hundreds of entries of banners are received from artistic entrants across the city, with the best hung along Nanaimo's streets for the months of summer.

ACCOMMODATIONS AND CAMPING

Under $50

A few of Nanaimo's older motels offer rooms under $50 outside of summer, but only **Nicol Street Hostel,** 65 Nicol St., 250/753-1188, falls into this price range year-round. In a converted house, this accommodation enjoys a convenient location three blocks from the train station and seven blocks from the bus depot. The hostel operates year-round, providing dormitory-style accommodations, as well as campsites, a kitchen, laundry, TV room, and bicycle rentals. Guests can get discounts at many local restaurants and attractions. All beds are $19; camping out back costs $9 per person. Register after 4 P.M.

$50–100

On an island of overpriced accommodations, two places, both on the same street in Nanaimo, stand out as being excellent value. The first of these, across from the waterfront and within easy walking distance of downtown and the Departure Bay ferry terminal, is the two-story **Buccaneer Inn,** 1577 Stewart Ave., 250/753-1246 or 877/282-6337, website www.buccaneerinn.com. Bedecked by a nautical-themed mural and colorful baskets of flowers, the motel is surrounded by well-maintained grounds, a sundeck, picnic tables, and a barbecue facility. The rooms themselves are spacious and brightly decorated, and each holds a desk, coffee-making facilities and a small fridge. The smallest rooms are $59 s, $64 d, while kitchen suites, some with gas fireplaces, range $89–119 s, $99–129 d. Friendly owner/operators provide a wealth of information on the local area (as does the motel website).

A few blocks toward downtown from the Buccaneer is the **Moby Dick Oceanfront Lodge,** 1000 Stewart St., 250/753-7111 or 800/663-

2116, website www.mobydicklodge.com. This four-story waterfront motel faces Newcastle Island, offering water views from every room. The rooms are extra large, and each has a kitchen and private balcony, making the rates of $70 s, $80 d extremely good value.

A bunch of other motels fall into the lower end of $50–100 price range, most along a short stretch of the old Highway 19 (Terminal Ave.) three km north of downtown. These include the **Bluebird Motel,** 995 Terminal Ave., 250/753-4151 or 877/764-3832, website www.theblue birdmotel.com, which charges $49 s, $59 d, and the nine-room **Colonial Motel,** 950 Terminal Ave., 250/754-4415, website www.colonial motel.ca, where rooms are $49 s, $69 d. Outside of summer, the best way to snag a cheap room is to cruise this strip looking for discounted rates posted out front.

Coming into the city from the south, **Days Inn Harbourview,** 809 Island Hwy. S, 250/754-8171 or 877/754-8171, website www.har bourviewdaysinn.com, features a large indoor pool, restaurant, and laundry; from $85 s, $95 d.

$100–150

As you'd expect, accommodations right downtown are more expensive than those farther out. The **Best Western Dorchester Hotel,** 70 Church St., 250/754-6835 or 800/661-2449, website www.dorchesternanaimo.com, offers water views and a rooftop terrace from a very central location. Rooms in this historic building are smallish, but they hold modern, sleek furnishings. Book online for discounts on the $120 s or d rack rates.

The **Coast Bastion Inn,** 11 Bastion St., 250/753-6601 or 800/663-1144, website www.coasthotels.com, is a full-service 179-room hotel with an exercise room, café and restaurant, lounge, and water views from every room. Advertised rates are from $134 s or d, but like other properties in this chain, search their website for packages that offer decent discounts, even in summer.

Seven km north of downtown, the three-story **Ramada on Long Lake,** 4700 Island Hwy. N, 250/758-1144 or 800/565-1144, website www.longlakeinn.com, overlooks a beautiful lake. The inn boasts a short stretch of private beach along the lakeshore; canoe rentals are available. Other amenities include an exercise room, sauna, spa, and a delightful waterfront café. Rooms are modern, and many have water views and kitchens; rates range 139–189 s or d including a light breakfast. At the north end of Long Lake is another of the city's finest hostelries, the **Four Points by Sheraton Nanaimo,** 4900 Rutherford Rd., 250/758-3000 or 800/325-3535, website www.fourpoints.com. Overlooking the lake, it features a nine-hole par-3 golf course, an indoor pool, an exercise room, and a restaurant. The rooms are chock-full of facilities and of a higher standard than you'd get in Vancouver or Victoria for $139 s or d.

Camping

Three commercial campgrounds lie within 10 km of city center, but the nicest surroundings are in the provincial park out on **Newcastle Island** (see Sights, above), connected to downtown by regular ferry service. The island isn't suitable for RVers, but it's ideal for those with a lightweight tent. Facilities include picnic tables and a barbecue shelter. If you don't want to cook, you can eat at the restaurant on the island. Sites are $12. For details call the park office at 250/391-2300.

The closest of the commercial campgrounds to downtown is **Westwood Lake RV Camping and Cabins,** 380 Westwood Rd., 250/753-3922. It's right on the edge of beautiful Westwood Lake, offering fishing, canoe rentals, a few short hiking trails, a barbecue area, game room, laundry, and hot showers. Unserviced sites are $17, hookups $20, cabins $55.

Living Forest Oceanside Campground, 6 Maki Rd., 250/755-1755, website www.camp ingbc.com, is on 20 forested hectares beside the braided mouth of the Nanaimo River south of downtown. The setting is delightful and facilities modern, including a laundry, general store, games room, and coin showers. Tent sites are $17, serviced sites $20–23, with the best of these enjoying water views.

Brannen Lake Campsites, 4220 Biggs Rd.,

250/756-0404 or 866/756-0404, offers sunny or shady lakeside sites on an operating beef ranch, complete with a petting zoo and playground. To get there, head north of town, turn left on Mostar Road, then right on Biggs Road. Sites are $15–18 per night.

FOOD

First things first. This is the place to try a delicious chocolate-topped **Nanaimo Bar,** a layered delicacy that originated in this city. When researching this edition, I headed for Commercial Street's long-time favorite bakeshop, the Scotch Bakery, only to find it was gone, replaced by a computer shop. Staff at Tourism Nanaimo quickly pointed me in the direction of the **Nanaimo Bakery,** 2025 Bowen Rd., for my annual Nanaimo Bar fix.

Cafés and Cheap Eats

Right on the harbor, in the Pioneer Waterfront Plaza, is **Javawocky,** 90 Front St., 250/753-1688, a modern coffeehouse with all the usual coffee drinks, great milkshakes, inexpensive cakes and pastries, and light lunchtime snacks. On a terrace overlooking the harbor is **Global Connections,** 10 Front St., 250/753-3366, offering a similar fare and water views from inside and out.

In the heart of downtown, a few greasy spoons make good stops for breakfast. Pick of the bunch is **Flo's Diner,** 187 Commercial St., 250/753-2148, complete with a counter, vinyl booths, and kitschy decorations. Breakfast portions are hearty, especially the filled omelets (as big as anywhere on the island), which are around $7–8. Also on Commercial St., up the hill from Flo's, is the **Modern Café,** 250/754-5022, which isn't, and down the hill is **Charlie's,** 250/753-7044,

© ANDREW HEMPSTEAD

VANCOUVER ISLAND

Troller's, down on the marina, provides the perfect setting for enjoying a meal of fish and chips.

where the windows are plastered with computer printouts advertising breakfast for $4.

Up Fitzwilliam Street from the center of town, in the Old Quarter, are a couple of quiet little cafés, including the **Wesley St. Restaurant,** 321 Wesley St., 250/755-4004, for more substantial meals and live jazz on Friday and Saturday evenings.

Seafood

Head down to the marina at the foot of Wharf Street for seafood straight from the fishing boats. You can buy salmon, halibut, cod, snapper, shrimp, crabs, mussels, or whatever the day's catch might be at very reasonable prices—perfect if you're camping or have a motel room with a kitchen (many local accommodations also have outdoor barbecue facilities). Also at the marina is **Troller's,** 250/741-7994, with tables and chairs set up around a small takeout counter on one of the arms of the floating dock. Expect to pay $6–8 for fish and chips.

Other Restaurants

Dinghy Dock Marine Pub, 250/753-2373, offers a unique dining experience; the floating restaurant is moored at nearby Protection Island. Well known for great food and plenty of seagoing atmosphere, the pub also hosts live entertainment on Friday and Saturday nights from May to September. It's open daily 11 A.M.–11 P.M., later on weekends. To get to the restaurant, take a ferry from Nanaimo Boat Basin. Ferries depart hourly 9:10 A.M.–11:10 P.M.; for information call 250/753-8244.

In the seaplane terminal on the waterfront (below the Bastion), the **Lighthouse Bistro,** 50 Anchor Way, 250/754-3212, is built over the water and has a large heated outdoor deck. The salmon chowder is excellent, served with delicious bread. Also on the menu are tasty appetizers, salads, burgers, sandwiches, croissants, pasta dishes, and good daily specials. Expect to pay $7–10 for a lunch entrée, $14–22 at dinner. It's open daily 11 A.M.–11 P.M. Upstairs is the **Lighthouse Pub,** with a similar menu and specials such as 25 cent wings daily 4–8 P.M.

In a renovated hotel building dating to 1889 is the **Globe Bar & Grille,** 25 Front St., 250/754-4910, offering the elegant decor of private club but with a more casual atmosphere and a reasonably priced menu of steak and seafood. If you don't feel like a full meal, it's okay to relax with a coffee or drink and choose from one of the many appetizers.

For some of the best Mexican food on the island, head for **Gina's Cafe,** behind the courthouse at 47 Skinner St., 250/753-5411. The building, a converted residence, is hard to miss—the exterior is painted shades of purple and decorated with a fusion of Mexican and maritime memorabilia. It's open daily for lunch and dinner.

TRANSPORTATION

Getting There

It's possible to get to Nanaimo by airplane, train, or bus, but most people arrive by car up Highway 1 from Victoria or by ferry from the mainland. **B.C. Ferries,** 250/386-3431 or, toll-free in B.C., 888/223-3779, operates a regular service between Vancouver and two of Nanaimo's three ferry terminals. Fares on both routes are the same: peak one-way travel costs adult $9.50, child $4.75, vehicle $33.50, motorcycle $16.75, bicycle $2.50, canoe or kayak $4. Limited reservations are taken at 604/444-2890 or 888/724-5223; $15 per booking. The **Nanaimo Seaporter,** 250/753-2118, meets ferries at both terminals, transporting passengers to downtown accommodations and the bus depot.

Ferries leave Vancouver's Tsawwassen terminal up to eight times a day for the two-hour trip to Nanaimo's **Duke Point** terminal, 20 minutes south of downtown, 250/722-0181. The Duke Point terminal opened in 1998, allowing passengers to bypass logjams of traffic through downtown Nanaimo with its direct link to the Vancouver Island Highway. The terminal itself is worthy of mention. Built at a cost of $50 million, it sits on a 10-hectare peninsula of land where lookouts, walking paths, and a cultural center keep Vancouver-bound passengers occupied while awaiting ferries.

Through downtown, at the north end of Stewart Avenue, is the **Departure Bay** terminal,

VANCOUVER ISLAND

250/753-1261. This facility contains a large lounge area with a café and large-screen TVs. Ferries from Vancouver's Horseshoe Bay terminal leave up to 11 times a day for Departure Bay. One of the vessels plying this route is the *Pacifi-Cat*, the newest and fastest boat in the B.C. Ferries fleet. The interior resembles a cruise ship, with most passengers congregating in the multi-level lounge area surrounded by wraparound windows.

Baxter Aviation, 250/754-1066 or 800/661-5599, and **Harbour Air,** 250/714-0900, fly daily between Vancouver and the seaplane base in downtown Nanaimo; $75 one-way.

The **Laidlaw** bus depot is at the rear of the Howard Johnson hotel on the corner of Terminal Ave. and Comox Rd., 800/753-4371. Buses depart regularly for points north and south of Nanaimo and west to Port Alberni and Tofino.

A great way to travel up the island is aboard the **E&N Railiner,** a scheduled train service that departs Victoria Mon.–Sat. at 8:15 A.M. and on Sunday at noon, running as far north as Courtenay. Get off at Nanaimo, spend a couple of hours exploring the city or Newcastle Island, then jump aboard the return service to Victoria that same afternoon. A same-day round-trip ticket costs $40. The station is on Selby St., up the hill from downtown, 250/383-4324 or 800/561-8630.

Getting Around

Nanaimo Regional Transit System buses run daily. The main routes radiate from the Harbour Park Mall (at the south end of downtown) north to Departure Bay, west to Westwood Lake, and south as far as Cedar. An all-day pass is $5. For schedule information call 250/390-4531.

Rental car agencies in Nanaimo include: **Avis,** 250/245-4166; **Budget,** 250/754-7368; **Discount,** 250/758-5171; **National,** 250/758-3509; and **Rent-a-wreck,** 250/753-6461.

SERVICES AND INFORMATION

The **post office** on Front St. in the Harbour Park Mall is open Mon.–Fri. 8:30 A.M.–5 P.M. **Nanaimo Regional General Hospital** is at 1200 Dufferin Crescent, 250/754-2141. If you need a **pharmacy** head for Pharmasave at 530 5th St., 250/753-8234. For maps, nautical charts, and books about Vancouver Island, visit **Nanaimo Maps and Charts,** 8 Church St., 250/754-2513. Numerous used bookstores can be found along Commercial Street.

Nanaimo is promoted to the world by **Tourism Nanaimo,** 250/756-0106 or 800/663-7337, website www.tourismnanaimo.bc.ca. The main **Nanaimo Visitor Info Centre** is north of downtown and off the main highway in the grounds of Beban Park at 2290 Bowen Road. More centrally located, within walking distance of the waterfront, is the **Downtown Nanaimo Information Centre,** at 82 Commercial St. 250/754-8531; open Mon.–Fri. 10 A.M.–8 P.M., Sat.–Sun. 10 A.M.–6 P.M.

GABRIOLA ISLAND

Like the Southern Gulf Islands, Gabriola (pop. 3,400) is partly residential, but also holds large expanses of forest, abundant wildlife, and long stretches of unspoiled coastline. The ferry from Nanaimo docks at Descanso Bay, on the east side of the island.

Take Taylor Bay Road north from the ferry terminal to access the island's best beaches, including those within five-hectare **Gabriola Sands Provincial Park.** Walk out to the park's southern headland to view sandstone cliffs eroded into interesting shapes by eons of wave action. The North and South Roads encircle the island, combining for a 30-km loop perfect for a leisurely bike ride. Many scenic spots invite you to pull off—at petroglyphs, secluded bays, and lookouts. **Drumbeg Provincial Park** protects the island's southeast corner, where a short trail through dense forest leads to a secluded bay.

Practicalities

The least expensive way to overnight on the island is by camping at **Gabriola Campground,** 595 Taylor Bay Rd., 250/247-2079. Facilities are limited (no showers or hookups), but it's a great little spot right on the ocean; $15 per night. Open April–Oct. only.

The island's nicest accommodation is **Marina's**

Hideaway, 943 Canso Dr., 250/247-8854 or 888/208-9850, a bed and breakfast overlooking Northumberland Channel one km from the ferry terminal. Each of the three guest rooms in this magnificent waterfront home has a king-size bed, gas fireplace, private entrance, and balcony. Rates are $110 s, $135 d.

B.C. Ferries, 250/386-3431, schedules 15 sailings daily between the terminal off Front St. in Nanaimo (downtown, across from Harbour Park

Mall) and Gabriola Island. The trip takes 20 minutes each way. The peak round-trip fare is adult $5.25, child $2.75, vehicle $13.50. For a taxi, call **Gabriola Island Cabs,** 250/247-0049. Basic services are available at Folklife Village, a little over one km from the ferry terminal on North Road. There you'll find a café, grocery store, and **Gabriola Island Visitor Info Centre,** 250/247-9332, website www.gabriolaisland.org, which is open mid-May to mid-September daily 9 A.M.–6 P.M.

Highway 4 to the West Coast

From Nanaimo, it's 35 km northwest up Highway 19 to one of Vancouver Island's main highway junctions, where Highway 4 spurs west to Port Alberni and the island's west coast. Follow Highway 4 to its end to reach **Pacific Rim National Park,** a long, narrow park protecting the wild coastal strip and some magnificent sandy beaches, and **Tofino,** a picturesque little town that makes the perfect base for sea kayaking, whale-watching, or fishing excursions.

HIGHWAY 4 TOWARD PORT ALBERNI

Englishman River Provincial Park

After turning off Highway 19, make your first stop here, where Englishman River—full of steelhead, cutthroat, and rainbow trout—cascades down from high Beaufort Range snowfields in a series of beautiful waterfalls. Within the park you'll find a picnic area, easy hiking trails to both the upper and lower falls, crystal-clear swimming holes, and plenty of campsites among tall cedars and lush ferns ($15 per night; no showers).

To get there, turn off Highway 4 on Errington Road, three km west of the highway junction, and continue another nine km, following signs.

Coombs

This small community comprises a row of old-fashioned country stores scattered around **Coombs Emporium and Frontier Town.** The shops sell everything from pottery planters, jewelry, and assorted knickknacks to tasty snacks

and cool drinks. Check out **Wood and Bone Crafts** for a unique souvenir, and cast your eyes toward the grass-covered roof of **Old Country Market,** where several goats can be seen contentedly grazing, seemingly oblivious to the amused, camera-clicking visitors.

Little Qualicum Falls Provincial Park and Vicinity

This 440-hectare park lies along the north side of the highway, 10 km west of Coombs. The park's main hiking trail leads alongside the Little Qualicum River to a series of plummeting waterfalls. Take your fishing pole along the riverside trail and catch a trout, stop for an exhilarating dip in one of the icy emerald pools, and stay the night in a sheltered riverside campsite ($15 per night; no showers).

The source of the Little Qualicum River is **Cameron Lake,** a large, deep-green, trout-filled body of water just outside the western park boundary. Magnificent old-growth forest encircles the lake, and at the west end is 136-hectare **MacMillan Provincial Park,** bisected by Highway 4. Here a 500-meter trail leads to majestic **Cathedral Grove,** a stand of 200- to 800-year-old Douglas firs that grow up to 70 meters high and 1.5 meters wide.

Mount Arrowsmith Regional Park

South of the highway, along a sometimes-rough 27-km logging road, this 489-hectare park offers several trails leading to the summit of 1,818-meter Mt. Arrowsmith.

PORT ALBERNI AND VICINITY

If you hit Port Alberni on a cloudy day, you won't know what you're missing—until the sky lifts! Then beautiful tree-mantled mountains suddenly appear, and Alberni Inlet and the Somass River turn a stunning deep blue. Situated at the head of the island's longest inlet, Port Alberni is an industrial town of 19,500 centered around the forestry industry. The town's three mills—lumber, specialty lumber, and pulp and paper—are its main sources of income. The town is also a port for pulp and lumber freighters, deep-sea vessels, and commercial fishing boats.

Despite all the industry, Port Alberni has much to offer, including a couple of interesting museums, nearby provincial parks, and a modern marina filled with both charter fishing boats and tour boats, including the famous MV *Lady Rose*.

Sights

Follow the signs from Highway 4 to brightly decorated **Alberni Harbour Quay** at the end of Argyle Street. For a great view of the quay, harbor, marina, inlet, and surrounding mountains, climb the clock tower. Also on the quay is the **Forestry Visitor Centre,** operated by the logging giant Weyerhaeuser, 250/720-2108, where you can view interpretive displays on logging, milling, and replanting, and arrange tours through local industry. It's open in summer daily 9:30 A.M.–5:30 P.M., the rest of the year Fri.–Sun. 11 A.M.–4 P.M. Through summer a **steam train** runs along the waterfront Sat.–Sun. 11 A.M.–4 P.M.; adults $3, children $2.

Find out more about the origins of the famous West Coast Trail, see a collection of native artifacts, or tinker with a variety of operating motorized machines from the forestry industry at the **Alberni Valley Museum,** on the corner of 10th Ave. and Wallace St., 250/723-2181. It's open Tues.–Sat. 10 A.M.–5 P.M. (Thursday until 8 P.M.); admission by donation.

MV Lady Rose

This vintage Scottish coaster has been serving the remote communities of Alberni Inlet and Barkley Sound since 1949 as a supply and pas-senger service. But because of the spectacular scenery along the route, the cruise is also one of the island's biggest tourist attractions. Depending on the time of year, orcas and gray whales, seals, sea lions, porpoises, river otters, bald eagles, and all sorts of seabirds join you on your trip through magnificent Barkley Sound. The vessel is also a great way to reach the remote fishing village of Bamfield (see below) and the only way to reach the Broken Group Islands (see the special topic Broken Group Islands).

Year-round, the MV *Lady Rose* departs Alberni Harbour Quay Tuesday, Thursday, and Saturday at 8 A.M., reaching Kildonan at 10 A.M. and Bamfield at 12:30 P.M., then departing Bamfield at 1:30 P.M. and docking back in Port Alberni at 5:30 P.M. In summer, sailings are also made to Bamfield on Sunday, with a special stop for kayakers in the Broken Group Islands (see the special topic). If you want to stay longer in Bamfield, accommodations are available (see below). June–Sept. an extra route is added to the schedule, with the vessel departing Monday, Wednesday, and Friday at 8 A.M. for the Broken Group Islands, arriving at Ucluelet at 1 P.M. for a 90-minute layover before returning to Port Alberni around 7 P.M. One-way fares from Port Alberni are: Kildonan $12, Bamfield $23, Broken Group Islands $20, Ucluelet $25. Children under 16 travel for half price. For further details contact the operators at 250/723-8313 or 800/663-7192, website www.ladyrosemarine.com. In summer the *Lady Rose* does a roaring business—book as far ahead as possible.

Fishing

Along with at least one other Vancouver Island town, Port Alberni claims to be the "Salmon Capital of the World." The fishing in Alberni Inlet is certainly world-class, but probably no better than a handful of other places on the island. The main salmon runs occur in fall, when hundreds of thousands of salmon migrate up Alberni Inlet to their spawning grounds.

To get the rundown on fishing charters head down to the full-service **Port Alberni Marina,** 5104 River Rd., 250/723-8022; open daily, in summer dawn to dusk, in winter 9 A.M.–5 P.M.

The owners, local fishing guides, have put together all kinds of printed information on local fishing. They know all the best spots and know how to catch the lunkers. Expect to pay $300 for two people, $330 for three for a six-hour guided morning charter; $200 for two, $220 for three, for a four-hour guided afternoon charter. The marina also rents boats (from $15 per hour or $90 per day, plus gas) and fishing rods ($12 per day), sells bait and tackle, and provides information about sportfishing/accommodations packages in the region.

The annual **Port Alberni Salmon Festival** fishing derby each Labour Day weekend (first weekend in September) draws anglers from afar in the hopes of winning over $60,000 in prize money. Crowds of fishing enthusiasts gather to watch thousands of pounds of salmon being weighed in at Clutesi Haven Marina, and multitudes of salmon-eaters throng to a three-day salmon barbecue. For details call 250/723-8165.

Della Falls

In the remote southern section of **Strathcona Provincial Park** (see Northern Vancouver Island, later in this chapter), difficult-to-reach Della Falls is accessible only from Port Alberni. The 440-meter waterfall northwest of town is one of the highest in North America, and getting to it requires a lot of effort: first by boat or canoe along Great Central Lake, then by a rough 16-km hike (eight hours each way) up the Drinkwater Creek watershed.

Accommodations and Camping

Whether you're in search of a tent site with water views, a cozy bed and breakfast, or a luxurious motel room, Port Alberni has something to suit, although Port Alberni motels are generally more expensive than those on other parts of the island.

Within walking distance of the quay is **Bluebird Motel,** 3755 3rd Ave., 250/723-1153 or 888/591-3888, which charges $65 s, $70 d. On

coho salmon

the main road through town is **Esta Villa Motel,** 4014 Johnston Rd., 250/724-1261 or 800/724-0844, a small accommodation with comfortable rooms for $75 s, $85 d. Right downtown, the **Coast Hospitality Inn,** 3835 Redford St., 250/723-8111 or 800/663-1144, is part of the upmarket Coast Hotels and Resorts chain, website www.coasthotels.com. Each of the large rooms is air-conditioned and features a comfortable bed and a writing desk; $130 s, $135 d.

The best camping is out of town, at **China Creek Park Marina and Campground,** right on Alberni Inlet, 250/723-9812. This one offers a choice of open or wooded full-facility sites ($16–28 per site), a marina, sailboard rentals, great views of the inlet from a sandy log-strewn beach, and lots of bald eagles for company. To get there take 3rd Avenue south to Ship Creek Road and follow it for 14 km. **Stamp River Provincial Park,** northwest of Port Alberni, enjoys a beautiful location on the river of the same name; $12 per site. To get there follow Highway 4 west, and immediately after crossing Kitsuksus Creek take Beaver Creek Road north for 14 km.

Food

At any time of day, the best place to find something to eat is down at Alberni Harbour Quay. At the entrance to the quay is **Blue Door Cafe,** 5415 Argyle St., 250/723-8811, a small old-style place that's a real locals' hangout. Breakfasts are huge; an omelet with all the trimmings goes for $6–7.50, and bottomless self-serve coffee is an extra buck. Open daily from 5 A.M. On the quay itself, **Turtle Island Fish & Chips,** 5440 Argyle St., 250/723-4227, features delicious salmon and chips for $8.50 as well as other seafood delicacies. Eat at the couple of tables supplied, or, better still, down on the grassy waterfront area. Through downtown to the west, the **Westwind Pub,** 4940 Cherry Creek Rd., 250/724-1324, is a nautical-themed bar with a good selection of reasonably priced meals.

Information

On the rise above town to the east is **Port Alberni Visitor Info Centre**, 2533 Redford St., 250/724-6535. This excellent facility is a great source of information on Pacific Rim National Park, transportation options to Bamfield, and all west coast attractions. It's open in summer daily 8 A.M.–6 P.M., the rest of the year Mon.–Fri. 9 A.M.–5 P.M. The best source of pre-trip planning is the Alberni Valley Chamber of Commerce website, www.avcoc.com.

BAMFIELD

One of the island's most remote communities, this tiny fishing village lies along both sides of a narrow inlet on Barkley Sound. Most people arrive here aboard the **MV *Lady Rose*** from Port Alberni (see above), but the town is also linked to Port Alberni by a rough 100-km logging road. It's well worth the trip out to go fishing, explore the seashore, or just soak up the atmosphere of this picturesque boardwalk village. Bamfield is also the northern terminus of the **West Coast Trail** (see Vicinity of Victoria, earlier in this chapter).

Practicalities

On the boardwalk, but across the channel from the road side of the village, **Bamfield Lodge** comprises self-contained cabins set among trees and overlooking the water. The cabins are $100 per night, which includes transfers. The lodge owners also operate a charter boat for fishing and wilderness trips.

Get to Bamfield aboard the **MV *Lady Rose,*** 250/723-8313 or 800/663-7192. This historic vessel departs Port Alberni's quay year-round on Tuesday, Thursday, and Saturday at 8 A.M., departing Bamfield for the return journey that same afternoon at 1:30 P.M. The fare is $23 each way.

WEST FROM PORT ALBERNI

Highway 4 west from Port Alberni meanders through unspoiled mountain wilderness, and you won't find a gas station or store for at least a couple of hours. The highway skirts the north shore of large Sproat Lake, whose clear waters draw keen trout and salmon anglers. Along the highway, camping at **Sproat Lake Provincial Park** is $17.50 per night. Provided they're not out squelching a fire, you can also see the world's largest water bombers—Martin Mars Flying Tankers—tied up here. Originally designed as troop carriers for World War II, only five were ever built and only two remain, both here at Sproat Lake. Used to fight wildfires, these massive flying beasts—36 meters long and with a wingspan over 60 meters—skim across the lake, each filling its tank with 27 tons of water.

Ninety-one km from Port Alberni, Highway 4 splits, leading eight km south to Ucluelet or 34 km north through Pacific Rim National Park to Tofino.

UCLUELET

A small town of 1,800 on the northern edge of Barkley Sound, Ucluelet (pronounced yoo-CLOO-let) was first established centuries ago by the Nuu-chal-nulth people as a fishing village. In the native language, the town's name means "People with a Safe Landing Place." During the last century or so, Ucluelet has also been a fur sealers' trading post and a logging and sawmill center. But fishing remains the steady mainstay, as evidenced by the town's resident fishing fleet and several fish-processing plants.

Today Ucluelet is obviously also benefitting from the tourism industry, netting a good share of all the west coast visitors. Many of these visitors also come for the fishing, particularly for chinook salmon (Feb.–Sept.) and halibut (May–July). The fall runs of chinook can yield fish up to 20 kilograms, and the town's busy charter fleet offers deep-sea fishing excursions as well as whale-watching trips.

Head south through town, passing **He-tin-kis Park,** where a short trail leads through a littoral rainforest to a small stretch of rocky beach, to the end of Peninsula Road, where a **lighthouse,** one of the most accessible along Canada's west coast, guides shipping along the coast. The **Wild Pacific Trail** links the lighthouse and the park.

VANCOUVER ISLAND

Practicalities

At unique **Canadian Princess Resort** on Peninsula Rd., 250/726-7771 or 800/663-7090, website www.obmg.com, you can spend the night aboard the 75-meter steamship *Canadian Princess,* which is permanently anchored in Ucluelet Harbour. The least expensive rooms aboard this historic gem are small and share bathroom facilities, but they're still good value at $65 s, $75 d. The resort also offers modern, more expensive onshore rooms and has a large fleet of boats for fishing charters. Most people staying here do so, on a multi-night fishing package. On the high side of Peninsula Rd. is **Peninsula Motor Inn,** 250/726-7751 or 888/368-5593, which is basic and charges $65 s, $75 d. Out of town, **Little Beach Resort,** 1187 Peninsula Rd., 250/726-4202, is a pleasant and quiet little spot within walking distance of a small sandy beach. Its 19 units go for $80–150 s or d. Fisherfolk congregate at **Island West Fishing Resort,** 160 Hemlock St., 250/726-7515, website www.islandwest resort.com, which has its own marina right on the inlet and serves as the base of operations for a wide range of charter boats. The resort also has a good restaurant and pub. In the height of summer, rooms—each with full kitchen—run from a reasonable $89 s or d. Waterfront RV parking (not suitable for tents) costs $25.

Holidaying anglers head to the pub or restaurant at Island West Fishing Resort, 250/726-7515. Locals congregate at **Smiley's,** 1922 Peninsula Rd., 250/726-4213, for breakfast, lunch, and dinner, and for its bowling lanes. The **Peninsula Restaurant,** in the front of the Peninsula Motor Inn at 1648 Peninsula Rd., 250/726-7751, which sports red vinyl booths and faded logging posters, offers a classic "Chinese and Canadian" menu (burgers from $3.50, entrées from $7).

Ucluelet Visitor Info Centre is just off Peninsula Rd. at 227 Main St., 250/726-7289. It's open daily in summer and Mon.–Fri. only the rest of the year.

PACIFIC RIM NATIONAL PARK

Named for its location on the edge of the Pacific Ocean, this park encompasses a long, narrow strip of coast that has been battered by the sea for eons. The park comprises three "units," each very different in nature and each accessed in different ways. The section at the end of Highway

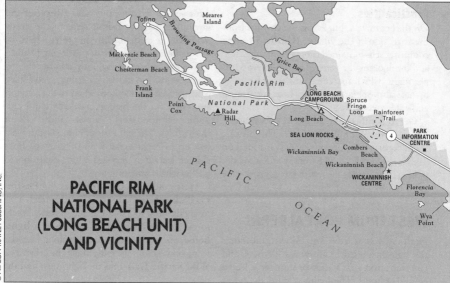

PACIFIC RIM
NATIONAL PARK
(LONG BEACH UNIT)
AND VICINITY

© AVALON TRAVEL PUBLISHING, INC.

4 is the **Long Beach Unit,** named for an 11-km stretch of beach that dominates the landscape. Accessible by vehicle, this is the most popular part of the park and is particularly busy in July and August. To the south, in Barkley Sound, the **Broken Group Islands Unit** (see the special topic) encompasses an archipelago of 100 islands, accessible by the MV *Lady Rose* from Port Alberni. Farther south still is the **West Coast Trail Unit,** named for the famous 77-km-long hiking trail between Port Renfrew and Bamfield (see Vicinity of Victoria, earlier in this chapter).

Flora and Fauna

Like the entire west coast of Vancouver Island, Pacific Rim National Park is dominated by littoral (coastal) rainforest. Closest to the ocean, clinging to the rocky shore, a narrow windswept strip of Sitka spruce is covered by salty water year-round. These forests of spruce are compact and low-growing, forming a natural windbreak for the old-growth forests of western hemlock and western red cedar farther inland. The old-growth forests are strewn with fallen trees and lushly carpeted with mosses, shrubs, and ferns.

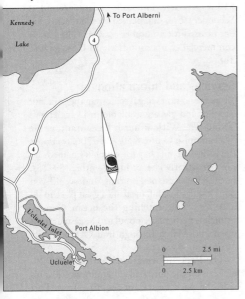

The ocean off western Canada reputedly holds more species of marinelife than any other temperate coast. Gray whales migrate up the coast each spring; seals and porpoises inhabit the park's waters year-round; sea lions overwinter on rocky offshore outcrops; and salmon spawn in the larger creeks through late fall. The tidal zone is the best place to search out smaller sea creatures—anemones, shellfish, and starfish are all colorful residents of the rocky shoreline.

The park's largest land mammal is the black bear, some of which occasionally wander down to the beach in search of food. Also present are blacktail deer, raccoons, otters, and mink. Bald eagles are year-round residents, but it's the migratory birds that arrive in the largest numbers—in spring and fall, thousands of Canada geese, pintails, mallards, and black brants converge on the vast tidal mudflats of **Grice Bay,** in the north of the park beyond the golf course.

Climate

Pacific Rim National Park receives heavy rainfall (3,000 millimeters annually), and the weather here can only be described as extremely changeable. It can be windy and wet in the morning, yet warm and dry in the afternoon—always carry extra clothes and raingear while exploring the park. In summer the average temperature is 15° C (59° F), and dense morning fog usually clears in the afternoon. In winter the park experiences a good proportion of its annual rainfall, and the average temperature is 6° C (43° F). In spring you can expect 10° C (50° F) days, 6° C days in autumn.

Long Beach

Ensconced between rocky headlands is more than 11 km of hard-packed white sand, covered in twisted driftwood, shells, and the occasional Japanese glass fishing float. Dense rainforest and the high snowcapped peaks of the Mackenzie Range form a beautiful backdrop, while offshore lie craggy surf-battered isles home to myriad marinelife. You can access the beach at many places, but first stop at the **Wickaninnish Centre,** 250/726-4212, which overlooks the entire beach from a protected southern cove. This is

VANCOUVER ISLAND

the place to learn about the natural and human history of both the park and the ocean through exhibits and spectacular hand-painted murals. The center is open mid-March to mid-October daily 10:30 A.M.–6 P.M.

Through summer Long Beach attracts hordes of visitors. Most just wander along the beach soaking up the smells and sounds of the sea, but some brave the cool waters for swimming or surfing. The waves here are reputed to be Canada's best; rent boards and wetsuits in Ucluelet and Tofino. In winter, hikers dress for the harsh elements and walk the surf-pounded beach in search of treasures, admiring the ocean's fury during the many ferocious storms.

Hiking

The most obvious place for a walk is Long Beach, but other options are worth consideration. From the Wickaninnish Centre, an 800-meter trail (15 minutes each way) leads south around a windswept headland, passing small coves and Lismer Beach, then descending a boardwalk to pebbly **South Beach.** Back up the hill, the **Wickaninnish Trail** leads 2.5 km (50 minutes each way) over to Florencia Bay. The beach along the bay can also be accessed by road off the Wickaninnish Centre access road. Continuing northwest toward Tofino, the **Rainforest Trail** traverses an old-growth littoral rainforest in two one-km loops (allow 20 minutes for each). Farther north, at the back of the Combers Beach parking lot, is the trailhead for the 1.5-km (30-minute) **Spruce Fringe Loop.** This trail leads along the beach past piles of driftwood and through a forest of Sitka spruce.

Camping

The park's one official campground fills up *very* fast every day through summer. But it's in a marvelous location behind **Green Point,** a beautiful bluff above the beach. Facilities include drive-in sites, washrooms, picnic tables, an evening interpretive program, and plenty of firewood, but no showers or hookups. Mid-March to mid-October, walk-in sites are $14 per night, semi-serviced $20; the rest of the year they're $12 and $18 respectively. The walk-in campground at Schooner Cove, still marked on some maps, has been closed for a number of years. The closest commercial campgrounds are in Ucluelet and Tofino.

Services and Information

There are no stores or gas stations in the park, but supplies and gas are available in Ucluelet and Tofino. The **Wickaninnish Restaurant,** in the Wickaninnish Centre, 250/726-7706, overlooks the wide sweeping bay for which it's named. It's not particularly cheap (lunch entrées $9–18), but the views are magnificent, and even if you don't indulge in a full meal, it's a great place to sip a coffee while watching the ocean. Sunday brunch is particularly popular. The restaurant is open mid-March through mid-October daily 10:30 A.M.–6 P.M.

The **Park Information Centre,** 250/726-4212, is on the north side of Highway 4 just inside the park boundary (coming from Port

© ANDREW HEMPSTEAD

The driftwood-strewn beaches of Pacific Rim National Park are great for beachcombing.

VANCOUVER ISLAND

THE BROKEN GROUP ISLANDS

These 100 or so forested islands in the mouth of Barkley Sound, south of Ucluelet, once held native villages and some of the first trading posts on the coast. Now they're inhabited only by wildlife, and visited primarily by campers paddling through the archipelago in canoes and kayaks. The islands offer few beaches, so paddlers come ashore in the many sheltered bays.

Marinelife abounds in the cool and clear waters; seals, porpoises, and gray whales are present year-round. Birdlife is also prolific. Bald eagles, blue herons, and cormorants are permanent residents, and large numbers of loons and Canada geese stop by on their spring and fall migration routes.

The archipelago extends almost 15 km out to sea from Sechart. The protected islands of **Hand, Gibraltar, Dodo,** and **Willis** all hold campsites and are good destinations for novice paddlers. Farther out, the varying sea conditions make a higher level of skill necessary. Predictably, a westerly wind blows up early each afternoon through summer, making paddling more difficult.

Everyone planning a trip to the islands should buy Marine Chart 3670 from Canadian Hydrographic Service, Chart Sales and Distribution Office, Institute of Ocean Services, 9860 W. Saanich Rd., P.O. Box 6000, Sidney, BC V8L 4B2; $11. The chart includes detailed navigational information on the islands and park, as well as a handy description of campsite facilities. Some islands are marked as having drinking water, but sources are unreliable so plan on bringing your own.

The best way to reach the Broken Group Islands is aboard the **MV Lady Rose** from Port Alberni or Ucluelet. Based in Port Alberni, this historic vessel departs Alberni Harbour Quay June–Sept., Monday, Wednesday, and Friday at 8 A.M., dropping canoeists and kayakers at the abandoned **Sechart Whaling Station.** The Lady Rose then continues to Ucluelet, departing that village at 2 P.M. and making another stop at Sechart before returning to Port Alberni. In July and August, an additional Sunday sailing departs Port Alberni at 8 A.M., stopping at Sechart and returning directly to Port Alberni. The one-way fare between Port Alberni and Sechart is $20; between Ucluelet and Sechart it's $13.

The company that operates the boat also rents canoes and kayaks ($35 and $35–50 per day, respectively), which are left at Sechart so you don't have to pay a transportation charge. If you bring your own canoe or kayak, the transportation charge is $15–20 each way. The trip out on this boat is worthwhile just for the scenery, with the Ucluelet sailing passing right through the heart of the archipelago. For further information and reservations (necessary in summer), call 250/723-8313 or 800/663-7192. **Subtidal Adventures,** 250/726-7336, offers a four-hour trip to the islands departing Ucluelet daily at 1:30 P.M.; $49 pp.

VANCOUVER ISLAND

Alberni, turn right toward Tofino at the Ucluelet/Tofino highway junction). It holds exhibits, displays, and lots of information. Open mid-March to mid-June daily 10:30 A.M.–6 P.M., mid-June through August 8 A.M.–8 P.M., September to mid-October 10 A.M.–6 P.M. For more information, contact the Superintendent, Pacific Rim National Park, P.O. Box 280, Ucluelet, BC V0R 3A0, 250/726-7721, website www.parkscanada.gc.ca/pacrim.

Park Fee

You're not charged a fee just to travel straight through the park to Tofino, but if you stop anywhere en route a strictly enforced charge applies. A two-hour permit is $3 per vehicle, a one-day permit is $8, and a season pass is $42. If you'll be traveling farther afield, consider the **Western Canada Annual Pass,** good for entry to all 11 of western Canada's national parks; $35 per person to a maximum of $70 per vehicle.

Tofino

The bustling fishing village of Tofino sits at the very end of a long narrow peninsula, with the only road access to the outside world being winding Highway 4. The closest town of any size is Port Alberni, 130 km to the east (allow at least two hours); Victoria is 340 km distant.

Originally the site of a native Clayoquot village, Tofino was one of the first points in Canada to be visited by Captain Cook. It was named in 1792 for Don de Vincent Tofino, a hydrographer with a Spanish expedition. Aside from contact with fur traders and whalers, the entire district remained basically unchanged for almost 100 years.

Fishing has always been the mainstay of the local economy, but Tofino is also a supply center for the several hundred hermits living along the secluded shores of the sound and for the hordes of visitors that come in summer to visit Pacific Rim National Park, just to the south. In winter it's a quiet, friendly community with a population of fewer than 1,500. In summer the population swells to several times that size and the village springs to life—fishing boats pick up supplies and deposit salmon, cod, prawns, crabs, halibut, and other delicacies of the sea, and cruising, whale-watching, and fishing boats, along with seaplanes, do a roaring business introducing visitors to the natural wonders of the west coast.

The town lies on the southern edge of sheltered **Clayoquot Sound,** known worldwide for an ongoing fight by environmentalists to save the world's largest remaining coastal temperate forest. Around 200,000 hectares of this old-growth forest remain; a number of new parks, including **Clayoquot Arm Provincial Park, Clayoquot Plateau Provincial Park, Hesquiat Peninsula Provincial Park, Flores Island Provincial Park,** and **Maquinna Marine Provincial Park** have resulted from the Clayoquot Sound Land Use Decision. An influx of environmentally conscious residents over the last two decades has added flavor to one of the west coast's most picturesque and relaxing towns. And due to a large number of aware residents who like Tofino exactly

the way it is, it's unlikely that high-rise hotels or fast-food chains will ever spoil this peaceful coastal paradise.

SIGHTS AND RECREATION
Sun, Sand, and Surf
If you fancy a long walk along a fabulous shell-strewn stretch of white sand, like to sit on craggy rocks watching the waves disintegrate into white spray, or just want a piece of sun all your own to lie in and work on your tan, head for **Chesterman Beach,** just south of Tofino. From that beach, at low tide you can walk all the way out to **Frank Island** to watch the surf pound the exposed side while the tide creeps in and cuts you off from civilization for a few hours. The turnoff (not marked) to Chesterman Beach is Lynn Road, on the right just past the Dolphin Motel as you leave Tofino. Follow the road and park at one of three small parking lots; the parking lot at the corner of Lynn and Chesterman Beach Roads is closest to Frank Island.

Surfers wanting to hit the water should head south of town to **Live To Surf,** 1182 Hwy. 4, 250/725-4464. The shop rents surfboards for $25 per day and wetsuits for $20, and offers lessons for $75 for two people. The staff will also tell you where the best surf can be found, and if there's no surf, they'll tell you how good it was last week. Check the website www.livetosurf.com for west coast surf reports.

Whale-watching
Each spring around 20,000 gray whales migrate between Baja and Alaska, passing through the waters off Tofino between March and May. Most of them continue north, but some stay in local waters through summer. Their feeding grounds are about 30 km up the coast at **Maquinna Marine Park,** accessible by a 20-minute boat trip. During the spring migration and some feeding periods, gray whales are also frequently sighted in the calm inland waters around **Meares Island,** just off Tofino.

© ANDREW HEMPSTEAD

Tofino marks the western end of the TransCanada Highway.

Whale-watching is one of the most popular activities in town, and companies search out whales to watch them cruise up the coast, diving, surfacing, and spouting. On the whale-watching trips, you'll likely spy other marinelife as well; look for sea lions and puffins sunning themselves on offshore rocks, dolphins and harbor seals frolicking in the bays and inlets, and majestic bald eagles gracefully swooping around in the sky or perching in the treetops. Trips depart mid-February to October and generally last 2–3 hours. Expect to pay about $50 per person. (See Local Charter Operators for contact numbers.)

Hot Springs
Pamper yourself and take a boat or floatplane to **Hotsprings Cove,** Vancouver Island's only hot spring. Water bubbles out of the ground at a temperature of 87° C (189° F), tumbles over a cliff, then drops down through a series of pools—each large enough for two or three people—and into the sea. Lobsterize yourself silly in the first

pool, or go for the ultimate in hot/cold torture by immersing yourself in the last pool, where at high tide you'll be slapped by breathtakingly refreshing ocean waves.

Several companies offer excursions out to the hot springs (see below for contact numbers), and although prices vary slightly, expect to pay around $70–80 for a six- to seven-hour trip departing around 10 A.M., with about three hours ashore at the hot springs and the chance to see whales en route. **Tofino Air,** based at the 1st Street dock, 250/725-4454, offers a scenic 15-minute flight to the hot springs by floatplane; from $85 per person round-trip, minimum three persons.

Local Charter Operators
The streets of downtown Tofino hold a profusion of charter operators offering a wide variety of trips. All of those listed below go whale-watching and head out to Hotsprings Cove. Other options include a tour of Meares Island and fishing charters. For details, head to any of the following: **Adventures Pacific,** 120 4th St., 250/725-2811 or 888/486-3466; **Chinook Charters,** 450 Campbell St., 250/725-3431 or 800/665-3646; **Jamie's Whaling Station,** 606 Campbell St., 250/725-3919 or 800/667-9913; **Remote Passages,** 71 Wharf St., 250/725-3330 or 800/666-9833; **Sea Trek,** 441 Campbell St., 250/725-4412 or 800/811-9155; **Seaside Adventures,** 300 Main St., 250/725-2292 or 888/332-4252; or the **Whale Centre,** at 411 Campbell St., 250/725-2132 or 888/474-2288 (head to the Whale Centre to see a 13-meter-long gray whale skeleton). Even with all these operators, business is brisk, so book ahead if possible.

Sea Kayaking
Exploring the waters around Tofino by sea kayak has become increasingly popular in recent years. **Tofino Sea Kayaking Company,** 320 Main St., 250/725-4222, website www.tofino-kayaking.com, has designed tours to meet the demand and suit all levels of experience. Excursions range from a 2.5-hour harbor paddle ($44 per person) to an overnight trip to a remote lodge on Vargas Island ($360 per person). The company's experienced staff will also help adventurous, independent pad-

VANCOUVER ISLAND

dlers plan an itinerary—many camping areas lie within a one-day paddle of Tofino. Single kayak rentals are $43 for one day or $35 per day for two or more days. Double kayaks are $74 and $65, respectively. Rental prices include all the accessories. At the company base, right on the harbor, is a shop selling provisions, accessories (such as marine charts), and a wide range of local literature. Also here are a coffee shop, bookstore, and a few rooms renting for $50 s, $60 d per room per night.

Eagle Aerie Gallery

This gallery, 350 Campbell St., 250/725-3235, features the excellent paintings, prints, and sculptures of Roy Henry Vickers, a well-known and highly respected Tsimshian artist. You can watch a video about the artist, then browse among the artworks—primarily native Canadian designs and outdoor scenes with clean lines and brilliant colors. If you fall for one of the most popular paintings but can't afford it, you can buy it in card or poster form. The gallery itself is built on the theme of a west coast native longhouse, with a carved and painted exterior and interior totem poles. Open in summer daily 9 A.M.–8 P.M., the rest of the year daily 9:30 A.M.–5:30 P.M.

Pacific Rim Whale Festival

Tofino and Ucluelet join together each spring to put on the annual Pacific Rim Whale Festival, which features educational shows and special events in the adjacent national park, a native song and dance festival, a parade, crab races, plays at the local theater, dances, concerts, a golf tournament, and a multitude of events and activities in celebration of the gray whale spring migration. The festival takes place the last two weeks of March. To receive a Pacific Rim Whale Festival package, including a calendar of events, whale-watching information, and accommodations brochures, call 250/725-3414.

ACCOMMODATIONS AND CAMPING

Tofino boasts plenty of accommodations, both in town and on the outskirts. But getting a room or campsite in summer can be difficult if you just turn up, so book as far ahead as possible. Without exception, all accommodations offer deeply discounted off-season rates.

Under $50

Tofino's least expensive accommodation is **Whalers on the Point Guesthouse,** 300 meters from downtown at 81 West St., 250/725-3443, website www.tofinohostel.com. Affiliated with Hostelling International, it is a world away from hostels of old, appealing to all travelers. The building is a stylish log structure, with a stunning waterfront location, of which the communal lounge area takes full advantage. Other facilities include a modern kitchen, laundry, large deck with a barbecue, game room, and bike rentals. Dorm beds are $22 for members ($24 for nonmembers). Private rooms with shared bathrooms cost $66 s or d ($70 for nonmembers) and ensuite rooms are $99 ($119 for nonmembers). Check-in is between 7 A.M. and noon and 5–11 P.M.

$50–100

Of Tofino's regular motels, least expensive is **Dolphin Motel,** on the highway into town, 250/725-3377, which charges $75 s, $79 d.

Continuing into town, **Tofino Swell Lodge** is just off the highway at 341 Olsen Rd., 250/725-3274. Above a busy marina, this seven-room motel offers well-decorated rooms, shared use of a fully equipped kitchen and living room (complete with stereo, TV, and telescope), and pleasant gardens with incredible views of Tofino Inlet, tree-covered Meares Island, and distant snowcapped mountains. Summer rates are $80 s, $95 d.

$100–150

Out of town to the south are a number of oceanfront resorts. Of these, **Middle Beach Lodge,** 250/725-2900, website www.middlebeach.com, offers the most unique west coast experience. It comprises two distinct complexes: "At the Beach," more intimate, with its own private beach, and the other, "At the Headland," with luxurious self-contained chalets built along the top of a rugged headland. A short trail links the two, and guests are welcome to wander between them.

Outdoor settings are scattered throughout the property. Rates "At the Beach" start at $105, ocean views from $140, and all rates include a gourmet continental breakfast served in a magnificent common room. Rates "At the Headlands" start at $140 rising to over $300. This part of the complex has a restaurant with a table d'hôte menu offered nightly.

The **Inn at Tough City,** right on the waterfront at 350 Main St., 250/725-2021, is a new lodging constructed with materials sourced from throughout the region. The bricks, all 30,000 of them, were salvaged from a 100-year-old building in Vancouver's historic Gastown, while stained glass windows, hardwood used in the flooring, and many of the furnishings are of historical value. The rooms are decorated in a stylish heritage color scheme, and beds are covered in plush down duvets. Summer rates are $140–175 s or d, discounted as low as $75 in winter.

$150–200

Tofino has many fine accommodations, so picking a favorite is difficult, but **Cable Cove Inn,** 201 Main St., 250/725-4236 or 800/663-6449, website www.cablecoveinn.com, is difficult to go past. It's tucked away in a quiet location overlooking a small cove, yet it's only a couple of hundred meters from the center of town. Well-furnished in a casual yet elegant style, each of the six rooms features a private deck and a fireplace. The least expensive room is $160 s or d, while the others, ranging $185–205, each have a hot tub. Outside of summer, rooms range $110–175. A continental breakfast is included in these rates. Book well in advance to be assured of a room.

In the best location in town, right beside the main dock, is **Himwitsa Lodge,** 300 Main St., 250/725-3319 or 800/899-1947, website www.himwitsa.com. No expense has been spared in the four contemporary upstairs suites, each with hot tub, comfortable lounge and writing area, TV and videocassette player, fully equipped kitchen, and private balcony with spectacular ocean views. Summer rates are $160–225 s or d with a two-day minimum; from $120 the rest of the year.

Out of town to the south is **Tin-Wis Resort Lodge,** 250/725-4495 or 800/661-9995, website www.tinwis.com. This beachfront accommodation sprawls across extensive grounds, with all rooms having views across Mackenzie Beach, and guests can take advantage of a spa facility and a popular in-house restaurant and lounge. Summer rates start at $175 s, $195 d, but for $20 extra, you get a suite with a king size bed and kitchen.

Camping

All Tofino's campgrounds are on the beaches south of town, but enjoying the great outdoors comes at a price in this part of the world, with some campsites costing over $50 a night. Best of the bunch is **Bella Pacifica Campground,** 250/725-3400, website www.bellapacifica.com, which is right on MacKenzie Beach and offers protected tent sites, full hookups, coin-operated showers, and a laundry. Sites are $26–34. Along the same stretch of sand, **Crystal Cove Beach Resort,** 250/725-4213, website www.crystalcovebeachresort.com, is one of the province's finest campgrounds. Facilities are modern, with personal touches such as complimentary coffee each morning and book exchange. Many of the sites are in a private heavily wooded area (unserviced $35, hookups $45) while others are right along the beach ($55).

OTHER PRACTICALITIES
Food

Tofino has grocery stores, fish and seafood stores, bakeries, and a variety of cafés and restaurants, many of them serving locally caught seafood. The **Common Loaf Bake Shop,** 180 1st St., 250/725-3915, is a favorite with locals (cinnamon rolls $1.35); sit outside or upstairs, where you'll have a magnificent view down Tofino's main street and across the sound. It's open daily 8 A.M.–6 P.M. Another popular café is the **Coffee Pod,** along the main highway at 4th St., 250/725-4246, serving healthy sandwiches, salads, and cakes and pastries.

The best views in town are from the nautical-themed **Sea Shanty,** 300 Main St., 250/725-2902, part of the Himwitsa Lodge complex above the marina. Breakfasts are around $7, pastas $13–15, and seafood delicacies—the bulk of the menu—over $18. In Weigh West Marine Resort's **Blue Heron Restaurant,** 634 Campbell St., 250/725-3277, you can savor delicious clam chowder with garlic toast for $6.50, and seafood or steak dinners for $13–19. In the same complex is a pub with inexpensive meals and water views. The **Loft,** 346 Campbell St., 250/725-4241, is open in summer daily 7 A.M.–8 P.M. for breakfast ($4–9), lunch ($6–11), and dinner ($9–21). The house specialty is west coast seafood, the atmosphere is relaxed, and the service is smart.

Transportation, Services, and Information

Laidlaw, 250/725-3101 or 800/318-0818, runs one bus daily between Victoria and Tofino.

The bus departs Victoria at 8:05 A.M. and Nanaimo at 11 A.M. before heading west along Highway 4, arriving in Tofino at 3:30 P.M. The return service departs Tofino at 4:10 P.M., arriving back in Nanaimo at 8:05 P.M. and Victoria at 11 P.M.

North Vancouver Air, 604/278-1608 or 800/228-6608, flies from its base near Vancouver's South Terminal to Tofino. Though it doesn't offer any scheduled flights, **Tofino Air,** based at the foot of 1st St., 250/725-4454, provides scenic floatplane flightseeing and charters.

The **post office,** a **laundromat,** and **Tofino General Hospital,** 250/725-3212, are all on Campbell Street. **Tofino Visitor Info Centre,** 121 3rd St., 250/725-3414, website www.tofinobc.org, is open in summer daily 9 A.M.–9 P.M., the rest of the year Mon.–Fri. 11 A.M.–4 P.M.

North from Nanaimo

Back on the east side of the island, the new Inland Island Highway north of the Highway 4 junction bypasses a stretch of coast that has developed as a popular holiday area, with many beaches, resorts, and waterfront campgrounds. The new route rejoins Highway 19 at Mud Bay.

Approximately halfway up the island is the **Comox Valley,** a popular year-round destination where you'll find more great beaches and fishing, and great downhill skiing and boarding on the back doorstep during the colder months.

PARKSVILLE TOWARD COURTENAY

Parksville

Golden sand fringes the coastline between Parksville (pop. 10,000) and Qualicum Beach. Parksville Beach claims "the warmest water in the whole of Canada." When the tide goes out along this stretch of the coast, it leaves a strip of sand up to a kilometer wide exposed to the sun. When the water returns, voilà—sand-heated water. **Rathtrevor Beach Provincial Park,** a 347-hectare chunk of coastline just south of Parksville, features a fine two-km-long sandy beach, a wooded upland area, nature trails, and bird-watching action that's particularly good in early spring, when seabirds swoop in for an annual herring feast. Plenty of campsites are available, but in summer line up early in the morning to stake your claim; walk-in sites $12, pull-throughs $18.50. Also on Rathtrevor Beach is three-story **Gray Crest Seaside Resort,** 1115 Island Hwy. E, 250/248-6513 or 800/663-2636, website www .graycrest.com, offering modern, kitchen-equipped units, some with a fireplace and hot tub; $120–178 s or d. Many other motels line

> *Golden sand fringes the coastline between Parksville and Qualicum Beach. Parksville Beach claims "the warmest water in the whole of Canada." When the tide goes out, it leaves a strip of sand up to a kilometer wide exposed to the sun. When the water returns, voilà—sand-heated water.*

this strip of coast, but none are particularly cheap. On the south side of Parksville, **Arbutus Grove Motel,** 1182 Island Hwy. E, 250/248-6422 or 888/667-7250, offers basic but clean and comfortable accommodations for $70 s or d.

On the southern outskirts of town, the **Parksville Visitor Info Centre,** 1275 Island Hwy. E, 250/248-3613, is open in summer daily 8 A.M.–8 P.M., the rest of the year Mon.–Fri. 9 A.M.–5 P.M. Adjacent to the information center is the outdoor **Craig Heritage Museum,** 250/248-6966, comprising historic buildings such as a post office and church; admission is free.

Qualicum Beach

This beach community (pop. 7,000) is generally quieter than Parksville, but it shares the same golden sands of Georgia Strait and attracts the same droves of beach-goers, sun worshippers, anglers, and golfers on summer vacation. The beachfront highway through town is lined with motels, resorts, and RV parks. The attractive downtown area, locally known as "the Village," is off the main highway and up a steep hill to the west. If you appreciate high-quality arts and crafts, detour off the main drag at this point and head for the **Old Schoolhouse Gallery and Art Centre,** 122 Fern Rd. W, 250/752-6133. The gallery occupies a beautifully restored 1912 building, while working artist studios below allow you a chance to see wood-carving, printmaking, pottery, weaving, painting, and fabric art in progress. Don't miss a stop at the gallery shop, where all kinds of original handcrafted treasures are likely to lure a couple of dollars out of your wallet.

At **Old Dutch Inn,** across from the water at 2690 West Island Hwy., 250/752-6914 or 800/661-0199, website www.olddutchinn.com,

VANCOUVER ISLAND

facilities include an indoor pool, sauna and whirlpool, restaurant, and high-standard rooms for $79–109 midweek, $89–119 weekends. The best camping is at **Qualicum Bay Resort,** north of Qualicum Beach at 5970 West Island Hwy., 250/757-2003 or 800/663-6899, website www.resortbc.com. Separated from the water by a road, facilities at this family-oriented resort include a manmade swimming lake, a playground, a games room, an ice cream stand, and a restaurant. Tent sites are $12, hookups $16–22, cabins and motel rooms $60–90 s or d.

For the complete rundown on this stretch of the coast, stop in at **Qualicum Beach Visitor Info Centre,** on the waterfront side of the highway, 250/752-9532, website www.qualicum.bc.ca.

Horne Lake Caves Provincial Park

Continue 11 km beyond Qualicum Beach and turn off at the Horne Lake Store, following the road for 16 km to this intriguing park where the Qualicum River drains into Horne Lake. The park encompasses a system of caves at the base of the Beaufort Range and also offers good swimming and fishing, canoe rentals, and camping for $18.50 per night. Several different guided tours of the caves are offered. The 90-minute tour of Riverbend Cave includes a short walk as well as underground exploration and explanation; adult $15, child $12. Two other caves are open for exploration without a guide. There's no charge for entering these caves, but you'll need a helmet and light source, which can be rented for $5. All caves are open mid-June to September daily 10 A.M.–4 P.M. For details call 250/757-8687.

Denman Island

Island-hoppers can catch the Denman Island ferry from Vancouver Island's **Buckley Bay** for a one-km, 10-minute trip across Baynes Sound to this quiet, mostly undeveloped island. Fishing, boating, and scuba diving are prime draws here, and you'll also find good beaches, parks, and an artisan community.

Just a short walk from the ferry, the downtown area boasts a number of early 20th century heritage buildings. Across the island, 23-hectare

Fillongley Provincial Park features forested trails, long stretches of beach, and campsites for $12. At **Boyle Point Provincial Park** in the south, an 800-meter loop trail (15 minutes round-trip) leads to a lookout with views across to Chrome Island, where a lighthouse stands.

Get to Denman Island with **B.C. Ferries,** 250/335-0323. The service runs hourly 7 A.M.–11 P.M., and reservations aren't necessary. Peak round-trip fare is adult $4.75, child $2.50, vehicle $11.75.

Hornby Island

Every hour, 8 A.M.–6 P.M., a small ferry departs the southern end of Denman Island for Hornby Island, a short, 10-minute run across Lambert Channel. The fares are the same as the Buckley Bay–Denman Island run. This small, seldom-visited island has great beaches, especially along crescent-shaped Tribune Bay, where the longest stretch of sand is protected by 95-hectare **Tribune Bay Provincial Park.** Continue beyond that park and take St. John's Point Road to 287-hectare **Helliwell Provincial Park,** on a rugged, forested headland where trails lead through an old growth forest of Douglas fir and western red cedar to high bluffs. Allow 90 minutes for the full five-km loop.

Neither of those provincial parks permits camping. Instead, stay at **Tribune Bay Campsite,** 250/335-2359, website www.tribunebay.com, on the beach; tent sites $24, electrical hookups $27. Right by the ferry dock is **Hornby Island Resort,** 4305 Shingle Spit Rd., 250/335-0136, which offers a marina and boat rentals, tennis courts, a restaurant and pub, and a laundry. RV camping is $20 per night, rooms in the main complex are $75 s or d, or stay in surrounding cabins for $725 per week.

COMOX VALLEY

The three communities of **Courtenay, Cumberland,** and **Comox** lie in the beautiful Comox Valley, nestled between Georgia Strait and high snowcapped mountains to the west. Welcome to the "Recreational Capital of Canada," where you can enjoy beaches, excellent downhill and cross-country skiing, fishing, golfing, and camping. The valley lies almost halfway up the island, 220 km from Victoria, but ferries also link it to the mainland.

Courtenay Sights

The valley's largest town and a commercial center for local farming, logging, fishing, and retirement communities, Courtenay (pop. 19,000) sprawls around the head of Comox Harbour. It's not particularly scenic but has a few interesting sights and plenty of accommodations. It was named for Captain George Courtenay, who led the original surveying expedition of the area in 1848.

As you enter Courtenay from the south, you pass all sorts of restaurants, the information center, and motel after motel. Continue into the heart of town and you come to the pleasing downtown area with its cobbled streets, old-fashioned lamps, brick planters full of flowers, and numerous shops. The main attraction downtown is **Courtenay and District Museum,** 207 4th St., 250/334-0686. Step back in time to visually relive the history of the Comox Valley from prehistoric times to the present. The highlight is a full-size replica of an elasmosaur. The original—12 meters long and 80 million years old—was found at the nearby Puntledge River. Other exhibits include a series of realistic dioramas and a replica of a bighouse containing many native artifacts and items, some formerly belonging to prominent chiefs. Finish up in the gift shop, which is well stocked with local arts and crafts. The museum is open May–Aug. daily 10 A.M.–4:30 A.M., the rest of the year Tues.–Sat. 10 A.M.–4:30 P.M.

From downtown, cross the bridge to the totem pole–flanked entrance to **Lewis Park,** at the confluence of the Puntledge and Tsolum Rivers. The two rivers join here to form the very short Courtenay River.

Cumberland Sights

Coal was first discovered in the Comox Valley in 1869, and by the mid-1880s extraction of the most productive seam was going ahead, near present-day Cumberland. The mine was operated by the Union Colliery Co., which brought in thousands of Chinese workers. Cumberland's Chi-

natown was once home to 3,000 people, second in size only to San Francisco's Chinatown. Mother Nature has taken her toll on the settlement—search out signs 1,500 meters west of Cumberland or ask for directions at the small museum on at 2680 Dunsmuir St., 250/336-2445. Admission is $3 and it's open daily 9 A.M.–5 P.M.

Comox Sights

In the small community of Comox, six km east of Courtenay, **Filberg Heritage Lodge and Park,** Comox Ave. at Filberg Rd., 250/339-2715, is worth a visit. The beautifully landscaped three-hectare grounds stretch along the waterfront and are open dawn to dusk year-round. Built by an early logging magnate, the lodge dates to 1929 and is open in summer daily 11 A.M.–5 P.M.; admission $3. You can visit farm animals at the petting zoo, then savor lunch or afternoon tea in the Filberg Teahouse. In early August, **Filberg Festival** features gourmet food, free entertainment, and unique arts and crafts from the best of B.C.'s artisans.

For insight into Canadian Air Force history, browse through **Comox Air Force Museum and Airpark,** at the entrance to Comox Air Force Base at the end of Ryan Rd., 250/339-8162. The museum isn't huge, but is chock-full of air force memorabilia. Outside the main building are four fighter planes. It's open in summer daily 10 A.M.–4 P.M., the rest of the year Sat.–Sun. 10 A.M.–4 P.M.

North of the ferry terminal, **Seal Bay Nature Park** protects one of the region's few undeveloped stretches of coastline. Trails lead through a lush forest of Douglas fir and ferns to a pleasant rocky beach. The park is on Waveland Road; take Anderton Road north from downtown Comox.

Summer Recreation

The heart of 250,000-hectare **Strathcona Provincial Park** is accessed from Highway 28 west of Campbell River (see Highway 28, below), but from Courtenay a gravel road climbs 35 km to **Forbidden Plateau,** a high alpine area in the extreme east of the park. The road ends at **Mt. Washington Alpine Resort.**

Between July and mid-October, the Eagle Express chairlift opens up higher elevations for hikers and bikers. To really experience the alpine environment, continue up to the plateau proper and an extensive network of trails and backcountry campgrounds. Ride the lift all day for adult $10, senior or child $8, or use the lift to access downhill mountain bike trails for $15 (mountain bike rental $15). For summer resort information call 250/338-1386; for winter information see below.

Comox Valley Kayaks, 2020 Cliffe Ave., 250/334-2628 or 888/545-5595, offers a sunset paddle for $35, three-hour sea-kayaking lessons for $40 per person, and full-day guided trips from $75. Or rent a kayak for some exploration by yourself, around the local waterways or out on nearby Denman and Hornby Islands; $35–63 for 24 hours. The company also rents canoes—great for nearby Comox Lake—for $28 per day.

Skiing and Snowboarding

In winter, you may be surprised to find all accommodations in Comox Valley fully booked. Off season for the rest of Vancouver Island is high season here, as hordes of skiers and snowboarders from the island and the mainland come to plant their poles on the slopes of two nearby winter resorts.

FORBIDDEN PLATEAU

This high plateau west of the Comox Valley was "forbidden" according to ancient legend. The village of Comox was threatened by Cowichan warriors many moons ago, so the Comox men sent their women and children up the mountain to be out of harm's way. When the danger was over, the men went up to collect their families, but they had disappeared without a trace—and were never seen again. Not knowing how or why the party disappeared off the face of the planet, the plateau became for the Comox a fearful and forbidden place. But judging by the number of skiers and hikers who explore Forbidden Plateau and return to tell the tale, the legend has been put to rest.

Mt. Washington Alpine Resort, 35 km northwest of Courtenay, attracts the fourth-largest number of skiers and boarders of any British Columbian resort. With a large self-contained base village, an annual snowfall of nine meters, and winter temperatures that never get too cold, the resort's popularity is no wonder. Six chairlifts serve 370 hectares with the vertical rise a respectable 500 meters and the longest run just under two km. Other facilities include a terrain park and a half pipe. Lift tickets are adult $44, senior $36, and child $23. A cross-country pass to the groomed trails of Paradise Meadows is $16.

Along with over 4,000 beds and an RV park, the base village contains restaurants and bars, a ski and snowboard school, and a couple of rental shops. For general resort information call 250/338-1386; for snow reports call 250/338-1515; for accommodations call 888/231-1499; on the Internet go to website www.mtwashington.bc.ca.

To the south, accessed along a different road, is **Forbidden Plateau Ski Area,** the island's first ski resort. It's a small day-use-only area great for families. You'll find a wide variety of terrain, fabulous views, a day lodge and ski and snowboard school, a chairlift, three T-bars, a rope tow, and a beginner's handletow. The lifts run Fri.–Sun. only. Downhill skiers and boarders pay $35 per day adult, $22 child; cross-country skiers pay $14 per day, which includes use of the chairlift to reach the beginning of the advanced trails. Ski and snowboard rentals are $25–35 per day, and lessons are available. For resort information call 250/334-4744; for snow reports call 250/338-1919.

Accommodations and Camping

The valley's least expensive motels are strung out along the highway (Cliffe Avenue) as you enter Courtenay from the south. Rates here are generally lower than on other parts of the island. The least expensive choice is **Courtenay Riverside Hostel,** 1380 Cliffe Ave., 250/334-1938. This budget accommodation offers private and shared rooms, public Internet access, a games room, and a reading room. Rates range $16–30 pp. A cheap motel is the **Anco Motel,** 1885 Cliffe Ave., 250/334-2451, with a heated outdoor pool; $50 s, $60 d, kitchens an extra $5. Offering excellent value on the same side of town is the **Kingfisher Oceanside Resort,** 4330 South Island Hwy., 250/338-1323 or 800/663-7929, website www.kingfisherspa.com, set around well-manicured gardens and a large heated pool right on the water. The resort also holds a spa facility, a lounge with outdoor seating, and a restaurant renowned for its West Coast cuisine (and a great Sunday brunch buffet). Accommodation choices are 28 regular rooms, each with a private balcony ($125 s, $130 d), or 18 new beachfront suites, each with a fireplace, hot tub, and kitchen (from $165 s or d). The 108-room **Coast Westerly Hotel** overlooks the Courtenay River at 1590 Cliffe Ave., 250/338-7741 or 800/668-7797, website www.coasthotels.com. It is one of the valley's finest accommodations, featuring an indoor pool, a fitness room, and a restaurant and pub. Rates are $139 s, $149 d.

In Comox, **Port Augusta Inn and Suites,** 2082 Comox Ave., 250/339-2277 or 800/663-2141, is close to everything and charges $70 s, $75 d.

Campers have a couple of choices in the Comox Valley. Along Lazo Rd., east of Comox, is **Seaview Tent and Trailer Park,** 250/339-3946, within walking distance of the beach. Unserviced sites are $20, hookups $21–28. Just north of the ferry terminal, **King Coho Fishing Resort,** 1250 Wally Rd., 250/339-2039, website www.king cohoresort.bc.ca, is popular with anglers (especially after the 1 August chinook opening). Its facilities include a boat ramp, boat rentals (from $14 per hour), guided charters, a tackle shop, and a weigh station. Tent sites are $15; serviced sites, some right on the waterfront, are $23–26.

Food

In downtown Courtenay, **Leung Grocery,** 456 5th St., 250/334-3824, is a local favorite serving food at a well-worn Formica counter. Across the road in more salubrious surroundings is **Union Street Grill,** 477 5th St., 250/897-0081. It's remarkably inexpensive, yet the portions are large. Breakfasts are around $5–8, lunches $4–9, and dinners from $8. Sunday brunch, from 10 A.M., is very popular. Another place for a cheap eat is

Betty's Place, on the waterfront below the information center, 250/897-1410.

Occupying one of Courtenay's original residences, the **Old House Restaurant,** 1760 Riverside Lane, 250/338-5406, sits among landscaped gardens right on the river. Downstairs is a casual restaurant/pub with a large outdoor deck, while upstairs is a more formal eatery with the ambience of an elegant country lodge. Both are open daily for lunch and dinner, with the Sunday brunch buffet (10 A.M.–2 P.M.; $15) filling the restaurant with hungry patrons.

Transportation

Getting to Courtenay by public transportation is easy. The most scenic way to arrive from Victoria is aboard VIA Rail's **E&N Railiner,** 250/383-4324 or 800/561-8630. This service terminates in Courtenay, departing Victoria Mon.–Sat. at 8:15 A.M., Sunday at noon. Similarly priced, **Laidlaw,** 250/334-2475 or 800/318-0818, runs buses three times daily between Victoria and Courtenay, continuing north to Campbell River.

B.C. Ferries, 250/386-3431, offers sailings four times daily between Comox and Powell River, allowing mainlanders easy access to midisland beaches and snow slopes and saving visitors to northern Vancouver Island from having to backtrack down to Nanaimo or Victoria. The regular one-way fare for this 75-minute sailing is adult $7.50, child $3.75, vehicle $25, motorcycle $12.50, bicycle $2.50, canoe or kayak $3. Round-trip travelers can save 15 percent by buying the **Circlepac** ticket, good for round-trip travel from mainland British Columbia as well as ferry connections along the Sunshine Coast.

Information

Comox Valley Visitor Info Centre, 2040 Cliffe Ave., 250/334-3234, website www.tourism -comox-valley.bc.ca, is on the main highway leading into Courtenay—look for the totem pole out front. It's open in summer daily 8:30 A.M.–6 P.M., the rest of the year Mon.–Fri. 9 A.M.–6 P.M. Information is also available at **Cumberland Visitor Info Centre,** 2755 Dunsmuir Ave., 250/336-8313.

VANCOUVER ISLAND

NORTH TOWARD CAMPBELL RIVER

An enjoyable place to pitch a tent, 137-hectare **Miracle Beach Provincial Park** is about three km off the main highway, 23 km north of Courtenay. Highlights include a wooded campground, sandy beach, good swimming and fishing, and nature trails. Look for porpoises and seals at the mouth of Black Creek, orcas in the Strait of Georgia, black-tailed deer, black bear, and raccoons in the park, and seabirds and crabs along the shoreline. In summer you can take a nature walk with a park naturalist, participate in a clambake or barbecue, or watch demonstrations and films at the Miracle Beach Nature House. Campsites cost $18.50 per night.

The road through the park ends at **Miracle Beach Resort,** 250/337-5171, website www .miraclebeachresort.com, a popular summer vacation getaway enjoyed by British Columbians for over 50 years. It's a delightful spot, adjacent to trails within the provincial park, and with modern facilities including free showers. Rates range from $15 for a tent site to $32 for a waterfront spot with full hookups.

A few km north of Miracle Beach and 18 km south of Campbell River is **Salmon Point Resort,** 2176 Salmon Point Rd., 250/923-6605, website www.salmonpoint.com, also offering great views of the Strait of Georgia and the snow-capped peaks of the Coast Mountains. Facilities are excellent, including a restaurant overlooking the water, a couple of recreation rooms (one for adults only), fishing guide service and tackle, boat rentals, a heated pool, heated bathrooms, and a laundry. All campsites sit among small stands of pines; tents $18, hookups $25–28.50. Cottages start at $75 per night.

Northern Vancouver Island

The northern section of Vancouver Island is mountainous, heavily treed, dotted with lakes, riddled with rivers and waterfalls, and almost completely unsettled. Just one main highway serves the region, though hundreds of kilometers of logging roads penetrate the dense forests. The gateway to the north is **Campbell River,** another small city that proudly calls itself the "Salmon Capital of the World." From this point north, the Island Highway follows a winding route over mountains and through valleys, first hitting the coast near **Telegraph Cove,** one of Canada's most photogenic communities and the departure point for orca-watching trips to the nutrient-rich waters of Johnstone Strait and Robson Bight. The island's northernmost town is **Port Hardy,** terminus for ferries heading north to Prince Rupert and the gateway to the wild west coast and **Cape Scott Provincial Park.**

CAMPBELL RIVER

This scenic resort town of 30,000 stretches along Discovery Passage 260 km north of Victoria and 235 km southeast of Port Hardy. Views from town—of tree-covered Quadra Island and the magnificent white-topped mountains of mainland British Columbia—are superb, but most visitors come for the superior fishing. The underwater topography creates the prime angling conditions; Georgia Strait ends just south of Campbell River, and Discovery Passage begins. The waterway suddenly narrows to a width of only two km between Vancouver and Quadra Islands, causing some of the strongest tides on the

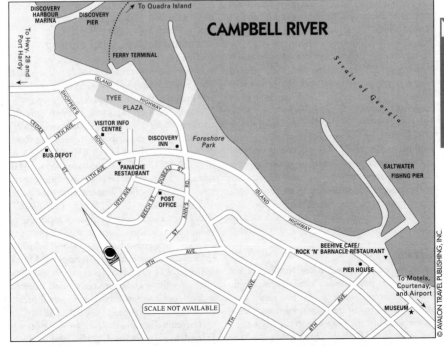

© AVALON TRAVEL PUBLISHING, INC.

coast, attracting bait fish, and forcing thousands of migrating salmon to concentrate off Campbell River, much to every angler's delight.

Sights

The best place to absorb some of the local atmosphere is **Saltwater Fishing Pier.** The 180-meter-long pier is fun to walk on whether you're into fishing or not. Its benches and protected shelters allow proper appreciation of the marina, strait, mainland mountains, and fishing action, even on wet and windy days. The pier also sports built-in rod holders, fish-cleaning stations, and colorful signs describing the fish you're likely to catch. Anglers of all sizes and ages spin cast for salmon, bottomfish, and the occasional steelhead, hauling them up in nets on long ropes. Rod rentals are available at the pier for $3.50 per hour, $9 per half-day, $17 per day. Don't forget, you also need a license.

The **Museum at Campbell River,** at the corner of Island Hwy. and 5th Ave., 250/287-3103, sits on four hectares overlooking Discovery Passage. First check out the photos and interesting written snippets that provide a look at Campbell River's early beginnings. Then feast your eyes on mystical artifacts, a huge collection of masks, exciting artwork, baskets, woven articles, carved-wood boxes, colorful button blankets, petroglyphs, and totem poles. Worth watching in the museum's theater is *Devil Beneath the Sea,* a documentary cataloging the destruction of nearby Ripple Rock by the world's largest non-nuclear explosion. The staff offers special cultural- and natural-history programs in summer. Finish up in the gift shop, where you can buy stunning native prints, masks, postcards, and other paraphernalia. Open May–Aug. daily 9 A.M.–5 P.M., the rest of the year Tues.–Sun. noon–4 P.M. Admission is $3.

Fishing

Salmon are pursued year-round in this area, but May–Oct. is peak season. Steelhead and freshwater cutthroat trout can also be caught year-round in the many freshwater lakes and rivers in the area, but the peak season for steelhead is Jan.–April, for freshwater trout March–May.

Start your research on fishing guides, equipment, and locations at the Visitor Info Centre. The staff stocks hundreds of brochures and will be happy to give you advice and point you in the right direction. Fishing from the Saltwater Fishing Pier is the easiest way to try to hook a big one, but you can also hire a professional guide through the information center.

If you're fishing between 15 July and 15 September, you may want to try qualifying for **Tyee Club** membership. This exclusive club, famous among anglers around the world, has been dedicated to upholding the traditional methods of sportfishing since 1924. Several rules must be followed in order to become a member: You have to preregister your intent to fish under club rules; troll from a rowboat in the mouth of the Campbell River without using a motor; use a rod between six and nine feet long, an artificial lure, and a line not more than 20 pounds pretested breaking weight; then catch a trophy-size tyee (a chinook weighing over 30 pounds). For more information, call the club at 250/287-2724.

Accommodations and Camping

As Campbell River is a resort, every kind of accommodation you could possibly want is here, from campgrounds and RV parks to luxury hotels and exclusive fishing lodges.

Along the highway south of town only the road separates several motels from Discovery Channel. Least expensive of these is **Big Rock Motel,** 1020 Island Hwy., 250/923-4211 or 877/923-4211, with small rooms for $55 s, $64 d, and a few kitchenettes for $70. Continuing north you'll come to the **Best Western Austrian Chalet,** 462 Island Hwy., 250/923-4231 or 800/667-7207, with a wide range of facilities including an indoor pool, a sauna, a restaurant and pub, and even a putting green. Rates start at $99 s, $109 d ($10 extra for an ocean view). **Super 8 Motel,** 340 Island Hwy., 250/286-6622 or 800/800-8000, website www.super8.com, offers a heated indoor pool and hot tub. A continental breakfast is included in the rates of $82 s, $88 d.

Through Campbell River to the north is **Friendship Inn Motel,** 3900 Island Hwy.,

250/287-9591, good value at $54 s, $62 d (head to the adjacent gas station for great potato wedges). Right downtown, **Coast Discovery Inn,** 975 Shopper's Row, 250/287-7155 or 800/663-1144, website www.coasthotels.com, is a full-service hotel with a fitness room, restaurant, and pub; from $135 s, $145 d.

Bed and breakfast accommodations are provided by **Pier House,** across from the Saltwater Fishing Pier at 670 Island Hwy., 250/287-2943. The old antique-filled house has a library and three guest rooms with shared or private bathrooms. Rates range $60–80 s, $80–100 d, including a cooked breakfast.

Many campgrounds line the highway south of town, but although they're close to the water, the surroundings are generally nothing special. One of the better choices is **Campbell River Fishing Village and RV Park,** 260 Island Hwy., 250/287-3630, with sites for $19–22. Less commercial options with limited facilities include **Elk Falls Provincial Park,** six km west of town on Hwy. 28, and **Loveland Bay Provincial Park,** on the shore of Campbell Lake 20 km west of town; $12 and $8, respectively.

Food

One of the best places to go for a meal is the **Bee Hive Cafe,** overlooking the marina at 921 Island Hwy., 250/286-6812. The house specialty is seafood, including clam chowder for $4.50 and fish and chips for around $9. Also on the menu are the usual burgers and salads, and cooked breakfasts ranging $5–9. It's open daily 6:30 A.M.–8 P.M. Above the Bee Hive Cafe, and with even better water views, is **Rock 'n' Barnacle Restaurant,** 915 Island Hwy., 250/286-6812. It offers good views and an upbeat, modern decor. The least expensive entrées, a variety of pastas, are $13.50. Salmon, cooked however you prefer, goes for $18.50. Open daily 5:30–10 P.M. The **Riptide Marine Pub,** 1340 Island Hwy., 250/830-0044, is divided into different sections, including a casual restaurant and a stylish lounge area with the elegant décor of an English gentlemen's club. Lots of seafood is offered, all at reasonable prices. Open daily for lunch and dinner.

Transportation

Campbell River Airport, off Erickson Rd. 20 km south of downtown, is served by **Pacific Coastal,** 800/663-2872, from Vancouver. For transportation between the airport and accommodations, call the **Campbell River Airporter** at 250/286-3000. From Victoria, **Laidlaw** operates three buses daily to Campbell River, with two continuing north to Port Hardy, one of which links up with the ferry to Prince Rupert. The bus depot, 250/287-7151, is on Cedar St. behind the Royal Bank.

Get around town by **Campbell River Transit System,** departing from Tyee Plaza via Shopper's Row. Pick up a schedule in the information center or call 250/287-7433; $1.75 per sector. Rental car agencies in Campbell River include: **Budget,** 250/923-4283; **National,** 250/923-1234; and **Rent-a-wreck,** 250/287-8353.

Services and Information

Park in the large parking lot of Tyee Plaza and you're within easy walking distance of all services, including the **post office** on Beech Street. Within the plaza itself are banks, supermarkets, restaurants, a laundromat, and a bookstore. Island Images gift shop in the plaza also has a post office outlet. The **hospital** is at 375 2nd Ave., 250/287-7111.

At the front of the Tyee Plaza parking lot is **Campbell River Visitor Info Centre,** 1235 Shopper's Row, 250/287-4636. Aside from tons of brochures, free tourist papers, and information on both the local area and Vancouver Island in general, the knowledgeable staff can answer just about any question on the area you could think up. It's open in summer daily 8 A.M.–8 P.M., the rest of the year Mon.–Fri. 9 A.M.–5 P.M. For other information contact **Campbell River Tourism,** 250/286-1616, website www.campbellriver tourism.com.

QUADRA ISLAND

A 10-minute ferry ride from downtown Campbell River takes you to this beautiful island, separated from the mainland by Discovery Passage. The ferry docks in the south of the island, where most of the population resides. This narrow peninsula widens in the north to a vast unpopulated area where wildlife such as black-tailed deer, raccoons, and squirrels are abundant. Marinelife around the shoreline is also widespread; orcas cruise Discovery Passage, and seals and sea lions are commonly spied in surrounding waters. Since Captain Vancouver first stepped ashore at Cape Mudge in 1792 to visit a native village, the island has seen much nonnative activity. It was settled well before the Campbell River area.

From the ferry, take Cape Mudge Road south to **Kwagiulth Museum,** in Cape Mudge Village, 250/285-3733. This excellent facility displays a wide variety of ceremonial dresses used in potlatches, as well as masks and other native artifacts. It's open in summer Mon.–Sat. 10 A.M.–4:30 P.M., Sunday noon–4:30 P.M., the rest of the year Tues.–Sat. 10 A.M.–4:30 P.M. Admission is adult $3, senior and child $2. Native petroglyphs found at the island's southern end have been moved to the museum grounds and can be viewed at any time.

At the island's southern tip, **Cape Mudge Lighthouse** was built in 1898 to prevent shipwrecks in the wild surging waters around the point. On the east coast is **Heriot Bay,** the name of both a cove and the island's largest community. Narrow Rebecca Spit, site of **Rebecca Spit Marine Park,** protects the bay from the elements. Roads lead north from Heriot Bay to the island's wild northern reaches, where you can go hiking to the low summit of **Chinese Mountain** (three km; allow one hour each way); around **Morte Lake** (five km; allow 90 minutes for the loop), and out to **Newton Lake** from Granite Bay (four km; 75 minutes each way).

Practicalities

Adjacent to Cape Mudge Lighthouse is **Tsa-Kwa-Luten Lodge,** 250/285-2042 or 800/665-7745, website www.capemudgeresort.bc.ca. Built by the local Kwagiulth people, the centerpiece of this magnificent waterfront lodge is the foyer, built in the style of a bighouse (a traditional meeting place) in locally milled woods. Each of the 35 spacious rooms is decorated in northwest native theme, and each has a private balcony with water views. Rates start at a reasonable

$125 s or d, with meal packages available. The lodge coordinates fishing charters and cultural activities, and its restaurant specializes in native foods. Another option is **Heriot Bay Inn,** Heriot Bay Rd., 250/285-3322, website www.heriotbayinn.com, a historic lodging with a full service marina, a restaurant, a pub with a great ocean side deck, and kayak and mountain bike rentals. Rooms are $75 s or d including breakfast and cottages cost $115 per night. The inn also offers a campground; $12 for tents, $17–19 with full hookups.

B.C. Ferries, 250/286-1412, offers services from Campbell River to the island, every hour on the hour 6 A.M.–11 P.M.; round-trip fare is adult $4.75, child $2.50, vehicle $12. For a cab, call **Quadra Taxi,** 250/285-3598.

CORTES ISLAND

Accessible by ferry from Quadra Island, Cortes Island (pronounced cor-TEZ—it was named by an early Spanish explorer) is a relatively remote place, closer to the mainland than to Vancouver Island. Few visitors venture out here. A couple of parks are among the island highlights. **Manson's Landing Provincial Park** is a beautiful little spot sandwiched between a large tidal lagoon and the forested shoreline of **Hague Lake.** And in the south of the island is **Smelt Bay Provincial Park,** another great spot for swimming, beachcombing, and taking in the unique island environment.

Practicalities

Accommodations on the island are limited, so unless you plan to camp, make reservations before coming over. **Smelt Bay Provincial Park,** 25 km from the ferry terminal, offers campsites for $12 per site. Closer to the terminal, **Gorge Harbour Marina Resort,** Hunt Rd., 250/935-6433, offers tent sites ($12) and full hookups ($19) beside the island's main marina, as well as four rooms ($70 s or d for bed and breakfast), bike and boat rentals, fishing charters, and a restaurant. Another accommodation choice is **Cortes Island Motel,** at Manson's Landing, 250/935-6363; $69 s, $79 d.

The ferry trip between Quadra and Cortes Islands takes 45 minutes. **B.C. Ferries,** 250/286-1412, operates scheduled service between the islands six times daily, with the first departing Quadra Island at 9 A.M. and the last departing Cortes Island at 5:50 P.M. Peak round-trip fare is adult $5.75, child $3, vehicle $14.50.

HIGHWAY 28

Running from the east coast to the west coast through the northern section of magnificent **Strathcona Provincial Park,** Highway 28 is another island road worth traveling for the scenery alone. The first place to stop is 1,087-hectare **Elk Falls Provincial Park,** six km west of Campbell River. Here you can follow beautiful forest trails to waterfalls, go swimming and fishing, and stay the night (April–Oct.) in a wooded campsite; $12 per night, no showers. Not far beyond the park, the highway parallels Upper Campbell Lake for 20 km before splitting, with the main highway continuing west to Gold River and a side road following the east shore of Buttle Lake into Strathcona Provincial Park.

Strathcona Provincial Park

British Columbia's oldest and Vancouver Island's largest park, Strathcona preserves a vast 250,000-hectare wilderness in the northern center of Vancouver Island. Vancouver Island's highest peak, 2,220-meter **Golden Hinde,** is within the park. The peak was named for Sir Francis Drake's ship, in which he circumnavigated the world in the 1570s (some believe he would have sighted the peak from his ship). The park's other superlative natural features include 440-meter-high **Della Falls,** one of North America's highest waterfalls (see Port Alberni and Vicinity, earlier in this chapter) and a 1,000-year-old, 93-meter-high Douglas fir, British Columbia's tallest known tree. Douglas fir and western red cedar carpet the valley, and wildflowers—lupine, Indian paintbrush, moss campion, and kinnikinnick—cover the high slopes. Resident mammals include black bears, wolves, wolverines, cougars, marmots, deer, and the island's only herd of elk. Cutthroat trout, rainbow trout, and Dolly Varden fill park's lakes. And all

kinds of birds soar the skies here, including the provincial bird, the Steller's jay.

You'll get a taste of Strathcona's beauty along Highway 28, but to get into the park proper turn south off Highway 28 halfway between Campbell River and Gold River. This access road hugs the eastern shore of **Buttle Lake,** passing many well-marked nature walks and hiking trails. One of the first is the 500-meter trail (10 minutes each way) to **Lupin Falls,** which are more impressive than the small creek across from the parking lot would suggest. Continuing south along the lakeshore past driftwood-strewn beaches, you'll come to the **Karst Creek Trail** (two-km loop; allow 40 minutes), which passes through a karst landscape of sinkholes and disappearing streams. At the lake's southern end, where the road crosses Thelwood Creek, a six-km trail (2.5 hours each way) climbs a steep valley to **Bedwell Lake** and surrounding alpine meadows.

As the road continues around the lakeshore, look for **Myra Falls** across the water. After passing through the Westmin Resources mining operation, the road ends on the edge of an old-growth forest. From this point, explore on foot by taking the **Upper Myra Falls Trail** (three km; one hour each way) to a lookout point above the falls.

Apart from numerous picnic areas along the shore of Buttle Lake, the only facilities within the park are two campgrounds. **Buttle Lake Campground** is beside Buttle Lake, just west of the junction of Highway 28 and the park access road. **Ralph River Campground** is farther south, on the shore of Buttle Lake. Both have pit toilets, picnic tables, and fire rings, and both charge $12.50 per night.

Gold River

Lying beyond the western edge of Strathcona Provincial Park at the confluence of the Gold and Heber Rivers, the town of Gold River (pop. 1,700) was built in 1965 to house employees of a pulp mill. It was the first all-electric town in Canada. Today it has lodgings, restaurants, stores, gas stations, and banking facilities.

   Peppercorn Trail Motel and RV Park, Mill Rd., 250/283-2443, charges $69 s or d for a very basic room and $18 for a campsite with hookups.

Of a higher standard, but significantly more expensive, is the 48-room **Ridgeview Motor Inn,** 395 Donner Court, 250/283-2277 or 800/989-3393; $95–130 s or d.

Find out about things to see and do in the region at **Gold River Visitor Info Centre,** along the main road (Highway 28) at Muchalat Dr., 250/283-2418, website www.village.goldriver .bc.ca. It's open daily 9 A.M.–4:30 P.M.

Nootka Sound and Beyond

Continue 14 km from Gold River to the dock at the end of Highway 28 and take a cruise up beautiful Nootka Sound on the **MV Uchuck III,** a converted World War II minesweeper. The vessel's primary purpose is dropping supplies at remote west coast communities and logging camps, but paying customers are more than welcome and are made to feel comfortable by the hardworking crew. The main sailing departs year-round every Tuesday at 9 A.M., arriving at **Tahsis** for a one-hour stopover at 1 P.M. before returning to the dock at 6 P.M.; adult $45, senior $41, child $22. A second sailing departs year-round Thursday at 7 A.M., heading out to the open ocean and up the coast to **Kyuquot.** This is an overnight trip, and accommodations are included in the price of $195 s, $310 d. A third sailing departs Wednesday at 10 A.M. in summer, visiting two points of historical interest: the spot where in 1778 Captain James Cook and his men became the first Europeans to land on the west coast, and **Friendly Cove,** where in 1792 Captain George Vancouver and Don Juan Francisco de la Bodega y Quadra negotiated possession of Nootka Sound territory. Fare for this sailing is adult $40, senior $37, child $20. One-way fares are available to all the above points for those exploring by sea kayak. For further information and reservations contact Nootka Sound Services, 250/283-2325, website www.mvuchuck.com.

Tahsis is also accessible by road from Gold River (70 km one-way), from where another logging road continues north to **Zeballos.** Gold was discovered in the region in the late 1700s, but it was over a century later, in 1924, that mining began on the Zeballos River. The mining took place inland, but the township grew on the ocean, where supplies were dropped off and the ore shipped out. Mining continued until 1948, but a road linking Zeballos to the outside world wasn't completed until 1970. Today, Zeballos is a quiet backwater, a base for commercial and recreational fishing boats, and home to a couple of small lodges. Call the local information center for all bookings, 250/761-4070, or go to the website www.zeballos.com.

NORTH TO PORT McNEILL

Highway 19, covering the 235 km between Campbell River and Port Hardy, is a good, fast road with plenty of straight stretches and not much traffic. Passing through kilometer after kilometer of relatively untouched wilderness, with only logged hillsides to remind you of the ugliness humanity can produce with such ease, it's almost as though you've entered another world, or at least another island. Stop at all the frequent rest areas for the very best views of deep blue mountains, white peaks, sparkling rivers and lakes, and cascading waterfalls.

Sayward

This small logging town (pop. 1,000) lies 15 km north of the Island Highway on Johnstone Strait. Down on the waterfront, the main attraction is the **log sort,** where cut logs from active logging areas are brought to be sorted for transportation south.

Nimpkish Valley

Continuing toward the north end of the island, the highway is one moment flanked by steep snowcapped mountains and gorgeous lakes, the next by bleak, desolate logged areas. In the Nimpkish Valley you'll pass the turnoff to **Ski Mt. Cain,** a small community-operated winter resort with two T-bars serving a vertical rise of 500 meters. The terrain is a good mix for all levels of ability, and the area's high snowfalls make it a hidden gem for hardcore powderhounds.

Telegraph Cove

Most visitors come to Telegraph Cove to go whale-watching on Johnstone Strait (see the special topic), but the village itself is well worth the eight-km detour from the highway. Built around a deep sheltered harbor, it's one of the last existing "boardwalk" communities on the island. Many of the buildings stand on stilts and pilings over the water, linked by a boardwalk.

Fewer than 20 people live here year-round, but the population swells enormously during late spring and summer when whale-watching, diving, and fishing charters do a roaring trade, canoeists and kayakers arrive to paddle along Johnstone Strait, and the campground opens for the season. Walk along the boardwalk, passing cabins, an art gallery, and a small store selling groceries, fishing tackle and licenses, bait, gas, oil, and souvenirs.

WHALE-WATCHING IN JOHNSTONE STRAIT

More than 50 whale-watching operations have sprung up around Vancouver Island in recent years, but the opportunity to view orcas (killer whales) close up in Johnstone Strait is unparalleled. These magnificent, intelligent mammals spend the summer in the waters around Telegraph Cove and are most concentrated in **Robson Bight,** where they rub on the gravel beaches near the mouth of the Tsitka River.

Stubbs Island Whale Watching pioneered whale-watching trips in the early 1980s and was involved in the establishment of **Robson Bight** as an ecological reserve. The company's two boats, *Lukwa* and *Gikumi,* depart Telegraph Cove on half-day whale-watching cruises daily from late May to early October. The experienced crew takes you out to view the whales in their natural habitat and to hear their mysterious and beautiful sounds through a hydrophone (underwater microphone). Both boats are comfortable, with covered areas and bathrooms.

The cost of the cruise is adult $65, senior or child $58.50. Make reservations as far ahead as possible at 604/928-3185 or 800/665-3066, website www.stubbs-island.com. Dress warmly and don't forget your camera for this experience of a lifetime.

Some of the cabins and houses on the boardwalk can be rented by the night, but they generally need to be reserved well in advance. The cabins are simply furnished, have kitchens, and enjoy an incredible setting; from $90 s or d for the most basic. Overlooking the bay, Wastell Manor has been restored, with the four well-furnished guest rooms ranging $145–175. Finally, a short walk from the village is a campground with wooded sites as well as showers, a laundromat, boat launch, and store. Sites are $18–23. For reservations at any of the above options, contact **Telegraph Cove Resorts,** 250/928-3131, website www.telegraph coveresort.com.

Port McNeill

The small coastal logging town of Port McNeill (pop. 3,000) lies on Broughton Strait 200 km from Campbell River. It's the regional headquarters for three logging companies and home of "the world's largest burl," on the main highway two km north of town at the entrance to a logging company office—you can't miss it. The center of town comprises a shopping plaza and industrial waterfront development. Stop at **Port McNeill Visitor Info Centre,** 1626 Beach Dr., 250/956-3131, for information on Alert Bay (see below).

ALERT BAY (CORMORANT ISLAND)

This fascinating village is the only settlement on crescent-shaped Cormorant Island, which lies in Broughton Strait 45 minutes by ferry from Port McNeill. The island's population of 600 is evenly split between natives and nonnatives.

Alert Bay holds plenty of history. Captain Vancouver landed there in the late 1700s, and it's been a supply stop for fur traders and gold miners on their way to Alaska, a place for ships to stock up on water, and home base to an entire fishing fleet. Today the village is one of the region's major fishing and marine service centers, and it holds two fish-processing and -packing plants. Half the island is owned by the Kwakiutl, whose powerful art draws visitors to Alert Bay.

Sights

All the island's numerous attractions can be reached on foot or by bicycle. Start by wandering through the village to appreciate the turn-of-the-century waterfront buildings and the colorful totems decorating **Nimpkish Burial Ground.**

For an outstanding introduction to the fascinating culture and heritage of the Kwakiutl, don't miss the **U'Mista Cultural Centre** on Front St., 250/974-5403. Built to house a ceremonial potlatch collection confiscated by the federal government after a 1921 ban on potlatches, the center contains masks and other Kwakiutl art and artifacts. Take a guided tour through the center, then wander at leisure past the photos and colorful displays to watch two award-winning films produced by the center—one explains the origin and meaning of the potlatch. The center also teaches local children the native language, culture, song, and dance. It's open year-round Mon.–Fri. 9 A.M.–5 P.M., Saturday noon–5 P.M. Admission is adult $7, senior $6, child $3.

Also on the north end of the island you'll find the **Indian Bighouse,** the world's second tallest totem pole (it's 52.7 meters high—the highest is in Victoria), and the historic century-old **Anglican Church.** Take a boardwalk stroll through the intriguing ecological area called **Gator Gardens** to see moss-draped forests, ghostly black-water swamps, and lots of ravens, bald eagles, and other birds. If you're still looking for something to do, consider a whale-watching cruise (June–Sept.) with **Sea Smoke Charters,** 250/974-5225; adults $70, children $55. The cruise lasts around six hours and includes a seafood lunch.

Practicalities

The island's least expensive accommodation is **Alert Bay Campground,** overlooking Broughton Strait, with a cookhouse and barbecues, 250/974-5213; campsites are $10–15 per night. Other choices include **Orca Inn,** 291 Fir St., 250/974-5322, website www.orcainn.com, which charges $60 s or d, and **Ocean View Cabins,** 390 Poplar St., 250/974-5457, comprising 12 kitchen-equipped cabins from $65 per night.

B.C. Ferries, 250/956-4533, runs to the island from Port McNeill many times daily. The peak round-trip fare is adult $5.75, children $3. You can take a vehicle over for $14.50 round-trip, but there's no real point as everything on the island is reachable on foot.

Across from the waterfront is **Alert Bay Visitor Info Centre,** 116 Fir St., 250/974-5213. It's open in summer daily 9 A.M.–6 P.M., the rest of the year Mon.–Fri. 9 A.M.–5 P.M.

PORT HARDY

Port Hardy (pop. 5,200) lies along sheltered Hardy Bay, on the edge of Queen Charlotte Strait. It's the largest community north of Campbell River and the terminus for ferries sailing the Inside Passage to and from Prince Rupert. The ferry is the main reason most people drive this far north, but Port Hardy is also a good base from which to explore the wild and untamed northern tip of the island or fish for salmon in the sheltered waters of "King Coho Country."

Sights and Recreation

As you enter the Port Hardy area, take the scenic route to town via Hardy Bay Road. You'll pass several original chainsaw woodcarvings and skirt the edge of peaceful Hardy Bay before entering downtown via Market Street.

One of the most enjoyable things to do in town is to stroll along the **seawalk** to **Tsulquate Park,** where you can appreciate native carvings and do some beachcombing if the tide is out. Many bald eagles reside around the bay, and if you're lucky you'll see them swooping about in the neighborhood. Also along the seawalk, you'll pass **Watchman's Bay,** where another chainsaw woodcarving holds representations of the fishing, logging, and mining industries that support the town, and **Carrot Park** with its unusual "Mile Zero Trans Carrot" sculpture. For years the residents of northern Vancouver Island pleaded for a link with the populated south. Throughout the years various governments made promises and "dangled the carrot" but never came through with the money required to complete the task. Eventually north islanders launched a massive Carrot Campaign, using every means possible to spread the word of their plight. When the campaign became an item on national radio and television, the government relented, kicking in "the rest of the carrot."

Another interesting place to spend a little time is the small **Port Hardy Museum,** 7110 Market St., 250/949-8143. Browse through a variety of artifacts and an old photograph collection, finishing up in the gift shop where you can buy books, postcards, T-shirts with native designs, and crafts by local artists. The museum is open Tues.–Sat. noon–4:30 P.M.

At **Quatse River Hatchery,** on Byng Rd.,

250/949-9022, you can observe incubation and rearing facilities for pink, chum, and coho salmon, as well as steelhead. The hatchery, open Mon.–Fri. 8 A.M.–4:30 P.M., is in the middle of a regional park on the scenic Quatse River. Good fishing on the river attracts droves of anglers year-round, but the Quatse is by no means the only fishing game in town. With so much water—both salt and fresh—surrounding Port Hardy, visiting fishermen probably won't know where to start. Ask at the local sporting-goods store on Market Street for the best fishing spots,

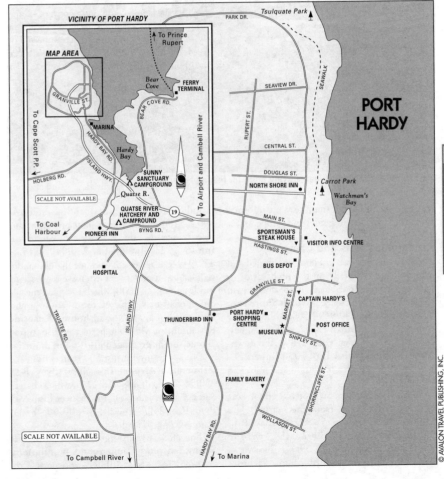

© AVALON TRAVEL PUBLISHING, INC.

VANCOUVER ISLAND

© ANDREW HEMPSTEAD

Port Hardy Marina is an ideal starting point for fishing adventures.

or take a fishing charter (inquire at the information center for current guides and skippers).

Accommodations and Camping

Accommodations in Port Hardy are limited and often fill up, especially on the night prior to ferry departures. Book ahead. Right downtown, the least expensive choice is **North Shore Inn,** 7370 Market St., 250/949-8500. Although the rooms aren't particularly large, each has a balcony with water views; $70 s, $78 d. Also downtown is **Thunderbird Inn,** 7050 Rupert St., 250/949-7767, with a restaurant and pub; $78 s, $84 d.

South of downtown, two hotels overlook Port Hardy's busy harbor from the marina. The **Quarterdeck Inn,** 6555 Hardy Bay Rd., 250/902-0455 or 877/902-0459, website www.quarterdeckresort.net, offers harbor views from each of its 40 smallish rooms. Facilities

include a fitness room, sauna, and a laundry. At $90 s, $100 d, including a light breakfast, this place is excellent value. The adjacent **Glen Lyon Inn,** 6435 Hardy Bay Rd., 250/949-7115 or 877/949-7115, website www.glenlyoninn.com, is older, but it underwent extensive renovations inside and out in 2000, which included the addition of 15 new units. All rooms are large and well equipped, and the in-house Oceanside Restaurant provides the perfect excuse to stay "home" in the evening; $90–120 s or d.

Out at the airport, just 500 meters from the terminal, is **Airport Inn,** 4030 Byng Rd., 250/949-9434 or 888/218-2224, which charges $80 s, $90 d. Farther out, the **Pioneer Inn,** 4965 Byng Rd., 250/949-7271 or 800/663-8744, charges $99 s, $109 d.

The closest camping to downtown is at **Sunny Sanctuary Campground,** near the ferry terminal turnoff at 8080 Goodspeed Rd.,

250/949-8111 or 866/251-4556. Facilities include a barbecue shelter, modern bathrooms, firewood and fire rings, and a small store. The open and treed sites are $16–21. Nearby, **Quatse River Campground,** right by the salmon hatchery on Byng Rd., 250/949-2395, provides endless fishing opportunities, shady sites, showers, and a laundromat. Sites are $20 with electricity, $16 without.

Food

Port Hardy doesn't offer a large variety of dining options. Wander around town and you'll soon see what there is. At **Captain Hardy's,** on Market St., 250/949-7133, the advertised breakfast specials are small and come on plastic plates, but cost only about $3.50. The rest of the day, this place offers good fish and chips from $5.

Dine at the **Oceanside Restaurant,** south of downtown in the Glen Lyon Inn on Hardy Bay Rd., 250/949-3050, for the opportunity to see bald eagles feeding right outside the window. The menu is fairly standard, but well-priced, with many seafood choices. It's open daily for breakfast, lunch, and dinner.

Getting There

Port Hardy Airport, 12 km south of town, is served by **Pacific Coastal,** 604/273-8666 or 800/663-2872, from Vancouver. It's a spectacular flight, with stunning views of the Coast Mountains for passengers seated on the plane's right side.

Airport facilities include parking ($2.50 per day), Budget and National rental car outlets, and a small café. **North Island Transportation,** 250/949-6300, offers twice-daily shuttle service between the airport and downtown accommodations.

Laidlaw, 250/949-7532, operates once-daily bus service up the length of the island, scheduled to correspond with ferry departures. The departure of the southbound bus links with ferry arrivals. The journey between Victoria and Port Hardy takes a painful nine hours and costs around $90 one-way. The depot is the North Island Transportation Ltd. ticket office at 7210 Market Street.

Continuing North by Ferry

Most people arriving in Port Hardy do so with the intention of continuing north by ferry to Prince Rupert and beyond. The ferry terminal is at Bear Cove, eight km from downtown Port Hardy. The *Queen of the North* departs Port Hardy at 7:30 A.M. every second day, arriving in Prince Rupert the same evening at 10:30 P.M. The service runs year-round, but departures are less frequent outside of summer. Peak one-way fare is adult $106, child 5–11 $53, vehicle $218, motorcycle $109, kayak or canoe $17.50, bicycle $6.50. (These peak-season fares are discounted up to 40 percent outside of summer.) A three-meal buffet package is offered for $40, and cabins cost $52 for the day. For reservations (as far in advance as possible in summer) contact **B.C. Ferries,** 250/386-3431 or, toll-free in B.C., 888/223-3779, website www.bcferries.com.

Prince Rupert is the northern terminus of the B.C. Ferries network. From there, you can head east along the Yellowhead Highway and explore northern British Columbia or jump aboard an Alaska Marine Highway ferry and continue north up the Inside Passage. (See Prince Rupert in the Northern British Columbia chapter).

Another option is the "Discovery Coast Passage." B.C. Ferries sails two routes through this area, both departing Port Hardy. The main one is via Shearwater, then east up Dean Channel to Ocean Falls and Bella Coola. Sailings depart in either direction around every three days in summer. One-way fares between Port Hardy and Bella Coola are adult $110, child 5–11 $55, vehicle $220, canoe or kayak $40.75, bicycle $15. To book, call B.C. Ferries at 250/386-3431 or, toll-free in B.C., 888/223-3779, website www.bcferries.com. (For more information on this route and the towns where stops are made, see Cariboo Country in the Central British Columbia chapter.)

Getting Around

The local **bus and taxi depot,** 7210 Market St., 250/949-6300, is also the base for **North Island Transportation Ltd.** Head here for all your transportation needs; the company can arrange transportation to the ferry terminal or airport and also acts as ticket agent for Island Coach Lines.

Information

Port Hardy Visitor Info Centre is by the waterfront at 7250 Market St., 250/949-7622. It's open in summer daily 8 A.M.–8 P.M., the rest of the year Mon.–Fri. 9 A.M.–5 P.M. The energetic staff will happily fill you in on everything there is to see and do in Port Hardy and the entire area. Collect maps (if you want to get off the beaten track, pick up the detailed Forest Service maps) and brochures and you're ready to explore.

CAPE SCOTT PROVINCIAL PARK

Cape Scott Provincial Park encompasses 22,566 hectares of rugged coastal wilderness at the northernmost tip of Vancouver Island. It's the place to go if you really want to get away from everything and everyone. Rugged trails, suitable for experienced hikers and outdoorspersons, lead through dense forests of cedar, pine, hemlock, and fir to 23 km of beautiful sandy beaches and rocky promontories and headlands.

To get to the park boundary, you have to follow 67 km of logging roads (remember that logging trucks always have the right of way), then hike in. Near the end of the road is a small Forest Service campground ($8 per night). The hiking trail to **Cape Scott Lighthouse** (23 km; about eight hours each way) is relatively level, but you'll need stout footwear. A cove east of the cape was once the site of an ill-fated Danish settlement. Around 100 Danes moved to the area in 1896, cutting themselves off from the rest of the world and forcing themselves to be totally self-sufficient. By 1930, the settlement was deserted, with many of the residents relocating to nearby Holberg.

A shorter alternative to the long trek out to the cape is the trail to beautiful **San Josef Bay** at the southern boundary of the park (2.5 km; 45 minutes each way).

Before setting off for the park, go by the Port Hardy Visitor Info Centre and pick up the park brochure and detailed logging-road maps for the area. Be well equipped for unpredictable weather, even in midsummer. Other sources of information include the BC Parks district office down the island in Parksville, 250/954-4600, and the website www.capescottpark.ca.

South of the park is rugged and remote **Raft Cove.** To get there turn off seven km before the park, following a rough 12-km logging road to a slight rise where the road ends. From this point, a narrow and rough trail leads 1.5 km to the cove.

Southwestern British Columbia

Once you've reluctantly decided to drag yourself away from Vancouver, you'll be confronted by a variety of things to see and do within a day's drive of the city.

Although British Columbia is best known for its mountains, a stretch of coastline northwest of Vancouver is a watery playground perfect for swimming, sunbathing on sandy beaches, canoeing and kayaking, beachcombing, scuba diving, boating, and fishing. Known as the **Sunshine Coast,** the region is reached by taking a ferry from Horseshoe Bay (west of North Vancouver) then continuing up Highway 101. The highway winds along the Strait of Georgia, passing seaside villages, provincial parks, and marine parks, and ending near **Powell River,** a large tourist town and service center. Powell River is the gateway to the paddler's paradise at **Desolation Sound** and on the **Powell Forest Canoe Route.**

Spectacular Highway 99, the aptly named **Sea to Sky Highway,** leads you northeast out of Vancouver along the edge of island-dotted **Howe Sound.** You'll pass numerous provincial parks before coming to the resort town of **Whistler.** This year-round outdoor-sports mecca offers outstanding opportunities

© ANDREW HEMPSTEAD

powder day, Whistler/Blackcomb

SOUTHWESTERN BRITISH COLUMBIA

To Kamloops

Cache Creek

Thompson River

Ashcroft

Lillooet

Gold Bridge

D'Arcy

Mount Currie

Nairn Falls
Provincial Park

Pemberton

Whistler

Brandywine Falls
Provincial Park

Garibaldi
Provincial
Park

Brackendale

THE CHIEF

Squamish

Howe
Sound

Gibsons

Sechelt

Egmont

Saltery Bay

Powell River

Texada
Island

Malaspina Strait

Vancouver

Island

To Victoria

Nanaimo

Georgia

Horseshoe Bay

VANCOUVER

Pitt
Lake

Golden Ears
Provincial
Park

Stave
Lake

Harrison
Lake

Harrison Hot Springs

Mission

Abbotsford

CANADA
UNITED STATES

Chilliwack

Hope

COQUIHALLA HWY.

Merritt

Lytton

Fraser River

Manning
Provincial
Park

15 mi

15 km

© AVALON TRAVEL PUBLISHING, INC.

SOUTHWESTERN B.C.

for hiking, biking, golfing, fishing, and other warm-weather pursuits. But it's best known for its alpine resort: Whistler/Blackcomb, boasting North America's highest lift-served vertical rise.

From Vancouver two routes head east—you can zip along the TransCanada Highway on the south side of the wide **Fraser River** or meander along slower Highway 7 on the north side of the river. Both highways take you through the lush, fertile, and obviously agricultural Fraser Valley, converging at **Hope.** After exploring Hope's spectacular canyon formations, you have another choice of routes: north along the Fraser River Canyon, northeast to Kamloops along the Coquihalla Highway, or east along Highway 3 to the picturesque lakes and alpine meadows of **Manning Provincial Park.**

The Sunshine Coast

The 150-km-long Sunshine Coast lies along the northeast shore of the Strait of Georgia between Howe Sound in the south and Desolation Sound in the north. This rare bit of sun-drenched Canadian coastline is bordered by countless bays and inlets, broad sandy beaches, quiet lagoons, rugged headlands, provincial parks, and lush fir forests backed by the snowcapped Coast Mountains. It's well worth visiting, whether on a day-trip from Vancouver, on the "circle route" to Vancouver Island and back, or on a relaxing extended vacation.

The twisty road north from Vancouver is punctuated by two ferry rides and offers delightful glimpses of wilderness islands in the Strait of Georgia. Settlement began here in the late 19th century, and as you work your way up this stretch of the coastline you'll notice the odd assortment of place-names left by Coast Salish natives and Spanish and British navigators.

Today the area is a recreation paradise. Boasting Canada's mildest climate, the Sunshine Coast enjoys moderately warm summers and mild winters, with only 940 mm of rain annually and 2,400 hours of sunlight—a few more hours than Victoria, the so-called provincial hot spot. Boaters and kayakers can cruise into a number of beautiful marine parks providing sheltered anchorage and campsites amid some of the most magnificent scenery along the west coast, or anchor at sheltered fishing villages with marinas and all the modern conveniences.

Traveling along the Coast

Although the Sunshine Coast is part of the mainland, a trip north entails two trips with **B.C. Ferries,** 604/669-1211 or, toll-free in B.C., 888/223-3779 (no reservations taken). From **Horseshoe Bay,** at the west end of Vancouver's north shore, ferries regularly cross Howe Sound to **Langdale,** the gateway to the Sunshine Coast. From there, Highway 101 runs up the coast 81 km to **Earls Cove,** where another ferry crosses Jervis Inlet to **Saltery Bay.** These trips take 40 and 50 minutes respectively and run approximately every two hours between 6:30 A.M. and 11:30 P.M. The ferry charge is adult $8, child $4, vehicle $27.75, motorcycle $14, bicycle $2.50, canoe or kayak $4, which includes one-way travel on both ferries or round-trip travel on just one ferry.

CIRCLEPAC

A special fare known as Circlepac has been designed expressly for those who want to explore both the Sunshine Coast and Vancouver Island on a loop trip. The fare includes passage on the ferry from Vancouver to Vancouver Island, on the ferry from Comox to Powell River, and on the two ferries along the Sunshine Coast, all at a savings of 15 percent off the individual one-way fares. The only catch is that travel is only allowed outside of peak hours. Request the Circlepac fare when you purchase the first sector.

SOUTHWESTERN B.C.

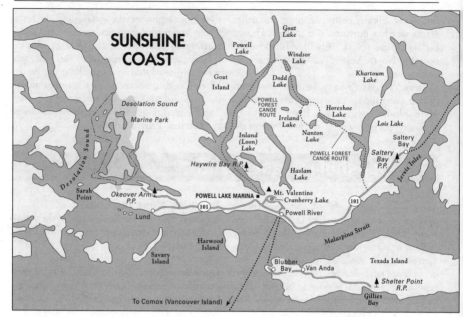

From the terminal at Saltery Bay, Highway 101 continues 35 km to Powell River. From here you can return along the same route, or loop back on Vancouver Island via the **Powell River–Comox ferry;** adult $7.50, child $3.75, vehicle $25, motorcycle $12.50, bicycle $2.50, canoe or kayak $3.50.

Gibsons

A delightful hillside community of 4,000 at the mouth of Howe Sound, Gibsons offers recreation galore. The town has two sections: the original 100-year-old fishing village around the harbor and a commercial corridor along the highway. Around the harbor, Gower Point Road is a charming strip of seafaring businesses, antique dealers, arty shops, and cafés (this was the setting for the popular 1970s TV series *The Beachcombers*). Down on the harbor itself is a marina and the pleasant Gibsons Seawalk, a 10-minute, scenic meander (lighted at night).

Elphinstone Pioneer Museum, 716 Winn Rd., 604/886-8232, features intriguing pioneer and Coast Salish native displays and holds what must be one of the largest seashell collections on

the planet (some 25,000). It's open in summer daily 9 A.M.–5 P.M. In August locals participate in a couple of salmon derbies and revel at the annual **Sea Cavalcade,** which features a swimming race from nearby Keats Island to Gibsons, a parade, and fireworks.

On the main road, **Cedars Inn,** 895 Hwy. 101, 604/886-3008 or 888/774-7044, features a heated outdoor pool, sauna, small exercise room, and restaurant; from $84 s, $88 d. On the same stretch of road is **Sunny Crest Motel,** 835 Hwy. 101, 604/886-2419, with very basic rooms from $50 s, $55 d.

Gibsons has a surprisingly good selection of eateries, most in the original part of town on a hill above the marina. For homestyle cooking at reasonable prices, try **Molly's Reach,** 647 School Rd., 604/886-9710. Food is also offered at the **Waterfront Restaurant,** 442 Marine Dr., 604/886-2831, overlooking the marina and open daily from 8 A.M.

Gibsons Visitor Info Centre, 668 Sunnycrest Rd., 604/886-2325, is along the main road through town but easy to miss—it's tucked away behind a Chevron gas station. Open daily 9

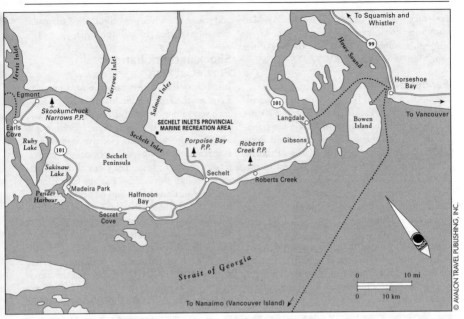

© AVALON TRAVEL PUBLISHING, INC.

A.M.–5 P.M. (Look for a new center to open early in 2003 at the east entrance to town.)

Roberts Creek

About nine km northwest of Gibsons you'll find the small artistic community of Roberts Creek (take the lower road off Highway 101), where arts-and-crafts appreciators can often snatch up a bargain. In an old-growth forest, **Roberts Creek Provincial Park,** 14 km northwest of Gibsons, holds hiking trails, waterfalls, a picnic ground, and a pebbly beach. Campsites are $12 per night.

Sechelt and Vicinity

The native cultural center and regional service center of Sechelt (pop. 7,800) perches on the isthmus of the Sechelt Peninsula between the head of Sechelt Inlet and the Strait of Georgia. Logging, fishing, and summer tourism support the town.

One of the area's nicest spots is **Porpoise Bay Provincial Park,** four km north of Sechelt via East Porpoise Bay Road. The park offers open grassy areas among forests of fir and cedar, and a broad sheltered sandy beach along the eastern shore of Sechelt Inlet. Hiking trails connect the beach with a day-use area and campground, and a woodland trail meanders along the bank of Angus Creek, where chum and coho salmon spawn in fall. The park is a handy base for kayakers and canoeists exploring Sechelt Inlets Provincial Marine Recreation Area. Porpoise Bay and the nearby rivers are also noted for good sportfishing, and oysters and clams are found along the inlet northwest of the park. The 84-site campground ($17.50) has hot showers. Also on Sechelt Inlet is **Porpoise Bay Charters,** 604/885-5950, a well-established company with kayak rentals and tours, diving charters, and a few waterfront cabins ($95 s or d).

Back in Sechelt, the **Driftwood Inn,** 5454 Trail Ave., 604/885-5811, features large rooms from $119 s, $139 d. At the inn, Pebbles Restaurant has water views. Out of town to the west, **Lord Jim's Resort Hotel** is an absolute waterfront complex overlooking Halfmoon Bay, 604/885-7038 or 877/296-4593, website www.lordjims.com. It features a wonderful restaurant (for the food and view), and rooms from $110 s, $130 d. **Sechelt Visitor Info Centre,**

SOUTHWESTERN B.C.

604/885-0662, is in the large Trail Bay Mall shopping complex along Hwy. 101. Open through summer 9 A.M.–6 P.M., the rest of the year Mon.–Fri. 9 A.M.–5 P.M.

Pender Harbour

Along the shores of Pender Harbour lie the villages of Madeira Park, Garden Bay, and Irvines Landing. Boating and ocean fishing are popular activities on this stretch of coast, and Ruby and Sakinaw Lakes—between Madeira Park and Earls Cove—are a trout fisher's delight in season. Canoeists head for the chain of eight lakes between Garden Bay and Egmont, where those casting a line will find good fishing for cutthroat trout May–October.

Pender Harbour is also orca habitat. These highly intelligent gentle giants, also known as killer whales, travel in pods of up to 100. Feeding on salmon found year-round in these waters, they grow up to nine meters long, weighing as much as eight tons. Keep your eyes on the water

and your camera ready to capture their triangular dorsal fins slicing through the water.

Skookumchuck Narrows Provincial Park

Just before Earls Cove, take the road north to Egmont, then the 3.5-km hiking trail (one hour each way) along Sechelt Inlet to this 123-hectare park. Meaning "Turbulent Water" in Chinook, Skookumchuck protects Narrows and Roland Points and the 400-meter-wide, rock-strewn waterway between them. The tides of three inlets roar through this narrow passage four times a day. The resulting rapids and eddies boisterously boil and bubble to create fierce-looking whirlpools—fascinating to see when your feet are firmly planted on terra firma, but very dangerous for inexperienced boaters unfamiliar with the tides. It's a particularly amazing spectacle during extreme tides in spring, when the rapids may reach as high as five meters and the water whooshes past at 20 kph. You'll also see abundant

© JIM BORROWMAN

Pacific whiteside dolphin

SOUTHWESTERN B.C.

marine creatures in tidal pools—it's a fascinating spot. Take a picnic lunch, pull up a rock, and enjoy the view.

Earls Cove

Earls Cove marks the end of this section of Highway 101. From here, B.C. Ferries offers regular service across Jervis Inlet to Saltery Bay. The 16-km crossing takes 50 minutes.

Saltery Bay and Vicinity

Less than two km from the Saltery Bay ferry terminal is 140-hectare **Saltery Bay Provincial Park,** one of the Sunshine Coast's diving hot spots. Waters off the park are accessible from the shore and are full of marinelife, including a three-meter bronze mermaid. The park also features good beaches and salmon fishing (from late April). Camping is $12 per night. Saltery Bay is named for a fish saltery that was nearby in the early 1900s.

From Saltery Bay, it's 31 km of winding road to Powell River. Along the way you'll cross Lois River, the outlet for large Lois Lake, and pass a string of coastal communities clinging to the rocky shoreline of Malaspina Strait.

POWELL RIVER

Situated between Jervis Inlet and Desolation Sound along the edge of Malaspina Strait, Powell River (pop. 16,500) is almost surrounded by water. The town is actually a municipality made up of four communities. **Townsite,** the original "Powell River," is occupied by an ugly waterfront pulp mill and a number of boarded-up buildings. A few kilometers south is **Westview,** Powell River's main service center, home to the ferry terminal and information center as well as accommodations and restaurants. The other two official communities are **Wildwood,** north of Townsite, and **Cranberry,** east of Townsite.

Powell River was named in 1885 after Dr. Israel Powell, Superintendent of Indian Affairs for B.C., who led the movement that brought B.C. into confederation with Canada in 1871. During the early years of the 20th century, logging of the tall and slender local trees began in the forests around Lois, Horseshoe, and Nanton Lakes, producing exceptionally fine flagpoles that were exported to the rest of the world. In 1912, Powell River became the first town in western Canada to manufacture newsprint.

Today Powell River holds one of the world's largest pulp and paper mill complexes and is a thriving center for the region's abundant outdoor-recreation opportunities, including salmon fishing (good year-round), trout fishing, scuba diving, sailing, canoeing, kayaking, and hiking.

Sights

One of the best ways to explore Powell River is on the Townsite Heritage Society walking tour through the historic section of town once owned by the local pulp and paper mill company. Tours are offered July and August, Wednesday at 7 P.M. and Saturday at 10 A.M. Call 604/483-3901 for bookings. The *Heritage Walk* brochure, available at the information center, will guide you around town at other times. The first commercial building was the original 30-room **Powell River Hotel,** completed in 1911. Most of the other buildings you'll see in the Townsite, north of the ferry terminal, were built between 1911 and 1939. This old section of Powell River is a shadow of its former self, with most businesses having moved south to Westview. But the town's reason for being—the pulp and paper mill complex—remains here. **Pacifica Papers** operates the mill, and tours are available in summer Mon.–Fri. four times a day. Call ahead at 604/483-3722 for reservations and meeting details.

Visiting the excellent **Powell River Historical Museum** across the road from Willingdon Beach (watch for the sign) on Marine Ave., 604/485-2222, is like wandering back in time. Peruse the vast collection of photographs (the province's third-largest archives) and other displays to find out about this seashore community and to see what the area was like before the town was established. Also see well-preserved artifacts, native carvings and baskets, the shanty home of a hermit who once lived along Powell Lake, and even sand from around the world. It's open in

SOUTHWESTERN B.C.

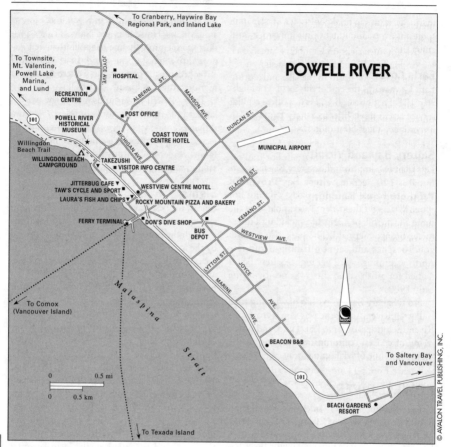

© AVALON TRAVEL PUBLISHING, INC.

summer daily 10 A.M.–5 P.M., the rest of the year Mon.–Fri. only.

Hiking

While most visitors to Powell River spend their time enjoying water-oriented sports, the hiking around town is also good—and chances are you'll have the trails to yourself.

From Powell River's municipal campground, the one-km **Willingdon Beach Trail** spurs north past interpretive boards describing natural features and the uses of old logging machinery. The trail ends at a viewpoint overlooking historic Townsite and the pulp operations. One of the most popular short local trails is the one-km hike up 182-

meter-high **Mount Valentine,** north of Cranberry. The trail leads to a stunning panoramic view of Malaspina Strait and the Strait of Georgia. Access is from the end of Crown Avenue: take Manson Avenue east to Cranberry Street, turn left, then turn right on Crown.

Another trail loops around **Inland Lake,** north of Powell River between Powell and Haslam Lakes. The wheelchair-accessible trail is 13 km round-trip, has bridges and boardwalks over swampy areas, and offers picnic sites at regular intervals. Minimal elevation gain is made; allow 3–4 hours. An interesting addition to this hike is a two-km spur leading to **Lost Lake;** follow the main trail clockwise from the parking lot 800 meters to the spur junction. To get to the trail-head from Westview, take Manson Avenue north for five km, turn right on Cranberry Street, then left on Haslam Street, from where a signposted logging road leads north to the lake and a primitive campground.

Completed in 1999 after seven years of volunteer labor, the **Sunshine Coast Trail** extends 180 km from Saltery Bay to Sarah Point, beyond Powell River and north of Lund. Most hikers complete just sections of the trail. For trail details head to website www.sunshinecoast-trail.com.

Canoeing and Kayaking

The sheltered Sunshine Coast provides plenty of opportunities for good lake and ocean canoeing or kayaking. The most popular canoe trip is the **Powell Forest Canoe Route** (see the special topic), while kayakers find solitude in Desolation Sound (see Vicinity of Powell River, below).

Wolfson Creek Ventures, 9537 Nassichuk Rd., 604/487-1699, website www.canoeing-bc.com, rents canoes for the Powell Forest Canoe Route. Prices range $26–33 for one day, or $23–26 per day for five or more days. The company also rents all the necessary accessories and fishing gear, provides free parking, and runs a shuttle service to and from the put-in ($60). Basic paddling courses start at $40, and fully guided overnight tours are available.

Although **Powell River Sea Kayak,** Malaspina Rd., 604/483-2160, outfits for the Powell Forest Canoe Route, kayaks are its specialty. Single and double kayaks for use around local waterways

POWELL FOREST CANOE ROUTE

This four- to eight-day backcountry canoe route is a great way to get away from it all, surrounding yourself with tree-covered lowlands and rugged mountain peaks while slipping through fjordlike lakes. Take side trips and you can extend the water distance from 80 km to more than 150 km, or just do one or two sections of the trail—all the major lakes can be reached by road.

To reach the put-in at **Lois Lake,** take Highway 101 east of Powell River 20 km to a logging road that branches north off the highway. Follow that road for one km, then turn right on the Branch 41 logging road and follow it seven km to a primitive lakeside campground. The route includes paddling along part of Lois Lake, then the lengths of **Horseshoe, Dodd, Windsor,** and **Goat Lakes** to **Powell Lake.** Powell Lake Marina is the most popular pull-out point.

In total, the route requires 57 km of paddling and 10 km of portaging. The longest single paddle is 28.5 km (but this can be broken up), and the longest portage is 2.5 km. Carry a tent, stove, and supplies, and stay at one of the 20 Forest Service recreation sites and camping areas along the route. Don't forget your fishing rod and tackle—all the lakes are stocked with cutthroat trout, and some hold rainbow trout and kokanee.

The route's major outfitter is **Wolfson Creek Ventures,** 9537 Nassichuk Rd., 604/487-1699, website www.canoeingbc.com. Canoe rentals range $26–33 for one day, $115–130 for five days. The company provides all accessories and free car parking, and shuttles paddlers to and from the route. A three-day guided paddle is $299 pp.

For a map and brochure describing the route in detail and to find out present water levels and campfire regulations contact the **Sunshine Coast Forest District** office at 7077 Duncan St., Westview, 604/485-0700, website www.gov.bc.ca/for, or drop by **Powell River Visitor Info Centre,** 4690 Marine Ave., Westview, 604/485-4701.

BOB RACE

SOUTHWESTERN B.C.

rent for $35–55 for one day, $60–90 for two days, additional days $20–35. Guided two-hour tours are $39, overnight sea-kayaking trips start at $200, and three-hour basic kayaking classes run from $40.

Scuba Diving

Known as the "Diving Capital of Canada," the Strait of Georgia provides divers with exceptionally clear, relatively warm water and more than 100 exciting dives mapped by local experts. Conditions are particularly excellent in winter, when visibility reaches 30 meters. Expect to see underwater cliffs and abundant marinelife, including sponges, giant octopuses, wolf eels, perch, ling cod, tubeworms, sea anemones, nudibranchs (including intriguing hooded nudibranchs), sea stars, crabs, and tunicates. Seals can be seen year-round, sea lions Nov.–April.

The highlight for wreck divers on the Sunshine Coast is the HMCS *Chaudiere*, sunk in 1993 to form an artificial reef. The hull provides a home for colorful marinelife, and giant holes have been cut through it to enable adventurous divers to do some inside exploration.

Diving gear and a list of charter operators are available at **Don's Dive Shop,** 6789 Wharf St., 604/485-6969; and **Good Diving & Kayaking,** under the Lund Hotel north of town, 604/483-3223. Beach Gardens Resort (see below) is a popular diver's hangout.

Fishing

With ocean to the west and lakes to the east, Powell River is a fishing fantasy come true. Saltwater fishing for chinook salmon is good year-round but particularly good in autumn and midwinter. Coho salmon usually arrive around April or May. Sport anglers also pursue red snapper, perch, flatfish, ling cod, and rockfish. Bring your own boat (launching ramps are free) or

> *The Strait of Georgia provides divers with exceptionally clear, relatively warm water. Conditions are particularly excellent in winter, when visibility reaches 30 meters. Expect to see underwater cliffs and abundant marinelife, including sponges, giant octopuses, wolf eels, perch, ling cod, tubeworms, sea anemones, nudibranchs, sea stars, crabs, and tunicates.*

charter one with or without a guide and equipment. Dangle a line from the wharf, docks, or breakwaters, or hurl it out from the shore; a saltwater fishing license is required.

Cutthroat trout inhabit more than a dozen local lakes, most of which are accessible by logging road. Many of the lakes are stocked with rainbow trout and kokanee, and in a couple you can also catch Dolly Varden. Note that you need separate fishing licenses for freshwater and saltwater fishing. Local tackle stores include: **Marine Traders,** 6791 Wharf St., 604/485-4624, and **Taw's Cycle and Sport,** 4597 Marine Ave., 604/485-2555.

Hotels and Motels

Powell River doesn't have a great number of regular motels, so try to reserve a room in advance or plan to camp or stay at a more expensive resort. A good cheapie is **Westview Centre Motel,** 4534 Marine Ave., 604/485-4023 or 877/485-4023, with basic rooms for $58 s, $68 d. The **Coast Town Centre Hotel,** 4660 Joyce Ave., 604/485-3000 or 800/663-1144, website www.coasthotels.com, has all the facilities of a full-service hotel, including a health club, restaurant, pub, and large courtyard complete with hot tub and gazebo. Rates start at $105 s, $115 d. **Beach Gardens Resort,** five km south of the ferry terminal at 7074 Westminster Ave., 604/485-6267 or 800/663-7070, features an indoor swimming pool, sauna, tennis courts, a fitness room, and a marina with boat rentals and divers' air; it's a great place to meet fellow scuba enthusiasts. The resort's restaurant offers lunchtime buffets and a pub. Rooms, most with water views, range $105–165 s or d.

Bed and Breakfast

One of the most attractive and relaxing lodgings in Powell River is **Beacon Bed and Breakfast,** 3750 Marine Dr. (two km south of the ferry terminal), 604/485-5563 or 800/485-5563, website www.beaconbb.com, which overlooks Malaspina Strait, Texada Island, and the peaks of Vancouver Island. Within the two-story waterfront home are three guest rooms, each with ocean views. Facilities include a lounge area overlooking the water and an outdoor hot tub. Rates are from $75 s, $85 d; the large Sunset Suite goes for $135 s or d.

Camping

Willingdon Beach Municipal Campground, on Marine Ave., 604/485-2242, enjoys a great waterfront location one km north of the ferry terminal. You'll find sheltered and very popular campsites along the beach, as well as a laundromat and washrooms with free hot showers. Basic tent sites are $15, hookups $16–20.

Canoeists find **Haywire Bay Regional Park** handy. It's seven km north of town on Powell Lake, at one end of the Powell Forest Canoe Route. The park's campground offers hot showers, a sandy beach, and a boat launch. Sites are $10. It's accessible by boat or canoe from Powell Lake Marina, and also by road; from the ferry terminal drive up Duncan Street, turn left on Manson Avenue and follow it for five km, then turn right on Cranberry Street and left on Haslam Street, from where a signposted logging road (on the left) leads north four km to Haywire Bay.

Food

Head to **Rocky Mountain Pizza and Bakery Co.,** 4471 Marine Ave., 604/485-9111, for great bakery items, coffee as strong (or as weak) as you like it, and daily newspapers. The rest of the day it's pizza, pizza, and more pizza.

Right by the ferry terminal is **Laura's Fish and Chips,** 4454 Willingdon Ave., 604/485-2252. It's a takeout only place, but the waterfront and a number of ideal picnic spots are just 100 meters away. At the entrance to Willingdon Beach, **Kathie's Kitchen** is always busy serving fish and chips, hamburgers, and the Sunshine Coast's best ice cream. The **Jitterbug Cafe,** 4643 Marine Ave. on the corner of Alexander St., 604/485-7797, occupies an old restored cottage with an outdoor deck offering views of Malaspina

Strait. In the same house is Wind Spirit Gallery, and many local artworks from the gallery are displayed in the café. The menu offers interesting yet remarkably inexpensive choices, such as a salad of fresh, locally grown greens covered in a strawberry vinaigrette ($4) and a delicious salmon pasta ($9). It's open for lunch Tues.–Sun. 11 A.M.–3 P.M. and for dinner Fri.–Sat. 5–8 P.M., with an 8:30 P.M. jam on Friday night and softer live music accompanying Saturday night diners.

There's no escaping the big city, even on the laid-back Sunshine Coast, so to fulfill your cravings for sushi head to **Takezushi,** open daily for lunch and dinner at 4701 Marine Dr., 604/485-4415. Aside from sushi, you can also choose from tempuras and teriyakis. Takeout is also offered.

At the marina overlooking Powell Lake, north of town, the **Shinglemill,** 604/483-2001, features dishes to suit all tastes; in the main restaurant entrées range $13–23.50. The nautically themed pub section offers less-expensive meals and great lake views. The restaurant is open daily for dinner while the pub is open daily 11 A.M.–11 P.M. Another popular place for seafood and fine cuisine is the **Beach Gardens Resort,** 7074 Westminster Ave., 604/485-6267, where the outdoor tables overlook Malaspina Strait. Sample the lunch buffet, salad bar, or bistro, or go for the formal sit-down dinner.

Transportation

Powell River Municipal Airport is east of town, off Duncan Street. **Pacific Coastal,** 604/483-2107 or 800/663-2872, flies at least three times daily between Powell River and its hub at the South Terminal of Vancouver International Airport.

The **bus depot,** on the corner of Joyce Ave. and Glacier St., is served by **Malaspina Coach Lines,** 604/485-5030. Malaspina runs twice daily in both directions between Powell River and Vancouver's Pacific Central Station.

The ferry terminal in Powell River is at the foot of Duncan St., right downtown. **B.C. Ferries** offers regular sailings between Powell River and Comox on Vancouver Island. One-way fares for the 75-minute sailing are adult $7.50, vehicle

$25, motorcycle $12.50, bicycle $2.50, canoe or kayak $4. You can't make reservations—just roll up and join the queue. For information call B.C. Ferries at 604/669-1211 or, toll-free in B.C., 888/223-3779, or call the local terminal at 604/485-2943.

Sunshine Coast Transit System, 604/885-3234, operates local bus service between Sunshine Coast communities; $1.50 per sector; no Sunday service.

Information

Powell River Visitor Info Centre is along the main strip of shops at 4690 Marine Ave., Westview, 604/485-4701, website www.discoverpowellriver.com. Coming off the ferry from Vancouver Island, drive up the hill to Marine Avenue and turn left; it's three blocks down on the right. Open in Mon.–Sat. 9 A.M.–9 P.M., Sunday 9 A.M.–5 P.M.; the rest of the year weekdays only.

VICINITY OF POWELL RIVER

Texada Island

A 35-minute ferry trip from the Powell River ferry terminal, Texada is one of the largest of the gulf islands (50 km from north to south and up to 10 km wide), but the permanent population is only 1,400 and services are limited. Originally home to a whaling station, the island has also housed a couple of mining operations and a distillery that supplied illegal liquor to the United States during Prohibition.

From the ferry terminal at Blubber Bay, the island's main road winds south for eight km to **Van Anda,** a historic village that once boasted saloons, an opera house, and a hospital. Take a walk along Van Anda's Erickson Beach to appreciate the island's natural beauty. Continuing south, the road leads to Gillies Bay and beyond to **Shelter Point Regional Park,** which has some short but enjoyable hiking trails and campsites for $12.

The 35-minute hop over to the island from Powell River with **B.C. Ferries,** 604/485-2943, costs adult $5.25, child $2.75, vehicle $13.50. Ferries depart about every two hours 8 A.M.–11 P.M.; no reservations taken.

Lund

Twenty-eight km north of Powell River, Highway 101 dead-ends on the old wooden wharf of Lund, a tiny fishing village founded in 1889 and named after the Swedish hometown of the first settlers. Lund lies on a secluded harbor backed by the magnificent peaks of the Coast Mountains. Although best known as the gateway to Desolation Sound, it's worth the trip out just for the relaxed atmosphere and surrounding beauty. Wander around the bustling marina, cruise over to the white sand beaches of Savary Island via water taxi (departs 4–5 times daily for $8 round-trip; 604/483-9749), or relax with a coffee at **Carvers Studio and Coffee House.** Dating to 1894, the historic **Lund Hotel,** 604/483-2400, underwent extensive renovations in 2001 and now offers small but comfortable rooms above a row of waterfront shops; from $85 s, $95 d. Dine inside or out on a deck offering magnificent water views.

Okeover Arm

The shallow, sheltered waters of Okeover Arm—a southern arm of Desolation Sound—provide the perfect environment for all kinds of prolific marinelife; try to time your visit with the receding tide. Access is via Malaspina Road, off Highway 101 south of Lund. Forested four-hectare **Okeover Arm Provincial Park** lies on the water; it's a small, rustic park with just a few undeveloped campsites ($12), a pit toilet, and a kayak-and boat-launching ramp, but it's a great spot to camp if you're into canoeing or kayaking.

North of the park on three hectares overlooking Okeover Arm, **Desolation Resort,** 2694 Dawson Rd., 604/483-3592 or 866/617-4444, website www.desolationresort.com, offers a wonderful escape at reasonable prices. Accommodation is in freestanding wood chalets set high above the lake edge on stilts.

All feature rich-colored wood furnishings, and even the smallest (the bottom half of one unit) has a king-size bed, large deck, kitchen, separate living and dining areas, and a barbecue. Rates range from just $120 for the unit detailed above to $270 for four guests sharing a two-bedroom, two-bathroom chalet. Fishing, canoeing, and kayaking are practically right out your door at the private marina.

Desolation Sound Marine Park

Desolation Sound was named by Captain Vancouver after his visit in 1792—he was obviously unimpressed, as the name implies. Today, 8,256 hectares of the sound are protected in the largest of British Columbia's 50 marine parks. The park also preserves over 60 km of shoreline, a number of offshore islands, the Gifford Peninsula, and a section of mainland that includes Unwin Lake. A wilderness-seeker's paradise, the park is totally undeveloped and without road access. The sound is a popular yachtie hangout and a haven for sea kayakers, who need to be totally self-sufficient here.

Good Diving and Kayaking, at the Lund Hotel, 604/483-3223, rents kayaks for $30–55 per day; transport the kayaks to Okeover Arm (see above) and you're on your way. **Powell River Sea Kayak,** on Powell Lake, 604/483-2410, offers similarly priced rentals and can organize drop-offs at Okeover Arm.

Sea to Sky Highway

The spectacular, aptly named Sea to Sky Highway (Highway 99) runs 105 km between Horseshoe Bay and Whistler. With the almost-vertical tree-covered **Coast Mountains** to the east and island-dotted **Howe Sound** to the west, this cliff-hugging highway winds precariously through a dramatic glacier-carved landscape.

The weather certainly affects what you see and how you feel about this part of British Columbia. On sunny days everything seems to be bright blue, emerald green, and sparkling clean; only water trickling down the roadside cliffs gives you the clue that it rains a bit around here. On the other hand, after a string of dull drizzly days, impressive waterfalls, one after another, plummet down those same cliffs right beside you to abruptly disappear underneath the highway, and the scenery merges into a magnificent blue-and-gray blur.

Along the road expect some tight corners, narrow stretches, and enough traffic to keep your concentration at an optimum. Be aware of potential hazards in bad weather (washouts can occur), and if you want to go slowly to absorb everything, use the slow-lane pullouts.

HORSESHOE BAY TOWARD SQUAMISH

Porteau Cove Provincial Park

On the east shore of Howe Sound, Porteau Cove is best known among the diving fraternity for its artificial reef of four sunken wrecks but also offers good swimming and fishing. In addition, the area's strong winds and lack of waves make for perfect windsurfing conditions. The park holds boat-launching and scuba-diving facilities, an ecology information center, picnic tables, and a waterfront campground for tents and RVs. The campground is open year-round; $18.50 per site per night March–Oct., free the rest of the year.

Furry Creek Golf and Country Club

North up Howe Sound beyond Porteau Cove is Furry Creek Golf and Country Club, 604/922-9461 or 888/922-9461, generally regarded as one of British Columbia's most scenic courses. Immaculately manicured, the course is bordered on one side by the driftwood-strewn beaches of Howe Sound and on the other by towering mountains. It is relatively short, at just over 6,000 yards, but water comes into play on many holes, including one where the green juts into the sound and is almost an island. On summer weekends, greens fees are $100, with the price of a round decreasing to $85 midweek and as low as $65 the rest of the year. Twilight rates reduce the costs further. All rates include valet parking, a locker, power cart, tees, and a towel.

Britannia Beach

Small Britannia Beach is worth a stop to visit the **B.C. Museum of Mining,** overlooking Howe Sound, 604/688-8735. In the early 1930s the

SOUTHWESTERN B.C.

Britannia Beach Mine was the British Empire's largest producer of copper, producing more than 600 million kg. Today it's not a working mine but a working museum. Ever wondered what it's like to slave away underground? Here's your chance to don a hard hat and raincoat, hop on an electric train, and travel under a mountain, without even getting your hands dirty. See fully functional mining equipment, along with demonstrations and displays on the techniques of mining. Then take a step into the past in the museum, where hundreds of photos and artifacts tell the story of the mine. Also here are a gift shop, restaurant, and gold-panning pool. Open mid-May to mid-October, daily 9 A.M.–4:30 P.M. The tour is adult $9.50, senior and student $7.50, children under five free.

Continuing North

Straddling the highway, 24-hectare **Murrin Provincial Park** provides good boating, fishing, swimming, and walking trails, as well as steep cliffs that attract novice and intermediate rock climbers. The park has picnic tables but no campsites. Farther up the highway, stop at 87-hectare **Shannon Falls Provincial Park** to view the spectacular 335-meter-high namesake falls from a platform at the base. You can picnic here or hike a few trails. No campsites are available, but just across the road is **Klahanie Campground and RV Park**, 604/892-3435. This pleasant campground has sites for $18–24 and an adjacent restaurant with spectacular views (open daily 6:30 A.M.–9 P.M.).

SQUAMISH

Squamish (pop. 16,500), 67 km north of Vancouver, enjoys a stunning location at the head of Howe Sound, surrounded by snowcapped mountains. It's a natural deep-water port and a "nuclear-weapons-free zone." The name Squamish is a native Coast Salish word meaning "Mother of the Wind"—the town gets stiff breezes year-round, delighting today's sailors and windsurfers.

The first white settlers made their home in the valley in 1888, logging the local giant cedar and fir trees for a living. Squamish quickly became a logging town, then a railroad town; at one time it was the southern terminus for the Pacific Great Eastern rail line. Today lumber is still the lifeblood of the area—the town holds four sawmills, and along **Mamquam Blind Channel** on the east side of town you can see logs being boomed in preparation for towing to other mills.

Town Sights

See around 65 vintage rail cars and engines in a mock working railyard, complete with a station garden, replica workers' home, and a restored station at the **West Coast Railway Heritage Park**, through Squamish on Industrial Way, one km from Hwy. 99, 604/898-9336. It's open May–Oct. daily 10 A.M.–5 P.M.; admission is included if you've come up on the *Royal Hudson*, otherwise it's $6 per person. Also in town is the **Squamish Valley Museum**, in a heritage house on 2nd Ave.; open Wed.–Sunday. Farther along 2nd Ave., at Victoria St., a colorful mural covers the exterior of the Ocean Pub, depicting the natural and human elements of life along the west coast.

Rock Climbing

Although Squamish has a reputation as an industrial town, it is also the center of a growing recreation-based economy. Leading the way is rock climbing on the 762-meter-high **Stawamus Chief**, clearly visible across the highway from downtown. The "Chief," as it's best known, is one of the world's largest granite monoliths. It formed around 100 million years ago as massive forces deep inside the earth forced molten magma through the crust—as it cooled, it hardened and fractured, creating a perfect environment for today's climbers. The face offers a great variety of free and aided climbing on almost 1,000 routes, which take in dikes, cracks, slabs, chasms, and ridges.

The Chief gained status as a provincial park in 1995, but facilities are still limited. Climbers camp at the base for $9 per night but head into town to the aquatic center to shower and soak in a hot tub ($3 per visit). If you've never climbed or

THE EAGLES OF BRACKENDALE

Squamish itself doesn't have a ton of sights, but if you're in the area during winter, **Brackendale,** just to the north along Highway 99, is definitely worth a stop. Through the colder months of the year, the riverflats behind this sleepy little town are home to a larger concentration of bald eagles than anywhere else on the face of the earth. Over 3,000 of these magnificent creatures descend on a stretch of the Squamish River between the Cheakamus and Mam-quam tributaries to feed on spawned out salmon that litter the banks. The dead fish are the result of a late-fall run of an estimated 100,000 chum salmon. The birds begin arriving in late October, but numbers reach their peak around Christmastime, and by early February the birds are gone.

The best viewing spot is from the dike that runs along the back of Brackendale. The best place to learn more about these creatures is the **Brackendale Art Gallery.** To get there, follow the main Brackendale access road over the railway tracks, take the first right and look for the gallery nestled in the trees on the right, 604/898-3333. The gallery is "Eagle Count Headquarters," open through January noon–5 P.M., weekends only the rest of the year, for slide presentations, talks, and other eagle-related activities. Guided walks to the site run through January and cost $35 pp.

bald eagle

BOB RACE

---

are inexperienced, consider using the services of **Squamish Rock Guides,** 604/898-1750, for a variety of courses with equipment supplied; expect to pay around $175 for a full day's instruction. **Vertical Reality,** 38154 2nd Ave., 604/892-8248, offers a full range of climbing equipment and sells local climbing guides.

Other Recreation and Events

At first it may be difficult to see past the industrial scars along Squamish's waterways, but on the west side of downtown a large section of the delta where the Squamish River flows into Howe Sound has escaped development. It comprises tidal flats, forested areas, marshes, and open meadows—and over 200 species of birds call the area home. Hiking trails lace the area, and there are three main access points: Industrial Road, the end of Winnipeg Street, and the end of Vancouver Street, all of which branch off Cleveland Avenue. Nearby Garibaldi Provincial Park (see below) offers many opportunities for more experienced hikers. For a bird's-eye view of the

area, take to the air from Squamish Municipal Airport with **Glacier Air Tours,** 604/898-9016.

Squamish celebrates two very different lifestyles at its major annual events. The last week of June is the **Squamish Adventure Festival,** a semi-social gathering of adventure-loving folk who come for the mountain biking, windsurfing, white-water kayaking, rock climbing, and even kite-flying. Then, early in August, Squamish is mobbed by loggers from around the world who congregate for the annual **Squamish Days Logger Sports,** 604/898-3500. Don't be too surprised to see people competing at racing up trees, rolling logs, and throwing axes. The show also includes an RV rally, Truck Loggers Rodeo, dances, pageants, and parades.

Accommodations

The best place to stay around Squamish is **Dryden Creek Resorts,** six km north of town (corner of Depot Rd.), 604/898-9726 or 800/903-4690, website www.drydrencreek.com. It's set on six hectares of landscaped parkland with Garibaldi Provincial Park as a backdrop. Each of the six

SOUTHWESTERN B.C.

suite-style studios has a cedar ceiling, large skylights, and a fully equipped kitchen with handcrafted cabinets. Rates of $75–85 s or d include complimentary coffee and chocolates. The resort's campground offers a choice of forested or creekside sites; unserviced sites $17.50, hookups $18–22.50.

Garibaldi Budget Inn, 38012 3rd Ave., 604/892-5204 or 888/313-9299, is one block from the main street and across from Squamish's infamous Ocean's Pub, but rooms go for just $49 s, $59 d ($76 with a kitchen) in the busy summer season. Also right downtown, **Howe Sound Inn,** 37801 Cleveland Ave., 604/892-2603 or 800/919-2537, website www.howe sound.com, is a stylish place with 20 spacious rooms from $105 s or d. The inn also has a restaurant and boasts an in-house brewery.

Information

For detailed information on Squamish, local provincial parks, and Whistler, follow the signs from the highway downtown to **Squamish Visitor Info Centre,** 37950 Cleveland Ave., 604/892-9244, website www.squamishchamber.bc.ca. It's open in summer daily 9 A.M.–5 P.M., the rest of the year Mon.–Fri. 9 A.M.–4 P.M. The Squamish Public Library is a large facility at 37907 2nd Ave., 604/892-3110, open daily except Friday.

NORTH TOWARD WHISTLER

Garibaldi Provincial Park

This beautiful park encompasses 195,000 hectares of pristine alpine wilderness east of Highway 99. Dominated by the snowcapped and glaciated Coast Mountains, the park reaches a high point at 2,678-meter **Mount Garibaldi,** named in 1860 after Italian soldier and statesman Giuseppe Garibaldi. Other park features include 2,315-meter **Black Tusk,** the **Gargoyles** (eroded

> *The trail to Brandywine Falls excites all your senses—magnificent frosty peaks high above, dense lush forest on either side, a fast, deep river roaring along on one side, the pungent aroma and cushiness of crushed pine needles beneath your feet. The falls plummet down a vertical lava cliff into a massive swirling plunge pool, then roar down a forest-edged river into a lake.*

rock formations reached by a trail from the park's southern entrance), and a 1.5-km-long lava flow above the west side of **Garibaldi Lake.**

Garibaldi is a true wilderness park, with road access only up to the park boundary. From late July through early September, the hiking is fabulous—through forests of fir, red cedar, hemlock, and balsam, across high meadows crowded with spectacular wildflowers, and past bright blue lakes, huge glaciers, and jagged volcanic peaks and lava flows. If you're in the right spot at the right time, you may see black and grizzly bears, mountain goats, and deer. And you'll certainly spy lots of marmots, chipmunks, squirrels, and birds. In winter and spring the park is thickly blanketed in snow, luring experienced crosscountry skiers. Snow can linger well into July, and the higher peaks are permanently mantled.

Between Squamish and Pemberton, five clearly marked entrance roads lead off Highway 99 to trailheads providing access into the five most popular areas of the park: **Diamond Head, Black Tusk/Garibaldi Lake, Cheakamus Lake, Singing Pass,** and **Wedgemount Lake.** Aside from these five areas, the rest of the park is untouched wilderness, explored only by mountaineers and experienced crosscountry skiers. All major trails have backcountry tent sites. For further park information contact the Garibaldi District Office, 604/898-3678.

Alice Lake Provincial Park

Alice Lake, surrounded by a 400-hectare park of open grassy areas, dense forests, and impressive snowcapped peaks, is particularly good for canoeing, swimming, and fishing for small rainbow and cutthroat trout. A 1.4-km (20-minute) trail encircles the lake while others lead to three smaller bodies of water. A campground with showers and picnic tables is open year-round;

walk-in sites are $15 while other sites are $18.50 per night March–Oct., free the rest of the time. The park entrance is 13 km north of Squamish and the lake just under two km from the highway.

Brandywine Falls Provincial Park

If you like waterfalls, stop at this 143-hectare park 45 km north of Squamish and follow the 300-meter, five-minute trail from the parking lot. It's the kind of trail that excites all your senses—magnificent frosty peaks high above, dense lush forest on either side, a fast, deep river roaring along on one side, the pungent aroma and cushiness of crushed pine needles beneath your feet.

The trail takes you to a viewing platform to see 66-meter-high **Brandywine Falls,** where the wa-

ters plummet down a vertical la massive swirling plunge pool, th forest-edged river into a lake. It' cent early in summer. The falls were name early part of this century by two railroad surveyors who made a wager on guessing the falls' height, the winner to receive bottles of, you guessed it, brandywine. From the trail to the falls you can also branch off on another trail that leads either to **Swim Lake** (400 meters; 10 minutes) or along the **Calcheak Trail** (four km; 70 minutes). Aside from hiking, the park is also a good spot for swimming and fishing. A campground near Highway 99 provides gravel campsites; $12 per night May–Oct., no charge the rest of the year.

Whistler

Magnificent snowcapped peaks, dense green forests, transparent lakes, sparkling rivers, and an upmarket, cosmopolitan village right in the middle of it all: Welcome to Whistler (pop. 9,000), one of the world's great resort towns, just 120 km north of Vancouver along Highway 99. The Whistler Valley has seen incredible development in recent years and is now British Columbia's third-most popular tourist destination (behind Vancouver and Victoria), attracting around 1.5 million visitors annually. The crowds and the costs might not be for everyone, but there *is* a great variety of things to in Whistler, and the village takes full advantage of magnificent natural surroundings, making a trip north from Vancouver well worthwhile at any time of year.

Best-known among skiers and boarders, the town is built around the base of one of North America's finest resorts, **Whistler/Blackcomb,** which comprises almost 3,000 hectares on two mountains accessed by an ultramodern lift system. A season stretching from November to May doesn't leave much time for summer recreation, but in recent years, the "off season" has become almost equally busy. Among the abundant summertime recreation opportunities: lift-served hiking and glacier skiing and boarding; biking through the valley and mountains; water activities

on five lakes; horseback riding; golfing on some of the world's best resort courses; and fishing, rafting, and jet-boating on the rivers. The more sedentary summer visitor can simply stay in bustling **Whistler Village** and enjoy a plethora of outdoor cafés and restaurants.

History

Although natives took advantage of the abundant natural resources of the Whistler Valley for thousands of years, and gold seekers passed through on their way to the Cariboo goldfields, the history of Whistler as a resort town doesn't *really* begin until the 1960s and is associated almost entirely with the development of the ski area. At this time the only development was a bunch of ramshackle summer holiday houses around Alta Lake (which was also the name of the "town"), pop. 300.

In 1964 the rough and treacherous road linking the valley to Vancouver was finally paved, and in 1965 the Garibaldi Lift Co. began constructing the first lifts on the west side of what was then called **London Mountain.** The lift system of that first season consisted of just one gondola and two T-bars. Still, skiers were impressed, and so were investors, who began plans for major base area facilities. The idea of a European-style

SOUTHWESTERN B.C.

-in, ski-out village was promoted throughout the 1970s, but it wasn't until 1980 that Whistler Village officially opened. The lift system on what became known as Whistler Mountain (after the shrill call of marmots that lived around its summit) had by this time expanded greatly, but the capacity of the resort doubled for the 1980–81 season with the opening of a resort on adjacent Blackcomb Mountain. In 1986 Intrawest bought Blackcomb from the original developer, Aspen Skiing Corporation, and it was evident to everyone that the future for the valley was bright. Each year onward saw one or both of the mountains construct more lifts, including 1986, when the first lift was opened above the treeline, and 1994, when the $12 million Excalibur gondola began operation.

Throughout the last two decades of the 20th century, on-mountain construction was overshadowed by developments in the valley below: Intrawest spent $25 million on base facilities at Blackcomb, some of the best-known names in the golf world were brought in to design championship-standard golf courses, in 1995 Whistler Village Centre opened, and the population increased 10-fold in 20 years.

In 1997 the inevitable happened, and the two mountains came under the control of one company, Intrawest, who bought Whistler Mountain to create the megaresort of **Whistler/ Blackcomb.** The company has continued to upgrade the lifts and skier facilities, but the basic integration of the two ski areas was in place well before the takeover.

Overdevelopment is an ongoing concern throughout the valley. The latest community plan has recommended capping the number of "beds" at 52,500, up from the current number of 42,000. The main reason for a cap on development is a lack of available land, but poor road access from Vancouver is also a contributing factor. But the demand for both motel rooms and residential lots is seemingly never-ending, pushing up the costs of living and staying in the village (empty lots rarely sell for less than $300,000, and existing homes start at $400,000). In addition, Whistler has been chosen as Canada's representative bid (with Vancouver) for the 2010

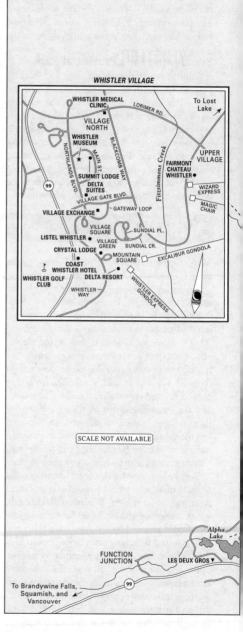

WHISTLER VILLAGE

SCALE NOT AVAILABLE

SOUTHWESTERN B.C.

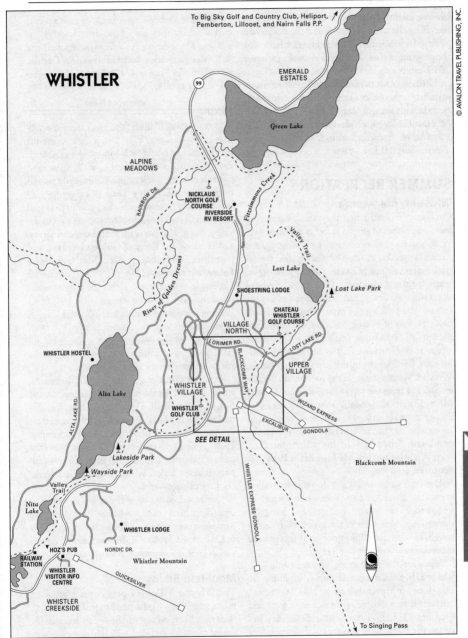

WHISTLER

To Big Sky Golf and Country Club, Heliport, Pemberton, Lillooet, and Nairn Falls P.P.

EMERALD ESTATES

Green Lake

ALPINE MEADOWS

RAINBOW DR.

NICKLAUS NORTH GOLF COURSE

RIVERSIDE RV RESORT

Fitzsimmons Creek

River of Golden Dreams

Valley Trail

Lost Lake

Lost Lake Park

SHOESTRING LODGE

CHATEAU WHISTLER GOLF COURSE

VILLAGE NORTH

LORIMER RD.

LOST LAKE RD.

WHISTLER HOSTEL

Alta Lake

BLACKCOMB WAY

UPPER VILLAGE

WHISTLER VILLAGE

WIZARD EXPRESS

ALTA LAKE RD.

WHISTLER GOLF CLUB

EXCALIBUR

GONDOLA

SEE DETAIL

Blackcomb Mountain

Lakeside Park

Wayside Park

Valley Trail

Nita Lake

WHISTLER LODGE

WHISTLER EXPRESS GONDOLA

MOON

RAILWAY STATION

HOZ'S PUB

NORDIC DR.

Whistler Mountain

WHISTLER VISITOR INFO CENTRE

QUICKSILVER

WHISTLER CREEKSIDE

To Singing Pass

© AVALON TRAVEL PUBLISHING, INC.

SOUTHWESTERN B.C.

Winter Olympic Games, with planned venues including the main ski resort and the Callaghan Valley, 15 km south of the village. Check out the progress of the bid at website www.vancouver 2010.com.

The best place to learn the full story of development in the valley is the **Whistler Museum,** near the bottom end of the village at 4329 Main St., 604/932-2019, which opens in summer daily 10 A.M.–4 P.M. and the rest of the year Thurs.–Sun. 10 A.M.–4 P.M.

SUMMER RECREATION
Whistler/Blackcomb

On the few months that they aren't covered in snow, the slopes of the ski resort come alive with locals and tourists alike enjoying hiking, guided naturalist walks, mountain biking, and horseback riding, or just marveling at the mountainscape from the comfort of the lifts. Die-hard skiers will even find glacier skiing here early in the summer (see the special topic Summer Skiing). Over 50 km of hiking trails wind around the mountains, including trails through the high alpine to destinations such as beautiful Harmony Lake (two km from the top of the gondola; Whistler Mountain) or to the toe of a small glacier (2.5 km from the top of the gondola; Whistler Mountain). It's also possible to rent snowshoes for $6 per hour to walk across areas of year-round snowpack. Or for an adrenaline rush, take the gondola up then bicycle down the mountain with **Whistler Backroads Mountain Bike Adventures,** 604/932-3111.

Even if it's a beautiful day down in the valley, expect the unexpected and take a warm wind- or waterproof coat in anticipation of a change in the weather. Also, some of the hiking trails can be rough, so wear good hiking boots if you plan to explore away from the main trails.

Rates for the sightseeing lifts are adult $22, senior $19, children free. Summer lift hours are mid-June to September daily 10 A.M.–5 P.M., during the first couple of weekends of June and October 11 A.M.–4 P.M. These dates vary between the mountains and are totally dependent on snow cover, or the lack of it. Dining facilities

are available on both mountains, or grab a picnic basket lunch from any of the delis down in the village. The best source of information is the **Whistler Activities and Information Centre,** 4010 Whistler Way, 604/932-2394, or call the resort direct at 604/932-3434 or 800/766-0449.

Hiking

The easiest way to access the area's most spectacular hiking country is to take a sightseeing lift up Whistler or Blackcomb Mountain (see above). But many other options exist. Walking around Whistler Valley you'll notice signposted trails all over the place. **Valley Trail** is a paved walkway/bikeway in summer, a cross-country ski trail in winter. It makes an almost complete tour of the valley, from Whistler Village to **Lost** and **Green Lakes,** along the **River of Golden Dreams,** and past three golf courses to **Alta, Nita,** and **Alpha Lakes,** and finally to Highway 99 in the Whistler Creekside area. If you'd rather do a short walk, head for Lost Lake via the two-km trail from Parking Lot East at the back of Whistler Village, or via the free Whistler Transit System bus from the middle of the village. Once at the beautiful lake, you can saunter along the shore, picnic, swim, or, in winter, cross-country ski.

Between Whistler and Blackcomb Mountains, a gravel road leads five km to the trailhead for the **Singing Pass Trail.** From the parking lot, this trail follows the Fitzsimmons Creek watershed for 7.5 km (allow 2.5 hours each way) to Singing Pass, gaining 600 meters in elevation. From the pass, it's another two km (40 minutes) to beautiful **Russet Lake,** where you'll find a back-country campground.

On the opposite side of the valley, an eight-km trail (three hours each way) leads from Alta Lake Road just north of the Whistler hostel up Twenty One Mile Creek to **Rainbow Lake.** The elevation gain is a strenuous 850 meters.

Mountain Biking

The Whistler Valley is a perfect place to take a mountain bike—you'd need months to ride all the trails here. Many of the locals have abandoned their cars for bikes, which in some cases are worth much more than their cars! You can see

M

SOUTHWESTERN B.C.

them scooting along **Valley Trail,** a paved walk/bikeway that links the entire valley and is the resident bicyclists' freeway. Another popular place for mountain bikers is beautiful **Lost Lake,** two km northeast of Whistler Village. In the last few years, the resort itself has developed a Mountain Bike Park for more adventurous riders. Using the lifts to access a vertical drop of 1,200 meters, it features three "Skill Centres," filled with obstacles for varying levels of skill; a Bikercross Course; and a variety of trails to the valley floor. Run the courses by yourself or join a group in a guided descent for $70 including bike rental.

If you didn't bring a bike, not to worry—they're for rent. Rental rates start at around $12 per hour, $30–70 per day. Or perhaps a guided bicycle tour of the local area sounds appealing—it's not a bad idea to have a guide at first. **Whistler Backroads,** Main St., Whistler Village North, 604/932-3111, offers tours throughout the valley, including down the slopes of the ski resort. Other rental outlets include: **Blackcomb Ski and Sport,** 4553 Blackcomb Way, 604/938-7788; **Can-ski Cycles,** 4573 Chateau Blvd., 604/938-7744; **Evolution,** 4122 Village Green, 604/932-2967; **Mountain Riders,** 4309 Skiers Approach, 604/932-3659; **Sportstop,** 4112 Golfers Approach, 604/932-5495; **Whistler Bike Co.,** 4050 Whistler Way, 604/938-9511; **Whistler Outdoor Experience Co.,** 8841 Hwy. 99, 604/932-3389; and **Wild Willies,** Nester's Square, 604/938-8836.

Water Sports

Sunbathers head for the public beaches along the shores of **Alta Lake**—watching all the windsurfers whipping across the water or beginners repeatedly taking a plunge is a good source of summer entertainment. Wayside Park at the south end of the lake has a beach, a canoe launch, an offshore pontoon, a grassy area with picnic tables, and hiking/biking trails. At Lakeside Park, also on Alta Lake, **Whistler Outdoor Experience Co.,** 604/932-3389, rents canoes for $18 an hour or $52 per half day, and kayaks for $15 an hour. It also offers adventure tours, including a 3.5-hour white-water rafting trip for $80 per person, a one-hour jet-boat trip for $75 per per-

son, and a three-hour horseback-riding trip for $65 per person. In winter it offers cross-country ski, heli-ski, and snowshoe adventures.

For a little white-water excitement, try river rafting with **Whistler River Adventures,** 604/932-3532, which provides guided scenic and white-water tours between the end of May and early September. Outings range from an easy float down the Green River for $65 per person to the white-water thrills of a full-day trip on the Elaho River for $135.

Golf

Whistler boasts four world-class championship golf courses, each with its own character and charm. The entire valley has gained a reputation as a golfing destination, with many accommodations offering package deals that include greens fees. Still, golfing at Whistler is as expensive as anywhere in the country. All the courses below hold a golf shop with club rentals ($30–40) and golfing apparel, and a clubhouse with dining facilities. The golfing season runs mid-May to October, so in late spring you can ski in the morning and golf in the afternoon.

Designed by Arnold Palmer, **Whistler Golf Club,** between Whistler Village and Alta Lake, 604/932-4544, offers large greens and narrow wooded fairways over a challenging 6,676-yard par-72 layout. Greens fees are $149 (the twilight rate of $99 is offered after 4 P.M.), cart rental is $35, and club rental costs from $35.

On the other side of the village is **Chateau Whistler Golf Club,** Blackcomb Way, 604/938-2092. Designed by renowned golf-course architect Robert Trent Jones Jr., this 6,635-yard course takes advantage of the rugged terrain of Blackcomb Mountain's lower slopes through holes that rise and fall with the lay of the land. Greens fees are $175, which includes the use of a cart equipped with a computerized yardage meter. After 3 P.M., rates drop to $125.

Nicklaus North, just north of Whistler Village, 604/938-9898, is the only course in the world that Jack Nicklaus, the architect, has lent his name to. The open course holds numerous water hazards, boasts 360-degree mountain vistas, and plays to a challenging 6,900 yards from the

SOUTHWESTERN B.C.

back markers. Greens fees are $205, which includes use of a driving range; twilight rate is $125 after 3 P.M.

Farther up the valley is **Big Sky Golf and Country Club,** 604/894-6106 or 800/668-7900, a lengthy par-72 course of over 7,000 yards; $150 per round with cart rental an additional $32.

Flightseeing

Nothing beats the spectacular sight of the Coast Mountains' majestic peaks, glaciers, icy-blue lakes, and lush mountain meadows from an unforgettable vantage point high in the sky. **Whistler Air,** 604/932-6615, will take you aloft in a floatplane from Green Lake, three km north of Whistler Village. A 30-minute flight over the glaciers of Garibaldi Provincial Park costs $85; a 40-minute flight over the Pemberton Ice Cap goes for $105; and a 70-minute flight landing on a high alpine lake runs $150. You can also charter the whole plane (minimum four people) for a remote backcountry adventure.

Helicopter rides are also available and will cost you from $80 per person for a 20-minute flight with either Whistler Air or **Mountain Helisports,** 604/932-2070. Both companies also offer heli-hiking and heli-picnic packages, and both base their choppers at a heliport 10 km north of Whistler Village.

SKIING AND SNOWBOARDING

No matter what your ability, the skiing at **Whistler/Blackcomb,** consistently rated as North America's No. 1 ski destination, makes for a winter holiday you won't forget in a hurry. Until the 1997–98 season, the ski area comprised two different resorts which in themselves boasted impressive statistics. Combined, they now overshadow all other North American resorts in terms of size and stature. The two lift-served mountains, Whistler and Blackcomb, are separated by a steep-sided valley through which Fitzsimmons Creek flows, with lifts converging at Whistler Village. Skiing is over 2,863 hectares (7071 acres), comprising more than 200 groomed runs, hundreds of unmarked trails through forested areas, three glaciers, and 12 bowls. Blackcomb and Whistler Mountains are 2,284 meters and 2,182 meters high respectively. The lift-served vertical rise of Blackcomb is 1,609 meters, the highest in North America, but Whistler is only slightly lower at 1,530 meters. (When Blackcomb and Whistler operated as separate entities, they boasted North America's highest and second-highest vertical rises.) In total, the resort has 33 lifts, including three gondolas, 12 high-speed quad chairlifts, five triples, one double, and 12 surface lifts. The terrain is rated Intermediate over 55 percent of the resort, with the remaining 45 percent split evenly between Beginner and Expert. Snowboarders are well catered to with four terrain parks and numerous half-pipes. The length of season is also impressive, running from November to May with the Horstman Glacier open for skiing for a few weeks of summer (see the special topic Summer Skiing).

The two mountains are similar not only in height but also size. Whistler offers 1,480 hectares of skiing, Blackcomb slightly less. From Whistler Village, a five-km-long gondola lifts skiers more than a vertical kilometer up Whistler Mountain (the one on the right as you look up at the resort from the valley floor) above the valley to east-facing slopes served by eight chairlifts and a T-bar. Over the back of the main mountain, the Harmony Express quad chairlift serves 400 hectares of bowl skiing. Much of Blackcomb Mountain is out of sight from the valley; over half the skiing is above the treeline, and over the back are two massive powder-filled bowls.

For many skiers, the resort can be overwhelming. Trail maps detail all marked runs but can't convey the vast size of the area. A great way to get to know the mountain is on an orientation tour; these leave throughout the day from various meeting points (ask when and where when you buy your ticket) and are free. **Whistler/Blackcomb Ski and Snowboard School,** 604/932-3434 or 800/766-0449, is the country's largest ski school and offers various lesson packages and programs, such as the Esprit, a three-day, women's-only "camp" that provides instruction in a variety of disciplines.

Lift tickets are adult $63, senior and youth

SUMMER SKIING

Just because the calendar, thermometer, and sun's angle say it's summer doesn't mean skiing is months away. Whistler/Blackcomb is one of just two North American resorts offering lift-served summer skiing. Between late June and early August (but very weather dependent), a T-bar on Blackcomb Mountain's **Horstman Glacier** opens up a small 45-hectare area with a vertical rise of 209 meters. The lift opens daily noon–4 P.M.; $39 per person includes lift transportation from the valley floor. The slopes can get crowded, with local and national ski teams in training and with visitors enjoying the novelty of summer skiing. But if it gets too bad, just go back to the valley floor for golf or water sports.

$54, child $32, and those under seven ski for free. For general resort information call 604/932-3434 or 800/766-0449; for snow reports call 604/932-4211 or, from Vancouver, 604/687-7507; for accommodation packages call 604/932-4222 or 800/944-7853. The resort's website is www.whistler-blackcomb.com.

Cross-Country Skiing

Many kilometers of trails wind through snow-covered terrain in the valley. Starting at Whistler Village and running in a long loop past Lost Lake and Green Lake is the **Valley Trail,** a paved walk/bikeway in summer that becomes a popular cross-country ski trail in winter. The biggest concentration of trails lies near Lost Lake and on the adjacent Chateau Whistler Golf Course. Most trails are groomed, while some are track set, and a five-km stretch is illuminated for night skiing. The trail system is operated by the **Whistler Nordic Cross-country Ski Club,** 604/932-6436, which collects a fee of $10 for a day pass from a ticket booth near Lost Lake, where you'll also find a cozy warming hut. The fairways of **Nicklaus North** are another popular cross-country skiing spot; $10 for a daily trail pass. Cross-country ski rentals are available from several shops in the village.

Heli-Skiing

Heli-skiing is offered by **Whistler Heli-skiing,** with a desk in the Crystal Lodge, 604/932-4105, which takes strong intermediates and expert adventurers high into the Coast Mountains to ski fields of untracked powder. Rates of $560 include a day's skiing (around 1,800 vertical meters), transportation to and from the heliport north of Whistler Village, a gourmet lunch, and the guide.

WET WEATHER RECREATION

Great Wall, under the Westbrook Hotel at 4340 Sundial Crescent, 604/905-7625, is an indoor climbing wall with varying degrees of slope and an overhang. It costs $15 for a day pass with instruction and equipment rental extra. Open daily 10 A.M.–10 P.M.

Pamper Yourself

Whistler Body Wrap, 4433 Sundial Pl. (next to the Keg Restaurant), Whistler Village, 604/932-4710, offers a wide variety of spa treatments, including massages, facials, body wraps, and salon services. A standard 25-minute massage costs $60, or a full day of treatments—including an herbal body wrap—and lunch costs from $320. **The Spa, Chateau Whistler,** 4599 Chateau Blvd., 604/938-2086, is a more luxurious facility styled on Romanesque surroundings. It offers all the same services but at a higher cost.

ENTERTAINMENT AND EVENTS

Entertainment

Throughout the year you can usually find live evening entertainment in Whistler Village. At **Buffalo Bill's** in the Timberline Lodge, 4122 Village Green, 604/932-6613, expect anything from reggae to rock. Another of the hottest nightspots, **Tommy Africa's,** 4216 Gateway Dr., 604/932-6090, is popular with the younger crowd, pumping out high-volume reggae across the valley's most popular dance floor.

Head to **Savage Beagle,** 4222 Village Square, 604/938-3337, nightly between 8 P.M. and 2 A.M. for dance, house, and alternative music. **Rogue Wolf,** downstairs in Tapleys Pub at 4068 Golfers

Approach, 604/932-4011, offers a similar scene. The **Boot Pub,** in the Shoestring Lodge out on Nancy Greene Way, 604/932-3338, offers some of the cheapest drinks in the valley and occasional live music. The **Garibaldi Lift Co. Bar & Grill,** 2320 London Lane, 604/905-2220, features live entertainment most nights—often blues and jazz—and good food at reasonable prices.

Black's Pub, on Mountain Square, 604/932-6945, offers more than 90 international beers and a quiet atmosphere in a small upstairs English-style bar. Other watering holes include **Crystal's Lounge** in the Crystal Lodge at 4154 Village Square, 604/932-2221, and the **Mallard Bar** at the Chateau Whistler Resort, 4599 Chateau Blvd., 604/938-8000.

Events

The winter season is packed with ski and snowboard races, but the biggest is the **World Ski & Snowboard Festival,** through mid-April, 604/905-3027, website www.wssf.com. This innovative event brings together the very best winter athletes for the World Skiing Invitational and the World Snowboarding Championship. These are only the flagships of this 10-day extravaganza, which also includes demo days, exhibitions, and a film festival.

Each weekend in May and June and daily through summer, the streets of Whistler come alive with street entertainment such as musicians, jugglers, and comedians. The last weekend of May is the official end of the ski season up on Blackcomb Mountain, with a **Slush Cup** and live music.

Canada Day, 1 July, is celebrated with a parade through Whistler Village. **Whistler Roots Festival,** the third weekend of July, brings together country, blues, Celtic, and world musicians for outdoor and indoor performances. The following weekend, the last in July, is the **Cactus Cup Mountain Bike Festival,** with demonstrations, lessons, guided rides, and racing.

On the second weekend of August, the valley hosts the **Whistler Classical Music Festival,** which includes a program of events ranging from Brass on a Raft to a concert by the Vancouver Symphony Orchestra high up on the slopes of Whistler Mountain. The **Alpine Wine Festival,** early in September, showcases the province's best wineries with daily wine-tasting at Pika's Restaurant, on Whistler Mountain. The streets come alive again the second weekend of September during the **Whistler Jazz and Blues Festival.**

During **Oktoberfest,** many restaurants and businesses dress themselves up in a Bavarian theme. The festival also features dancing in the streets, and, of course, a beer hall.

ACCOMMODATIONS AND CAMPING

Whistler's accommodations range from a hostel and inexpensive dorm beds to luxury resort hotels. It's just a matter of selecting one to suit your budget and location preference. Skiers may want to be right in Whistler Village or by the gondola base in Whistler Creekside so they can stroll out their door, strap on skis, and jump on a lift. (The term "slopeside" describes accommodations within a five-minute walk of the lifts.)

Accommodation pricing in Whistler is very complex. The best advice is to shop around using the phone or Internet. Contact the lodgings themselves, then the booking agencies listed below to get a comparison. Winter is most definitely high season, with the week after Christmas and all of February and March a high season within a high season, especially for lodgings within walking distance of the lifts or that are self-contained and capable of sleeping more than two people. These are also the accommodations that discount most heavily outside of winter. Search out Delta Whistler Village Suites at website www.delta-whistler/village, type in a February date and then a July date under reservations—a bargain in July and over the top in winter.

If you plan on skiing or golfing, a package deal is the way to go. These can be booked directly through many accommodations, but the following agencies offer a wider scope of choices. **Whistler Central Reservations,** 604/664-5625 or 800/944-7853, website www.whistler -resort.com, is the official reservation agency of

Tourism Whistler, or make bookings through one of the following: **Champagne Chalets of Whistler,** 604/938-1184 or 800/465-3754, website www.sportpak.com; **Powder Resort Properties,** 604/932-2882 or 800/777-0185, website www.powderresorts.com; **Rainbow Retreats Accommodations,** 604/932-2343, website www.rainbowretreats.com; or **Whistler Chalets,** 604/932-6699 or 800/663-7711, website www.whistlerchalets.com. For Internet-active, Whistler-bound travelers, discounted hotel rooms and condos can be rented through website www.accommodation/auction.com.

Although winter is peak season, rates quoted below are for summertime.

Under $50

Hostelling International—Whistler, Alta Lake Rd., 604/932-5492, website www.hihostels.com, is on the western shore of Alta Lake, boasting magnificent views across the lake to the resort. It's relatively small (just 32 beds), with facilities including a communal kitchen, dining area, and big, cozy living area. Bike and canoe rentals are available. It's understandably popular year-round; members $18.50 per night, nonmembers $23.50. Check-in is 8–11 A.M. and 4–10 P.M. To get there from the south, take Alta Lake Road to the left off Highway 99 and watch for the small sign on the lake side of the road. **Whistler Transit System** buses depart Whistler Village and run right past the hostel door.

The **Shoestring Lodge,** 7124 Nancy Greene Dr., White Gold Estates (north of the Village on the right side of the highway), 604/932-3338 or 877/551-4954, website www.shoestringlodge.com, is a popular local pub with dorm beds for $21 per night and $105 per week through summer, rising to $32 and $139 in winter.

Scattered through Whistler are club-owned lodges open to nonmembers when beds are available. Best of the bunch is UBC-owned **Whistler Lodge,** 2124 Nordic Dr., 604/932-6604. It has a large kitchen and lounge area, and an outdoor deck with barbecue facilities. You provide your own bedding and towels. Dorm beds are $23.50 in summer, slightly higher in winter. Check-in is 4–10 P.M.

$50–100

There's not too much on offer in Whistler in this price bracket—it's either a dorm bed or an expensive hotel room. The exception is the **Shoestring Lodge,** 7124 Nancy Greene Dr., 604/932-3338 or 877/551-4954, website www.shoestringlodge.com, detailed above for its dormitories. It also has small double rooms (which can get noisy) with ensuite bathrooms, TV, and daily housekeeping. Summer rates are $80 per night or $280 for a full week. It's out of the village, but pub downstairs serves meals.

$100–150

Crystal Lodge, 4154 Village Green, 604/932-2221 or 800/667-3363, website www.crystallodge.com, stands out as excellent value in the heart of the action of Whistler Village. The spacious rooms have a homely feel and guests have the use of an outdoor hot tub and heated pool. Rates start at $120 s or d for a regular hotel-style room, rising to $180 for a suite with a private balcony. Winter rates start at over $200.

$150–200

On the edge of the village and adjacent to one of the valley's best golf courses is **Coast Whistler Hotel,** 4005 Whistler Way, 604/932-2522 or 800/663-5644, website www.coastwhistlerhotel.com. Each of the 194 rooms is simply but stylishly decorated in pastel colors. Facilities include a heated outdoor pool, exercise room, hot tub, restaurant, and bar. Summer rates start at a reasonable $159 (from $109 in spring and fall), but the winter rate of $285 s or d is a little steep considering you're away from the ski lifts.

Closer to the action, **Listel Whistler,** 4121 Village Green, 604/932-1133 or 800/663-5472, website www.listelhotel.com, is a self-contained resort complete with a year-round outdoor pool, outdoor hot tub, laundry facility, bistro, and wine bar. The contemporary styled rooms are $199 s or d through much of year, rising to $399 in February and March. Check the Listel website for specials.

Delta Hotels and Resorts has two properties in the village. With the best location of any lodging,

SOUTHWESTERN B.C.

right where the gondolas for both Whistler and Blackcomb converge, is **Delta Whistler Resort,** 4050 Whistler Way, 604/932-1982 or 800/515-4050, website www.delta-whistler.com. This 288-room hotel has a full-service health club with an outdoor pool, two restaurants, and a bar. Rack rates through summer are from $180 s or d, while in February rooms start at $450. Across the village, **Delta Whistler Village Suites,** 4308 Main St., 604/905-3987 or 888/299-3987, website www.delta-whistler.com, combines the conveniences of a full-service hotel with more than 200 kitchen-equipped units—the only such property in Whistler; from $180 s or d outside winter. In both cases, check the website for promotional deals.

Over $200

Summit Lodge, 4359 Main St. (off Northlands Blvd.), 604/932-2778 or 888/913-8811, website www.summitlodge.com, is a luxurious European Alps-style boutique hotel. Each of the 81 units features comfortable furnishings, a slate floor, a fireplace, a balcony, and a small kitchen. Off-season rates start at $300 s or d, rising to $450 in winter.

    Fairmont Chateau Whistler, at the base of Blackcomb Mountain in Upper Village, 604/938-8000 or 800/441-1414, website www.fairmont.com, is Whistler's most luxurious lodging, with its own championship golf course, a health club with the best equipment money can buy, tennis courts, and all the facilities expected of one of the world's best accommodations. The massive lobby is decorated in the style of a rustic lodge, but the rooms couldn't be more different. Each is elegantly furnished and offers great mountain views. In the low season (late spring and fall) rooms start at $270 s or d; peak summer rates start at $340 s or d, winter rates at $400 s or d.

Camping

Enjoying a pleasant location just over two km north of the village, **Riverside RV Resort** is the only campground within town boundaries. This new facility (opened 2001) offers a modern bathroom complex, hot tub, laundry, small general store, and a shuttle service. Sites range $35–55,

Delta Whistler Village Suites

© ANDREW HEMPSTEAD

with a small wooded area set aside for walk-in tent campers. Cabins are $100–150. Reserve a site at 604/905-5533 or 877/905-5533, website www.whistlercamping.com.

    Out of town, the closest campgrounds are in **Brandywine Falls Provincial Park,** 11 km south, and **Nairn Falls Provincial Park,** 28 km north. Both are open April–Nov. and charge $12 per night. For more facilities, **Dryden Creek Resorts,** 50 km south (just north of Squamish), 604/898-9726 or 800/903-4690, is a good option; unserviced sites $17.50, hookups $20–22.50.

FOOD

Breakfast on the Mountain

Through the ski season, Whistler/Blackcomb offers breakfast on the mountain, as well as the chance to hit the slopes before the lifts officially open. On Blackcomb, it's coffee and cakes in the **Rendezvous Restaurant** for $7.50, while over on Whistler, a full buffet breakfast in **Pika's Restau-**

rant is $15. These breakfast deals must be paid for in conjunction with a lift pass, and lifts open at 7:30 A.M. for diners.

Cafés

One of the best places in Whistler Village for breakfast is **Chalet Deli,** 4437 Sundial Place, 604/932-8345. Light breakfasts cost from $5 and the service is fast and efficient. The rest of the day the deli is a great choice for hamburgers and healthy sandwiches and salads. Open daily from 7:30 A.M. Scattered through the village are a number of coffeehouses, including **Starbucks,** 4295 Blackcomb Way, 604/938-0611; **Moguls Coffee Bean,** 4208 Village Square, 604/932-1918; and **Grabbajabba,** in Village North at 4390 Lorimer Rd., 604/932-3213. If you've been visiting the information center at the entrance to town, cross the road to the **Southside Deli,** 2102 Lake Placid Rd., 604/932-3368, for a well-priced cooked breakfast or light meal.

North American

For steaks, seafood, a salad bar, fresh hot bread, and plenty of food at a reasonable price, the **Keg Restaurant,** at Whistler Village Inn, 4429 Sundial Place, 604/932-5151, is a sure thing. Expect to pay from $12 for an entrée; open daily from 5:30 P.M. The rustic decor and great Canadian food at **Garibaldi Lift Co. Bar & Grill,** at the base of the Whistler Village gondola, 604/905-2220, has been a big hit since opening in 1995. The bar and sundeck are popular après-ski hangouts, and by around 8 P.M. everyone's back for dinner. For western-style atmosphere, head to the **Longhorn Saloon and Grill** at 4290 Mountain Square, 604/932-5999, or the **Rodeo Bar and Grill** at the Listel Whistler, 4121 Village Green, 604/932-1133. **Citta,** 4217 Village Stroll in Whistler Village, 604/932-4177, offers all the usual pizza, pasta, and salads at reasonable prices; open daily for lunch and dinner. Near Whistler Creekside, **Hoz's Pub,** 2129 Lake Placid Rd., 604/932-5940, is renowned for good pub food, such as fish and chips from $8.50 and ribs from $16; open daily from 11:30 A.M. In the same complex, the **Creekside Grill,** 604/932-4424,

is a small restaurant with burgers around $10 and steaks from $20.

Hy's, in the Delta Whistler Village Suites at 4308 Main St., 604/905-5555, undoubtedly offers the best steaks in the valley. The scene is up-market, with elegant tables set within rich-colored wood walls. Starters range $8–12 with steaks starting at $27.

European

For great Greek food, **Zeuski's Taverna,** 4314 Main St., Town Plaza, Village North, 604/932-6009, is open daily for lunch and dinner and is always busy. For something different, sample the souvlaki cooked on the barbecue.

Restaurant entrepreneur Umberto Menghi operates numerous eateries in Vancouver and two restaurants in Whistler Village. Both are reasonably priced with menus influenced by the cuisine of Tuscany. Check out **Il Caminetto di Umberto,** 4242 Village Stroll, 604/932-4442, and **Trattoria di Umberto,** 4417 Sundial Place, 604/932-5858. The former, named for a fireplace that has been replaced by more tables, has a warm, welcoming atmosphere and a long menu of pastas from $18. The latter is less expensive and attracts a more casual crowd.

Ristorante Araxi, 4222 Village Square, Whistler Village, 604/932-4540, consistently wins awards for its traditional Italian menu, which takes advantage of produce from around the Lower Mainland. It also boasts an extensive wine list. In the same price range is **Quattro,** 4319 Main St., 604/905-4844, a casual dining room set around a busy bar and a crackling fireplace. This restaurant features elegant furnishings and a menu inspired by the cuisine of northern Italy.

One of the valley's finest restaurants is **Val d'Isere,** 4433 Sundial Place, Whistler Town Plaza, 604/932-4666, open daily from 5:30 P.M. The atmosphere is elegant and intimate, with classic French dishes the specialty. Expect to pay from $20 for an entrée and revel in an impressive wine list. More casual is **Les Deux Gros,** one km west of Whistler Creekside on Alta Lake Rd., 604/932-4611, dishing up classic French country fare Tues.–Sun. 5:30–10:30 P.M.

Asian

Reasonably priced Mongolian fare is on the menu at **Mongolie Grill,** 4295 Whistler Way, Whistler Village, 604/938-9416; open daily from 11:30 A.M. **Whistler Garden** in the luxurious Delta Whistler Resort, 4050 Whistler Way, 604/938-9781, is a large Chinese restaurant featuring a dim sum lunch and a Cantonese-inspired regular menu; open daily.

TRANSPORTATION

Getting There

Vancouver International Airport, 130 km to the south, is the main gateway to Whistler. **Perimeter,** 604/266-5386 (Vancouver) or 604/905-0041 (Whistler), provides bus service between the two up to five times daily; $53 each way. Buses make stops at some Vancouver hotels and a short rest stop at pretty Shannon Falls. **Greyhound,** 604/932-5031, runs six buses daily between Vancouver's Pacific Central Station at 1150 Station St. and Whistler Village; $22 one-way, $35 round-trip, with connections from the airport. A schedule is posted at website www.whistlerbus.com.

The scheduled **BC Rail** passenger service between Vancouver and Prince George stops at Whistler. Extra trains are run in summer, making a day trip to Whistler possible. They depart from 1311 W. 1st St., North Vancouver, daily at 7 A.M. and depart the Whistler terminal, on Lake Placid Rd. near Whistler Creekside, for the return journey at 4 P.M. The trip takes two and a half hours each way, allowing plenty of time to explore the village. A day trip costs $106, which includes return train travel, breakfast and dinner aboard the train, a lunch voucher, and a gondola ride. For those who want to stay longer or provide their own meals, the cost is $39 each way. For all BC Rail information call 604/984-5246 or 800/663-8238, website www.bcrail.com.

Getting Around

Once you're in Whistler, getting around is pretty easy—if you're staying in Whistler Village, everything you need is within easy walking distance. **Whistler Transit System,** 604/932-4020, operates extensive bus routes throughout the valley

daily 6 A.M.–midnight. Routes radiate from Village Exchange in Whistler Village south to Whistler Creekside and as far north as Emerald Estates on the shore of Green Lake. Fare is $1.50 (exact change only) except for travel on the Village Loop, which is free (and probably the only thing in the valley that *is* free). An all-day pass costs $4.50. Through summer Whistler Transit runs a shuttle between Whistler Village and Lost Lake every 15 minutes.

For a cab call **Sea to Sky Taxi,** 604/932-3333, or **Whistler Taxi,** 604/938-3333.

Rental car agencies in Whistler include **Budget,** 604/932-1236, and **Thrifty,** 604/938-0302.

SERVICES AND INFORMATION

In Whistler Village you'll find a post office, banks, a currency exchange, laundromat, supermarket, and liquor store. **Whistler Medical Centre** is at 4380 Lorimer, 604/932-3977. **Whistler Public Library,** 4329 Main St., 604/932-5564, is open Mon.–Tues. and Thursday 10 A.M.–8 P.M., Fri.–Sun. 10 A.M.–5 P.M.

Information

Tourism Whistler promotes the resort town throughout the world via the Internet (www.tourismwhistler.com) and at all major ski and travel shows. It also operates Whistler Central Reservations, 604/664-5625 or 800/944-7853, for all accommodation bookings.

On entering Whistler from the south, look for **Whistler Visitor Info Centre** on the right-hand side of the road at 2097 Lake Placid Rd., Whistler Creekside, 604/932-5528. A map outside the center shows the Whistler Valley in detail, including hiking trails (with length and elevation gain), downhill and cross-country ski areas, overnight shelters, vehicle and tent campgrounds, fishing, hiking, picnic spots, canoe and kayak portages, and more. The center is open year-round daily 9 A.M.–5 P.M.

Four newspapers are good sources of local information: *Whistler Journal* (published every three months), which has a detailed map of Whistler Valley; the *Question* (daily Mon.–Thurs.); *Whistler this Week* (Friday); and the weekly *Pique*.

The Gold Nugget Route

The route north between Whistler and Lillooet is best traveled in good weather—the scenery is so spectacular you don't want to miss *anything*. See white-topped peaks all around you and big glacier-colored rivers. If you have the time, stop at provincial parks along the way for always-good scenery and outdoor activities.

Make your first stop north of Whistler **Nairn Falls Provincial Park,** on the banks of Green River, where a wooded trail leads to a waterfall. Stay overnight at the campground; open April–Nov., $12 per site May–Oct., free the rest of the year.

Pemberton

A small logging town and service center surrounded by mountains, trees, lakes, and rivers, Pemberton sits in the fertile Pemberton Valley 32 km north of Whistler. Best known for its potatoes, locals affectionately call the area "Spud Valley." It's only a short distance south of the Lillooet River, a main transportation route to the Cariboo during the 1860s' gold-rush days. Today's visitors mostly leave their gold pans at home, coming mainly to fish or to hike in the beautiful valleys around Pemberton.

The summer-only **Pemberton Visitor Info Centre** is back out of town on Hwy. 99, 604/894-6175.

North to Lillooet

From Pemberton you can take one of three routes to Lillooet. Whichever route you decide on, it's important to note that the weather can change rapidly, and even in summer you might find yourself traveling through a sudden snowstorm at higher elevations. However, the scenery makes the effort worthwhile. You'll see beautiful lakes, fast rivers, summer wildflowers, deep-blue mountains, steep ravines, never-ending forests, and vistas in every shade of green imaginable.

Campgrounds and picnic areas mark all the best locations.

The most direct way—the route once taken by fortune seekers heading toward the Cariboo goldfields—is paved Highway 99. A few kilometers out of Mount Currie, the highway begins switchbacking, as it climbs abruptly into the Coast Mountains and crests at a 1,300-meter-high pass. Just before the pass is 1,460-hectare **Joffre Lakes Provincial Park,** where a 500-meter (10-minute) trail leads to Lower Joffre Lake. The trail continues beyond the first lake, making an elevation gain of 400 meters before reaching the main body of water, 10 km (three hours) from the highway.

From the pass, Highway 99 loses over 1,000 meters of elevation in its descent to Lillooet. Along the way is narrow **Duffey Lake** (the highway itself is referred to locally as the "Duffey Lake Road"), backed by the steep-sided Cayoosh Range. At the north end of the lake is a provincial park with camping ($12 per night).

The second route (summer only) spurs north through Mt. Currie following the Birkenhead River, passing the turnoff to 9,755-hectare **Birkenhead Lake Provincial Park,** then descending to **D'Arcy.** Beyond this point, the road can get extremely rough, so check conditions in town before setting out.

The third, northernmost, and longest route, over 200 km of mostly unpaved road (also summer only), climbs north along the Lillooet River through Pemberton Meadows, over Hurley Pass, and to the historic mining communities of **Gold Bridge** and **Bralorne** before closely following the shore of Carpenter Lake in an easterly direction back to Lillooet.

For information on **Lillooet,** the confluence of the three above routes, see the beginning of the Cariboo Country section of the Central British Columbia chapter.

East from Vancouver

FRASER VALLEY

When you leave Vancouver and head due east, you travel through the most built-up and heavily populated area of British Columbia, skirting modern cities, residential suburbs, and zones of heavy industry. However, it's not an unattractive area—the main roads follow the mighty Fraser River through a fertile valley of rolling farmland dotted with historic villages, and beautiful mountains line the horizon in just about any direction.

You have a choice of two major routes. The TransCanada Highway, on the south side of the Fraser River, speeds you out of southeast Vancouver through Abbotsford and scenic Chilliwack to Hope. Slower, more picturesque Highway 7 meanders along the north side of the Fraser River through **Mission,** named after a Roman Catholic mission school built in 1861. The town is now known for its Benedictine monastery, which offers a retreat center open to the public. The highway then passes the access road to **Harrison Hot Springs** and crosses over the Fraser River to Hope. In summer you can pick and choose from an endless number of roadside stands selling fresh fruit at bargain prices—the raspberries in July are delectable.

Fort Langley National Historic Site

In 1827, the Hudson's Bay Company established a settlement 48 km upstream from the mouth of the Fraser River as part of a network of trading posts, provision depots, and administrative centers that stretched across western Canada. The original site was abandoned in 1838 in favor of another, farther upstream, where today the settlement has been re-created. It was the abundance of fur-bearing mammals that led to the region's settlement originally, but within a decade salmon had become its mainstay. Through its formative years, the fort played a major role in the development of British Columbia. Out its gates have vamoosed native fur and salmon traders, adventurous explorers who opened up the interior, company traders, and fortune seekers heading for the goldfields of the upper Fraser River. When British Columbia became a crown colony on 19 November 1858, the official proclamation was uttered here in the "big house." In the process, Fort Langley was declared capital of the colony, but one year later, the entire colonial government moved to the more central New Westminster.

Today the restored riverside trading post springs to life as park interpreters in period costumes animate the fort's history. Admission is adult $5, child $2.50. It's open in March–Nov. 10 A.M.–5 P.M., closed the rest of the year. The park is within walking distance of Fort Langley village, where many businesses are built in a heritage style and you'll find dozens of antique shops, boutiques, restaurants, and cafés along its main tree-lined street.

To get there, follow Highway 1 for 50 km east from downtown Vancouver and head north toward the Fraser River from Exit 66 on 232nd Street then Glover Road. From the highway it's five km to downtown Fort Langley; the fort itself lies a few blocks east of the main street. It's well signposted from Highway 1, but the official address is 23433 Mavis St., Fort Langley, 604/513-4777.

East toward Hope

Beyond Langley is the city of **Abbotsford,** where there's a worthwhile detour north from Highway 1 to delightful **Clayburn Village** (access is east along Clayburn Road, which intersects with Highway 11 six km north of Highway 1), originally a company town for a local brickworks. As you'd expect, most of the neat houses are built of brick, providing a local atmosphere a world away from the surrounding modern subdivisions. Head to the local general store for delightful Devonshire tea. It is possible to continue east through Clayburn to **Sumas Mountain Provincial Park** (ask directions at the local general store), or take Exit 95 from Highway 1 to Sumas Mountain Road, then take Batts Road, which

SOUTHWESTERN B.C.

climbs steadily up the mountain's southern slopes. From the end of this service road, it's a short climb to the 900-meter summit of Sumas Mountain, from where views extend north across the Fraser River and south across a patchwork of farmland to Washington's snowcapped Mt. Baker. From the pull-out one km from the end of road, a hiking trail descends for 1.5 km to forest-encircled Chadsey Lake and a lakeside picnic area.

Continuing east along the TransCanada Highway, **Cultus Lake Provincial Park,** 11 km south of Chilliwack, holds a warm-water lake surrounded by mountains—a good spot for swimming, picnicking, or camping. The park's campground is open year-round; $18.50 per night March–Oct., free the rest of the year.

From Chilliwack, it's a further 36 km east along the south bank of the braided Fraser River to Hope, but it is also possible to cross the river via Highway 9 and backtrack a few kilometers to the following attractions.

Kilby Historic Store and Farm

This historic site, 604/796-9576, lies on the north side of the Fraser River 40 km east of Mission and six km west of Agassiz (look for the inconspicuous sign close to Harrison Mills). It is off the beaten track and often missed by those unfamiliar with the area. The fascinating museum/country store, which operated until the early 1970s, is fully stocked with all the old brands and types of goods that were commonplace in the 1920s and '30s. On the two-hectare riverside grounds are farm equipment, farm animals, a gift shop, and a café serving delicious homestyle cooking. It's open April–Nov. daily 11 A.M.–5 P.M.

Around the corner, you can picnic, swim, and fish at **Harrison Bay.**

Harrison Hot Springs

A popular resort self-described as "The Spa of Canada," Harrison Hot Springs (pop. 1,100) lies on the sandy southern shores of southwestern B.C.'s largest body of water, **Harrison Lake,** 125 km east of Vancouver. Coast Salish were the first to take advantage of the soothing water,

then in the late 1850s gold miners stumbled across the springs, and by 1886 the St. Alice Hotel, B.C.'s first resort, was enticing guests with a large bathhouse.

Due to a historical agreement, only the Harrison Hot Springs Resort has water rights, but the hotel operates **Harrison Public Pool,** right downtown on the corner of Harrison Hot Springs Rd. and Esplanade Ave., 604/796-2244. Scalding 74° C (165° F) mineral water is pumped from its source, cooled to a soothing 38° C (100° F), then pumped into the pool. One-time admission is adult $7.50, senior and child $5.50, or you can swim and soak all day for $9 and $6, respectively. The pool is open in summer daily 8 A.M.–9 P.M., the rest of the year daily 9 A.M.–9 P.M.

The lake itself provides many recreation opportunities, with good swimming, sailing, canoeing, and fishing for trout and coho salmon. Through town to the north is 1,220-hectare **Sasquatch Provincial Park,** named for a tall, hairy, unshaven beast that supposedly inhabits the area. The park extends from a day-use area on the bank of Harrison Lake to two picturesque tree-encircled lakes, each with road access, short hiking trails, and day-use areas. On the second weekend of September, Harrison Hot Springs hosts the **World Championship Sand Sculpture Competition,** 604/796-3425, website www.harrisand.org, a gathering of sand sculptors aiming to create a masterpiece that will crown them world champion (and net a share of the $37,000 prize money). Each team has 100 man-hours to complete its sculpture, with the judging taking place on Sunday afternoon. The event is unique in that the inland venue has no tides to wash away the sculptures, which stay in place for a month after judging.

The aforementioned lakeside **Harrison Hot Springs Resort,** 100 Esplanade, 604/796-2244 or 800/663-2266, website www.harrison resort.com, is the town's most elegant accommodation, offering guests use of a large indoor and outdoor complex of mineral pools, complete with grassed areas, lots of outdoor furniture, and a café. Other facilities include boat and

SOUTHWESTERN B.C.

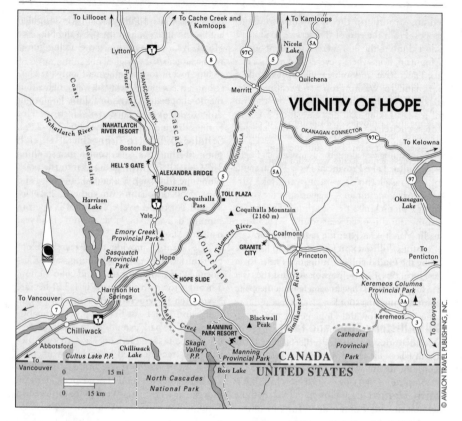

VICINITY OF HOPE

canoe rentals, sailing lessons, and a restaurant and lounge bar. Most of the 300 rooms have a private balcony, many with spectacular views across the lake. Rates range $160–240. Within walking distance of the public hot pool and lake is **Glencoe Motel,** 259 Hot Springs Rd., 604/796-2574, which charges $60 s, $70 d. The pick of three campgrounds along the road into town is **Bigfoot Campgrounds,** 670 Hot Springs Rd., 604/796-9767 or 800/294-9907, which features large shaded sites, free showers, a laundry, and a game room; tent sites $16, hookups $18–22. Camping at **Sasquatch Provincial Park,** north of town, is $12.50 per night.

Harrison Hot Springs Visitor Info Centre is beside the main road into town, 604/796-3425. It's open in summer daily 8 A.M.–6 P.M.

HOPE AND VICINITY

Locals say "all roads lead to Hope"—and they're right. On a finger of land at the confluence of the Fraser and Coquihalla Rivers, 158 km east of Vancouver, Hope (pop. 7,000) really is a hub. The TransCanada Highway and Highway 7 from Vancouver, the Coquihalla Highway to Kamloops, and Highway 3 from the Okanagan all meet at Hope. Don't be put off by first impressions of the town itself. Surrounded by magnificent mountains and rivers, with a couple of great wilderness areas only a short drive away and an abundance of recreational opportunities, Hope is a great place to spend some time.

Simon Fraser, after whom the Fraser River was named, stopped in this area in 1808 after

HOLLYWOOD COMES TO HOPE

Late in 1981, Hollywood came north to Hope to film the first Rambo movie, *First Blood.* The multimillion-dollar blockbuster starring Sylvester Stallone transformed the quiet streets of Hope into a movie set. Buildings were constructed just to be blown away, and local businesses were renamed to suit the film. The wilderness action scenes were shot almost entirely in Coquihalla Canyon, east of town. More recently, *K-2, Shoot to Kill,* and *White Fang II* were filmed in and around Hope.

leading the first expedition south down Fraser River Canyon. By 1848 Fort Hope had been set up by the Hudson's Bay Company as a fur-trading post. With the discovery of gold in the canyon in 1858, Hope became a busy stopping point and meeting spot for adventurers and fortune seekers. How did Hope get its name? No one really knows, but most theories revolve around various explorers or settlers feeling some kind of hope at reaching the river junction at which the town lies.

Town Sights

To find out more about the history of Hope, visit **Hope Museum,** 919 Water Ave., 604/869-7322, in the same building as the information center. The museum's comprehensive collection of pioneer artifacts is displayed in several recreated settings, including a kitchen, bedroom, parlor, schoolroom, and blacksmith shop. Other exhibits focus on local native crafts and on artifacts from the original Fort Hope and gold-rush days. Outside, climb on the Hope Gold Mill, a restored gold-ore concentrator from the Coquihalla area. The museum is open May–June daily 9 A.M.–5 P.M., July–Aug. daily 8 A.M.–8 P.M.

While you're discovering the downtown area, check out the authentic **Japanese garden** in Memorial Park beside the town hall. The garden was constructed to commemorate Tashme, a World War II internment camp for Japanese-Canadians that was east of Hope. Also don't miss

the tree-stump art in Memorial Park. The eagle holding a salmon in its claws (in front of the district office) was carved from a tree with root rot, and it was one of the original tree-stump works of art. As the years go by, more and more carvings (28 at last count) are added by chainsaw artist Pete Ryan. During summer look for him in the park, working on his latest creation.

Othello-Quintette Tunnels

These five huge tunnels through a steep gorge of **Coquihalla Canyon** were carved out of solid granite by the Kettle Valley Railway, completing a route for the company's steam locomotives between Vancouver and Nelson. The tunnels opened in 1916, but the line was plagued by snow, rock slides, and washouts, and closed for repairs more often than it was open. It was eventually abandoned in 1959. By 1962 the tracks and four steel bridges over the awesome Coquihalla River gorge had been removed. Today a short, tree-shaded walk takes you from the **Coquihalla Canyon Provincial Park** parking lot to

© ANDREW HEMPSTEAD

SOUTHWESTERN B.C.

the Othello-Quintette tunnels

the massive, dark tunnels, now a popular tourist attraction. Stroll through them and over the sturdy wooden bridges to admire the gorge and the power and the roar of the Coquihalla River below. To get to the tunnels from downtown, take Wallace Street to 6th Avenue and turn right. Turn left on Kawkawa Lake Road, crossing the Coquihalla River Bridge and railway tracks. At the first intersection take the right branch, Othello Road, and continue until you see a sign to the right (over a rise and easy to miss) pointing to the recreation area. The tunnels are closed Nov.–April.

On the way up to the tunnels, **Kawkawa Lake** is a pleasant body of water with a high concentration of kokanee and a lakeside picnic area.

Skagit Valley Provincial Park

This remote wilderness of 32,577 hectares southeast of Hope is bordered to the east by Manning Provincial Park and to the south by the U.S.–Canada border. Access is along the Silver-Skagit Road, which branches south off Flood Hope Road four km southwest of Hope. This rough gravel road climbs steadily for 39 km to the park entrance, then continues 22 km farther to the international border and road's end at **Ross Lake Reservoir.**

Through the park, the road follows the Skagit River, which flows northward from Ross Lake Reservoir through a magnificent valley cloaked in spruce, pine, aspen, and maple. Black bears, cougars, wolves, coyotes, deer, beavers, and over 200 species of birds are all present within the park.

Outdoor enthusiasts can hike trails suited mainly to overnight excursions. Skagit River Trail begins just east of where the park access road crosses the river, following the river downstream for 15 km (allow five hours) to a day-use area beside Highway 3. Fishing in the Skagit River is good for Dolly Varden and rainbow trout. The access road is dotted with day-use areas, including Shawatum, six km from the park entrance, which was the site of a bustling town with saloons, restaurants, a sawmill, and a daily newspaper—until it was discovered that the only gold found in the area had been planted.

Within the park are two campgrounds; **Silvertip** is three km from the park entrance, while **Ross Lake** is near the end of the road. Over the border, within the boundary of Ross Lake National Recreation Area, is **Hozomeen Campground.** All sites are $11. Another option for camping is **Silver Lake Provincial Park,** six km along the park access road from Hope; $12.50.

Hope Slide

On Highway 3, about 18 km southeast of Hope, the effects of one of nature's amazing forces can be seen. On 9 January 1965, a minor earthquake caused a huge section of mountain to come crashing down, filling the bottom of the Nicolum Creek Valley, destroying about three kilometers of the Hope-Princeton Highway, and killing four motorists. The highway, viewpoint, and parking area are built over the Hope Slide, but you can still see the slide's treeless boundaries along the south side of the valley.

Accommodations and Camping

Hope's newer accommodations are east of the TransCanada Highway on Old Hope–Princeton Way, but a couple of choices are downtown. Best value of these is **Park Motel,** 832 4th Ave., 604/869-5891 or 888/531-9933, charging $60 s, $65 d. Similarly priced is the **Best Continental Motel,** 860 Fraser Ave., 604/869-9726, which also has a restaurant.

Out on Old Hope–Princeton Way, **Royal Lodge Motel,** 604/869-5358 or 877/500-6620, has rooms for $50 s, $55 d, with kitchens an extra $5. The much newer **Alpine Motel,** 604/869-9931 or 877/9931, offers large, comfortably furnished rooms, a pool, and a pleasant setting; from $70 s, $76 d. In a beautiful spot four km north of Hope, **Beautiful Lake of the Woods Resort,** TransCanada Hwy., 604/869-9211 or 888/508-2211, sits on a lake with views of the surrounding mountainscape. Rooms are fairly basic, but facilities include a restaurant and canoe rentals. Rates are $57 s, $67 d.

Along the road up to the tunnels, **Coquihalla Campground,** Kawkawa Lake Rd., 604/869-7119 or 888/869-7118, sits right beside the river.

Trees surround most sites, and facilities include hot showers, a barbecue area, laundry, and game room. Unserviced sites are $17, hookups $19–22.

Food

Chinese **Kan-Yon Restaurant,** 800 3rd Ave., 604/869-2212, looks unremarkable from the outside, but dishes are well-prepared and portions generous. Combination dinners run $9–13, and most entrées are under $12; open daily 8 A.M.–11 P.M. The **Home Restaurant,** in a stylish two-story building at 665 Old Hope–Princeton Way, 604/869-5241, is recommended for delicious entrées such as ribs, chicken, and steaks. Expect to pay around $25 per person for a three-course meal.

Information

Hope Visitor Info Centre is right downtown at 919 Water Ave., 604/869-2021, website www.hopechamber.bc.ca. It's open daily 9 A.M.–5 P.M., with extended summer hours of 8 A.M.–8 P.M. The friendly staff can help you decide which of the routes to take out of Hope, but might also convince you to stay in town a little longer.

FRASER RIVER CANYON

From Hope, the old TransCanada Highway runs north along the west bank of the fast-flowing Fraser River. Although the new Coquihalla Highway is a much shorter option for those heading for Kamloops and beyond, the old highway offers many interesting stops and is by far the preferred route for those not in a hurry. Head north through downtown Hope, cross the Fraser River, take the first right and you're on your way.

The first worthwhile stop is 15-hectare **Emory Creek Provincial Park,** 15 km from Hope. Stopping at this quiet riverside park, it's hard to believe that a little over 100 years ago it was the site of Emory City, complete with saloons, a brewery, a large sawmill, and all the other businesses of a bustling frontier gold town. The city had virtually disappeared by the 1890s, and today no hint of its short-lived presence remains. Wander along riverside trails, try some fishing, or stay at one of the wooded campsites ($12).

Yale

This small town of 200 has quite a history. It started off as one of the many Hudson's Bay Company posts, then became a transportation center at the head of the navigable lower section of the Fraser River—the terminus of one of the largest sternwheeler operations on the west coast. Enormous Lady Franklin Rock blocked the upriver section to steamer traffic, so all goods heading for the interior had to be carried from this point by wagon train along the famous Cariboo Wagon Road.

In 1858 Yale was a flourishing gold-rush town of 20,000, filled with tents, shacks, bars, gambling joints, and shops. But when the gold ran out so did most of the population, and Yale dwindled to the small forestry and service center it has been for 100 years. If you want to find out

WHITE-WATER RAFTING

The Thompson and Fraser Rivers offer some of Canada's most exciting white-water rafting, and both are run commercially by a number of companies. The town of **Lytton,** at the confluence of the two rivers, is home to a couple of companies, with others spread south along the TransCanada Highway.

Whichever operator you go with, and whichever river you choose to run, you'll be in for the trip of a lifetime. The Thompson is known for its high water, the mighty Fraser for its spectacular canyon and obstacles such as Hell's Gate. Those looking for an extra thrill also run the Nahatlatch, a tributary of the Fraser.

All companies include a great lunch (such as a salmon barbecue) and all transfers, charging around $100–120 for a full day. Other options are overnight trips (from $250) and weeklong floats from deep in the interior (from $1,300).

From south to north, companies include: **Fraser River Raft Expeditions,** Yale, 604/863-2336 or 800/363-7238; **REO Rafting,** Boston Bar, 604/461-7238 or 800/736-7238; **Kumsheen Raft Adventures,** Lytton, 604/455-2296 or 800/663-6667; and **Hyak Adventures,** Lytton, 604/734-8622 or 800/663-7238.

more about Yale's historic past, the gold rush, the Cariboo Wagon Road, and railway construction, visit the **Yale Museum,** on Douglas St., 604/863-2324, and the adjacent historic 1863 **St. John's Church.** The museum is open in summer Wed.–Sat. 9:30 A.M.–5:30 P.M.

Stay in town at the 12-room **Fort Yale Motel,** 604/863-2216; $45 s or d. Or head back down the highway 12 km to the campground at **Emory Creek Provincial Park.** Along the TransCanada Highway is a small **information booth,** 604/863-2324, open through summer daily 9 A.M.–6 P.M.

Alexandra Bridge

The treacherous Fraser Canyon posed a major transportation obstacle between the trails from the south and the interior. Several routes across the river were attempted, including a canoe crossing, a cable ferry, and the 1848 Anderson Bridge trail from Fort Yale to Spuzzum.

The gold rush of the 1850s and the onslaught of gold miners and mule trains on the route increased the need for a safe river crossing. In 1863, Alexandra Bridge, 22 km north of Yale, was completed. However, with the successful completion of the Canadian Pacific Railway line through the canyon, the bridge and the Cariboo Wagon Road fell into disrepair.

The popularity of the automobile forced engineers to construct a new suspension bridge in 1926. The new bridge used the original abutments and lasted right up to 1962, when it was replaced by today's bridge on Highway 1. **Alexandra Bridge Provincial Park** now protects a section of the old Cariboo Wagon Road, including the old bridge. The trail down to the bridge makes a good place to get out and stretch your legs.

Hell's Gate

At well-known Hell's Gate, the Fraser River powers its way through a narrow, glacially carved, 34-meter-high gorge. When Simon Fraser saw this section of the gorge in 1808 he called it "the Gates of Hell" and the name stuck. In 1914 a massive rock slide rocketed down into the gorge, blocking it even further and resulting in the almost total obliteration of the sockeye salmon

population that spawned farther upstream. In 1944 giant concrete fishways were built to slow the waters and allow the spawning salmon to jump upstream—the river soon swarmed with salmon once again. Today you can cross the canyon aboard the 25-passenger **Hell's Gate Airtram,** 604/867-9277, which runs through summer daily 9 A.M.–6 P.M.; adult $10.50, senior $9, child $6.50. Across the river you can browse through landscaped gardens, learn more about the fishway and salmon, or sink your teeth into a fresh salmon at the **Salmon House Restaurant** (same telephone number as the Airtram).

North toward Cache Creek

Another small town with a gold-rush history, **Boston Bar** is today a popular white-water rafting mecca for those brave enough to float the Fraser River's roaring rapids. A bridge crossing at Boston Bar accesses the **Nahatlatch River,** renowned for white-water kayaking. Along quieter stretches of this river are some great fishing spots, three lakes, and numerous primitive campgrounds. **REO Rafting Adventure Resort,** 16 km along this road, 604/461-7238 or 800/736-7238, website www.reorafting.com, offers a few campsites for $15 and tent cabins from $50, or stay in a log cabin, and take a raft trip, with all meals included, for $160 pp for one night. As the name suggests, the resort is the base for REO Rafting, but horseback riding, rock climbing, and guided hiking are also offered.

Continuing up the canyon, the narrow highway winds northward for 34 km to **Lytton,** a historic village at the confluence of the Fraser and Thompson Rivers, before spurring eastward and following the Thompson River. This route eventually reaches Cache Creek, the gateway to Cariboo Country (see the Central British Columbia chapter), and continues on to the major interior city of Kamloops.

COQUIHALLA HIGHWAY

Opened in late spring 1986, the Coquihalla Highway is the most direct link between Hope and the interior of British Columbia. It saves at least 90 minutes by cutting 72 km from the trip between Hope and Kamloops and bypassing the TransCanada Highway's narrow, winding stretch along the Fraser River Canyon. Along the 190-km route are many worthwhile stops, but only one that's compulsory—a toll plaza at Coquihalla Pass, 115 km from Hope, where $10 is collected from each vehicle.

The highway ascends and descends through magnificent mountain and river scenery to dry semiarid grasslands. You'll cruise through the valleys of the Lower Coquihalla River and Boston Bar Creek, climb to the 1,240-meter summit of Coquihalla Pass near Coquihalla Lake, descend along the Coldwater River, then climb the Coldwater's eastern valley slope to Merritt. From Merritt the highway climbs the valleys of the Nicola River and Clapperton Creek to join the Trans-Canada Highway eight km west of Kamloops.

Merritt

This town of 8,000 in the Nicola Valley, 115 km north of Hope, provides the only services along the Coquihalla Highway. It's also the exit point for those heading east to the Okanagan on the Okanagan Connector.

Make your first stop off the highway at **Merritt Visitor Info Centre,** on a high point east of the highway, 250/378-2281. Upstairs in this large log building is an intriguing forestry exhibition, and behind the building is the **Godey Creek Hiking Trail,** which takes you 1.4 km (25 minutes) each way to a lookout cabin. The center is open year-round daily 9 A.M.–5 P.M.

Each July, **Merritt Mountain Music Festival** attracts tens of thousands of country-music lovers for a weekend of concerts featuring the biggest names in country music. For information and tickets call 604/860-1470.

Since the Coquihalla Highway opened, many motels have been built around Merritt. But by far the best choice is one of the originals, the **Quilchena Hotel,** on Nicola Lake, 23 km east of town on Hwy. 5A (take Exit 290), 250/378-2611, website www.quilchena.com. Built in 1908, this grand old three-story hostelry features a café, restaurant, and antique-decorated rooms. The hotel sits beside a beautiful lake where you can go swimming or rent a boat and go fishing. Horse-

back riding and mountain bike rentals are also offered. Rates are $71–99 s or d. If you'd prefer the luxury of modern amenities, consider **Days Inn— Merritt,** 3350 Voght St. (one km north from the main highway exit), 250/378-2292 or 800/665-7117, website www.daysinn.com, which has an outdoor pool, a hot tub, a restaurant, and a bar; from $74 s, $82 d.

MANNING PROVINCIAL PARK

This spectacular 70,844-hectare park in the Cascade Mountains, 64 km east of Hope along Highway 3, stretches down to the Canada–U.S. border. Highway 3 makes a "U" through the park—from the northwest to south to northeast corners. But to really appreciate the park, you need to get off the highway—take in the beautiful bodies of water, drive up to a wonderful stretch of high alpine meadows, or hike on the numerous trails. Within the park are two major watersheds; the Skagit River flows west to the Fraser River, and the Similkameen River flows east into the Columbia River. The many tributaries of these two rivers flow down from the highest peaks of the rain-drenched Cascade Mountains, through dense subalpine forests of Engelmann spruce, Douglas fir, western red cedar, and hemlock to the valley through which Highway 3 runs. Wildlife is abundant, including populations of black bear, moose, elk, coyote, and beaver.

Summer Recreation

A highlight of the park is the paved road immediately across Highway 3 from Manning Park Resort; it climbs steadily to **Cascade Lookout,** a viewpoint offering a magnificent 180-degree panoramic view. Beyond the lookout, the road turns to gravel and continues climbing for nine km, ending at a parking lot beneath 2,063-meter Blackwall Peak. From this area of flower-filled alpine meadows, views extend over the park's remote northern boundary. Take time to soak up the color by taking one of the short trails originating from the parking lot. Or hike **Heather Trail** (10 km each way; allow three hours) to Three Brothers Mountain. If you're there between late July and mid-August, you won't believe what you'll see—a rich yellow, orange, and white carpet of wildflowers as far as you can see.

Along Highway 3 are some short self-guided nature trails, including a 700-meter walk (20 minutes) through a stand of ancient western red cedars. The trailhead is Sumallo Grove day-use area, 10 km east of where Highway 3 enters the park from the west. Just east of the Visitor Information Centre, on the south side of the road, is the 500-meter (10-minute) **Beaver Pond Trail.** If you notice people arriving on foot in this parking lot with worn soles, bent backs, and great big smiles on their faces, give them a pat on the back—they may have just completed one of the world's greatest long-distance hikes. The **Pacific Crest Trail** runs 3,860 km from the U.S.–Mexico border to this small and undistinguished trailhead.

During the summer months you can fish in rivers, streams, and lakes for Dolly Varden and rainbow trout (get a license first) or explore **Lightning Lake** in a canoe; lakeside rentals cost $12 per hour. At **Manning Park Corral,** next to Manning Park Resort, 250/840-8844, you can go on a one-hour trail ride for $25, or spend all day on horseback with a hearty trailside lunch thrown in for $118.

Skiing

The park gets plenty of dry snow for good downhill and cross-country skiing. At **Manning Park Resort,** 11 km west of Manning Park Resort along Gibson Pass Rd., downhill enthusiasts can take advantage of a 437-meter vertical rise served by two chairlifts, a T-bar, and a rope tow. Most runs are for intermediate skiers, but novices and experts will also find suitable terrain. Lift tickets are adult $31, senior $20, child $19, under six free. On-hill facilities include a cafeteria, ski school, and ski rentals (from $25 for a full day). A free shuttle bus transfers guests to the ski area from Manning Park Resort, which offers winter packages from $129 for two nights' midweek accommodations and two days' skiing. In winter, RVers can stay in one of the ski area's upper parking lots. For ski resort and packages information call 250/840-8822 or 800/330-3321, website www.manningparkresort.com; for ski conditions call the Vancouver Snowphone at 604/689-7669.

Along with 190 km of wilderness trails, cross-country skiers can enjoy 30 km of groomed trails for $14 per day. Cross-country skis rent for $15 per day.

Manning Park Resort

In the heart of the park on Highway 3, Manning Park Resort, 250/840-8822 or 800/330-3321, is a full-service lodging providing comfortable hotel rooms, cabins, and triplexes, as well as a dining room, self-serve cafeteria, small grocery store, and an open fireside lounge. Other facilities include saunas, an indoor pool, a TV room, a fitness center, tennis courts, a coin-operated laundry, and a gift shop. Through summer, rooms in the main lodge are $99 s or d, and chalets with kitchens range $119–149. The rest of the year rates are reduced, with rooms from $64.

Camping

The park's four campgrounds hold a total of 355 sites; in summer, get in early to be assured of snagging one. Each campground provides drinking water and toilets. Firewood is available for a fee. The most popular is **Lightning Lake,** two km west of Manning Park Resort on Gibson Pass Rd., which has showers; $18.50 per night. Others include **Coldspring Campground,** on Hwy. 3 two km west of the resort; **Hampton Campground,** on Hwy. 3 four km east of the resort; and **Mule Deer Campground,** a further four km east. These three charge $12 per night.

Information

The park's **Visitor Information Centre** is one km east of Manning Park Resort, 250/840-8836, website www.elp.gov.bc.ca/bcparks. Inside you'll find displays on recreation opportunities and on the area's natural and cultural history, as well as maps and detailed information about park facilities. The center is open in summer daily 8:30 A.M.–4:30 P.M.; weekdays only the rest of the year. In July and August park interpreters offer guided walks, interesting slide shows, and evening talks at the amphitheater on Gibson Pass Road; scan information boards around the park or inquire at the Visitor Information Centre to see what's on.

CONTINUING TOWARD THE OKANAGAN VALLEY

From the eastern boundary of Manning Provincial Park, Highway 3 follows the Similkameen River north to Princeton, then turns sharply to the southeast to Osoyoos, at the southern end of the Okanagan Valley, a total distance of 158 km. Between the Manning Provincial Park and Princeton, stop along the highway at **Similkameen Falls,** where the Similkameen River rushes over a narrow escarpment. The adjacent campground costs $12 per night.

Princeton

At the confluence of the Similkameen and Tulameen Rivers, surrounded by low tree-covered hills, lies the small friendly ranching town of Princeton (pop. 3,000). **Princeton and District Pioneer Museum,** 167 Vermilion Ave., 250/295-7588, features pioneer artifacts from Granite City (see below), Chinese and Interior Salish artifacts, and a good fossil display; open Mon.–Fri. 1–5 P.M. Another local attraction is **Castle Park,** on the northeast side of town, where the 75-year-old stone-and-concrete ruins of a cement plant lie beside twinkling One Mile Creek. Around, through, and over these magnificent ruins grow trees, wild roses, lilacs, and lupines. Take a look at the concrete paths and steps leading down from the back of the administrative building to the ruins—the concrete is loaded with fossilized shells. The ruins are now part of a commercial campground, and tours are run throughout summer. To get there from Princeton, cross the bridge at the north end of Bridge Street, turn right on Old Hedley Road, cross Highway 5, turn left on Five Mile Road, then continue until the sign to the park leads you right. You'll pass a small lake before coming to the park entrance.

Just a short stroll from downtown, **Riverside Motel,** 307 Thomas Ave. at the north end of Bridge St., 250/295-6232, was built in 1934 as a hunting and fishing lodge. The aptly named motel is right beside the river, and in the height of summer the water level drops to expose a small beach and shallow swimming hole. Ask the owner to show you a photo of the place taken in 1937—the

cabins still look exactly the same. Each basic cabin has a toilet, a shower, and a kitchen with a fridge, stove, cooking utensils, crockery, and cutlery. Rates are a very reasonable $30–38 s, $36–44 d. **Princeton Castle Resort & RV Park,** on Hwy. 5A three km north of town, 250/295-7988 or 888/228-8881, website www.castleresort.com, features sites alongside a small creek in a treed setting. Sites are $14–18, cabins from $65.

For a meal, head downtown to the **Princeton Hotel** at 258 Bridge St., 250/295-3355; order bistro-style at the small window across from the bar.

Princeton Visitor Info Centre is at the west entrance to town, 250/295-3103, and is open year-round 8:30 A.M.–4:30 P.M., daily in summer but Mon.–Fri. only the rest of the year.

Coalmont

If you want to see some impressive canyon scenery off the main tourist drag, cross the river at the north end of Princeton's Bridge Street and turn left, heading west toward Coalmont (about 18 km) and Granite City (20 km). Coalmont came to the forefront when gold-rush activity moved from Granite City (see below) to this village in 1911. Today, you can't help but notice that the town's residents have a sense of humor. The welcoming sign states that Coalmont has no industry but plenty of activity in the form of sleeping and daydreaming. It also claims Coalmont has a hot, cold, wet, and dry climate, warns traveling salesmen to stay away, and advises single women that their safety is not guaranteed due to the predominance of bachelors. The attractive old **Coalmont Hotel** (circa 1911) still stands, along with quite a number of homes—some with backyards crammed with eclectic collections of rusting mine machinery.

Granite City

At the stop sign in Coalmont, continue straight ahead to Granite Creek, turn left on Hope Street, right over the creek, then follow the road until you reach the remains of Granite City, a ghost town. After the discovery of a gold nugget in Granite Creek back in 1885, a 13-saloon goldrush city sprang to life on this spot. Soon it was the third-largest city in the province, supporting a population of over 2,000. It's on the right just after the first road intersection, but it's easy to miss because there isn't much left—just a few fallen-down cabins among wild lilac bushes and trees. It's up to your imagination to re-create the good ol' days.

If you continue along Rice Road you'll end up at the B.C. Forest Service's **Granite Creek Recreation Site**, a gorgeous place to picnic or camp. Tree-shaded campsites with picnic tables line the creek in a large daisy- and cow-filled meadow. Pit toilets are nearby. The fee is $8 per night.

Continuing East from Princeton on Highway 3

From Princeton, Highway 3 takes you on a scenic route through the beautiful **Similkameen River Valley**, which holds lots of places to camp, in either provincial parks or private campgrounds. Between Princeton and Keremeos the road follows the Dewdney Trail, a 468-km mule track used in the 1860s to connect Hope with the Kootenay goldfields. This stretch itself has also been a major mining area, supplying a fortune in gold, silver, nickel, and copper over the years. One of the richest mines was the Nickel Plate Gold Mine, north of **Hedley.** There's been talk for many years now of opening up the mine for public inspection, but a treacherous road that snakes up from the valley floor is the major stumbling block. To immerse yourself in the history of the mining era wander around the tree-lined streets of Hedley or consider staying at **Colonial Inn B&B**, Hwy. 3, 250/292-8131, a guest house for the Nickel Plate mine dating from the mining era. Most of the six rooms have a private bathroom, and a cooked breakfast is included in the rates of $70 s, $80 d.

The landscape east of Princeton is different from that to the west, but the change is most pronounced east of Hedley—from tall, tree-cov-

The landscape east of Princeton is different from that to the west, but the change is most pronounced east of Hedley—from tall, tree-covered mountains through rolling hills covered in sagebrush and lush irrigated orchards around Keremeos to desert (complete with lizards, cactus, and rattlesnakes) around Osoyoos.

ered mountains through rolling hills covered in sagebrush and lush irrigated orchards around Keremeos to desert (complete with lizards, cactus, and rattlesnakes) around Osoyoos on the Canada–U.S. border.

Cathedral Provincial Park

Wilderness hikers and mountaineers should not miss the turnoff to this spectacular 33,000-hectare park just west of Keremeos. A 21-km gravel road leads into the park, ending one km beyond the base camp for privately owned **Cathedral Lakes Lodge.** Guests get a lift 16 km uphill to the resort; everyone else has to walk. For this reason most park visitors stay at the resort, which provides accommodations, meals, use of canoes, a recreation room and hot tub, and transportation to and from the base camp. The minimum stay is a two-day package; original cabins are $115–140 per night while rooms in the main lodge are $170–190. For reservations call 250/226-7560 or 888/255-4453, website www.cathedral-lakes-lodge.com.

About 50 km of wilderness trails lead from the resort to a variety of striking and enticingly named rock formations, including Stone City, Giant Cleft, Devil's Woodpile, Macabre Tower, Grimface Mountain, Denture Ridge, and Smokey the Bear. Wander through meadows waving with dainty alpine flowers, climb peaks for tremendous views, fish for trout in sparkling turquoise lakes, capture on film immense glacier-topped mountains. For general park information, call 250/494-6500.

Keremeos

As you approach mountain-surrounded Keremeos from the west, the road is lined with lush irrigated orchards and fruit stands, one after another, which is probably what inspired the town's claim to fame as the "Fruit Stand Capital of Canada." Keremeos has one of the longest growing seasons in the province. Try a tastebud-tingling fruit-juice shake in summer; recommended is the second-to-last stand as you head east out of town. Harvest dates are mid-June to mid-July for cherries; mid-July to early August for apricots; mid-July to early September for peaches; mid-August to mid-September for pears; early August to mid-October for apples; early to mid-September for plums; early September to early October for grapes.

The town's main historic attraction is the **Grist Mill**, 250/499-2888, a restored water-powered mill built in 1877. This is where pioneer Similkameen Valley settlers used to grind locally produced wheat into flour. Take a guided tour of the mill any day of the week from mid-May to October (closed the rest of the year), then try your hand at the many informative and entertaining hands-on displays in the museum and visitor center, or relax in the tearoom overlooking the gardens. Admission is $4.50. To get there, go through town on the main highway, turn north on Highway 3A toward Penticton, then right at the Historic Site sign on Upper Bench Road.

Another local highlight, although it takes some effort to reach, is 20-hectare **Keremeos Columns Provincial Park.** The park is named for a 90-meter cliff of remarkable hexagonal basalt columns rising from a lava base just outside the park boundary. The columns were supposed to be in the park but because of a surveying accident actually stand on private land. Access the viewpoint by taking a steep eight-km logging road off Highway 3 about four km north of town (turn right at the Keremeos cemetery), then take another steep eight-km hike (allow at least three hours one-way) across private property; ask for permission and trail details at the house at the end of the paved road.

Okanagan Valley

This warm, sunny valley 400 km east of Vancouver extends 180 km between the U.S.–Canada border in the south and the TransCanada Highway in the north. Lush orchards and vineyards, fertile irrigated croplands, low rolling hills, and a string of beautiful lakes line the valley floor, where you'll also find 40 golf courses, dozens of commercial attractions, and lots and lots of people—especially in summer.

The Okanagan Valley's three main cities—**Penticton, Kelowna,** and **Vernon**—are spread around long, narrow **Okanagan Lake** and collectively hold the bulk of interior British Columbia's population. Numerous smaller communities also ring the lakeshore, doubling or tripling in size between May and September when hordes of vacationers turn the valley into one big resort. Most of these summer pilgrims are Canadians from cooler climes, who come in search of guaranteed sunshine, lazy days on a beach, and a take-away tan. In winter, the valley draws pilgrims of another sort—skiers and snowboarders on their way to the world-class slopes flanking the valley.

All the credit for developing the Okanagan into

Harvest Golf Club, Kelowna

© ANDREW HEMPSTEAD

To Kamloops

To Sicamous

Enderby

97

Armstrong

97A

SILVER STAR
MOUNTAIN
RESORT

HISTORIC O'KEEFE RANCH ★

OKANAGAN VALLEY

5A

Vernon

6

To The Kootenays

Fintry
Provincial Park

Ellison
Provincial Park

Kalamalka Lake

To Merritt
and Vancouver

97

Aspen
Grove

Pennask Lake
Provincial Park

Winfield

Bear Creek
Provincial Park

CRYSTAL
MOUNTAIN

OKANAGAN 97C CONNECTOR

Kelowna

Westside

BIG WHITE SKI
RESORT

Westbank

Peachland

Okanagan Lake

97

Okanagan Lake
Provincial Park

Okanagan
Mountain
Provincial
Park

Coalmont

Summerland

Naramata

Princeton

Sun-Oka Beach
Provincial Park

APEX MOUNTAIN
RESORT

3

Hedley

Penticton

Skaha Lake

33

3

Similkameen

3A

Okanagan Falls

To Hope
and Vancouver

97

Keremeos

River

Oliver

0   15 mi

0   15 km

Mt. Kobau
(1874 m)

To Grand Forks

Cathedral
Provincial Park

3

Spotted Lake

Osoyoos Lake

3

Osoyoos

CANADA

UNITED STATES

© AVALON TRAVEL PUBLISHING, INC.

Canada's fruit basket goes to the original planter, Father Charles Pandosy, a French oblate priest who established a mission in the Kelowna area in 1859. Within a couple of years he had successfully introduced apple trees to the district. The trees positively blossomed under his care, thanks to the valley's long five-and-a-half-month growing season, over 2,000 hours of sunshine a year, relatively mild winters, and the ready availability of water. Soon fruit orchards of all types were springing up everywhere, and today the Okanagan Valley region produces 30 percent of Canada's apples, 60 percent of its cherries, 20 percent of its peaches, half of its pears and plums, and all the apricots in the country.

OSOYOOS

This town of 4,300 is nestled on the west shore of **Osoyoos Lake,** Canada's warmest freshwater lake (up to 24° C, 75° F in summer). The town also boasts Canada's highest year-round average temperature.

Sights

Away from the valley floor and its many orchards, the landscape is surprisingly arid. In one particular area, a 100-hectare "pocket desert" has the distinction of being Canada's driest spot, receiving less than 300 millimeters of precipitation annually. It is a desert in the truest sense, complete with sand, cacti, prickly pear, sagebrush, lizards, scorpions, rattlesnakes, and other desert dwellers, including 23 invertebrates found nowhere else in the world. Learn more about this unique landscape at the **Desert Centre,** 250/495-2470 or 877/899-0897, a research and interpretive facility. Admssion of adult $5, senior $4, child $2, includes a guided walk along a 1,500-meter-long boardwalk. To get there follow Highway 97 north from Osoyoos, and take 146th Avenue to the west.

For a bird's-eye view of the lake, take Highway 3 west from town 12 km, then follow a 20-km gravel road to the 1,874-meter summit of **Mount Kobau.** Short trails there lead to viewpoints of the Similkameen and Okanagan Valleys. Along the section of Highway 3 before the

turnoff, watch for **Spotted Lake,** a bizarre natural phenomenon on the south side of the road. As summer progresses and the lake's water evaporates, high concentrations of magnesium, calcium, and sodium crystallize, forming colorful circles.

Practicalities

In summer, Osoyoos Lake attracts hordes of boaters, water-skiers, anglers, windsurfers, and sun worshippers, so getting accommodations can be difficult. **Avalon Motel,** on Hwy. 3 between the information center and downtown, 250/495-6334 or 800/264-5999, is a clean and comfortable accommodation with smallish rooms for $65 s, $70 d and self-contained suites for $120. Boasting a great location down on the lakeshore is **Holiday Inn Sunspree Resort,** Hwy. 3, 250/495-7223 or 877/786-7773, website www.holidayinnosoyoos. It offers 85 rooms, many overlooking the resort's private beach, as well as a rooftop garden, fitness center, boat rentals, and a restaurant. Rates start at $119 s or d (although the least expensive rooms are fairly small). Also on the lakeshore are several older resort motels, including **Desert Motor Inn,** 7702 62nd Ave., 250/495-6525 or 877/495-6525, which charges $75–98 per room. At the **Poplars Motel,** 6404 67th St., 250/495-6035, guests have use of a private beach; from $95 s or d per night. **Haynes Point Provincial Park** protects an extremely narrow low-lying spit that juts into Osoyoos Lake south of downtown. Camping in the park is $18.50 per night.

Walk down Main Street and take your pick from various cafés and the usual smattering of Italian and Chinese restaurants. **Beans Desert Cafe,** 8323 Main St., 250/495-7742, features a good range of coffee concoctions in a modern setting. More traditional fare is offered down on the spit at **Osoyoos Burger House,** where hamburgers cost $3.50–6.

In a parking lot at the corner of Highways 3 and 97 is **Osoyoos Visitor Info Centre,** 250/495-7142 or 888/676-9667. It's open 8:30 A.M.–4:30 P.M. daily in summer and Mon.–Fri. the rest of the year.

Penticton

One of the Okanagan's three major population centers, Penticton (pop. 33,000) lies between the north end of Skaha Lake and the south end of Okanagan Lake. The city gets its name from the nomadic Salish natives, in whose tongue Penticton means "Place to Stay Forever."

Approaching from the south, you'll see a roadside plaque honoring pioneer Thomas Ellis, who arrived in the valley in 1886, built a great cattle empire, and planted the area's first orchard. Today fruit orchards are everywhere. Penticton's nickname is Peach City; the annual **Peach Festival** celebrates the harvest in mid-August with a week of sailboat races, parades, games, and entertainment. Penticton also participates in the **Okanagan Wine Festival**, the first weekend of October, another fruitful event.

SIGHTS AND RECREATION

Along Okanagan Lake

Wander west along the tree-shaded shores of Lake Okanagan to see the **SS** *Sicamous,* the last Canadian Pacific Railway sternwheeler to work on Okanagan Lake. The *Sicamous* operated from 1914 to 1951; now it rests on the lakeshore at the end of the beach and houses a museum. It's open in summer daily 7 A.M.–7 P.M.; admission $4. The adjacent **rose garden** is worth a stroll to see perfect blooms and manicured lawns, and to read all the stats on the **Okanagan Lake Dam** and flood-control system. Next to the rose garden are a **miniature golf course** and a bicycle-rental outfit.

If you wander east from the tourist center along Lakeshore Drive, you'll come to the **Art Gallery of the South Okanagan,** 199 Front St., 250/493-2928; open Tues.–Fri. 10 A.M.–5 P.M., Sat.–Sun. 1–5 P.M. The craft shop is a good place to pick up creative treasures and handmade souvenirs. If you're visiting on a Sunday you can get in on afternoon tea. Continue east from the gallery to the local **marina**—another enjoyable spot for a lakeside stroll.

Penticton Museum

This museum, at 787 Main St., 250/490-2451, houses an excellent collection of western Canadiana, covering natural history, local native peoples, the fur-trading days, railways, early Chinese residents, and sternwheelers. It also features an enormous taxidermy section; mining, ranching, and ghost-town artifacts and treasures; and assorted military miscellany. Allow at least an hour or two in here. The museum is open Mon.–Sat. 10 A.M.–5 P.M.

To Okanagan Mountain Provincial Park

A 14 km secondary road runs northeast out of Penticton, skirting the east side of Okanagan Lake and passing through the small community of **Naramata.** Stop here at **Lang Vineyards,** on Gammon Rd. (follow the signs from Naramata Rd.), 250/496-5987, to sample or buy quality wines available only at the vineyard.

Continue through Naramata and up into the mountains, where the road fizzles out near the south border of undeveloped 10,512-hectare Okanagan Mountain Provincial Park. The only way to get into this piece of untouched wilderness is to walk or boat over. Hike in for the day for a picnic, some fishing, or to explore the 24 km of trails. Be sure to bring warm clothes—it gets cold up here even when it's warm and balmy down in Penticton. The park has no facilities.

Commercial Attractions

Okanagan Game Farm, eight km south of Penticton on Hwy. 97, 250/497-5405, contains over 1,000 animals from around the world, including lions, bears, giraffes, and snakes. Admission is adult $8, child $6, under five free. Open daily 8 A.M.–dusk. From Penticton north you'll no doubt notice that water-slide mania has hit the Okanagan hard—even the Travelodge in Penticton has an indoor water slide. If you're in the mood for a bit of slip slidin' away, try **Wonderful Waterworld,** 225 Yorkton Ave., 250/492-8121; open daily, adult $17.50, child $14.

OKANAGAN VALLEY

Skiing and Snowboarding

Sunniest of the Okanagan resorts is **Apex Mountain Resort,** 33 km west of Penticton, which provides 605 vertical meters and 56 runs over 450 hectares. The slopes are served by a T-bar and two chairlifts, one of which—the Quickdraw Express—zips skiers and boarders to the summit of 2,178-meter Beaconsfield Mountain and opens up most of the expert terrain. Boarders are catered to with a terrain park and half-pipe, or you can slide downhill on an inflatable tube in the tube park. The epicenter of the western-style base village is Mountainside Lodge, a day-use facility with eateries, a lounge, a ski and snowboard school, and a rental outlet. The resort is open daily December to mid-April, with one run open for night skiing on Wednesday, Friday, and Saturday. Lift tickets are adult $44, senior $37, child $29, kids under seven free. For resort information call 250/292-8222; for accommodation packages call 877/777-2739; on the Internet, search out www.apexresort.com.

Cross-country skiers head to Apex Mountain's 12 km of trails around the base area, or to **Nickel Plate Nordic Centre,** six km from the resort, featuring 30 km of groomed trails and 20 km of backcountry trails.

On-mountain accommodations are available at **Holiday Inn Sunspree Resort,** 250/292-8121 or 800/387-2739, which charges $120 s or d. Many Penticton accommodations offer great packages from $50 per person.

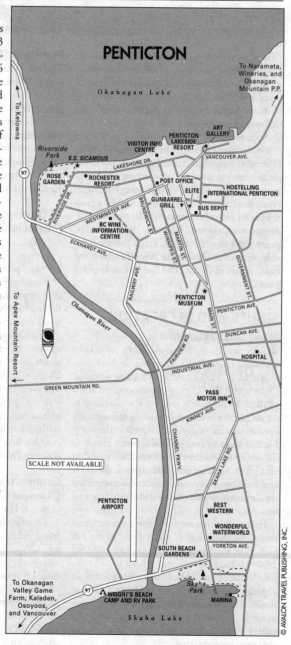

PENTICTON

© AVALON TRAVEL PUBLISHING, INC.

Events

Penticton seems to have festivals, parades, events, or competitions going on throughout the year. The biggest event is the annual **Peach Festival,** 800/663-5052, held on the first weekend of August; it's a tradition going back more than 50 years. Events include peach tasting, the crowning of Miss Penticton, a classic auto show, a sandcastle competition, fireworks, and nightly entertainment in Gyro Park.

Other annual happenings include **Mid-Winter Break-Out** in mid-February, which includes everything from ice-carving to a Polar Bear Dip, 250/490-3078; the **Spring Wine Festival,** 250/861-6654, website www.owfs.com, hosted by many local wineries in late April; the **Penticton Highland Games,** 250/493-1257, the first Sunday of July in Kings Park; the **Ironman Canada** triathlon the last Sunday in August, 250/493-5922; and the **Pentastic Hot Jazz Festival** the second weekend of September, 800/663-100, website www.pentastic-jazz.com. Two major wine festivals are a valley highlight; for details see the Kelowna section, below, or check the website www.owfs.com.

ACCOMMODATIONS AND CAMPING

Under $50

As you'd expect in a resort town, the only accommodation under $50 is in a dormitory. **Hostelling International—Penticton,** 464 Ellis St., 250/492-3992, website www.hihostels.bc.ca, occupies a historic residence close to the heart of downtown. Facilities include a kitchen, laundry, bike rentals, and an outdoor barbecue area; $16 per night for members of Hostelling International, $20 for nonmembers, and private rooms for $40 s or d.

$50–100

The least expensive of several lodgings on Lakeshore Drive, close to both the lake and downtown, is the 36-room **Rochester Resort,** at 970 Lakeshore Dr., 250/493-1128 or 800/567-4904. All units have a kitchen and there's a communal barbecue area for guest use;

$79 s, $89 d. Another bunch of motels lies south of downtown, within walking distance of Skaha Lake. Least expensive of these is **Pass Motor Inn,** 2307 Skaha Lake Rd., 250/492-0323 or 800/670-8062, which charges from $69 s, $79 d.

$100–150

Best Western Inn at Penticton, 3180 Skaha Lake Rd., 250/493-0311 or 800/668-6746, website www.bestwestern.com, offers an indoor pool in tropical surroundings, an outdoor pool, and a barbecue area. Rooms feature modern furnishings and the suites have kitchens; from $119 s or d.

$150–200

For a million-dollar lake view, consider the six-story **Penticton Lakeside Resort,** 21 Lakeshore Dr. W, 250/493-8221 or 800/663-9400, website www.rpbhotels.com, the only accommodation right on the lake. The full-service hotel has over 200 rooms, an indoor pool overlooking the lake, a whirlpool, saunas, two tennis courts, a bar with a lakeside deck, and a restaurant. In July and August rooms start at $189, rising to $240 for a hot tub suite. Prices go down from there, to as low as $100 in the depths of winter.

Camping

All Penticton's commercial campgrounds are south of downtown around the north end of Skaha Lake. They're very popular in summer, so make reservations in advance if possible. The least-crowded seems to be **Wright's Beach Camp RV Park,** Hwy. 97, 250/492-7120, which is a little bit surprising as it's right on the lake and many sites are shaded. Sites are $22–32 per night. Across from Sudbury Beach and adjacent to Hwy. 97 is **South Beach Gardens,** 3815 Skaha Lake Rd., 250/492-0628, which charges $16 for an unserviced site and $20–25 for hookups. RV hookups are also offered year-round up at Apex Mountain Village, 33 km west of Penticton. The cost is $17.50 per vehicle, but you'll need plenty of quarters for the showers.

OKANAGAN WINES

Okanagan wines receive acclaim worldwide, although this success is only recent. In fact, it was doubted that quality grapes could be grown north of the 49th parallel until the late 1980s, when most of the original vines were ripped out and replaced with classic European varietals. The valley's climate—long summer days and cool nights—produces small grapes with a higher-than usual sugar content, creating intensely flavored and aromatic wines. A wide variety of red and white wine grapes are planted, with the reds thriving in the warmer south end of the valley, where Merlot, Cabernet Franc, and Pinot Noir grapes produce the best local wines. The entire wine-making process in the Okanagan has been one of experimentation, and along the way more unusual varietals such as Ehrenfelser and Auxerrois have been grown with suc-

Okanagan Valley winery

© ANDREW HEMPSTEAD

cess, make tasting local wines all the more interesting.

The best introduction to the valley's vino offerings is the **British Columbia Wine Information Centre,** 888 Westminster Ave., 250/490-2006. As much a wine shop as anything else, it offers plenty of information along with wine tour maps and knowledgeable staff to set you off in the right direction. It's open in summer daily 9 A.M.–5:30 P.M. The closest wineries to Penticton are northeast of the city along Naramata Road, including renowned **Hillside Estate,** 1350 Naramata Rd., 250/493-6294, with an impressive three-story wooden building holding the main winery. Hillside is known for its Pinot Noir, but it also produces an unusually dry but fruity Riesling. Open for tours daily 10 A.M.–6 P.M. and for lunch daily from 11 A.M.

OTHER PRACTICALITIES

Food

Many Penticton restaurants feature outdoor eating areas, allowing diners to take advantage of the mild climate. One of the most popular of these is **Okanagan Surf & Turf,** the signature restaurant of the Penticton Lakeside Resort, 21 Lakeshore Dr. W, 250/493-8221. The adjacent bar also serves food, and both places have an outdoor deck area overlooking the lake.

On Main Street between Okanagan and Skaha Lakes are several decent eateries. For home cooking at inexpensive prices, try the family-style **Elite Restaurant,** right downtown at 340 Main St., 250/492-3051. Good-value daily specials (soup or salad, main course, dessert, and coffee)

go for around $7–8. Open daily 7 A.M.–9 P.M. In the same vicinity, the **Gunbarrel Grill,** 399 Main St., 250/490-0573, is a second-story restaurant with views across downtown from an outdoor eating area. It's open daily for breakfast, lunch, and dinner, with the lunchtime "pasta of the day" and nightly grills highlights.

In Kaleden, south of Penticton, the **Historic 1912 Restaurant,** 250/497-6888, provides the opportunity to enjoy some of the valley's best food in a historic lakefront location. The menu takes advantage of fresh local produce wherever possible, changing as different fruits and vegetables become available. It was the latter, a huge platter of sautéed seasonal vegetables for $19, that caught my eye when eating here. The house specialties are gourmet dinners for two or four, such as chateaubriand tenderloin carved at your table for $95 (serves two), complete with a starter and dessert.

Transportation

Visitors flying into the Okanagan use Kelowna Airport, to the north (see below). The **Greyhound Bus Depot** is at 307 Ellis St., 250/493-4101. Greyhound offers daily buses south to Osoyoos, linking up with services along Highway 3, and north through the Okanagan Valley to Salmon Arm on the TransCanada Highway.

Getting around town is easy on **Penticton Transit System,** 250/492-5602. Rental cars are available at nearby Kelowna Airport; otherwise contact one of the following local agencies: **Avis,** 250/493-8133; **Budget,** 250/493-0212; **National,** 250/493-7288; **Rent-a-wreck,** 250/492-4447; or **Thrifty,** 250/493-2224. The **Bike Barn,** downtown at 300 Westminster Ave. W, 250/492-4140, rents mountain bikes; from $9 for the first hour, $7 for the second hour, $30 a day.

Services and Information

Penticton Regional Hospital is on Carmi Ave. (east off Main St.), 250/492-4000. The **post office** is on the corner of Winnipeg St. and Nanaimo Avenue.

You can't miss the **Penticton Visitor Info Centre** north of downtown right on the shore of Okanagan Lake, 250/493-4055 or 800/663-5052, website www.penticton.org. It's open in summer daily 8 A.M.–8 P.M., the rest of the year Mon.–Fri. 9 A.M.–5 P.M., Sat.–Sun. 10 A.M.–4 P.M. If it's closed when you're there, you can still orient yourself to local surroundings with the gigantic town map and directory outside the entrance.

NORTH OF PENTICTON

Highway 97 links Penticton and Kelowna, running along the west side of Okanagan Lake for the entire 60 km. The first worthwhile stop is tiny **Sun-Oka Beach Provincial Park,** which offers trees galore, picnic tables, beaches, and good swimming.

Summerland

As you enter picturesque Summerland, nestled between Giants Head Mountain and the lake 16 km north of Penticton, turn west (away from the lake) at either of the stoplights and follow the signs to Prairie Valley Station, the departure point for **Kettle River Railway,** 250/494-8422 or 877/494-8424. This steam train, dating to the early 1900s, runs along a historic 10-km stretch of track, through orchards and vineyards, and over a 75-meter-high trestle bridge. Departures are mid-May to mid-Oct. Sat.–Mon. at 10:30 A.M. and 1:30 P.M., with additional trips in July and August on Thursday and Friday. The fare is adult $14, senior $13, child $10.

Another interesting stop is **Summerland Sweets** factory on Canyon View Rd., 250/494-0377, to see syrups, jams, and candy being made from fresh and frozen fruit; from Highway 97 take the Dunn Street or Arkell Road exit west, turn right on Gartrell Road, left on Happy Valley Road, right on Hillborn Street, then left on Canyon View Road.

Sumac Ridge Estate, one km north of Summerland on the lake side of the highway, 250/494-0451, was British Columbia's first estate winery. Today, this well-recognized name appears on a wide variety of red and white wines, including an award-winning Cabernet Franc and one of the Okanagan's few sparkling wines. Tours and tastings are offered May–Oct. daily 10 A.M.–4 P.M. on the hour, and a bistro is open daily for lunch.

Continuing toward Kelowna

On the way to Kelowna you'll pass two entrances to **Okanagan Lake Provincial Park,** a grassy, beach-fringed park popular for boating and swimming. Ponderosa pines line the shore while exotic trees such as maple and oak shade dozens of picnic tables. Camping is $18.50 a night April–October.

Farther along is the community of **Peachland.** Crammed between a rocky bluff and Okanagan Lake, Peachland was founded in 1808 by Manitoba entrepreneur and newspaperman John Robinson, who came to the Okanagan in search of mining prospects but turned his talents to developing the delicious locally grown dessert peaches.

Kelowna

British Columbia's largest city outside the Lower Mainland and Victoria, Kelowna (pop. 96,000) lies on the shores of 170-km-long Okanagan Lake, approximately halfway between Penticton in the south and Vernon in the north. The city combines a scenic location among semiarid mountains with an unbeatable climate of long, sunny summers and short, mild winters. The low rolling hills around the city hold lush terraced orchards, and the numerous local vineyards produce some excellent wines. Visitors flock here in summer to enjoy the area's sparkling lakes, sandy beaches, numerous provincial parks, and golfing; in winter they come for great skiing and boarding at nearby Big White Ski Resort.

History

For thousands of years before the arrival of the first Europeans, the nomadic Salish peoples inhabited the Okanagan Valley, hunting (*kelowna* is a Salish word for grizzly bear), gathering, and fishing. The first European to settle in the valley was an oblate missionary, Father Pandosy, who established a mission on the southern outskirts of present-day downtown Kelowna in 1859. Since the first apple trees were planted at the mission, Kelowna has thrived as the center of the Okanagan fruit, vegetable, and vineyard industry (the valley is Canada's largest fruit-growing region).

In 1960, Kelowna's population stood at 24,000, and began expanding soon after as wide-scale forestry, agriculture, and tourism took hold. As local services have improved, the region has become more attractive to older, retired people. Since the opening of the Okanagan Connector in 1986, traveling time between Vancouver and Kelowna has been cut from around

Kelowna combines a scenic location among semiarid mountains with an unbeatable climate of long, sunny summers and short, mild winters. The low rolling hills around the city hold lush terraced orchards, and the numerous local vineyards produce some excellent wines.

six hours to under four hours, and the population has literally exploded, with the number of wineries doubling since the mid-1980s, luxurious resorts being built along the lake, new golf courses opening every year, and exclusive subdivisions carving away land formerly given over to agriculture.

SIGHTS

Along the Waterfront

Right downtown, beautiful **City Park** is the largest of Kelowna's many parks. Its 14 lakefront hectares hold lots of flowers and large shady trees, expansive lawns, and a long sandy beach. You can rent a boat, houseboat, and fishing equipment at one of several marinas. Waterskiing and parasailing are also popular activities. Near the entrance to the park is the large, sparkling-white, attention-grabbing Dow Reid sculpture *Sails*, as well as a replica of the famed lake-dwelling serpent, Ogopogo (see the special topic).

At the south end of the park is one end of the **Okanagan Lake Bridge.** Built in 1958, this 1,400-meter-long floating bridge, anchored to the lakebed in 24 spots, is the only such structure in Canada.

A promenade leads north from the Ogopogo statue past a large marina and a prime waterfront site undergoing redevelopment. Beyond the construction is the **Grand Okanagan,** the Okanagan's most luxurious accommodation. Even if you can't afford a lakefront suite, the resort holds a bar and restaurant with water views, and full spa services. Beyond the resort, the promenade crosses a small lock, which allows boaters to travel between the higher water level of an artificial lagoon and the lake itself.

OKANAGAN VALLEY

Other Downtown Sights

Kelowna Museum, 470 Queensway Ave., 250/763-2417, is opposite the post office; look for the brightly painted totem pole marking the entrance. The museum holds a mishmash of fascinating displays, including horse-drawn carriages; fossils found in the Princeton area; indigenous arts, crafts, clothing, jewelry, beads, and furs; children's books and games; radio equipment; pioneer artifacts; re-creations of an 1861 Kelowna trading post and a Chinese store; and a display of the interior of a Salish winter dwelling. It's open in summer Mon.–Sat. 10 A.M.–5 P.M., the rest of the year Tues.–Sat. 10 A.M.–5 P.M. Admission is by donation.

Behind the museum is **Kasugai Gardens.** Built with the cooperation of Kelowna's Japanese sister city, Kasugai, the gardens are a quiet retreat from the downtown business district; admission is free and the gates are locked at dusk. **Kelowna Art Gallery,** 1315 Water St., 250/762-2226, is a modern facility hosting touring exhibitions and maintaining a permanent collection of contemporary and historical works by artists from throughout the province. It's open Tues.–Sat. 10 A.M.–5 P.M., Sunday 1–5 P.M.; admission is by donation.

In an old downtown packinghouse, complete with exposed red-brick walls and hand-hewn wooden beams, the **B.C. Orchard Industry Museum,** 1304 Ellis St., 250/763-0433, tells the story of the local orchard industry through rare photographs, displays, and a hands-on discovery corner. It's open Tues.–Sat. 10 A.M.–5 P.M. In the same building, the **Wine Museum,** 250/868-0441, has information on local wineries and tours, and sells the finished product. It's open Mon.–Sat. 10 A.M.–5 P.M., Sunday noon–5 P.M.

Benvoulin Heritage Park

This park surrounds a Gothic revival Benvoulin Church, which dates to 1892, east of downtown at 2279 Benvoulin Road. The church and a historic residence also within the grounds are closed to the public, but it is the garden that holds most interest. It is a "xeriscape" garden, which are designed to take advantage of the local climate and environment. In this case, plants grown here require little moisture, reflective of problems encountered by professional and amateur gardeners along the entire valley.

Pandosy Mission Provincial Heritage Site

Farther south along Benvoulin Road is the site of the mission established by Father Pandosy in 1859. The route meanders through lush irrigated farmlands and orchards, past nurseries, fields of grass-munching horses, and large country homes with picture-perfect flower and vegetable gardens. Father Pandosy, an oblate priest, operated a church, school, and farm here, ministering to natives and whites until his death in 1891. His mission claimed a lot of "firsts"— first white settlement in the Okanagan Valley, first school in the valley, first fruit and vine crops in the valley, and first Roman Catholic mission in the B.C. interior. Not much has changed within the broken down wooden fences that

one of the original buildings at Pandosy Mission

© ANDREW HEMPSTEAD

hold the mission—four of the eight buildings on-site date to Pandosy's era, including a chapel and barn. The mission is open daily from 8 A.M. to dark, and the $2 donation includes an informative tour of the buildings, grounds, and antique farming equipment.

Wineries

Viticulture has been a mainstay of the Okanagan's economy for almost a century, but it has really taken off in the last decade, with local wines exported and winning awards worldwide. Most of the local wineries welcome visitors with tours and free tastings year-round (but call ahead outside of summer to check hours). Due to the popularity of visiting the wineries, most now charge a small fee for tasting.

One of the province's oldest wineries, in operation since 1932, is **Calona Vineyards,** downtown at 1125 Richter St., 250/762-9144. There's no actual vineyard, just a large winery that uses grapes grown throughout the valley. Calona offers tours throughout the year at 2 P.M. (more frequently in summer), with tastings and sales in a room set up as a cellar, open 9 A.M.–7 P.M.

Across Okanagan Lake from Kelowna is **Mission Hill Family Estate,** 1730 Mission Hill Rd., Westbank, 250/768-7611, high atop a ridge and surrounded by vineyards with stunning lake views. Mission Hill, British Columbia's most successful winery, completed massive expansions in 2001, including a 45-meter-high bell tower, open for the public to climb. Tours depart three times daily, each ending with an informal tasting session at the Wine and Food Interpretation Centre. Open daily 10 A.M.–7 P.M. At nearby **Quail's Gate Estate Winery,** 3303 Boucherie Rd., 250/769-4451, the Reserve Pinot Noir is a signature wine—enjoy a glass or two alfresco at the winery bistro. Winery tours are conducted daily at 11 A.M., 1 P.M., and 3 P.M.

Back on the main highway, farther south is **Hainle Vineyards Estate Winery,** 5355 Trepanier Bench Rd., Peachland, 250/767-2525. Walter Hainle was a pioneer in the development of ice wines, and while this is the style that the

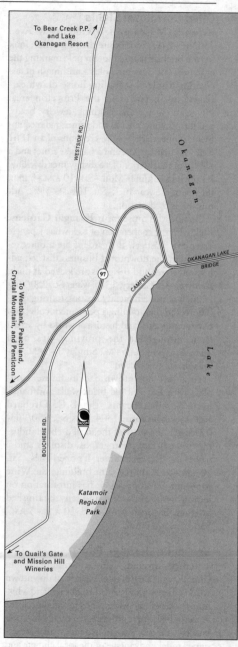

Knox Mountain Park
KNOX MOUNTAIN DR.

CROWLEY AVE.

KELOWNA

To Winfield, Okanagan Golf Club, Airport, and Vernon

TRAIN STATION

WESTERN BUDGET MOTEL

HIGH RD.

GLENMORE RD.

LEATHEED RD.

Waterfront Park

RICHTER ST.

ETHEL ST.

GORDON DR.

GLENMORE DR.

DAYS INN

33

★ SUN-RYPE PRODUCTS

BERNARD AVE.

ELLIS ST.

BEST WESTERN INN KELOWNA

City Park

COAST CAPRI HOTEL

BUS DEPOT

To Big White Ski Resort and Grand Forks

HARVEY AVE.

SEE "DOWNTOWN KELOWNA" MAP

ABBOTT ST.

97

SUTHERLAND AVE.

CARMELLE'S RESTAURANT

WENRICK CRES.

CADDER AVE.

SPRINGFIELD RD.

HOSPITAL

Mission Creek Regional Park

KELOWNA LAND & ORCHARD COMPANY

HOSTELLING INTERNATIONAL KELOWNA

★ BENVOULIN HERITAGE PARK

DUNSTER RD.

PANDOSY ST.

BENVOULIN RD.

EAST KELOWNA RD.

SPORTS RENT

EAST KELOWNA RD.

SIESTA MOTOR INN

K.L.O. RD.

LANFRANCO

Mission Creek

Gyro Beach

THE HARVEST GOLF CLUB

Rotary Beach

HIAWATHA RV PARK

★ PANDOSY MISSION PROVINCIAL HISTORIC SITE

MANTEO RESORT

McCULLOCH RD.

HOTEL ELDORADO

SCALE NOT AVAILABLE

MICHAELBROOK RANCH GOLF COURSE

To Cedar Creek Estate Winery and Okanagan Mountain P.P.

To Kettle Valley Railway and Gallagher's Canyon Golf & Country Club

© AVALON TRAVEL PUBLISHING, INC.

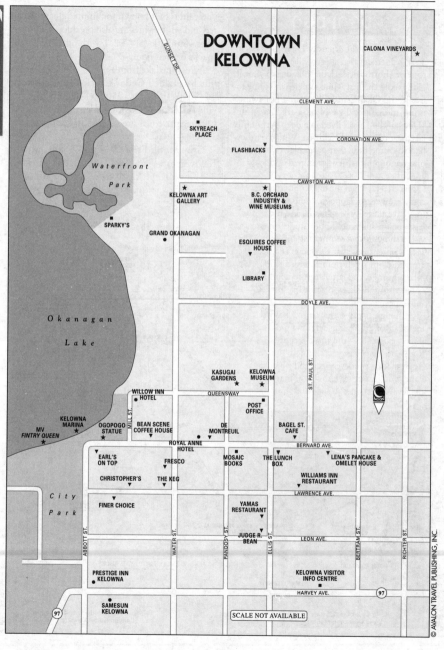

DOWNTOWN KELOWNA

CALONA VINEYARDS

CLEMENT AVE.

SKYREACH PLACE

CORONATION AVE.

FLASHBACKS

CAWSTON AVE.

Waterfront Park

KELOWNA ART GALLERY

B.C. ORCHARD INDUSTRY & WINE MUSEUMS

SPARKY'S

GRAND OKANAGAN

ESQUIRES COFFEE HOUSE

FULLER AVE.

LIBRARY

DOYLE AVE.

Okanagan Lake

KASUGAI GARDENS

KELOWNA MUSEUM

ST. PAUL ST.

Moon

QUEENSWAY

WILLOW INN HOTEL

POST OFFICE

MILL ST.

KELOWNA MARINA

OGOPOGO STATUE

BEAN SCENE COFFEE HOUSE

DE MONTREUIL

BAGEL ST. CAFE

MV FINTRY QUEEN

ROYAL ANNE HOTEL

BERNARD AVE.

EARL'S ON TOP

FRESCO

MOSAIC BOOKS

THE LUNCH BOX

LENA'S PANCAKE & OMELET HOUSE

CHRISTOPHER'S

THE KEG

WILLIAMS INN RESTAURANT

LAWRENCE AVE.

City Park

FINER CHOICE

YAMAS RESTAURANT

ABBOTT ST.

WATER ST.

PANDOSY ST.

JUDGE R. BEAN

ELLIS ST.

LEON AVE.

BERTRAM ST.

RICHTER ST.

PRESTIGE INN KELOWNA

KELOWNA VISITOR INFO CENTRE

97

SAMESUN KELOWNA

HARVEY AVE.

97

SCALE NOT AVAILABLE

© AVALON TRAVEL PUBLISHING, INC.

OGOPOGO

Ogopogo is the friendly Loch Ness–style sea serpent that allegedly lives on the bottom of "bottomless" Lake Okanagan. Local natives told the first white settlers who came to live in the Okanagan Valley that a fast-swimming monster called N'ha-a-tik, meaning "Devil of the Lake," lived in a deep part of the lake near present-day Kelowna. Whenever they had to canoe near that particular point, they unceremoniously threw an animal overboard as a sacrifice.

Since 1942, when the mysterious monster became known as Ogopogo, thousands of sightings have allegedly been made, and the creature has been the subject of feature stories on the television shows *Unsolved Mysteries* and *Inside Edition.* Consensus is that Ogopogo is a snakelike creature with small humps, green skin, and a nice big smile, the latter feature confirmed by enterprising locals who print his image on T-shirts, posters, and postcards.

Although many times a prize has been put up for anyone providing definitive proof of Ogopogo's existence—the most recent is $2 million—no one has yet claimed the reward. Anyway, keep your eyes open and your camera at hand; you just never know, you may be one of the few (sober) ones to spot him.

vineyard is best known for, limited quantities of red and white wines are also produced. It's open Tues.–Sun. 10 A.M.–5 P.M. with lunch and light snacks offered noon–3 P.M.

Across the lake from the above wineries is the much-heralded **Cedar Creek Estate Winery,** 5445 Lakeshore Dr., 250/764-8866, where the vineyards and extensive gardens overlook Lake Okanagan. Tours are offered in summer daily 11 A.M.–4 P.M.

Gray Monk Estate Winery, 22 km north of Kelowna on Camp Rd., Winfield, 250/766-3168, is a family affair most recognized for its German-style wines, including Gewürztraminer and a Pinot Gris. Tours are offered April–Oct. on the hour 11 A.M.–4 P.M., the rest of the year on Sunday at 2 P.M.

Other Agricultural and Industrial Tours

You could probably spend a couple of weeks taking one tour a day around Kelowna—orchard tours, vineyard tours, fruit-factory tours, forestry tours, and industrial tours. One that all tour-lovers will enjoy is the free 30-minute tour of **Sun-Rype Products,** 1165 Ethel St., 250/860-7973, which shows you how apple juice, applesauce, and pie fillings are created. Tours are offered June–Sept. Mon.–Fri. 9 A.M.–3 P.M. **Kelowna Land and Orchard Co.,** 3002 Dunster Rd., 250/763-1091, for which K.L.O. Road is named, is a 60-hectare apple orchard that was established in 1904. Tours of the orchard aboard a tractor-drawn wagon depart daily at 11 A.M., 1 P.M., and 3 P.M. Onsite are a store and teahouse.

If you have your own transportation, take the self-guided **McCulloch Forest Tour** along a short forest route southeast of Kelowna; pick up a brochure with a map to various points of interest at the information center.

© ANDREW HEMPSTEAD

RECREATION

On the Lake

During the warm and sunny months of summer, Okanagan Lake comes alive with a colorful array of watercraft, fishermen, and swimmers out on the water, and sunbathers dot the surrounding sandy beaches. The busiest spot is the stretch of sand fronting City Park, right downtown. Beyond the beach's northern end, you can rent watercraft from **Sparky's,** in front of the Grand Okanagan Lakefront Resort, 250/862-2469; rent small power boats at **Kelowna Marina,** 250/861-8001, or go parachuting behind a boat with **Kelowna Parasail Adventures,** 250/868-4838, for $45 per person.

In the same vicinity, the paddlewheeler **MV Fintry Queen,** 250/763-2780, moored at the foot of Bernard Ave., makes a fun and stylish way to see some of Lake Okanagan. In summer, afternoon cruises depart Mon.–Sat. at noon and Sunday at 2 P.M., and evening cruises depart Mon.–Fri. at 7:30 P.M., Saturday at 9 P.M., and Sunday at 5:30 P.M. All cruises last two hours, except for the weekend evening sailings, which last three hours. All cost adult $10, senior $8.50, child $6 with the option of dinner ($18.50 per person extra) on evening cruises. The *Fintry Queen* did not operate in 2001, so call ahead.

Gyro Beach and adjacent **Rotary Beach** are beautiful stretches of sand south of downtown along Lakeshore Drive. Less crowded are the beaches in **Okanagan Mountain Provincial Park,** farther south.

Sports Rent, 3000 Pandosy St., 250/861-5699, rents kayaks from $25 per day, canoes for $35 per day, as well as wetsuits.

Hiking and Biking

Now abandoned, the **Kettle Valley Railway** grade winds around the back of Kelowna; it was constructed in 1914 to connect the Kootenays city of Nelson to the main CPR line. Today it's a great destination for hikers or those with reliable mountain bikes. To get there take K.L.O. Road to McCulloch Road, turn south (right) and then south (right) again, following Myra Forest Service Road for 8.5 km. From the parking lot at this point, it's under one km to the first of 18 trestles spanning 12-km-long Myra Canyon, where the rail line was carved into the mountainside.

The cacti-covered top of **Knox Mountain** offers great lake and city views. A hiking trail and a paved road popular with bicyclists both lead to the summit. To get there head north out of town along the lakeshore, passing pretty, lakeside Sutherland Park (good views of Crown Forest Mill and log rafts), then take Knox Mountain Drive up to Knox Mountain Park, stopping at Crown Viewpoint on the way to the top.

Trails lead off the summit in all directions, and in May the mountain swarms with activity as cars and motorcycles race up the mountain during the **Knox Mountain Hill Climb.**

Golfing

Many of Canada's best resort-style golf courses lie in and around Kelowna. These courses, combined with a mild climate and relatively well-priced greens fees, make the Okanagan one of the country's finest golfing destinations. All the courses listed below offer club rentals, power carts (generally around $30), and on-course dining facilities. **Okanagan Reservations,** 250/493-3200 or 800/663-1900, website www.okres.bc.ca, offers golf packages from $70 per person per night.

The **Harvest Golf Club,** 250/862-3103 or 800/257-8577, sitting on terraced land southeast of downtown, offers golfers views back across the city and lake. This 7,109-yard course features fairways lined with fruit trees, large greens, lots of water hazards, and a magnificent clubhouse. Greens fees are $85; the twilight rate is $55. Get there by taking K.L.O. Road east from Pandosy Street.

Continue east from the Harvest Golf Club and you'll eventually reach **Gallagher's Canyon Golf & Country Club,** one of Canada's finest golf courses. Not particularly long, this immaculately manicured course snakes through a canyon and opens up to fairways lined with mature pine trees. It is a par-72 course that plays to 6,800 yards. Greens fees are $80 a round, or pay $55 after 4 P.M. For bookings call 250/861-4240.

North of town and opposite the airport is **Okanagan Golf Club,** 250/765-5955, a residential and resort complex featuring 36 of the valley's finest holes. Designed by Jack Nicklaus's company, **The Bear** opened for the 1999 season while **The Quail,** featuring multitiered fairways and large elevations, has been a long-time local favorite. Both courses play to a par of 72 and are just under 7,000 yards from the back tees. Greens fees are $85 and $75 respectively, with a discounted twilight rate of $45 for each course.

South of downtown on Gordon Dr., **Michaelbrook Ranch Golf Club,** 250/763-7888, is home to a unique putting course, complete with 18 par 2–5 holes and even water hazards.

Okanagan Valley Wine Train

This new venture runs north from Kelowna through the heart of orchard country then through some of the province's finest ranching land to Armstrong. Passengers can travel in regular rail carriages, but most opt for the themed carriages, such as "Hollywood," "Western," "Blues & Jazz" or "Rock 'n' Roll." The fare is adult $65, child $32.50, which includes a meal and a Las Vegas–style show in Armstrong. The trip departs in summer daily at 5:30 P.M. (Sunday at 11 A.M.) and takes just over five hours. For bookings call 250/712-9888 or 800/674-8725.

Fun Parks

Head across the floating bridge to access the following two attractions. **Mariner's Reef Waterpark & Slides,** in Westbank, 250/768-5141, is open May–Sept. daily; adult $18, children 4–6 $12, three and under free. Also in Westbank is **Old MacDonald's Farm,** on Hwy. 97, 250/768-5167, where you'll find a variety of farm animals and exotic animals, as well as mini-golf and pony rides. Open May–Sept.; adult $9, senior or child $7.50.

Skiing and Snowboarding

Of the two alpine resorts near Kelowna, largest by far is **Big White Ski Resort,** 57 km east of Kelowna on Hwy. 33. One of the Okanagan's three major winter resorts and B.C.'s second largest, Big White has seen much expansion over the last few years. Construction of a new high-speed detachable quad chairlift on the Westridge

face almost doubled the terrain to 850 hectares and added over 100 meters to the area's vertical rise, now over 725 meters. The resort is served by 13 lifts, including a gondola and four high-speed quad chairs. Lifts operate December through mid-April daily 8:30 A.M.–3:30 P.M., and for night skiing and boarding Tues.–Sat. 5–9 P.M. Lift tickets are adult $48, senior $33, 70 and over and under five free. Adjacent to the main lift-served area is Happy Valley Adventure Centre, a tube park with its own lift. Big White is also home to a terrain park, half pipe, cross-country trails, and an ice-skating rink. On-mountain facilities in the 9,000-bed base village include rental shops, a ski and snowboard school, accommodations, restaurants and cafés, and a large mall. For general resort information call 250/765-3101; for Big White Central Reservations call 250/765-8888 or 800/663-2772; for snow conditions call 250/765-7669; on the Internet go to www.bigwhite.com.

Since 1967 when the first chairlift was installed, **Crystal Mountain,** 28 km west of Kelowna, 250/768-5189, has grown to be a family favorite. With three lifts and 20 runs over a 210-meter vertical rise, most of the slopes are suitable for beginners and intermediates. The small area also features a snowboard park with a half-pipe and jumps. Other facilities include a rental shop, ski and snowboard school, and cafeteria. Tickets are adults $29, senior $14.50, child $21. The lifts operate Wed.–Sun., with night skiing and boarding Wed.–Sat. until 9 P.M.

Nightlife

Enjoy a drink overlooking Okanagan Lake in the stylish lounge at the **Hotel Eldorado,** 500 Cook Rd., 250/763-7500. Right downtown, **Sgt. O'Flaherty's,** in the Royal Anne Hotel at 348 Bernard Ave., 250/860-6409, is a friendly pub with bands churning out a variety of music styles nightly from 9 P.M. **Flashbacks,** 1268 Ellis St., 250/861-3039, is a local favorite for dancing into the early hours; open weekends only.

Lake City Casino is in the Grand Okanagan at 1310 Water St., 250/860-9467. Don't expect the ritz and glitz of Las Vegas, though—this is gambling Canadian style, with the action restricted to slot machines, blackjack, roulette, Caribbean stud poker, and mini baccarat, and everyone's ushered out the front door at 2 A.M.

Sunshine Theatre, 250/763-4025, puts on three to four plays throughout the summer; pick up a schedule at the information center. The **Uptown Cinema Centre** screens films at 1521 Water St., 250/762-0099.

Festivals and Events

The **Spring Wine Festival,** 250/861-6654, website www.owfs.com, is somewhat less pretentious than the fall equivalent, with many wineries not normally open to the public offering tours and tasting sessions through late April. On the first weekend of May, the **Apple Blossom Festival** coincides with the beginning of the apple-picking season. The event features fun family events out at the Kelowna Land and Orchard Company on Dunster Road. The **Knox Mountain Hill Climb,** North America's longest paved motor-vehicle hill climb, has been contested annually since 1957; it's on in late May.

Throughout July, the mobile **Mozart Festival** takes place, with classical performances at venues throughout the city, including at local churches and museums. Each of the 10 concerts costs $15 per person and can be booked by calling 250/762-3747. **Parks Alive** is another summertime music event, this one held through July and August at city parks Wed.–Sat. nights; expect everything from classical to country. The second weekend of July, wander down to the marina at the Hotel Eldorado to admire watercraft displayed at the **Antique and Classic Boat Show;** call 250/763-8603 for details. On the first weekend of August, the Sunshine Theatre Co., 250/763-4025, presents the **Kelowna Comedy Festival** at various indoor and outdoor venues. Held on streets, in parks, and at venues through the city, the **Kelowna Fringe Festival,** 250/763-1661, brings eclectic modern theater productions late in August.

The valley's biggest event is the **Fall Wine Festival,** held annually over 10 days from the last full weekend of September to celebrate the end of the grape harvest. Thousands of visitors participate in food and wine tastings, releases of new wines, cooking classes, and art displays with

all sections of the industry participating. For a schedule of activities, call 250/861-6654, website www.owfs.com. The **apple harvest** is celebrated during the same period at the B.C. Orchard Museum, 1304 Ellis St., 250/763-0433, with apple tastings and displays.

ACCOMMODATIONS AND CAMPING

Under $50

Hostelling International—Kelowna is at 2343 Pandosy St., 250/763-6024, website www.hihostels.bc.ca. It's a rambling old house, with 30 beds, an outdoor deck and barbecue facility, public Internet access, a communal kitchen, a laundry room, and a TV room, all within one block of the beach and a 10-minute walk from downtown. Dorm beds are $15 per night for members of Hostelling International, $19 for nonmembers. **Samesun Kelowna** is a three-story, purpose-built backpacker lodge right downtown at 245 Harvey St., 250/763-5013 or 888/562-2783, website www.samesun.com. Inside the distinctive three-story building are 120 beds, many in private rooms, with communal kitchens, bathrooms, a large lounge area, and public Internet access. Out back is a pleasant grassed barbecue area and a beach volleyball court. Rates are $19.50 for a dorm bed, $44 s or d in a private room. Pickups from the bus depot are free, drop-offs a reasonable $2. The owners of the Samesun operate another backpacker lodge up at Big White Ski Resort, 57 km east of town, 250/765-2100 or 888/595-6411. They are busiest in winter but most enjoyable without the crowds in summer. Off-season (outside of winter) rates are $15 per person for a dorm bed and $19.50 per person d.

Kelowna's only motel under $50 is the **Western Budget Motel,** 2679 Hwy. 97 N, 250/763-2484, which charges from $45 for a basic room.

$50–100

Aside from the Samesun Kelowna, the least expensive place to stay right downtown is the old **Willow Inn Hotel,** 235 Queensway Ave., 250/762-2122 or 800/268-1055, offering large rooms, each with a writing desk and lounge. Summer rates are $85 s, $95 d, from $55 s, $65 d the rest of the year. South of downtown, the **Siesta Motor Inn,** 3152 Lakeshore Rd., 250/763-5013 or 800/663-4347, www.siestamotorinn.com, offers a beachside atmosphere one block from the water. Rooms open onto a wide balcony overlooking a courtyard and pool. Rates range $94–128 s or d; many rooms have kitchenettes.

$100–150

Built in 1926 and moved to its present location in 1989, the **Hotel Eldorado,** 500 Cook Rd., south of downtown along Pandosy St., 250/763-7500, website www.eldoradokelowna.com, is a delightful lakeside accommodation offering just 20 rooms, each furnished with antiques and many offering a lake view and private balcony. Hotel facilities include a lakefront café, a restaurant, a lounge, and a marina with boat rentals. Summer rates range $139–179, with only the more expensive rooms having water views.

Highway 97 (also known as Harvey Avenue) north of downtown holds many motels tucked between shopping malls, gas stations, and fast-food restaurants. Along this strip is **Days Inn Kelowna,** 2469 Hwy. 97 N, 250/868-3297 or 800/337-7177, website www.daysinn.com, with large, modern rooms decorated in Santa Fe style, as well as an outdoor pool and hot tub; the smallest rooms cost $109 s or d, but it's worth an extra $20 for a much-larger suite. As at all Days Inns, rates include a light breakfast. Across the road and back toward downtown a few blocks, **Best Western Inn Kelowna,** 2402 Hwy. 97 N, 250/860-1212 or 888/860-1212, website www.bestwestern.com, features rooms of a high standard, a restaurant and lounge, complimentary coffee, and an outdoor pool; $129 s, $139 d. Continuing back toward the city center is the **Coast Capri Hotel,** 1171 Hwy. 97 N, 250/860-6060 or 800/663-1144, a full-service hotel with a heated pool, hot tub, sauna, coffee shop, fine dining restaurant, pub, and nightclub. Rates start at $125 s, $135 d.

$150–200

Right downtown, the **Prestige Inn Kelowna,** 1675 Abbott St., 250/860-7900 or 877/737-

8443, website www.prestigeinn.com, has spacious, elegantly furnished rooms as well as a fancy restaurant and lounge, an exercise room, and an indoor pool; from $150–180 s or d.

Overlooking the same stretch of lake as the Hotel Eldorado is the colorful and modern **Manteo Resort,** 3766 Lakeshore Rd., 250/860-1031 or 888/462-6836, website www.manteo.com. This self-contained complex includes a 78-room hotel and guest and resident facilities such as a private beach, marina with boat rentals, pool complex with a water slide, tennis courts, a small movie theater, a lounge with billiard table, and a barbecue area. Rates start at $195 s or d for a standard hotel room ($225 with a water view), but villas that sleep six can be rented for $450 per night. Outside of summer, bed and breakfast is under $150 per couple.

Over $200

The grandest of Kelowna's accommodations is **The Grand Okanagan,** a sprawling lakeside

The grandest of Kelowna's accommodations is the Grand Okanagan, right on the lakefront.

© ANDREW HEMPSTEAD

development right downtown and integrated with local walking paths. Along the lake side of the resort is a convoluted lagoon, with its own private lock and watercraft rentals, while farther along are eateries and a bar with outdoor seating. Inside, once past the cavernous lobby, you'll find a fitness center, spa services, restaurants, a lounge bar, and 205 luxuriously appointed rooms. In summer, standard rooms are $259 s or d, with suites from $325. The best deals are the packages, which include, for example, breakfast, dinner, and a room upgrade for an additional $70. Off-season rates start at $159 room only. It's at 1310 Water St., 250/763-4500 or 800/465-4651, website www.grandokanagan.com.

Lake Okanagan Resort, on the west side of Okanagan Lake 17 km north along Westside Rd., 250/769-3511 or 800/663-3273, website www.lakeokanagan.com, sprawls over 100 hectares of absolute waterfront property. It offers tennis courts, a par-3 golf course, swimming pools, a full-service marina, and horseback riding. In the main lodge is a restaurant open daily for dinner, a more casual café where dining alfresco is the order of the day, a poolside bar, and an upstairs lounge. The spacious units are each kitchen-equipped and have a private balcony, but are in need of an upgrade. Between mid-June and mid-Sept., a two-night package including one dinner and one breakfast is $284 pp, discounted to $184 the rest of the year.

Camping

The closest campground to downtown is **Hiawatha RV Park,** 3787 Lakeshore Rd., 250/861-4837 or 888/784-7275, website www.hiawatharvpark.com. It has a tenting area, showers, a laundromat, game room, and playground; tent sites $30, hookups $37–40.

Most of the other commercial campgrounds are on the west shore of Okanagan Lake at Westbank. They include: **Happy Valley Resort,** 4026 Pritchard Dr., 250/768-7703; **Green Bay Resort,** 1375 Green Bay Rd., 250/768-5543; and **West Bay Beach,** 3745 West Bay Rd., 250/768-3004. All charge $30–35 per site and offer coin-operated showers and full hookups.

Two provincial parks in the vicinity of Kelowna offer camping. The closest is **Bear Creek Provincial Park,** across the bridge from downtown and then nine km north on Westside Road. With 122 sites nestled under cottonwood trees, this park is a world away from the busy nearby commercial campgrounds, but arrive early in the day to ensure a site; $18.50 per night includes showers. Campers also enjoy a short beach and trails that cross back over Westside Road and into desert-like terrain above the lake. **Fintry Provincial Park** lies a further 23 km north along Westside Road in the same beachside setting as Bear Creek, although the campground is less developed; $18.50 per night. A trail leads from the campground to a deep canyon along Shorts Creek.

FOOD

Downtown Kelowna has a great number of dining choices, for everything from a quick coffee to a full meal, but many of the city's finer restaurants are away from the business core, along quiet country roads or at the many golf clubs.

Downtown Cafés

The business of breakfast doesn't get going until around 8 A.M. in the downtown area, but one exception is **Lena's Pancake & Omelet House,** 553 Bernard St., which opens its doors at 6:30 A.M.—the perfect place for a meal after an early morning walk along the lakefront; cooked breakfasts start at $3.99. Back toward the lake is the friendly little **Lunch Box,** 509 Bernard St., 250/862-8621, open Mon.–Fri. 8 A.M.–8 P.M. and Saturday 9 A.M.–4 P.M. A full cooked breakfast is just $4, healthy muffins and sandwiches are on the menu for lunch, and in the evening no main dish is over $12. Diagonally opposite is the black-and-green decorated **Bagel St. Café,** 526 Bernard St., part of a chain of big city-style coffeehouses that originated in Vancouver. If you're browsing for a book at **Mosaic Books,** back toward the lake at 411 Bernard St., follow the aroma of freshly brewed coffee to the adjacent coffee bar. Away from Bernard Street, the following cafés are all within the downtown core. **Judge R. Bean,** 1654 Ellis St., is a specialty coffee shop in an old brick building with a row of outdoor table settings shaded by roadside trees; open weekdays from 6:30 A.M. and from 8 A.M. on weekends. **Esquires Coffee House** is tucked away at the base of a multilevel parkade (opposite the entrance to the library) on Ellis Street. It a popular spot with local businesspeople, who come for coffee, cakes, and healthy sandwiches to eat in or to go. Continue toward the waterfront to reach the Grand Okanagan Lakefront Resort; on the street side of the complex is **Mind Grind,** 1340 Water St., 250/763-2221, another trendy little coffee shop.

Family-Style Dining

Opposite City Park, **Earl's on Top,** upstairs at 211 Bernard Ave. (corner of Abbott St.), 250/763-2777, does a booming business, deservedly. The atmosphere features a shiny, black-and-white decor with flashy neon lighting (nothing beats a neon palm tree) and a mass of plants. Grab a table on the rooftop garden patio and absorb the lake view, or just pretend you're outside (not hard to do with all the plants). The menu offers a wide variety of soups, salads, burgers, chicken, seafood, steak, and pasta dishes—even tapas. Lunch ranges $5–12, dinner $6–20. Earl's is open Sun.–Mon. 11:30 A.M.–11 P.M., Tues.–Sat. 11:30 A.M.–midnight. The **Keg Restaurant,** downtown at 1580 Water St., 250/763-5435, is open daily 4–11 P.M., offering a 60-item salad bar, steaks, seafood, prime rib, and steak or chicken fajitas. Expect to pay $8–19 for a main course.

Crepes

Carmelle's Restaurant, 1836 Underhill Rd., 250/762-6350, gives you the option of sitting in the bright nonsmokers' room with picture windows and a view of orchards and hills across the road, or the darker smokers' room with a large open fireplace. A relaxing atmosphere, plenty of candles, and low-hanging orange-tassled lampshades suspended over each table invite quiet conversation while you tuck in to tantalizing crepes for $11–19, other main dishes for $8–19, and sinful dessert crepes for $4–7. Open for lunch Mon.–Fri. 11:30 A.M.–2 P.M. and for dinner daily from 5 P.M.

Other Restaurants

One of Kelowna's best restaurants is the **Finer Choice,** 237 Lawrence Ave., 250/763-0422, an elegant dining room decorated with antiques and oozing old-world charm. The waitpersons are attentive and the food well prepared; expect to pay $16–25 for the mostly North American-inspired dinner entrées. Open Mon.–Fri. for lunch and daily for dinner.

The atmosphere at **Christopher's,** across the road at 242 Lawrence Ave., 250/861-3464, is much different, with a light and breezy decor. But the seasonal steak and seafood dishes are also excellent. Open daily for lunch and dinner. Farther east along the same street is the **Williams Inn,** with table settings spread over two stories of a restored heritage house at 526 Lawrence Ave., 250/763-5136. The menu features lots of B.C. seafood and game, but the European training of the chefs is reflected in the style of dishes offered. Most dinner mains are around $20. Open daily for lunch and dinner.

Also downtown, **de Montreuil Restaurant,** 368 Bernard St., 250/860-5508, is a starkly decorated yet stylish restaurant. The menu offers many mouthwatering choices, such as an Australian rack of lamb basted in fresh rosemary and garlic. The table d'hôte menus offer the best value—two courses for $30, three for $36, and four for $41. It's open weekdays for lunch, daily for dinner, and also for Sunday brunch.

Fresco, 1560 Water St., 250/868-8805, is the latest addition to Kelowna's dining scene. In the surrounds of a heritage commercial building are elegant table settings, a bar, and comfortable sofas. The menu is typically West Coast, but more adventurous than you'd expect this far from Vancouver. Mains range $20–26 while Signature Collection dishes are $42.

For tangy Greek food, locals recommend **Yamas Restaurant,** 1630 Ellis St., 250/763-5823. The authentic Greek atmosphere features blue-and-white furnishings and plenty of greenery. Open daily for a lunch buffet and from 5:30 P.M. for dinner; $9–14 for dinner entrées. A belly dancer performs on Saturday nights.

OKANAGAN VALLEY

SERVICES AND INFORMATION

Transportation

Kelowna Airport, the province's third busiest, is 15 km north of downtown along Hwy. 97. It's served by **Air B.C.,** 250/542-3302, and **West-Jet,** 800/538-5696, both of which offer daily flights to and from Vancouver, Calgary, and Edmonton.

Greyhound, 2366 Leckie Rd., 250/860-3835 or 800/661-8747, provides bus service throughout the Okanagan and beyond. Local buses are run by **Kelowna Regional Transit System.** Get schedule and route information from the downtown terminal, Bernard Ave. at Ellis St., 250/860-8121.

For a taxi, call **Kelowna Cabs,** 250/762-4444, or **Checkmate Cabs,** 250/861-1111. Another taxi service is offered by **City View Water Taxi,** 250/860-6300, which makes pick-ups at points around the lake, such as the Hotel Eldorado, from where the fare to downtown is $25. A 30-minute lake tour is $45.

Rental car agencies include: **Avis,** 250/491-9500; **Budget,** 250/860-7825; **Hertz,** 250/765-3822; **National,** 250/762-0622; **Rent-a-wreck,** 250/763-6632; and **Thrifty,** 250/868-2151. All these agencies have vehicles out at the airport, but call in advance to ensure availability, especially in midsummer and during the ski season.

Sports Rent, 3000 Pandosy St., 250/861-5699, rents mountain bikes for $7–10 per hour and $21–30 per day.

Other Services

The **post office** is right downtown on Queensway Avenue. **Mosaic Books,** 411 Bernard Ave., 250/763-4418 or 800/663-1225, is an independent bookseller that has been serving the valley for over 30 years. As well as an excellent collection of western Canadian titles, it has a wide selection of magazines and an in-house coffee bar. It's open Monday 8 A.M.–6 P.M., Tues.–Fri. 8 A.M.–9 P.M., Saturday 9 A.M.–6 P.M., Sunday 11 A.M.–5 P.M. The eye-catching, semicircular building on Ellis St. is **Kelowna Library,** open Monday 10 A.M.–5:30 P.M., Tues.–Thurs. 10 A.M.–9 P.M., Fri.–Sat. 10 A.M.–5:30 P.M.

Kelowna General Hospital is on the corner of Strathcona Ave. and Pandosy St., 250/862-4000.

Information

Kelowna Visitor Info Centre is at 544 Harvey Ave. (Hwy. 97 N), 250/861-1515, website www.kelownachamber.org. It's open in summer daily 8 A.M.–7 P.M. (weekends from 9 P.M.), the rest of the year daily 9 A.M.–5 P.M. Coming into town from the south on Highway 97, continue up Harvey Avenue for five blocks, then turn left on Richter Street at the traffic lights and go back one block (free parking). A good map for immediate orientation is posted outside the center; it also incorporates a legend of motels and attractions. On the west side of Lake Okanagan is **Westbank Visitor Info Centre,** 2375 Pamela Rd., 250/768-3378.

Vernon and Vicinity

The city of Vernon (pop. 35,000) lies between Okanagan, Kalamalka, and Swan Lakes, at the north end of the Okanagan Valley 50 km from Kelowna. The city itself holds little of interest; the surrounding area boasts the main attractions. Among the area highlights: many sandy public beaches; local provincial parks; Silver Star Mountain Resort, a year-round recreation paradise east of the city (see below); and fishing in more than 100 lakes within an hour's drive of the city.

History

When gold was discovered at Cherry Creek (now Monashee Creek), east of Vernon, a small gold rush resulted. But some of the miners noticed the agricultural potential of the Vernon area and decided to plant instead of pan. Forbes George Vernon, after whom the town was named in 1887, was one of these early settlers. Another, Cornelius O'Keefe, was bound for gold in the Cariboo when he noticed the area's lush growth of bunchgrass—prime feed for cattle and horses—and decided to stay put and establish a ranch. Between the 1860s and 1870s, a number of large ranches sprang up. By 1890 over 4,000 head of cattle were mowing the bunchgrass on the rangelands around Vernon.

When construction began on the Shuswap and Okanagan Railroad connecting Vernon with the Canadian Pacific Railway mainline at Sicamous, Vernon began to grow. By 1891, the year the first passenger train puffed into town, Vernon had evolved from a sleepy little cattle community into a thriving town of 500 residents. That same year, Lord Aberdeen bought the Coldstream Ranch from Forbes George Vernon, subdivided it, and sold the parcels at affordable prices, thereby encouraging settlement. He also promoted the idea of growing

Cornelius O'Keefe was bound for gold in the Cariboo when he noticed the area's lush growth of bunchgrass—prime feed for cattle and horses—and decided to stay put and establish a ranch. By 1890 over 4,000 head of cattle were mowing the bunchgrass on the rangelands around Vernon.

trees in the area. Vernon became a city in 1892, which makes it the oldest city in the B.C. interior or fifth-oldest in the province.

SIGHTS AND RECREATION

In Town

Greater Vernon Museum and Archives, 3009 32nd Ave. (corner 31st St., behind the clock tower and fountain), 250/542-3142, holds photos from the early 1900s and a large collection of pioneer and native artifacts. Displays cover natural history, recreation, period clothing, and steamships. The museum is open in summer Mon.–Sat. 10 A.M.–5 P.M., the rest of the year Tues.–Sat. 10 A.M.–5 P.M. In the same vicinity is **Vernon Public Art Gallery,** 3228 31st Ave., 250/545-3173, featuring works by local artists as well as touring exhibitions. Open Mon.–Fri. 10 A.M.–5 P.M., Saturday noon–4 P.M.

Polson Park, off Hwy. 97 at 25th Ave., has a Chinese teahouse and Japanese garden, but most people go to stare at the spectacular floral clock—nine meters wide, made up of more than 3,500 plants, and the only one of its kind in western Canada.

Historic O'Keefe Ranch

Established in 1867, the O'Keefe Ranch, 13 km north of Vernon toward Kamloops on Hwy. 9, 250/542-7868, was one of the Okanagan's first cattle ranches. Today you can tour the opulent, fully furnished O'Keefe Mansion and other noteworthy outbuildings, including a furnished old log house that was the O'Keefes' original home; a working blacksmith's shop; the still-in-use St. Ann's Church, where services have been held since 1889; a fully stocked general store where you can buy postcards and old-fashioned candy; and

OKANAGAN VALLEY

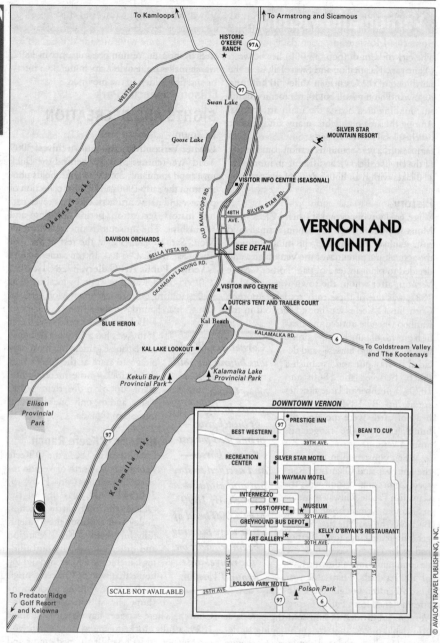

To Kamloops

To Armstrong and Sicamous

HISTORIC
O'KEEFE
RANCH

97A

97

Swan Lake

SILVER STAR
MOUNTAIN RESORT

Goose Lake

WESTSIDE

Okanagan Lake

VISITOR INFO CENTRE (SEASONAL)

48TH
AVE.

SILVER STAR RD.

OLD KAMLOOPS RD.

**VERNON AND
VICINITY**

DAVISON ORCHARDS

SEE DETAIL

BELLA VISTA RD.

OKANAGAN LANDING RD.

VISITOR INFO CENTRE

DUTCH'S TENT AND TRAILER COURT

BLUE HERON

Kal Beach

KALAMALKA RD.

6

To Coldstream Valley
and The Kootenays

KAL LAKE LOOKOUT

Kekuli Bay
Provincial Park

Kalamalka Lake
Provincial Park

Ellison
Provincial
Park

97

Kalamalka Lake

DOWNTOWN VERNON

97

BEST WESTERN

PRESTIGE INN

BEAN TO CUP

39TH AVE.

RECREATION
CENTER

SILVER STAR MOTEL

HI WAYMAN MOTEL

INTERMEZZO

POST OFFICE

MUSEUM

32ND AVE.

GREYHOUND BUS DEPOT

KELLY O'BRYAN'S RESTAURANT

ART GALLERY

30TH AVE

38TH ST.

21ST ST.

18TH ST.

POLSON PARK MOTEL

25TH AVE.

Polson Park

97

6

SCALE NOT AVAILABLE

To Predator Ridge
Golf Resort
and Kelowna

© AVALON TRAVEL PUBLISHING, INC.

the Chinese cook's bunkhouse. If you worked up an appetite in your explorations, visit the **Homestead Restaurant,** open daily for lunch and weekends for dinner.

The ranch is open mid-May to early October daily 9 A.M.–5 P.M., until 7 P.M. in July and August; admission adult $6.50, senior $5, child $4.50.

Davison Orchards

Dozens of farms surround Vernon, but one in particular, Davison Orchards, west of downtown off Bella Vista Rd., 250/549-3266, is worth a visit. Set on a sloping hill with views extending across Kalamalka Lake and up the Coldstream Valley, this family-operated business is a hive of tourist activity throughout the warmer months. A self-guided walk leads through a garden where everything from cucumbers to cantaloupe is grown, a wagon tour traverses the entire 20-hectare property (daily 6 P.M.), and there's a Critter Corral, a café with outside dining, an ice cream stand, and, of course, a fruit and vegetable market. It's open daily 8 A.M.–8 P.M.

Ellison Provincial Park

Follow Okanagan Landing Road (from 25th Avenue off Highway 97) west to access the northern reaches of Okanagan Lake and this 200-hectare lakefront park, 16 km from downtown. Most of the park is on a bench, with trails leading to and along the rocky shore. Ellison is best known by divers as B.C.'s first freshwater marine park. Enjoy shallow-water snorkeling and diving, weed beds full of life, underwater rock formations, a plastic bubble "Dive Dome," a deep-water wreck, and beach showers. Camping is $15.

Kal Beach is a wonderful spot to cool off on a summer's day.

© ANDREW HEMPSTEAD

Kalamalka Lake

If you've driven up to Vernon from Kelowna, this was the beautiful lake that Highway 97 paralleled for much of the way. It's known as a "marl" lake, because as summer warms the water, the limestone bedrock forms crystals that reflect the sunlight, creating a distinctive aquamarine color that is all the more stunning with surrounding parched hills as a backdrop. The continuously changing emerald and turquoise water and surrounding mountain panorama is best appreciated from **Kal Lake Lookout,** five km back toward Kelowna along Highway 97. Just south of the information center, a steep road winds down to the lakeshore and fine **Kal Beach,** fringed by trees. Parking is across the railway line from the beach (access is under the rail bridge) and costs $1 for the day. Also on the beach is a concession and, at the east end, a pub with a huge deck. Continue beyond the beach for eight km to **Kalamalka Lake Provincial Park.** This 978-hectare park has trails leading through the grassland to a sandy beach.

Golfing

South of Vernon off Highway 97 is 27-hole **Predator Ridge Golf Resort,** 250/542-3436 or 888/578-6688, one of Canada's best resort-style courses. Set on a high plateau, this links-style course takes advantage of natural hazards and undulates with the lay of the land. From the back markers, it plays 7,114 yards and to a par of 73, but is rated at 75.4, an indication of its challenging nature. Through the day rates are $95 for 18 holes, while the twilight rate is $40.

Festivals and Events

In early February, Vernon and nearby Silver Star spring to life to celebrate **Vernon Winter Carnival** with parades, sleigh rides, ice sculptures, hot air balloon rides, and the "Over the Hill Downhill" team ski race at Silver Star. Get all the event information and dates at the information center.

Two of the local attractions detailed above host events through the year. The highlights are an **Old Time Fair** at Historic O'Keefe Ranch in mid-July and the Apple Harvest Hoedown and Pumpkin Festival in mid-Sept. and mid-Oct., respectively, at Davison Orchards. Local rodeos are held at Falkland on the third weekend of August and in Armstrong on the weekend closest to 1 September.

ACCOMMODATIONS AND CAMPING

$50-100

Polson Park Motel, 3201 24th Ave., 250/549-2231 or 800/480-2231, is the least expensive of Vernon's 20-odd motels. Across from Polson Park, the three-story motel has an outdoor pool and rooms from $45 s, $55 d. Continuing north along Highway 97 (32nd Street) through the center of Vernon are more motels, including inexpensive **Silver Star Motel,** 3700 32nd St., 250/545-0501, which charges from $45 s, $50 d, $65 for a kitchenette. **Hi Wayman Motel,** 3500 32nd St., 250/545-2148 or 877/667-0599, is similarly priced.

$100-150

On the north side of downtown, **Best Western Vernon Lodge,** 3914 32nd St. 250/545-3385 or 800/663-4422, website www.rpbhotels.com, has spacious, stylishly decorated rooms overlooking an enclosed three-story tropical atrium. Other facilities include an indoor pool with a whirlpool, a café, a restaurant, and a pub; $109 s, $119 d. In the same vicinity, the **Prestige Inn,** 4411 32nd St., 250/558-5991, offers a high standard of rooms, each comfortable and stylishly furnished; from $139 s, $149 d in summer and under $100 the rest of the year.

Camping

Dutch's Tent and Trailer Court, three km south of downtown on Kalamalka Rd., 250/545-1023, is only 400 meters from Kal Beach and Kalamalka Lake. The park has hot showers, a laundromat, and a snack bar. Tent sites are $18, hookups $19–23.

Two provincial parks within a 15-minute drive of downtown provide campsites. Sixteen km southwest of town on Okanagan Landing Road is **Ellison Provincial Park,** on the east shore of Okanagan Lake ($15 per night), while south along Highway 97 toward Kelowna, **Kekuli Bay Provincial Park** sits right on Kalamalka Lake, but it's open to the elements ($18.50).

OTHER PRACTICALITIES

Food

The dining choices in Vernon have improved vastly in recent years, as has the coffee scene. The best coffee joint is **Bean to Cup,** in a converted residential house at 3903 27th St., 250/503-2222. It offers a wide range of hot drinks and light meals, best enjoyed on the heated patio; open daily 6 A.M.–midnight.

At **Kelly O'Bryan's Restaurant,** 2933 30th Ave., 250/549-2112, tuck in to burgers, steak, seafood, salads, and pasta; open daily 11 A.M.–midnight. **Intermezzo,** 3206 34th Ave., 250/542-3853, has a casual yet somewhat romantic setting and is a locals' favorite for its wide choice of pastas. Daily specials are the best value—usually around $15 for two courses. For more of a dinnertime splurge try the **Garden Grill** at the Best Western Vernon Lodge, 3914 32nd St., 250/545-3385. The dining room is set in a lush tropical garden with a stream flowing through the middle, and the menu features continental cuisine with nightly specials. Open daily, for lunch from 11 A.M. and dinner from 5 P.M.

The **Blue Heron** is a few km west of downtown, but well worth the drive. It sits right on Okanagan Lake, and a large deck right on the water is the most popular of the pub's three dining areas. The menu is fairly standard, with lots of dishes to share, but as it's off the tourist path, prices are reasonable. The Blue Heron is at 7673 Okanagan Landing Rd., 250/542-5550.

Services and Information

The **Greyhound** bus depot is on the corner of 30th St. and 31st Ave., 250/545-0527. For local bus information and schedules, contact **Vernon Regional Transit System,** 250/545-7221.

The **post office** is on the corner of 31st St. and 32nd Avenue. **Vernon Visitor Info Centre** is in a spruced up heritage house on Highway 97 at the south end of town, 250/542-3256 or

800/665-0795, website www.vernontourism.com; open daily 8:30 A.M.–6 P.M., till 6:30 P.M. in summer. If you're driving in from the north, make a stop at the seasonal Info Centre at 6326 Hwy. 97 N.

SILVER STAR MOUNTAIN RESORT

For summer or winter recreation, head up to Silver Star Mountain Resort, 22 km northeast of Vernon (take 48th Avenue off Highway 97). The views of Vernon as you climb the mountain are worth the fairly long, steep drive, and the resort at the top offers great skiing and snowboarding, a variety of summer recreation, and a colorful gold-rush-era-style, fully self-contained village. The resort can be contacted at 250/542-0224 or on the Internet at www.silverstarmtn.com; book accommodations and packages through central reservations, 800/663-4431.

Summer Activities

Silver Star offers the biggest range of summer recreation of any alpine resort in the interior. Starting at the end of June, a chairlift runs from the village to the top of Silver Star Mountain (1,915 meters) for terrific views of Vernon and surrounding lakes. Much of the alpine area around the summit is protected by 8,714-hectare **Silver Star Provincial Park;** pick up a hiking guide in the village. The summer lift operates until September daily 10 A.M.–4 P.M.; $8 per ride, or buy an all-day pass for $24. To learn more about the mountain's natural history, take the naturalist-led three-hour wildflower tour each Sunday at 1 P.M.; $18 per person, which includes a chairlift ride. Mountain-bike rentals are $10.50 for one hour, $17.50 for two hours, and $24.50 for four hours. If you want to spend the day riding the mountain trails on a bike, pay $42 for an all-day lift pass and the use of a bike. A Trail Pass is an additional $5. Also in summer you can go horseback riding on beautiful trails adjacent to the village. A one-hour ride is $27 per person, two hours $45, and an evening wiener roast is also $45. Within the village itself is disc golf, a climbing wall, and an aquatic center.

Skiing and Snowboarding

From November through April, skiers and boarders mob Silver Star, coming for great terrain and the facilities of an outstanding on-hill village. The two main faces—Vance Creek, good for beginners, and Putnam Creek, for intermediates and experts—are served by five chairlifts and a couple of T-bars. The resort's 80 runs cover 1,135 hectares with a vertical rise of 760 meters. Lift tickets are adult $46, senior $32, child $24; those over 70 and under six ski free. For snow reports call 250/542-1745. Through winter a shuttle bus operates between Kelowna Airport and the mountain; book through central reservations, 800/663-4431.

Silver Star Cross-country Centre features 35 km of groomed and set tracks, while beyond these are 50 km of backcountry trails. A day pass is $12 per person; rentals are available for an additional $15.

Accommodations

The base village contains numerous types of accommodations; book year-round through central reservations, 800/663-4431, or contact each accommodation directly. The rates quoted below are for summer, which is low season. Through winter, expect to pay double (except at the Samesun property).

Least expensive is **Samesun Silver Star,** 888/562-2783, website www.samesun.com, Canada's only ski-in, ski-out backpacker lodge. Facilities include a modern communal kitchen, plenty of table space for dining and 140 beds in dorms and private rooms. Dorm beds are $19.50, private rooms $49.50.

The **Kickwillie Inn,** 250/542-4548 or 800/551-7466, website www.pinnacles.com, is part of the adjacent and much larger Pinnacles Suite Hotel, but has the better value rooms; from $90 s or d with a kitchen. The **Lord Aberdeen Hotel,** 250/542-1992 or 800/553-5885, website www.lordaberdeen.com, also offers self-contained suites, and is similarly priced. The most luxurious on-mountain lodging is **Silver Star Club Resort,** 250/549-5191 or 800/610-0805, website www.silverstarclubresort.com, which offers standard hotel rooms and self-contained suites spread through three buildings. Guests enjoy use of all facilities at the nearby National Altitude Training Centre. Summer rates start at $85 s or d, rising to $125 for a suite.

The Kootenays

The wild and rugged Kootenays region of British Columbia lies east of the Okanagan Valley and south of the TransCanada Highway. It is bordered by the United States to the south and Alberta to the east. Three north-to-south-trending mountain ranges—the **Monashees, Selkirks, and Purcells**—run parallel to each other across the region, separated by lush green valleys and narrow lakes up to 150 km long. The snow-capped mountains and forested valleys abound with wildlife, including large populations of deer, elk, moose, black bear, and grizzly bear.

Europeans first entered the Kootenays in the late 1800s, searching for precious metals such as gold, silver, lead, and zinc, all of which were found in large quantities. While many of the boomtowns from this era have slipped into oblivion, others live on; **Sandon** is a ghost town, **Fort Steele** survives as a heritage theme park complete with costumed performers, and the grand old city of **Nelson** is today a heritage masterpiece, its streets lined with restored buildings.

At the southern end of the Monashee Mountains in the West Kootenays, delightful **Rossland** perches on the flanks of an extinct volcano and was once home to one of the world's richest gold mines. In the East Kootenays, highways follow the Rocky Mountain Trench north from the population center of **Cranbrook** to the Bavarian city of **Kimberley** and on to wilderness areas, hot springs, and the famous national parks of the Canadian Rockies.

© ANDREW HEMPSTEAD

Dutch Creek Hoodoos, just south of Fairmont Hot Springs

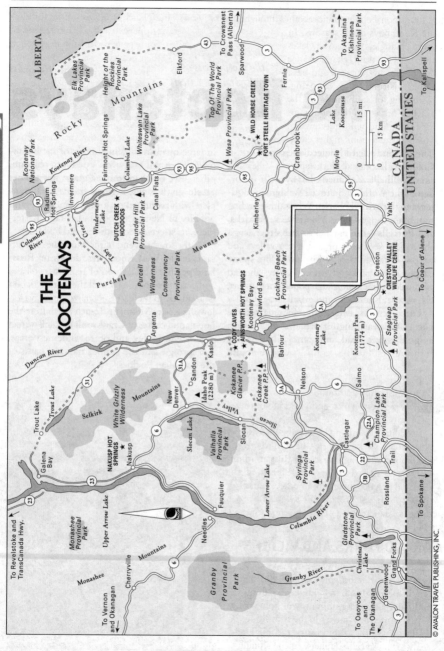

THE
KOOTENAYS

ALBERTA

Rocky

Mountains

Elk Lakes Provincial Park
Height of the Rockies Provincial Park
Whiteswan Lake Provincial Park
Top Of The World Provincial Park
Wasa Provincial Park

To Crowsnest Pass (Alberta)
To Akamina Kishinena Provincial Park
To Kalispell

Elkford
Sparwood
Fernie

WILD HORSE CREEK
FORT STEELE HERITAGE TOWN

Lake Koocanusa

Kootenay National Park
Kootenay River
Fairmont Hot Springs
Columbia Lake
Thunder Hill Provincial Park
DUTCH CREEK HOODOOS

Radium Hot Springs
Invermere
Windermere Creek
Windermere Lake

Canal Flats

Cranbrook

Columbia River

Purcell

Purcell Wilderness Conservancy Provincial Park

Mountains

Kimberley

Moyie

Yahk

CANADA
UNITED STATES

Duncan River

Argenta

Kaslo

CODY CAVES
AINSWORTH HOT SPRINGS
Crawford Bay
Kootenay Bay

Lockhart Beach Provincial Park

Galena Bay

Trout Lake

Selkirk

White Grizzly Wilderness

Mountains

Sandon
New Denver
Idaho Peak (2280 m)

NAKUSP HOT SPRINGS
Nakusp

Slocan Lake

Valhalla Provincial Park

Slocan

Balfour

Kokanee Glacier P.P.
Kokanee Creek P.P.

Nelson

Kootenay Lake

Kootenay Pass (1774 m)

Stagleap Provincial Park

CRESTON VALLEY WILDLIFE CENTRE

Creston

To Coeur d'Alene

To Revelstoke and TransCanada Hwy.

Monashee Provincial Park

Upper Arrow Lake

Fauquier

Needles

Cherryville

Monashee

Mountains

To Vernon and Okanagan

Lower Arrow Lake

Syringa Provincial Park

Castlegar

Champion Lake Provincial Park

Salmo

Trail

Rossland

Columbia River

Gladstone Provincial Park

Granby Provincial Park

Granby River

Christina Lake

Greenwood
Grand Forks

To Osoyoos and The Okanagan

To Spokane

15 mi
15 km

© AVALON TRAVEL PUBLISHING, INC.

Recreational opportunities abound throughout the Kootenays in all seasons. In summer, anglers flock to the lakes and rivers for trout, char, kokanee salmon, freshwater cod, and bass. Other visitors enjoy canoeing, swimming, or sunbathing on the beaches, or take to the mountains for hiking and wildlife-viewing. Much of the region's higher elevations are protected in rugged and remote parks, including the spectacular **Valhalla, Kokanee Glacier, Top of the World,** and **Purcell Wilderness Conservancy Provincial Parks.** While these natural

> *In colder months the mountains of the Kootenays catch a phenomenal amount of snow, turning the whole region into a winter wonderland.*

preserves offer plenty of opportunities for day-trippers, it takes extended back-country trips to fully experience their beauty.

In colder months the mountains of the Kootenays catch a phenomenal amount of snow, turning the whole region into a winter wonderland. You won't find any major resorts here; however, three small but legendary ski areas—**Red Mountain, Whitewater,** and **Fernie**—attract adventurous powderhounds with some of North America's highest snowfalls and steepest lift-served slopes.

West Kootenays

Clustered on the edge of the Monashee Range in the western Kootenays are several communities that seem a world away from the hustle and the bustle of the nearby Okanagan Valley. Grand Forks, Rossland, Trail, and Castlegar all boomed at the turn of the 20th century, when thousands of gold-hungry prospectors descended on the slopes of Red Mountain. Today Red Mountain draws more powderhounds than prospectors, and lakes, rivers, parks, and peaks are the area's main attractions.

In addition to mining history, the West Kootenays are also known as the home of the Doukhobors, a religious sect of Russian immigrants who arrived in the early 1900s to till the land and practice their faith in peace. Aspects of their unique culture and lifestyle can be seen today in Grand Forks and elsewhere in the region.

GRAND FORKS AND VICINITY

Perched above the confluence of the Granby and Kettle Rivers, Grand Forks (pop. 4,200) started out as a Hudson's Bay Company trading post and later became a mining town, home to the largest nonferrous smelter in the British Empire. At the turn of the 20th century, the rough-and-ready town was full of miners, ranchers, and land

speculators. But then a very different group arrived in the valley.

The Doukhobors, a religious sect practicing pacifism and vegetarianism, fled persecution in their Russian homeland and set up communes in British Columbia in the early 1900s. They kept a low profile—farming, making everything they needed, and operating many successful communal enterprises. The sect added a contrasting element to the area's social mix until Doukhobor leader Peter Verigin died in 1924. After his death, the sect's way of life deteriorated, and the communes dispersed. Today many Doukhobor descendants live in Grand Forks. Although they no longer live in communal villages, they still follow their beliefs and speak Russian, which is taught in local schools. To find out more about the intriguing Doukhobor lifestyle, visit **Mountain View Doukhobor Museum,** a 1912 Doukhobor communal farmhouse on Hardy Mountain Rd., 250/442-8855, or **Doukhobor Heritage Centre,** 6110 Reservoir Rd., 250/442-3523, with similar displays.

Grand Forks also features a mix of historic turn-of-the-century homes and restored civic buildings. Downtown's **Boundary Museum,** 7370 5th St., 250/442-3737, displays mining artifacts, historic photos, and pioneer memorabilia. It's open June–Oct. daily 10:30 A.M.–4:30 P.M.

Grand Forks is the gateway to remote **Granby Provincial Park.** This 40,845-hectare park protects the upper reaches of the Granby River along with an old-growth forest of red cedar. The park is well off the beaten path, and access is recommended only in a four-wheel-drive vehicle. To get there, head north out of Grand Forks; take the left fork 40 km from town, then another left fork at the 59-km mark and again at the 60-km mark. The road ends at the park boundary, a further five km to the north. Get more information from the Forest Service office in Grand Forks, 250/442-5411.

In a pleasant setting on the west edge of town, **Pinegrove Motel,** 209 Central Ave., 250/442-8203, offers rooms from $80 s, $90 d (with a huge discount for travelers aged 50 or older). Campers gravitate to the riverside **municipal campground,** at the end of 5th Street. Showers and hookups are offered; $12–18 per night. Adjacent to the museum on 5th St. is **Grand Forks Visitor Info Centre,** 7362 5th St., 250/442-2833, website www.boundary.bc.ca; open year-round Mon.–Fri. 9:30 A.M.–4:30 P.M.

Christina Lake

This 19-km-long lake, 25 km east of Grand Forks along Highway 3, is a summer mecca for folks from throughout the West Kootenays, who come for the lake's warm waters and fishing for rainbow trout, bass, and kokanee. On the western edge of town is **Christina Lake Golf Club,** a pleasant 18-hole layout; greens fees are $38, or play after 4 P.M. for $28.

All commercialism is confined to the lake's southern end. The best-value motel is the **New Horizon Motel,** along the highway at the eastern edge of town, 250/447-9312 or 888/859-0159; rooms are spacious and comfortable, and although the summer rate is $76 s, $86 d, at any other time of the year rooms are under $60. The best of many commercial campgrounds at Christina Lake is **Cascade Cove RV Park,** 1290 River Rd., 250/447-6662, which offers tent sites for $15 and serviced sites for $18–21. To the north, at the opposite end of the lake, **Texas Creek Campground** is within 39,322-hectare **Gladstone Provincial Park,** with 49 unserviced sites for $12.

ROSSLAND

Clinging to the slopes of an extinct volcanic crater deep in the tree-covered Monashee Mountains, Rossland (pop. 4,500) was once a gold-rush boomtown known as "The Golden City." The precious yellow metal was discovered on 1,580-meter Red Mountain by Joe Moris in 1890. Moris, like thousands of other prospectors unaware of the nearby wealth, had been traveling eastward on the Dewdney Trail to goldfields farther away. He nevertheless staked five claims on Red Mountain, the richest of which, Le Roi, later sold for $3 million. When word got out, thousands of diggers rushed in, and the township of Rossland was born. The town's population peaked at 7,000 in 1897. At that time, the city boasted four newspapers, 40 saloons, and daily rail service south to Spokane. By 1929, the mountain had yielded six million tons of ore worth $165 million. Today, tourism supplies the bulk of Rossland's gold; the town serves as a mecca for mountain-bike enthusiasts and adventurous skiers and boarders.

Sights

Downtown Rossland is a picturesque place full of historic buildings and old-fashioned street lamps. Pick up a *How to find your way around the twisting, hilly, scenic, tree-lined, and sometimes confusing (because it's situated on the side of a mountain—which is really what makes this place so great) streets and trails of Rossland* pamphlet from the museum, library, or downtown shops, and hit the streets.

Fire razed Rossland three times during its heyday, so it's ironic that the city is home to the **B.C. Firefighters Museum,** Queen St. and 1st Avenue. Housed in the 1900 fire hall, the museum is open weekdays 10 A.M.–4 P.M.

One km west of downtown, **Rossland Museum,** Hwy. 3B and Columbia Ave., 250/362-7722, stands at the entrance to the famous Le

OLAUS JELDNESS

In the late 1890s, after the first frantic summer of gold mining on Red Mountain, a group of prospectors put on a winter carnival, including a ski race down the slopes of Red Mountain. The organizer was Olaus Jeldness, a legendary Norwegian who had prospected all over the western United States before moving north of the border. Jeldness admitted that the mountain was "far too steep and the snow conditions too extreme" for a proper race. But it went ahead nevertheless. First the competitors hiked all the way to the summit. Then Jeldness gave the signal to go before strapping on his own skis and schussing off after the rest of the field. Despite their head start, Jeldness easily passed the other racers to become Canada's first national champion. His wooden skis and trophies are housed in the Western Canada Ski Hall of Fame in the Rossland Museum.

Jeldness was the first of many heroes to have skied the legendary slopes of "Red"—the mountain has been a breeding ground for more members of the Canadian National Ski Team than any other resort, not bad considering the adjacent town has just 4,500 residents.

Roi mine and offers exhibits on the area's lustrous geological and human history. The museum also holds the Western Canada Ski Hall of Fame, which honors such luminaries as Olaus Jeldness—instigator of the local ski craze— and champion skier Nancy Greene, a local heroine who won a gold medal in the 1968 Olympics. The museum is open summers daily 9 A.M.–5 P.M. Admission is adult $4, senior $3, child $1.50.

To experience the day-to-day life of the early hardrock miners, tour **Le Roi Gold Mine,** next to the museum complex. Outside the mine sit a gigantic compressor, a simulated mine shaft, and large pieces of mining machinery. The gold mine itself, just up the path, provides an introductory course in local geology with its displays of mineral veins, dikes, faults, and old and new mining equipment. The 45-minute tour includes detailed explanations of how ore is mined, trammed, drilled, and blasted, and tells

you how to differentiate igneous, metamorphic, and sedimentary rocks. Museum admission is included in the tour cost of adult $9, senior $6, child $3.50.

Mountain Biking

Each spring, Rossland comes alive with pedal power as mountain-bike enthusiasts take advantage of the maze of old logging and mining trails surrounding the city. Now known as the "Mountain Bike Capital of Canada," Rossland has hosted both the Canadian and North American championships. Rent bikes from **The Powderhound,** 2040 Columbia Ave., 250/362-5311.

Red Mountain

The site of what was once one of the world's richest gold mines is now part of an alpine resort offering some of North America's most challenging lift-served runs. Facilities on the mountain have certainly improved since the days of Olaus Jeldness, but Red Mountain is no megaresort. Nevertheless, the skiing and boarding are still world-class. While two mountains provide opportunities for all ability levels, the resort holds most appeal for experts. The heart-stopping face of Red Mountain is the star of the show. But adjacent Granite Mountain offers a vertical rise of 880 meters and almost unlimited intermediate, expert, and extreme skiing and boarding, mostly on unmarked trails through powder-filled glades. Lift tickets are adult $42, senior $27, child under 12 $22, and those six and under ski for free. For resort information call 250/362-7700; for local accommodation reservations call 800/663-0105; website www.ski-red.com.

Across the road from the resort, **Blackjack** nordic area offers 50 km of groomed tracks. Cross-country skiers can also explore the many old logging roads in the area.

Ram's Head Inn

One of Canada's premier small lodges lies in the woods at the base of Red Mountain. Primarily designed for wintertime, the Ram's Head Inn offers 14 guest rooms—each with private bath—a dining area, game room, sauna, outdoor hot tub, and a spacious communal lounge with luxurious chairs and a large fireplace. In winter (book well ahead), two-night packages go for $220–264 per person and seven-night packages are $700–826, including luxurious accommodations, breakfasts, and lift passes. In summer, the lodge charges a reasonable $66 s, $ 76 d, with breakfast extra. For reservations call 250/362-9577 or 877/267-4323, website www.ramshead.bc.ca.

Other Accommodations

Also up at the resort is the **Red Shutter Inn,** 250/362-5131, a cozy little bed and breakfast with shared bathrooms, a lounge area, and hot tub; summer rates are $45 s, $55 d. Winter rates are double. Backpackers are catered to at **Mountain Shadow Hostel,** upstairs, right downtown at 2125 Columbia Ave., 250/362-7160 or 888/393-7160; $17–20 per person per night. The premier downtown accommodation is the **Uplander Hotel,** 1919 Columbia Ave., 250/362-7375 or 800/667-8741, website www.uplanderhotel.com, with a restaurant and lounge; summer rates are $79–99 s or d.

Food

Each morning, locals converge on the **Sunshine Cafe,** 2116 Columbia Ave., 250/362-5070, for hearty cooked breakfasts from $6. The rest of the day, the café offers a diverse menu including Mexican and Indian dishes. **Goldrush Books and Espresso,** 2063 Washington St., 250/362-5333, sets a few tables around bookshelves full of local and Canadian literature. Another good coffeehouse is **Alpine Grind,** 2207 Columbia Ave., 250/362-2280. For more substantial fare, head up the hill to **Mountain Gypsy Cafe,** 2167 Washington St., 250/362-3342, a funky little restaurant decorated with local artwork and open for lunch and dinner daily.

On the ski hill access road, the **Rock Cut Neighbourhood Pub,** 250/362-5814, is busiest in winter, but opens year-round. It offers typical pub fare, smartly presented and well priced. Enjoy the mountain surroundings by eating on the heated deck.

Information

Rossland Visitor Info Centre is out of town in the museum complex south of downtown at the corner of Hwy. 3B and Columbia Ave., 250/362-7722 or 888/448-7444. It's open in summer only daily 9 A.M.–5 P.M.

TRAIL AND VICINITY

Sprawling along both sides of the mighty Columbia River, Trail (pop. 8,000) lies 10 km and 600 vertical meters below Rossland. It's probable that neither your first nor your subsequent impression of Trail will be positive. The world's largest lead and zinc smelter dominates the downtown area, its 120-meter-high smokestacks belching thick plumes of smoke into the atmosphere 24 hours a day. The smelter is the foundation of Consolidated Mining and Smelting Co. (Cominco), one of the world's largest mining companies, and poor Trail is often described as "Cominco with a town built around it." Head to the **Cominco Interpretive Centre,** downtown at 1199 Bay Ave., to learn about the smelting process. Free tours of the **Cominco complex** show you the area where ores are melted and separated and tell you about the byproducts, such as fertilizers, converted from the wastes. The tours depart from the interpretive center, but to book a tour call the information center at 250/368-3144.

Trail Visitor Info Centre, downtown at 1199 Bay Ave., 250/368-3144 or 877/636-9569, is open 9 A.M.–5 P.M. daily in summer, weekdays only the rest of the year.

Champion Lakes Provincial Park

Escape the smokestacks in this 1,426-hectare park, 23 km east along Highway 3B toward Nelson, then a few km farther along the access road. The park encompasses a chain of three small lakes nestled in the Bonnington Range. Hiking trails connect the lakes; First Lake, accessed from a trail at road's end, is the least busy. Camping is $15.

Salmo toward Creston

East of Trail on Highway 3, the small village of Salmo (pop. 1,100) features old-fashioned wooden buildings, a small museum (open in summer daily 1–5 P.M.), and streets decorated in summer with huge hanging flower baskets bursting with brilliant color. The promise of quick fortune brought prospectors to gold diggings in the Salmo River watershed through the 1860s, but as in so many other boomtowns in the Kootenays, the riches were short-lived. Those who stayed in the area turned to logging cedar and pine from the surrounding Selkirk Mountains as a source of income.

About 35 km east of Salmo, at 1,133-hectare **Stagleap Provincial Park,** travelers can pause to picnic by Bridal Lake or go for a short hike.

Continuing east from there, you'll crest 1,774-meter **Kootenay Pass** (the highest paved highway pass in the country) and drop down the other side into Creston (see Kootenay Lake and Creston, below).

CASTLEGAR

Though endowed with the rich history of the Doukhobors, Castlegar (pop. 7,400) is not a particularly attractive place. Spread out along the barren Columbia River Valley, it's a real cross-

roads town. Here the Kootenay River drains into the much larger Columbia River, Highway 3 passes through east to west, Highway 3A leads north to Nelson, and Highway 22 leads south to Rossland and Trail. The town is also the major air gateway for the Kootenays.

The area's first nonnative residents, the Doukhobors, arrived in 1908. These pacifist Russian immigrants planted orchards, built sawmills, and even operated a jam factory while living in segregated villages along the valley floor. Many of their descendants still live in the area. Today, mining, transportation, and hydroelectric-power production sustain the local economy.

Doukhobor Sights

Castlegar's major attraction is the **Doukhobor Village Museum,** on the east side of the river along Hwy. 3A, 250/365-6622. The village allows a glimpse of the traditional lifestyle of these intriguing Russian immigrants. The $4 admission includes a guided tour, led by Doukhobor descendants, through the main building and the

THE KOOTENAYS

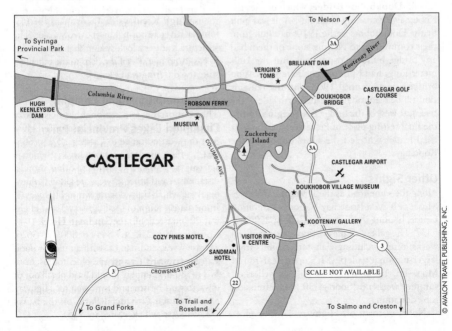

© AVALON TRAVEL PUBLISHING, INC.

simply furnished brick dwellings and outbuildings. Along the way you'll see some of the sect's artifacts, including handwoven clothing, crocheted bedspreads and shawls, a barn full of antique farming implements, and carved wooden spoons and ladles. Also featured is a historic photo collection of the original Doukhobor settlements in Saskatchewan and British Columbia. The museum is open daily 9 A.M.–6 P.M.

Zuckerberg Island, at the confluence of the Kootenay and Columbia Rivers, was the home of Russian immigrant Alexander Zuckerberg, who came to Castlegar to teach Doukhobor children in 1931. Connected to the mainland by a 150-meter suspension bridge, the tree-covered two-hectare island is interesting to explore. A one-km trail passes a full-scale model of a *ckukuli* (native winter pit house), as well as a Hiroshima memorial, Russian orthodox chapel house, cemetery, log house, and many other Zuckerberg creations. To get there, turn off Highway 22 at 9th Street, turn left on 7th Avenue, then immediately right.

While you're in a Russian frame of mind, visit the old **Doukhobor Bridge,** which crosses the Kootenay River along Highway 3A. It was built by the Doukhobors in the 1910s as a link from their community to Nelson; none of them had any bridge-building experience, but the 100-meter-long, hand-poured concrete suspension bridge was used until 1968, and the remains can still be seen today. On the north side of the river just west of the bridge lies **Verigin's Tomb,** the final resting place of Peter Verigin, the spiritual leader who led the Doukhobors to the Kootenays.

Other Sights

Along the same road as the Doukhobor Village Museum is West Kootenay National Exhibition Centre, housing the **Kootenay Gallery,** 250/365-3337. The gallery displays a good variety of artworks, often including elaborate exhibits from larger national galleries. It's open year-round Mon.–Fri. 10:30 A.M.–4:30 P.M., as well as on summer weekends noon–4:30 P.M. Admission is by donation.

North of town off Highway 3A, the enor-

suspension bridge to historic
Zuckerberg Island

mous **Hugh Keenleyside Dam** spans the Columbia River to form Lower Arrow Lake. The structure features a lock system that allows boats to pass from one side of the dam to the other, despite the differing water levels.

Accommodations and Camping

The comfortable and reasonably priced **Cozy Pines Motel,** 2100 Crestview Crescent (on Hwy. 3 at the west entrance to Castlegar), 250/365-5613, offers spotless rooms with kitchenettes starting at $50 s, $55 d. Most other motels, restaurants, and other services are along Columbia Ave., which links downtown to Highway 3. Immediately south of the Highway 3 and Highway 22 intersection is the **Sandman Hotel,** 1944 Columbia Ave., 250/365-8444 or 800/726-3626, website www.sandman.ca, with an indoor pool, a 24-hour restaurant, and 132 older rooms; from $72 s, $80 d. Campers should head north out of town toward Nelson and turn west off Highway 3A to **Syringa Provincial Park,** on the banks of Lower Arrow Lake. Sites are $15.

Services and Information

Castlegar Airport, along Hwy. 3A, is the Kootenays' air transportation hub. It's served by **Air B.C.,** 888/247-2262, and **Canadian Regional,** 800/665-1177. **Budget** has a rental desk out at the airport, 250/365-5733.

Castlegar Visitor Info Centre is off Columbia Ave. at 1995 6th Ave., 250/365-6313. It's open daily 8 A.M.–7 P.M. in summer, Mon.–Fri. 9 A.M.–5 P.M. the rest of the year.

THE SLOCAN VALLEY

The historically rich Slocan Valley, or "Silvery Slocan," nestles snugly between the Slocan and Valhalla Ranges of the Selkirk Mountains. In the 1890s the valley sprang into the limelight when silver was discovered at Sandon. It's much quieter today, offering many pic-turesque towns and an abundance of outdoor-recreation opportunities.

New Denver

Western gateway to "Silver Country," this picturesque town of 600 is on Slocan Lake, opposite Valhalla Provincial Park. Originally called Eldorado and renamed after Denver, Colorado, the town reached its mining peak in the 1890s.

Today the main street is lined with funky false-front stores and pioneer-style buildings left over from the prosperous silver days. Visit the **Silvery Slocan Museum** to find out all about New Denver's heyday. It's on the corner of 6th St. and Bellevue Dr., 250/358-2201; open July to early September.

Down on the lake within easy walking distance of the main street, **Sweet Dreams Guesthouse,**

THE KOOTENAYS

© ANDREW HEMPSTEAD

Heritage buildings line the streets of New Denver.

702 Eldorado St., 250/358-2415, website www.newdenverbc.com, offers large rooms and a cooked breakfast for $45 s, $70–85 d. Out of New Denver to the south, **Silverton Resort,** 250/358-7157, website www.silvertonresort.com, lies right on the edge of Slocan Lake. The log cottages line the waterfront, with the Loft Cottage literally on the water. Rates range $90–140 s or d. Campers can head to a **municipal campground** with full hookups on the south side of the town ($13–16), or to **Rosebery Provincial Park,** on Wilson Creek six km north of town ($12).

New Denver Visitor Info Centre is off the main street at 101 Eldorado St., 250/358-2719; open July–Aug. daily 9 A.M.–5 P.M.

Valhalla Provincial Park

This 49,893-hectare park preserves the high peaks, deep valleys, and magnificent alpine lakes between the Valhalla Range of the Selkirk Mountains on the west and the west shores of Slocan Lake on the east. The most imposing peaks are in the south of the park, where spectacular spires rise above alpine meadows to a height of 2,800 meters.

Roads come to an abrupt end at the north and south ends of the park, so the most popular access is by boat from New Denver or Slocan, across the lake. An eight-km lakeshore trail also connects Slocan with the west shore. There, hiking trails lead into the heart of the park. The most rewarding and popular is the **Beatrice Lake Trail,** 12.5 km each way. Like all trails starting from the lake, elevation gain is steady; you'll climb just under 1,000 vertical meters as you pass Little Cahill and Cahill Lakes and enter the massive cirque in which Beatrice Lake lies. From the backcountry campground at the lake, a vast wilderness is yours to explore. Another trail, one of the park's steepest, begins across Slocan Lake from New Denver and climbs **Sharp Creek.** Elevation gain is 1,400 meters, most of it made in the final push to a point overlooking **New Denver Glacier.**

The best source of trail and transportation information is **Valhalla Wilderness Society,** 307 6th Ave., New Denver, 250/358-2333, a group of local environmentalists who were instrumental in the establishment of the park and who have gone

VALHALLA WILDERNESS SOCIETY

Originally founded to lobby for the establishment of Valhalla Provincial Park, the Valhalla Wilderness Society has more recently been instrumental in convincing the B.C. government to designate the Khutzeymateen Valley, north of Prince Rupert, as Canada's first grizzly bear sanctuary. Closer to home, the small organization also successfully campaigned for the creation of the White Grizzly Wilderness. Its latest crusade is for the protection for the habitat of the Kermode bear in the north of the province; log onto website www.savespiritbear.org for details.

The society's headquarters, in New Denver at 307 6th St. (under the Valhalla Trading Post sign), holds a small retail outlet selling books, posters, calendars, and shirts. For more information on the society contact the Valhalla Wilderness Society, P.O. Box 329, New Denver, BC V0G 1S0, 250/358-2333.

on to crusade for further parks throughout the province. At the society's office you can pick up a copy of the detailed *Trail Guide to Valhalla Provincial Park.*

Sandon

The original Slocan Valley boomtown, Sandon once was a thriving town of 5,000 people. After the discovery of silver on the slopes of Idaho Peak, Sandon grew quickly and at one time boasted 24 hotels, 23 saloons, banks, general stores, mining brokers' offices, and a newspaper. Its main link to the outside world was the Kaslo & Slocan Railway, built in 1895 to connect Sandon with sternwheeler transportation on Kootenay Lake.

Sandon was destroyed by fire in 1902, but quickly rebuilt and incorporated as a city in 1908. The Great Depression of 1929 put an end to the heyday, but the town remained the "soul of the Silvery Slocan" until the spring of 1955. That year the creek running through town flooded, sweeping away most of the city and leaving a ghost town. Today you can count the population on two hands.

The best place to start a visit to Sandon is the 1900 city hall, where the *Sandon Walking Tour Guide* is sold ($1). The brochure details all the original structures—only a fraction of which remain—with a map that makes exploring on foot more enjoyable. Up the creek from city hall are **Sandon Museum,** where exhibits bring the old town back to life, and **Silversmith Mine Powerhouse,** which still supplies power to the few remaining residents and retains its title as western Canada's oldest operating hydroelectric plant. Also on this side of the creek is the road to 2,280-meter **Idaho Peak.** The road is very rough, passable only in July and August. From the end of the 12-km road, a steep one-km trail leads to the summit and spectacular 360-degree views of the Kootenays.

Along the north side of Carpenter Creek, buildings in various states of disrepair line a road leading to the mining area of Cody. On the same side of the creek, the **K&S Historic Trail** follows the route taken by the old wood-burning engines of the Kaslo & Slocan Railway as they carried rich silver ore from Sandon to Kaslo. The railway was destroyed by fire in 1910. The hiking trail, 5.6 km each way, passes several mining sites and provides fabulous views of the **New Denver Glacier,** across Slocan Lake in Valhalla Provincial Park.

The only services in Sandon are a souvenir shop in the old city hall and the **Tin Cup Cafe,** which was built as a private home in 1895 and is now open for coffee and light snacks. It's on the north side of Carpenter Creek at the far end of town.

NAKUSP

Forty-eight km northwest of New Denver, Nakusp (pop. 1,800) was established during the mining-boom years. Today the small town is best known for its hot springs and its stunning location on Upper Arrow Lake at the foot of the Selkirk Mountains.

Nakusp Museum, on 6th Ave., features an odd but intriguing collection of items, including pre-dam photos of the towns now flooded beneath the Arrow Lakes. It's open July and August only daily 9 A.M.–5 P.M.; admission $1.

Favorite summer activities include mountain biking along surrounding logging roads, fishing and swimming in Upper Arrow Lake, and golfing at **Nakusp Golf Course,** 250/265-4531.

Nakusp Hot Springs

To get to these hot springs take Highway 23 north out of town for one km, then follow the sign-posted road along Kuskanax Creek for 12 km. Admission is adult $6, senior and child $5. The pools are open in summer daily 9:30 A.M.–10 P.M., the rest of the year daily 10 A.M.–9:30 P.M. For information call 250/265-4528.

To see the source of the springs, take the sandy 500-meter trail that starts behind the pools. You'll cross the river and clamber through damp rainforest crammed with ferns and mosses, then come to an impressive waterfall where you can smell the sulfur from the springs.

Practicalities

Kuskanax Lodge, 515 Broadway, 250/265-3618 or 800/663-0100, has 48 bright and breezily decorated rooms; $89 s or d. **Nakusp Village Campground,** on 8th St., 250/265-4019, has large shaded sites, coin-operated showers, and firewood within walking distance of the beach and the main street; unserviced sites $15, powered sites $18. Campers can also head 10 km south of town to **McDonald Creek Provincial Park,** which has fewer facilities but a better location; $12.

Accommodations are also offered up at the hot springs, but it can get busy during summer. The campground, 250/265-4528, features a grassy tent area and wooded vehicle campsites beside Kuskanax Creek; sites, some with hookups, are $15–18. At **Nakusp Hot Springs Cedar Chalets,** 250/265-4505, each of the units has a kitchen and private bathroom. Most are $75 s or d, but the smallest, tucked behind the rest, costs just $50.

Another nearby resort, this one with its own private hot springs, is **Halcyon Hot Springs Resort,** 32 km north of Nakusp, 250/265-3554 or 888/689-4699, website www.halcyon-hotsprings .com. Accommodations are in cabins ($70 s or d) and luxurious lakeside chalets ($145–205), or you can camp ($24.50 per site).

The place to be seen in Nakusp is the **Broadway Deli Bistro,** 408 Broadway St. W, 250/265-3767, where you'll find great coffee and a constant stream of muffins coming out of the oven. Sit by the door to catch all the gossip as the locals wander in. It's open daily at 7 A.M. **Manor Restaurant,** 311 Broadway, 250/265-4433, serves Canadian and Chinese food ($5–10). Open daily 7:30 A.M.–9 P.M.

Nakusp Visitor Info Centre occupies the small building with the big yellow paddlewheel at 92 6th Ave., 250/265-4234 or 800/909-8819. It's open in summer daily 8 A.M.–4 P.M., the rest of the year on weekdays only.

WEST TO THE OKANAGAN

From Nakusp, Highway 6 follows Lower Arrow Lake south to Fauquier, where it jumps the lake (you'll take the free ferry) and continues northwest to Vernon, a total distance of 195 km.

Fauquier consists of a gas station, golf course, and **Arrow Lake Motel,** 250/269-7622 or 888/499-5222, featuring lake views and small but comfortable rooms for $45 s, $55 d. The ferry across Lower Arrow Lake operates every 30 minutes 5 A.M.–10 P.M., crossing the lake to **Needles,** a ferry landing and nothing more.

Cherryville and Vicinity

From Needles, Highway 6 ascends steeply to the high peaks of the Monashee Mountains and the village of Cherryville. Along the main street, the **Monashee Woolen Mill,** 250/547-6040, opened in 1998 as a mill complex using antique machinery and old-time techniques. Materials come from locally raised sheep, as well as alpacas and musk oxen. The owners give tours, and you can try your hand at spinning. A small on-site store sells everything from raw materials to a variety of finished products. It's open Mon.–Fri. 8:30 A.M.–3 P.M. Cherryville is also the jumping-off point for remote 7,513-hectare **Monashee Provincial Park.** Access is north along 46-km Sugar Lake Rd. then on foot along a rough 12-km trail.

From Cherryville, Highway 6 descends to the **Coldstream Valley,** where you'll see field crops, orchards, and low, rolling hills; paddocks where horses frolic in fluorescent-green grass; rustic old barns in various degrees of disrepair; and well-loved old homes. At **Lumby** a road leads 37 km northeast to **Mabel Lake Provincial Park,** with a tree-shaded picnic area and camping for $12 per night.

For information on Vernon, see the Okanagan Valley chapter.

Nelson

The elegant city of Nelson (pop. 9,700) lies in a picturesque setting on the West Arm of Kootenay Lake, 660 km east of Vancouver. Its relaxed pace, hilly tree-lined streets, and turn-of-the-century architectural treasures have helped attract an eclectic mix of jaded big-city types, artists, and counterculture seekers. But while the city itself is uniquely charming, the surrounding wilderness of the Selkirk Mountains is Nelson's biggest draw. The area's many lakes provide excellent fishing, sailing, and canoeing, as well as some of British Columbia's best inland beaches. Trails suitable for hikers of all fitness levels lace Kokanee Glac-ier Provincial Park's alpine reaches. Old logging and mining trails attract happy hordes of mountain-bikers. And nearby hot springs provide a welcome relief at the end of a hard day's play. In addition, when the snow starts flying, powder-hounds flock to Whitewater Ski & Winter Resort for some of North America's best lift-served powder skiing and boarding.

History

After the discovery of copper and silver deposits on Toad Mountain in 1886, Nelson sprang up as a small mining camp along the banks of Ward

THE KOOTENAYS

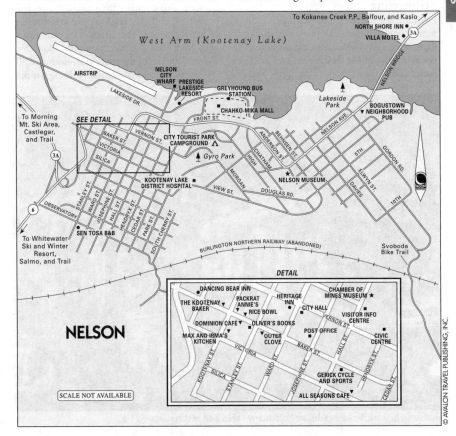

NELSON

SCALE NOT AVAILABLE

© AVALON TRAVEL PUBLISHING, INC.

Creek. The early mines proved profitable and the town expanded rapidly. Construction of a smelter began at the end of 1895, and wagon roads, railroads, and steamboat routes were developed to serve the local mining boom. Soon Nelson became the commercial and cultural center of the Kootenays, at its peak boasting 23 hotels and six saloons. Although mining operations waned by the turn of the century, silver had left a grand impact on Nelson. It was the first city in the province to operate an electric power plant (on Cottonwood Creek), and the smallest city in the country to have a streetcar system.

SIGHTS
Architecture

Nelson has 350 designated heritage buildings, more per capita than any other city in British Columbia, save Victoria. Most can viewed by walking around the downtown core between Baker and Vernon Streets. Pick up the detailed

Heritage Walking Tour or *Heritage Motoring Tour* brochures from the information center. The walking-tour brochure details 26 downtown buildings, including the 1909 courthouse on Ward Street and the impressive stone-and-brick 1902 city hall on the corner of Ward and Vernon Streets.

Museums

Nelson's two museums are both worth visiting. **Nelson Museum,** 402 Anderson St., 250/352-9813, concentrates on local history, with displays covering native peoples, explorers, miners, traders, early transportation, Nelson's contribution to World War I, and the Doukhobors (a Russian religious sect that settled in the Kootenays). It also contains the *Ladybird,* a record-breaking speedboat designed prior to the advent of hydroplanes in the 1950s. The museum is open Mon.–Sat. 1–6 P.M. in summer, Mon.–Sat. 1–4 P.M. the rest of the year. Admission is $2.50.

To absorb some of Nelson's mining history,

Nelson's historic buildings today hold many cafés and restaurants.

© ANDREW HEMPSTEAD

cruise past the mining artifacts, mineral displays, and historic photos at the free **Chamber of Mines Museum,** next to the information center on Hall St., 250/352-5242. It's open Mon.–Fri. 1–5 P.M.

Nelson Artwalk

Organized by the local arts council, Nelson's annual Artwalk highlights the work of up to 100 local artists. Throughout summer, works are displayed city-wide at various venues such as restaurants, hotels, the theater building, art galleries, and even the local pool hall. On the last Friday of every month, receptions are held at each of the venues. The receptions feature live entertainment, refreshments, and the artists themselves, on hand to discuss their work. A brochure available at the information center and motels and galleries around town contains biographies of each featured artist, tells where his or her work is displayed, and provides a map showing you the easiest way to get from one venue to the next. Drop by the information center or call 250/352-2402 for details.

PARKS AND RECREATION

City Parks

For a good view of the city and lake, head to **Gyro Park,** beyond the east end of Vernon Street. **Lakeside Park,** another pleasant green spot, is by Nelson Bridge and has a sandy beach, tennis courts, and a picnic area.

Hiking and Biking

The best nearby hiking is in **Kokanee Glacier Provincial Park** (see Kootenay Lake and Creston section), but the bed of the Burlington Northern Railway, built in 1893, provides an interesting nine-km trek right on Nelson's back doorstep. Access the railway from the top end of South Cherry Street. The many old logging and mining roads surrounding the city are great for mountain biking; one favorite is the **Svoboda Bike Trail,** accessed along Elwyn Street beyond the college. For bike rentals and a trail map, head to **Gerick Cycle and Sports,** 702 Baker St., 250/354-4622.

Fishing

Kootenay Lake holds kokanee, Dolly Varden, and rainbow trout, and the lake's feeder streams also provide good fishing opportunities. Contact the information center for registered fishing guides.

Those content to view fish rather than catch them can watch spawning kokanee at the mouth of **Kokanee Creek,** 20 km northeast of town on Highway 3A, and at **Redfish Creek,** five km farther northeast, where an interpretive center offers displays describing the kokanee's lifecycle. Kokanee are landlocked salmon. Instead of migrating in from the ocean like their anadromous cousins, kokanee spend their lives in the larger lakes of British Columbia's interior, spawning each summer in the rivers and streams draining into the lakes.

Skiing and Snowboarding

Legendary powder makes **Whitewater Ski & Winter Resort** a mecca for ski bums in the know. The small resort 19 km south of Nelson sits beneath a string of 2,400-meter-high peaks. The peaks catch an amazing amount of snow and deposit it in enough bowls and glades to keep most experts happy for days. Three double chairlifts access 18 marked trails; the Summit Chair, with a vertical rise of 410 meters, opens up the best powder-packed slopes. The area's abundant snowfall makes for a long season, but conditions are best in February and March. Whitewater has no on-mountain accommodations—just the lifts and a day lodge with a cafeteria, rental shop, and ski/snowboard school. Lift tickets are adult $37, senior $28; children under six ski free. For resort information call 250/354-4944; for snow reports call 250/352-7669; for accommodations packages call 800/666-9420. On the Internet, register through the resort's website, www.ski whitewater.com, and you'll be sent an email when there's fresh powder.

Morning Mountain Ski Area, 250/352-9969, provides good family fun, with runs geared to beginning and intermediate skiers and boarders. Facilities include a T-bar, day lodge, rental shop, and ski school. The area offers night skiing Tues.–Fri. and day skiing Sat.–Monday. To get there, head out toward Castlegar and take Blewitt Ski Hill Road.

New for the 2001–02 season, Whitewater developed an 18-km network of groomed cross-country ski trails through the Hummingbird Valley, or head to **Apex-Busk Cross-country Ski Area,** off Hwy. 6, 12 km south of Nelson.

ACCOMMODATIONS AND CAMPING

Under $50

Right downtown, the **Dancing Bear Inn,** at 171 Baker St., 250/352-7573, website www.dancing bearinn.com, offers clean and comfortable accommodations at a very reasonable price. Affiliated with Hostelling International, the nicely renovated inn is a lot more than a regular hostel (and was voted Canada's best by Hostelling International in 2000). It features a cozy lounge area with a TV, reading material, information on local attractions and restaurants, and a cupboard full of board games. Other facilities include Internet access, kitchen, laundry, and lockers. The dorm-style rooms are spacious, with a maximum of six beds in each. A few doubles and a single room are also available. Members of Hostelling International pay $17 per night, nonmembers $20; private rooms are $40–46 d. Dancing Bear Inn packages combine a round of golf or a day's skiing at White-water for a very reasonable $50 per person.

$50–100

Right downtown, the 1898, four-story **Heritage Inn,** 422 Vernon St., 250/352-5331, is a city landmark. It provides attractive, recently refurbished rooms, some with lake views, for $65–84 s, $75–94 d, including breakfast in the downstairs restaurant.

The pick of Nelson's many bed and breakfasts is **Sen Tosa B&B,** uphill from downtown at 402 Observatory St., 250/354-1993. It offers three comfortable guest rooms and particularly delicious breakfasts. Guests have use of a communal living area and a pleasant garden with an outdoor hot tub. Rates are $65 s, $75 d.

The following choices are out of the city to the north. Directly across Nelson Bridge from down-

town are **Villa Motel,** 250/352-5515 or 888/352-5515, website www.thevillamotel.com, and **North Shore Inn,** 250/352-6606 or 800/593-6636, both offering rooms of a high standard for $60 s, $70 d. If you don't mind being farther from the action, check out **Duhamel Motel,** eight km northeast of Nelson on Hwy. 3A, 250/825-4645. Each of the four units has a kitchenette, and across the road is a sandy beach; $56 s, $63 d.

$100–150

The construction of the **Prestige Lakeside Resort,** 701 Lakeside Dr., 250/352-7222, website www.prestigeinn.com, is the first stage in the redevelopment of Nelson's waterfront. This resort features a spa facility, fitness center, swimming pool, private marina, restaurants, and lakeside rooms from $149 s or d and theme suites from $209.

Camping

Right downtown, **City Tourist Park** on the corner of High and Willow Streets, 250/352-9031, isn't particularly impressive. It's surrounded by houses and its sites are closely spaced; $15–22 per night, open in summer only. A much better choice is the lakeside **Kokanee Creek Provincial Park,** 20 km northeast of Nelson on Hwy. 3A, 250/825-4421. Although the large park offers more than 100 sites, it's often full; the beautiful location makes this one of the Kootenays' most popular campgrounds. Unserviced sites are $18.50. If the park is full, continue eight km farther northeast to Balfour, where you'll find two commercial campgrounds.

FOOD AND DRINK

Nelson's reputation as a center of good eating has come ahead in leaps and bounds during recent years, but a few old Chinese places hang on along Baker Street and remain open later than all the other restaurants listed below. The best place for breakfast is the **General Store Restaurant** in the Heritage Inn, 422 Vernon St., 250/352-5331. Cooked breakfasts are huge, especially the omelets (from $6.50), which come piled high with delicious hash browns. Open daily 7:30

A.M.–8:30 P.M. Open early and a great place for a relaxing coffee is the **Dominion Café,** 334 Baker St., 250/352-1904.

The counterculture of Nelson is evident at the café inside **Packrat Annie's** bookstore, 411 Kootenay St., 250/354-4646, where a wide cross-section of the local community wanders in for herbal tea, muffins, or lunch. **The Kootenay Baker,** 295 Baker St., 250/352-2274, offers a great selection of breads and cakes.

Restaurants

For the cheapest meal in town and the chance to view Nelson's alternative-lifestylers, head to the **Rice Bowl,** 301 Baker St., 250/354-4129, where you can get six pieces of sushi for $4 or the delicious Thai noodle salad for $7. The freshly squeezed juices are also good. The **Outer Clove,** 536 Stanley St., 250/354-1667, is typical of Nelson's better restaurants, appealing to modern tastes but in a relaxed, low-key environment. The emphasis is on garlic (it's even an ingredient in a couple of the desserts), with tapas from $5 (you'd need three for a filling meal) and dinners $10.50–16. All lunch items are under $10. It's open Mon.–Sat. 11:30 A.M.–9:30 P.M.

Tucked into a back alley behind the main street is **All Seasons Cafe,** 620 Heritage Lane, 250/352-0101, a small yet stylish place known for its wine list. Lunch is well-priced, but dinner is most popular, with a menu ranging from vegetarian Japanese to West Coast salmon. The best pizza in town comes straight from the wood-fired oven at **Max & Irma's Kitchen,** 515 Kootenay St., 250/352-2332, open for lunch and dinner. Order your favorite off the standard menu ($10 and up) or pay $6 for a base and build your own from a large assortment of mouthwatering toppings. Down on the water, the Prestige Lakeside Resort, 701 Lakeside Dr., 250/352-7222, holds a couple of eateries: soak up the sun on the outdoor patio of the **Elephant Mountain Bar & Grill** or savor Pacific Northwest cuisine in the casual elegance of the **Broiler Steakhouse.**

Drink

The **Heritage Inn,** 422 Vernon St., 250/352-5331, is the center of Nelson's after-dark scene.

This old hotel contains **Mike's Place,** a bar that comes alive with a disco Wed.–Sat. from 10 P.M., as well as the elegant **Library,** with tapestried chairs by a fireplace, books to read, and an elaborate draped ceiling—the perfect place to head to for a quiet drink. Down on the water, the bar in the **Prestige Lakeside Resort,** 701 Lakeside Dr., 250/352-7222, has an expansive deck that catches the afternoon sun. Another popular drinking hole is **Bogustown Neighbourhood Pub,** toward the Nelson Bridge at 712 Nelson Ave., 250/354-1313, with a fireplace and outdoor patio. The pub's intriguing name was coined by miners who were attracted to the city for its supposed wealth but were never paid.

SERVICES AND INFORMATION

Transportation

Although a prime chunk of lakeside real estate, right in town, is taken up by a small airstrip, no scheduled flights serve Nelson. The closest commercial airport is at Castlegar, 45 km away. **Nelson Mountain Air,** 250/354-1456, is a local flightseeing operation that departs from Nelson City Wharf; a flight to and around Kokanee Glacier costs $125 per person.

Long-distance bus transportation is provided by **Greyhound.** The depot is at the Chahko-Mika Mall, 1112 Lakeside Dr., 250/352-3939. From Vancouver, buses come into Nelson via Castlegar, then continue east to Cranbrook via Salmo.

Local car rental agencies include: **Rent-a-wreck,** 250/352-5122; **Thrifty,** 250/352-2811; and **Whitewater Motors Ltd.,** 250/352-7202. For details of local bus transportation, call **Nelson Regional Transit System** at 250/352-8201.

Other Services

Kootenay Lake District Hospital is immediately east of downtown at 3 View St., 250/352-3111. The **post office** is at 514 Vernon Street. For quality arts and crafts, drop by the **Craft Connection,** 441 Baker St., 250/352-3006, a co-op owned and operated by local artists and craftspersons; closed Sunday. **Packrat Annie's,** 411 Kootenay St., sells books, tapes, and CDs, and offers good people-watching opportunities.

Information

Search out local literature at **Oliver's Books,** 398 Baker St., 250/352-7525. All the information you'll need on Nelson and the Kootenays is available at **Nelson Visitor Info Centre,** 225 Hall St., 250/352-3433, website www.discovernelson.com.

It's open in summer Mon.–Fri. 8:30 A.M.–6 P.M. and Sat.–Sun. 10 A.M.–6 P.M., the rest of the year Mon.–Fri. 8:30 A.M.–4:30 P.M. For information on the Kootenays' provincial parks, head north 20 km to the **West Kootenay Visitor Centre** at Kokanee Creek Provincial Park, 250/825-4421.

Kootenay Lake and Creston

Heading first north, then east from Nelson, Highway 3A follows a narrow arm of Kootenay Lake before coming to the main, 100-km-long body of water at Balfour. From there, you have a choice of routes. You can cross Kootenay Lake by ferry and follow the east shore of the lake down to Creston, or you can continue north up the west shore of the lake, passing through Ainsworth Hot Springs and Kaslo before arcing back west to Slocan Valley and Arrow Lake.

Kokanee Creek Provincial Park

This 257-hectare park 20 km northeast of Nelson features a great beach and one of the Kootenays' most popular campgrounds. Short trails crisscross the park, and kokanee—a landlocked species of salmon—spawn in Kokanee Creek at the end of summer (access is from the visitor center). The epicenter of the action occurs along the park's one-km-long sandy beach, backed by a shallow lagoon and a large grassed area dotted with picnic tables. The large campground's sites have showers, but no hookups, and they fill fast through summer; $18.50 per night. A visitor center, open in summer 9 A.M.–9 P.M., holds displays on local ecosystems, trail reports for Kokanee Glacier Provincial Park, and other useful information.

Kokanee Glacier Provincial Park

Straddling the highest peaks of the Selkirk Mountains, this 32,035-hectare mountain wilderness park can be seen from downtown Nelson. The steep and narrow gravel roads into the park are often impassable until late June, and the hiking trails remain snow-covered even later; check road and trail conditions at the visitor center in the park before setting off. But don't let these things

discourage you from visiting. This is one of B.C.'s premier provincial parks, filled with magnificent scenery and abundant wildlife and providing some unrivaled opportunities for backcountry travel.

The park is named for a massive glacier that, along with two other glaciers and 30 lakes, feeds dozens of creeks and rivers flowing west to Slocan Lake and east to Kootenay Lake. Almost entirely above 1,800 meters, the park's environment is very different from the valley floor—dominated by barren peaks and, for a few short weeks in the middle of summer, meadows of lush subalpine wildflowers.

The heart of the park is too steep and rugged to be penetrated by roads, so all the best features must be reached on foot. The main access is via an unsealed road that spurs off Highway 3A 20 km from Nelson and follows Kokanee Creek 16 km to **Gibson Lake.** A 2.5-km trail circles the lake, but the best hiking is farther afield. From Gibson Lake, it's four km uphill to beautiful **Kokanee Lake.** There the trail flattens out, continuing three km to Kaslo Lake and a further two km to a backcountry campground ($5 per person) and **Slocan Chief Cabin,** a century-old structure that sleeps 12 ($15 per person). Total elevation gain along this trail is 600 meters, but most of this is gained in the moderately steep ascent to Kokanee Lake. From the cabin, those experienced in alpine travel have many opportunities for exploring surrounding peaks and Kokanee Glacier.

The park can also be accessed from a rough, 24-km unsealed road that begins six km west of Kaslo and ends at the **Joker Millsite** trailhead. From here a steep five-km trail leads to Slocan Chief Cabin and a five-km trail (elevation gain

450 meters) goes to a backcountry campground at **Joker Lakes,** two beautiful bodies of water in a glacial cirque surrounded by towering peaks.

Because of the park's remote location, it's vital to pick up information on road and hiking-trail conditions (in years of high snowfall, some hiking trails are impassable until late July) at the **visitor center** in Kokanee Creek Provincial Park, 250/825-4421; open in summer 9 A.M.–9 P.M. The center can provide you with detailed directions to other park access points and give you up-to-the-minute information on which trails, if any, are closed due to bear activity.

Balfour

The picturesque village of Balfour lies at the junction of the north, south, and west arms of Kootenay Lake. Here you can easily while away the better part of a day, enjoying beautiful lake views from a waterfront café or watching the local community of partially tame Canada geese honking for handouts down on the beach.

Back in the 1890s, sternwheelers plied the lake, dropping off prospectors and supplies at isolated mining camps and settlements along its shores. But completion of the railway in the early 1900s quickly put most of the sternwheelers out of action. Today one public ferry remains, and it's "North America's longest free ferry ride." The 45-minute trip across Kootenay Lake from Balfour to Kootenay Bay offers majestic lake and mountain scenery and makes a good route to Creston and points east (see Across Kootenay Lake, below).

AINSWORTH HOT SPRINGS

Overlooking Kootenay Lake from a hillside 17 km north of Balfour, these springs were discovered in the early 1800s by local natives who found that the hot, odorless water (high in magnesium sulfate, calcium sulfate, and sodium carbonate) helped heal their wounds and ease their aches and pains. Today the springs have been commercialized and include a main outdoor pool, a hot tub, steam bath, and cold plunge pool. Rates are $7.50 for a single entry or $12 per day. The pools are open year-round, with summer

hours 10 A.M.–9:30 P.M. (from 8:30 A.M. for resort guests).

If you want a bit more pampering, stay at **Ainsworth Hot Springs Resort,** 250/229-4212 or 800/668-1171, website www.hot naturally.com, which features exercise and massage rooms, a lounge, and a licensed restaurant overlooking the main pool and beautiful Kootenay Lake. Room rates are $118 s or d, but you'll pay $138–158 for a lake view. Rates start at $80 in the off season.

Cody Caves Provincial Park

High above the hot springs, this cave system was discovered by prospector Henry Cody in the 1890s. Made up of several large chambers totaling 800 meters in length, the caves also hold an underground creek that drops over 11-meter Cody Falls. Experienced spelunkers can explore the caves unguided, but others will want to join a tour with **Hiadventure Corp.,** 250/353-7425. Based at the caves' entrance, this company offer tours through summer 10 A.M.–5 P.M. Cost is adult $12, child $8. To get to the caves, turn off Highway 31 just north of Ainsworth Hot Springs, follow a narrow 15-km gravel road to a trailhead, then hike 20 minutes.

KASLO AND VICINITY

Tree-lined streets graced by elegant late 19th century architecture, lake and mountain views from almost every street, and the world's oldest passenger sternwheeler tied up at the wharf make Kaslo (pop. 1,100), 70 km north of Nelson, a worthwhile stop. Another of the Kootenays' great boomtowns, Kaslo began as a sawmill community in 1889. But nearby silver strikes in 1893 quickly turned the town into a bustling city of 3,000 and an important commercial hub; a railway brought silver down from Sandon to Kaslo, where it was loaded onto steamers and shipped out to Creston and the outside world. The town's 1898 city hall is one of only two wooden buildings in the country that are still the seats of local government.

Sights

Drydocked by the lakefront stands the 50-meter-long **SS *Moyie,*** the last Canadian Pacific Railway

THE KOOTENAYS

sternwheeler to splash up Kootenay Lake. Built in 1897 and launched the following year at Nelson, the grand old red-and-white vessel was used for transportation of passengers, freight, and mail right up until its retirement in 1957. Today the ship serves as a museum containing a fine collection of photos, antiques, and artifacts of the region. It's open daily in summer 9:30 A.M.–5 P.M.; admission adults $5, seniors $4, children $3.

Practicalities

Right downtown, the **Kaslo Motel,** 330 D Ave., 250/353-2431 or 877/353-2431, website www.kaslomotel.com, charges $45–52 s or d; some rooms have small kitchens. A few km north of Kaslo, the **Lakewood Inn,** Kohle Rd., 250/353-2395, website www.lakewoodinn.com, has been taking in guests since the 1920s. Lakefront cabins are $70–90, while campers pay $12–20.

Kaslo Visitor Info Centre, 324 Front St.,

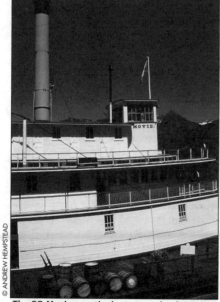

The SS Moyie was the last sternwheeler on Kootenay Lake.

250/353-2525, is open mid-May to mid-Oct. daily 9 A.M.–8 P.M.

North from Kaslo

Highway 31 leads north from Kaslo to **Galena Bay,** 50 km south of Revelstoke. The road parallels Kootenay Lake before turning to gravel and climbing into the Selkirks. A turnoff to the east, 32 km north of Kaslo, loops around the north end of Kootenay Lake to **Argenta.** Founded by two Quaker families from Argenta, California, in the early 1950s, this quaint hamlet has no tourist facilities but is worth the short detour from Highway 31.

The highlight of the road north from the Argenta turnoff is **Trout Lake,** a narrow body of water surrounded by 2,000-meter-high peaks. The lake's outlet, at its extreme southern end, is a spawning area for rainbow trout; you'll also find a small provincial park and camping. From this point the road gets pretty rough, climbing high above the lake and winding around steep gullies. At the north end of the lake is the remote community of Trout Lake, the center of a short-lived gold rush.

White Grizzly Wilderness

Straddling the Selkirk Mountains north of Highway 31A, this area protects 137,000 hectares of mountainous terrain that is prime territory for grizzly bears. Within the boundary of this wilderness zone, further protection to native habitat is provided by **Goat Range Provincial Park,** accessible along an old logging road north from New Denver. The best way to visit the area is on a guided hike with the Valhalla Society in New Denver, 307 6th Ave., 250/358-7789. The full-day trip begins with a one-hour slide show teaching species identification and safe travel in bear country. Then it's out into the field to visit an uninhabited black bear den and hike along the Whitewater Glacier Trail, from which grizzlies can often be seen at a safe distance across the valley. Tour cost is adults $40, children $20. For further information on the area, including a topographical map showing trails ($4), head to the Valhalla Society headquarters in New Denver.

© ANDREW HEMPSTEAD

THE KOOTENAYS

ACROSS KOOTENAY LAKE TO CRESTON

From Balfour, the world's longest free ferry ride takes you across Kootenay Lake to **Kootenay Bay.** Launched in 2000, the *Osprey* offers lots of outside spots at which to sit and soak up the surrounding mountain panorama.

Crawford Bay

From the ferry dock, Highway 3A traverses a low ridge before dropping into Crawford Bay, a small community sandwiched between the Purcell Mountains and the water. Artisan outlets have put this village of 200 on the map. On the left as you descend the hill is **North Woven Broom,** 250/227-9245, western Canada's only traditional broom manufacturer. The raw materials (from California and Mexico) are handcrafted into brooms using 19th-century methods. Stop in anytime and you're likely to find craftspeople hard at work and eager to share their knowledge of this lost art. The workshop is crammed with brooms of all shapes and sizes, ranging in price $24–58. A little farther along is **Kootenay Forge,** 250/227-9467, a traditional blacksmith shop where you can watch artisans practicing this ancient trade; open daily 9 A.M.–5 P.M.

Also at Crawford Bay is **Kokanee Springs Golf Resort,** 250/227-9226 or 800/979-7999, one of the province's most picturesque courses. Featuring water views, forested fairways, huge greens, large elevation drops, and colorful flower beds around the tee boxes, it is not only a beautiful place to golf, it's also very challenging. Greens fees are a very reasonable $55 ($52 weekends). The course is open late April to early October.

The pick of local accommodations is **Wedgwood Manor,** 250/227-9233 or 800/862-0022. Set on 20 beautiful hectares adjacent to the golf course and within walking distance of a beach, this 1910 home offers six heritage-style rooms, each with a private bathroom. Guests can relax in the library or in the extensive gardens. Rates are $79 s, $99–125 d. Right on the golf course is **Kokanee Springs Lodge,** 250/227-9226 or 800/979-7999, website www.kokaneesprings.com. The 26

rooms are decorated in a stylish deep blue color, offset by the natural colors of wooden trim and furniture. High season rates start at $130 s or d, but most guests stay as part of a golfing package.

South along Kootenay Lake

From Crawford Bay, it's 80 km of lake-hugging road to Creston. Along the way you'll pass small clusters of houses and a number of resorts. **Mountain Shores Marina & Resort,** 13 km from Crawford Bay, 250/223-8258, is a lakefront resort with a pool and marina. Campsites are crowded, but the location is superb. Tent sites are $18, hookups $20–24. Continuing south, **Lockhart Beach Provincial Park** has a small campground with sites for $12 per night.

CRESTON

In a wide, fertile valley at the extreme southern end of Kootenay Lake lies Creston, a thriving agricultural center of 4,900. Although the town is south of the Kootenays' most spectacular mountains, the scenery is still impressive; the Selkirk Mountains flank the valley to the west, while the Purcell Mountains do the same to the east. No mineral riches have been found around Creston, but the lure of gold and silver farther afield drew hopefuls through the valley, turning it into a prime transportation link across British Columbia's remote southern interior. As the town grew, agriculture became the mainstay of the local economy. Fruit stands lining Highway 3 as it enters Creston from the west are a sign of the district's most obvious industry; apples, strawberries, apricots, plums, and peaches are all sold at roadside stands.

Creston Valley Wildlife Management Area

This 7,000-hectare wildlife reserve lies 10 km west of Creston, 250/428-3259, extending from Kootenay Lake to the Canada–U.S. border. Protecting vital resting grounds along the Pacific Flyway, the site provides a haven for more than 250 species of birds, including a large population of osprey, a flock of the rare Forester's tern, and a nesting colony of western grebe. Start a visit at the park's wildlife center, where displays focus on the abundant birdlife, as well as on mammals and reptiles present in the reserve. It's open May–Aug. daily 8 A.M.–6 P.M., April and October Wed.–Sun. 9 A.M.–4 P.M. From the center, hiking trails lead along areas of wetland to a 10-meter-high bird-watching tower. Admission to the center is $3, and you can take a guided canoe trip for just $5 per person. Special events through the year coincide with various natural cycles, such as the spring Osprey Festival.

Other Sights

Creston & District Museum, on the west side of town and south across the railway tracks at 219 Devon St., 403/428-9262, is home to a Kutenai canoe, unlike any other in North America, but similar to the style used by the Gilyaki people in Russia, leading ethnologists to speculate about the possible links. The museum is open in summer daily 10 A.M.–3:30 P.M. West of the museum is **Kootenay Candles,** 1511 Northwest Blvd., 250/428-9785, where candles are handcrafted and sold at a factory retail outlet.

Creston is home to the **Columbia Brewery,** 1220 Erickson St., 250/428-9344, producer of British Columbia's popular Kokanee beer. Tours

Protecting vital resting grounds along the Pacific Flyway, Creston Valley Wildlife Management Area provides a haven for more than 250 species of birds, including a large population of osprey, a flock of the rare Forester's tern, and a nesting colony of western grebe.

are offered in summer Mon.–Fri. at 9:30 A.M., 11:30 A.M., 1 P.M., and 2:30 P.M. At the brewery entrance is Kokanee Beer Gear, a retail shop open weekdays 9:30 A.M.–4 P.M.

Practicalities

Right downtown, the aptly named **Downtowner Motor Inn,** 1218 Canyon St., 250/428-2238 or 800/665-9904, sports an easily recognized blue and white exterior; $46 s, $51 d. **Scottie's RV Park,** 1409 Erickson Rd., 250/428-4256 or 800/982-4256, enjoys a pleasant treed setting across the road from the Columbia Brewery. Tent sites are $15.50, hookups $17.50–20.50.

The busiest place in town each morning is **Creston Valley Bakery,** 113 10th Ave., 250/428-2661, where you'll find plenty of tables and a large selection of freshly baked cakes and pastries. Formerly specializing in just fine coffees, **Kootenay Rose,** 129 10th Ave., 250/428-7252, is now open Mon.–Sat. for dinner. The menu is packed with healthy vegetarian dishes.

Creston Visitor Info Centre is at the east end of town at 1711 Canyon St., 250/428-4342. It's open in summer daily 9 A.M.–6 P.M., the rest of the year weekdays 9 A.M.–4:30 P.M.

East Kootenays

In the southeastern corner of the province, the East Kootenays encompass the Purcell Mountains and the upper reaches of the Columbia River, with the Rocky Mountains rising abruptly from the Columbia Valley to the Continental Divide and the British Columbia–Alberta border to the west. The crossroads of the region is the service center of **Cranbrook**, from where Highway 3 heads west to **Fernie** and the neighboring province of Alberta, and Highway 93/95 parallels the Columbia River northward through a region dotted with golf courses, hot springs, and many provincial parks.

History

For 2,000 years before the first Europeans arrived, the Kootenay tribe lived in the Columbia Valley, hunting, gathering, and making trips over the Rockies to hunt buffalo on the Albertan plains. In 1807 David Thompson, an explorer for the fur-trading North West Company, found his way over Howse Pass and set up Kootenay House trading post at the north end of Windermere Lake. During the next 50 years the region was explored and mined, its animals trapped by fur traders, its people preached to and baptized by missionaries. But it wasn't until 1863 that settlers showed much interest in the rugged, mountainous terrain. At the shout of "Gold!" along Wild Horse Creek, miners swarmed into the area. First the town of **Fisherville** sprang up along the banks of the gold-bearing creek, then **Galbraith's Ferry** was established nearby on the edge of the Kootenay River. In 1888, Galbraith's Ferry was renamed **Fort Steele** to honor North West Mounted Police Superintendent Sam Steele, who built the first NWMP post west of the Rockies on the site.

In 1893 North Star Mine opened in **Kimberley** and began yielding riches in the form of lead, zinc, and silver. Fort Steele was the commercial center of the region until 1898, when the Canadian Pacific Railway (CPR) bypassed it in favor of Cranbrook. Fort Steele then declined as Cranbrook flourished.

EAST FROM CRESTON

From Creston, the Crowsnest Highway (Highway 3) crosses the **Purcell Mountains** and descends to Cranbrook, the region's largest town. The distance between the two towns is a little over 100 km.

Yahk

Yahk grew into a thriving lumber town in the 1920s but was abandoned by the 1930s. Today empty houses and hotels line the streets, but the pioneer **museum** keeps history alive with its displays of household artifacts and costumes from the past. Tiny nine-hectare **Yahk Provincial Park** lies beside the rushing Moyie River east of town. Fishing in the river is good for rainbow trout and Dolly Varden; camping is $12 per night (this campground has only 26 sites, so arrive in early afternoon to be assured of a spot).

South of Yahk is the **Kingsgate port of entry**, open daily 24 hours.

Moyie

North from Yahk, Highway 3/95 parallels the Moyie River to its source at **Moyie Lake**, a deep-blue body of water backed by cliffs. Halfway along the lake, Moyie, once boasting a population of 1,500, today holds nothing more than a few historic buildings, a pub, and a small general store; the 1904 church on Tavistock St. and the fire hall beside the highway are among the original survivors. Miners working the nearby St. Eugene Mine for lead and silver were the first settlers. The old mine is visible back up the hill by wandering down to the lakeshore, or take Queens Avenue east out of town and look for tailings.

Around 13 km north of town is 91-hectare **Moyie Lake Provincial Park**, which has a sandy swimming beach, short interpretive trails, and the chance to view kokanee spawning on gravel river beds. The large campground has semi-private sites, hot showers, and a weekend interpretive program; $18.50 per site.

CRANBROOK

Crossroads of the eastern Kootenays, Cranbrook (pop. 19,000) nestles at the base of the Purcell Mountains 106 km east of Creston and provides spectacular views eastward to the Canadian Rockies. The city itself has few tourist attractions, but with all the surrounding wilderness and nearby Fort Steele Heritage Town, it's a good base for further exploration. Cranbrook also claims to be British Columbia's sunniest town, with 2,224 hours of sunshine annually.

History

Originally a campsite for Kootenay natives, the area's first European landowners were the Galbraiths, who ran the ferry across the Kootenay River at Fort Steele. In the 1880s the family sold their holdings to Col. James Baker, who met with little success in his initial attempts to es-

tablish a townsite here. But Baker's fortunes turned around quickly when the Canadian Pacific Railway ran its line right through the struggling settlement. The town rapidly grew, and in 1905 the city of Cranbrook was incorporated. Today this service and transportation center is the region's major city and has an economy based on forestry, mining, ranching, and the new College of the Rockies.

Canadian Museum of Rail Travel

Cranbrook's main attraction, this museum is on a siding of the main CPR line directly opposite downtown on Van Horne St., 250/489-3918. It's expanded greatly in recent times and in early 2002 moved south a few hundred meters along the rail line to a restored railyard building. Still, most of the displays are outdoors, spread along three 300-meter-long sets of track, including the only surviving and restored set of special

Canadian Museum of Rail Travel

© ANDREW HEMPSTEAD

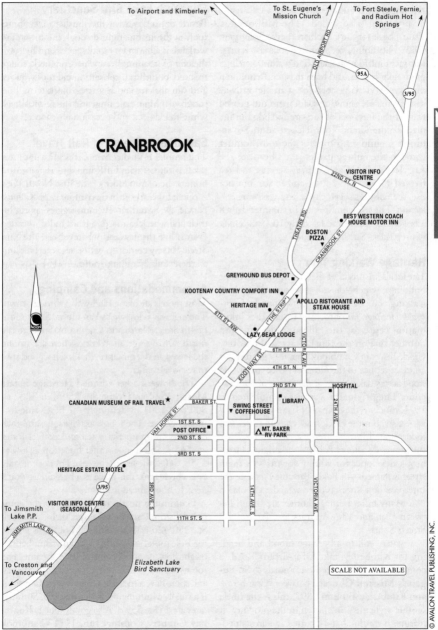

To Airport and Kimberley

To St. Eugene's Mission Church

To Fort Steele, Fernie, and Radium Hot Springs

95A

3/95

CRANBROOK

OLD AIRPORT RD

VISITOR INFO CENTRE

22ND ST. N

THEATRE RD

BEST WESTERN COACH HOUSE MOTOR INN

CRANBROOK ST.

BOSTON PIZZA

GREYHOUND BUS DEPOT

KOOTENAY COUNTRY COMFORT INN

HERITAGE INN

"THE STRIP"

APOLLO RISTORANTE AND STEAK HOUSE

8TH ST. NW

LAZY BEAR LODGE

VICTORIA AVE.

KOOTENAY ST.

6TH ST. N

4TH ST. N

2ND ST. N

HOSPITAL

LIBRARY

24TH AVE.

CANADIAN MUSEUM OF RAIL TRAVEL

BAKER ST.

SWING STREET COFFEEHOUSE

VAN HORNE ST.

1ST ST. S

POST OFFICE

2ND ST. S

MT. BAKER RV PARK

3RD ST. S

HERITAGE ESTATE MOTEL

3/95

VISITOR INFO CENTRE (SEASONAL)

3RD AVE. S

14TH AVE. S

VICTORIA AVE.

11TH ST. S

To Jimsmith Lake P.P.

JIMSMITH LAKE RD

To Creston and Vancouver

Elizabeth Lake Bird Sanctuary

SCALE NOT AVAILABLE

MOON

© AVALON TRAVEL PUBLISHING, INC.

THE KOOTENAYS

railway cars from the Trans-Canada Limited, a luxury train (also called "The Millionaires' Train") built for the Canadian Pacific Railway in 1929. The dining, sleeping, and solarium lounge cars sport inlaid mahogany and walnut paneling, plush upholsteries, and brass fixtures. Restoration displays, a viewing corridor, a model railway display, a slide show, and a 45-minute guided tour of the interiors of cars are included in the price of the Grand Tour Ticket; adult $6, senior $5, child $3.50. After the tour, wander through the railway garden then head for the **Argyle Dining Car** to enjoy scones and tea (served 11:30 A.M.–2 P.M.) and to see, but not use, the railway's silver, china, and glassware collection. The museum is open in summer daily 8 A.M.–8 P.M., spring and fall daily 10 A.M.–6 P.M., winter Tues.–Sat. noon–5 P.M.

Heritage Walking Tour

The locals are proud of their downtown heritage buildings, which you can view on a self-guided walking tour by picking up the handy *Cranbrook Heritage Tour* brochure from either information center or the railway museum (stop number one on the tour). Start at the Rotary Clock Tower in Cranbrook Square—the tower is an exact replica of the old post office tower that stood across Baker Street at the corner of 10th Avenue. The original tower was demolished in 1971, much to the dismay of Cranbrook preservationists, but the clock from the old tower was incorporated into the replica. You can still see the home of Colonel Baker—the original Cranbrook developer for whom downtown's main street is named—in Baker Park off 1st St. S; the Interpretation Room is open weekdays 9 A.M.–5 P.M. Many other heritage homes are found between 10th and 13th Avenues and 1st and 4th Streets South.

If you're still in a heritage mood and heading for Kimberley, take Old Airport Road (a continuation of Theatre Road) north to **St. Eugene's Mission Church,** between Cranbrook and Kimberley. Built in 1897, this is the finest Gothic-style mission church in the province; it features beautiful, hand-painted Italian stained-glass windows.

Elizabeth Lake Bird Sanctuary

Beside the highway at the southern city limits (park at the information center), this large area of wetlands is a haven for many species of waterfowl, including Canada geese, and teal, ringneck, scaup, redhead, bufflehead, goldeneye, and ruddy ducks. You can also see coots, grebes, black terns, and songbirds. Mammals present include muskrats, white-tailed deer, and occasionally moose.

Sam Steele Days

The annual four-day Sam Steele Days festival takes place on the third weekend in June and honors the commander of the first North West Mounted Police post in this region. Expect a huge parade, the Sweetheart Pageant, loggers' sports, bicycle and wheelchair races, a truck rodeo, sporting events, live theater, and whatever else the Sam Steele Society comes up with each year. Find out all the details by calling 250/426-4161.

Accommodations and Camping

Most motels are along Highway 3 through town. The highway is known as Van Horne Street south of 4th Street North and Cranbrook Street to the north. On average, motel prices here are among the lowest in the province, making it a good spot to rest overnight.

The flower-basket-adorned **Heritage Estate Motel,** 362 Van Horne St., 250/426-3862 or 800/670-1001, is definitely the best value-for-money choice. The rooms are spacious, and each contains complimentary tea and coffee. Rates are $45 s, $52 d in summer but drop as low as $35 s, $40 d the rest of the year. I'm not the only one who regards this place as a bargain, so you'll need to book ahead in summer.

Continuing north, in the heart of the commercial strip, **Lazy Bear Lodge,** 621 Cranbrook St., 250/426-6086 or 888/808-6086, is an old roadside motel snazzed up with log trim, beds of bright flowers, and a colorful coat of paint. The rooms remain basic but each has a coffeemaker, and some have a fridge and microwave. Out front is a small swimming pool for guest use. Summer rates are $55 s, $59 d. Also good value is **Kootenay Country Comfort Inn,** 1111 Cranbrook St., 250/426-2296 or 800/862-2823, where the country-style rooms are priced from $52 s, $56 d. Kitchenettes start at $60. **Best Western Coach House Motor Inn,** 1417 Cranbrook St. N, 250/426-7236 or 800/528-1234, offers an outdoor pool, dining room, and cocktail lounge, and charges from $68 s, $75 d. A few blocks back toward the city, the **Heritage Inn,** 803 Cranbrook St., 250/489-4301 or 888/888-4374, website www.heritageinn.net, is Cranbrook's largest accommodation, with over 100 spacious but older rooms. Facilities include an indoor pool, a small fitness room, a sauna, two restaurants, a cocktail lounge, and a nightclub; $89 s, $98 d includes an unusually late midday checkout.

One of the area's most attractive campgrounds is in 12-hectare **Jimsmith Lake Provincial Park,** four km off the main highway at the southern outskirts of the city. The park's wooded campsites rent for $12 per night; open May–September. Downtown, **Mt. Baker RV Park,** at the corner of 14th Ave. and 1st St. S, 250/489-0056, provides grassy tent sites for $15 and hookups for $17–20. A stream and waterfall flow nearby, and hot showers are available.

Food

For good coffee, fresh muffins, and light snacks head to **Swing Street Coffeehouse,** 16 11th St. S, 250/426-5358; open daily from 8:30 A.M.

Cranbrook lacks outstanding restaurants, but a few longtime favorites offer reliable food and service. One of these is **Apollo Ristorante and Steak House,** 1012 Cranbrook St., 250/426-3721. The Apollo offers a salad bar, steaks, seafood, Italian dishes, and 25 varieties of pizza. Expect to pay $6 and up at lunch, from $13 in the evening. Open daily. Motel dining is best at the family-style restaurant in the **Best Western Coach House Motor Inn,** 1417 Cranbrook St. N, 250/426-7236. It's open throughout the day with a buffet dinner offered on weekends. **Boston Pizza,** 1201 Cranbrook St. N, 250/489-2822, has separate lounge and restaurant sections, with nightly specials in both, including half price pasta on Tuesday after 5 P.M.

Transportation

Cranbrook Airport, on the north side of town off Hwy. 95A, is served by **Air B.C.,** 888/247-2262, and **WestJet,** 800/538-5696. Both offer daily flights between Cranbrook and Vancouver. The **Greyhound** bus depot is at 1229 Cranbrook St., 250/426-3331 or 800/661-8747. Bus service runs at least once daily east to Fernie, Sparwood, and into Alberta; west to Creston and Castlegar; and north to Kimberley, Radium Hot Springs, and through Kootenay National Park to Banff and on to Calgary.

Rental car agencies include: **Avis,** 250/489-1115; **Budget,** 250/489-4371; **National,** 250/489-0911; and **Rent-a-wreck,** 250/426-3004. For a cab call **Star Taxi** at 250/426-5511.

Services and Information

Cranbrook Regional Hospital is off 2nd St. on 24th Ave. N, 250/426-5281. The **post office** is downtown on the corner of 10th Ave. and 1st St. South.

Cranbrook has two information centers, one at each end of the city. The main **Cranbrook Visitor Info Centre** is at 2279 Cranbrook St. N, 250/426-5914 or 800/222-6174. It's open in summer daily 8:30 A.M.–7 P.M., the rest of the year Mon.–Fri. 9 A.M.–5 P.M. At the southern entrance to the city is a seasonal center open in summer daily 9 A.M.–5 P.M.

FERNIE AND VICINITY

Fernie (pop. 5,200) nestles in the Elk Valley 100 km east of Cranbrook on Highway 3. The town itself is a coal-mining and forestry center offering little of visitor interest, but in winter one of British Columbia's great little alpine resorts comes alive nearby. Town center is a couple of blocks south of the highway, holding the usual array of historic buildings and small-town shops. Look for an impressive red-brick courthouse on 4th Avenue and a good bakery on 2nd Avenue. About 12 km south of town is 259-hectare **Mount Fernie Provincial Park,** where hiking trails lead along a picturesque creek and to a waterfall.

Fernie Alpine Resort

This is another of British Columbia's legendary winter resorts, boasting massive annual snowfalls, challenging skiing and riding, and uncrowded slopes. Fernie has long held a reputation throughout the west as a hidden gem, and development was minimal until the late 1990s, when the resort was bought by the Resorts of the Canadian Rockies, which also owns resorts such as Lake Louise. New lifts opened soon after and the base facilities were expanded. One thing that remains the same is the fantastic terrain, all 1,215 hectares of it. The lift-serviced area lies under a massive ridge that catches an incredible nine meters of snow each year, filling a wide open bowl with enough of the white fluffy stuff to please all powderhounds. A few runs are groomed, but the steeper stuff—down open bowls and through trees—is the main attraction. The resort's total vertical rise is 857 meters, with many of the challenging slopes at higher elevations and in Cedar and Timber Bowls. Lift tickets cost adult $56, senior $45, child $15; under six ski free. The resort is open mid-December through mid-April, but the best conditions are in January and February. In July and August, one chairlift operates, opening up hiking and mountain biking terrain. Hikers pay $8 per ride, or $21 for a day pass. Use the lift to take the hard work out of mountain biking for $26 for a full day. Bikes can be rented at the base village for $25–40. Other summer activities include horseback riding, dog carting (a summer version of mushing), guided hikes, tennis, and photography courses. Accommodations are available on the hill, and visitors with RVs are offered hookups and shower facilities. The resort is 14 km south of Fernie. For information call 250/423-4655 or surf the Internet to www.skifernie.com; for snow reports call 250/423-3555.

Practicalities

Fernie has a variety of accommodation options, most offering packages though winter. The least expensive place to stay is **Raging Elk Hostel,** 892 6th Ave., 250/423-6811, website www.ragingelk.com. A converted motel, this hostel is an associate of Hostelling International, and although basic it provides all the usual hostelling facilities, including a communal kitchen and laundry. Each dormitory holds 4–10 beds and has

its own bathroom. The few private rooms have twin beds or one double bed and also a TV. Rates range $15–17 for a dorm bed or $25–30 s, $35–40 d in a private room. These rates include a pancake breakfast. **Super 8 Motel,** one km west of downtown at 2021 Hwy. 3, 250/423-6788 or 800/800-8000, website www.super8.com, charges from $66 s, $80 d. **Park Place Lodge,** 742 Hwy. 3, 250/423-6871 or 888/381-7275, website www.parkplacelodge.com, is a modern three-story hotel along the main road. Amenities include spacious and elegant rooms opening to an atrium, the Red Rock Bistro, and a pub. Summer rates are from a reasonable $99 s, $109 d, with golf and ski packages starting from $85 per person.

Up at the resort, **Griz Inn Sport Hotel,** 250/423-9221 or 800/661-0118, website www.grizinn.com, offers 45 kitchen-equipped suites, an indoor pool, hot tub, and restaurant. Through winter, room rates start at $105 s or d, while off-season rates (outside the busy winter season) drop as low as $65.

The best bet for campers is 12 km south at **Mount Fernie Provincial Park.** Facilities are limited, but the treed setting more than makes up for it; $12 per night. RV sites at **Fernie Alpine Resort** are $15–20 per night.

Jamochas Coffee House is the pick of many local caffeine joints. It's set back from the highway at 851 7th Ave., 250/423-6977. This place also has some delicious homemade soups. Overlooking the Elk River at the west end of town, **Rip and Richard's Restaurant,** 250/423-3002, serves standard fare, including hearty cooked breakfasts from $6, burgers from $6.50, and dinners from $10. From the deck, you'll enjoy panoramic views all the way across to the resort.

Fernie Visitor Info Centre is through town to the north, 250/423-6868. It's open Mon.–Fri. 8:30 A.M.–4:30 P.M.

Akamina–Kishinena Provincial Park

Bordering Glacier National Park (Montana, U.S.) and Waterton Lakes National Park (Alberta), this remote tract of 10,921 hectares protects the extreme southeastern corner of British Columbia. The park is named for its two main waterways, which flow southward into Montana. This was the main reason for the park's recent creation, as now, alongside Waterton Lakes National Park, entire watersheds of Glacier National Park are protected. The landscape has changed little in thousands of years, since the Kootenay rested in the open meadows beside Kishinena Creek before crossing the Continental Divide to hunt bison on the prairies. The only access to the park is on foot from one of two trailheads. The most popular and easiest access is from the east via Akamina Parkway in Waterton Lakes National Park. From near the end of Akamina Parkway (the trailhead is signposted) it's 1.5 km to the park border, from where trails lead past stunning alpine lakes to the park's more remote corners. You can also access the area at the end of an unsealed road that leaves Highway 3 16 km south of Fernie. The road leads 110 km into the Flathead River Valley, where trails climb along Akamina Creek into the park. The best source of information is the Kootenay District office for BC Parks, 250/422-4200.

Sparwood

Thirty kg northeast of Fernie, Sparwood (pop. 4,300) began as three separate coal-mining towns: Michel, Middletown, and Natal. In the 1960s, a resurgence of civic pride saw the old towns demolished and replaced by the new center of Sparwood.

The coal seams and part of the mining operations can be seen on the ridge high above Sparwood, but a more eye-catching element of the local industry is the world's largest truck, which sits beside Highway 3 in the center of town. Beside the truck is **Sparwood Visitor Info Centre,** 250/425-2423, where you can arrange a tour of the mines. **Mountain Shadows Campground,** set among trees immediately south of town, 250/425-7815, adjoins the local golf course and holds the trailhead for a four-km hiking trail. Unserviced sites are $12, hookups $14–20, which includes the use of hot showers.

Elkford

Surrounded by towering peaks, this coal-mining community of 3,000 lies 35 km north of Sparwood on Highway 43, which continues north to remote Elk Lakes Provincial Park. Abundant recreation opportunities in the area include fishing in the Elk River, wildlife viewing, and hiking and mountain biking on hundreds of kg of logging and mining roads. In winter, these same roads are a mecca for snowmobilers. The community has few services, but you'll find a

© ANDREW HEMPSTEAD

Sparwood is home to the world's largest truck.

small **municipal campground** within walking distance of downtown. At the corner of Highway 43 and Michel Rd. is **Elkford Visitor Info Centre,** 250/865-4614 or 877/355-9453, a good source of local road and trail information.

Elk Lakes Provincial Park

This 17,245-hectare park encompasses rugged wilderness 87 km north of Elkford. Glaciers shaped the terrain here; their remnants can still be seen along the park's west border. The main access road ends in the provincial park, which borders Kananaskis Country in Alberta. From the main parking lot, a trail leads one km to Lower Elk Lake and another kilometer or so to Upper Elk Lake. At the lower lake, a narrow trail climbs 135 meters to a lookout. Steep snowcapped peaks surround the stunningly beautiful upper lake, and several avalanche paths end right at water's edge. Fishing in the lower lake is productive for Dolly Varden and cutthroat trout. The park's only facility is a primitive campground at the main trailhead; $5 per night. For further information contact the local BC Parks office at 250/422-2400.

FORT STEELE AND VICINITY

Gold miners first poured into the area north of Cranbrook when gold was discovered in Wild Horse Creek in 1865. The miners crossed the Kootenay River by ferry at a site that became known as Galbraith's Ferry. The fare to cross the river was a steep $5 per person and $10 per loaded pack animal.

In 1887, a year before the first bridge was constructed, the North West Mounted Police established a post on the riverbank. Superintendent Sam Steele and his 75 Mounties settled landownership disputes between local natives and new ranchers, easing friction and maintaining order. When silver and lead discoveries were made in the East Kootenays in the 1890s, Fort Steele grew rapidly. The town became a social, administrative, and supply center for the region, and served as a busy river-traffic hub for sternwheelers carrying ore and supplies to American refineries. However, the glory and bustle were

short-lived. When the railway bypassed the town in 1898, putting Cranbrook on the map instead, Fort Steele's population plummeted—to a miserable 500 people by 1905.

Fort Steele Heritage Town

Today Fort Steele lives again. At Fort Steele Heritage Town you'll see over 60 restored, reconstructed, fully furnished buildings, including log barracks, hotels, a courthouse, jail, museum, dentist's office, ferry office, printing office, and a general store crammed to the rafters with intriguing historical artifacts. In summer, the park staff brings Fort Steele back to life with appropriately costumed working blacksmiths, carpenters, quilters, weavers, bakers, ice-cream makers, and many others. Hop on a stagecoach or a steam train, heckle a street politician, witness a crime and testify at a trial, watch a silent movie, and view operatic performances in the Opera House.

The grounds are open year-round. From mid-May to early October, the action takes place daily 9:30 A.M.–5:30 P.M. Admission is adults $6, seniors and youths $4, children $2, families $13. Once inside, some shows cost extra. One of the highlights is Fort Steele Follies, a professional 1880s'-style live-theater company performing a musical comedy at the Wild Horse Theatre, 250/426-5682. Showtimes are summer only Tues.–Sun. at 2 P.M. and 8 P.M. Afternoon shows cost adult $9, senior $7, while the evening shows are slightly more expensive. For general information on Fort Steele Heritage Town call 250/417-6000.

A few commercial facilities surround the main entrance to Fort Steele. The largest is **Fort Steele Resort and RV Park,** 250/489-4268, website www.fortsteele.com, which offers a heated pool, showers, laundry, and a barbecue and cooking facility. Unserviced sites are $18, serviced sites $22–26.

Wild Horse Creek

To get to the original Wild Horse Creek diggings, continue north from Fort Steele and take the logging road to Bull River and Kootenay Trout Hatchery. Fisherville—the first township in the East Kootenays and once home to over 5,000 miners—was established at the diggings in 1864 but was relocated upstream when it was discovered that the richest seam of gold was right below the main street.

About five km from the highway is Wild Horse Graveyard. From this point you can hike a section of Wild Horse Creek to see a number of historic sites, including the Chinese burial ground, the site of the Wild Horse post office, the remains of Fisherville, and the diggings. It takes about two hours to do the trail, allowing for stops at all the plaques along the way. Hikers here can also saunter down the last 2.5 km of

the Dewdney Trail, imagining all the men and packhorses, loaded to the hilt, that once struggled from the Fraser Valley to the East Kootenays in search of fortune.

KIMBERLEY

Kimberley (pop. 7,000), 31 km north of Cranbrook on Highway 95A, is a charming little town, with no commercial strip or fast food outlets, just streets of old stucco mining cottages with a downtown that's been "Bavarianized." In fact, Kimberley is also known as the "Bavarian City." Most of the local shops and businesses,

THE KOOTENAYS

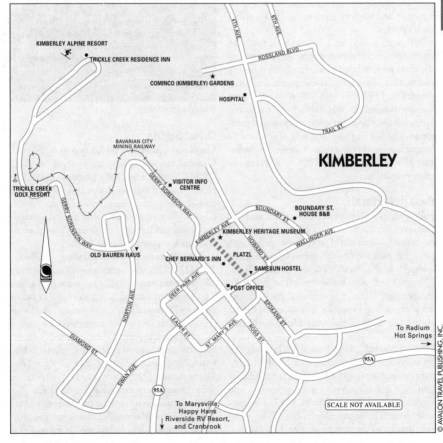

KIMBERLEY

KIMBERLEY ALPINE RESORT
TRICKLE CREEK RESIDENCE INN
COMINCO (KIMBERLEY) GARDENS
HOSPITAL
4TH AVE.
6TH AVE.
ROSSLAND BLVD.
TRAIL ST.
BAVARIAN CITY MINING RAILWAY
GERRY SORENSON WAY
VISITOR INFO CENTRE
TRICKLE CREEK GOLF RESORT
GERRY SORENSON WAY
BOUNDARY ST.
BOUNDARY ST. HOUSE B&B
KIMBERLEY AVE.
KIMBERLEY HERITAGE MUSEUM
HOWARD ST.
WALLINGER AVE.
OLD BAUREN HAUS
CHEF BERNARD'S INN
PLATZL
SAMESUN HOSTEL
DEER PARK AVE.
POST OFFICE
NORTON AVE.
LEADER ST.
ST. MARY'S AVE.
ROSS ST.
SPOKANE ST.
To Radium Hot Springs →
DIAMOND ST.
SWAN AVE.
95A
95A
To Marysville, Happy Hans Riverside RV Resort, and Cranbrook
SCALE NOT AVAILABLE

© AVALON TRAVEL PUBLISHING, INC.

and many of Kimberley's homes, have been decorated Bavarian-style with dark wood finish and flowery trim, steep triangular roofs, fancy balconies, brightly painted window shutters, and flower-filled window boxes. The Bavarianization occurred in the 1970s, when a group of local businesspeople devised the idea to attract tourists. They did such a good job of luring visitors that many Europeans found Kimberley appealing and joined the town's resident population—the European-style delis and restaurants you see downtown are mostly authentic. Strolling the pedestrian-only Bavarian Platzl, you'll feel as though you've just driven into a village high in the Swiss Alps. Even the local car dealership looks like a chalet where you'd expect to find bell-wearing cows and brightly dressed milkmaids rather than vehicles.

Although named for a famous South African diamond mine, Kimberley boomed as a result of the silver and lead deposits unearthed on nearby North Star Mountain. The deposits were discovered in 1892, and by 1899 over 200 claims had been staked. As was so often the case, only operations run by larger companies proved profitable. The last of these, and one of the world's largest lead and zinc mines, Cominco's **Sullivan Mine,** closed in late 2001 as reserves became exhausted.

Bavarian Platzl

Follow signs to Kimberley city center and the Platzl on Spokane Street. This is the focus of downtown—a cheerful, red-brick, pedestrian plaza complete with babbling brook, ornamental bridges, and the "World's Largest Cuckoo Clock" ("Happy Hans" pops out and yodels on the hour). Shops, many German restaurants, and delis line the plaza, selling European specialties. At the far end of the Platzl, **Kimberley Heritage Museum,** 250/427-7510, houses mining-history exhibits, a stuffed grizzly bear, a hodgepodge of artifacts, and displays relating to all the locally popular outdoor sports. One of the latter exhibits honors Kimberley hero Gerry Sorensen, the world's fastest downhill skier in 1982. The museum is open in summer Mon.–Sat. 9 A.M.–4:30 P.M., the rest of the year Mon.–Sat. 1–4 P.M.

© ANDREW HEMPSTEAD

Bavarian Platzl

Other Sights

Cominco Gardens, also known as Kimberley Gardens, enjoys a hilltop location off 4th Ave., 250/427-2293. Originally planted in 1927 to promote a fertilizer developed by Cominco, the one-hectare gardens now hold close to 50,000 flowers. Admission is $3. After a stroll through the flower garden, refresh yourself next door at **Garden Treasures** teahouse (see below).

The **Bavarian City Mining Railway,** 250/427-2929, was constructed from materials salvaged from mining towns around the province. The seven-km track climbs a steep-sided valley, crosses a 70-meter-long trestle bridge, and stops at particularly impressive mountain viewpoints, the original townsite, the now-closed Sullivan mine entrance, and other points of interest before terminating near the base village of Kimberley Alpine Resort. The train operates up to six times daily through summer; adult $7, child $3.

On the southern outskirts of Kimberley is the community of **Marysville,** where you can stop and stretch your legs at **Marysville Falls.** From the parking lot at the bridge, walk downstream 800 meters through the woods—passing wild roses and other assorted wildflowers—to a series of small waterfalls and one large fall.

Golfing

The Columbia Valley is one of British Columbia's premier golfing destinations, and while most of the best courses are farther north, Kimberley is home to the newly opened par-72, 6,896-yard **Trickle Creek Golf Resort,** which lies along the lower slopes of North Star Mountain at the base of Kimberley Alpine Resort. The resort course–style layout is generally regarded as one of the best in the valley, featuring huge elevation changes (such as the par 3 11th hole, which drops over 20 meters from tee to green) and stunning mountain scenery. Greens fees are $89, or play twilight rates for $54. For further information and tee times call 250/427-5171 or 888/874-2553. Dating to 1924, **Kimberley Golf Course,** in Marysville, 250/427-4161, is much shorter at just 6,000 yards, but fairways lined with mature ponderosa pines and small greens add to the challenge. Greens fees are $38.

Kimberley Alpine Resort

From early December to early April, this resort provides great skiing and snowboarding on a wide variety of slopes four km west of downtown. Soon after the acquisition by Resorts of the Canadian Rockies, what was traditionally a small hill oriented toward families became the scene of much expansion, mostly in the base area. Currently there are 67 named runs covering 738 hectares, with a maximum vertical rise of 751 meters. The longest run covers more than six kg. Most beginners and intermediates will be content on the well-groomed main slopes, while more experienced skiers and boarders will want to head to the expert terrain served by the Easter Chair. Night skiing is offered Tues.–Sat., and ski/snowboard rentals and lessons are available. Additional facilities at the resort include two snowboard parks, a cross-country ski area, an ice-skating rink, accommodations, and restaurants. Lift tickets are adult $45, senior $27, child $15 (children six and younger ski free).

Summer activities include chairlift rides, hiking, mountain biking, and luge rides; head to the Adventure Desk in the Marriott Hotel, 250/427-6743, for details.

For general information call 250/427-4881 or try website www.skikimberley.com; for snow reports call 250/427-7332; and for accommodation packages call 800/258-7669.

Events

Several annual events in Kimberley draw crowds. Look for **Winterfest** in mid-February, an **International Old Time Accordion Championship** in the Platzl the second week of July, followed a week later by **Julyfest** (musical comedy, a pancake breakfast, a parade, and various Bavarian-themed events. On the first weekend of September, Kimberley kicks up its heels at the **International Folk Festival.** Get a complete list of local events from the information center.

Accommodations and Camping

If you plan on golfing or a winter vacation in Kimberley, contact **Kimberley Vacations,** 250/427-4877 or 800/667-0871, website www .kimberleyvacations.bc.ca, for the best package deals. Otherwise contact one of the following choices.

If you don't mind being a couple of kg out of town, **Travellaire Motel,** toward Marysville at 2660 Warren Ave., 250/427-2252 or 800/477-4499, provides excellent value. It's only a small place, but it has recently been totally renovated and decked out with new beds and furniture. There's also a barbecue area for guest use. Rates are $46 s, $54 d, or pay an extra $5 for a room with a small kitchenette. On the Platzl, right downtown, **Chef Bernard's Inn,** 250/427-4820 or 800/905-8338, offers basic rooms for $60 s or d. Many of Kimberley's best restaurants are right at the front doorstep. **Trickle Creek Residence Inn** is a Marriott property at the base of Kimberley Alpine Resort, 250/427-5175 or 877/282-1200, website www.skikimberley.com. This stunning log and stone structure holds 80 spacious rooms, each with a kitchen, balcony, and fireplace. Guest facilities include a fitness center and a year-round outdoor heated pool. Sum-

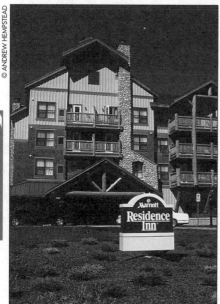

© ANDREW HEMPSTEAD

Kimberley's best accommodation, the
Residence Inn, is up at the alpine resort.

mer rates are $149 s or d for a studio room and
$169 for a one-bedroom suite. Check the website
for golf and ski packages.

One block from downtown, **Boundary St.
House B&B,** 89 Boundary St., 250/427-3510,
is a 1920s' house decorated with antiques. Rates
are $55 s, $70 d, including a cooked breakfast.

The old Happy Hans Campground was a victim of new development at the base of the alpine
resort, and now **Happy Hans Riverside RV Resort** enjoys a new name reflecting its new location
seven km south of downtown on Hwy. 95A and
then three km west along St. Mary's River Rd.,
250/427-2929, website www.happyhans.com.
Tent sites are $16, hookups $20–24.

Food

European gourmet specialties, predominantly
German, are available all around town. The
Gasthaus, in the Platzl, 250/427-4851, features
German lunches, such as goulash, from $6, and
German dinner specialties, such as bratwurst,

rheinischer sauerbraten, wienerschnitzel, and
kassler rippchen for $10–16. It's open daily except
Tuesday, 11:30 A.M.–10 P.M. For breakfast, head
to **Chef Bernard's,** also in the Platzl, 250/427-
4820. It's inexpensive and servings are hearty.
Kimberley City Bakery, a Swiss bakery, tearoom, and sidewalk café in the Platzl, 250/427-
2131, is open daily from 8:30 A.M. Away from
the Platzl, **Old Bauren Haus,** on the way up to
the resort at 280 Norton Ave., 250/427-5133,
features Bavarian specialties and plenty of atmosphere. It's in a post-and-beam building originally constructed about 350 years ago in
southern Bavaria. The building was taken apart,
shipped to Canada, and painstakingly rebuilt.
It's open for dinner only and closed Tuesday.

If you've had enough of the old Bavarian
theme, head to the **Ozone Pub** in the Hotel
Kootenay at the bottom end of the Platzl,
250/427-7744, where you'll find Canadian-style
pub meals and live entertainment most nights.

Garden Treasures, at Cominco Gardens,
250/427-0501, serves a classic afternoon tea, accompanied by desserts and delectables such as
fresh-baked scones with jam. Prices are reasonable
and the atmosphere, inside a real greenhouse, is
delightful; the stunning pink-and-green interior
is complemented by hanging plants, flowery
tablecloths, and views of the distant mountains
and gardens. Summer hours are 10 A.M.–6 P.M.
daily.

Information

For more information on Kimberley and the surrounding area, drop by **Kimberley Visitor Info
Centre,** 115 Gerry Sorensen Way, 250/427-
3666. It's open in summer daily 9 A.M.–7 P.M., the
rest of year Mon.–Fri. 9 A.M.–5 P.M.

CONTINUING NORTH
TOWARD INVERMERE

This stretch of highway passes through a deep valley chock-full of commercial facilities like world-
class golf courses, resorts, and hot springs. The
low elevation makes for relatively mild winters
and an early start to the summer season. And
with the Purcell Mountains on one side and the

Rockies on the other, the valley certainly doesn't lack for scenery.

Wasa Provincial Park

Unlike the several backcountry parks in the area, 144-hectare Wasa Provincial Park, 30 km north of Kimberley, is easily accessible off the main highway. The lake is warm, making for good summer swimming; fishing is possible but only so-so. Facilities include picnic tables, a nature trail, and swimming and water-sports areas. The park is open year-round, but the $15 camp fee is collected only May–September.

Whiteswan Lake Provincial Park

Continuing north, the Rockies close in and the scenery becomes unbelievably beautiful. Twenty-eight km north of Skookumchuck, an unsealed logging road takes off east into the mountains, leading to 1,994-hectare Whiteswan Lake Provincial Park. The road climbs steadily from the highway, entering Lussier Gorge after 11 km. Within the gorge, a steep trail leads down to **Lussier Hot Springs.** Two small pools have been constructed to contain the hot (43° C, 109° F) and odorless water as it bubbles out of the ground and flows into the Lussier River. Within the park itself, the road closely follows the southern shoreline of first **Alces Lake** and then the larger **Whiteswan Lake.** The two lakes attract abundant birdlife; loons, grebes, and herons are all common. They also attract anglers, who come for great rainbow trout fishing. Both lakes are stocked, and they have a daily quota of two fish per person. Camping is at one of four campgrounds within the park; $12 per site.

Top of the World Provincial Park

If you thought the scenery around Whiteswan Lake was wild and remote, wait till you see this 8,790-hectare wilderness a rough 52 km from

The dominant peak in Height of the Rockies Provincial Park is 3,460-meter Mount King George, which is flanked by massive hanging glaciers on its north- and east-facing slopes. Mountain goats thrive on all massifs, while the remote valleys are home to high concentrations of elk and grizzly bears.

Highway 95 (turn off the Whiteswan Lake access road at Alces Lake). You can't drive into the park, but it's a fairly easy six-km hike from the end of the road to picturesque **Fish Lake,** the park's largest body of water. The trail climbs alongside the pretty Lussier River to the lake, which is encircled with Engelmann spruce and surrounded by peaks up to 2,500 meters high. The hike to the lake gains just over 200 vertical meters and makes a good day trip. Trails from the lake lead to other alpine lakes and to a viewpoint that allows a good overall perspective on the high plateau for which the park is named. Fish Lake is productive for cutthroat trout and Dolly Varden. Camping is at one of four designated areas ($5), or stay in the large cabin nestled in trees beside Fish Lake ($15).

Height of the Rockies Provincial Park

This long, narrow, 58,205-hectare park protects a remote 50-km-long section of the Canadian Rockies east of Highway 93/95. It is bordered by Elk Lakes Provincial Park and Elk Lakes Recreation Area to the east, but access is from the east and the final approach must be made on foot, meaning it is not a destination for the casual day-tripper. Mountains dominate the landscape, with 26 peaks—some of which remained unnamed until recently—rising over the magical 10,000-foot (3,050-meter) mark. They lie in two distinct ranges, the **Royal Group** in the north and the **Italian Group** in the south. The dominant peak is 3,460-meter **Mount King George,** in the Royal Group, which is flanked by massive hanging glaciers on its north- and east-facing slopes. Mountain goats thrive on all massifs, while the remote valleys are home to high concentrations of elk and grizzly bears.

The park can be reached from two directions. Neither is signposted, so before setting out for the park, it's wise to get hold of a good map of the area; local information centers and Forest Service offices can supply these. The following directions are intended only as a guide. **Connor Lake** is the most popular destination in the south of the park. It is reached by passing through Whiteswan Lake Provincial Park (see above) and continuing along a rough logging road that parallels the White River to its upper reaches. (The most important intersection to watch for is 11 km from Whiteswan Lake; stay right, immediately crossing the river.) At the end of the road, a tortuous 72 km from Highway 93/95, is a small area set aside for tents and horse corrals. From this trailhead it's an easy walk up Maiyuk Creek and over a low ridge to Connor Lake, with the Italian Group in plain view to the north and Mt. Forsyth to the southwest. Along the lakeshore is a primitive campground and a rustic cabin. Small **Queen Mary Lake** lies in the western shadow of the impressive Royal Group. It is generally the destination only of those on horseback or mountaineers continuing into the Royal Group. It is reached by turning off Highway 93/95 at Canal Flats and following a logging road up the Kootenay River watershed. The first 48 km follow the Kootenay itself, then the road turns westward, climbing along the south side of the Palliser River a further 35 km to the end of the road. From this point it's a 12-km slog up a forested valley, with numerous creek crossings, to the lake.

To reserve the cabin at Connor Lake or for general park information call the East Kootenay District office of BC Parks at 250/422-2400.

Canal Flats

The small lumber-mill town of Canal Flats lies between the Kootenay River and Columbia Lake. David Thompson, the first European explorer in this neck of the woods, crossed from the lake to the river in 1808, naming the flat McGillivray's Portage. In 1889 the two waterways were connected by a canal with a single lock, but the passage was so narrow and dangerous that only two steamboats ever got through.

North of Canal Flats, the highway passes 44-hectare **Thunder Hill Provincial Park,** which overlooks turquoise-and-blue Columbia Lake, then approaches and passes the weirdly shaped **Dutch Creek Hoodoos,** a set of photogenic

rock formations carved over time by ice, water, and wind.

Fairmont Hot Springs

Kootenay natives used these springs as a healing source for eons prior to the arrival of Europeans, but they wouldn't recognize the place today. Surrounding the site is **Fairmont Hot Springs Resort,** comprising a four-star resort, golf courses, a ski resort, and an airstrip long enough to land a Boeing 737.

Despite all the commercialism, the hot springs are still the main attraction. Their appeal is simple; unlike most other springs, the hot water bubbling up from underground here contains calcium, not sulfur with its attendant smell. The pools are a magical experience, especially in the evening. Lazily swim or float around in the large warm pool, dive into the cool pool, or sit 'n' sizzle in the hot pool and watch the setting sun color the steep faces of the Canadian Rockies immediately behind the resort. Admission is

© ANDREW HEMPSTEAD

It's impossible to miss the Dutch Creek Hoodoos driving north from Canal Flats.

adult $7, child $5.50. For an additional fee, spa treatments, herbal wraps, and massages are offered. The pools are open daily 8 A.M.–10 P.M.

Most scenic of the resort's two 18-hole golf courses is **Riverside.** The course is relatively short, but multiple water hazards, including the Columbia River winding through the layout, create a challenge for all levels of golfer. The river, surrounding mountains, bunkers filled with pure-white silica, well-manicured fairways and greens, and an award-winning layout combine to make this one of Canada's best resort courses. Greens fees are $65 for 18 holes. The other course, **Mountainside,** meanders through the forest adjacent to the resort itself; greens fees are $55.

Behind the hot springs is **Fairmont Hot Springs Ski Area,** unique in western Canada in that access is restricted to resort guests. The terrain is limited to an area served by one chairlift and a platter, but the mountain vistas and the unique opportunity to soak in hot springs after a day on the slopes make a winter trip to Fairmont worthwhile. The resort also has a short half-pipe for snowboarders as well as rentals and a ski/snowboard school. The resort is laced with cross-country ski trails, and horse-drawn sleigh rides are offered whenever there's snow on the ground.

A lodge with upmarket accommodations and a campground make up the rest of the resort complex. Rooms in the lodge are $159–265 s or d, with the more expensive having a loft and kitchen. Discounted ski, golf, and spa packages are often available; check the website below. In the off-season, rooms go for less than $100. Campers have a choice of over 300 sites spread around tree-shaded grounds, all just a one-minute stroll from the hot pools. Unserviced sites are $18 while hookups range $23–36 (no tents), discounted outside of summer and open year-round. For all resort information and bookings call 250/345-6311 or 800/663-4979, website www.fairmontresort.com.

INVERMERE AND VICINITY

The next area to lure travelers off Highway 93/95 is **Windermere Lake.** Overlooking the lake, the town of **Invermere** (pop. 3,200) is the commercial center of the Columbia Valley. The lake and surrounding wilderness is a recreational playground, especially popular among landlocked Albertans. The area was the site of an 1807 post set up by David Thompson to trade with Kootenay natives (a small plaque along the road to Wilmer marks the exact spot), the first such trading post along the Columbia River. The first official town in the valley, known as Athalmer, was alongside the outlet of Lake Windermere, but continual flooding led to the town's expansion on higher ground. The original townsite is now a popular recreation area, where a pleasant grassy area dotted with picnic tables runs right down to a sandy beach and the warm, shallow waters of the lake. It's on the left as you travel along the Invermere access road. On the approach to town is **Windermere Valley Museum,** 622 Third St., 250/342-9769, where the entire history of the valley is contained in seven separate buildings. The main street itself (7th Avenue) is lined with restored heritage buildings and streetlights bedecked with hanging baskets overflowing with colorful flowers.

Panorama Resort

Recent years have seen a big push at promoting Panorama, in the Purcell Mountains immediately west of Invermere, as a year-round destination by its owners, Intrawest. The resort has a long way to go before becoming the "next Whistler," also owned by Intrawest, but Panorama Mountain Village, comprising a redeveloped base area, a residential subdivision, an open-air gondola to move visitors between the two main villages, a year-round water park, and a resort-style golf course, is just the first step in future plans. **Greywolf Golf Course,** which opened amid much fanfare for the summer of 1999, is a challenging 7,140 yards from the back tees, with water coming into play on 14 of the 18 holes, including the signature 6th hole, "the Cliffhanger," which requires an accurate tee shot across a narrow canyon to a green backed by towering cliffs. Greens fees are $105, dropping to $75 for twilight rates. Also during the warmer months, there are white-water rafting and inflatable kayak trips down Toby Creek, horseback riding, and, in the village itself, tennis and a swimming pool.

It was skiing that first put Panorama on the map, mainly due to the fact that the resort boasts the third-highest vertical rise of all North American winter resorts (1,200 meters), behind only Whistler/Blackcomb, also in British Columbia, and Big Sky, Montana. Despite the impressive relief, Panorama offers slopes suitable for all levels of expertise, including an additional 800 hectares that have opened since the 1995–96 season. Lift tickets are adult $48, child $32. For snow reports call 250/345-6413.

The village is also home to **R.K. Heli-ski,** 250/342-3889 or 800/661-6060, which operates out of its own "heli-plex," complete with a lounge and restaurant. The company is one of the few heli-ski operations that specialize in day trips. Their 135 named runs are spread through 2,000 square kg of the Purcell Mountains.

Purcell Wilderness Conservancy Provincial Park

If you take the road west from Invermere beyond Panorama Resort, you'll end up nine km from the boundary of Purcell Wilderness Conservancy, a 106,290-hectare wilderness straddling the heart of the rugged Purcell Mountains. No roads and few trails penetrate the preserve. The end of the road is the trailhead for a 61-km hike—up Toby Creek, over 2,256-meter Earl Grey Pass, and along the Hamill Creek watershed. The trail ends on Kootenay Lake, six km east of Highway 31, 40 km north of Kaslo.

Practicalities

Invermere holds motels, eateries, grocery stores, gas stations, a Greyhound bus depot, and a laundry. The motels downtown are a bit overpriced; the best option is **Delphine Lodge,** 250/342-6851, a couple of kg north in the historic village of Wilmer. Restored to its former glory, this 19th-century hotel has been converted to a boutique bed and breakfast. The six guest rooms share bathrooms but are comfortable, and guests have the use of a private garden, lounge, and library. Rates of $55 s, $65–80 d include breakfast. If you prefer motel-style lodging, **Best Western Invermere Inn,** 1310 7th Ave., 250/342-9246 or 800/661-8911, offers the best rooms in town, as well as a restaurant and bar; $95 s, $105 d. Accommodations in Panorama Mountain Village are all relatively new; they can be booked through the resort at 250/342-6941 or 800/663-2929, website www.panorama resort.com.

The usual array of fast-food joints line the access road into town, but Invermere is also home to **Strand's,** one of the best non-city restaurants in the province. It's contained in a restored heritage house, with diners seated in small intimate rooms and offered a seasonal menu that often includes delicacies such as trout, salmon, and venison. It's at 818 12th St. (up the hill from 7th Ave.), 250/342-6344, and opens daily at 5 P.M.

At the turnoff to town is **Invermere Visitor Info Centre,** 250/342-2844; open July–Aug. daily 9 A.M.–5 P.M. The website www.adventure valley.com provides information about local recreational opportunities.

Canadian Rockies

The highest peaks of the Canadian Rockies form British Columbia's eastern boundary, separating the province from neighboring Alberta. On the British Columbia side of the Canadian Rockies (often called the **BC Rockies**) are **Kootenay** and **Yoho National Parks** and the gateway towns of **Radium Hot Springs** and **Golden,** respectively. The two national parks may lack the bustling resort towns of their famous Albertan neighbors, Banff and Jasper, but they boast the same magnificent mountain vistas, glacially fed streams and rivers, unlimited hiking opportunities, and abundant wildlife.

Many factors combine to make the Canadian Rockies so beautiful. The peaks themselves exhibit drastically altered sedimentary layers visible from miles away, especially when accentuated by a particular angle of sunlight or a dusting of snow. Between the peaks lie numerous cirques—basins gouged into the mountains by glaciers. These cirques fill with glacial meltwater each spring, creating lakes that shimmer a trademark translucent green. And thanks to a climate that keeps the treeline low and the vegetation relatively sparse, fantastic views of the wide sweeping valleys are assured.

Encompassing close to 20,000 square kilometers of Mother Nature's finest offerings, Kootenay and Yoho, along with neighboring Banff and Jasper National Parks (both of which lie across the Continental Divide in Alberta) have been declared a World Heritage Site by UNESCO. For detailed coverage of

© PROVINCE OF BRITISH COLUMBIA

above Takakkaw Falls, Yoho National Park

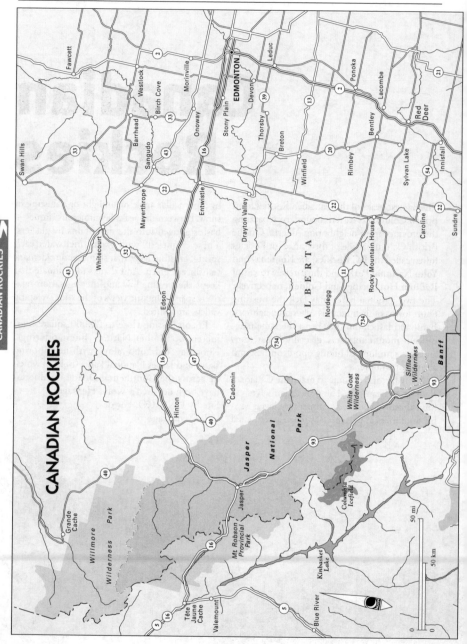

CANADIAN ROCKIES

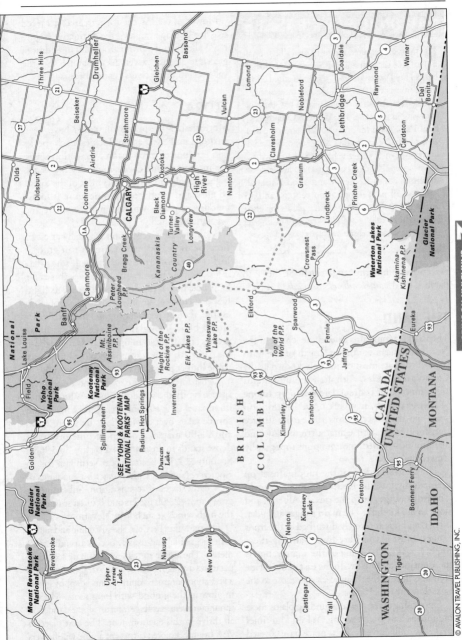

© AVALON TRAVEL PUBLISHING, INC.

CANADIAN ROCKIES

NATIONAL PARK PASSES

Permits are required for entry into all national parks of the Canadian Rockies. A **National Parks Day Pass** is adult $5, senior $4, child $2 to a maximum of $10 per vehicle. It is interchangeable between parks and valid until 4 P.M. the day following its purchase. The **Western Canada Annual Pass,** good for entry to all national parks west of Manitoba, is adult $35, senior $27 to a maximum of $70 per vehicle ($54 for two or more seniors). Both types of pass are available at the entrances to Kootenay and Yoho National Parks, at all park information centers, and at campground fee stations. Annual passes can also be bought by calling 800/748-7275 or online at the Parks Canada website, www.parkscanada.gc.ca.

the entire mountain range north of the 49th parallel, see *Moon Handbooks: Canadian Rockies.*

THE LAND

The Rocky Mountains extend the length of the North American continent; north of the 49th parallel they are most commonly known as the **Canadian Rockies.** Although the mountains are composed of bedrock laid down up to one billion years ago, it wasn't until 100 million years ago that forces below the earth's surface transformed western Canada from a lowland plain into the varied, mountainous topography seen today.

The western ridges of the mountains drop dramatically into the Rocky Mountain Trench. The **front ranges** lie to the east, in Alberta, and slope to the foothills. The **main ranges** are older, higher, and not as severely disturbed as the front ranges; most glaciers are found among these mighty peaks. The spine of the main range is the **Continental Divide.** To the east of the divide all waters flow to the Atlantic Ocean; those to the west flow into the Pacific.

Since rising above the surrounding plains these mountains have been eroding. At least four times in the last million years sheets of ice have covered much of the land, filling valleys and rounding

off lower peaks. As the ice retreated it carved massive U-shaped valleys, the distinctive Kootenay Valley being a prime example. In addition, glacial meltwater carved deep channels into the valleys, and many rivers changed course.

FLORA

More than 700 species of plants have been recorded in the Canadian Rockies. Each species falls into one of three distinct vegetation zones: the **montane zone** covers the valley floors; the higher **subalpine zone** covers most of the forested area; and the highest **alpine zone** is found among the peaks, where climate is severe and vegetation limited.

Montane-zone vegetation is usually at elevations below 1,350 meters, but it can grow at higher elevations on sun-drenched, south-facing slopes. As fires frequently affect this zone, lodgepole pine is the dominant species; its tightly sealed cones open only with the heat of a forest fire, thereby regenerating the species quickly after a blaze. Douglas fir is the zone's climax species and is found in open stands throughout the parks. Aspen is common in older burn areas, while limber pine thrives on rocky outcrops.

Dense forests of white spruce and Engelmann spruce typify the subalpine zone. White spruce dominates to 2,100 meters, while Engelmann spruce takes over at elevations between 2,100 and 2,400 meters. Lodgepole pine occurs in dense stands in areas affected by fire. In 1968 a fire burned 2,500 hectares near Vermilion Pass in Kootenay National Park; today it's a good area to view early stages of regeneration. Subalpine fir grows above 2,200 meters and is often stunted by the high winds at such lofty elevations.

The transition between the subalpine and alpine zones is gradual and usually occurs around 2,300 meters. The alpine zone's severe climate sees temperatures averaging below zero, strong winds, and a very short summer. Alpine plants adapt by growing low to the ground with long roots. Mosses, mountain avens, saxifrage, and an alpine dandelion all thrive in this environment. The best place to view brightly colored carpets of alpine wildflowers is Kindersley Summit in Kootenay National Park.

FAUNA

The Canadian Rockies provide a spectacular backdrop for viewing a great variety of mammals, many of which can be spotted from the roadside. Spring and fall are the best times of year for wildlife-viewing. The big-game animals have moved below the snow cover of the higher elevations and the crowds have thinned out. Winter also has its advantages. Although bears are hibernating, herds of elk winter at lower elevations, coyotes are often seen roaming around highways, bighorn sheep have descended from the heights, and wolf packs can occasionally be seen along Kootenay River Valley. In summer, with the onslaught of millions of visitors, the larger mammals tend to move away from the more heavily traveled tourist areas. It then becomes a case of knowing when and where to look for them.

Ungulates

Four species of deer inhabit the British Columbia side of the Canadian Rockies. Elk can be seen along the highways through Kootenay and Yoho National Parks. White-tailed deer can be seen throughout the mountains. Mule deer are less common but are easily recognized by their large floppy ears. Moose, although not common, can occasionally be seen feeding on aquatic plants along the major drainage systems.

In summer, mountain goats feed in alpine meadows. Unlike most large mountain-dwelling mammals, these surefooted creatures don't migrate to lower elevations in winter but stay sheltered on rocky crags where wind and sun keep the vegetation snow free. Often confused with the goat is the darker bighorn sheep. The thick horns on the males of this species often curl 360 degrees.

© ANDREW HEMPSTEAD

Besides people, elk are the most common large mammals in the Canadian Rockies.

Predators

Coyotes are widespread along all major valley corridors, where they find an abundance of small game. The lynx population fluctuates greatly; look for them in the backcountry during winter. Cougars, the largest local members of the cat family, are very shy. Wolves had been driven close to extinction by the early 1950s, but today at least 10 packs have been reported through the four contiguous parks of the Canadian Rockies.

Bears

Black bears are common in both national parks. They are most often spotted in spring, when they first come out of hibernation. At that point, snow blankets much of the mountains and the bears are forced to lower elevations to feed, often along the edge of the highway.

During late spring grizzlies are occasionally seen crossing highways at higher elevations. For the most part they remain in remote mountain valleys, and if they do see, smell, or hear you they'll generally move away.

The chance of encountering a bear face-to-face in the backcountry is remote. To lessen chances of an encounter even further, follow these simple precautions: never hike alone or at dusk; make lots of noise when passing through heavy vegetation; keep a clean camp; and read the pamphlets available at all park information centers. At each center, daily trail reports list recent bear sightings. Report any bears you see to the nearest park information center.

Birds

Over 200 species of birds have been recorded in the area, but most are shy and live in heavily wooded areas. One species that definitely isn't shy is the gray jay. This fearless marauder haunts campgrounds and picnic areas, scavenging food right off your picnic table. Similar in color, but larger, is the **Clark's nutcracker,** which lives in higher, subalpine forests. Other common residents include the jet-black raven and the black-and-white magpie.

Several species of grouse inhabit the area. Most common is the downy ruffled grouse, seen in montane forest. The blue grouse and spruce grouse are found at higher elevations, as is the white-tailed ptarmigan, which lives above the treeline (watch for them along higher elevations of the Stanley Glacier Trail in Kootenay National Park). **Woodpeckers** can often be heard drilling for dinner in the subalpine forests.

Radium Hot Springs and Vicinity

One of two main western gateways to the Canadian Rockies is the small town of Radium Hot Springs (pop. 700), which lies at the junction of Highways 93 and 95, 140 km north of Cranbrook and a spectacular two-hour drive through Kootenay National Park from the famous resort town of Banff. Its setting is spectacular; most of town lies on benchlands above the Columbia River, from where the panoramic views take in the Rockies to the east and the Purcell Mountains to the west. As well as providing accommodations and other services for mountain visitors and highway travelers, Radium is a destination in itself for many. Aside from the town's namesake (see Kootenay National Park, below), the area boasts a wildlife-rich wetland, two excellent golf courses, and many other recreational opportunities.

SIGHTS AND RECREATION

Columbia River Wetland

Radium sits in the Rocky Mountain Trench, which has been carved over millions of years by the Columbia River. From its headwaters south of Radium, the Columbia flows northward through a 180-km-long wetland to Golden, continuing north for a similar distance before reversing course and flowing south into the United States. The wetland by Radium holds international significance, not only for its size (26,000 hectares and up to two km wide), but for the sheer concentration of wildlife it supports. Over 100 species of birds live among the sedges, grasses, dogwoods, and black cottonwoods surrounding the convoluted banks of the Columbia. Of special interest are blue herons in large numbers and ospreys in one of the world's highest concentrations. The wetland also lies along the Pacific Flyway, so particularly large numbers of ducks, Canada geese, and other migratory birds gather here in spring and autumn.

The **Wings over the Rockies Bird Festival** celebrates northbound spring migration the first week of May in conjunction with International Migratory Bird Day. The festival features ornithologist speakers, field trips on foot and by boat, workshops, and events tailored especially for children, all of which take place throughout the valley. For details call 888/933-3311.

Golfing

Radium Hot Springs supports two golf courses and is marketed around western Canada as a golfing destination. Aside from the excellent resort-style courses and stunning Canadian Rockies scenery, golfers here enjoy the area's mild climate. Warm temperatures allow golfing as early as April and as late as October—a longer season than is typical at other mountain courses.

The 36-hole **Radium Resort** is a highlight of golfing the Columbia River Valley, comprising two very different courses. One of them, the 6,767-yard, par-72 Springs Course, is generally regarded as one of the province's top 10 resort courses. It lies between the town and steep cliffs that descend to the Columbia River far below. Immaculately groomed fairways following the land's natural contours, near-perfect greens, and over 70 bunkers filled with imported sand do little to take away from the surrounding mountainscape. Greens fees are a Canadian Rockies bargain at $60 for 18 holes (discounted to $55 midweek). Call 250/347-6200 or 800/667-6444 for tee times. The resort's second course, the Radium Course, is much shorter (5,300 yards and par 69), but tighter and still challenging. It is nestled in the shadow of the Rockies to the south of Radium, circling the resort's other facilities, which include accommodations (see below) and tennis courts. For tee times, call 250/347-6266 or 800/667-6444.

Other Recreation

Radium is a base of operations for recreation opportunities outside the park. White-water rafting trips are offered by **Kootenay River Runners,** 250/347-9210; from $68 for a half-day trip, $105 full-day. Horse fanciers can rent a ride at **Longhorn Stables,** one km north of town, 250/347-9755.

CANADIAN ROCKIES

ACCOMMODATIONS AND CAMPING

Radium, despite its small population, has over 30 motels, an indication of its importance as a highway stop for overnight travelers. Radium's main strip of motels is along the access road to Kootenay National Park. Each comes alive with color in summer, trying to outdo the other with floral landscaping.

$50–100

Kootenay Motel is along Hwy. 93, up the hill from the junction of Hwy. 95, 250/347-9490 or 877/908-2020. The rooms are very basic (but air-conditioned) and rent from $48 s, $55 d, $10 extra for a kitchenette. Also on-site is a barbecue area and pleasant gazebo.

Up the hill a little, across the road, and similarly priced, is **Valley View Motel,** 250/347-9565 or 800/688-6138, with a pleasant outdoor barbecue area; from $60 s, $65 d.

Back across the road from the Valley View is the **Alpen Motel,** 250/347-9823 or 888/788-3891, website www.alpenmotel.com, which is probably the best-value accommodation in town (and arguably has the best and brightest flowers out front).

The rooms are modern and the rates right; $69 s or d in spring and fall and $89 s or d in summer. The Alpen is closed Nov.–February.

Continuing toward the national park entrance is the **Gables Motel,** Hwy. 93, 250/347-9866 or 877/387-7007, where each of the smallish rooms has mountain views and is well-furnished; $79 s or d.

A number of older motels lie in the residential streets west of Hwy. 93/95. Least expensive is the **Ritz Motel,** 4883 Stanley St., 250/347-9644 or 877/347-9644. It's an older motel but the rooms are large, with separate sleeping areas. Some have kitchens and are air-conditioned. Rates range $50–60 s, $55–65 d.

Although it has undergone renovations, the **Pinewood Motel,** 4870 Stanley St., 250/347-9529 or 888/557-5567, still offers rooms at a reasonable $60–70 s or d; $75 with a kitchen.

The best of the bunch on the west side of the highway is the **Park Inn,** 4873 Stanley St., 250/347-9582 or 800/858-1155, website www.parkinn.bc.ca, which features an indoor pool and a covered barbecue area. Standard rooms are $70 s, $75 d, while those with kitchenettes are $80 s, $85 d.

Over $100

South of town, **Radium Resort,** 250/347-9311 or 800/667-6444, website www.radiumresort.com, features two 18-hole golf courses as well as a health club, indoor pool, restaurant, and lounge. Regular motel rooms range $160–190, while kitchen-equipped condos sleeping up to six people start at $240 per night. Golf, ski, and spa packages lower rates considerably, especially before and after summer's peak season.

Radium's newest accommodation, the **Prestige Inn,** opened for the 2001 summer season right at the town's main intersection at 7493 Main St. W, 250/347-2300 or 877/737-8443, website www.prestigeinn.com. Facilities include a fitness room, indoor pool, spa services, a restaurant, and a lounge bar. Summer rates are from $219 s or d, but these rates are almost halved in winter.

Camping

Within Kootenay National Park, but accessed from Highway 93/95, is **Redstreak Campground** (see Kootenay National Park, below). The closest commercial camping is at **Canyon RV Resort,** on Hwy. 95, 300 meters north of the Hwy. 93/95 junction, 250/347-9564, website www.canyon-rv.com. Sites are spread along a pleasant creek, and all facilities are provided; $20–25 per night. **Spur Valley Resort,** 18 km north of Radium along Hwy. 95, 250/347-9822, has sites set around a large grassy area; $15–20 per night, self-contained cabins $64. Recreation facilities include a nine-hole golf course and tennis courts.

FOOD

The town of Radium Hot Springs holds several good choices for a food break. Give all the fast-food places out by the highway junction a miss and head to **Springs at Radium Restaurant,** at the golf course on Stanley St. (on the west side of the highway), 250/347-9311. The view from the deck, overlooking the Columbia River and Purcell Mountains, is nothing short of stunning. The food is good and remarkably inexpensive; in the morning, for example, an omelet with hash browns and toast is just $7.50. Lunch and dinner are also well priced, with a massive Caesar salad for $6.50 and main meals $10–18.50.

Back in town, **Back Country Jack's,** Main St. W, 250/347-0097, serves up steak, ribs, and chicken. And Jack's delivers anywhere in Radium. Across the road, **Horsethief Creek Pub and Eatery,** Main St. E, 250/347-6400, serves up

good pub-style fare. As always, **Husky House Restaurant,** at the corner of Highways 93 and 95, 250/347-9811, offers diners a good solid menu of typical Canadian fare at reasonable prices. This one is open daily 6:30 A.M.–10:30 P.M. Just around the corner is **Screamer's,** the place to hang out with an ice cream on a hot summer's afternoon.

INFORMATION

On the east side of Highway 93/95 and at the south end of the commercial strip is **Radium**

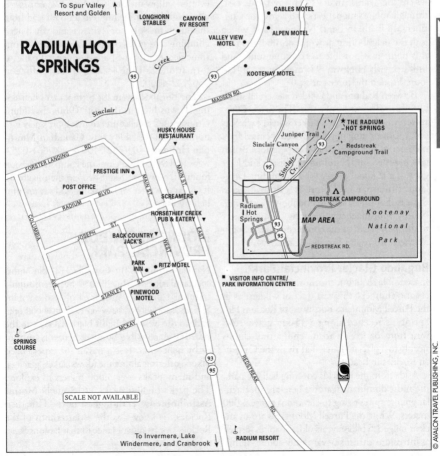

© AVALON TRAVEL PUBLISHING, INC.

CANADIAN ROCKIES

Hot Springs Visitor Info Centre, 250/347-9331 or 800/347-9704, website www.rhs.bc.ca. This building is also home to the national park information center. It's open weekdays year-round and in the busier summer months Mon.–Thurs. 9 A.M.–5 P.M., Friday 9 A.M.–8 P.M., Sat.–Sun. 10 A.M.–6 P.M.

NORTH FROM RADIUM ALONG HIGHWAY 95

From Radium, most travelers head into Kootenay National Park (see below), but another option is to continue north for 105 km to Golden, from where the TransCanada Highway heads east, through Yoho National Park and across the Continental Divide to Banff National Park, which is in the neighboring province of Alberta. From this point it is possible to continue south and link up with Highway 93, making a 350-km loop through the three parks.

Between Radium and Golden are several small, historic towns worthy of a stop. The first is **Edgewater,** where a farmers' market is held each Saturday. Continuing north is **Brisco.** Named for a member of the 1859 Palliser expedition, Brisco was founded on the mining industry and later grew as a regional center for surrounding farmland. Brisco General Store is a throwback to those earlier times, selling just about everything. Nearby **Spillimacheen,** meaning "White-water" to the natives, sits at the confluence of the Spillimacheen River and Bugaboo Creek.

Bugaboo Glacier Provincial Park

Inaccessible to all but the most experienced hikers and climbers, this vast tract of wilderness in the Purcell Mountains northwest of Radium Hot Springs is reached along a 45-km gravel road west from Brisco. At road's end, a trail climbs steeply to a glaciated area that rivals the Canadian Rockies in beauty.

Aside from the icefields covering half the park, the most dominant features here are spectacular granite spires rising to elevations above 3,000 meters. While the Purcell Mountains are an ancient range 1.5 billion years old, the spires formed as intrusions thrust skyward only about 70 mil-

lion years ago. Since then, erosion has shaped them into today's granite needles towering over the surrounding icefields.

For nearly 100 years the Bugaboos have been a mecca for climbers, but first ascents have been made as recently as the 1970s. In 1972, the Alpine Club of Canada built the **Conrad Kain Hut** as a base for hikers and climbers wanting to explore the park. The hut, equipped with stoves and bunk beds for 50 people, is named for the first mountaineer to climb the highest spire. It's a strenuous five-km hike from the end of the road, up a valley carved by the retreating Bugaboo Glacier. The trail gains around 700 meters in elevation; allow at least two hours. Camping is also possible near the hut. No set trails lead from the hut to the spires or icefields, and you'll need climbing and glacier-travel experience to continue deeper into the park. For general park information, call the local BC Parks office at 250/422-4200.

The Bugaboos were the birthplace of heli-skiing. It was here in the mid-1960s that Hans Gmoser used a helicopter to transport skiers into normally inaccessible areas. **Canadian Mountain Holidays,** 403/762-7100 or 800/661-0252, website www.cmhski.com, the company Gmoser founded, now has a lodge deep in the Bugaboos. It's open in winter for heli-skiing and summer for heli-hiking.

MOUNT ASSINIBOINE PROVINCIAL PARK

Named for one of the Canadian Rockies' most spectacular peaks, this 39,050-hectare, roughly triangular park lies northeast of Radium Hot Springs, sandwiched between Kootenay National Park to the west and Banff National Park to the east. It's inaccessible by road; access is on foot or by helicopter. It is a haven for experienced hikers, offering alpine meadows, lakes, glaciers, and many peaks over 3,000 meters to explore. The park's highest peak, 3,618-meter **Mount Assiniboine** (seventh-highest in the Canadian Rockies), is known as the "Matterhorn of the Rockies" for its resemblance to that famous Swiss landmark.

The peak is named for the Assiniboine people, who ventured into this section of the Canadian Rockies many thousands of years prior to European exploration. The mountain was sighted and named by a geological survey team in 1885, but it wasn't until 1901 that the first ascent was made.

Lake Magog is the destination of most park visitors. Here you'll find the park's only facilities and the trailheads for interesting and varied day hikes. One of the most popular walks is the Sunburst Valley/Nub Ridge. From Lake Magog, small Sunburst Lake is reached in about 20 minutes, then the trail continues in a northwesterly direction for a short distance to Cerulean Lake. From the lake's outlet, the trail descends slowly along the Mitchell River to a point four km from Lake Magog. At this point, take the right fork, which climbs through a dense subalpine forest to Elizabeth Lake, nestled in the southern shadow of Nub Peak, the southern end of a high ridge that extends northward to Nestor Peak. From this point, instead of descending back to Cerulean Lake, take the Nub Ridge trail, which climbs steadily for one km to a magnificent viewpoint high above Lake Magog. From this point it's just under four km, downhill all the way, to the valley floor. The total length of this outing is 11 km, and as elevation gained is only just over 400 meters, the trail can be completed in four comfortable hours.

Mount Assiniboine is named for the Assiniboine people, who ventured into this section of the Canadian Rockies many thousands of years prior to European exploration. The mountain was sighted and named by a geological survey team in 1885, but it wasn't until 1901 that the first ascent was made.

Approaching the Park on Foot
Three trails provide access to **Lake Magog,** the park's largest body of water. The most popular comes in from the northeast, starting at Sunshine Village in Banff National Park and leading 29 km via Citadel Pass to the lake. Not only is this trail spectacular, but the relatively high elevation of the trailhead (2,100 meters) makes for a less strenuous approach. Another approach is from the east, in Kananaskis Country (Alberta). The trailhead is at the southern end of Spray Lake;

take the Mt. Shark turnoff 38 km south of Canmore. By the time the trail has climbed the Bryant Creek drainage to 2,165-meter Assiniboine Pass, all elevation gain (450 meters) has been made. At 27 km, this is the shortest approach, but its elevation gain is greater than that of the other two trails. The longest and least-used access is from Highway 93 at Simpson River in Kootenay National Park. This trail climbs the Simpson River and Surprise Creek drainages and crosses 2,270-meter Ferro Pass to the lake for a total length of 32 km.

The Easy Way In
If these long approaches put visiting the park out of your reach, there's one more option: you can fly in by helicopter from the Mt. Shark Helipad, across the border in Alberta at the southern end of Spray Lake, Kananaskis Country. Helicopter access is restricted to Wednesday, Friday, and Sunday. Those staying at the lodge pay $100 per person each way, including a 30-pound per person baggage limit, while campers pay $110 per person each way with a 40-pound baggage limit. **Alpine Helicopters,** 403/678-4802, operates the flights, but bookings (including for campers) must be made through Mt. Assiniboine Lodge, 403/678-2883, Mon.–Fri 8 A.M.–2 P.M. If you're planning on hiking into the park, Alpine Helicopters will fly your gear in for $1.50 per pound.

Park Practicalities
Lake Magog is the park's main facility area. Not that the park offers *that* many facilities. A designated camping area on a low ridge above the lake's west shore provides a source of drinking water and pit toilets. Open fires are prohibited. Sites are $5 per person per night. Also at the lake are the **Naiset Cabins,** $15 per person per night (no bookings taken). **Mt. Assiniboine Lodge,** 403/678-2883, was built in 1928 by the Canadian Pacific Railway and is owned by

BC Parks but managed privately. Sleeping up to 30 people in six rooms and six cabins, accommodations are rustic but comfortable, and the rate of $170–220 per person per day includes all meals.

The best source of pre-trip planning is the BC Parks website, www.elp.gov.bc.ca/bcparks. The local BC Parks district office can be contacted at 250/442-4200. For information on the condition of trails leading into the park, drop by the Kootenay, Lake Louise, or Banff park information centers.

Kootenay NationalPark

Shaped like a lightning bolt, this narrow 140,600-hectare park lies northeast of Radium Hot Springs, bordered to the east by Banff National Park and Mount Assiniboine Provincial Park and to the north by Yoho National Park. Highway 93, extending for 94 km through the park, provides spectacular mountain vistas, and along the route you'll find many short and easy interpretive hikes, scenic viewpoints, hot springs, picnic areas, and roadside interpretive exhibits. The park isn't particularly noted for its day-hiking opportunities, but backpacker destinations such as Kaufmann Lake and the Rockwall rival almost any other area in the Canadian Rockies.

Day-use areas, a gas station and lodge, and three campgrounds are the only roadside services inside the park; Radium Hot Springs, at the junction of Highways 93 and 95 (see above), is the park's main service center. The park is open year-round, although you should check road conditions in winter, when avalanche-control work and snowstorms can close Highway 93 for short periods of time.

THE LAND

Kootenay National Park, on the western side of the Continental Divide, straddles the Main and Western Ranges of the Canadian Rockies. As elsewhere in the Canadian Rockies, the geology of the park is complex. Over the last 70 million years, these mountains have been pushed upward—folded and faulted along the way—by massive forces deep beneath the earth's surface. They've also been subject to erosion that entire time, particularly during the ice ages, when glaciers carved U-shaped valleys and high cirques into the landscape. These features, along with glacial lakes and the remnants of the glaciers themselves, are readily visible in the park today.

The park protects the upper headwaters of the **Vermilion** and **Kootenay Rivers,** which drain into the Columbia River south of the park.

Flora

In the lowest areas of the park, in the Kootenay River Valley, Douglas fir and lodgepole pine find a home. Along the upper stretches of the Vermilion River Valley, where the elevation is higher, Engelmann spruce thrive, while immediately above lie forests of subalpine fir. The treeline in the park is around 2,000 meters above sea level. This is the alpine, where low-growing species such as willow and heather predominate. For a short period each summer, these elevations come alive with color as forget-me-nots, avens, and avalanche lilies flower. Of special interest is the Vermilion Pass Burn, where fire destroyed 24 square km of forest in 1968. Lodgepole pine is the dominant species here.

Fauna

Large mammals tend to remain in the Kootenay and Vermilion River Valleys. White-tailed deer, mule deer, moose, black bears, and elk live year-round at these lower elevations, as do bighorn sheep, which can be seen at mineral licks along Highway 93. The park's population of grizzlies currently numbers around 10; they generally remain in the backcountry but are occasionally sighted in spring high on roadside avalanche slopes.

HISTORY

Although their traditional home was along the river valley to the south, the indigenous Kootenay people regularly came to this area to enjoy the hot springs—a meeting place for mountain and plains bands. Natives called the springs Kootemik, meaning "Place of Hot Water." Early European visitors warped "Kootemik" into "Kootenay" and applied the name to the local residents. The natives traveled as far east as the Paint Pots area, to collect ocher for ceremonial painting purposes.

In 1905 Randolph Bruce, an Invermere businessman, persuaded the Canadian government and Canadian Pacific Railway to build a road linking the Columbia River Valley to the prairie transportation hub of Calgary so that western produce could get out to eastern markets. Construction of the difficult **Banff-Windermere Road** began in 1911. But with three mountain ranges to negotiate and deep, fast-flowing rivers to cross, the money ran out after the completion of only 22 km. To get the highway project going again, the provincial government agreed to hand over an eight-km-wide section of land along both sides of the proposed highway to the federal government. In return, the federal government agreed to finance completion of the highway. Originally called the Highway Park, the land became known as Kootenay National Park in 1920. The highway was finally completed in 1922, and the official ribbon-cutting ceremony was held at Kootenay Crossing in 1923; a plaque marks the spot.

> *Although their traditional home was along the river valley to the south, the indigenous Kootenay people regularly came to this area to enjoy the hot springs—a meeting place for mountain and plains bands. Natives called the springs Kootemik, meaning "Place of Hot Water." Early European visitors warped "Kootemik" into "Kootenay."*

DRIVING HIGHWAY 93

Climbing eastward from the town of Radium Hot Springs, Highway 93 (still known locally as the Banff-Windermere Highway) enters the boundary of Kootenay National Park at narrow Sinclair Canyon, a natural gateway to the wonders beyond. After squeezing through the canyon, the highway emerges at the actual springs that give the town of Radium Hot Springs its name.

Radium Hot Springs

This was a popular destination for the early Kootenay people, who, like today's visitors, came to enjoy the odorless mineral water that gushes out of the foot of Redstreak Mountain at 44° C (111° F) three km northeast of the town of the same name. Englishman Roland Stuart purchased the springs for $160 in 1890 and built rough concrete pools to contain the water. Development continued when a visiting millionaire—impressed by the improvement in his paralysis after soaking in the springs—contributed more money to the project. Originally known as Sinclair Hot Springs, after an early settler, the name was changed to Radium in 1915 for the high level of radioactivity in the water. With the declaration of Kootenay National Park in 1922, ownership reverted to the government.

Today, the water is diverted from its natural course into the commercial pools, including one that is Canada's largest. Steep cliffs tower directly above the hot pool, whose waters are colored a milky blue by dissolved salts, which include calcium bicarbonate and sulfates of calcium, magnesium, and sodium. The hot pool (39° C, 97° F) is particularly stimulating in winter, when it's edged by snow and covered in steam—your head is almost cold in the chill air, but your submerged body melts into oblivion.

The entire complex saw multiyear renovations through the second half of the 1990s, which included relining the pools, upgrading surrounding facilities, constructing an observation deck by the source of the springs, and relocating the main park information center. Summer hours are daily 9 A.M.–11 P.M., the rest of the year noon–9 P.M.

CANADIAN ROCKIES

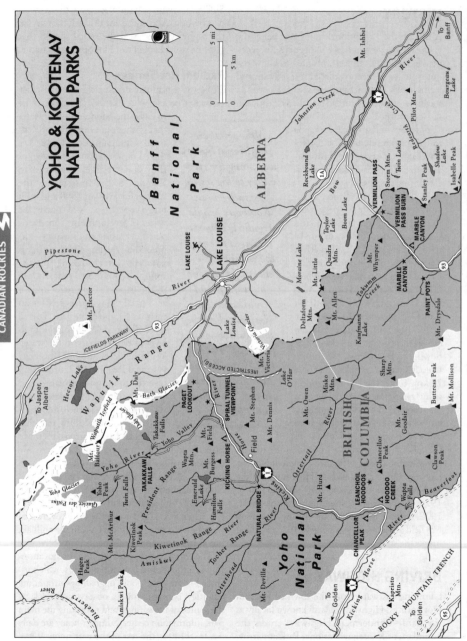

YOHO & KOOTENAY
NATIONAL PARKS

5 mi

5 km

0

Banff National Park

ALBERTA

Pipestone River

To Banff

Mt. Ishbel

Johnston Creek

Bow River

Pilot Mtn.

Bourgeau Lake

Rockbound Lake

1A

VERMILION PASS

Storm Mtn.

Twin Lakes

Shadow Lake

Isabelle Peak

Stanley Peak

VERMILION PASS BURN

MARBLE CANYON

93

Taylor Lake

Boom Lake

Quadra Mtn.

Mt. Whymper

MARBLE CANYON

Moraine Lake

Mt. Little

Mt. Allen

Tokumm Creek

PAINT POTS

Mt. Drysdale

LAKE LOUISE

LAKE LOUISE

Lake Louise

Victoria Glacier

Mt. Victoria

Deltaform Mtn.

Kaufmann Lake

Mt. Hector

ICEFIELDS PARKWAY

93

Bow River

Hector Lake

Waputik Range

To Jasper, Alberta

Mt. Daly

Bath Glacier

PAGET LOOKOUT

SPIRAL TUNNEL VIEWPOINT

Mt. Stephen

Mt. Dennis

Mt. Owen

Ottertail River

Sharp Mtn.

Mt. Goodsir

Buttress Peak

Mt. Mollison

BRITISH COLUMBIA

Misko Mtn.

Lake O'Hara

(RESTRICTED ACCESS)

Kicking Horse River

Waputik Icefield

Mt. Balfour

Daly Glacier

Takakkaw Falls

Yoho Valley

Mt. Field

Mt. Burgess

KICKING HORSE

Wapta Mtn.

TAKAKKAW FALLS

President Range

Yoho Peak

Twin Falls

Yoho Glacier

Glacier des Poilus

Mt. McArthur

Kiwetinok Peak

Hagen Peak

Amiskwi Peak

Emerald Lake

Hamilton Falls

NATURAL BRIDGE

Field

Kiwetinok Range

Tocher Range

Otterhead River

Amiskwi River

Mt. Deville

Yoho National Park

Mt. Hurd

LEANCHOIL HOODOOS

HOODOO CREEK

CHANCELLOR PEAK

Chancellor Peak

Clawson Peak

Wapta Falls

Beaverfoot River

Kicking Horse River

To Golden

Kapristo Mtn.

To Golden/Radium

ROCKY MOUNTAIN TRENCH

95

Blackberry River

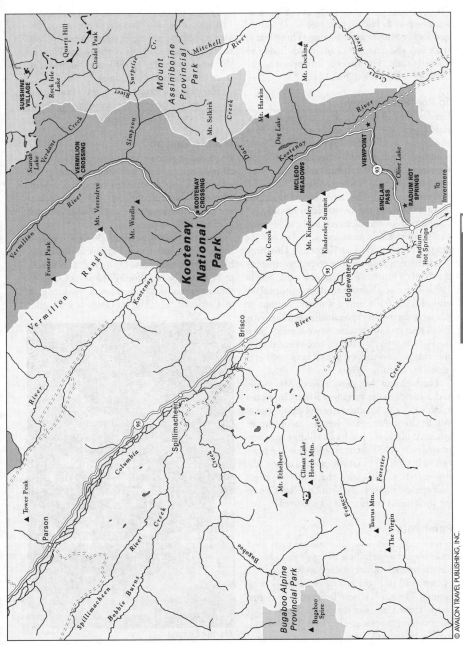

© AVALON TRAVEL PUBLISHING, INC.

CANADIAN ROCKIES

Admission is $6 for adults (day pass $8.25), $5 for seniors and children (day pass $7.25). Towel and locker rentals are available. Three hiking trails link the complex to the park's Redstreak Campground. For springs information, call 250/347-9485 or 800/767-1611.

To Kootenay Valley

Leaving the hot springs, the road parallels Sinclair Creek, crests 1,486-meter Sinclair Pass, and passes small Olive Lake, which is ringed with bright yellow wildflowers in summer. At **Kootenay River Viewpoint** a splendid view overlooks the wild Kootenay River Valley 250 vertical meters below and the snowcapped mountains along the Continental Divide.

The highway then descends to the valley floor, passes two riverside picnic areas, and crosses the pretty Kootenay River at **Kootenay Crossing.** The official ribbon-cutting ceremony opening the Banff-Windermere Road took place here in 1923. Today you'll find a roadside historical exhibit, hiking trails, and a warden's station. As you cross the river and pass small, green Kootenay Pond, your eyes will revel in views of milky-green rivers, lush grassy meadows, tree-covered hills, and craggy, snowcapped peaks; keep your eyes peeled for mountain goats.

The highway then climbs over a low saddle and descends to the Vermilion River. On the descent, you'll pass a particularly nice picnic spot at Wardle Creek. Across the river, the mountainside is scarred black, the result of a wildfire that devastated over 4,000 hectares of forest in the summer of 2001. Left to take its natural course, the fire spread south along the Simpson River drainage and down to the Vermilion River, burning itself out as the first winter snow fell.

Paint Pots

A scenic one-km trail (20 minutes each way) leads over the Vermilion River to this unique natural wonder: three circular ponds stained red, orange, and mustard yellow by oxide-bearing springs. The natives, who believed that animal spirits resided in these springs, collected ocher from around the pools. They mixed it with animal fat or fish oil then used it in ceremonial body- and rock-painting. The ocher had a spiritual association and was used in important rituals. Europeans, seeing an opportunity to "add to the growing economy of the nation," mined the ocher in the early 1900s and shipped it to paint manufacturers in Calgary.

Several much longer hiking trails lead off the Paint Pots trail, including one of many routes to the Rockwall (see Hiking, below).

Marble Canyon

Be sure to stop and take the enjoyable self-guided trail, one km each way, that leads along this ice-carved, marble-streaked canyon. The walk takes only about 30 minutes or so, yet, as one of several interpretive plaques says, it takes you back over 500 million years.

From the parking lot, the trail follows a fault in the limestone and marble bedrock through Marble Canyon, which has been eroded to depths of 37 meters by fast-flowing Tokumm Creek. As the canyon narrows, water roars down through it in a series of falls. The trail ends at a splendid

© ANDREW HEMPSTEAD

Marble Canyon

viewpoint where a natural rock arch spans a gorge. Marble Canyon is also the trailhead for the Kaufmann Lake Trail (see below).

East to the Continental Divide

Continuing eastward from Marble Canyon, Highway 93 climbs steadily to the **Vermilion Pass Burn.** Lightning started the fire that roared through this area in 1968, destroying thousands of hectares of trees. Lodgepole pine, which requires the heat of a fire to release its seeds, and fireweed were the first plant species to sprout up through the charred ground. From the highway everything seems pretty dead, but along the 0.8-km **Fireweed Trail** you'll see the growth of a new forest on the floor of the old.

The burn area is immediately west of the Continental Divide, which the highway crosses at an elevation of 1,640 meters. The divide marks the border between Kootenay National Park to the west and Banff National Park in Alberta to the east. From the divide, it's 11 km to Highway 1, from which point the Town of Banff lies 29 km southeast and Lake Louise lies 27 km northwest.

HIKING

Some 200 km of trails lace Kootenay National Park. Hiking opportunities range from short interpretive walks (see Sights, above) to challenging treks through remote backcountry. All trails start from Highway 93 on the valley floor, so a strenuous climb is required to reach the park's high alpine areas, especially those in the south. For this reason, many hikes require an overnight stay in the backcountry.

Juniper Trail

- Length: 3.2 km (one hour) round-trip
- Elevation gain: 90 meters
- Rating: easy

Named for the abundance of juniper along one section, this trail traverses a variety of terrain in a relatively short distance. You'll pass Sinclair Creek, an avalanche slope, and a lookout offering views of the Windermere Valley and the Purcell Mountains. The trail begins on the north side of the road just beyond the park information center

and rejoins the highway 1.5 km farther into the park. There you can retrace your steps back to the start or return along the highway.

Kindersley Summit

- Length: 10 km (four hours) one-way
- Elevation gain: 1,050 meters
- Rating: difficult

The elevation gain on this strenuous day hike will be a deterrent for many, but views from the summit make up for the pain endured along the way. The trailhead is 10 km up Highway 93 from the park's west gate. From this point the trail climbs through a valley for about three km, then switchbacks up across avalanche paths and through more forest before emerging at an alpine meadow on Kindersley Pass. The final two-km slog gets you 200 meters higher, to an elevation of 2,400 meters at Kindersley Summit, a saddle between two slightly higher peaks. This is where the scenery makes the journey worthwhile. You'll enjoy views west to the Purcell Mountains, east to the Continental Divide, and, most spectacularly, north over the Kootenay River Valley. An alternate return route to the valley floor follows Sinclair Creek down from Kindersley Summit. This cuts a couple of km off the return distance.

Dog Lake

- Length: 2.6 km (40 minutes) one-way
- Elevation gain: 80 meters
- Rating: easy

Dog Lake is no Mona Lisa, but it is a popular and easily reached destination, especially for those staying in McLeod Meadows Campground (if you're not camping, park at the picnic area 500 meters to the south). The trail first crosses the wide Kootenay River by footbridge. Then it hops a low ridge over to the shallow lake, which is fringed by marshes at the north end.

Floe Lake

- Length: 10.4 km (3.5 hours) one-way
- Elevation gain: 730 meters
- Rating: moderate-difficult

Of all the lakes in Kootenay National Park, this would have to be the most beautiful. Unfortunately, reaching it requires a strenuous day trip or

CANADIAN ROCKIES

CANADIAN ROCKIES

an overnight expedition. From the parking lot 70 km up Highway 93 from Radium Hot Springs, the trail follows Floe Creek, ascending the watershed through a forest of lodgepole pine and making many switchbacks before leveling off 400 meters before the lake. Nestled in a glacial cirque, the gemlike lake's aquamarine waters reflect the Rockwall, a sheer limestone wall rising 1,000 meters above the far shore. In fall, stands of stunted larch around the lakeshore turn brilliant colors, adding to the incredible beauty.

The Rockwall

- Length: 54 km (three days) round-trip
- Elevation gain: 760 meters
- Rating: moderate-difficult

This is one of the classic hikes in all the Canadian Rockies. The Rockwall is a 30-km-long east-facing escarpment that rises over 1,000 meters from an alpine environment. Four different routes provide access to the spectacular feature;

The trail to Dog Lake takes about 40 minutes each way.

© ANDREW HEMPSTEAD

each begins along Highway 93 and traverses a steep valley to the Rockwall's base.

The most popular trail starts at the Paint Pots and follows Helmet Creek 12 km to spectacular 365-meter Helmet Falls. A further 2.4 km takes you to the beginning of the Rockwall trail and a campground, the first of five along the route. The trail then follows the Rockwall in a southeasterly direction for 30 km, passing magnificent glaciers, waterfalls, and lakes before ending at Floe Lake (see above), 10.4 km from the highway.

The Tumbling Creek and Numa Creek drainages provide alternative access routes to the Rockwall and require similar elevation gains. The elevation gain noted above is for the initial climb from the highway; along the route ascents are made to four additional passes, with elevation gains ranging 280–830 meters. Hikers will need to make arrangements for shuttle transportation between the beginning and end of this route—about 13 km apart—or allow extra time to hike back.

As elsewhere in the park, all hikers spending the night in the backcountry must register and pick up a permit ($6 per person per night) at either of the park information centers.

Kaufmann Lake

- Length: 15 km (five hours) one-way
- Elevation gain: 570 meters
- Rating: moderate

The overnight backpack trip to this beautiful lake in the extreme north end of the park begins at Marble Canyon parking lot. The trail follows Tokumm Creek the entire distance, passing through a forest of lodgepole pine before entering an open meadow and crossing many small waterways. Most elevation gain is made in the final two km, as the trail switchbacks up to the glacial cirque holding Kaufmann Lake. Peaks jutting as high as 3,400 meters surround the exquisite lake. Two campgrounds lie at the end of the trail.

Stanley Glacier

- Length: 4.6 km (two hours) one-way
- Elevation gain: 365 meters
- Rating: moderate

Although this glacier is no more spectacular than

those alongside the Icefields Parkway just a few km away, the sense of achievement of traveling on foot makes this trail well worth the effort. From the trailhead on Highway 93, three km west of the park's eastern boundary, the trail crosses the higher reaches of the Vermilion River. It passes through an area burned by devastating fires in 1968 and climbs steadily until reaching a narrow rock-filled basin and the main glacier viewpoint. It's possible to continue another km up the valley to within 500 meters of the glacier's toe, but the going gets rough.

PRACTICALITIES
Kootenay Park Lodge
This small lodge at Vermilion Crossing, 65 km from Radium Hot Springs, 403/762-9196, website www.kootenayparklodge.com, is the only accommodation in the heart of the park. Although no railway passes through the park, the lodge was built by the CPR in 1923. It consists of 10 log cabins, a restaurant, a gas station/grocery store, and an information center. Each rustic cabin has a bathroom, small fridge, and a coffeemaker; rates range $85–105, depending on cabin size. The lodge is open mid-May to September.

Camping
The park's largest camping area is **Redstreak Campground** in the extreme southwest (vehicle access from Hwy. 93/95 on the south side of Radium Hot Springs township), which holds 242 sites, showers, and kitchen shelters. Trails lead from the campground to the hot springs, town, and a couple of lookouts. In summer, free slide shows and talks are presented by park naturalists five nights a week and typically feature topics

such as wolves, bears, the park's human history, or the effects of fire. Unserviced sites are $16, hookups $21. Fire permits cost $4 per site per night. This facility is open mid-May through early October.

The park's two other campgrounds—**McLeod Meadows,** 27 km from the west gate, and **Marble Canyon**—are much smaller and offer fewer facilities (no hookups or showers). They're open June–Aug., and all sites are $13. Hikers planning overnight trips in the backcountry must register at either of the park information centers and pick up a permit ($6 per person per night).

Information
Kootenay Park Information Centre recently moved for the third time in as many years. It's now at the base of the access road to Redstreak Campground, in the town Radium Hot Springs, 250/347-9615. Here you can collect a free map with hiking trail descriptions; find out about trail closures and campsite availability; get the weather forecast; browse through a gift shop; buy topographical maps ($11 each) and national park fishing licenses ($6 for seven days); and register for overnight backcountry trips. It's open in summer daily 9 A.M.–7 P.M., the rest of the year weekdays only 9 A.M.–5 P.M. A smaller park-operated center is in **Kootenay Park Lodge,** along Hwy. 93 in the middle of the park. It's open April–May, Fri.–Sun. 11 A.M.–6 P.M.; June–Sept., daily 10 A.M.–7 P.M.; and the early part of October Fri.–Sun. 11 A.M.–6 P.M.

For further park information, write the Superintendent, Kootenay National Park, P.O. Box 220, Radium Hot Springs, BC V0A 1M0, call 250/347-9615, or check out the website www.parkscanada.gc.ca/kootenay.

Yoho National Park

Yoho, a Cree word of amazement, is a fitting name for this 1,313-square-km national park on the western slopes of the Canadian Rockies. East of Golden, the TransCanada Highway bisects the park. Kootenay National Park lies immediately to the south, while Banff National Park (Alberta) borders Yoho to the east.

Yoho is the smallest of the four contiguous Canadian Rockies national parks, but its wild and rugged landscape holds spectacular waterfalls, extensive icefields, a lake to rival those in Banff, and one of the world's most intriguing fossil beds. In addition, you'll find some of the finest hiking in all of Canada on the park's 300-km trail system.

Within the park are four lodges, four campgrounds, and the small railway town of **Field,** offering basic services. The park is open year-round, although road conditions in winter can be treacherous, and occasional closures occur on Kicking Horse Pass. The road out to Takakkaw Falls is closed through winter, and it often doesn't reopen until mid-June.

THE LAND

The park extends west from the Continental Divide to the western main ranges of the Rocky Mountains. The jagged peaks along this section of the Continental Divide—including famous Mt. Victoria, which forms the backdrop for Lake Louise—are some of the park's highest. But the award for Yoho's loftiest summit goes to **Mount Goodsir** (3,562 meters), southwest of the Continental Divide in the Ottertail Range.

The park's only watershed is that of the **Kicking Horse River,** which is fed by the Wapta and Waputik Icefields. The Kicking Horse, wide and braided for much of its course through the park, flows westward, joining the mighty Columbia River at Golden. The park's many individual geological features of interest—such as Takakkaw and Twin Falls, Natural Bridge, Leanchoil Hoodoos, Emerald Lake, and Lake O'Hara—are covered under Sights and Recreation, below.

Flora

Elevations within the park cover a range of more than 2,500 meters, making for distinct vegetation changes. Douglas fir is the climax species at lower elevations, but lodgepole pine dominates areas affected by fire. Western red cedar, hemlock, and the delightful calypso orchid can be found in the damp valley around Emerald Lake. At higher elevations, where temperatures are lower and precipitation is higher, the familiar subalpine forests of Engelmann spruce and subalpine fir thrive. The northernmost extent of larch exists around Lake O'Hara. Larch is a conifer (evergreen), but its needles turn a stunning orange in fall—a photographer's delight. Above the treeline, where wind and rain have deposited soil, wildflowers such as heather, Indian paintbrush, and arnica create a carpet of color for a few short weeks midsummer.

Fauna

The animals for which Yoho is best known are fossilized in beds of shale and have been dead for over 500 million years. But they still create great interest for the role their remains have played in humanity's understanding of life on earth in prehistoric times. (See the special topic Burgess Shale.)

Large mammals are not as common in Yoho as in Kootenay National Park, simply because the terrain is so rugged. Valleys are inhabited by mule deer, elk, moose, and black bears, as well as a wide variety of smaller mammals. Porcupines are common along Yoho Valley Road. The park has a healthy population of grizzly bears, but sightings are relatively rare as the grizz tends to remain in remote valleys far from the busy TransCanada Highway corridor. Much of the park is above the treeline, where noisy marmots and pikas find a home, along with mountain goats. Around 200 bird species have been recorded within the park.

HISTORY

The Kootenay and Shuswap tribes of British Columbia were the first humans to travel through the rugged area that is now the national park. It's believed the men hid their families in the mountains before crossing over to the prairies to hunt buffalo and to trade with other tribes. On their return they set up seasonal camps along the Kicking Horse River to dry the buffalo meat and hides. They used a more northern route than that taken by travelers today, crossing the divide at Howse Pass and descending to the Kootenay Plains beyond the present-day junction of Highways 93 and 11.

The first Europeans to explore the valley of the Kicking Horse River were members of the 1858 Palliser Expedition, which set out to survey the west and report back to the British govern-ment on its suitability for settlement. The party approached from the south, climbing the Kootenay and Vermilion watersheds of present-day Kootenay National Park before descending to Wapta Falls. It was here that the unfortunate expedition geologist, Dr. James Hector, inadvertently gave the Kicking Horse River its name. While walking his horse over rough ground, he was kicked unconscious and took two hours to come to, by which time, so the story goes, other members of his party had begun digging his grave.

Guided by outfitter Tom Wilson, Maj. A.B. Rogers (for whom Rogers Pass to the west is named) surveyed Kicking Horse Pass in 1881. His favorable report to the Canadian Pacific Rail-

BURGESS SHALE

High on the rocky slopes above Field is a layer of sedimentary rock known as the Burgess Shale, which contains what are considered to be the world's finest fossils from the Cambrian period. The site is famous worldwide, for it has unraveled the mysteries of a major stage of evolution.

In 1909, Smithsonian Institution paleontologist Charles Walcott was leading a pack train along the west slope of Mt. Field, on the opposite side of the valley from the newly completed Spiral Tunnel, when he stumbled across these fossil beds. Encased in the shale, the fossils are of marine invertebrates around 530 million years old. Generally fossils are the remains of vertebrates, but at this site some freak event—probably a mudslide—suddenly buried thousands of soft-bodied animals (invertebrates), preserving them by keeping out the oxygen that would have decayed their delicate bodies. Walcott ex-cavated an estimated 65,000 specimens from the site. Today, paleontologists continue to uncover perfectly preserved fossils here—albeit in far fewer numbers than in Walcott's day. They've also un-covered additional fossil beds, similar in makeup and age, across the valley, on the north face of Mt. Stephen.

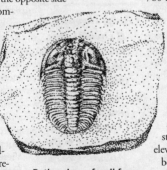

Bathyuriscus fossil from neighboring Mt. Stephen

BOB RACE

Protected by UNESCO as a World Heritage Site, the two research areas are open only to those ac-companied by a licensed guide. The Yoho–Burgess Shale Foundation guides trips to both sites mid-July to mid-September. The access to "Walcott's Quarry" is along a strenuous 10-km trail that gains 760 meters in elevation. Trips leave Fri.–Mon. at 8 A.M. from the trading post at the Field inter-section, returning around 6:30 P.M.; $48.15 per person. Trips to the Mt. Stephen Fossil Beds depart Saturday and Sunday at 10 A.M., returning around 4:30 P.M.; $26.75 per person. The trail to the Mt. Stephen beds is shorter, but equally steep and strenuous, gaining 520 meters of elevation in three km. The trails to both sites are unrelenting in their elevation gain —you must be fit. Reservations are a must; call 800/343-3006 Mon.–Fri. be-tween 10 A.M. and 3:30 P.M., or email burgshal@rockies.net. For further information con-tact Yoho–Burgess Shale Foundation, P.O. Box 148, Field, BC V0A 1G0, 250/343-6006, website www.burgess-shale.bc.ca.

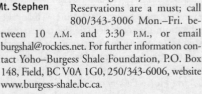

CANADIAN ROCKIES

way led to this route being chosen for the much-awaited transcontinental railway. The railbed was laid in 1884, and its grade was terribly steep; the first train to attempt the run suffered a brake failure and derailed, killing three workers. In 1909, after dozens more wrecks and derailments, the CPR rerouted the steepest section of the line through the Spiral Tunnels (see below). The highway now follows the original rail grade.

The small township of Field started as a railway maintenance depot at the bottom of treacherous "Big Hill." In 1886 the Canadian Pacific Railway opened Mt. Stephen House in Field, as a dining stop for customers of the railway and to encourage visitors to this side of the mountains. The CPR then built lodges at several natural attractions in the area, including Emerald Lake Lodge in 1902, Lake O'Hara Lodge in 1913, and Wapta Lodge Bungalow Camp in 1921.

The coming of the railway was a prime catalyst in the formation of Yoho National Park. Upon the opening of the railway line in 1886, 26 square km of land around the base of Mt. Stephen were set aside as Mt. Stephen Park Reserve, Canada's second national park. In 1901 the reserve was expanded, and after three further boundary changes, the park of today came into being in 1930. Mining of lead, zinc, and silver continued until 1952, and today remnants of the Monarch and Kicking Horse mines can still be seen on the faces of Mt. Stephen and Mt. Field, respectively.

ROAD-ACCESSIBLE SIGHTS

As with all other parks of the Canadian Rockies, you don't need to travel deep into the backcountry to view the most spectacular features—many are visible from the roadside. The sights below are listed from east to west, starting at the park boundary (the Continental Divide). An alternative to taking the TransCanada Highway over Kicking Horse Pass is to travel Highway 1A, which begins from the road up to Lake Louise,

Along Highway 1A is Divide Creek, which does exactly that—the creek splits in two, with one side flowing west to the Pacific Ocean and the other east to the Atlantic Ocean.

rejoining the main highway just a couple of kilometers into the park. Along this road is **Divide Creek,** which does exactly that—the creek splits in two, with one side flowing west to the Pacific Ocean and the other east to the Atlantic Ocean.

Spiral Tunnel Viewpoint

The joy CPR president William Van Horne felt upon completion of his transcontinental rail line in 1886 was tempered by massive problems along a stretch of line west of Kicking Horse Pass. "Big Hill" was less than five km long, but its gradient was so steep that runaway trains, crashes, and other disasters were common. A trail from Kicking Horse Campground takes you past the remains of one of those doomed trains.

Nearly a quarter century after the line opened, railway engineers and builders finally solved the problem. By building two spiral tunnels down through two km of solid rock to the valley floor, they lessened the grade dramatically and the terrors came to an end. Today, the TransCanada Highway follows the original railbed. Along the way is a viewpoint with interpretive displays telling the fascinating story of Big Hill.

Yoho Valley

Fed by the Wapta Icefield in the far north of the park, the **Yoho River** flows through this spectacularly narrow valley, dropping more than 200 meters in the last kilometer before its confluence with the Kicking Horse River. The road leading up the valley passes the park's main campground, climbs a *very* tight series of switchbacks, and emerges at **Upper Spiral Tunnel Viewpoint,** which offers a different perspective on the tunnel described above. A further 400 meters along the road is a pullout for viewing the confluence of the Yoho and Kicking Horse Rivers—a particularly impressive sight as the former is glacier-fed and therefore silty, while the latter is lake-fed and clear.

Yoho Valley Rd. ends 14 km from the main highway at **Takakkaw Falls,** officially Canada's

TAKAKKAW FALLS

The torrent, issuing from an icy cavern, rushes tempestuously down a deep, winding chasm till it gains the verge of the unbroken cliff, leaps forth in sudden wildness for a hundred and fifty feet, and then in a stupendous column of pure white sparkling water, broken by giant jets descending rocket-like and wreathed in volumed spray, dashes upon the rocks almost a thousand feet below, and, breaking into a milky series of cascading rushes for five hundred feet more, swirls into the swift current of the Yoho River.

—**Sir James Outram,**
In the Heart of the Canadian Rockies

M uch discussion is made of which is Canada's highest waterfall. Della Falls, on Vancouver Island, also in British Columbia, is 440 meters,

but this drop is broken by a ledge. Takakkaw Falls is considerably lower, at 254 meters, but the drop is unbroken, which, officially, makes it Canada's highest. There is one thing of which there is no doubt: Takakkaw Falls will leave you breathless, much as it did famous alpinist Sir James Outram, and everyone who has viewed the spectacle since.

Takakkaw Falls

© PROVINCE OF BRITISH COLUMBIA

highest waterfall and unofficially the most impressive in the Canadian Rockies. The falls are fed by the Daly and Des Poilus Glaciers of the Waputik Icefield, which straddles the Continental Divide. Meaning "wonderful" in the language of the Cree, Takakkaw tumbles 254 meters over a sheer rock wall, creating a spray bedecked by rainbows. It can be seen from the parking lot, but it's well worth the easy 10-minute stroll over the Yoho River to appreciate the sight in all its glory.

Natural Bridge

Three km west of Field is the turnoff to famous Emerald Lake (see below). On your way out to the lake, you'll first pass another intriguing sight. At Natural Bridge, two km down the road, the Kicking Horse River has worn a narrow hole through a limestone wall, creating a bridge. Over time, the bridge will collapse and, well, it won't be such an intriguing sight anymore. A trail leads to several viewpoints—try to avoid the urge to join the idiots clambering over the top of the bridge.

Emerald Lake

Outfitter Tom Wilson stumbled upon stunning Emerald Lake while guiding Maj. A.B. Rogers through the Kicking Horse River Valley in 1881. He was led to the lake by his horse, which had been purchased from natives. He later surmised that the horse had been accustomed to traveling up to the lake, meaning that the horse's former owners must have known about the lake before the white explorers arrived.

One of the jewels of the Canadian Rockies, the beautiful lake is surrounded by a forest of Engelmann spruce, as well as many peaks over 3,000

CANADIAN ROCKIES

meters. It is covered in ice most of the year but comes alive with activity for a few short months in summer, when hikers, canoeists, and horseback riders take advantage of the magnificent surroundings. **Emerald Sports,** on the shore of Emerald Lake, 250/343-6377, rents canoes and small boats for $30 per hour or $45 all day. Fishing in Emerald Lake isn't world-class, but there are some trout in the waters and Emerald Sports offers fishing tackle for rent or sale. Also at the lake is **Emerald Lake Stables,** a trail riding outfit. A one-hour trip around Emerald Lake costs $28. Two-hour rides are $44, three-hour rides $55, lunch rides $80, and all-day rides with dinner go for $105.

LAKE O'HARA

"In all the mountain wilderness the most complete picture of natural beauty is realized at O'Hara Lake." So said alpinist Walter Wilcox in 1904, after having traveled throughout the Canadian Rockies. Visitors today are no less in awe of the lake. Nestled in a high bowl of lush alpine meadows, Lake O'Hara is surrounded by dozens of smaller alpine lakes and framed by spectacular peaks permanently mantled in snow. As if that weren't enough, the entire area is webbed by a network of hiking trails radiating from the lake in all directions; the longest is just 7.5 km, making Lake O'Hara an especially fine hub for day-hiking. The best area day hikes are detailed below.

The lake has been a popular destination since the early 1900s, when the CPR began constructing trails and built a small lodge in a lakeside meadow. The lodge has since been moved and now sits right on the lakeshore, providing comfortable accommodations (see below). Also at the lake are a campground and warden's cabin. Trail maps are available for $8 at the Lake O'Hara Lodge or the park information center.

Access to the lake is by shuttle bus from a parking lot 15 km east of Field and three km west of the Continental Divide. Buses run four times daily between mid-June and the end of September. Reservations are taken up to three months in advance from 20 March at the Field Visitor Centre, 250/343-6433. The reservation fee is $10

per booking and the fare is $12 per person round-trip. Six places are allotted each day on a first-come, first-served basis; show up the day *before* you want to go, but be at the visitor center before it opens at 8 A.M. as there's usually a line for these tickets. You can also walk up the 11-km access road to the lake in about three and a half or four hours; the elevation gain is 420 meters.

Lake Oesa

- Length: 3 km (one hour) one-way
- Elevation gain: 250 meters
- Rating: easy-moderate

With the Continental Divide peaks of Mt. Victoria (3,464 meters) and Mt. Lefroy (3,423 meters) as a backdrop, this small aqua-colored lake surrounded by talus slopes is one of the area's gems. The trail begins on the north side of Lake O'Hara, nearly opposite the lodge, and climbs past a number of small lakes before entering the cirque in which Lake Oesa lies.

Opabin Plateau Circuit

- Length: 5.9 km (two hours) round-trip
- Elevation gain: 250 meters
- Rating: easy-moderate

Separated from Lake Oesa by 2,848-meter Mt. Yukness, this plateau high above treeline is dotted with small lakes. The time given above is an absolute minimum, for it's easy to spend an entire day exploring the alpine plateau and scrambling around the surrounding slopes. From the trailhead, 300 meters southeast of Lake O'Hara Lodge, the trail passes Mary Lake, climbing steeply and reaching the plateau in a little over two kilometers. The trail loops through the plateau before descending back into the subalpine forest and finishing on the Lakeshore Trail 600 meters from the lodge.

Lake McArthur

- Length: 3.5 km (80 minutes) one-way
- Elevation gain: 300 meters
- Rating: easy-moderate

This trail begins along the main access road, 200 meters north of Lake O'Hara Lodge. It crosses an open meadow, disappears into a dense forest of Engelmann spruce and subalpine fir, then climbs up to Schäffer Lake. At a junction beyond that lake, the left fork leads to Lake McArthur and the right fork to McArthur Pass. It's a steep final ascent to the lake, but the trail levels off and slopes gently down for the final 400 meters. Surrounded on two sides by steep cliffs, the large lake is fed by McArthur Glacier and reaches depths of over 80 meters.

Cathedral Basin

- Length: 7.5 km (2.5 hours) one-way
- Elevation gain: 300 meters
- Rating: moderate

The trail out to Cathedral Basin is the longest in the Lake O'Hara area, yet it's still an easy day trip for most people. From the Lake O'Hara campground the trail heads northwest, crossing Morning Glory Creek at the 2.4-km mark then passing large Linda Lake. The final ascent to Cathedral Basin makes a wide loop through an area of ancient rockslides. From this point, the magnificent panorama of the Lake O'Hara area and the backdrop of the Continental Divide are laid out to the southeast.

YOHO VALLEY HIKING

The valley for which the park is named lies north of the TransCanada Highway. As well as the sights discussed above, it provides many fine opportunities for serious day-hikers to get off the beaten track.

Twin Falls

- Length: 8 km (2.5 hours) one-way
- Elevation gain: 300 meters
- Rating: moderate

This trail takes over where the road through the Yoho Valley ends. Starting at the Takakkaw Falls parking lot, it continues up the Yoho River to Twin Falls, passing many other waterfalls along the way. At spectacular Twin Falls, water from the Wapta Icefield divides in two before plunging off an 80-meter cliff. Mother Nature may work in amazing ways, but sometimes she needs a helping hand—or so the Canadian Pacific Railway thought. In the 1920s, the company dynamited one of the channels to make the falls more sym-

metrical. **Twin Falls Chalet** was built below the falls by the CPR in 1923 and today offers hikers light snacks through the middle of the day.

Yoho Pass

- Length: 4.7 km (two hours) one-way
- Elevation gain: 530 meters
- Rating: moderate

The trail to Yoho Pass, which can be combined with the Iceline Trail (see below), begins on the west side of Whiskey Jack Hostel, 500 meters before the Takakkaw Falls parking lot. It leads 3.7 km to picturesque, spruce-encircled Yoho Lake, then continues another easy kilometer to the pass. The pass is below treeline, so views are limited. But from this point it's 5.5 km and an elevation loss of 530 meters down to Emerald Lake; six km and an elevation gain of 300 meters to spectacular Burgess Pass; or 2.4 km north, with little elevation gain or loss, to an intersection with the Iceline Trail.

Iceline Trail

- Length: 6.4 km (2.5 hours) one-way
- Elevation gain: 690 meters
- Rating: moderate-difficult

Constructed in 1987, the Iceline Trail is one of the most spectacular day hikes in the Canadian Rockies. The length given above is from the trailhead at Whiskey Jack Hostel to the highest point along the trail. In the middle of this stretch you'll reach the trail's highlight—the four-km traverse of a moraine below Emerald Glacier. Views across the valley improve as the trail climbs to its 2,220-meter crest. Many day-hikers return from this point, although officially the trail continues into Little Yoho River Valley. Another option is to continue beyond Celeste Lake and loop back to Takakkaw Falls and the original trailhead, a total distance of 18 km.

EMERALD LAKE HIKING
Emerald Lake Loop

- Length: 5.2 km (less than two hours) round-trip
- Elevation gain: minimal
- Rating: easy

CANADIAN ROCKIES

One of the easiest yet most enjoyable walks in Yoho is around the park's most famous lake. The trail encircles the lake and can be hiked in either direction. The best views are from the western shoreline, where a massive avalanche has cleared away the forest of Engelmann spruce. Across the lake from this point, Mt. Burgess can be seen rising an impressive 2,599 meters.

Hamilton Falls

- Length: 800 meters (40 minutes) one-way
- Elevation gain: 60 meters
- Rating: easy

The trail to these falls begins from the Emerald Lake parking lot, down the hill from the bridge to the lodge. It's an easy walk through a forest of Engelmann spruce and subalpine fir to a viewpoint at the base of the falls. A little farther along, the trail begins switchbacking steeply and offers even better views of the cascade.

The trail continues beyond the waterfall to **Hamilton Lake,** which lies in a small glacial cirque a steep 880 vertical meters above Emerald Lake. Total distance from Emerald Lake to Hamilton Lake is 5.5 km (2.5 hours) one-way.

Emerald Basin

- Length: 4.5 km (less than two hours) one-way
- Elevation gain: 280 meters
- Rating: easy-moderate

The trail to the delightful Emerald Basin begins from the west shore of Emerald Lake, 1.5 km from the main parking lot. From there it's a steady three-km climb through a subalpine forest to the basin, which, chances are, you'll have to yourself. The most impressive sight awaiting you is the south wall of the President Range, towering 800 vertical meters above.

HIKES IN OTHER AREAS OF THE PARK

Aside from Ross Lake, which is accessed from Highway 1A, the hikes detailed below are along the TransCanada Highway. (The hike to the world-famous Burgess Shale is detailed in the special topic.)

Ross Lake

- Length: 1.3 km (20 minutes) one-way
- Elevation gain: minimal
- Rating: easy

This small lake is easily reached from a trail that begins along Highway 1A just west of the Great Divide and two km east of the TransCanada Highway. The trailhead is relatively high, making the short trip an easy way to access a subalpine lake.

Paget Lookout

- Length: 3.5 km (90 minutes) one-way
- Elevation gain: 520 meters
- Rating: moderate

Beginning from a trailhead at the Wapta Lake picnic area five km west of the Continental Divide, the trail to this viewpoint is moderately strenuous but worthwhile for the panorama of the Kicking Horse River Valley. The first kilometer traverses a forest of Engelmann spruce. Then the trail breaks out above treeline just below the lookout, the site of an abandoned fire tower. As an alternative, branch right 1.4 km along the trail and continue two km to **Sherbrooke Lake,** which is fed by the Waputik Icefield.

Hoodoo Trail

- Length: 3 km (60–90 minutes) one-way
- Elevation gain: 460 meters
- Rating: moderate

Hoodoos are found in varying forms throughout the Canadian Rockies, but this outcrop, officially known as the Leanchoil Hoodoos, is among the most impressive. Hoodoos are formed by the erosion of relatively soft rock from beneath a cap of harder, more weather-resistant rock. Although these examples require some effort to reach, their intriguing appearance makes the trip worthwhile. The trail begins from Hoodoo Creek Campground, 23 km southwest of Field. The first half of the trail is relatively flat, leaving all the elevation gain to be made in the last, painful 1.5 km.

Wapta Falls

- Length: 2.4 km (45 minutes) one-way
- Elevation loss: minimal
- Rating: easy

CANADIAN ROCKIES

This trail begins from the end of a two-km access road leading south off the TransCanada Highway in the park's extreme southwestern corner. It follows an old fire road for a bit, then narrows for the easy stroll through thick forest to a viewpoint above the falls. A steep descent leads to a lower viewpoint.

ACCOMMODATIONS AND CAMPING

Emerald Lake Lodge

The extensive grounds of this grand, luxury-class accommodation lie along the southern shore of one of the Canadian Rockies' most magnificent lakes. The original lodge was built in 1902 in the same tradition as the Chateau Lake Louise and Banff Springs Hotel—as a playground for wealthy railway travelers. No original buildings remain (although the original framework is made use of in the main building). In 1986 the lodge underwent considerable renovation and expansion. It now boasts 85 rooms and cabins, as well as a hot tub and sauna, swimming pool, restaurant, lounge, and café. Guests can also go horseback riding, or go boating and fishing on Emerald Lake. The units are large, and many of the more expensive ones are on the lakefront. Rates range $300–460 per night, with sharp discounts in the off season. For bookings, call 250/343-6321 or 800/663-6336, website www.crmr.com.

Kicking Horse Lodge

In the small railway town of Field, simple yet elegant Kicking Horse Lodge, 100 Centre St., 250/343-6303 or 800/659-4944, website www.kickinghorselodge.net, offers 14 well-furnished rooms, a large comfortable lounge, and a restaurant (open in summer only). Summer rates range $118–144 s or d (off-season discounts are up to 50 percent)—great value for the Canadian Rockies.

Cathedral Mountain Lodge and Chalets

Comprising 21 rustic cabins alongside the Kicking Horse River, this is the most basic of the park's accommodations. Original cabins cost $135 s or d, while larger, newer cabins, each with a small kitchen, range $169–189. A restaurant and grocery store are on the premises. The lodge is open mid-May to the end of October. For bookings, call 250/343-6442. In the off season call 403/762-0514; website www.cathedral mountain.com.

Lake O'Hara Lodge

This lodge set around beautiful Lake O'Hara allows hikers not equipped for overnight camping the opportunity to explore the backcountry on leisurely day hikes. Located 11 km from the highway, guests arrive via shuttle bus from a parking lot three km west of the Continental Divide and 15 km east of Field. The 15 cabins, each with a private bathroom, are spread around the lakeshore, while within the main lodge are eight rooms, most of which are twins and share bathrooms. Rates of $375–500 d include all meals. Between February and April, the eight rooms in the main lodge are available for cross-country skiers. The lodge books up well in advance; for reservations call 250/343-6418 (call 403/678-4110 in the off season) or check the website www.lakeohara.com.

Hostel

Between mid-June and September Hostelling International operates **Whiskey Jack Hostel** near Takakkaw Falls. Formerly cabins used by the CPR, then staff quarters for a privately run lodge that was destroyed by an avalanche, the hostel provides basic dormitory accommodations for up to 27 guests, who have use of a communal kitchen and showers. Members of Hostelling International pay $13 per night, nonmembers $17. Book through Banff International Hostel at 403/762-4122.

Camping

The park's main camping area is **Kicking Horse Campground,** five km northeast of Field along the road to Takakkaw Falls. Facilities include coin-operated showers ($1), flush toilets, and kitchen shelters. All sites are unserviced; $18 per night. The campground is open mid-May to

CANADIAN ROCKIES

early October. Back toward the TransCanada Highway, an overflow area with more limited facilities is also open for winter camping. At the end of the same road, **Takakkaw Falls Campground** is designed for tent campers only. Park at the very end of the road and load up the carts with your gear for a pleasant 400-meter walk along the valley floor. No showers are provided, and the only facilities are pit toilets and picnic tables; $13 per site.

Hoodoo Creek Campground, along the TransCanada Highway 23 km southwest of Field, provides sheltered private spots among the trees; $14 per night. A few hundred meters farther west is the turnoff to **Chancellor Peak Campground,** beside the Kicking Horse River; $13 per night.

Just north of **Lake O'Hara** is a 30-site campground with two kitchen shelters and woodstoves. Camping is $6 per person per night. Reservations for sites can be made at 250/343-6433 in conjunction with the shuttle service (see Lake O'Hara above). A few sites are left open on a first-come, first-served basis.

Primitive wilderness campsites are scattered throughout the backcountry. Users must obtain a permit from the park information center; $6 per person per night.

FOOD

At Emerald Lake Lodge, overlooking the water, **Cilantro on the Lake** is a casual café featuring magnificent views from tables inside and out. The menu is varied—you can sit and sip a coffee or have a full lunch. Pastas range $8–15, grills are

around $20, and sandwiches and salads $6–10. (The corn and potato chowder is particularly good.) Up the hill, within the main lodge, is a more formal dining room and a bar.

In Field, the **Kicking Horse Lodge,** 250/343-6303, has a small restaurant with views over the valley floor. It features a short but varied menu and is open throughout the day in summer only. Across the road is a general store offering hot takeout meals.

SERVICES AND INFORMATION

Transportation

Transportation to the park is limited. **Greyhound,** 800/661-8747, stops in Field three to four times daily on its route along the TransCanada Highway between Banff and Golden, from where it continues west to Vancouver.

Information

The main source of information about the park is the **Field Visitor Centre** on the TransCanada Hwy. at Field, 250/343-6783. This is also the place to book the bus trip up to Lake O'Hara, pick up backcountry camping permits, buy topographical maps, and find out schedules for the interpretive programs. The center is open in peak summer season daily 8 A.M.–7 P.M., May–June and September daily 9 A.M.–5 P.M., the rest of the year 9 A.M.–4 P.M. For more information, write Superintendent, Yoho National Park, P.O. Box 99, Field, BC V0A 1G0, or surf the Net to www.parkscanada .gc.ca/yoho. For park road conditions call 403/762-1450.

Golden

From the western boundary of Yoho National Park, the TransCanada Highway meanders down the beautiful Kicking Horse River Valley to Golden (pop. 5,400), which lies at the confluence of the Kicking Horse and Columbia Rivers. The town makes a good central base for exploring the region, being just a short drive from both Yoho National Park to the east and Glacier National Park to the west. Golden is historically a logging and railway town, but it has been gaining a reputation in recent years for its many recreational opportunities. This has been brought in by a surge in popularity of white-water rafting down the Kicking Horse River and the development of what was a community-owned ski hill into a world-class four-season resort.

SIGHTS AND RECREATION

Take Highway 95 off the TransCanada Highway to the old section of town, a world away from the commercial strip along the main highway. There's not really much to see in town, although you may want to check out the small museum on 14th Street. The **Columbia River Wetland** (see Radium Hot Springs, earlier in this chapter) extends as far north as Golden. One easily accessible point of the wetlands is **Reflection Lake,** on the southern outskirts of Golden. Here you'll find a small shelter with a telescope for viewing the abundant birdlife.

White-Water Rafting

Anyone looking for white-water rafting will want to run the Kicking Horse River. The rafting season runs late May–Sept., with river levels at their highest in late June. The Lower Canyon, immediately upstream of Golden, offers the biggest thrills, including a three-km stretch of continuous rapids. Upstream the river is tamer but still makes for an exciting trip, while even farther upstream, near the western boundary of Yoho National Park, it's more a float—a good adventure for the more timid visitor. Most companies offer the option of half-day (from $58) or full-day (from $74) trips.

Whitewater Voyageurs, based at the Golden Rim Motor Inn, 1416 Golden View Rd. (just off the TransCanada Hwy. east of downtown), 250/344-7335 or 800/667-7238, is one of the original operators. It offers half- and full-day trips as well as transportation from Lake Louise. **Alpine Rafting,** 250/344-6778 or 888/599-5299, has an office by the Husky gas station in Golden. It offers a wide variety of trips, including an easy float and a trip down the Lower Canyon. Transportation from Banff and Lake Louise is an extra charge. Also based in Golden is **Wet 'n' Wild Adventures,** 250/344-6546 or 800/668-9119. Alberta-based companies providing transportation from Lake Louise and Banff include **Rocky Mountain Rafting,** 250/344-6979 or 888/518-7238, and **Wild Water Adventures,** 403/522-2211 or 888/647-6444.

Kicking Horse Mountain Resort

When Golden's local mill closed in the mid-1990s, the economy sagged, and one of the first things sold off was the local community ski hill, Whitetooth. A massive redevelopment program slated for completion in 2007 was begun, with the first stage of the Kicking Horse Mountain Resort, 866/754-5423, website www.kicking horseresort.com, opening for the inaugural 2000–01 season. This comprised an eight-person gondola, the Golden Eagle Express, which rises an impressive 1,260 meters and opens up over 2,000 hectares of terrain previously only accessible to heli-skiers. Other new facilities include a day lodge, with a ski school, rental outlets, and a café. The access road was paved in 2001 and next up is the construction of luxurious ski-in, ski-out hotels, condominiums, and restaurants. Lift tickets are adult $49, senior $38, child $19.25.

The Golden Eagle Express is open for sightseeing through summer, with hiking and mountain biking trails leading along a high ridge and winding down to the base area. A day pass is adult $18, senior and child $14.

Access is signposted through downtown

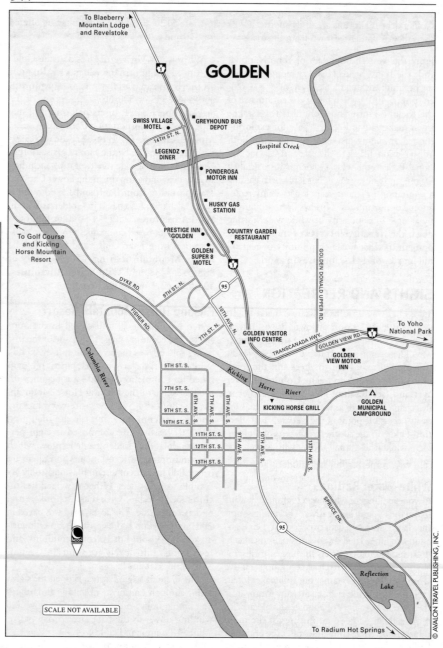

GOLDEN

To Blaeberry
Mountain Lodge
and Revelstoke

SWISS VILLAGE
MOTEL

14TH ST. N.

GREYHOUND BUS
DEPOT

Hospital Creek

LEGENDZ
DINER

PONDEROSA
MOTOR INN

HUSKY GAS
STATION

To Golf Course
and Kicking
Horse Mountain
Resort

PRESTIGE INN
GOLDEN

COUNTRY GARDEN
RESTAURANT

GOLDEN
SUPER 8
MOTEL

GOLDEN DONALD UPPER RD.

DYKE RD.

9TH ST. N.

FISHER RD.

7TH ST. N.

10TH AVE. N.

GOLDEN VISITOR
INFO CENTRE

To Yoho
National Park

Columbia River

TRANSCANADA HWY.

GOLDEN VIEW RD.

GOLDEN
VIEW MOTOR
INN

Kicking   Horse   River

5TH ST. S.

7TH ST. S.

6TH AVE. S.

7TH AVE. S.

8TH AVE. S.

KICKING HORSE GRILL

GOLDEN
MUNICIPAL
CAMPGROUND

9TH ST. S.

10TH ST. S.

11TH ST. S.

9TH AVE. S.

10TH AVE. S.

12TH ST. S.

13TH ST. S.

13TH AVE. S.

SPRUCE DR.

MOON

Reflection
Lake

SCALE NOT AVAILABLE

To Radium Hot Springs

© AVALON TRAVEL PUBLISHING, INC.

Golden (the main runs are easily spotted across the valley as you enter town from the east).

Golfing

Rated as one of Canada's finest public courses is **Golden Golf and Country Club,** a challenging 6,800-yard, 18-hole course set in a forested section of the valley through town and to the north. Water comes into play on many holes, with streams and lakes to catch wayward shots. Facilities include a driving range, club and power cart rentals, and an RV park. Greens fees are $50, or there's a $40 twilight rate. For tee times, call 250/344-2700.

ACCOMMODATIONS AND CAMPING

It's easy to find a place to stay in Golden—the town holds over 20 motels, most of which lie right along the TransCanada Highway.

$50–100

Ponderosa Motor Inn, on the TransCanada at the west entrance to town, 250/344-2205 or 800/881-4233, website www.ponderosa motorinn.bc.ca, has older rooms, but it's on two hectares of landscaped gardens, with impressive mountain views, a hot tub, a picnic area, and a playground, making it good value at just $78 s, $88 d ($55–65 outside summer).

Golden Super 8 Motel, 1047 TransCanada Hwy., 250/344-0888 or 800/800-8000, website www.super8.com, is a modern air-conditioned facility where breakfast is included in the rates of $90 s or d.

Blaeberry Mountain Lodge, nine km north of Golden along Hwy. 1 then seven km farther north along Moberly School Rd., 250/344-5296, website www.blaeberrymountainlodge.bc.ca, is on a 62-hectare property amongst total wilderness. Rooms are in the main lodge or self-contained cabins, with plenty of activities available to guests. Standard rooms with shared bathroom are $60 s or d, and the cabins, which have a rustic kitchen and wood-burning stove, sleep

four, are $120. Breakfast and dinner are offered for $10 and $20 respectively.

$100–150

Next door to the Super 8 is **Prestige Inn Golden,** 1049 TransCanada Hwy., 250/344-7990 or 877/737-8443, website www.prestigeinn.com, where you'll find the town's highest-standard rooms, along with views that extend well down the Columbia Valley. Amenities include an indoor pool, hot tub, fitness center, lounge, and restaurant. Rates range $149–169 s or d, discounted from $109 in winter.

Camping

Down beside the Columbia River you'll find **Golden Municipal Campground,** on 9th St. S (turn at the one traffic light in town), 250/344-5412. It's a quiet place with adequate facilities, including a pool and tennis court next door. Unpowered sites are $13, powered sites $15. Golfers can stay out at the golf course in a specially developed area for $12 per night.

OTHER PRACTICALITIES

Food

All the usual fast-food places line the TransCanada Highway, but it's worth taking the time to search out the following two restaurants. Overlooking the river from a quiet downtown location is the **Kicking Horse Grill,** 1105 9th St. S, 250/344-2330. Constructed of rough-cut logs complete with bulging burls, the building itself is interesting. The menu changes with the seasons, but always offers distinctly international dishes ranging from paella to sushi. All but the beef dishes are under $20. Taking a little longer to reach is **Eagle Eye's Restaurant,** high above town at the 2,350-meter summit of Kicking Horse Mountain Resort, 250/439-5400. As you'd expect, the views are stunning, set off by a stylish timber and stonework interior. The menu is distinctly west coast, with lots of B.C. produce and game. Lunch is well-priced (mostly under $15), while dinner is a more extravagant affair (mains all under $30). Down on the highway, **Legendz Diner,** on the west side of the TransCanada Hwy., 250/344-5059, is the best of a bad bunch. As the name suggests, it's a 1950s-style diner complete with attentive staff and good, filling meals from $7.

Services and Information

Scheduled flights between Vancouver (Boundary Bay Airport) and Golden are operated by **Montair,** 604/946-6688; check the website www.mont air.com for the cheapest fares. **Greyhound** stops beside the Esso gas station up to four times daily on its TransCanada route. Call the Banff depot, 403/344-6172 or 800/661-8747, for a schedule. Local rental car companies include **Hertz,** 250/344-2966, and **National,** 250/344-9899. For a cab call **Mt. Seven Taxi,** 250/344-5237.

Golden Visitor Info Centre is off the highway in the old railway station building at 500 10th Ave., 250/344-7125 or 800/622-4653. It's open year-round weekdays 8:30 A.M.–4:30 P.M.

Central British Columbia

Ranging from the western slopes of the Rocky Mountains to the Pacific Ocean, central British Columbia holds such varied natural features as the massive Fraser River, the lofty peaks of the Cariboo and Coast Mountains, and the deeply indented coastal fjords around Bella Coola.

The region's history is dominated by colorful sagas of Canada's biggest gold rush, when over 100,000 miners and fortune seekers passed through the area on their way to the goldfields. But the best remembered man in these parts was not a miner but an explorer. In 1793, Alexander Mackenzie left the Fraser River for the final leg of his epic transcontinental journey. Fourteen days later he reached the Pacific Ocean, becoming the first person to cross the continent.

Today the most heavily traveled route through central B.C. is the TransCanada Highway, which for the purposes of this book also forms the region's southern boundary. In the east of the province, the highway bisects **Glacier National Park,** a small but spectacular park of glaciers and towering peaks. Heading west from the park, the highway passes the heli-skiing hub of **Revelstoke** and the watery playground of **Shuswap Lake** before coming to the large population center of **Kamloops.**

© ANDREW HEMPSTEAD

Echo Valley Guest Ranch Resort in Cariboo Country

From Kamloops, two highways lead north. Highway 5 accesses **Wells Gray** and **Mount Robson Provincial Parks,** the former a vast forested wilderness and the latter named for one of the most spectacular mountain peaks in all of Canada. The other route, Highway 97, runs through **Cariboo Country,** best-known for the 1860s' gold-rush town of **Barkerville,** now completely restored and one of the highlights of a trip north.

Glacier National Park

Encompassing 135,000 hectares of the Selkirk Mountains west of the Rocky Mountain Trench, this park is a wonderland of jagged snowcapped peaks, extensive icefields, thundering waterfalls, steep-sided valleys, and fast-flowing rivers. The TransCanada Highway bisects the park, cresting at 1,327-meter **Rogers Pass.** From this lofty summit, Golden is 80 km east and Revelstoke is 72 km west.

Those from south of the 49th parallel probably associate the park's name with the American national park in Montana. The two parks share the same name and glaciated environment, but the similarities end there. In the "other" park, buses shuttle tourists here and there and the backcountry is crowded with hikers. Here in the Canadian version, commercialism is almost totally lacking and use of the backcountry is blissfully minimal.

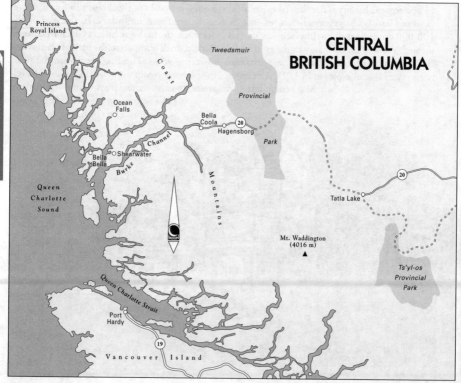

The best place to start a visit to the park is **Rogers Pass Information Centre.** Looking south from the center, you can see the **Illecillewaet, Asulkan,** and **Swiss Glaciers.** As far as actual "sights" go, driving through the park you'll be surrounded by one of the most awe-inspiring panoramas visible from any Canadian highway. Each roadside viewpoint seems to outdo the last. You can also get out of the car and go hiking to get a better feeling for the park, but most of the trails here entail strenuous climbs.

Through-traffic excepted, permits are required for entry into Glacier National Park; they're available from the information center. A one-day permit is $5 per person to a maximum of $10 per vehicle, and an annual Great Western Pass, good for entry to all 11 of western Canada's national parks, is $35 per person to a maximum of $70 per vehicle.

THE LAND

Regardless of whether you approach the park from the east or west, you'll be climbing from a valley only 600 meters above sea level to 1,327-meter Rogers Pass in under 15 km. The pass is not particularly high, but it's impressive. Surrounding peaks, many topping 3,000 meters, rise dramatically from the pass and draw massive amounts of precipitation from eastward-moving clouds. The resulting heavy snows feed more than 400 glaciers and permanently cloak some 14 percent of the park's landscape in snow and ice. Most of the glaciers lie in the park's southern half. Notable among them are Deville Icefield, which surrounds 3,393-meter Mt. Dawson, the park's highest peak, and Illecillewaet Icefield, whose glacial arms can be viewed up close from hiking trails starting at the Illecillewaet Campground.

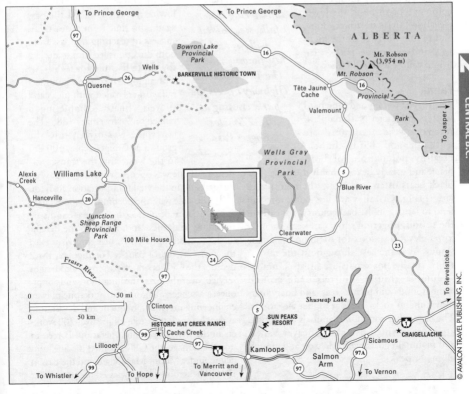

© AVALON TRAVEL PUBLISHING, INC.

CENTRAL B.C.

Flora

Three distinct vegetation zones can be seen within the park—montane (600–1,300 meters), subalpine (1,300–1,900 meters), and alpine (1,900 to 3,000-plus meters). The montane forest supports a lush variety of tree species, including mountain hemlock, subalpine fir, Engelmann spruce, western red cedar, western hemlock, lodgepole pine, whitebark pine, western white pine, black cottonwood, Douglas fir, aspen, and white birch.

Flower lovers will be impressed by the 600 species of flowering plants that have been identified within the park. The best time to see wildflowers in the high meadows and forests is early August, though an amazing profusion of color sweeps through the lower elevation forests starting in June, and in July the edge of the highway and avalanche paths turn bright yellow with wild lilies.

Fauna

The rugged terrain and long hard winters in Glacier National Park mean that resident mammals are a tough and hardy bunch. Healthy populations of both black and grizzly bears inhabit the park. The black bears often feed along the roadside in late spring. Grizzlies are less common and tend to remain in the backcountry, but early in the season, lingering snow can keep them at lower elevations; look for them on avalanche slopes. As is the case throughout the mountains, smaller mammals are most common. Columbia ground squirrels hang around campgrounds and picnic areas, and hoary marmots inhabit rocky areas at higher elevations. The only other common mammals in the park are moose, which live along Beaver Valley, and mountain goats, which live on and around all major peaks.

HISTORY

In a scenario familiar throughout western Canada, the proclamation of Glacier National Park was influenced by the Canadian Pacific Railway's desire to see tourists use its rail line. For CPR engineers, finding a passable train route through the Columbia Mountains proved a formidable challenge. The major obstacle was not the elevation, but the threat of avalanche; extremely high snowfalls in the area were coupled with narrow valleys and steep approaches from both east and west, all attributes spelling danger.

Encompassing 135,000 hectares of the Selkirk Mountains west of the Rocky Mountain Trench, Glacier National Park is a wonderland of jagged snowcapped peaks, extensive icefields, thundering waterfalls, steep-sided valleys, and fast-flowing rivers. The TransCanada Highway bisects the park, cresting at 1,327-meter Rogers Pass.

In 1881 Maj. A.B. Rogers, chief engineer of the CPR, scaled Rogers Pass from the west, along the Illecillewaet River. The following year he climbed the pass again, this time from the east. His success in reaching the pass from both directions led him to declare the route feasible for a railway. Through the next three summers rail workers toiled with picks and shovels, finally completing a railbed on 7 November 1885. The last spike was driven into the ground at Craigellachie, 100 km to the west, and the transcontinental rail line was opened, with Rogers Pass an integral link in the vital transportation corridor.

To coincide with the opening, a national park was proclaimed, protecting the pass and surrounding wilderness and, much to the delight of the cash-strapped CPR, bringing visitors to the area—by rail of course. For the next three decades the CPR operated passenger and freight services over the pass, thrilling thousands of pioneer passengers. Unfortunately, despite railway engineering ingenuity, frequent and devastating avalanches took their toll, killing over 200 workers in the first 30 years of operation. Forced to stop the carnage, the CPR rerouted the line, tunneling under Mount Macdonald and the pass in 1916. The rerouted line bypassed the park's most spectacular scenery, and the number of visitors to the park dropped dramatically. To lessen the gradient still further, a new tunnel replaced the old in 1988. At 14.5 km, it's North America's longest railway tunnel.

TransCanada Highway

In the early 1950s, a new team of engineers tackled the same problem—this time in an effort to build a highway across the pass. The tunnel approach that had worked for the railway was deemed impractical for a highway, so a new solution to the avalanche danger was required. In 1962 a route through the national park and over the pass was completed—this time with the addition of concrete snowsheds over sections of the highway. At the same time, the world's largest mobile avalanche-control program was created to stave off danger. Experts constantly monitor weather and snow conditions so they can accurately predict when and where avalanches will occur. Then they close the highway and dislodge potential slides with mobile howitzers, thereby stabilizing the slopes.

HIKING

The park's 21 hiking trails cover 140 km and range from short interpretive walks to long, steep, difficult climbs. Aside from the interpretive trails, most gain a lot of elevation, rewarding the energetic hiker with outstanding views. Along flat ground, reasonably fit hikers can usually cover three kilometers (or more) in an hour, but on Glacier National Park's steep trails, up to double that time should be allowed. Opportunities for long-distance backcountry trips are limited to the far eastern end of the park. If you're planning an overnight trip into the backcountry you need to register and pick up a permit ($6 per person per night) from the information center. Remember, many of the park's high-elevation trails are covered in snow until well into July.

The two most popular interpretive trails are the **Abandoned Rails Interpretive Trail** (one km; 20 minutes round-trip), which starts to the west of the information center, and the **Meeting of the Waters Trail** (one km; 25 minutes round-trip),

which starts behind Illecillewaet Campground, four km south of the information center. The first four trails detailed below also start at Illecillewaet Campground.

Avalanche Crest

- Length: 4.2 km (2.5 hours) one-way
- Elevation gain: 800 meters
- Rating: moderate-difficult

This trail begins behind the Illecillewaet Campground, four km south of Rogers Pass Information Centre. As you face the large information board, the trail leads off to your left, climbing steeply through a subalpine forest for the first three km, then leveling out and providing stunning views below to Rogers Pass and south to Illecillewaet and Asulkan Glaciers.

Great Glacier

- Length: 4.8 km (two hours) one-way
- Elevation gain: 320 meters
- Rating: easy-moderate

Of the trails beginning from the Illecillewaet Campground, the Great Glacier Trail has the least elevation gain. But hard-core hikers will get the opportunity to scramble up rocky slopes to the toe of the Illecillewaet Glacier, 340 vertical meters higher.

Asulkan Valley

- Length: 6.5 km (four hours) one-way
- Elevation gain: 930 meters
- Rating: moderate-difficult

While elevation on this trail is similar to others in the steep-sided Illecillewaet River Valley, it is gained over a longer distance, meaning a less strenuous outing. Nevertheless, a full day should be allowed round-trip. From the back of Illecillewaet Campground, the trail follows Asulkan Brook through a valley of dense subalpine forest. Whereas other trails lead to panoramic overlooks, the highlight of this trail's final destination is a view of the immense icefield rising high above you.

Abbott Ridge

- Length: 5 km (3.5 hours) one-way
- Elevation gain: 1,040 meters

• Rating: difficult

Winding up the west slope of a steep valley, this trail is for the physically fit; the gradient averages 20 percent. For the first 2.5 km, wide switchbacks lead up to Marion Lake. The trail then continues upward to a high treeless ridge offering views extending eastward across the Illecillewaet Icefield and adjoining glaciers. The ridge itself rises a further 150 meters to the 2,454-meter summit of Mt. Abbott.

Balu Pass

• Length: 5 km (3.5 hours) one-way
• Elevation gain: 1,020 meters
• Rating: difficult

From the information center parking lot, this trail climbs steeply and steadily between 2,606-meter Mt. Cheops to the south and a ridge of 2,700-meter peaks to the north. As elevation is gained, the valley closes in and the trail becomes steeper, finally ending at a pass 2,300 meters above sea level.

Hermit

• Length: 2.8 km (two hours) one-way
• Elevation gain: 940 meters
• Rating: difficult

This trail begins from the west side of the highway one km north of the information center. It climbs *very* steeply through a subalpine forest, breaking out above the treeline and ending at a view of glaciated peaks towering 1,000 meters above. Snow lingers on this trail well into July, so check conditions before heading out.

Copperstain

• Length: 16 km (seven hours) one-way
• Elevation gain: 1,225 meters
• Rating: difficult

The Beaver Gravel Pit, 12 km northeast of Rogers Pass Information Centre, is the trailhead for two overnight hikes, including this one to alpine meadows flanked by 2,320-meter Bald Mountain and 2,606-meter Copperstain Mountain. The climb is steady at first, ascending the Beaver

The snowcapped peaks of Glacier National Park can be seen from the highway.

© ANDREW HEMPSTEAD

CENTRAL B.C.

River Valley for four km, then branching north along Grizzly and Copperstain Creeks for the final painful ascent to the meadows. Also from the gravel pit, a 42-km trail leads up the Beaver River Valley to the park's extreme southeast corner. Backcountry camping is allowed anywhere along these two trails, but register first at the information center.

ACCOMMODATIONS AND CAMPING

Glacier Park Lodge

This lodge at Rogers Pass is a Best Western affiliate and the only motel in the park. It offers 50 midsize rooms, a restaurant, café, and heated outdoor pool. Summer rates are from $115 s, $125 d; off-season rates are considerably lower. Within the hotel is a 24-hour café and a restaurant offering a reasonably priced breakfast, lunch, and dinner buffet. For bookings call 250/837-2126 or 800/528-1234, website www.glacier parklodge.ca. Motels of a similar standard but with much lower rates can be found in Golden, 80 km to the east, and Revelstoke, 72 km to the west.

Camping

Illecillewaet Campground, 3.5 km south of Rogers Pass, is open late June to September. Facilities include kitchen shelters, flush toilets, picnic tables, firewood, and an evening interpretive program. Sites are not particularly private, and the surrounding peaks and towering cedar trees mean little sunshine before noon, but the campground is the perfect base for exploring as it's the trailhead for the park's main concentration of hiking trails. All sites are $13. When this campground fills, campers are directed to an overflow area in the nearby Sir Donald Picnic Area. Smaller **Loop Brook Campground** holds just 20 sites and also costs $13 per night. It's three km beyond the Illecillewaet Campground toward Revelstoke; open July–September.

With just 80 campsites in the entire park and

TIME TRAVEL

Glacier National Park falls within two time zones. If you pass through the park westbound, turn your watch *back* one hour to **Pacific time.** If you're eastbound, turn it *forward* one hour to **mountain time.**

no reservations taken, chances are good that both campgrounds will be full if you arrive late in the afternoon. If that's the case, head 40 km west to **Canyon Hot Springs Resort,** 250/837-2420, website www.canyonhotsprings.com, where you'll find hot springs, showers, a laundry, and a restaurant. Unserviced sites are $20, serviced sites $27, basic sleeping cabins $48, and self-contained chalets from $95. Open May–September.

INFORMATION

Rogers Pass Information Centre, 250/837-7500, is 1.2 km north of the actual pass and resembles the old-fashioned snowsheds that once protected the railroad from avalanches. The center's fascinating displays focus on the park's natural and human history. Videos on various aspects of the park are shown on the television (the viewing area by the fireplace is a great spot to while away time waiting for the clouds to lift), and the center's theater screens *Snow War,* an award-winning documentary on avalanche protection. Staff members provide information on trail conditions and closures, conduct interpretive programs, and lead guided hikes. The center is also the only place in the park to buy park passes, necessary for those planning any hiking or camping. (Rangers regularly check for passes at all trailheads.) If you already have an annual pass, it must be presented for admission to the information center. Hours are 8 A.M.–7 P.M. daily during the peak summer season, 9 A.M.–5 P.M. daily the rest of the year. For road conditions through the park call 250/837-6867. The park's official website is www.parkscanada.gc.ca/glacier.

Revelstoke

Revelstoke lies 72 km west of Rogers Pass at the confluence of the Illecillewaet River and the mighty Columbia, surrounded by mountains—the Monashees to the west and the Selkirks to the east. The setting couldn't be more spectacular.

An 1850s' gold rush along the Columbia River brought the first Europeans to the area, but the town really began to grow with the coming of the railroad in the 1880s. In fact, the city is named for Lord Revelstoke, who provided funding for completion of the Canadian Pacific Railway's line through town. Finally, the TransCanada Highway came to town earlier this century, helping turn Revelstoke into today's midsize city of 8,500.

The town holds a couple of museums, but the main attractions are farther afield, including two massive dams, a national park on the back doorstep, and great skiing and snowboarding on Mt. Mackenzie.

SIGHTS

The TransCanada Highway makes a lazy loop around the back of Revelstoke, missing downtown completely. It's well worth the detour to downtown, not just for the best dining and accommodations, but to enjoy the laid-back atmosphere of a small city that has done an excellent job of preserving its heritage. The downtown core has been rejuvenated and centers around the appealing, all-brick Grizzly Plaza. Southwest from the plaza along Mackenzie Avenue are many frontier-style false fronted buildings and the art deco-style Roxy Theatre. Pick up the *Heritage Walking & Driving* brochure for routes that take in the highlights of downtown's many old buildings.

Museums

Railway buffs shouldn't miss **Revelstoke Railway Museum,** a re-creation of an early Canadian Pacific Railway station. Reflecting the importance of this mode of transportation in Revelstoke's history, the museum centers around

a massive 1948 steam locomotive and Business Car No. 4, the ultimate in early rail-travel luxury. Admission is adult $5, senior $4, child $2.50. Open in summer daily 9 A.M.–7 P.M., the rest of the year Mon.–Fri. 1–4 P.M. It's on Victoria Rd., between the TransCanada Highway and downtown, 250/837-6060.

Revelstoke Museum, in an imposing two-story old post office building on the corner of Boyle Ave. and 1st St., preserves plenty of pioneer memorabilia and a great collection of historical black-and-white photos, and offers displays on local industries, early Chinese miners, and skiing on Mt. Mackenzie. Upstairs is the local **art gallery.** Open in summer Mon.–Sat. 10 A.M.–5 P.M., the rest of the year Mon.–Fri. 1–4 P.M. Admission is by donation.

Dams

The 1,900-km Columbia River, North America's third-longest, is controlled by many dams. Four of these are in British Columbia and two are in the vicinity of Revelstoke. The dams also provide the necessary water for two massive hydroelectric operations. These two generating stations are each capable of producing 1,800 megawatts of electricity—or, combined, 30 percent of the province's needs.

Revelstoke Dam, eight km north of the city on Highway 23, was completed in 1985. It's 470 meters wide, 175 meters high, and contains over two million cubic meters of concrete. The massive reservoir behind the dam stretches over 100 km and covers 11,000 hectares. Nestled in the valley below the dam is the generating station. Exhibits at the two-story **Revelstoke Dam Visitor Centre,** above the generating station, explain the valley's history and the operation and impact of the dams. From the center, a high-speed elevator whisks visitors to the top of the dam for an excellent view. The center is open weekdays only, in summer 8 A.M.–7 P.M., the rest of the year 9 A.M.–5 P.M. Admission is free.

Upstream of Revelstoke Dam is **Mica Dam,** 140 km by road to the north. This dam is much

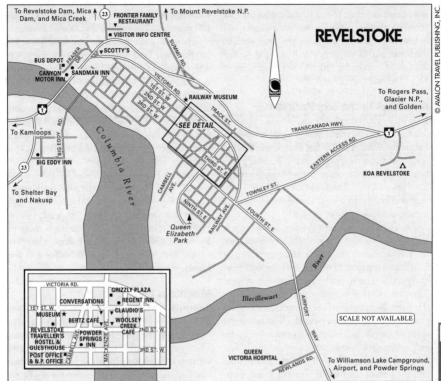

© AVALON TRAVEL PUBLISHING, INC.

CENTRAL B.C.

larger, rising 240 meters (North America's highest earth-filled dam), stretching 792 meters at the crest across the Columbia River Valley, and containing 14.8 trillion cubic meters of water in 200-km-long **Kinbasket Lake.** The lake extends north to Valemount and south to a point just north of Golden. **Mica Dam Visitor Centre** is open in summer daily 8 A.M.–8 P.M., late spring and early fall 9 A.M.–5 P.M.; tours of the powerhouse are offered at 11 A.M. and 1:30 P.M.

A gas station and a commercial campground, both 74 km north of Revelstoke, are the only facilities along this stretch of Highway 23.

MOUNT REVELSTOKE NATIONAL PARK

Visitors to this 26,000-hectare national park can experience a high alpine environment without any strenuous hiking; the main access road into the park, Meadows in the Sky Parkway, climbs abruptly from the valley bottom, gaining nearly 1,500 meters of elevation before reaching a high alpine meadow over 2,000 meters above sea level.

The park protects the highest peaks of the **Clachnacudiann Range,** a northern arm of the Selkirk Mountains. The forested slopes of the range come to an icy apex around the Clachnacudiann Glacier and surrounding peaks, such as **Mt. Coursier** and **Mt. Inverness,** both 2,637 meters high. The park's diverse vegetation includes forests of ancient cedar along the Illecillewaet River, subalpine forests of Engelmann spruce and fir on higher slopes, and finally, above the treeline, meadows of low-growing shrubs that come alive with color for a few weeks in midsummer.

As with all Canadian national parks, a permit

is required for entry; in this case it applies only for travel on the Meadows in the Sky Parkway (see below). Permits are issued at the park gate, at the lower end of the parkway. A one-day permit is adult $4, senior $3, child $2 to a maximum of $8 per vehicle.

Meadows in the Sky Parkway

East of Revelstoke the TransCanada Highway follows the Illecillewaet River, the park's southern boundary. Along this 25-km stretch you'll pass a couple of short interpretive trails, but the park's beauty is best appreciated from Meadows in the Sky Parkway, a 26-km road that leaves the highway and climbs to a high alpine meadow—the most spectacular part of the park.

The road is very steep, gaining well over one kilometer of elevation as it climbs seemingly endless hairpin bends through a subalpine forest of Engelmann spruce, hemlock, and the odd towering cedar. The summit area is snowed in until July, so try to plan your trip after this time. Over the years, high usage of the summit area created problems, so a few years back the final kilometer to the summit was blocked to private vehicles and a free shuttle-bus service established. The bus runs between a parking lot at Balsam Lake and the end of the road at Heather Lake. It operates daily 10 A.M.–4:20 P.M. in summer, starting as soon as the snow melts off the road—usually late July at the earliest. It's also possible to walk this final stretch; the trail climbs 90 meters in elevation and takes around 20 minutes each way. From the top, the panoramic view takes in the Columbia River Valley and the distant Monashee Mountains.

Hiking

The park doesn't have an extensive network of hiking trails—just 10 marked trails totaling 65 km in length. Most take under an hour and are posted with interpretive panels. Along the Trans Canada Highway, the 500-meter-long **Giant Cedars Boardwalk** (allow 10 minutes) traverses a meadow before disappearing into an ancient cedar forest and then along a sparkling creek. Farther west along the highway is the trailhead for **Skunk**

Cabbage Interpretive Trail, which leads 1.2 km (20 minutes) down to the Illecillewaet River.

The park's most demanding trail is the 10-km **Summit Trail,** which begins—or, more sensibly, ends—at the entrance to the park and runs to the Balsam Lake warden's cabin. The trail makes an elevation gain of 1,200 meters, so allow at least three and a half hours for this strenuous uphill slog. The eight-km **Lindmark Trail** is equally strenuous, gaining 950 meters in elevation as it traverses up to Balsam Lake from the lookout eight km from the park gate.

Heather Lake is the trailhead for the one-km (round-trip) **Meadows in the Sky Trail,** which features signs explaining the flora of the fragile alpine environment. From the east side of Heather Lake, a nine-km trail leads through alpine meadows to the **Jade Lakes.** Along the route, short side trails lead to **Miller** and **Eva Lakes.**

Mountain Bike Tours

Summit Cycle Tours, 250/837-3734 or 888/700-3444, takes the hard part out of a mountain-biking trip through the national park. The company's tours start with a van ride to the summit of Meadows in the Sky Parkway, where you'll spend some time exploring the alpine environment. Then the tour proceeds downhill on a ride back to the valley floor. The tour lasts four hours and costs $69 per person, including lunch.

Park Information

The park's main gate is closed from 10 P.M. until 7 A.M., prohibiting access. Although backcountry camping is allowed in designated areas (permit required; $6 per person per night), no campgrounds or services lie within the park. Revelstoke is home to the park's **administration office,** in the post office building at 313 3rd St., 250/837-7500. It's open year-round Mon.–Fri. 8:30 A.M.–4:30 P.M. Ask here about the park's evening interpretive program. Other sources of information are **Rogers Pass Information Centre,** in nearby Glacier National Park, and the website www.parkscanada.gc.ca/revelstoke.

RECREATION

Skiing and Snowboarding

The local downhill resort is **Powder Springs,** on the lower slopes of Mt. Mackenzie. The resort's two chairlifts, one T-bar, and one rope tow serve a vertical rise of 350 meters. Facilities include ski and snowboard rentals, a ski school, cafeteria, and bar. The season generally lasts from mid-December to late March, and adult lift tickets are $32. A massive expansion plan is finally underway, and eventually a gondola will whisk skiers from Revelstoke itself to the summit of Mt. Mackenzie. In the meantime, it's possible to ski the mountain's higher slopes with **CAT Powder Skiing,** From the Powder Springs day lodge, a Sno-Cat takes skiers high above the lift-served slopes for an average 4,000–5,000 vertical meters of powder skiing a day. Packages include skiing, accommodations, and all meals, and cost around $1,050 for two days, $1,420 for three days. The same company operates the ski hill and the CAT skiing operation, as well as the downtown Powder Springs Inn. Contact numbers for all three are 250/837-5151 or 800/991-4455, website www.catpowder.com.

Nestled between the Selkirk and Monashee Mountains, Revelstoke is also the center of much heli-skiing. **Selkirk Tangiers Heli-skiing,** 250/837-5378 or 800/663-7080, website www.selkirk-tangiers.com, operates from town, offering all-inclusive packages—including seven days heli-skiing (over 30,000 vertical meters), accommodations (at the Hillcrest Resort Hotel), and meals—from around $6,200. Three- and five-day packages are also offered, and early-season discounts apply.

CMH Heli-skiing, 403/762-7100 or 800/661-0252, website www.cmhski.com, has heli-skiing lodges scattered throughout the remote backcountry of British Columbia, but in Revelstoke, the company's guests stay right downtown at the Regent Inn and are whisked off daily for the mountains.

Entertainment

In July and August, free entertainment takes place nightly at the **Grizzly Plaza bandshell,** at the bottom end of Mackenzie Avenue. Whether it be comedy or country, crowds of up to a couple of hundred gather, sitting in plastic chairs, snagging a table at a surrounding restaurant, or just standing in the background. For music and dancing of a more formal nature, the young crowd heads for **Big Eddy Inn,** 2108 Big Eddy Rd., 250/837-9072. For a quieter evening, head to the **One Twelve Lounge,** in the Regent Inn at 112 1st St., 250/837-2107, or the poolside lounge at the **Sandman Inn** on the TransCanada Hwy., 250/837-5271.

ACCOMMODATIONS AND CAMPING

Under $50

The best value of all accommodations in town is the **Revelstoke Traveller's Hostel and Guesthouse,** within easy walking distance of downtown at 400 2nd St. W, 250/837-4050 or 888/663-8825, website www.hostels.bc.ca. Providing a true home away from home, this heritage house has been fully restored, complete with hardwood floors and comfortable beds with linen. The 26 double and twin rooms share bathrooms, kitchen facilities, a laundry, free Internet access, and a game room. Rates are $17 pp for members of Hostelling International, $19 pp for nonmembers. The hosts have a wealth of knowledge about Revelstoke and the adjacent national park. Bike rentals are also available. Check in at the office across 2nd Street.

$50–100

Downtown, the **Powder Springs Inn,** 200 3rd St. W, 250/837-5151 or 800/991-4455, website www.catpowder.com, is a renovated motel with comfortable beds in large rooms, a hot tub, and a restaurant/bar. It's a base for a Sno-Cat skiing operation (see Skiing and Snowboarding, above), so is busiest in winter. The rooms are great value year-round; $70 s or d in summer (and as low as $40 the rest of the year, with skiing packages equating to free skiing).

Out on the highway are many more motels, including the **Canyon Motor Inn,** 1911 Fraser

Dr., 250/837-5221 or 888/837-5221, which has a restaurant. Rates are $65 s, $85 d.

Like others in the chain, the **Sandman Inn,** 1821 Fraser Dr., 250/837-5271, website www.sandman.ca, is right on a busy highway, with a heated pool and a 24-hour restaurant, $90 s, $95 d.

$100–150

Right downtown, the elegantly restored **Regent Inn,** 112 1st St. E, 250/837-2107 or 888/245-5523, website www.regentinn.com, serves as the wintertime base of CMH Heli-skiing. The inn offers comfortable, well-furnished rooms, a restaurant, café, bar, and guest lounge. Rates are $99 s, $114 d, including breakfast.

Camping

KOA Revelstoke is off the TransCanada Highway six km east of downtown, 250/837-2085 or 800/562-3905. The well-kept campground offers grassy sites, lots of trees, a swimming pool, propane-filling facilities, a well-stocked store, free hot showers, laundry facilities, and a main lodge that looks like a Swiss chalet. Unserviced sites are $20.50, full hookups $25. It's open mid-April to mid-October.

Quiet **Williamson Lake Campground** lies on the edge of a warm lake perfect for swimming. Shaded grassy sites, hot showers, a picnic shelter, and fire pits are all just above the shoreline. Sites are $14.50–18. The campground is seven km south of town on Airport Way, 250/837-5512 or 888/676-2267.

Finally, along Highway 23 between Revelstoke and Shelter Bay are three provincial parks offering sites for $12.

FOOD

Downtown

Bertz Outdoor Equipment and Cafe, 217 Mackenzie Ave., 250/837-6575, is, as the name suggests, the combination of a café and a camping store. Lunch is busiest, with healthy salads, soups, and sandwiches on the menu. On the same block, toward the bandshell, **Conversations,** 205 Mackenzie Ave., 250/837-4772,

serves up gourmet coffees and light meals in a relaxed atmosphere. Across the road from these two, the **Woolsey Creek Café,** 212 Mackenzie St., 250/837-5500, has a warm, friendly atmosphere, but is always full and noisy with locals enjoying a wide range of well-prepared and remarkably inexpensive dishes. I had the Spanish Seafood Paella ($9) while researching this edition, and it was as good as city restaurants where you'd expect to pay double the price. It's open daily from 8 A.M., with breakfasts and lunches under $8 and dinners all under $12.

Claudio's, 204 Mackenzie Ave., 250/837-6743, is typical of small town Italian restaurants across the continent, complete with widely spread tables with plenty of elbow room; red, white, and green paper tablecloths; and the local radio station playing in the background. The menu is also typical, with pizza, pasta, and meat dishes ranging $13–18 and daily specials somewhere in between. Claudio's also has a few tables on the sidewalk.

The stylish decor and relaxed atmosphere of **One Twelve Restaurant,** at the Regent Inn, 112 1st St., 250/837-2107, make it a popular place to go if you're in the mood for a bit of a splurge. Open from 5:30 P.M. but closed Sunday. In the same inn, open daily, is **Dapper Dan's Pub,** offering Mexican food, burgers, soups, and salads for $6–8.

Out on the Highway

I feel almost guilty listing the following two restaurants with so many good choices downtown, but they've both been listed in the previous five editions of this book, and so for the sake of hurried highway travelers only, they shall remain. For breakfast, head to **Scotty's,** 250/837-4464, behind the Shell gas station. The service is fast and efficient, and six bucks will get you the daily special or most any cooked meal on the menu. Across the road is the **Frontier Family Restaurant,** 250/837-5119, a typical roadside diner with an atmosphere that lives up to its name. The wood interior is decorated with red-and-white checkered curtains, cowboy boots, hats, antlers, and cattle horns; the waitresses wear jeans; and a sign outside says "Y'all come back, y'hear!" On top of all that, the food is good. Huge breakfasts cost around $7 (try the "Hide-yer-plate-flapjacks"). Lunch is similarly priced, and dinner is $12–16.

SERVICES AND INFORMATION

Greyhound buses come through Revelstoke four to seven times daily in both directions along the TransCanada Highway. The depot is by the Sand-man Inn at 1899 Fraser Dr., 250/837-5874.

Queen Victoria Hospital is on Newlands Rd. (off Airport Way), on the southeast side of town,

250/837-2131. The **post office** is a couple of blocks from downtown at 307 3rd Street.

Revelstoke Visitor Info Centre is downtown at 204 Campbell Ave., 250/837-5345 or 800/487-1493. It's open in summer daily 8 A.M.–7 P.M., the rest of the year Mon.–Fri. 8:30 A.M.–4:30 P.M. On the TransCanada Highway, in front of the Frontier Family Restaurant, is a sea-sonal information center open in summer daily 7 A.M.–7 P.M. The **Revelstoke National Park ad-ministration office** is in the post office building at 313 3rd St., 250/837-7500. It's open year-round Mon.–Fri. 8:30 A.M.–4:30 P.M.

West toward Kamloops

Continuing west along the TransCanada Highway from Revelstoke, it's 104 km to the major center of Salmon Arm. The first stop along the way should be intriguing black **Summit Lake,** lying in a heavily forested ravine and fed by a waterfall that plunges over a cliff face high above. A few km farther west is similarly black **Victor Lake,** also fed by a water-fall. Shoreside **Victor Lake Provin-cial Park** makes a good spot for a picnic.

Three Valley

Several attractions on the next stretch of road compete for your tourist dollar. On the shore of Three Valley Lake is the well-marked **Three Valley Gap** "ghost" town, a rebuilt pioneer commu-nity with more than 20 historic buildings moved to the site from around the province. The town is open April–Oct. 8 A.M.–dusk; ad-mission $7.50. In the same complex is **Three Valley Lake Chateau,** a large motel (160 rooms) overlooking extensive gardens and the lake. Amenities include a café, restaurant, and indoor pool. Standard rooms are $95 s, $105 d, while the Cave theme room—complete with

At Craigellachie, on 7 November 1885, a plain iron spike joined the last two sections of Canadian Pacific's transcontinental rail line, finally connecting Canada from sea to sea. A cairn with a plaque and a piece of railway line marks the spot.

stone walls, roof, fireplace, and bathroom—is $145 s or d. For more informa-tion or reservations, call 250/837-2109 or 888/667-2109, website www.3valley.com.

The next commercial attrac-tion, eight km west, is **Enchanted Forest,** 250/837-9477, where a trail through towering trees me-anders past more than 250 hand-crafted figurines to fairyland buildings. It's open daily through summer from 8 A.M. until sunset; admission is adult $6, child $4.

The next venture along the highway, **Beardale Castle Minia-tureland,** 250/836-2268, takes miniature appreciators through sev-eral European towns and villages, into the world of nursery rhymes and fairy tales, and on into the world of trains. It's open daily May–Sept.; ad-mission is adult $6, child $4.

The Last Spike

At **Craigellachie,** signs point off the highway to the Last Spike. It was here on 7 November 1885 that a plain iron spike joined the last two sections of Canadian Pacific's transcontinental rail line, finally connecting Canada from sea to

CENTRAL B.C.

sea. A cairn with a plaque and a piece of railway line marks the spot. Nearby are picnic tables and **Craigellachie Station,** an information center open May–October.

Sicamous

This town of 3,000, 62 km west of Revelstoke, lies on the shore of **Shuswap Lake** and is known as the "Houseboat Capital of Canada." The lake itself is a convoluted body of water with four distinct arms, edged by secluded beaches, rocky coves, 25 marine parks, and more than 1,000 km of shoreline. Houseboating is the number-one activity in these parts, and Sicamous is headquarters to major agencies, including: **Blue Water Houseboats,** 250/836-2255 or 800/663-4024; **Three Buoys Houseboat Vacations,** 250/836-2403 or 800/663-2333, website www.threebouys.com; and **Twin Anchors Houseboat Vacations,** 250/836-2450 or 800/663-4026, website www.t winanchors.com. Expect to pay from $150 per boat per day, more for those that sleep more than four people. The season runs May–Oct. with peak season being summer school holidays.

SALMON ARM

Known as the "Gem of the Shuswap," Salmon Arm (pop. 15,000) lies along the Salmon Arm of Shuswap Lake, surrounded by lush farmland and forested hills. Legend has it that the name was coined in the days when the rivers here were chockablock with salmon. Farmers used to spear the fish with pitchforks and use them for fertilizer.

Sights

From downtown, follow the Salmon Arm Wharf signs to lakeside **Marine Park,** where picnic tables dot the lawns and colorful flower boxes hang from the lampposts. The attractive **Salmon Arm Wharf,** the largest marina structure in British Columbia's interior, lures you out over the water, past a boat-launching area, a snack bar, and businesses renting motorboats and houseboats.

Two km east of Salmon Arm on Highway 97B, **R.J. Haney Heritage Park** holds the town's main attractions. Here you'll find the **Salmon**

Arm Museum, 250/832-5243, which relates the town's early history through a slide show, photo albums, and the adjacent **Haney House,** an early 20th century farmhouse on beautiful, parklike grounds. Also in the park is a blacksmith's shop, an old fire hall, and a historic gas station. The park is open through summer, daily 10 A.M.–5 P.M. Admission is $4.

For excellent views of Shuswap Lake, take **Fly Hills Scenic Drive,** which starts almost opposite the Salmon River Motel and RV Park on the TransCanada Highway west of town. From the highway, turn onto 40th Street and follow the scenic route signs: right on 10th Avenue, left on Salmon Valley Road, right on Christensen Road, left on 5th Avenue, left on 60th Street, right on 15th Avenue, then on up a Forest Service road into the Fly Hills. The road gets pretty rough in sections, but the higher you go, the better the views become.

Accommodations and Camping

Salmon River Motel and RV Park, one km west of Salmon Arm, 250/832-3065, offers 10 rooms of a reasonable standard for $54 s, $65 d, $5 extra for a kitchenette. Out back are a few tree-shaded campsites with hookups; $19.50. Closer to town is the Best Western–affiliated **Villager West Motor Inn,** 61 10th St. SW, 250/832-9793, with an indoor pool; $70–90 s or d. The landscaped **KOA Salmon Arm,** just south of the TransCanada Hwy. along Hwy. 97B, 250/832-6489, features hot showers, a laundry, heated pool and hot tub, store, miniature golf, playground, and petting zoo. Tent sites are $23, full hookups $31, and rustic cabins $45.

Food

Near the Greyhound bus depot at 995 Lakeshore Dr., 250/832-9447, the **Hideaway Pub and Bistro** offers typical pub food throughout the day and nightly specials such as prime rib on Friday night. **Minos Greek House,** 720 22nd St. NE, off the TransCanada Hwy. east of town, 250/832-2079, is where the locals splurge on southern European cuisine; mains start at $12.50.

Services and Information

The **Greyhound** bus depot is on 10th St. W (behind the Village West Mall on the Trans-Canada Hwy.), 250/832-3962. **Shuswap Air,** 250/832-8830, offers flightseeing and scheduled flights between Salmon Arm and Vancouver. All flights arrive and depart from the airport at the east end of 20th Avenue.

Salmon Arm Visitor Info Centre, 751 Marine Park Dr., 250/832-2230 or 877/725-6667, is open in summer daily 9 A.M.–6 P.M., the rest of the year Mon.–Fri. 9 A.M.–5 P.M. Another source of information is **Tourism Shuswap,** 800/661-4800, website www.shuswap.bc.ca.

CONTINUING WEST

Squilax

Squilax lies at the turnoff to Roderick Haig-Brown Provincial Park, 48 km west of Salmon Arm. The town's one remaining building was originally a general store and is now the Hostelling International–affiliated **Squilax General Store Hostel,** 250/675-2977. The hostel office and a store selling organic products are in the building, while the dorm beds and communal kitchen are in three railway cabooses (the living quarters for railway workers in days gone by). The carriages sit on a short stretch of rail line overlooking the west end of Shuswap Lake. Rates are $15 for members and $19 for nonmembers.

Adams River Sockeye Run

Turn off at the Squilax Bridge to get to 988-hectare **Roderick Haig-Brown Provincial Park,** named for noted British Columbian conservationist and writer Roderick Haig-Brown but best known for protecting in its entirety the Adams River sockeye salmon run, North America's biggest such run. The salmon runs occur annually, but every four years (2002, 2006, etc.) a dominant run brings up to two million fish congregating in the river. These salmon are near the end of their four-year lifecycle, having hatched in the same section of the Adams River four years previously. Unlike other species, after hatching sockeye spend up to two years of their life in a "nursery" lake, which in the case of the Adams River run is Shuswap Lake. It is estimated that in conjunction with dominant runs 15 million Adams River sockeye enter the Pacific, with about 10 million running back toward their birthplace, of which just one in five make it past fishing nets to their birthplace. After an arduous 500-km swim from the Pacific Ocean, the salmon spawn on shallow gravel bars here during the first three weeks of October (numbers generally peak in the second week).

Forested with Douglas fir, cottonwood, birch, hemlock, and cedar, the park flanks the Adams River between Adams Lake and Shuswap Lake, protecting the spawning grounds in their entirety. Undoubtedly, October 2002 is the best time to visit in the near future, but at other times, the park is still interesting and interpretive boards describe the salmon run you've missed. Large mammals are common, interesting canyons dot the riverbank, fishing is good, and hikers can traverse a 40-km-long network of trails.

CENTRAL B.C.

Kamloops

Kamloops (pop. 80,000), 110 km west of Salmon Arm and 355 km northeast of Vancouver, is the province's sixth-largest city and a main service center along the TransCanada Highway. The city holds a few interesting sights but is certainly no scenic gem—the surrounding landscape is dominated by barren parched rolling hills. The downtown area, however, lies along the south bank of the Thompson River and is set off by well-irrigated parkland.

Entering the city from the west, the Trans-Canada Highway descends the Aberdeen Hills, passing shopping malls, motels, and Kamloops Visitor Info Centre. The highway bypasses downtown; take Columbia Street West to get to the city center. From the east, the TransCanada Highway parallels the Thompson River through almost 20 km of industrial and commercial sprawl.

History

The Secwepemc, whose descendents are now known as Shuswap, were the first people to live in this region, basing their lifestyle on hunting and salmon fishing. They knew the area as T'kumlups, meaning "Meeting of the Rivers." The first nonnative settlement occurred in 1812, when the North West Company established a fur-trading post at the confluence of the north and south branches of the Thompson River. Prospectors began arriving in 1858, followed by entrepreneurs who began setting up permanent businesses. Over the ensuing years all kinds of colorful characters have passed through or lived in Kamloops—fur traders, explorers, gold miners, cattle ranchers, railway builders, and farmers. Around the time of the town's founding, sternwheelers plied the Thompson River, dropping off passengers and collecting lumber. But the arrival of the railway in Kamloops contributed the most to the region's development; the Canadian Pacific Railway line was completed in 1885. Settlers flocked in on the trains; lumber and cattle were chugged out. The Canadian Northern Railway (now the Canadian National Railway) was completed in 1915, and Kamloops became a major transportation center. Today the local economy revolves around the forest-products industry, copper mining, cattle and sheep ranching, and tourism.

SIGHTS

Kamloops Museum and Art Gallery

Excellent displays at **Kamloops Museum,** 207 Seymour St., 250/828-3576, cover local native culture, the fur trade (peek in the reconstructed fur trader's cabin), pioneer days, natural history (many stuffed and mounted critters), industry, and transportation. You'll see a furnished turn-of-the-century living area, a stable complete with tack and carriage, a blacksmith shop, paddlewheels, old wall clocks and cameras, and a 15-minute slide presentation on the city's history.

Kamloops Art Gallery, 465 Victoria St., 250/828-3543, features an impressive collection of more than 1,000 works by contemporary artists in all sorts of media—quite a contrast to the museum.

Entry to both the museum and gallery are free. Hours are also the same; summer Mon.–Fri. 9 A.M.–8 P.M., Saturday 10 A.M.–5 P.M., and Sunday 1–5 P.M., the rest of the year Tues.–Sat. 9:30 A.M.–4:30 P.M.

Secwepemc Museum & Heritage Park

A living-history museum dedicated to the Shuswap tribe, this cultural attraction offers numerous exhibits focusing on the Shuswaps' traditions and rich mythology. Among the highlights are an archaeological site dating back 2,000 years, a re-created Shuswap winter village, a salmon-fishing station, a garden filled with native plants for food and medicinal purposes, and a re-creation of a traditional summer shelter. To get to the park, follow Highway 5 north across the Thompson River and take the first right. It's open Mon.–Fri. 8:30 A.M.–4 P.M.

KAMLOOPS

To Sun Peaks Resort, Wells Gray P.P., and Mt. Robson P.P.

HALSTON AVE.

8TH ST.

PAUL LAKE RD.

To Paul Lake P.P. and Harper Mountain Ski Area

To Airport

KWAN'S

FORTUNE DR.

TRANQUILLE DR.

ROMA'S

Thompson River

RIVERSIDE PARK

RED BRIDGE

LORNE ST.

RAILWAY STATION

D'AGOSTINO RESTAURANT

LANSDOWNE ST.

BAGEL ST. CAFÉ

POST OFFICE

ART GALLERY

SMORGASBORD

KAMLOOPS HOSTEL

ELEMENTS CAFÉ

PLAZA HERITAGE HOTEL

EXECUTIVE INN

SEYMOUR ST.

KAMLOOPS MUSEUM

BATTLE ST.

1ST AVE.

2ND AVE.

3RD AVE.

FOUNTAIN MOTEL

6TH AVE.

NICOLA ST.

COLUMBIA ST.

OVERLANDER BRIDGE

LANSDOWNE ST.

MT. PAUL WAY

ATHABASCA ST.

RED BRIDGE

S. Thompson River

SEE DETAIL

LORNE ST.

WANDA SUE DEPARTURE TERMINAL

SECWEPEMC NATIVE HERITAGE PARK

SUMMIT DR.

SEYMOUR ST.

BATTLE ST.

PAVILION THEATRE

RIVER ST.

STORMS

HOSPITALITY INN

SAGEBRUSH MOTEL

COLUMBIA ST. W

1ST AVE.

2ND AVE.

3RD AVE.

6TH AVE.

NICOLA ST.

COLUMBIA ST.

9TH AVE.

12TH AVE.

To Kamloops Wildlife Park, Campground, and Salmon Arm

HOSPITAL

DOUGLAS ST.

NOTRE DAME DR.

ACCENT INNS KAMLOOPS

TRANSCANADA HWY.

SAGEBRUSH THEATRE

GREYHOUND BUS DEPOT

LAVAL CR.

SUMMIT DR.

VISITOR INFO CENTRE

To Cache Creek, Coquihalla Hwy., and Vancouver

ALPINE MOTEL

5A

To Merritt

SCALE NOT AVAILABLE

© AVALON TRAVEL PUBLISHING, INC.

CENTRAL B.C.

Admission is adult $6, senior $4, child $3. For more information call 250/828-9801.

Kamloops Wildlife Park

This nonprofit park is primarily a wildlife rehabilitation center, but among the more than 150 furry inhabitants are many species of mammals from western Canada, including a couple of grizzly bears, wolves, cougars, and lynx. Other attractions are a huge visitor center, a glass-walled beehive, and, for the kids, a petting zoo and miniature steam train. The park is beside the TransCanada Highway,16 km east of Kamloops, 250/573-3242. Admission is adult $8, senior and child $5. Open daily through summer 8:30 A.M.–8 P.M., the rest of the year 8 A.M.–4 P.M.

River Cruise

One of the best ways to appreciate the city and some of its history is to take a cruise down the Thompson River on the *Wanda Sue,* a reconstructed sternwheeler. The boat departs through May–Sept. daily at 1:30 P.M. and weeknights at 6:30 P.M. from the terminal at the Old Yacht Club Public Wharf on River Street. Light meals and alcoholic beverages are available onboard during the two-hour cruise. Tickets cost adult $11.50, senior $10.50, child $6.50; get your ticket from the wharf ticket office up to one hour before sailing. For current times and more information, call 250/374-7447.

RECREATION

Paul Lake Provincial Park

This small 402-hectare provincial park northeast of Kamloops is a relaxing, grassy, tree-shaded spot to take a picnic, go swimming in warm Paul Lake, or camp. And the drive out there, following Paul Creek past scrub-covered rolling hills and flower-filled meadows, is an enjoyable ramble through the countryside. At the park's picnic area and beach you'll find picnic tables, toilets, and changing rooms. The campground offers basic sites for $12. To get there, head north of Kamloops five km on Highway 5, then 17 km east on Paul Lake Road.

Sun Peaks Resort

This resort, formerly known as Tod Mountain, is north of the city along Highway 5, 250/578-7222, website www.sunpeaksresort.com. In the last decade it has evolved from a medium-sized local ski hill to a year-round resort, with ongoing development both on the slopes and at the base village, where a golf course spreads out along the valley floor.

In summer, the Sunburst Express lift takes the hard work out of reaching the alpine for hikers and bikers. From the top of this lift, it's easy to descend back to the village on foot in less than an hour, but if the weather is good, consider exploring higher elevations, including the 2,152-meter summit of Mt. Tod. Mountain bike enthusiasts have a variety of options, but the most popular destination is McGillivray Lake, accessed along a wide 6.2-km trail from the village. Ride the lift all day for $12 ($26 with a mountain bike). Other activities include golfing a nine-hole course (a second nine hole course is slated to open in 2003), tennis, horseback riding, and fishing. The most popular of a packed event schedule are the **Alpine Blossom Festival** in late July, an outdoor performance by the **Kamloops Symphony Society** the first weekend of August, and the **Canadian Mountain Bike Festival** over two weeks in early August.

High season for the resort is wintertime, when two high-speed lifts whisk skiers up the mountain. One of these—the Sunburst Express—links up with three more lifts that access intermediate and expert terrain above the treeline as well as an easy eight-km cruising run back to the village. The total vertical rise is 882 meters over almost 1,000 hectares of terrain. Facilities at the resort include eateries, a rental shop, and the Snow Sports School. Lift tickets are adult $49, senior $34, child $27; discounted multiday and half-day tickets available. On-mountain accommodations packages are good value—from $75 per person per night including a lift ticket. For room reservations call 800/807-3257. For snow reports call 250/578-7232.

Harper Mountain

Smaller and closer to the city than Sun Peaks is locally owned Harper Mountain, 23 km from

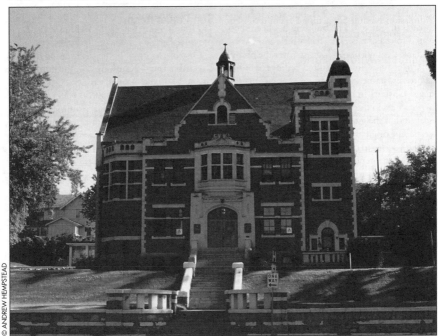

Hostelling International—Kamloops

© ANDREW HEMPSTEAD

CENTRAL B.C.

downtown along the road out to Paul Lake Provincial Park, 250/372-2119. It's a family-oriented area with a vertical rise of 425 meters served by three lifts. The hill is open in winter daily (one chairlift only midweek) and for night skiing Wed.–Fri. until 10 P.M. On weekdays, the main chairlift operates only after 12:30 P.M. On weekends, lift tickets are adult $28, senior or child $19. During the week they're a little cheaper. Facilities include a day lodge, rentals, ski school, and groomed cross-country trails. For daily ski reports call 250/828-0336.

Entertainment

Two River Junction is a nightly dinner and musical revue presented for the entertainment of overnighting passengers on the Rocky Mountaineer, but anyone is welcome to attend. It tells the story of Billy Miner, a U.S. stagecoach robber who, it is claimed, coined the phrase "Hands Up!" and spent the last years of his life in the Kamloops region. The revue is $29 pp, $49 with the buffet-style dinner. Call 250/314-1631 for times and locations. The amateur and professional musicians of the **Kamloops Symphony Society** regularly present classical and pop performances at the **Sagebrush Theatre,** 821 Munro St., 250/372-5000. The main season is Oct.–April, but the first weekend of August the orchestra performs outdoors at Sun Peaks Resort (see above). **Western Canada Theatre** presents live theatrical productions by top Canadian actors, producers, and designers. Performances take place in the **Pavilion Theatre,** down by the river at 1025 Lorne St., 250/372-3216.

ACCOMMODATIONS AND CAMPING

Under $50

Built in 1909, the Old Courthouse is now home to **Hostelling International—Kamloops,** 7 W.

Seymour St., 250/828-7991, one of the grandest hostels in Canada. The building has been renovated to make hostellers feel a little more comfortable than the original "guests," yet the historic charm remains in the vaulted ceilings, winding staircases, stained glass windows, and Canadian flags. Upstairs in the main courtroom you can write letters in the witness stand, sit in the judge's seat to sign the guest register, or relax in the jury seats. The original jail cells now hold bathrooms. And if you try to do any ironing, you'll be sent to solitary confinement—where the ironing board is. Dorm beds are $16 for members, $20 for nonmembers, and private rooms are $35–45.

$50–100

Least expensive downtown is the **Fountain Motel,** 506 Columbia St., 250/374-4451 or 800/253-1569, website www.fountain.kamloops.com, which offers a higher standard of rooms than the exterior may suggest; $56–62 s or d and kitchenettes an extra $10. Other similarly priced choices lie along a wide sweeping bend of Columbia St. W between the TransCanada Hwy. and downtown. Least expensive of these is **Sagebrush Motel,** 660 Columbia St. W, 250/372-3151, with a pool and restaurant; $48 s, $53 d. Of a higher standard, and with more facilities, is the **Hospitality Inn,** 500 Columbia St. W, 250/374-4164 or 800/663-5733, website www.hospitalityinn.kamloops.com. Rates start at $85 s, $88 d, and for a few extra bucks you get a view.

On the western approach to the city are many newer accommodations aimed at the passing highway traveler. These offer clean and comfortable no-frills accommodations but no particular bargains. Among them, **Alpine Motel,** 1393 Hugh Allan Dr., 250/374-0034 or 800/270-1260, offers standard rooms from $70, or suites with kitchen and hot tub for a few dollars more.

$100–150

Just off the highway near the west side access to downtown, **Accent Inns Kamloops,** 1325 Columbia St. W, 250/374-8877 or 800/663-0298, website www.accentinns.com, charges $119 s, $129 d for a modern and spacious room, with

guests having use of an outdoor pool, hot tub, and fitness room. Check the website of this small provincial chain for discounted rates.

One of the city's better accommodations is **Executive Inn—Kamloops,** in the heart of the city and home to a small casino at 540 Victoria St., 250/372-2281 or 800/663-2837, website www.stockmenshotel.com. Summer rates are from $130 s, $145 d, but rates are considerably lower the rest of the year. Also right downtown is the **Plaza Heritage Hotel,** 405 Victoria St., 250/377-8075 or 877/977-5292, first opened in 1928 as one the Interior's finest accommodations. Its restoration and opening as a boutique hotel is only recent. The 68 rooms feature rich woods, a heritage color scheme, and comfortable beds covered in plush duvets. At street level is the Heritage Restaurant and a stylish lounge bar. The smallest rooms are $100 s, $120 d, with suites for $159 s or d.

Camping

Heading out of Kamloops to the east, 16 km from downtown, **Kamloops Waterslide and RV Park,** 9115 TransCanada Hwy., 250/573-3789, offers full hookups, coin-operated showers, a laundry, hot tub, and grocery store, and is next door to the wildlife park. Unserviced sites are $16, hookups $18–25.

The city's most scenic campground is at **Paul Lake Provincial Park,** north of Kamloops five km on Highway 5, then 17 km east on Paul Lake Road. Facilities are basic (no hookups or showers), but the setting makes up for it. All sites are $12.

FOOD

Downtown

Sitting on one of downtown's busiest streets is the **Bagel Street Café,** 428 Victoria St., 250/372-9322. Bagels and other pastries and hearty soups can be enjoyed either inside in a welcoming environment or at sidewalk table settings. Another good lunch spot is **Smorgasbord,** 225 7th Ave., 250/377-0055, which is not a smorgasbord as the British know it, but a small café offering a wide range of soups, salads, and sandwiches, with a daily special offering the best value. It's open Mon.–Sat. 7 A.M.–5 P.M. Offering similar home-cooked fare as well as more substantial dishes such as cottage pie is **Elements Café,** 229 Victoria St., 250/372-1341. This place is also open for dinner (all mains under $8), and there's a jazz jam Thursday night.

D'Agostino Restaurant, 258 Victoria St., 250/372-1111, offers a lunch menu featuring burgers from $6, salads from $3, and pasta dishes from $6. The dinner menu offers more of the same at a slightly higher price, as well as steaks, seafood, and all-you-can-eat specials (around $10). Beyond the *Wanda Sue* dock is **Storms,** 1502 River St., 250/372-1522, one of Kamloops' best restaurants. The elegant setting includes tables set on an outdoor deck overlooking the river. The menu features classic European and North American dishes, such as a succulent rack of lamb roasted in Dijon mustard and fresh rosemary for $23. Other mains start at $14, or just soak up the river atmosphere with a platter of appetizers for $19. Open daily for lunch and dinner.

Tranquille Road

Aside from downtown, the next biggest concentration of restaurants is along Tranquille Road, heading north toward the airport. Most are family-style restaurants with relaxed atmosphere and plenty of parking. Typical of these is **Roma's,** 311 Tranquille Rd., 250/554-2022, featuring a pizza-and-pasta menu and fast, efficient servers in a cavernous room with only a few tables. Dinner mains start at $10. It's open Mon.–Sat. for lunch and daily for dinner. Continuing north, **Kwan's,** 501 Tranquille Rd., 250/376-3328, serves up a Chinese buffet lunch for just $7.

SERVICES AND INFORMATION
Transportation
Kamloops Airport is on Airport Rd., seven km

northwest of city center; follow Tranquille Rd. through the North Shore until you come to Airport Rd. on the left. **Air B.C.,** 888/247-2262, offers scheduled flights between Kamloops and Vancouver.

The railway station is right downtown at the north end of 3rd Avenue. **VIA Rail,** 800/561-8630, runs scheduled service three times weekly west to Vancouver and east to Jasper. Kamloops is also the overnight stop for **Rocky Mountaineer Railtours,** 800/665-7245, a summer-only luxurious rail trip between Vancouver, Jasper, and Banff (see Transportation in the On the Road chapter for more details).

The **Greyhound** bus depot is at 725 Notre Dame Dr., off Columbia St. W at the west end of town, 250/374-1212 or 800/661-8747. Greyhound provides daily service to most parts of the province.

Local bus transportation is provided by **Kamloops Transit System;** adult fare is $1.50, while a day pass is $4.50. For a schedule and route information, call 250/376-1216. Taxi companies include: **Kami Cabs,** 250/554-1377, and **Yellow Cabs,** 250/374-3333. For a rental car, call **Budget,** 250/374-7368; **Discount,** 250/372-7170; **Hertz,** 250/376-3022; **National,** 250/374-5737; or **Rent-a-wreck,** 250/374-7788.

Other Services and Information
The **Royal Inland Hospital** is at the south end of 3rd Ave. at 311 Columbia St., 250/374-5111. The **post office** is at 301 Seymour Street. **Kamloops Visitor Info Centre** is beside the TransCanada Highway on the western outskirts of town (at Hillside Rd. opposite the Aberdeen Mall), 250/374-3377 or 800/662-1994, website www.city.kamloops.bc.ca. It's open in summer daily 8 A.M.–8 P.M., the rest of the year Mon.–Fri. 8:30 A.M.–4 P.M. The local tourism association's website is www.venturekamloops.com.

North to Mount Robson

From Kamloops, Highway 5 follows the North Thompson River to Tete Jaune Cache on Highway 16. This stretch of highway is part of the most direct route between Vancouver and Jasper National Park, and is also worthwhile for two excellent provincial parks—**Wells Gray,** a vast wilderness of rivers and mountains, and **Mount Robson,** protecting a spectacular peak that is the highest point in the Canadian Rockies.

Clearwater

The small town of Clearwater (pop. 1,600), 125 km north of Kamloops, is the gateway to Wells Gray Provincial Park. A few motels, restaurants, gas stations, services, and an information center are on the highway; the rest of the community is off the highway to the south.

Jasper Way Inn Motel, on the old highway, two blocks north of Hwy. 5, 250/674-3345, lies on the shores of Dutch Lake. From its wildflower-edged garden, views extend across the lake to tree-covered hills on the far shore and snowcapped mountains in the distance. Basic rooms start at $50 s, $55 d, with one- and two-bedroom units up to $90. Camping is most pleasant within the nearby provincial park, but an alternative is the year-round **Dutch Lake Resort,** 361 Ridge Rd., 250/674-3351 or 888/884-4424, website www.dutchlake.com, where tent camping is $20 and hookups range $25–27. Cabins range $74–129.

At the turnoff to Wells Gray Provincial Park is **Clearwater Visitor Info Centre,** 250/674-2646; open daily through summer 8 A.M.–6 P.M., the rest of the year weekdays 9 A.M.–5 P.M.

WELLS GRAY PROVINCIAL PARK

Snow-clad peaks, extinct volcanoes, and ancient lava flows. Amazing waterfalls—so many the park is often referred to as the "Waterfall Park." Icy mineral springs, subalpine forest, and flower-filled meadows. An abundance of lakes and rivers where anglers can fish to their heart's content for rainbow trout and Dolly Varden.

With so much to see and do, Wells Gray Provincial Park is a must-see detour on the route between Kamloops and Jasper. The main access road into the 540,000-hectare park leads north from Clearwater for 36 km to the park boundary. From there it continues 11 km to one of the park's highlights, Helmcken Falls, where it turns to gravel and continues another 16 km to its end at Clearwater Lake. Apart from three campgrounds, the park has no services.

Sights and Hikes

Just inside the park boundary on the road up from Clearwater, a short trail leads to a colorful lava canyon where 61-meter-high **Spahats Creek Falls** plummets over multicolored bedrock. The narrow ribbon of water flows into a wide pool before merging with the Clearwater River.

Continuing through the park, take a signposted gravel road to the west to **Green Viewing Tower** atop Green Mountain. The viewpoint provides panoramic views of a volcanic cone and many spectacular, rugged peaks, including snow-covered Garnet Peak, highest in the park.

Wells Gray is best known for its waterfalls, the two most spectacular of which are accessible by road. Southernmost is **Dawson Falls,** four km into the park, where the **Murtle River** cascades over a 90-meter-wide and 20-meter-high ledge. A little farther along the main road is the **Mush Bowl** (or Devil's Punchbowl), where the river has carved huge holes in the riverbed. But save some film for incredible **Helmcken Falls,** British Columbia's fourth-highest falls, where the Murtle River cascades off the edge of Murtle Plateau in a sparkling, 137-meter-high torrent to join the Clearwater River. In winter, the frozen falls create an enormous ice cone as tall as a 20-story building.

For an enjoyable short walk from the road (20 minutes each way), hike the one-km trail out to **Ray Farm,** former home of one of the area's first settlers. John Bunyon Ray cleared his farm out of the wilderness in 1912, and he and his wife raised a family in this isolated spot. The picturesque abandoned farm buildings sit among rolling

CENTRAL B.C.

meadows full of wildflowers. From the farm, another short trail leads to a mineral spring.

Continuing north up the road, a 500-meter trail (10 minutes each way) winds through a stand of towering cedar trees to **Bailey's Chute,** a narrow rapids-filled passage between two lakes. In fall, large numbers of chinook salmon battle the torrent, trying in vain to leap up the chute. After a number of valiant attempts, they're washed back downstream to the gravel beds where they spawn and die.

Back out on the road and continuing north, you'll soon come to **Clearwater Lake** at road's end. One of the park's six major lakes, Clearwater Lake was created when an ancient lava flow blocked the valley. In summer, **Clearwater Lake Tours,** 250/674-2121, runs a four-hour motorboat cruise from Clearwater Lake Campground to the north end of the lake, where you'll have views of adjacent **Azure Lake.** Tours depart at 10 A.M.; adult $45, senior $36, child $28. The company also rents canoes for those who would rather propel themselves the 50 km to Azure Lake; $35 a day or $160 a week, drop-offs available via water taxi anywhere on Clearwater Lake. This overnight trip is popular with paddlers, the only hitch being a 500-meter portage between the two lakes. Numerous wilderness campsites line the shores of both lakes.

The center of the park and the rugged northern reaches are accessible only on foot; they contain a vast wilderness of tall peaks, dense forests, and lakes and rivers. This is where the animals like to hang out—mountain goats, caribou, moose, mule deer, and black and grizzly bears. Access into the east side of the park is by a 24-km gravel road off Highway 5, just north of the community of Blue River. From the trailhead at the end of the road it's a 2.5-km hike (40 minutes) to **Murtle Lake,** the park's largest freshwater lake.

Accommodations and Camping

Between Clearwater and the park boundary, **Wells Gray Guest Ranch,** 250/674-2792, is surrounded by grassy meadows full of wildflowers and grazing horses. Activities organized for guests include horseback riding, canoeing, whitewater rafting, and fishing. Well-furnished, kitchen-equipped cabins rent for $115 per night. The ranch also has a restaurant and saloon. **Helmcken Falls Lodge,** 250/674-3657, website www.helmckenfalls.com, is also on the park access road, offering similar activities and accommodations. Cabins rent for $116–143 per night, while the camping fee of $19–27 includes hookups and hot showers.

Each of the three campgrounds inside the park has drinking water, toilets, and picnic tables; $12 per site. Heading up the road from the village of Clearwater, you'll pass, in order, **Dawson Falls Campground, Falls Creek Campground** (with spacious riverside sites), and finally **Clearwater Lake Campground,** which is almost at the end of the road, right on the lake, and is the first to fill each night.

Information

Park information is available at **Clearwater Visitor Info Centre** in Clearwater, 250/674-2646. The center sells two invaluable guidebooks to the park: *Exploring Wells Gray Park* and *Nature Wells Gray.* Another source of information is the Thompson River District office of BC Parks, in Kamloops, 250/851-3000.

CONTINUING TOWARD MOUNT ROBSON

Blue River

Although right on busy Highway 5, 215 km north of Kamloops, this one-time railway division point has remained small, holding just a few hundred residents along with services for passing travelers. But with the Cariboo Mountains to the north, Wells Gray Provincial Park to the west, and the northern reaches of the North Thompson River just to the east, the town makes a great base for exploring British Columbia's unspoiled interior wilderness. Closer in, Lake Eleanor offers a good beach and swimming right in the heart of town. And just over the rail line from downtown, at the confluence of the Blue and North Thompson Rivers, await myriad hiking trails.

TERRY FOX

Terry Fox is a name that is sure to come up at some point on your Canadian travels. In 1977, as a college-bound teenager, Fox lost his right leg to cancer. On 12 April 1980, after three years of training, with next to no sponsorship and little media coverage, he set off from Newfoundland on his **Marathon of Hope,** with the aim of raising money for cancer research. After running over 5,000 km in 144 days, a recurrence of the cancer forced him to stop just outside Ontario's Thunder Bay. Cancer had begun spreading to his lungs, and on 28 June 1981, aged just 22, he died. As his run had progressed, the attention had grown, and, more importantly, the donations poured in. In total, his Marathon of Hope raised $24 million, far surpassing all goals.

The legacy of Terry Fox lives on in many ways, including 2,650-meter **Mount Terry Fox,** along the Yellowhead Highway; the **Terry Fox Run,** an annual fall event in many Canadian towns; Vancouver's **Terry Fox Plaza** and a tribute in the adjacent B.C. Sports Hall of Fame and Museum; and an annual $5 million scholarship fund.

The **Mike Wiegele Resort,** at the north end of town, offers heli-skiing in the surrounding Monashee and Cariboo Mountains. The company has been featured in many ski movies and attracts an international clientele. During summer, the resort is a base for heli-hiking, glacier-based heli-skiing, heli-fishing, heli-biking, and boring old flightseeing (from $100 pp) in the same mountain ranges. Other summer activities centered at the lodge include mountain biking, fishing, and tennis. In the height of summer, luxurious motel-style rooms cost $175 s or d, while freestanding, self-contained lakeside chalets are $225. The main lodge holds the Powder Max Dining Room as well as a health club. For resort information call 250/673-8381 or 800/661-9170, website www.wiegele.com.

Glacier Mountain Lodge, 250/673-2393, is another stylish Blue River accommodation, this one offering 33 well-appointed guest rooms.

Summer rates of $85 s, $100 d, including a breakfast buffet, make this place good value. The least expensive place to stay in town is **Blue River Campground,** 250/673-8203, where sites range $14–22 per night. The campground is within walking distance of Lake Eleanor and the town's services.

Valemount and Vicinity

North of Blue River, Highway 5 follows the North Thompson River through the Cariboo Mountains to Valemount, 30 km south of the Yellowhead Highway. Valemount is a base for Canadian Mountain Holidays (CMH). **CMH Heli-hiking,** 403/762-7100, website www.cmh-hike.com, offers packages including transportation to a remote lodge, accommodations, helicopter flights to alpine hiking areas high above treeline, hiking gear, and gourmet meals, all for $1,734 per person for three nights. For heli-skiing details, check the CMH website, www.cmhski.com. A good local accommodation is the **Alpine Inn,** 250/566-4471 or 877/566-4471, which charges $80 s, $90 d. **Irvin's Park and Campground,** one km north of town, is suited mostly for RVs and trailers; $23–29 per rig.

From the Yellowhead Highway junction north of Valemount, Prince George is 270 km to the west, and the British Columbia–Alberta border is 77 km east. Although most of the distance to the border is through Mount Robson Provincial Park (see below), two worthwhile stops lie between the highway junction and the park. The first of these is **Rearguard Falls,** a one-km hike (20 minutes each way) from the highway. Eight km downstream from the falls—some 1,200 km up the Fraser River from the Pacific Ocean—is a spawning grounds for Pacific salmon; many of the hardy fish make it all the way to the falls. Farther east along the highway is a viewpoint for 2,650-meter **Mount Terry Fox** (see the special topic Terry Fox).

MOUNT ROBSON PROVINCIAL PARK

Spectacular Mount Robson Provincial Park was created in 1913 to protect 224,866 hectares of steep canyons and wide forested valleys; icy lakes, rivers, and streams; and rugged mountain peaks permanently blanketed in snow and ice. Towering over the park's western entrance is magnificent 3,954-meter **Mount Robson,** highest peak in the Canadian Rockies. The park lies along the Continental Divide, in British Columbia, adjacent to Jasper National Park. The main watershed is the Fraser River, one of British Columbia's most important waterways. From within the park it flows northwest to Prince George then southward through the heart of the province to drain into the Pacific Ocean at Vancouver. Highway 16, from where many roadside sights present themselves, splits the park in two, but for many visitors it is the famous Berg Lake Trail to which they are attracted.

Flora and Fauna

The elevation differences with the park are as great as anywhere else in the Canadian Rockies, giving a great variety of flora and fauna. The main service center lies in a forested valley at an elevation of just 840 meters, right in the heart of the montane. The oft-photographed view of Mt. Robson from the visitor center is framed by a stand of trembling aspen across a cleared meadow, but the most common tree at this elevation, and one that covers the valley floor, is Douglas fir. Western red cedar and hemlock thrive in damp sections of the park. As with the rest of the Canadian Rockies, the subalpine is dominated by Engelmann spruce and, at higher elevations, subalpine fir. The alpine zone in the park begins at around 2,400 meters.

In spring black bears are often seen feasting on dandelions by the roadside, but their larger relative, the grizzly, rarely makes an appearance in the busy valley through which Highway 16 winds. Elk, moose, and mountain goats are also present, as are many smaller critters. Over 170 bird species have been identified, with the rare harlequin duck a special joy to watch as it passes though the park each spring.

History

Local Shuswap natives called Mt. Robson Yuh-hai-has-hun ("Mountain of the Spiral Road")

for its layered appearance. Historians guess that the peak's European name honors a member of the Hudson's Bay Company, though details of the christening have been lost to history.

Mountaineers were attracted to the challenge of climbing Mt. Robson at the very beginning of this century, but the first official ascent took place in 1913, the same year the park as we know it today was created. Led by Swiss guide Conrad Kain, the first ascent party was made up of members of the Alpine Club of Canada. Although this was the first official summit climb, the summit had been attempted four years earlier by Rev. George Kinney and friends. Kinney thought he'd made the summit, but he was climbing the summit ridge in a heavy fog; a cairn and a message recording the names of the members of Kinney's climbing team were later found on the ridge about 100 vertical meters from the top.

Roadside Sights

If you're approaching the park from the west along Highway 16, you'll see **Mount Robson** long before you reach the park boundary, provided the weather is cooperating. It's impossible to confuse this distinctive peak with those that surround it—no wonder it's known as the "Monarch of the Canadian Rockies." Once inside the park boundary, the highway climbs gradually to the main facility area, where you'll find a visitor center, campgrounds, a gas station, and a restaurant. On a clear day the panorama from this lump of commercialism is equal to any sight in British Columbia. The sheer west face of Mt. Robson slices skyward just seven km away across a flower-filled meadow. This is as close as you can get to the peak in your car.

From the park's only service area, the highway climbs steeply then parallels photogenic **Moose Lake.** Waterfalls on the far side of the lake create a scenic backdrop. The Moose River drains into the Fraser River at **Moose Marsh,** a good spot for wildlife watching at the southeast end of the lake. Moose often feed here at dawn and dusk, and waterfowl are present throughout the day. Continuing westward, the highway crosses the upper reaches of the Fraser River before passing long and narrow Yellowhead Lake at the foot of

MOUNT ROBSON PROVINCIAL PARK

Calumet Ridge

Calumet Peak

Mumm Peak

Mural Glacier

Mt. Phillips

ROBSON PASS

Upright Mtn.

Toboggan Falls

Berg L.

Rearguard Mtn.

Reef Icefield

Whitehorn Mtn.

Emperor Falls

Robson Cirque

River

Mt. Robson

Resplendent Mtn.

Rainbow Range

Kinney Lake

Mt. Kain

Mt. Robson Provincial Park

Sufficurrent Glacier

Robson

EMPEROR RIDGE
ROBSON RIVER

MT. ROBSON VISITOR CENTRE

HWY

ROBSON MEADOWS

River

Mt. McNaughton

MOUNT ROBSON LODGE

MOUNTAIN RIVER LODGE

Fraser

16 YELLOWHEAD

Tête Jaune Cache

16

Moose Lake

Moose Marsh

Mt. Terry Fox

Mt Terry Fox Provincial Park

The Comb

Swift Creek

Sleeper Mountain

Sleeper Creek

Creek

Valemount

5

McLennan River

0   5 mi

0   5 km

Canoe River

Kinbasket Lake

Yellowjacket Creek

To Kamloops

© AVALON TRAVEL PUBLISHING, INC.

CENTRAL B.C.

MOON

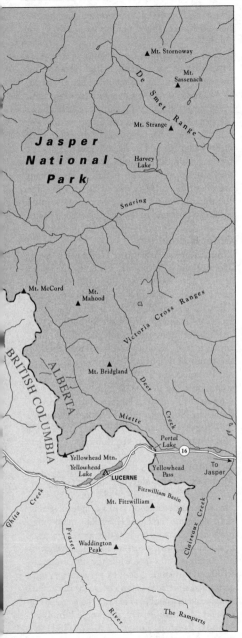

2,458-meter **Yellowhead Mountain.** Finally, Highway 16 exits the park at the 1,066-meter **Yellowhead Pass,** on the British Columbia–Alberta border 60 km east of the visitor center. It's the lowest highway pass over the Continental Divide. Right before the pass is picturesque **Portal Lake,** with a small lakeside picnic area.

Berg Lake Trail

- Length: 19.5 km (eight hours) one-way
- Elevation gain: 725 meters
- Rating: moderate-difficult

This is the most popular overnight hike in the Canadian Rockies, but don't let the crowds put you off—the hike is well worth it. Beautiful aqua-colored Berg Lake lies below the north face of Mount Robson, which rises 2,400 meters directly behind the lake. Glaciers on the mountain's shoulder regularly calve off into the lake, resulting in the icebergs that give the lake its name. It's possible to traverse the trail's first section and return the same day, but to get all the way to Berg Lake and back you need to stay in the backcountry overnight. Along the route are seven primitive campgrounds, including three along the lakeshore. Overnight hikers must register at the visitor center and pay a camping fee of $6 per person per night. Only 75 campsites lie along the trail. Bookings for these sites are taken at the visitor center or through BC Parks at 800/689-9025. Book early as the quota fills quickly.

From the trailhead two km north of the visitor center along a narrow access road, the trail follows the Robson River 4.5 km through dense subalpine forest to glacially fed **Kinney Lake.** There the trail narrows, crossing the fast-flowing river at the eight-km mark and climbing alongside it. The next four km, through the steep-sided Valley of a Thousand Falls, are the most demanding, but views of four spectacular waterfalls ease the pain of the 500-vertical-meter climb. The first glimpses of Mount Robson come soon after reaching the head of the valley, from where it's a further one km to the outlet of Berg Lake, 17.5 km from the trailhead. The first of three lakeside campgrounds is two km from this point.

CENTRAL B.C.

© ALEC PYTLOWANY

Mount Robson

east to the Continental Divide and west to the Selwyn Range. Allow two hours each way for this hike.

The other option is the 13-km (each way) **Fitzwilliam Basin Trail,** which requires an overnight stay in the backcountry. Elevation gain is 950 meters, so it's a fairly demanding trail. From the trailhead on the south side of Highway 16, three km east of Lucerne Campground, the trail climbs steadily for six km to the confluence of Rockingham and Fitzwilliam Creeks. Although easy to follow, the remaining seven km along the northern slopes of 2,911-meter Mt. Fitzwilliam are rough going. After ascending a steep ridge the trail all but dissipates, but many camping spots can be found in the wide lake-filled basin.

Other Recreation

Mount Robson Adventure Holidays, based at Mount Robson Adventure Centre (by the visitor center), 250/566-4386 or 800/882-9921, conducts "gentle adventure" tours within the park. These include rafting ($45), canoeing on Moose Lake ($44), and an easy float trip ($40).

Flightseeing by fixed-wing aircraft and helicopter is from Valemount, 20 km west then 22 km south on Highway 5 from the visitor center. **Premier Air,** 250/566-4901, offers flightseeing over the area for $75 per person for 40 minutes, $130 for 70 minutes. More expensive is flightseeing by helicopter; **Robson Helimagic,** 250/566-4700, charges $169 per person for a 36-minute flight up to Mt. Robson.

Accommodations and Camping

Mountain River Lodge, four km west of the visitor center, 250/566-9899 or 888/566-9899, website www.mtrobson.com, is in a delightful setting right alongside the Fraser River. The main lodge holds five rooms, each with a different character, a balcony, and private bathroom. The smallest of the rooms is $80 s or d while the other four are $100; rates include a cooked breakfast. A self-contained riverfront cabin costs $90 per night, with breakfast available at an extra charge. One km beyond Mountain River Lodge is the turnoff for **Mount Robson Lodge,** 250/566-4821 or 888/566-4821, with 18 freestanding cabins

While the panorama from the lake is stunning, most hikers who have come this far want to spend some time exploring the area. From the north end of the lake, trails lead to Toboggan Falls and more mountain views, to the head of Robson Glacier, and to Robson Pass, which opens up the remote northern reaches of Jasper National Park.

If the walk in seems too ambitious, **Robson Helimagic,** 250/566-4700, makes drop-offs at Robson Pass from Valemount every Monday and Friday; $169 per person (minimum four).

Other Hikes in the Park

Aside from the busy trail to Berg Lake, the park holds only two other established trails. The shortest of the two ascends the slopes of 2,458-meter **Yellowhead Mountain.** From the trailhead across the rail line at Yellowhead Lake it's a steady climb through subalpine forest to the first viewpoint at the one-km mark. Another three km and a total elevation gain of 720 meters brings you to flower-filled meadows and panoramic views extending

($70–125 s or d); meals available. The closet motel accommodation to the park is in Valemount.

Within the park are five campgrounds with road access. Three of these are park operated. Closest to the visitor center is **Robson River Campground,** while across the road is **Robson Meadows Campground.** Both have flush toilets and showers but no hookups; $17.50 per site. In the east is the more rustic **Lucerne Campground,** where sites are $12. **Emperor Ridge Campground,** 250/566-8438, is a small commercial facility right behind the visitor center; $14.50 per site including hot showers but no hookups. **Robson Shadows Campground** is part of Mount Robson Lodge. It also has showers but no hookups. It's five km west of the visitor center, 250/566-4821. Sites are $14.50 per night.

Information

At the park's western entrance, **Mount Robson Visitor Centre,** 250/566-9174, features informative natural-history slide shows, an evening interpretive program, and trail reports updated daily. The center stocks the brochure *Mount Robson Provincial Park,* which provides sufficient information if you're only driving through the park. Hikers and climbers can pick up more detailed trail descriptions and topographical maps ($11) at the center. Hours are mid-June to mid-September daily 8 A.M.–8 P.M., mid-May to mid-June and mid-September to mid-October daily 8 A.M.–5 P.M., closed the rest of the year. Another source of information is the BC Parks' Mount Robson Area Office in Valemount, 250/566-4325, and the website www.elp.gov.bc.ca/bcparks.

CENTRAL B.C.

Cariboo Country

The wild, sparsely populated Cariboo region extends from Kamloops north to Prince George and west to the Pacific Ocean. Its most dramatic natural features are the mountain ranges rising like bookends to either side. In the west, the **Coast Mountains** run parallel to the coast and rise to a height of 4,016 meters at **Mount Waddington.** In the east, the **Cariboo Mountains** harbor numerous alpine lakes, high peaks, and several provincial parks.

Between the two ranges flows the **Fraser River,** which is flanked to the west by expansive plateaus home to British Columbia's biggest ranches. This is cowboy country, where horseback holidays and the famous Williams Lake Stampede are the main visitor drawcards. This was once gold-rush country—most of the region's towns began as stopping places along the Gold Rush Trail. Those such as **100 Mile House** owe their names to the trail but have remained small, while others, such as **Williams Lake** and **Quesnel,** have continued to grow and are service centers for the ranching and forestry industries. The only coastal access in Cariboo Country is via Highway 20, which runs through **Tweedsmuir Provincial Park** to **Bella Coola,** at the head of a long fjord.

CACHE CREEK

A town born with the fur trade at a spot where traders cached furs and food supplies, Cache Creek was once the largest town between Vancouver, 337 km to the south, and Kamloops, 80 km to the east. But since the new Coquihalla Highway opened, the town is but a shadow of its former self. It still lies on the most direct route between the south and north ends of the province, and travelers not willing to pay the $10 toll on the Coquihalla Highway still pass through, even though it costs them at least an extra $5 in gas.

The surrounding desertlike climate is intriguing; sagebrush and cacti grow on the relatively barren volcanic landscape, and tumbleweeds blow through town. Due to the town's former highway prominence, the main drag is lined with motels, roadside diners, and gas stations.

Historic Hat Creek Ranch

Between 1885 and 1905, the Cariboo Wagon Road bustled with stagecoaches and freight wagons. One of the few sections of the original road still open to the public is at Hat Creek Ranch, 11 km north of Cache Creek on Highway 97. Many of the original buildings—some dating as far back as 1861—still stand, and visitors can watch the blacksmith at his forge, appreciate a collection of antique farm machinery, enjoy a picnic lunch in the orchard, or take a guided tour of the ranch house. Admission to the ranch is free, but a donation is requested after touring the house. The ranch is open mid-May to mid-Oct. daily 10 A.M.–6 P.M. For more information call 250/457-9722.

© BC RAIL

The luxurious Whistler Northwind passes through the heart of Cariboo Country.

CENTRAL B.C.

Accommodations

The **Sage Hills Motel**, 1390 Hwy. 97, 250/457-6451 or 888/794-4949, is one of many local motels that would have filled every night before the highway was rerouted. Today, it's seen better days, but the owners try their best, keeping the place clean and planting a colorful bed of flowers out front each spring. Rates are $45 s or d, while units with kitchens are $55. Similar is the **Desert Motel**, 1069 TransCanada Hwy., 250/457-6226 or 800/663-0212, which is air-conditioned and has a small outdoor pool; $52 s, $58 d. The best campground in town is **Brookside Campsite**, at the base of steep cliffs east of town, 250/457-6633. Facilities are excellent and sites are $14–19.

LILLOOET

This historic town of 2,100 was founded as Mile 0 of the 1858 Cariboo Wagon Road—also known as the Gold Rush Trail—which led north to the Barkerville and Wells goldfields. Several towns along the Gold Rush Trail—70 Mile House, 100 Mile House, and 150 Mile House, among them—were named for their distance up the wagon road from Lillooet.

With thousands of prospectors passing through in the mid-1800s, Lillooet was the scene of its own gold rush. Originally known as Cayoosh Flat, the town was renamed in the mid-1860s. (The new name was a misspelling of Leel-wat, the name of a tribe of natives who lived to the north.) By this time the city held some 16,000 residents, making it the second-largest population center north of San Francisco and west of Chicago. But like all other boomtowns, the population explosion was short-lived. As all the most productive local goldfields were worked dry, prospectors continued north on the Cariboo Wagon Road or east on the Dewdney Trail.

A row of rusty farming relics out front marks **Lillooet Museum**, on Main St. at 8th Ave., 250/256-4308. Inside are ore samples and details about the one-time boomtown's mining history and growth. It's open May through mid-October daily 11 A.M.–4 P.M. Then saunter along wide Main Street and pretend you're back in the gold-rush era—which won't be hard if you happen to be here in June during **Only in Lillooet Days**. During this weeklong celebration, the town re-creates the Old West with all sorts of entertaining events. Lillooet is also home to the unique **Sheep Pasture Golf Course**, 250/256-4484, a nine-hole layout on a working sheep farm. It's five km southwest of town.

Practicalities

One block up the hill from the museum, **4 Pines Motel**, 108 8th Ave., 250/256-4247 or 800/753-2576, website www.4pinesmotel.com, charges $46 s, $60 d. **Cayoosh Creek Campground** is a barren spot near the south end of town, where Cayoosh Creek drains into the much larger Fraser River. Facilities include hot showers and hookups. Sites are $12–18.

For a meal, head to **Lillooet Inn Restaurant**, 687 Main St., 250/256-0028, open every day from 6:30 A.M.

Along the main drag at 8th Ave. is **Lillooet Visitor Info Centre** (in the museum building), 250/256-4308; open in summer daily 11 A.M.–4 P.M.

CLINTON TO 100 MILE HOUSE

Clinton

Originally called 47 Mile House, the old-fashioned town of Clinton lies 40 km north of Cache Creek on Highway 97. The original roadhouse, opened in 1861 at the junction of the original Cariboo Wagon Road and the new route north from Yale, burned down in 1958. Until the fire, the roadhouse was the site of the annual **Clinton Ball**, a fancy-dress wingding that attracted people from all over the area each May. The ball continues to this day but in other locations.

South Cariboo Historical Museum, on the main drag through town (Highway 97), 250/459-2442, occupies an old schoolhouse made of handmade bricks fired locally in the 1890s. The museum contains pioneer belongings, guns, historical photos, native and Chinese artifacts, freight wagons, and all sorts of items from the gold-rush days. It's open in summer Mon.–Fri. 10 A.M.–6 P.M.

A nearby natural attraction worth seeing is Painted Chasm, in 3,067-hectare **Chasm**

ECHO VALLEY GUEST RANCH RESORT

As a travel writer I've been lucky enough to travel throughout the world, but when it came to choosing a spot to honeymoon, it was difficult go past Echo Valley Guest Ranch Resort, right on our back doorstep. And it exceeded our expectations in every way. Deep in the heart of Cariboo Country, the resort provides the opportunity to immerse yourself in western culture while indulging in the luxury of an upmarket lodge. The emphasis is on horseback riding, with lessons and guided rides scheduled each day, but there are plenty of other things for to do, such as a four-wheel-drive excursion into the nearby Fraser River Canyon, watching a falcon trainer at work, and learning about native culture. The centerpiece of the sprawling property is an impressive main lodge, built entirely of glistening spruce logs. Inside is a comfortable lounge area, the communal dining room overlooking an open kitchen, and a downstairs billiards and TV room. Adjacent is an impressive Baan Thai structure, with full spa services, and the Pavilion, for quiet contemplation. Rooms in the main lodge are beautifully fur-

nished, and each has a private balcony, while the Honeymoon Cabin sits high above a deep ravine and has a wraparound deck complete with hot tub. Dining is ranch style, at a couple of long tables with plenty of interaction between guests. But the food is anything but chili and beans from a one-time chef to European royalty.

As you'd expect, staying at Echo Valley isn't cheap (from $300 per person per night), but it's a very special place, one that will stay will us for many years to come. For more information on the ranch or to make reservations call 800/253-8831, website www.evranch.com.

© ANDREW HEMPSTEAD

Echo Valley Guest Ranch Resort

Provincial Park, eight km north of town. Glacial meltwater has carved a deep box canyon out of mineral-laden volcanic bedrock. It's quite a spectacle when the sunlight brings out the color and sparkle of the minerals.

The huge log structure on the main street is **Cariboo Lodge Resort,** 250/459-7992 or 877/459-7992, website www.cariboolodge bc.com, featuring comfortable guest rooms ($70–80 s or d), a restaurant, café, and western-style pub. **Clinton Visitor Info Centre** occu-

pies a beautiful 1910 house on the main street of town, 250/459-2640; open May–Aug. daily 9 A.M.–5 P.M.

North to 100 Mile House

North of Clinton, a gravel road leads west off the highway into the ranch country of the Fraser Plateau. Up this road about 40 km is 332-hectare **Big Bar Lake Provincial Park,** which offers fishing for rainbow trout and swimming in both the lake and the adjacent river; campsites $12.

Also in the vicinity is the enormous **Gang Ranch.** Started in the 1860s, the ranch was at one time North America's largest and today spreads over 400,000 hectares.

Back on the main highway, between 70 Mile House and 100 Mile House are several turnoffs leading to hundreds of lakes, big and small. All information centers in Cariboo Country stock the invaluable *Cariboo-Chilcotin Fishing Guide.* Updated annually, the booklet features essential fishing information (where, when, and with what) for many of the lakes, plus maps, camping spots, and even recipes for the ones that didn't get away. The other provincial park between Clinton and 100 Mile House is at 32-km-long **Green Lake,** 19 km east of Highway 97. This emerald-colored shallow lake lies along an old Hudson's Bay Company fur-brigade trail; you can see traces of the trail along the lake's shoreline. The park has a shaded lakeside picnic area and a campground ($12 per night).

Passing through 100 Mile House, it's difficult to miss the **South Cariboo Visitor Info Centre,** 250/395-5353 or 877/511-5353. Look for the world's largest cross-country skis out front. The center is open year-round Mon.–Fri. 8:30 A.M.–4:30 P.M.; longer hours in summer. At the north end of town, one of the original Cariboo stagecoaches is on display. And bird-watchers might want to detour a couple of kilometers west of town to an eight-hectare wetlands reserve where waterfowl are prolific. A smaller wetland lies directly behind the information center, with signage depicting the many species that are often present.

Toward Williams Lake

Three km north of 100 Mile House, a road heads east off the highway, leading 30 km to **Ruth Lake,** which is stocked with rainbow trout; 44 km to six-hectare **Canim Beach Provincial Park,** with campsites for $12; 70 km to **Canim River Falls,** between Canim and Mahood Lakes; and 86 km to the western border of **Wells Gray Provincial Park** (see North to Mount Robson, earlier this chapter), where you'll find a primitive campground.

Back out on the highway and continuing

north, you'll come to 19-km-long **Lac La Hache,** named for a trader who dropped his axe in the water. This is one of the most picturesque bodies of water in Cariboo Country, known by anglers for its populations of kokanee and lake trout. At the lake's south end is the small community of Lac La Hache, with a small museum and information center on the east side of the highway. At the lake's north end, a provincial park offers campsites for $12.

The next main turnoff, at **150 Mile House,** takes you on a 65-km scenic drive (the last 10 km are unpaved) northeast to **Horsefly Lake Provincial Park,** which offers swimming, campsites ($12), and, in late August, a sockeye salmon run. In 1859, the first gold strike in the Cariboo region was made nearby. Continuing out to the end of the access road you'll come to the much larger **Quesnel Lake.**

WILLIAMS LAKE

Originally bypassed by the builders of the Cariboo Wagon Road because of protests from a stubborn landowner, Williams Lake (pop. 11,500), 95 km north of 100 Mile House, has ironically become the Cariboo region's largest city. No one knows for sure how the city got its name, but the most popular theory is that it was named after Shuswap chief Will-yum, who kept the peace as best he could between the valley's indigenous people and early white settlers. Today the ranching and forestry center is best known for the Williams Lake Stampede, one of Canada's biggest rodeos.

History

When gold seekers poured into the Cariboo in 1860, Williams Lake became a regional postal center and headquarters for the gold commissioner. It was destined for boomtown status until the Cariboo Wagon Road bypassed the town in 1863, thus terminating the small community's reason for being.

Despite the town's uncertain future, William Pinchbeck decided to stay in the valley. He and fellow settler William Lyne started a large farm that supplied the gold camps with bacon, ham,

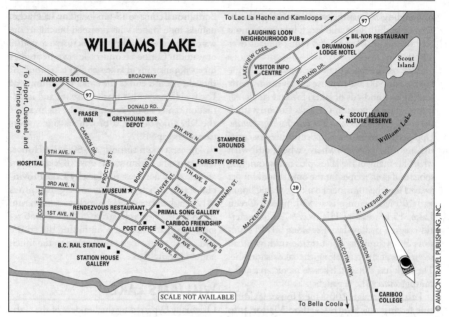

WILLIAMS LAKE

To Lac La Hache and Kamloops
97
LAUGHING LOON
NEIGHBOURHOOD PUB
BIL-NOR RESTAURANT
DRUMMOND
LODGE MOTEL
Scout
Island
LAKEVIEW CRES.
VISITOR INFO
CENTRE
BORLAND DR.
BROADWAY
To Airport, Quesnel, and Prince George
JAMBOREE MOTEL
97
DONALD RD.
FRASER
INN
GREYHOUND BUS
DEPOT
CARSON DR.
8TH AVE. N.
SCOUT ISLAND
NATURE RESERVE
Williams Lake
5TH AVE. N
STAMPEDE
GROUNDS
HOSPITAL
PROCTOR ST.
BORLAND ST.
OLIVER ST.
7TH AVE. S
FORESTRY OFFICE
3RD AVE. N
5TH AVE. S
20
MUSEUM
BARNARD ST.
MACKENZIE AVE.
S. LAKESIDE DR.
COMER ST.
RENDEZVOUS RESTAURANT
PRIMAL SONG GALLERY
1ST AVE. N
POST OFFICE
CARIBOO FRIENDSHIP
GALLERY
HODGSON RD.
CHILCOTIN HWY.
3RD AVE. S
4TH AVE. S
B.C. RAIL STATION
2ND AVE. S
STATION HOUSE
GALLERY
CARIBOO
COLLEGE
SCALE NOT AVAILABLE
To Bella Coola

© AVALON TRAVEL PUBLISHING, INC.

fresh vegetables, and flour, as well as whiskey from their own distillery. In addition to being a farmer, Pinchbeck acted as the local judge, lawyer, and doctor.

In September 1919 the Pacific Great Eastern Railway (now BC Rail) ran tracks around the lake, and Williams Lake came back to life. To celebrate the event, the town held a large picnic and rodeo—the first Williams Lake Stampede. By 1920 the town had hotels, stores, and homes, and ranchers were thrilled to be able to put their cattle on the train instead of herding them south on cattle drives.

Sights

The highlight of the large **Museum of the Cariboo Chilcotin,** 113 4th Ave. N, 250/392-7404, is the BC Cowboy Hall of Fame and associated rodeo, ranching, and Stampede displays. Other exhibits include historical photos, remains of the Chinese settlement at Quesnel Forks, and all kinds of picks, pans, and axes from the gold-mining days. The museum is open in summer Mon.–Sat. 10 A.M.–4 P.M., the rest of the year Tues.–Sat. 11 A.M.–4 P.M. Admission is $2.

Many stores in town sell the painting, pottery, weaving, photography, and jewelry of local artisans. These include: **Station House Gallery,** in the original railway station at 1 Mackenzie Ave. N, 250/392-6113; **Cariboo Friendship Society,** 99 3rd Ave. S, 250/398-6831, featuring native artwork; and **Primal Song Gallery,** 369 Oliver St., 250/392-7171, holding the distinctive works of local artist Andrew Kiss.

On the eastern outskirts of the city, **Scout Island Nature Centre,** 250/398-8532, is surrounded by wetlands that serve as a staging area for migratory waterfowl. Colorful displays inside the center catalog the surrounding ecosystem, but the idea is to get out into the wetlands. Wander along one of the short hiking trails or climb the observation tower for a bird's-eye view of the wild landscape. The center is open in summer Mon.–Fri. 9 A.M.–4 P.M., Sunday 1–4 P.M.

Outdoor Recreation

Opportunities for outdoor recreation abound in the area. One of many ranches offering horseback riding is **Springhouse Trails Ranch,** on Dog Creek Rd., about 20 km southwest of town off Hwy. 20, 250/392-4780. Horse rental is $18 an hour or $75 per day, and you can stay out on the ranch overnight (see below).

The region's diverse waterways provide plenty of opportunities for boating. Numerous gently flowing streams and serene lakes make perfect spots for canoe and kayak discovery trips, while the Fraser River provides opportunities for exciting rafting trips. **Chilko River Expeditions,** 250/398-6711 or 800/967-7238, offers a full-day trip in rafts and inflatable kayaks for $93 per person. Fishing in local waters is rewarding, yielding a variety of trout, steelhead, Dolly Varden, and kokanee (although the fishing in Williams Lake itself is poor). The booklet *Cariboo-Chilcotin Fishing Guide,* available at the information center, details the region's most productive lakes.

Plenty of winter activities keep locals and passers-through from getting cabin fever. Cross-country skiers use 30 km of wooded trails on **Bull Mountain,** about 20 km north on Highway 97. Downhill skiers head to **Mt. Timothy Ski Area,** 25 km east of Lac La Hache, 250/395-3772 or 250/392-1446 for snow reports, which offers 25 runs and a vertical rise of 250 meters. Snowmobiling and ice fishing are two other locally popular winter pastimes.

Williams Lake Stampede

On the first weekend of July, the town comes alive as the best cowboys in the land compete in the Williams Lake Stampede, one of Canada's largest rodeos with $100,000 up for grabs. The whole town dresses up for the occasion; the locals put on Western garb, and the shopfronts are decorated accordingly. The highlight of each day's action is the rodeo, when cowboys compete for big bucks in bareback riding, saddle-bronc riding, calf-roping, steer-wrestling, chuckwagon racing, and the crowd favorite, bull riding. Scheduled around these traditional rodeo events are cow-milking contests, barrel racing, tractor pulls, cattle penning, chariot races, raft races, a parade, barn dances, all-you-can-eat breakfasts and steak-outs, and a host of other decidedly Western-flavored activities.

Stampede headquarters is below the main grandstand. This is where you can purchase tickets and Stampede memorabilia; many of the event posters have become collectors' items. For general Stampede information, call 250/398-8388; for tickets, call 800/717-6336; website www.williamslakestampede.com.

Accommodations and Camping

The least expensive motels are along Highway 97 on the city's northeastern and western outskirts. Off the highway at the north end of town is **Jamboree Motel,** 845 Carson Dr., 250/398-8208, which charges $52 s, $57 d. One block closer to downtown is **Fraser Inn,** 285 Donald Rd., 250/398-7055 or 800/452-6789, website www.fraserinn.com, a full-service hotel with a whirlpool, sauna, exercise room, gift shop, pub, and restaurant. Rooms are $75–92 s or d. Pick of the lot is **Drummond Lodge Motel,** on Hwy. 97 one km east of downtown, 250/392-5334 or 800/667-4555. It's set picturesquely on extensive grounds overlooking the lake, and each of the well-decorated rooms comes with complimentary coffee and plenty of TV channels. Rates are $75 s, $80 d. RVers can set up their rigs out back for $26 per night. Barbecue facilities are available.

If a ranching vacation is more your style, consider **Springhouse Trails Ranch,** 20 km southwest of town on Dog Lake Rd., 250/392-4780, website www.springhousetrails.com, where horseback riding is $18 an hour. The basic but comfortable rooms are $61 s, $69 d, and all-inclusive package deals are available from $125 per person per day, including accommodations, meals, and riding. You can also camp here for $21 a night, with hookups.

The best campground in the area is **Wildwood Campsite,** about 13 km north of the city center, 250/989-4711. Facilities include full hookups, washrooms and showers, a laundry, and a general store; $15–20 per site. During the Stampede, camping is permitted on the Stampede grounds.

Food

Williams Lake lacks outstanding eateries but has no shortage of typical family-style restaurants.

One of these is the **Great Cariboo Steak Company,** in the Fraser Inn at 285 Donald Rd., 250/398-7055, open on weekdays from 6 A.M., Saturday from 7 A.M., Sunday from 8 A.M. Breakfast ranges $5–10; all-you-can-eat lunch buffets are $10; sandwiches, croissants, and burgers run $6.50–9; and dinner prices range from $8.50 for the all-you-can-eat salad bar to $14–21 for steak, prime rib, chicken, seafood, and pasta dishes. On the northern edge of town, the **Laughing Loon Neighbourhood Pub,** 1730 S. Broadway, 250/398-5666, offers a wide-ranging menu of beef, chicken, and pork dishes in a welcoming atmosphere. The building itself is new, but decor is heritage-style.

For Chinese food try the locally recommended **Bil-Nor Restaurant,** east of the information center on Hwy. 97 S, 250/392-4223, which is open daily for dinner but busiest on weekends, when a buffet is offered.

Services and Information

Williams Lake Airport, 13 km northwest of downtown, is served by **Air B.C.,** 888/247-2262, offering flights to and from Prince George, Vancouver, and Kamloops. The **Greyhound** bus depot is just off Highway 97 at 215 Donald Rd., 250/398-7733. Daily services run north to Prince George and south to Vancouver. Williams Lake is also on the **BC Rail** route between Vancouver and Prince George; for reservations call 250/398-3799. The local outlet of **National** can be reached by calling 250/392-2976.

Williams Lake Visitor Info Centre is beside Hwy. 97 at 1148 Broadway, 250/392-5025. It's open in summer daily 8 A.M.–6 P.M., the rest of the year Mon.–Fri. 9 A.M.–5 P.M.

HIGHWAY 20

Highway 20 west of Williams Lake leads 485 km to Bella Coola, the only road-accessible town along the 500 km of coastline between Powell River and Prince Rupert. The highway is paved less than half its length; the rest of the way it's mostly all-weather gravel and can be slow going in spots. But experiencing the vast and varied wilderness of the **Chilcotin Coast** is worthy of as

much time as you can afford. And with the 1996 resumption of ferry service between Bella Coola and Port Hardy, you'll only need to make the trip one-way. Services along Highway 20 are spaced at regular intervals, but don't take the trip too lightly; make sure your vehicle is in good condition and carry tools and spare tires to alleviate the necessity of an expensive tow-truck ride.

West from Williams Lake

The road west from Williams Lake meanders through the Fraser River Valley before beginning a steady climb to the **Chilcotin Plateau,** the heart of British Columbia's ranching country. The landscape is open—most of the land has been cleared by generations of ranchers.

The first worthwhile detour is **Junction Sheep Range Provincial Park,** which lies at the end of a 20-km unpaved road that branches south off Highway 20 at Riske Creek, 47 km west of Williams Lake. The triangular park protects 4,573 hectares of mostly semi-arid grasslands between the Fraser and Chilcotin Rivers. The confluence of these two major rivers forms the southern tip of the park and can be reached on foot in well under one hour from the end of the access road. The park is also home to around 600 bighorn sheep.

Back on Highway 20, the first community with services is **Alexis Creek,** 114 km west of Williams Lake. Beside the Chilcotin River, 10 km west of Alexis Creek, is **Bull Canyon Provincial Park,** with campsites for $12 a night. Continuing west, the highway follows the Chilcotin River for 60 km to Chilanko Forks; here a spur road leads 10 km north to **Puntzi Lake.** At this picturesque body of water are a number of low-key fishing resorts, including **Poplar Grove Resort,** 250/481-1186 or 800/578-6804, website www.poplargrove resort.com, which features small lakeside cabins, each with basic cooking facilities and shared washrooms. Rates are $45–80 s or d, or you can camp for $15 per night. The lake is best known to anglers for its large population of kokanee.

Chilko Lake

The road narrows and turns to gravel, passing the small community of Tatla Lake and the turnoff to remote **Ts'yl-os Provincial Park.** Ts'yl-os is the native Chilcotin name for the park's highest peak, 3,066-meter Mt. Tatlow, but its most magnificent feature is 84-km-long, glacially fed Chilko Lake, which is ringed by the highest glaciated peaks of the Coast Mountains. The park is home to a wide variety of wildlife, including grizzly and black bears, bighorn sheep, and, at higher elevations, mountain goats. Fishing in the lake is legendary for rainbow trout (to six pounds). The park access road parallels the lake's northeast shore, and here you'll find a number of accommodations. The best of these, 60 km south of Highway 20, is **Chilko Lake Resort,** 250/481-3333, website www.chilkolake.com. Right on the lake, this lodge offers boat and canoe rentals, horseback riding, a pool, tennis, a hot tub and sauna, a restaurant, and a bar. Rates are $160 pp, including meals. Also at the north end of the park is a small provincial park campground; $9 per night.

Toward the Coast

From Tatla Lake, Highway 20 continues westward, climbing steadily to **Nimpo Lake,** where you'll find more small resorts. **Stewart's Lodge,** 250/742-3388 or 800/668-4335, website www.stewartslodge.com, offers cabins of varying standards on Nimpo Lake ($55–165 s or d), as well as eight "outpost" cabins at remote lakes throughout the Chilcotin region.

From this point, it's 10 km west to **Anahim Lake,** where fishing is good for rainbow trout, then a steady climb of another 30 km to 1,524-meter **Heckman Pass** over the Coast Mountains. Continuing west across the pass, you face with **"The Hill."** This infamous descent from Heckman Pass to the Bella Coola Valley drops nearly the full 1,524 meters in less than 10 km. Be prepared for numerous switchbacks and a gradient as steep as 18 percent.

Tweedsmuir Provincial Park

At nearly a million hectares, this is British Columbia's largest provincial park. Roughly triangular, the park is bounded by Ootsa Lake on the north, the high peaks of the Coast Mountains on the west, and the Rainbow Range—so named

for its colorful volcanic formations—on the east. Within these boundaries lies an untouched landscape, wild and remote, holding numerous river systems, forested valleys, alpine meadows, waterfalls, and glaciers. Most of those park highlights are accessible only on foot.

Although the park's resident populations of large mammals are high, viewing opportunities are limited. Black and grizzly bears, mountain goats, caribou, wolves, and moose are all present, but they tend to remain well away from the highway. In early fall, grizzlies can occasionally be seen feeding on spawned-out salmon along the Atnarko River. Highway 20 meanders through the southern section of the park, but aside from two campgrounds and a handful of picnic areas along this route, the park is devoid of facilities.

The park's trail system is not extensive, and most established routes require an overnight stay in the backcountry. One exception is a trail to a series of kettle ponds formed by a receding glacier that stalled many thousands of years ago. This trail is four km (70 minutes) each way, beginning from a picnic area 16 km west of Atnarko River Campground. At the other end of the spectrum, the 16.5-km trek to **Hunlen Falls** is a park highlight for experienced backcountry hikers. These falls tumble 260 meters into a narrow canyon from the north end of Turner Lake. The trail is steep, gaining around 1,500 meters and snaking through more than 60 switchbacks in one six-km section. To get to the trailhead, take the gravel road south from the bottom of The Hill.

Another popular activity is fishing; Atnarko and Bella Coola Rivers are productive for salmon, and the larger lakes are filled with trout, Dolly Varden, and whitefish.

Campgrounds are on the north bank of the Atnarko River (at the base of The Hill) and 30 km west at Fisheries Pool. Facilities at both include pit toilets, drinking water, and picnic tables; $12 a night. **Tweedsmuir Air Services,** 250/742-3388, is based at Nimpo Lake and offers charter flights and drop-offs within the park, as well as flightseeing trips over Hunlen Falls (from $80 per person). The best source of park information is the **BC Parks office** at 281 1st Ave. N in Williams

Lake, 250/398-4414. **Williams Lake Visitor Info Centre** also offers park information.

(For more details about the north end of the park, see West from Prince George in the Northern British Columbia chapter.)

BELLA COOLA

The urge to see what's at the end of the road brings many travelers over The Hill and down to Bella Coola (pop. 800). Here the Bella Coola River drains into North Bentinck Arm, a gateway to the Inside Passage and the Pacific Ocean. The town lies in a coastal valley that was originally the home of the Nuxalk tribe. On 22 July 1793, Alexander Mackenzie reached the coast here, simultaneously becoming the first nonnative to see the area and the first person to cross continental North America. That latter feat earned him a place in history as one of the world's greatest explorers.

It wasn't until 1894 that permanent settlement of Bella Coola Valley began in earnest. That year a group of Norwegians arrived and, seeing the fjords and snow-capped peaks, were reminded of home. They settled inland at a spot on the river they named Hagensborg.

Although the Hudson's Bay Company established a post at Bella Coola in 1869, it wasn't until 1894 that permanent settlement of Bella Coola Valley began in earnest. That year a group of Norwegians arrived and, seeing the fjords and snowcapped peaks, were reminded of home. They settled 15 km inland at a spot on the river they named Hagensborg.

Sights and Recreation

Bella Coola Museum, housed in a schoolhouse and surveyor's cabin, 250/799-5767, features artifacts of early Norwegian settlers and the Hudson's Bay Company; open June–September. It's open Mon.–Sat. 10 A.M.–5 P.M. and admission is $2. Over in Hagensborg, the many hand-hewn timber buildings still standing are testament to the construction skills of the early settlers.

Aside from the above historic sites, there's plenty of outdoor recreation to keep visitors busy. Unfortunately, most of the action is out on the water and requires the services of a boat charter company (not cheap). Fishing is the most popu-

lar activity; expect to pay from $75 per hour for four persons. Those with a sense of history will want to visit **Mackenzie Rock,** in the Dean Channel, where Alexander Mackenzie, in his own words, "mixed up some vermillion and melted grease and inscribed in large characters on the face of the rock on which we slept last night, this brief memorial: Alexander Mackenzie, from Canada, by Land, the Twenty Second of July, One Thousand Seven Hundred and Ninety Three." For charter information, call **Bella Coola Outfitting,** 250/799-0066.

Practicalities

Right on the river is **Bella Coola Motel,** Clayton St., 250/799-5323, with clean and comfortable rooms each with a full kitchen for $80 s, $85 d. Similarly priced is the **Bella Coola Valley Inn,** Mackenzie St., 250/799-5316 or 888/799-5316, which also has a restaurant and bar. In Hagensborg, **Bay Motor Hotel,** 250/982-2212 or 888/982-2212, was renovated in 1995 and also has a restaurant and bar; $69–79 s or d. Bella Coola's only campground is in Hagensborg; **Gnome's Home Campground and RV Park,** 250/982-2504, has unserviced sites for $12 and serviced sites for $16–21.

Both Bella Coola and Hagensborg have a couple of restaurants.

Bella Coola Visitor Info Centre, 250/799-5919, is open in summer daily from 9 A.M. to around 7 P.M. Other services in Bella Coola include gas stations, a post office, and a hospital.

DISCOVERY COAST PASSAGE

In 1996, **B.C. Ferries** resumed sailings between Port Hardy (Vancouver Island) and a number of remote communities off the coast of Bella Coola, including Bella Coola itself. The *Queen of Chilliwack* makes the 22-hour sailing June–Sept., with departures from Bella Coola and Port Hardy approximately every three days. Peak one-way fares are adult $110, child 5–11 $55, vehicle $220, canoe or kayak $40.75, bicycle $15. To book, call B.C. Ferries at 250/386-3431 or, toll-free in B.C., 888/223-3779, website www .bcferries.com.

Shearwater

B.C. Ferries makes a number of stops between Port Hardy and Bella Coola, but only for a couple of hours each time, so if you want to get off, plan on overnighting until the next ferry comes by. The most interesting stop is **Shearwater,** on Denny Island. Shearwater is an old cannery village that has also been a logging camp, a base for flying boats patrolling the coast during World War II, and a stop for major shipping lines. The community was sold off to a private enterprise and today operates as **Shearwater Marine Resort,** 250/957-2666 or 800/663-2370, website www.shearwater.ca, catering to up to 50 guests at a time. The accommodations are fairly basic, and aimed toward anglers, but the resort does have a marina with boat rentals and fishing charters, kayak rentals, a general store, a restaurant, and a bar. Rates are $65–75 s, $75–90 d, with the least expensive rooms sharing bathrooms.

Ocean Falls

Ocean Falls, another stop on the B.C. Ferries Discovery Coast Passage route, lies on the mainland northeast of Shearwater, but it's accessible only by ferry or by air from Bella Coola. At one time 3,000 people called Ocean Falls home, but when the local pulp and paper mill closed in 1980 after 62 years of operation, most people moved out. Today, the town is a skeleton of its former self; many multistory buildings and a large hotel remain, along with 100 residents. It's an interesting place to walk around; if you decide to stay the night your only option is **Inga's Place,** 250/289-3234, which offers three guest rooms (shared baths). Rates are $60 s, $70 d, which includes a cooked breakfast.

QUESNEL

Back inland, Highway 97 north from Williams Lake takes you to Quesnel. The town (pop.

8,500) began during the Barkerville gold rush of the 1860s. Prospectors traveling north on the Fraser River disembarked at the confluence of the Fraser and Quesnel Rivers, and a town sprang up on the site. Today the town's economy continues to thrive, with an asphalt plant that opened in 1998 adding to the local ranching, mining, and, especially, forestry industries; Two Mile Flat, east of downtown, is North America's most concentrated wood-products manufacturing area. The town has a museum worth visiting, but the region's major attractions, Barkerville Historic Town and Bowron Lakes Provincial Park (see East from Quesnel, below), are out of town to the east along Highway 26.

Sights

At **Heritage Corner,** Carson Ave. and Front St., you can see the Old Fraser Bridge, the remains of the steamer *Enterprise,* a Cornish waterwheel used by gold miners, and the original Hudson's Bay Store. To learn all about Alexander Mackenzie or the gold-rush days, head to **Quesnel and District Museum,** Highway 97 at Carson Ave., 250/992-9580, which holds almost 20,000 artifacts. It's open in summer daily 8 A.M.–4:30 P.M.; admission $3. The scenic four-km (allow 75 minutes) **Riverfront Trail** loops around the downtown core, with plaques honoring early residents; start at any point along the river.

Eight km west of Quesnel on Baker Drive are the geologically intriguing, glacially eroded hoodoos at the small, day-use **Pinnacles Provincial Park.** Another local provincial park is **Ten Mile Lake,** 11 km north of town. Fishing is regarded as good for rainbow trout, and there's a large beaver dam near the day-use area.

Billy Barker Days

The main event in Quesnel is the Billy Barker Days celebration, named for the prospector who made the first gold strike in the Cariboo. Over the third weekend of July, downtown streets are closed to traffic in favor of an outdoor crafts fair, parade, and dancing. Residents casually stroll around town in period costumes from the gold-mining days—men in cowboy hats, women in slinky long dresses with brightly feathered hats.

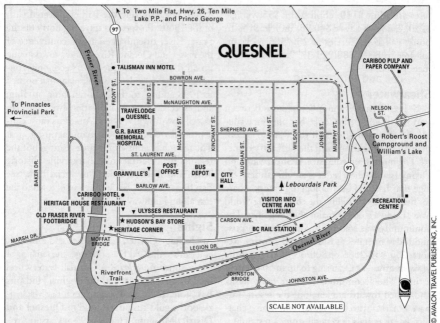

QUESNEL

To Two Mile Flat, Hwy. 26, Ten Mile Lake P.P., and Prince George

97

TALISMAN INN MOTEL

BOWRON AVE.

CARIBOO PULP AND PAPER COMPANY

To Pinnacles Provincial Park

FRONT ST.

REID ST.

McNAUGHTON AVE.

NELSON ST.

TRAVELODGE QUESNEL

G.R. BAKER MEMORIAL HOSPITAL

McCLEAN ST.

KINCHANT ST.

SHEPHERD AVE.

CALLANAN ST.

WILSON ST.

JONES ST.

MURPHY ST.

To Robert's Roost Campground and William's Lake

ST. LAURENT AVE.

BAKER DR.

GRANVILLE'S

POST OFFICE

BUS DEPOT

CITY HALL

VAUGHAN ST.

97

CARIBOO HOTEL
HERITAGE HOUSE RESTAURANT

BARLOW AVE.

Lebourdais Park

OLD FRASER RIVER FOOTBRIDGE

ULYSSES RESTAURANT

VISITOR INFO CENTRE AND MUSEUM

RECREATION CENTRE

MARSH DR.

MOFFAT BRIDGE

HUDSON'S BAY STORE
HERITAGE CORNER

CARSON AVE.

BC RAIL STATION

Quesnel River

LEGION DR.

Riverfront Trail

JOHNSTON BRIDGE

JOHNSTON AVE.

Fraser River

SCALE NOT AVAILABLE

© AVALON TRAVEL PUBLISHING, INC.

The Quesnel Rodeo is one of some 150 events staged during the festival; a detailed schedule is available at the information center or by calling the organizing committee at 250/992-1234.

Accommodations and Camping

Right downtown is the **Cariboo Hotel,** 254 Front St., 250/992-2333 or 800/665-3200. Built in 1896, this historic inn has been restored with modern furnishings; rates of $60 s, $65 d include a continental breakfast. Three blocks north, the **Travelodge—Quesnel,** 524 Front St., 250/992-7071 or 800/665-6995, is an older-style place, but the rooms are spacious and it has a small indoor pool; $65 s, $70 d. Continuing north and across Highway 97 is the **Talisman Inn,** 753 Front St., 250/992-7247 or 800/663-8090, website www.talismaninn.bc.ca. Most of the 86 rooms are of a standard quality for the price ($65 s, $75 d), although the larger rooms, with more modern furnishings and particularly spacious bathrooms, a microwave, and a toaster are best value ($80 s, $93 d; a light breakfast is included in all rates).

For campers, the best bet is to head north 11 km to 260-hectare **Ten Mile Lake Provincial Park,** where sites are $15 a night. Closer to town is **Robert's Roost Campground,** on the west side of Dragon Lake, 250/747-2015 or 888/227-8877. To get there, take Highway 97 south, turn east on Gook Road, and go to the end. Amenities include showers, a laundry, boat rentals, and a beach with swimming. Unserviced sites are $17, serviced sites $18–24, kitchenette units $65 s or d.

Food

For a full meal or just a coffee and cake, head to the **Heritage House Restaurant,** 102 Carson Ave., 250/992-2700, in a historic log building that dates to 1867, when it was used as a Hudson's Bay Company trading post. Prices are right, and everything served is fresh and healthy. A popular coffeehouse is **Granville's,** 383 Reid St., open daily from 8 A.M. **Savala's Steak House,** 240 Reid St., 250/992-9453, offers an extensive salad bar as well as steaks, spareribs, pizza, and other Italian dishes. The salad bar alone is $7, while entrées start at $10. **Ulysses Restaurant,** 122 Barlow Ave., 250/992-6606, specializes in southern European cuisine. A hearty plate of pasta or souvlaki is around $11–16.

Services and Information

Quesnel is served by air, rail, and bus transportation. **Air B.C.,** 888/247-2262, flies daily between Quesnel and Vancouver. The airport is off Highway 97 on the northern outskirts of town. **BC Rail** trains stop at Quesnel daily on their run between Vancouver and Prince George. The station is on Carson Ave., directly opposite the information center. And then there's **Greyhound,** which offers daily bus service to and from everywhere; the depot is at 365 Kinchant St., 250/992-2231.

Quesnel Visitor Info Centre is beside Lebourdais Park at 705 Carson Ave., 250/992-8716 or 800/992-4922, website www.city.quesnel.bc.ca. It's open daily 8 A.M.–8 P.M. in summer and Mon.–Fri. 8:30 A.M.–4:30 P.M. the rest of the year.

EAST FROM QUESNEL

Cottonwood House Provincial Historic Park

About 28 km east of Quesnel on Highway 26, this park preserves a former roadhouse built in 1864. In addition to the old guesthouse, structures at the site include a barn, stable, and other outbuildings. You'll also find an interpretive center and displays of old farming equipment. In summer, carriage rides are a main attraction. The park is open early June to mid-September daily 8 A.M.–8 P.M. Admission is free. For more information call 250/992-3997.

Wells and Vicinity

A few kilometers before reaching Barkerville Historic Town, Highway 26 passes the village of Wells, which offers accommodations, a restaurant, a pub, and a general store. Life in the village revolves around the historic 1933 **Wells Hotel,** 2341 Pooley St., 250/994-3427 or 800/860-2299, website www.wellshotel.com. Rooms are in the original hotel or in a new wing, but all are well-furnished and good value

at $75–120 s, $85–130 d including a continental breakfast.

Barkerville Historic Town

In 1862 Billy Barker struck gold on Williams Creek, in the north of Cariboo Country, 88 km east of Quesnel. One of Canada's major gold rushes followed, as thousands of prospectors streamed in to what soon became known as Barkerville. The area turned out to be the richest of the Cariboo mining districts, yielding over $40 million in gold. By the mid-1860s Barkerville's population had peaked at over 10,000. But fortunes began to fade after the turn of the 20th century. In 1916 Barkerville was destroyed by fire. Although the town was quickly rebuilt, the gold played out soon thereafter, and many of the miners lost interest and moved on.

A hundred years after the first strike, the provincial government decided to make the town a heritage site and re-create its boomtown atmosphere. Today, Barkerville, 85 km east of Quesnel, holds over 120 authentically restored buildings. Historic reenactments take place throughout summer, when the town's shops, stores, and restaurants all operate in a century-old time warp. Highlights include the town bakery, which sells some of the most mouthwatering baked goods in the province; the stagecoach rides, a big hit with the kids; and the musical comedy performances at the Theatre Royal, presented two to three times daily (adults $9).

The park is open year-round daily 8 A.M.–8 P.M., although many of the attractions and rides operate in summer only and for shorter hours; admission is adult $8, senior $6.25, child $2.25. For more information call 250/994-3332.

BC Parks runs three campgrounds (with hot showers) within the historic site; sites are $15 a night. You can also spend the night in one of two historic buildings within the town. **Kelly House,** 250/994-3328, is a heritage home where three guest rooms with shared bathrooms are $85 s, $95 d, which includes a cooked breakfast. The other option is the 1890s **St. George Hotel,** 250/994-0008 or 888/246-7690, which has been fully restored and offers seven rooms, some of which share bathrooms; all are tastefully furnished with comfortable beds and authentic antiques. Rates are $100–179 s, $120–189 d, which includes a cooked breakfast.

Bowron Lake Provincial Park

Best known for its wilderness canoe circuit, Bowron Lake Provincial Park encompasses 121,600 magnificent hectares of forests, lakes, and rivers in the Cariboo Mountains. To get there, take Highway 26 east of Quesnel toward Barkerville, but just past Wells take a signposted gravel road to the north.

The park boundary follows a chain of six major lakes—Indianpoint, Isaac, Lanezi, Sandy, Spectacle, and Bowron—and some smaller lakes and waterways that, roughly, form a diamond-shaped circuit. Campsites, cabins, and cooking shelters are strategically spaced along the way. To circumnavigate the entire 116-km route takes 7–10 days of paddling and requires seven portages, the most difficult being a 2.5-km hike uphill from the starting point. As well as being proficient in the use of canoes, those attempting the route should be well prepared for backcountry travel and wet weather. July and August are the most popular months; try to avoid departing on a weekend if you like solitude. September is one of the most colorful months, with lakeside trees in their fall colors.

Before setting out on the circuit, paddlers must obtain a permit from the BC Parks Registration Centre at the end of the park access road. Permits cost $150 per canoe. The center is open 15 May–30 Sept. daily 7 A.M.–8 P.M. A limited number of persons are permitted on the circuit at any given time. Reserve a spot by calling 250/387-1642 or 800/435-5622 as far in advance as possible. The reservation fee is $19.26 per canoe. A small number of spots are reserved each day for "drop ins," but the sensible course of action is to reserve as far ahead as possible. For general park information, contact the local BC Parks district office at 281 1st Ave. N, Williams Lake, 250/398-4414, or check the website www.elp.gov.bc.ca.

At the very end of the access road is a provincial park campground with 25 sites for $12 each (no hot showers). The alternatives are two privately owned lodges near the end of the park access road. Both are right on Bowron Lake and offer a variety of accommodations as well as canoe rentals ($10 per hour, $40 per day), full outfitting services for those doing the lake circuit, and meals. Taking in guests since the 1930s, **Bowron Lake Lodge,** 250/992-2733, website www.bowronlakelodge.com, has the better location of the two, including its own private sandy beach. Motel-style rooms are $60–75 s or d and camping is $20. The other accommodation, **Beckers Lodge,** 250/992-8864 or 800/808-4761, website www.beckers.bc.ca, sits on a high bluff with panoramic lake views.

Northern British Columbia

Wild, remote northern British Columbia extends from the Yellowhead Highway (Highway 16) north to the 60th parallel. Its mostly forested landscape is broken by two major mountain ranges—the Rockies and the Coast Mountains—and literally thousands of lakes, rivers, and streams. Wildlife is abundant here; the land is home to moose, deer, black and grizzly bears, elk, Dall's sheep, and mountain goats.

The region's largest city is **Prince George**, a forestry and service center 780 km north of Vancouver in the heart of a recreational paradise. From Prince George, the Yellowhead Highway runs west to the towns of **Vanderhoof, Burns Lake, Smithers,** and **Terrace,** all jumping-off points for fishing and boating adventures on surrounding lakes and rivers.

The western terminus of the Yellowhead Highway is **Prince Rupert,** a busy coastal city at the north end of the B.C. Ferries network and a stop on the Alaska Marine Highway. It's northern B.C.'s sole coastal city; north of here the coastline is part of Alaska.

Off the coast from "Rupert" are the **Queen Charlotte Islands,** part of British Columbia yet entirely unique. The islands beckon adventure, with legendary fishing, great beachcombing, ancient Haida villages, and a typical laid-back island atmosphere.

© ANDREW HEMPSTEAD

Salmon Glacier, near the coastal town of Stewart, is one of the highlights of Northern British Columbia.

NORTHERN B.C.

NORTHERN BRITISH COLUMBIA

ALBERTA

To Edmonton

To Quesnel and Williams Lake

To Fort Liard (NWT)

To Watson Lake (Yukon)

Atlin

Telegraph Creek

Mount Edziza Provincial Park

CASSIAR

Stikine River

Spatsizi Plateau Wilderness Provincial Park

Tatlatui Park

ALASKA HWY.

Mucho Lake Provincial Park

Stone Mountain Provincial Park

Wokkpash Recreation Area

Fort Nelson

ALASKA HWY.

Rocky Mountains

Williston Lake

Takla Lake

Trembleur Lake

Babine Lake

Burns Lake

Houston

Smithers

New Hazelton

Terrace

Kitimat

Prince Rupert

HWY. 37A

Stewart

Hyder

Coast Mountains

Fort St. John

Dawson Creek

Chetwynd

Hudson's Hope

Mackenzie

Tumbler Ridge

Monkman Provincial Park

Prince George

Fort St. James

Stuart Lake

Vanderhoof

UNITED STATES ALASKA

Queen Charlotte Islands

100 mi
100 km
0

© AVALON TRAVEL PUBLISHING, INC.

Two routes head north off the Yellowhead Highway. The **Stewart-Cassiar Highway** begins west of Prince George and parallels the Coast Mountains, passing the turnoff to the twin towns of **Stewart** and **Hyder** and some remote provincial parks. It ends at its junction with the other route north—the famous **Alaska Highway.** Mile Zero of the Alaska Highway is at **Dawson Creek,** northeast of Prince George. From there the highway winds through kilometer after kilometer of boreal forest, past lakes and mountains to the great northland of Alaska.

Prince George

British Columbia's seventh-largest city, Prince George (pop. 78,000) lies roughly at the geographical center of the province, at the confluence of the historically important Fraser and Nechako Rivers. The 1,360-km-long Fraser is the province's longest river, while the Nechako is the Fraser's third-largest tributary. Together the two rivers flow for 50 km within the city limits.

History
Early trappers and explorers used the rivers as transportation routes into the northern reaches of the province. When they discovered the region's wealth of wolf, fox, lynx, mink, wolverine, otter, and muskrat, they quickly established forts and trading posts by rivers and lakes so that furs could be sent out and supplies could be brought in. In 1807, Simon Fraser of the North West Company began construction of Fort George—named after then-reigning King George III of England—near the confluence of the Fraser and Nechako Rivers. The North West Company merged with the Hudson's Bay Company in 1821, and Fort George was operated as a Hudson's Bay Company post until 1915.

The railroad reached the area in 1908, and in 1915 the Grand Trunk Pacific Railway platted the townsite of Prince George a few km south of the original Fort George. The new town went on to become a major logging, sawmill, and pulp-mill town, the center of the white spruce industry in British Columbia's central interior. Hundreds of sawmills started cutting local timber, and Prince George became the self-proclaimed "Spruce Capital of the World." The city has continued from strength to strength, and has grown to become northern British Columbia's economic, social, and cultural center.

SIGHTS
Connaught Hill Park
The best place to start a Prince George sightseeing trip is the top of Connaught Hill, which affords a panoramic view of the city. To get there from downtown, take Queensway Street south, turn right on Connaught Drive, then right again on Caine Drive. At the summit are grassy tree-shaded lawns, picnic spots, and several well-kept gardens bursting with color in summer.

Fort George Park
The site where Simon Fraser established Fort George in 1807 is today preserved as 36-hectare riverside Fort George Park. Trails lead through the park along the Fraser River and to the Indian Burial Grounds. Park highlights include the Fraser–Fort George Regional Museum (see below) and the original **Fort George Railway Station,** just across from the museum, where on summer weekends and holidays noon–4 P.M., weather permitting, a miniature steam train provides rides along a kilometer or so of track; $2 per person. Next to the rail station is an old schoolhouse—if it's locked, peek in through the window at row after row of old-fashioned desks.

Fraser–Fort George Regional Museum
This museum in Fort George Park, 250/562-1612, is an excellent place to discover the fascinating natural and human history of Prince George and the lifestyle and culture of the indigenous Carrier tribe. Exploration Place, at the

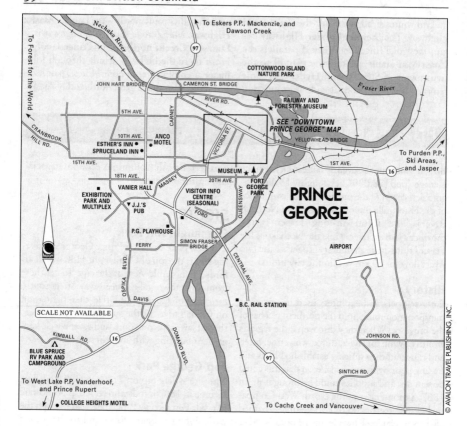

To Eskers P.P., Mackenzie, and Dawson Creek

Nechako River

To Forest for the World

JOHN HART BRIDGE

CAMERON ST. BRIDGE

COTTONWOOD ISLAND NATURE PARK

RAILWAY AND FORESTRY MUSEUM

Fraser River

RIVER RD.

CRANBROOK HILL RD.

5TH AVE.

CARNEY

SEE "DOWNTOWN PRINCE GEORGE" MAP

YELLOWHEAD BRIDGE

10TH AVE.

ANCO MOTEL

VICTORIA ST.

ESTHER'S INN
SPRUCELAND INN

15TH AVE.

To Purden P.P., Ski Areas, and Jasper

MUSEUM

1ST AVE.

18TH AVE.

20TH AVE.

FORT GEORGE PARK

VANIER HALL

MASSEY

PRINCE GEORGE

EXHIBITION PARK AND MULTIPLEX

VISITOR INFO CENTRE (SEASONAL)

QUEENSWAY

J.J.'S PUB

FORD

P.G. PLAYHOUSE

FERRY

SIMON FRASER BRIDGE

AIRPORT

OSPIKA BLVD.

CENTRAL AVE.

DAVIS

SCALE NOT AVAILABLE

B.C. RAIL STATION

KIMBALL RD.

16

DOMANO BLVD.

JOHNSON RD.

BLUE SPRUCE RV PARK AND CAMPGROUND

97

To West Lake P.P., Vanderhoof, and Prince Rupert

SINTICH RD.

COLLEGE HEIGHTS MOTEL

To Cache Creek and Vancouver

© AVALON TRAVEL PUBLISHING, INC.

NORTHERN B.C.

museum entrance, is filled with modern exhibits that go beyond the meaning of a museum in the usual sense. Here you'll find a technological dinosaur display, a small IMAX-style theater, high-speed Internet terminals, and many hands-on exhibits. As for the museum proper, the self-guided-tour pamphlet available at the main entrance gives you the opportunity to explore the facility at your own pace; allow at least an hour.

Among the items on display are many stuffed and mounted specimens of wild animals and birds native to British Columbia—including two towering grizzly bears in the foyer—fine crafts of the local Carrier people, an impressive stern-wheeler anchor, snowshoes, guns, horrific animal traps and other relics of the fur trade, artifacts from early sawmilling days, an old buggy, mock-

ups of early business establishments, and a hands-on Science Centre. The museum is open year-round, daily 10 A.M.–5 P.M. Admission is a worthwhile adult $7.95, senior $5.95, child $4.95 and for an extra $2 pp entry to the SimEX theater is included.

Prince George Railway and Forestry Museum

This outdoor museum catalogs Prince George's industrial history. Take a self-guided tour through some of the antiquated railway cars and buildings, clamber on retired railway equipment, and chug back in time via the black-and-white photo displays and assorted memorabilia. It's open daily 10 A.M.–6 P.M. Admission is adult $3.50, senior $3, child $2. To get there from downtown, take Highway 16 east to the River Road exit (just before the Yellowhead Bridge over the Fraser River) and continue north down River Road one km to the museum. For more information call 250/563-7351.

Cottonwood Island Nature Park

Just down River Road from the railroad museum is the entrance to beautiful 33-hectare Cottonwood Island Nature Park—one of Prince George's 16 city parks and a beautiful spot for a quiet stroll or picnic. The park lies beside the Nechako River, which overflows each spring; over time, sediment from the overflow has built up an island. The park's dominant feature is an extensive forest of northern black cottonwood trees. In spring sticky buds cover the cottonwoods, and in summer the air is thick and the ground white with seed-bearing tufts of fluff. You'll see all sorts of birds, and might spy the occasional beaver, fox, or moose. The park's trail system is extensive; the short walk between the main parking lot and the river is popular.

Eskers Provincial Park

This 3,979-hectare park 40 km northwest of Prince George (access is off Highway 97 along Pine Marsh Rd.) is named for the park's main features. The eskers, or long gravel ridges, were deposited by a receding glacier at the end of the last ice age. Fifteen km of hiking trails lead around Circle Lake to two viewing platforms and through forests of aspen, lodgepole pine, and Douglas fir.

Forestry Sights

Forestry is the heart and soul of Prince George's economy. In summer, **Canfor,** the largest Canadian-owned forest products company, offers tours of its operations. The four-hour tour takes in the climate-controlled seedlings nursery; the sawmill, where logs are processed into dimension lumber; and the pulp mill, where high-quality pulp is produced for paper manufacturers around the world. The tour is free, but visitors are required to wear long pants and closed-toe shoes for safety. Tours depart from the seasonal Visitor Info Centre (corner of Highways 16 and 97)

weekdays at 1 P.M.—they're very popular, so book ahead at 250/563-5493.

Forest for the World, a 106-hectare recreation area set aside for forest demonstrations, hiking, and cross-country skiing, was established in 1986 to commemorate Prince George's 75th anniversary. To get there, take 15th Avenue to the west end of the city, continue onto Foothills Boulevard, and turn left on Cranbrook Hill Road, which steeply climbs Cranbrook Hill. At the signs for Forest for the World, turn left on Kueng Road and continue to the end. From the parking lot, trails lead to Shane Lake (10 minutes one-way), where beavers and waterfowl are present, and to a hilltop viewpoint northwest of Shane Lake (15 minutes one-way).

Galleries

The architecturally stunning **Two Rivers Art Gallery,** 725 Civic Plaza, 250/614-7800, is Prince George's newest cultural attraction. The large permanent collection is the main drawcard, but temporary shows that change every four to five weeks are included in the admission fee. It's also a good place to buy high-quality local artwork at a reasonable price. Look for paintings, sculpture, pottery, beadwork, woven and painted silk items, and jewelry. Hours are daily 10 A.M.–5 P.M. (until 9 P.M. Wed.–Fri.), but closed Monday outside of summer. Entry is adult $4.50, senior and child $3.75.

To see and buy all sorts of native arts and crafts, head for the **Native Art Gallery** in the Native Friendship Centre, 1600 3rd Ave., 250/614-7726. Throughout summer you can watch experienced carvers and painters teaching their students. Moccasins, jewelry, carvings, hand-printed cards, and sweatshirts with native designs are all for sale. The gallery is open year-round Tues.–Sat. 10 A.M.–4:30 P.M.

RECREATION
Summer Activities

Prince George is a convenient base for a wide range of outdoor pursuits. Anglers probe the area's lakes and rivers for trout, char, salmon, steelhead, Dolly Varden, whitefish, sturgeon,

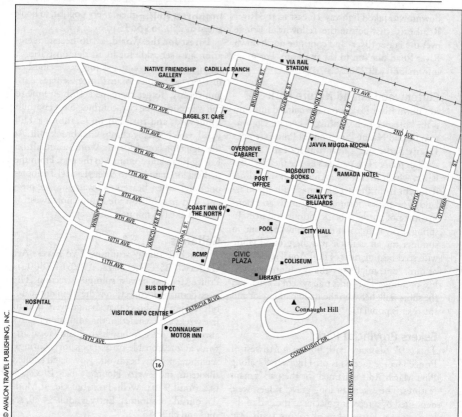

© AVALON TRAVEL PUBLISHING, INC.

and grayling. The lakes also provide enjoyable canoeing and boating. Wildlife watchers will have a field day scanning the woods for black and grizzly bears, elk, mountain goats, bighorn sheep, woodland caribou, wolves, deer, and moose. In spring, autumn, and winter, visit the unique **moose viewing area** near Tabor Mountain to see these enormous wild vegetarians in their natural habitat.

Hikers can follow the **Heritage River Trail** through the city, past interpretive signs detailing local natural history. The clearly marked gravel trail, open to hikers, joggers, cyclists, and cross-country skiers, runs between Cameron Street Bridge and Carrie Jane Gray Park. You can make an 11-km loop of it if you complete the circuit by following Carney Street. Ask for the *Heritage River Trails* pamphlet at the information centers.

Those who prefer to get off the beaten track should instead request the *Prince George and Area Hiking Guide,* which describes seven trails in the area. One of the most popular of those listed in the guide is **Fort George Canyon Trail,** a 4.5-km path through a canyon (striking in autumn) southeast of West Lake Provincial Park. To get there go west along Highway 16, turn south (left) on Blackwater Road, then east (left) on West Lake Road.

Skiing and Snowboarding

The closest alpine skiing and boarding to Prince

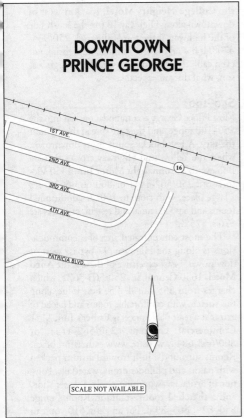

DOWNTOWN PRINCE GEORGE

1ST AVE.

2ND AVE.

(16)

3RD AVE.

4TH AVE.

PATRICIA BLVD.

SCALE NOT AVAILABLE

George is 30 km east at **Tabor Mountain,** while **Purden Lake Ski Area** is a further 25 km east. Both are small family-oriented resorts with under 300 meters vertical rise and no overnight accommodations. Both have ski and snowboard schools and rentals. Near Pine Pass, 195 km north of the city along Highway 97, is **Powder King Mountain Resort,** (see Along the Crooked River in the North from Prince George section, below).

Cross-country skiers can find beautiful spots to ski just about anywhere in the area—try **Fort George Park** or **Cottonwood Island Nature Park** downtown, any of the nearby abandoned logging roads, or an overnight ski to **Raven Lake.** Get more details at the main Prince George Visitor Info Centre.

Indoor Activities

Four Seasons Leisure Pool, at the corner of the Civic Plaza at 700 Dominion St., 250/561-7636, is open daily 6:30 A.M.–11 P.M.; admission of adult $6 allows use of the pools, saunas, hot tub, and water slide, as well as participation in several daily aqua-fitness classes. Waterslide fanatics will want to head to **Fantasy North Waterslide,** at Esther's Inn, 1151 Commercial Dr., 250/562-4131.

To shoot pool in a clean and bright setting, head to **Chalky's Billiards,** 511 George St., 250/564-1283. Prince George also offers bowling alleys, roller rinks, and curling rinks.

ENTERTAINMENT

Performing Arts

Excellent live-theater productions are regularly staged at **Prince George Playhouse,** junction of Highways 16 and 97, 250/563-8401. **Studio 2880,** 2880 15th Ave., 250/562-4526, is the local arts center, operated by the Community Arts Council. It hosts many cultural activities, acts as a ticket office for events, and organizes workshops, art classes, concerts, ballets, special events, and two major craft markets each year. In 800-seat **Vanier Hall,** at Prince George Secondary School, 2901 Griffiths, 250/562-6441, you can take in a concert by the **Prince George Symphony Orchestra** or one of many visiting performers. Touring musicians and other entertainers perform in the **Civic Centre,** 855 Dominion St., 250/561-7723.

Prince George's two main entertainment venues are the 2,500-seat **Coliseum,** in Civic Plaza, and the 5,000-seat **Multiplex,** in Exhibition Park, 250/561-7777.

To find out what's going on in town, pick up the local newspaper or inquire at one of the information centers.

Drinking and Dancing

Of the city's many pubs and nightclubs, one of the most popular is **Steamers,** 2595 Queensway St., 250/562-6654, with typical pub meals and bands playing most weekends. For country music, it's impossible to go past the **Cadillac**

NORTHERN B.C.

Ranch, 1380 2nd Ave., 250/563-7720, with a mixture of bands and DJ music, but it's always hard-core country and always busy. There's a regular disco in the **Coast Inn of the North,** 770 Brunswick St., 250/563-0121, or for a quiet drink head to the lounge bar in the **Ramada Hotel,** 444 George St., 250/563-0055.

FESTIVALS AND EVENTS

Prince George is certainly not short on year-round celebrations and goofy seasonal events; ask at the information centers for a free events calendar. In early January, the **Fete d'hiver** is a winter carnival featuring logging sports, scuba diving, dogsledding, and car races on the ice at nearby Tabor Lake. One month later the city goes berserk with a 10-day **Snow Daze,** featuring a snow ball and snow golf in bright crazy costumes, knurdling (jousting using padded poles), bed races on ice, and other hog-wild events. It's all finished off with a fireworks display. For details of these winter festivals call Prince George Festivals at 250/564-3737.

In May, the warmer half of the annual events calendar kicks off with the biennial (even years) **Forest Expo,** held at Exhibition Park. The expo, North America's largest forestry exposition, is interesting even for those not involved in the industry, especially the displays of new technology. For dates and other details call 250/563-8833, website www.forestexpo.bc.ca.

On the middle weekend of August, the **Fringe Festival,** 250/564-5556, attracts a good range of performers from throughout Canada to venues through the city. The following weekend, the largest of Prince George's festivals kicks off. A 10-block stretch of George Street is sealed off to vehicular traffic, as crowds converge for live entertainment, a food festival, arts and crafts, and a wide variety of free fun; 250/564-3737.

ACCOMMODATIONS AND CAMPING

Under $50

With no hostels, Prince George holds just one accommodation that falls into this price range. It's

the **College Heights Motel,** five km west of downtown along Highway 16 (on the south side of the highway at the top of the rise), 250/964-4708. It has no toll-free number, no website, not even cable TV, but for $33 s, $38 d in high season, what do you expect?

$50–100

Most Prince George accommodations fall into the $50–100 range, and they are spread throughout the city. A few blocks south from downtown, where the Yellowhead Highway crosses Patricia Boulevard, is **Connaught Motor Inn,** 1550 Victoria St., 250/562-4441 or 800/663-6620. It's a large place, with close to 100 air-conditioned rooms and a pool, sauna, and restaurant. Rates are $70 s, $75 d.

The most concentrated area of accommodations is along the Highway 97 bypass west of downtown. Least expensive of these is the **Anco Motel,** 1630 Central St., 250/563-3671, which charges from $55 s or d. The best value along this stretch, with comfortable rooms and a load of extras at a reasonable price, is **Esther's Inn,** 1151 Commercial Crescent, 250/562-4131 or 800/663-6844, website www.esthersinn.bc.ca. Rooms surround a lush tropical atrium packed with palms and philodendrons, waterfalls, Polynesian artifacts, swimming pools, a water slide, and a thatched-roof restaurant. Rooms range $56–82 s, $63–89 d. For an extra $10 you can have a room with a kitchen.

$100–150

The **Ramada Hotel,** 444 George St., 250/563-0055 or 800/830-8833, website www.ramada .ca, is an unattractive but distinctive red-brick building in the heart of downtown. Amenities include a restaurant, lounge, pub, pool, sauna and whirlpool, casino, gift shop, and covered parking. Rack rates are a scary $200 s or d, but you'd be crazy to pay this much; call or check the website, and you should be able to find a room for around $120, even in summer. In the same price category and also centrally located is the 193-room **Coast Inn of the North,** 770 Brunswick St., 250/563-0121 or 800/663-1144, website www.coasthotels.com. This full-service hotel has

NORTHERN B.C.

a smallish fitness room, an indoor pool, a sauna, and three in-house eateries (including a Japanese restaurant). Summer rates are $145 s, $155 d, but like the Ramada, check the Coast Hotels website for perpetually discounted rooms.

Camping

Privately operated **Blue Spruce RV Park and Campground** is on Kimball Rd., five km west on Highway 16 from the junction of Highway 97, 250/964-7272. It's a popular spot, filling up each night during the busy summer months. Each site has a picnic table and a barbecue grate, and the facilities include spotlessly clean heated bathrooms, a coin-operated laundry, a swimming pool, mini-golf, and a playground. Unserviced sites are $15, hookups $18–22.50. The closest provincial park to Prince George is at **Purden Lake,** 55 km east of the city on Highway 16. The picturesque lake has a small stretch of sandy beach and offers fishing for rainbow trout and burbot. Sites are $12 a night.

FOOD

Coffeehouses

Javva Mugga Mocha, 304 George St., is a stylish, big-city type of coffeehouse right downtown. A few blocks from downtown is **Bagel Street Cafe,** 1493 3rd Ave. at Victoria Street. It's small—just one long row of stools—and gets crowded when workers from the government offices across the road are on a break, but it's inexpensive; coffee $1.50, hearty lunches from $5.

Restaurants

An excellent place for lunch is **Papaya Grove Restaurant** in Esther's Inn, 1151 Commercial Crescent, 250/562-4131. You can choose from among three different seating areas: under a thatched roof, around the pool, or in the bar. All are enclosed within a massive tropical indoor atrium. A set menu is offered, but the buffet is the most popular choice. The daily lunch buffet (11 A.M.–2 P.M.) is around $10, with a different theme each day. Sunday brunch is particularly good; for $15.95 you get all the usual breakfast choices, along with salmon, prawns, roast beef, and a

staggering number of desserts. The dinner buffet is $16.95 Sun.–Thurs., $19.95 on Friday and Saturday when prime rib is served.

Foodteller, 508 George St., 250/562-0450, breaks the stereotype of a northern restaurant. The well-traveled owners have brought the best of their experiences in dining around the world to the city, offering a wide range of classic North American and European dishes served in a stylish setting. Dinner mains run $16–27. Another popular spot for a splurge is the **Log House Restaurant,** overlooking Tabor Lake nine km east of downtown, 250/963-9515. It's decorated in a typical northern style—the walls are crammed with antiques and trophy heads. Both the food and service are excellent. It's open daily for dinner from 6 P.M. The menu is typically West Coast, with mains ranging $16.50–24.

TRANSPORTATION

Air

The airport is about 18 km east of town and is served by **Air B.C.,** 888/247-2262, and **WestJet,** 800/538-5696. Both these airlines fly daily to Vancouver and other regional centers, with Air B.C. also flying to Calgary. The **Airporter** bus, 250/563-2220, provides shuttle service between the airport and downtown.

Train

VIA Rail operates transcontinental service from Prince George west to Prince Rupert and east through Jasper and Edmonton to Toronto and beyond. The VIA Rail station is on 1st Ave. between Brunswick and Quebec Streets, 250/564-5233 or 800/561-8630.

Through summer **BC Rail** runs the *Cariboo Prospector* and more luxurious *Whistler Northwind* trains between Vancouver and Prince George via Whistler. The BC Rail station is out of town on the southeast side of the city, off Terminal Blvd., 250/564-9080 or 800/663-8238.

Bus

The **Greyhound** bus depot is at 1566 12th Ave. (corner of Victoria St.), just across from Tourism

Prince George, 250/564-5454 or 800/661-8747. Greyhound runs regularly scheduled services from Prince George south to Kamloops and Vancouver (via Williams Lake and Quesnel); west along the Yellowhead Highway to Terrace and Prince Rupert; north to Dawson Creek via Chetwynd; and east along the Yellowhead Highway to Jasper and Edmonton.

Getting Around

The **Prince George Transit System** operates buses throughout the city daily except Sunday. Pick up a current *Prince George Rider's Guide* from the information centers or call 250/563-0011 for an automated timetable. Prince George **handyDART,** 250/562-1394, provides door-to-door transportation for disabled passengers unable to use the regular bus service.

For a cab call **Prince George Taxi,** 250/564-4444. Car-rental agencies in town include: **Budget,** 250/563-2662; **National,** 250/564-4847; and **Thrifty,** 250/564-3499.

SERVICES AND INFORMATION

Services

Prince George Public Library, 887 Dominion St., 250/563-9251, also has a good display of native art and artifacts; open Mon.–Thurs. 10 A.M.–9 P.M., Fri.–Sat. 10 A.M.–5:30 P.M., Sunday (in winter only) 1–5 P.M. **Mosquito Books,** 1209 5th Ave., 250/563-6495, features a great selection of local and northern British Columbia literature, as well as major Canadian newspapers; closed Sunday.

The main **post office** is on the corner of 5th Ave. and Quebec Street. **Prince George Regional Hospital** is at 2000 15th Ave., 250/565-2000 (routine calls) or 250/565-2444 (emergencies). A private health clinic deals with walk-in problems; turn off 15th Ave. on Edmonton by the hospital. The RCMP is on the corner of Brunswick and 10th Ave., behind the library, 250/562-3371.

Information

Tourism Prince George, 250/562-3700 or 800/668-7646, website www.tourismpg.bc.ca, operates two information centers. The main one is at the corner of Victoria St. and Patricia Blvd.; open year-round Mon.–Fri. 8:30 A.M.–5 P.M., Saturday 9 A.M.–4 P.M. The other one is at the corner of Highways 16 and 97, handy if you're coming into the city from the south or west; open summers only daily 9 A.M.–8 P.M.

M

NORTHERN B.C.

West from Prince George

VANDERHOOF

The first town west of Prince George is Vanderhoof (pop. 4,500), a service center for the Nechako Valley and British Columbia's geographical center (the exact spot is marked by a cairn five km east of town). Vanderhoof grew as a stop on the Grand Trunk Pacific Railway. Today it's a prosperous farming and logging town.

Sights

The 1914 building at the corner of Highway 16 and Pine Ave. houses **Vanderhoof Community Museum,** 250/567-2991. The museum displays mounted specimens of birds and animals, pioneer equipment, blacksmithing tools, a rock collection, and plenty of local history from gold-rush and pioneer days. It's open daily 10 A.M.–5 P.M.; admission $2. The museum is on the grounds of a **Heritage Village,** which consists of 11 restored heritage buildings, among them a jail, 1922 schoolhouse, and a restored gambling room. Also in the village is the **OK Cafe,** where you can tuck in to hearty homemade soup and rolls, salads, and tasty pie and ice cream. It's inside a heritage-style building decorated with old-fashioned wallpaper and frilly curtains.

Vanderhoof's town symbol is the Canada goose. You can see these beautiful birds and other waterfowl in spring and fall at their transient home, **Nechako Bird Sanctuary,** along the banks of the Nechako River. Access it via the wooden bridge at the north end of Burrard Avenue, the town's main street.

If you want to get away from the main highway for a couple of hours, take a 100-km detour south along a good gravel road (Nechako Avenue, then Kenney Dam Road) to **Kenney Dam,** once the world's largest earth-filled dam. From the far side of the dam, a 1.2-km trail (20 minutes each way) leads downriver to 18-meter-high **Cheslatta Falls** and a picnic area.

Recreation

Rivers and lakes dot the region, making fishing a prime local pastime. Pick up a copy of the local *Recreation and Fishing Guide* from the information center. Another must-have for those who want to escape the main highway is the *Vanderhoof Forest District Recreation Map* ($3). It details the Nechako River watershed south of Vanderhoof, including forest roads, trails, recreation sites, campsites, and other facilities.

Practicalities

Inexpensive accommodations are available at the **Hillview Motel,** 250/567-4468, and the **Coachlight Motel,** 250/567-2296. Both are on Highway 16 at the east side of town and charge from $55 s, $65 d. The Coachlight also offers RV hookups for $14. Similarly priced, but right downtown and home to Vanderhoof's best restaurant, is **North Country Inn,** 2575 Burrard Ave., 250/567-3047; $59 s, $65 d.

Riverside Park Campground, 250/567-4710, enjoys a pleasant setting beside the Nechako River. Turn north off Highway 16 onto Burrard Avenue and continue through town; the campground is to the west side of Burrard Avenue. Showers and firewood are supplied; $14 per night.

For delicious food at reasonable prices head to the comfortable **North Country Inn,** 2575 Burrard Ave., 250/567-3047, where the restaurant is in a stunning alpine-style log building. Breakfasts are hearty and cost from $5; lunch is mostly burgers and sandwiches ranging $5–9. In the evening the soup and salad bar is $8, and steak, seafood, and pasta dinners run $10–29. Try the delicious chicken lasagna.

Vanderhoof Visitor Info Centre is at 2353 Burrard Ave., 250/567-2124 or 800/752-4094. It's open daily 8:30 A.M.–6 P.M. in summer and Mon.–Fri. 9 A.M.–5 P.M. the rest of the year.

FORT ST. JAMES

A sealed road leads 60 km north from Vanderhoof to Fort St. James (pop. 2,200), the earliest nonnative settlement in northern British Co-

NORTHERN B.C.

lumbia. It's worth a detour up from the Yellow-head Highway to check out several sights of interest in the area.

Fort St. James National Historic Site

In the early 1800s, Fort St. James was the chief fur-trading post and capital of the large and prosperous district of New Caledonia—the name originally given to central B.C. by Simon Fraser.

When Fraser first arrived at Stuart Lake he was working for the North West Company, expanding the fur trade west of the Rockies and trying to find a water route to the Pacific. He established the fort among the cooperative local Carrier tribe in 1806. The natives did not fear the white man—they desired his iron, tools, weapons, and exotic jewelry. But establishment of the fort changed their lifestyle forever. In 1821, the fort became a Hudson's Bay Company outpost and continued to operate until the early 20th century.

Today the beautifully restored fort forms the centerpiece of a historic park that holds Canada's largest collection of original fur trade buildings. Enter the fort through the Visitor Reception Centre, which holds displays on pioneer explorers, fur traders, and the indigenous Carrier people. An audio recording and a map trace the route of the early explorers, and a slide show fills you in on the restoration of the fort's original buildings. Free guided walking tours leave from the center May–September. In July and August, characters dressed in pioneer garb lurk in the log-constructed general store, the fish cache, the single men's bunkhouse, the main house, and the veggie garden. You're actively encouraged to get into the spirit of things and play along. Tell them you've just arrived by canoe, want to stay the night in the men's house, and need a good horse and some provisions . . . then see what happens!

> *In the early 1800s, Fort St. James was the chief fur-trading post and capital of the large and prosperous district of New Caledonia—the name originally given to central B.C. by Simon Fraser. Today the beautifully restored fort forms the centerpiece of a historic park.*

Most of the park is open only in the summer season, mid-May through September daily 9 A.M.–5 P.M. The reception center, 250/996-7191, is open the rest of the year as well Mon.–Fri. 8:30 A.M.–4:30 P.M. Admission to the park is free.

Other Local Sights

Aside from the historic park, you can cruise west along the lakefront, first along Stuart Drive, then Lakeshore Drive. You'll pass Our Lady of Good Hope Catholic Church, built in 1873, and the **Russ Baker Memorial** (Baker was a local bush pilot who founded Pacific Western Airlines.) Bush pilots played an important role during the early days of mining, fur trapping, and forestry in this area. Pictographs are found along the lake's northern shore but can only be reached by boat.

The area's natural attractions also make the side trip to Fort St. James worthwhile. Start with **Stuart Lake** itself, the province's seventh largest body of water. The lake is more than 90 km long and up to 13 km wide. It's known to produce rainbow trout up to seven kilograms and lake char up to 13 kilograms, as well as lake trout, whitefish, and kokanee. So break out the rod and reel, or go swimming, sailing, or windsurfing.

North of Fort St. James, Germanson Landing North Road (well-maintained gravel) leads to the **Takla-Nation Lakes** region—a favorite with hikers and campers in search of untouched wilderness, and with anglers wanting to pull grayling, char, rainbow trout, and Dolly Varden from the region's dozens of fish-filled lakes. Others canoe or take small motor boats along waterways used by pioneer explorers. Canoeists often travel the 100-km route through the Nation Lakes chain. And locals say it's possible, using a small motorboat, to travel 290 km through the Takla Lake system from Fort St. James, taking 7–10 days. The third very popular way of getting into the backcountry is by floatplane—to rustic lodges and remote fishing camps.

Many good hiking trails wander away from the local area—try the three-km (one hour) each way **Mt. Pope Trail** northwest of town, which takes you to the summit for views of Stuart Lake and surrounding mountains. Get details on this and other trails at the local information center.

In winter, **Murray Ridge Ski Hill,** 30 km north of Fort St. James, offers 19 designated runs on a 570-meter vertical rise, as well as a day lodge, rental shop, ski school, and snack bar. The season runs from mid-December to mid-April, with lifts operating Friday through Monday. Other winter activities popular in the area include cross-country skiing, snowmobiling, and ice fishing.

Practicalities

The best place to stay in the area is **Stuart Lodge,** Stones Bay Rd., 250/996-7917, on the shore of Stuart Lake five km west of Fort St. James. The complex's six kitchenette cottages are well priced at just $60 s, $66 d. If you'd prefer to be in town, stay at the **New Caledonia Motel,** 167 Douglas Ave., 250/996-8051, which charges $50 s, $55 d in the old wing and $59 s, $64 d for the newer rooms.

Paarens Beach Provincial Park and **Sowchea Bay Provincial Park,** west of Fort St. James, both offer lakeside tent and vehicle camping, swimming, fishing, picnic areas, and washrooms; open May–Sept. with an $12 nightly fee for campers.

To get the scoop on the entire area, stop at **Fort St. James Visitor Info Centre,** 115 Douglas Ave., 250/996-7023. It's open Mon.–Fri. 8:30 A.M.–4:30 P.M. in May, June, and September, and daily 8 A.M.–6 P.M. in July and August.

FORT FRASER TO FRASER LAKE

Heading west from Vanderhoof, the Yellowhead Highway passes through low rolling terrain to Fort Fraser, one of the province's oldest communities; Simon Fraser established the former fur-trading post in 1806.

Continuing west, the highway crosses the wide Nechako River, passing the turnoff to 191-hectare **Beaumont Provincial Park.** The park offers boating on Fraser Lake, a short interpretive trail, and a campground open May–Oct.; $15 per site. It also marks the eastern edge of an area known as the **Lakes District,** comprising more than 300 fish-filled lakes. Traveling this stretch of the highway in summer you'll notice all the vehicles hauling canoes, kayaks, or small fishing boats.

The town of Fraser Lake (pop. 1,400), 60 km west of Vanderhoof, lies on a chunk of land sloping gently down to its namesake lake. In winter, trumpeter swans settle in at each end of the lake. In summer, a salmon run on the **Stellako River**—a short stretch of water between Fraser and Francois Lakes—draws scores of eager anglers. Overlooking Fraser Lake, **Piper's Glen Resort,** 250/690-7565, website www.pipersglenresort.com, features a grassy lakeshore camping area with full hookups and showers; $13–18 per night for campers, $40 s or d in basic self-contained cabins. **Fraser Lake Visitor Info Centre,** along the highway through town, 250/699-8844, offers tourism information and a small museum out back. It's open July–Aug. daily 8 A.M.–6 P.M.

Just west of Fraser Lake, a turnoff leads south to **Francois Lake,** another popular fishing hole. **Glenannan Tourist Area,** at the lake's east end, boasts a handful of resorts providing everything an angler could possibly desire. **Francois Bay Resort,** 250/699-6551, rents motorboats and rustic cabins for $40–50 per night and campsites for $14–17 per night.

BURNS LAKE AND VICINITY

The first thing you see when you enter Burns Lake is an enormous chainsaw-carved trout with the inscription "Three Thousand Miles of Fishing!" That pretty much sums up what attracts visitors to the town and surrounding Lakes District.

Like other towns along the Yellowhead Highway, Burns Lake (pop. 2,100) grew after construction of the Grand Trunk Pacific Railway. Many buildings from those early railroad days remain, and **Deadman's Island** in Burns Lake got its name from an accident that killed two workers during the railway's construction. The one-hectare island is the province's smallest provincial park.

Sights

Continue west along the highway through town for about one kilometer until you come to the green-and-white **Heritage Centre,** comprising a museum and the local information center. The museum is housed in a 1919 home whose furnished rooms contain an odd assortment of articles, including a collection of foreign currency, memorabilia from an old ship (viewed through a porthole), and typewriters that have seen better days. Open daily 1–5 P.M.; admission $2.

Ask at the adjacent information center for a map showing all the heritage buildings around town. Of particular note is the **Bucket of Blood,** a historic fur-trading depot and gambling den where a murder occurred during a poker game. It's on the corner of Highway 16 and 5th Avenue. You'll also discover many gift shops where paintings and beadwork by the local Carrier bands are on display.

For a wonderful view of the area, follow 5th Avenue up the hill out of town, then take the turnoff to **Boer Mountain Forestry Lookout.** Rockhounds might prefer to head 6.5 km south of town to **Eagle Creek Agate Opal Site,** one of the province's few opal deposits. From the parking lot, a four-km trail (one hour each way) leads to the creekside deposit and an intriguing outcrop of hoodoos.

Fish Fantasies

More than 300 lakes dot the high country between the Fraser and Skeena watersheds, and all are renowned fishing spots. To even mention all the lakes and their fishing possibilities would take a whole other book. Ask at the information center for the free *Burns Lake 3,000 Miles of Fishing* map and information sheet. The center also stocks brochures on local fishing resorts and guides, boat rentals, and floatplane adventures.

Burns Lake itself offers excellent fishing for rainbow, eastern brook, and cutthroat trout, as well as kokanee, chinook salmon, steelhead, lake

char, and other species. The area between Burns Lake and Tweedsmuir Provincial Park is dotted with resorts and rustic lodges, most catering primarily to anglers.

Practicalities

Wanakena Motel, on the east end of town before Highway 16 descends to the main street, 250/692-3151 or 888/413-3151, is an older place, but rooms are clean; $50 s, $55 d, kitchenettes an extra $5. For something a bit more upmarket, stay at the 44-room **Burns Lake Motor Inn,** Hwy. 16 W, 250/692-7545 or 800/663-2968, which charges $65–70 s or d.

KOA Burns Lake is off Highway 16 on Freeport Rd., about seven km east of Burns Lake, 250/692-3105. Its picturesque tent sites lie up in a forested area, and each site has a picnic table. The large RV section below is out in the open and has full hookups, free showers, a laundromat, store, and gift shop. Unserviced sites are $16, hookups $18–22. The nearest provincial park with a campground is along a gravel road north of Burns Lake. **Ethel F. Wilson Provincial Park** is on Pinkut Lake, 24 km along this road; $12 a night.

A locally recommended eatery is the **Panhandle Restaurant,** 710 Yellowhead Hwy., 250/692-3316, serving reasonably priced Chinese dishes; open daily for dinner. Across the highway from Lakeview Mall, **Mulvaney's Pub,** 250/692-3078, offers salads, burgers, and hearty pub-style meals at reasonable prices.

Burns Lake Visitor Info Centre is in the Heritage Centre west of downtown, 250/692-3773. It's open through summer Mon.–Fri. 8 A.M.–7 P.M., Sat.–Sun. 9 A.M.–5 P.M. As well as town information, the staff provides hints on the best fishing spots and directions to Tweedsmuir Provincial Park.

TWEEDSMUIR PROVINCIAL PARK (NORTH)

The town of Burns Lake is not only near British Columbia's smallest provincial park (Deadman's Island in Burns Lake), it also happens to be the northern gateway to the largest: 981,000-hectare

Tweedsmuir Provincial Park. The park extends over 200 km from north to south. Its northern boundary, formed by **Ootsa** and **Whitesail Lakes,** is accessed along a network of gravel roads south from Burns Lake. The only road *within* the park is Highway 20 (see Cariboo Country in the Central British Columbia chapter).

Most of the park's northern section is made up of the **Quanchus Mountain Range,** holding many peaks topping 1,900 meters, and the **Nechako Plateau,** which is riddled with lakes and streams. Wildlife abounds. If you're in the right place at the right time you can see caribou, mountain goats, moose, black and grizzly bears, mule deer, wolves, smaller mammals such as hoary marmots and wolverines, and many birds. The lakes are filled with fish, including rainbow trout, kokanee, mountain whitefish, and burbot.

Aside from fishing, the most popular activity in the park's northern reaches is boating, canoeing, or kayaking the circular route through Ootsa, Whitesail, Eutsuk, Tetachuck, and Natalkuz Lakes. Some portaging is required. Ootsa Lake is the main access to the park, but the shoreline has been described as a forest of drowned trees and floating hazards—very dangerous, with few places to land when frequent strong winds funnel across the lakes. Some channels have been cut through the dead trees to emergency landing areas; follow the large yellow diamond signs. Because of the strong winds, keep as close to the shoreline as possible. May is the windiest month.

Practicalities

Wilderness campsites sprinkle some of the lakes within the park. To get to Ootsa Lake, follow Highway 35 for 16 km south from Burns Lake to Francois Lake, take the free vehicle ferry across Francois Lake, then continue south another 44 km to the settlement of Ootsa Lake. To get *into* the park itself, you'll need a canoe, kayak, motorboat, or chartered floatplane. **Lakes District Air Services,** based along Francois Lake Rd., 250/692-3229, flies charters year-round—on floats in summer and skis in winter. Rates are $365 per hour for the three-passenger Cessna 185, and $480 per hour for the six-passenger Beaver. This company also owns a cabin in the

park at Tesla Lake. The cabin sleeps four and comes equipped with cooking facilities, hot showers, and a couple of small motorboats. It rents for $1,800 for four people for four days, including the flight out; you supply your own food, sleeping bags, and fishing gear.

Before visiting the park, contact the Skeena District office of BC Parks in Smithers, 250/847-7320, check the website www.elp.gov.bc.ca/bcparks, or stop by Burns Lake Visitor Info Centre.

TOPLEY TO TELKWA
Babine Lake
At Topley, 51 km west of Burns Lake, a side road leads north to 177-km-long Babine Lake, the province's largest natural lake and yet another spot known for producing trophy-size rainbow trout, Dolly Varden, kokanee, coho salmon, and whitefish. The rivers flowing in and out of the lake also splash with fish, including rainbow trout, steelhead, and salmon.

Topley Landing, 30 km from the Yellowhead Highway, is a former trapping and trading center dating back to the 1700s. Beyond the landing, over the Fulton River, is 148-hectare **Red Bluff Provincial Park,** named for iron-impregnated cliffs nearby. The park's small campground enjoys a picturesque riverside location, but facilities are limited; $12 per night.

The road terminates at **Granisle,** formerly a company town where life revolved around a copper mine. In 1992 the mine closed, many residents moved out, and a developer moved in, attempting to attract retirees and holidaymakers. The preexisting mining-employee accommodations were refurbished to be sold as condominiums, and the former Granisle Village Inn was revamped and renamed the **Grande Isles Resort.** The resort, 250/697-6322 or 800/671-4475, website www.grandeislesresort.com, is excellent value, with comfortable kitchenette units from $70 s or d. The sockeye salmon run in August and September, but other than that there's little reason to come out here. A free municipal campground is one km south of town. Firewood and pit toilets are provided.

© ANDREW HEMPSTEAD

Fishing draws many visitors to Babine Lake.

Houston

Like Burns Lake, Houston's welcoming sign also proudly bears a carved fish—this time a steelhead. Houston calls itself "Steelhead Country," for the only species of trout that migrates to ocean. The forestry town of 4,000 lies at the confluence of the Bulkley and Morice Rivers in the stunning Bulkley Valley, which enjoys the snowcapped Telkwa and Babine Ranges for a backdrop. As in the rest of this region, the local fishing is superb. At the information center pick up a copy of the local forestry district recreation map ($3), which shows all the area's rivers, lakes, logging roads, and campgrounds. The best steelhead fishing is in the Morice River—take the highway west toward Smithers, turn left at the Northwood Pulp Mill sign, and continue about 1.6 km to the end. At the dirt road turn right (at the bridge). Both bait fishing and fly-fishing are popular here.

Motels in town include **Houston Motor Inn,** 250/845-7112 or 800/994-8333, and **Pleasant Valley Motel,** 250/845-2246 or 888/311-7766. Both are on the highway, and both charge from $56 s, $62 d. Camp at the Houston Motor Inn; $14–22.

Houston Visitor Info Centre is on the highway at Benson Ave., 250/845-7640—look for the huge fishing rod in the parking lot. It's open in summer daily 9 A.M.–5 P.M., weekdays only the rest of the year.

Telkwa

As you continue west, the scenery just keeps getting better. You'll pass open fields and rolling, densely forested hills, all the while surrounded by snowcapped mountains peeking tantalizingly out of clouds. The neat little village of Telkwa lies at the confluence of the Bulkley and Telk-

NORTHERN B.C.

wa Rivers. Several species of anadromous fish make spawning runs up the rivers here at various times of year—spring chinook salmon in late June, coho salmon in August, and steelhead between fall and freeze-up. The area also appeals to canoeists, offering stretches of water to suit novices through intermediates.

Many of the buildings in the village were put up between 1908 and 1924. The Telkwa Museum Society puts out a *Walking Tour Through Historic Telkwa* brochure, which describes each of the buildings. On the highway through town, the **Douglas Motel,** 250/846-5679, is one of the best places to stay between Prince George and the coast. It offers a beautiful riverside setting and is surrounded by gardens. Motel rooms are $70 s, $75 d, while self-contained log cabins, complete with fireplaces, are $85 s, $95 d. Nearby **Tyhee Lake Provincial Park** has a good swimming beach, picnic facilities, and a campground with hot showers ($17.50 per site May–Sept., free the rest of the year).

SMITHERS AND VICINITY

The Coast Mountains surround the town of Smithers (pop. 5,800), while the splendid 2,560-meter Hudson Bay Mountain towers directly above. It's a vibrant community with some excellent accommodations, fine restaurants, and interesting arts-and-crafts shops. Hiking trails close to town lead to a magnificent glacier, intriguing fossil beds, and a remote recreation area.

Town Sights

With a backdrop of magnificent mountains, it's no surprise that Main Street is done up in a Bavarian theme. Visitors shop here for native crafts and tourist paraphernalia. The grand old 1925 courthouse, at the junction of the Yellowhead Highway and Main St., is home to **Bulkley Valley Museum,** 250/847-5322, and **Smithers Art Gallery,** 250/847-3898. The museum spotlights the valley's history with plenty of black-and-white photos and pioneer equipment. The gallery exhibits local artwork. Both the museum and gallery are open in summer Mon.–Sat. 11 A.M.–5 P.M.

Driftwood Canyon Provincial Park

Many millions of years ago, the Bulkley Valley had a subtropical climate. The area north of where Smithers now lies was a low wetland of swamps and shallow lakes. Over eons, deposited sediments covered and preserved the remains of the plants and animals that died in the water. Around a million years ago, a lava flow covered the entire region. But then during the last ice age, melting ice carved out a canyon that sliced right through the ancient wetlands, exposing the fossil beds.

Most of the fossils here are from plants, but insect and fish fossils have also been uncovered, including some of the world's oldest known trout fossils. A short walk from the road leads to a viewing platform over the east bank of Driftwood Creek, where interpretive panels describe the site's significance. Excavated specimens can be viewed in the Bulkley Valley Museum. The park is 17 km northeast of town; take Highway 16 three km east, head north on Old Babine Lake Road, turn left on Telkwa High Road, then right on Driftwood Road.

Babine Mountains Provincial Park

From Driftwood Canyon, Driftwood Road continues five km to a parking lot—the trailhead for trails leading into Babine Mountains Provincial Park. The park protects 32,400 hectares of the Skeena Mountains, a remote wilderness dominated by rugged peaks, alpine plateaus, and glacier-fed lakes and rivers. The park is accessible only on foot, but you don't need to travel too far into the park to reach the best parts. From this trailhead, the **McCabe Trail** leads eight km (three hours) one-way to the alpine meadows between Mounts Hyland and Harvey, while the **Silver King Basin Trail** climbs steadily through a subalpine forest for nine km (three hours) one-way to another alpine meadow. The wildflower-filled meadows come alive with color in mid-July.

Kathlyn Glacier and Vicinity

About eight km west of Smithers on the Yellowhead Highway, take the **Hudson Bay Mountain Lookout** turnout for magnificent views of the mountain and the quickly receding Kathlyn Glacier on its north face. In the same vicinity,

NORTHERN B.C.

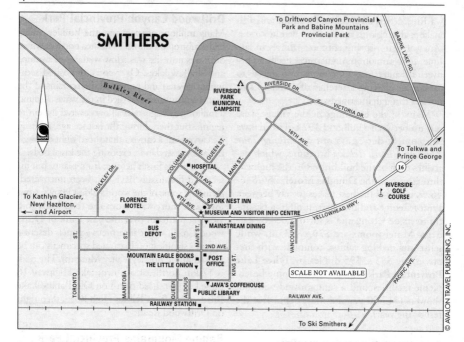

SMITHERS

To Driftwood Canyon Provincial Park and Babine Mountains Provincial Park

BABINE LAKE RD.

Bulkley River

RIVERSIDE DR

RIVERSIDE PARK MUNICIPAL CAMPSITE

VICTORIA DR.

To Telkwa and Prince George

16TH AVE

16TH AVE

QUEEN ST.

COLUMBIA

MAIN ST.

HOSPITAL

6TH AVE.

7TH AVE.

6TH AVE.

16

RIVERSIDE GOLF COURSE

To Kathlyn Glacier, New Hazelton, and Airport

BULKLEY DR.

FLORENCE MOTEL

STORK NEST INN

MUSEUM AND VISITOR INFO CENTRE

YELLOWHEAD HWY.

ST.

ST.

ST.

BUS DEPOT

MAIN ST.

MAINSTREAM DINING

VANCOUVER

2ND AVE.

TORONTO

MANITOBA

MOUNTAIN EAGLE BOOKS

THE LITTLE ONION

POST OFFICE

KING ST.

PACIFIC AVE.

SCALE NOT AVAILABLE

QUEEN

ALDOUS

JAVA'S COFFEEHOUSE

PUBLIC LIBRARY

RAILWAY AVE.

RAILWAY STATION

To Ski Smithers

© AVALON TRAVEL PUBLISHING, INC.

turn south off the highway at Lake Kathlyn Road to the trailhead for **Glacier Gulch,** a strenuous 1,000 vertical meters above the parking lot. The trail is only six km one-way, but allow at least three hours to reach the toe of Kathlyn Glacier. Just 500 meters along the trail is dramatic **Twin Falls,** a worthy destination in itself. Beyond the Glacier Gulch trailhead, Lake Kathlyn Road ends, appropriately enough, at **Lake Kathlyn,** a photogenic body of water at the base of Hudson Bay Mountain.

Ski Smithers

This 120-hectare winter resort on Hudson Bay Mountain is mostly geared to beginners and intermediates, but a few of the 19 designated runs challenge more experienced skiers and boarders. Four lifts serve a vertical rise of 600 meters and 120 hectares of mostly intermediate terrain. Facilities include two day lodges, a rental shop, and a ski and snowboard school. A day pass is adults $33, senior $22, child $18; those under six and over 60 ski free. For resort infor-

mation call 250/847-2058, for a snow report call 250/847-2550, or go to website www.skismithers.com. Cross-country skiers can choose from a 2.5-km marked trail on the mountain or the 10-km **Pine Creek Loop** on the road to the resort. To get to the mountain take either Main Street or King Street south onto Railway Avenue and turn left; the base area is 23 km from downtown Smithers.

Accommodations and Camping

Because skiers and snowboarders from throughout the north flock to the slopes of Hudson Bay Mountain when the snow falls, the local lodgings are apt to be as busy in winter as in summer. The upscale **Stork Nest Inn,** north of the highway at 1485 Main St., 250/847-3831, website www.storknestinn.com, is styled on a Bavarian lodge. It features comfortable rooms, a cooked breakfast, and airport transfers; $65 s, $70 d. Save a few bucks by staying at the **Florence Motel,** 4160 Hwy. 16, 250/847-2678, but it's a bit rough around the edges; $45 s, $50 d.

Riverside Park Municipal Campsite is beside the Bulkley River, north of town. It's open May–Oct., providing shaded sites and river fishing only minutes from downtown. Facilities include showers and a kitchen shelter but no hookups; sites are $12 per night. **Riverside Golf Course,** along the Yellowhead Hwy. east of town, 250/847-3229, has better facilities and is within the bounds of a golf course; unserviced sites $15, serviced sites $17–20.

Food

Specialty coffees and a fine selection of light meals draw locals to the cavernous **Java's Coffeehouse,** 3735 Alfred Ave., 250/847-5505. **The Little Onion,** 1089 Main St., 250/847-6121, is a great little restaurant with a stylish yet uncomplicated decor. The short but varied menu is priced similarly to big-city restaurants of similar standard. Dinner mains range $11–17.50. It's open weekdays for lunch and Mon.–Sat. for dinner.

At busy **Mainstream Dining,** 1338 Main St., 250/847-4567, you'll find pizza (the large "small" starts at around $12), a good salad bar (try the tangy house dressing), and an assortment of tasty Italian dishes, ribs, steaks, and seafood. Main courses range $8–17. Finish it off with gourmet Italian ice cream.

Services and Information

Smithers Airport, right beside Highway 16, four km west of town, is served by **Air B.C.,** 888/247-2262. The **Greyhound** bus depot is on Highway 16, west of the information center, 250/847-2204. **Thrifty** has a limited number of rental vehicles at the airport; 250/847-5569.

Smithers Visitor Info Centre is upstairs in the museum building at the corner of Main St. and the Yellowhead Hwy., 250/847-5072 or 800/542-6673, website www.bulkley.net/~smicham. It's open daily 9 A.M.–6 P.M. in summer and Mon.–Fri. 8:30 A.M.–4:30 P.M. the rest of the year. A good source of northern literature is **Mountain Eagle Books,** 1237 Main St., 250/847-5245.

Continuing West from Smithers

The next place to stop and stretch your legs is the viewpoint at **Moricetown Canyon,** where the 500-meter-wide Bulkley River funnels and roars its way down through a 15-meter-wide canyon. Salmon desperately hurl themselves up these spectacular rapids in autumn. Below the canyon the river pours into a large pool, one of the best fishing spots in the area.

The canyon is part of **Moricetown Indian Reserve,** which recognizes an area that has been a Carrier village site for more than 5,000 years. Villagers still fish the canyon using traditional spears and nets; look for the locals congregated around the canyon in summer.

Continuing west, the scenery changes dramatically; suddenly pine trees line the Bulkley River and cover the hills and mountains. About 50 km from Smithers, a four-km gravel road to the north leads to 307-hectare **Ross Lake Provincial Park,** named for a lake with crystal-clear waters full of trout and Dolly Varden. The backdrop is one of forested hills and spectacular snowcapped peaks. In the early mornings you can hear loons; in the evenings beavers slide into the water, slapping their tails. Facilities include a boat-launching area (no powerboats allowed), barbecue pits, picnic tables, and pit toilets. The park is a day-use area only, with no campsites.

NEW HAZELTON AND VICINITY

It's easy to be confused by the three Hazeltons—Hazelton, New Hazelton, and South Hazelton—situated at the most northerly point on the Yellowhead Highway. As usual, the arrival of the Grand Trunk Pacific Railway caused the confusion. The original Hazelton (called Old Town) was established 50 years or so before the railway came. The other two Hazeltons were founded because each of their respective promoters thought he owned a better spot for a new railway town. Today the largest of the three small communities is New Hazelton (pop. 900), a service center watched over by spectacular Mt. Rocher Deboule (French for "Mountain of the Rolling Rock").

Hazelton

From New Hazelton, Highway 62 leads about eight km northwest to Hazelton. Along the way it crosses the one-lane **Hagwilget Suspension**

Bridge, 79 meters above the turbulent Bulkley River. Stop and read the plaque about the original footbridge—made from poles and cedar rope—that once spanned the gorge here; you'll be glad you live in modern times.

At the junction of the Bulkley and Skeena Rivers, Hazelton has retained its unique 1890s-style architecture and pioneer settlement atmosphere. Along the waterfront sit a museum (open daily 10 A.M.–5 P.M.), a landing with river views, and a café.

'Ksan Historical Village and Museum

'Ksan, which means "Between the Banks," is an authentically reconstructed Gitksan village on the outskirts of Hazelton, 250/842-5544. In the main building is a museum, featuring cedar boxes and cedar-bark mats, woven and button blankets, masks, coppers (the most valuable single object a chief possessed), rattles used by shamans, and an art gallery with changing exhibitions. In the adjacent gift shop are the works of on-site artists. Beyond the museum is the main village. To best appreciate the Gitksan culture, join one of the fascinating guided tours.

Admission to the museum and grounds is $2, and tours are adult $8. Tours leave every hour on the hour, visiting the burial house, food cache, smokehouse, community houses, and the 'Ksan artists' carving shop and studio. You'll see traditional northwest coast carved interiors, paintings and painted screens, totem poles, and fine examples of native artifacts, arts and crafts, tools and implements, and personal possessions. And you'll learn how the people lived and all about their beliefs and legends. The village is open May to mid-October daily 9 A.M.–6 P.M. On Friday nights from mid-July to mid-August, performances of traditional Gitksan song and dance take place starting around 8 P.M. Admission is adult $8.50, child $6.

Kispiox

The traditional Gitksan village of Kispiox lies 16 km north of Hazelton along Kispiox Valley Road (turn off on the Smithers side of Hazelton). Sights include a large group of red cedar **totem poles** near the confluence of the Skeena and Kispiox Rivers and the locally operated, log-constructed **Kispiox Salmon Hatchery.** The hatchery can rear 500,000 salmon fry per year. It's open daily 8 A.M.–5 P.M.

The Seven Sisters

These impressive peaks lie west of New Hazelton, immediately south of the junction of the Yellowhead Highway and Highway 37. From the highway you'll get only occasional glimpses of the range; for the best panorama take Highway 37 north across the Skeena River, turn west (left) toward Cedarvale, and stop after about 10 km at the picnic area by Sedan Creek.

Several trails also lead to good views of the peaks. The one-km **Gull Creek Trail** climbs about 200 vertical meters from the trailhead at Gull Creek, which is signposted along Highway 16. Serious hikers can take any of a number of routes up into the heart of the range, but each is a strenuous slog. The easiest to follow is **Coyote Creek Trail,** an old mining road beginning from where Highway 16 crosses Coyote Creek. The nine-km road ends at a few cabins often used by climbers. From there it's a six-km climb along a rough trail that becomes increasingly difficult to follow. The trail ends on a high alpine ridge at the base of a large icefield.

Practicalities

Along the highway through New Hazelton is the **28 Inn,** 250/842-6006 or 877/842-2828, a motel complex with large rooms, a restaurant, and a pub. Rooms are $53 s, $58 d.

Between the highway and "Old" Hazelton is the log **Hummingbird Restaurant,** 250/842-5628, the best spot for a meal in all the Hazeltons. The wood interior is decorated with etched glass and hanging lamps, and you'll be dazzled by the million-dollar picture-window view of Mt. Rocher Deboule. Tiny hummingbirds flit back and forth between the feeders outside the windows. At lunch, expect to pay around $6–9 for sandwiches, hamburgers, or a huge taco salad. At dinner choose from steaks, chicken, and pasta dishes, all for around $14. It's open daily from 11 A.M. until at least 10 P.M.

Hazelton Visitor Info Centre is at the intersection of Highways 16 and 62, 250/842-6071. It's open June–Sept. daily 8 A.M.–7 P.M. and holds a display detailing local history.

TERRACE AND VICINITY

Terrace (pop. 13,500) lies on the Yellowhead Highway, 580 km west of Prince George and 146 km east of Prince Rupert. The city is built on a series of steep terraces along the beautiful Skeena River, the province's second-largest river system, and is completely surrounded by the spectacular Hazelton and Coast Mountains. The town offers basic tourist services and little else. But the surrounding area makes up for it with a mix of intriguing sights, beautiful parks, and outstanding recreation opportunities.

Originally home of the Tsimshian, "Those Who Taste the Rain," the site that is now Terrace was founded by George Little in 1911. Little's sawmill operation got a boost with the arrival of the railway in 1914; his logs were used for railroad ties. Today the

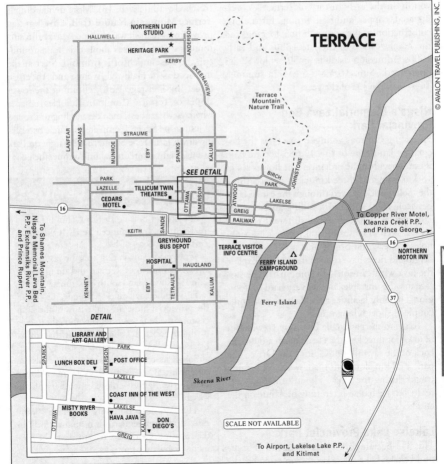

© AVALON TRAVEL PUBLISHING, INC.

NORTHERN B.C.

forestry industry still forms the basis for the city's economy.

Heritage Park

At this outdoor-indoor museum, 4113 Sparks St. (north of downtown up Skeenaview St.), 250/615-3000, a one-hour guided tour takes you through an old, beautifully furnished log hotel, a dance hall, a barn, and six authentic log cabins dating from between 1910 and 1955. Some of the cabins are furnished; others contain historical artifacts or collections of antique farming and mining equipment. The guide fills you in on the early history of Terrace—covering gold, copper, and lead mining, fur trading, construction of the telegraph line, logging, and the homesteaders of the late 1800s and early 1900s. Admission is adults $3.50, senior $2. It's open Wed.–Sun. 10 A.M.–6 P.M. in summer, Tues.–Sat. the rest of the year.

Nisga'a Memorial Lava Bed Provincial Park

Protecting Canada's youngest lava flow, the fascinating landscape of this 17,683-hectare park is unique within the province. The flow is about 18 km long and three km wide; experts think the molten rock spewed through the earth's crust between 1650 and 1750, killing an estimated 200 natives. You can see all different types of lava, as well as crevasses, spiky pinnacles, sinkholes, craters, and bright blue pools where underground rivers have risen to the surface. Explore the lava with caution—in some parts the surface may be unstable, and it's very hard on footgear. The only facilities are a day-use area and a couple of short hiking trails.

To get to the park, take Highway 16 west out of town for three km, then head north around the back of the sawmill on Kalum Lake Drive. The park is 78 km along this road; watch for logging trucks during the week. The information center in Terrace has an interesting brochure on the lava beds.

Lakelse Lake Provincial Park

This 354-hectare park at the north end of beautiful Lakelse Lake offers good swimming beaches, boating, fishing, and a hiking trail through an old-growth forest of towering spruce, cedar, and hemlock. Also here are a large campground (see below) and a shaded picnic area. To get there, take Highway 37 south toward Kitimat for 26 km.

Hiking

In addition to those at the parks mentioned above, many other trails in the area tempt hikers. For an easy stroll, take the three-km path (50 minutes or less) around **Ferry Island,** in the middle of the Skeena River east of downtown (reached via Highway 16). More demanding is **Terrace Mountain Nature Trail,** a five-km trail providing great views of the city and the surrounding area. It takes about two hours round-trip, because much of it is uphill. Start at the intersection of Halliwell Avenue and Anderson Street (by Heritage Park), climbing the lower slopes of Terrace Mountain to a cleared area where views are best, then descending to the end of Johnstone Street. Complete the circle by walking down Johnstone Street, turning right on Park Avenue, right again on Kalum Avenue, then con-

THE ELUSIVE KERMODE

Little known outside British Columbia is the Kermode (pronounced kerr-MO-dee), an elusive subspecies of black bear (*Ursus americanus kermodei*) inhabiting only the vast tract of wilderness north of Terrace and uninhabited Princess Royal Island south of Kitimat.

First studied by Francis Kermode, director of the provincial museum at the turn of the 20th century, the bear was originally thought to be a distinct species. It's slightly larger than other black bears, has a different jaw structure, and, although its color varies, some individuals are pure white. These white bears are not albinos, merely the lightest-colored members of the species.

The Tsimshian called the Kermode "Spirit Bear" and often rendered it in human form in their artwork. Once close to extinction, the Kermode is now fully protected.

tinuing straight onto Skeenaview Avenue back to the trailhead.

Farther afield, consider scenic **Clearwater Lakes Trail,** which begins from Highway 37, 27 km south of Terrace. The trail leads 1.8 km to Little Clearwater Lake, then another 700 meters to Big Clearwater Lake. The two lakes are linked by a shallow creek, along the banks of which are many good picnic spots and berries to pick in season. From the same parking lot, a trail leads 1.8 km to a lookout with outstanding views of Lakelse Lake.

To get the rundown on all the best hikes in the area, ask for the handy *Terrace Hiking Trails* brochure at the information center.

Fishing

The Skeena River is chock-full of salmon, as well as a variety of other fish. Steelhead can be caught April–May and Aug.–October. Chinooks make their upstream migration in late May and again July through August. Coho salmon run from August to early fall. Be sure to get a license and read up on the latest rules and regulations before hitting the rivers and lakes. You can pick up a list of local guides and outfitters from the information center.

Skiing and Snowboarding

Shames Mountain offers a vertical rise of 550 meters and virtually guaranteed good snow coverage. In the opening season (1990–91) an amazing 2,400 cm of snow fell at the resort—nearly twice as much as at any other resort in North America. Current facilities include a day lodge, ski and snowboard school, chairlift, T-bar, and rope tow, but Shames Mountain has big expansion plans for the future. Lift tickets are adult $32, senior $21, child $16. Lifts operate between Christmas and early April Wed.–Sun. only. For further resort information, phone 250/635-3773 or call the Snowphone at 800/663-7754.

Galleries

Northern Light Studio, 4820 Halliwell Ave., 250/638-1403, is an art studio, gallery, and shop featuring custom framing, stained glass, native art, British Columbia jade, fine silver jewelry,

and original paintings. It's open Mon.–Sat. 9:30 A.M.–5:30 P.M. Behind the studio is a small Japanese garden. The basement floor of **Terrace Public Library,** 4610 Park Ave., 250/638-8177, holds a community art gallery offering exhibitions that change monthly. It's open Tues.–Sat. noon–3 P.M. and 7–9 P.M., Sunday 1–4 P.M.; closed Monday.

Accommodations

The less expensive motels are strung out along Highway 16 on the eastern and western outskirts of the city. To the west, your best bet is **Cedars Motel,** 4830 Hwy. 16, 250/635-2258, which is nothing special but charges only $46 s, $48 d. On the other side of town is **Copper River Motel,** three km east at 4113 Hwy. 16, 250/635-6124 or 888/652-7222, set up for anglers, with fishing supplies and guides, 4WD rentals, and free ice. Rooms are clean and have coffee- and tea-making appliances. On the down side are the paper-thin walls. Summer rates are from $60 s, $65 d; a kitchen is available for an extra $10.

Right downtown is the upmarket **Coast Inn of the West,** 4620 Lakelse Ave., 250/638-8141 or 800/663-1144, website www.coasthotels.com, where each of the 60 air-conditioned rooms is decorated in stylish pastel colors. Facilities include a White Spot family restaurant and lounge, and a nearby aquatic center is open to guests. Rooms are $145 s, $155 d, but check the website for discounts.

Camping

On Ferry Island in the Skeena River, just over three km east of downtown, **Ferry Island Campground,** 250/615-3000, offers sheltered sites among birch and cottonwood trees, berry bushes, and wildflowers. A few sites have excellent views of the river and mountains, and a hiking trail runs through the woods and around the island. Facilities include picnic tables and shelters, fire grates, firewood, and pit toilets, but no showers. A few sites have electrical hookups. Unserviced sites are $12 per night, powered sites are $14.

A short drive from Terrace three provincial

parks have campgrounds. **Kleanza Creek Provincial Park,** site of a short-lived gold rush, is 20 km east of Terrace on Highway 16; $12 a night. In the opposite direction, 50 km west of the city on Highway 16 is **Exchamsiks River Provincial Park;** $12 a night. **Lakelse Lake Provincial Park,** 16 km south of Terrace along Highway 37, is the most developed of the three parks, offering a sandy beach, safe swimming, an interpretive amphitheatre, hot showers, and flush toilets. Sites are $17.50 a night.

Food

One of the most popular places to go for breakfast is the **Northern Motor Inn,** near the Chevron gas station on Highway 16 just east of Terrace, 250/635-6375. Large omelets, hash browns, toast, and coffee run around $7–8. The rest of the day, head to **Hava Java,** 4621 Lakelse Ave., for your daily quota of caffeine in a big-city coffeehouse atmosphere. Just down the street is the **Lunch Box Deli,** 4716 Lazelle Ave., 250/635-3696, good for sandwiches.

For delicious Mexican food, head downtown to **Don Diego's,** 3212 Kalum St., 250/635-2307, where many tables catch the evening sun. It's a small, bright restaurant with lots of plants and Mexican wall hangings. Lunch is $6–9 (the shrimp crepes are superb). Dinner entrées start at around $10. It's always busy, so you may have to wait for a table. Hours are Mon.–Sat. 11 A.M.–9 P.M., Sunday 10 A.M.–2 P.M. and 5–9 P.M.

Transportation

Terrace and Kitimat Airport is on Highway 37 eight km south of Terrace. Both **Air B.C.,** 888/247-2262, and Terrace-based **Hawk Air,** 866/429-5247, offer daily scheduled flights to Vancouver. **VIA Rail** trains pass through town three times a week en route to Prince Rupert. The train station is just a small building on Railway Road that opens only when a train arrives or leaves. For more rail information, call VIA Rail direct at 800/561-8630. The **Greyhound** bus depot is at 4620 Keith Ave., 250/635-4428. Greyhound offers daily service west to Prince Rupert and east to Prince George. The only northward public transportation is with **Sea-**port **Limousine,** 250/636-2622, which makes runs to Stewart. Call **Hertz** at 250/635-6866 for a rental car.

Information

Terrace Visitor Info Centre, 4511 Keith Ave., 250/635-2063 or 800/499-1637, website www.terracetourism.bc.ca, is beside Highway 16 on the east side of town. It's open through summer Mon.–Fri. 8:30 A.M.–8 P.M. and Sat.–Sun. 9 A.M.–8 P.M., the rest of the year Mon.–Fri. 9 A.M.–5 P.M. The helpful staff will happily load you down with brochures and pamphlets and tell you everything there is to do in the area. For local literature and a good selection of Canadiana, head downtown to **Misty River Books,** 4710 Lakelse Ave., 250/635-4428.

KITIMAT

The planned industrial community of Kitimat (pop. 12,000), at the northern end of Douglas Channel 62 km south of Terrace, was founded by the aluminum giant **Alcan** (Aluminum Company of Canada) in the 1950s. Canada's largest industrial endeavor at the time, the project included one of the world's largest aluminum smelters, a company town to serve the workers, and a massive hydroelectric scheme on the Nechako River. The hydroelectric project intended to redirect the river's course to a power station at Kemano, then use the electricity generated there to run the Kitimat smelter. The government kicked in millions of dollars upgrading the region's infrastructure, but only the first stages of the hydroelectric project were ever completed. Intense pressure from environmentalists and native organizations forced the provincial government to cancel the rest of the project in 1995.

Tours

The highlight of a visit to B.C.'s self-proclaimed "Aluminum City" is a guided industrial tour. The town's Alcan smelter, **Kitimat Works,** produces 270,000 tons of aluminum products worth $350 million annually. Tours, offered in summer Mon.–Fri. at 10:30 A.M. and 1:30 P.M., start with an audiovisual presentation, then it's into a bus for

NORTHERN B.C.

a drive around the works and down to the wharf. Tours are free, but book ahead at 250/639-8259.

Methanex, Kitimat's newest industry and northern British Columbia's only **petrochemical plant,** offers tours Monday and Wednesday at 3 P.M. Bearded men (or women) are not permitted on this tour. Book at 250/639-9292. Eurocan's **pulp and paper mill** tour is conducted Tuesday and Thursday at 10 A.M. and 2 P.M. No children under 12; 250/639-3407.

If all this industrial hooey gives you a headache, get back to nature at **Kitimat River Fish Hatchery,** 250/639-9616, which releases 11 million trout and salmon annually. Tours are conducted three times daily through summer.

Other Sights

In **Radley Park,** along the Kitimat River, stands the province's largest living tree, a 50-meter-high, 500-year-old Sitka spruce. It's behind the Riverlodge Recreation Centre. The **Centennial Museum,** 293 City Centre, 250/632-7022, tells the story of the planned town and displays historic and native artifacts; a gallery features locally produced artwork. It's open June–Aug., Mon.–Sat. 10 A.M.–5 P.M., the rest of the year Mon.–Fri. 10 A.M.–5 P.M., Sat.–Sun. noon–5 P.M.

Practicalities

City Centre Motel, right downtown at 480 City Centre, 250/632-4848 or 800/663-3391, features comfortable rooms, each with a fully equipped kitchen and tea- and coffee-making facilities. Rates run a reasonable $55 s, $58 d. **Radley Park Campground** has a riverside setting, showers, a few hookups, and a kitchen shelter; $11–15.50 a night.

For the best breakfast in town, head to **The Chalet,** 852 Tsimshian Blvd., 250/632-2662. **Rosario's,** 607 Legion St., 250/632-4980, serves up pizza, pasta, and steaks nightly until 10 P.M.

Kitimat Visitor Info Centre is at the north entrance to town at 2109 Forest Ave., 250/632-6294 or 800/664-6554, website www.sno.net/kcoc.

WEST TOWARD PRINCE RUPERT

The 147-km stretch of the Yellowhead Highway between Terrace and Prince Rupert rivals any stretch of road in the province for beauty. For almost the entire distance, the highway hugs the north bank of the beautiful Skeena River (Skeena is a Gitksan word for "River of Mist"). On a fine day, views from the road are stunning—snow-dusted mountains, densely forested hillsides, ponds covered in yellow water lilies, and waterfalls like narrow ribbons of silver, snaking down vertical cliffs from the snow high above. In some sections the highway shrinks to two extremely narrow lanes neatly sandwiched between the railway tracks and the river—drive defensively.

Exchamsiks River Provincial Park, on the north side of the highway 50 km west of Terrace, features a grassy picnic area where the deep green Exchamsiks River drains into the much larger Skeena River. Camping is $12 a night. As the highway continues westward, the Skeena widens, eventually becoming a tidal estuary. Sandbars and marshes, exposed at low tide, are a mass of colorful mosses, and wading birds feed in shallow pools. Keep an eye out for bald eagles on the sandbars or perched in the trees above the highway.

Just over 110 km from Terrace, the highway leaves the river and meanders inland past high forested cliffs to **Prudhomme Lake,** on the north side of the highway. The lake holds a number of forested islands and is flanked by a small provincial park; campsites $12.

Prince Rupert

Prince Rupert (pop. 18,000) lies on hilly Kaien Island 726 km west of Prince George. It's one of Canada's major west coast ports, and life here revolves around the ocean. The city boasts a large fishing fleet and is a major water transportation hub; from here you can catch ferries south to Vancouver Island, west to the Queen Charlotte Islands, or north to Alaska. The city itself holds an odd but intriguing mixture of cultural icons—Pacific Northwest native totem poles, old English coats of arms and street names, modern highrise hotels and civic buildings—all crammed together on the edge of the Pacific Ocean.

The city has always been a hub for travelers but has never been seen as a destination in itself. That began changing in the early 1990s, with the redevelopment of Cow Bay, and in 1999 the first cruise ship arrived at the newly constructed Atlin Dock. The area south along the waterfront from Cow Bay is still a wasteland of railyards and disused docks, but work has already begun on sprucing up this part of the city, and it will continue for many years to come. Plan to spend at least a day in the area, visiting the excellent museum, exploring an old cannery village, or maybe taking a harbor tour.

History

For at least 5,000 years, Kaien Island and the vicinity have been inhabited by the Coast Tsimshian, whose lives were traditionally dominated by fishing and food gathering. They followed the spring and summer salmon and oolichan runs, returning every season to the same village sites. Trade networks were established, artistic traditions emerged, and a class system evolved. Before 1790 the region was among the most heavily populated areas on British Columbia's coastline.

When Europeans arrived on the northwest coast, the local Tsimshian, eager to cash in on fur trading, moved to Fort Simpson, a Hudson's Bay Company post north of Prince Rupert. For a time, they continued to hold their traditional potlatches—days-long festivals filled with feasting, storytelling, and dancing in elaborate costumes and masks. But in 1884, the government, swayed by church lobbyists who claimed the practice was evil, banned potlatching, and this crucial, millennia-old element of the Tsimshians' economic, trade, and social structure effectively died out.

Prince Rupert was the brainchild of Charles M. Hays, general manager of the Grand Trunk Pacific Railway. In 1902, Hays devised a plan to build a rail line from North Bay, Ontario, to a new port on the central B.C. coast—a port he hoped would rival Vancouver and become *the* Pacific port for Canada. In 1914 the railway was completed, but unfortunately, Hays never saw it. He went down with the *Titanic* in 1912. The new city was named after pioneer English business magnate and adventurer Prince Rupert.

After World War I, fishing and fish processing became important parts of the city's economy,

PORT ESSINGTON

Port Essington, originally a Tsimshian site called Spokeshute, was established as a shipping settlement at the mouth of the Skeena River south of Prince Rupert. The settlement was serviced by sternwheelers and riverboats, and supplied Hudson's Bay Company brigades and ports. As the fur trade declined through the 1800s, the salmon industry here grew. The area soon had 12 canneries—mainly staffed by Chinese, Japanese, and native laborers.

The town flourished during fishing seasons and boasted hotels, restaurants, stores, and a red-light district. In the 1890s, miners stopped in on their way to northern Canadian goldfields, and the inevitable missionaries came to try to enforce Christianity. The port's boom days lasted until the arrival of the Grand Trunk Pacific Railway, when canneries were built near the railhead at Prince Rupert and Port Essington was abandoned. Today only charred fragments remain.

PRINCE RUPERT

SEE "DOWNTOWN PRINCE RUPERT" MAP

Prince Rupert Harbour

Seal Cove

SEAL COVE RD.

BELL'S RD.

- HARBOUR AIR
- VANCOUVER ISLAND HELICOPTERS

6TH AVE E

11TH AVE E

FREDERICK ST.

GEORGE HILLS WAY

PRINCE RUPERT BLVD

5TH AVE E

Cow Bay

MCBRIDE

2ND AVE

8TH AVE W

9TH AVE W

SUMMIT AVE.

PARK AVE.

11TH ST.

Morse Creek

ANCHOR INN

PARK AVE. CAMPGROUND

■ HOSPITAL

■ CIVIC CENTRE

■ EARL MAH AQUATIC CENTRE

★ OLDFIELD CREEK HATCHERY

Oldfield Creek

Hays Creek

WANTAGE RD.

▲ Mt. Hays (732 m)

Butze Rapids

16

To Port Edward, Ridley Island, Prudhomme Lake P.P., and Terrace

BC FERRIES TERMINAL

ALASKA MARINE HWY.

To Ketchikan

To Digby Island (Airport)

To Port Hardy

SCALE NOT AVAILABLE

© AVALON TRAVEL PUBLISHING, INC.

NORTHERN B.C.

and during World War II Prince Rupert became a shipbuilding center and an American army base. Tourism started in the '60s with the commencement of the B.C. and Alaska ferry services. Today, fishing is still the mainstay of the economy; up to 2,000 fishing vessels cruise the coast in search of salmon, herring, lingcod, sole, and halibut. Their total annual catch averages some 7,000 tons. Prince Rupert also boasts four fish-processing plants, extensive deepwater-port facilities, grain and coal terminals, and a thriving wood-products industry.

SIGHTS

Museum of Northern British Columbia

You can easily spend several hours at this fascinating museum, which occupies the distinctive post-and-beam building on the corner of 1st Ave. W and McBride St., 250/624-3207. Exhibits trace the history of Prince Rupert from 5,000-year-old Tsimshian settlements through fur-trading days to the founding of the city in 1914 as the western terminus of the Grand Trunk Pacific Railway. Many of the most fascinating displays spotlight the Coast Tsimshian natives—their history, culture, traditions, trade networks, and potlatches. Among the Tsimshian artifacts on display: totem poles, pots, masks, beautiful wooden boxes, blankets, baskets, shiny black argillite carvings, weapons, and petroglyphs.

Admission to this excellent museum is adult $5, child $1. The museum and the information center out front are both open early June through early September Mon.–Fri. 9 A.M.–8 P.M. and Sunday 9 A.M.–5 P.M., the rest of the year Mon.–Sat. 10 A.M.–5 P.M. (Beside the information center is a pleasant park with views across to Digby Island.)

Other Town Sights

Right by the Museum of Northern British Columbia is **Pacific Mariner's Memorial Park**, a grassed area with benches strategically placed for the best ocean views. A statue of a mariner staring out to sea is surrounded by plaques remembering those lost at sea. Also in the park is the *Kazu*

Maru, a small fishing boat that drifted across the Pacific from Japan after its owner was lost. It washed up on the Queen Charlotte Islands in 1987, two years after it was reported missing. On the other side of the museum to the memorial park and beside the fire hall is the **Firehall Museum,** 250/627-4475, which features a 1925 REO Speedwagon along with various other fire-fighting memorabilia. It's open Tues.–Sat. 9 A.M.–5 P.M., except when there's a fire being fought in town. From this museum, continue south along 1st Avenue, then head to the foot of 2nd Street, which ends harborside. Here you'll find the **Kwinitsa Station Railway Museum,** 250/627-1915, housed in a small railway station—one of only four such remaining buildings that were once part of a chain of 400 identical stations along the Grand Trunk Railway. Displays tell the story of the railway and its implications for Prince Rupert. It's open in summer daily 9 A.M.–noon and 1–5 P.M.

If you find modern architecture interesting, you may want to walk around the **Civic Centre,** corner McBride St. and Wantage Rd.—look for the three brightly painted totem poles out front. Adjacent to the Civic Centre is the ultramodern **Prince Rupert Performing Arts Centre,** also worth a visit. You can take a guided tour through its muted purple-and-orange interior by appointment; call 250/627-8888. In the same vicinity, along Wantage Rd. is **Oldfield Creek Hatchery,** 250/624-6733, a salmon-raising facility open for tours. On the same side of the city but a little farther out (just south of the industrial park) is **Butze Rapids.** The churning water of these reversing tidal rapids produces lots of floating foam, which local Tsimshian natives called *kaien*—hence the name Kaien Island, upon which the city of Prince Rupert stands. The rapids are reached along a 2.4-km trail (about 40 minutes each way).

North Pacific Cannery Village Museum

South of Prince Rupert in Port Edward is the oldest remaining cannery village on North America's west coast. Dating to 1889, the village is now classified as a historic site. You can find out

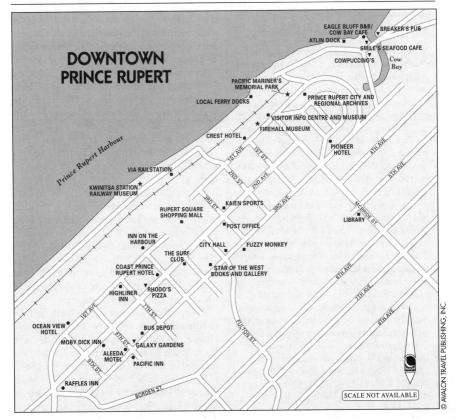

DOWNTOWN
PRINCE RUPERT

Prince Rupert Harbour

EAGLE BLUFF B&B/
COW BAY CAFE
BREAKER'S PUB
ATLIN DOCK
SMILE'S SEAFOOD CAFE
COWPUCCINO'S
Cow Bay
PACIFIC MARINER'S
MEMORIAL PARK
LOCAL FERRY DOCKS
PRINCE RUPERT CITY AND
REGIONAL ARCHIVES
VISITOR INFO CENTRE AND MUSEUM
FIREHALL MUSEUM
CREST HOTEL
PIONEER
HOTEL
VIA RAILSTATION
KWINITSA STATION
RAILWAY MUSEUM
KAIEN SPORTS
RUPERT SQUARE
SHOPPING MALL
LIBRARY
POST OFFICE
INN ON THE
HARBOUR
CITY HALL
FUZZY MONKEY
THE SURF
CLUB
COAST PRINCE
RUPERT HOTEL
STAR OF THE WEST
BOOKS AND GALLERY
HIGHLINER
INN
RHODO'S
PIZZA
OCEAN VIEW
HOTEL
BUS DEPOT
MOBY DICK INN
GALAXY GARDENS
ALEEDA
MOTEL
PACIFIC INN
RAFFLES INN
BORDEN ST.

1ST AVE.   1ST ST.   2ND ST.   2ND AVE.   3RD ST.   3RD AVE.   4TH AVE.   5TH AVE.   McBRIDE ST.   5TH AVE.   6TH AVE.   7TH AVE.   8TH AVE.   FULTON ST.   7TH ST.   8TH ST.   9TH ST.

SCALE NOT AVAILABLE

© AVALON TRAVEL PUBLISHING, INC.

everything you've ever wanted to know about fish, the fishing industry, canning—even which fish tastes the best (locals say it's red snapper every time). You're free to stroll at your own pace along the boardwalk through the riverside cannery settlement with its many original buildings, but a variety of guided tours are offered and included in the admission charge. Also included is the *Skeena River Story*, a live performance and slide show presented through summer daily at 11:30 A.M., 1 P.M., 2:30 P.M., and 4 P.M. The village is open May–Sept. daily 9 A.M.–6 P.M., the rest of the year Wed.–Sat. 10 A.M.–4 P.M. Admission to the museum and village is $8, good for credit on purchases of $8 or more in the cannery stores. For further information, call 250/628-3538.

To get to the village, head out of Prince Rupert on the Yellowhead Highway and take the first road to the right after leaving Kaien Island. Local buses run from downtown Prince Rupert to Port Edward several times a day on weekdays, twice a day on Saturday. Fare to Port Edward proper is $1.75 each way, but to get to the cannery—another 6.5 km down the road—you have to specifically tell the driver your destination when you board in Rupert and pay an extra $1.

Harbor Tours, Ferries, and Boat Charters

The best way to see the harbor is on an **Archeological Harbour Tour** operated by the Museum of Northern British Columbia, corner 1st Ave. W and McBride St., 250/624-3207.

THE KHUTZEYMATEEN

Officially protected as a provincial park, the Khutzeymateen is a rugged and remote 44,300-hectare tract of wilderness 50 km northeast of Prince Rupert that is Canada's only grizzly bear sanctuary. To the Tsimshian people, the area was known as the K'tzim-a-Deen, which translates to "The Long Inlet Surrounded by a Steep Valley." To Canadian conservationists the name Khutzeymateen is synonymous with one of their earliest victories—a 1984 decision to set aside a 385,000-hectare area where grizzly bears would be safe from hunters. In 1994, further protection was given with the proclamation of a provincial park where grizzly numbers were highest within the no-hunting zone. The park extends from the upper reaches of Khutzeymateen Inlet to the 2,000-meter-high peaks of the Kitimat Range, protecting the tidal zone at the head of the inlet where grizzly bears, fresh out of hibernation in May and June, come down to the water's edge to feed on sedges and grasses. Through summer, the bears remain in the area, feeding in the salmon-rich Khutzeymateen and Kateen Rivers.

Permits are required for entry to the sanctuary; these can be obtained in advance from the Skeena District Office of BC Parks, Bag 5000, Smithers, BC V0J 2N0, 250/847-7320. All visitors must then register at the floating ranger station, moored near the estuary.

Due to the inaccessibility of the region, most visitors arrive on a guided trip. **West Coast Launch,** 250/627-9166, runs visitors into the area from Prince Rupert for $125 pp, but most of the six-hour trip is spent traveling. Longer tours are run by **Sunchaser Charters,** P.O. Box 1096, Prince Rupert, BC V8J 4H6, 250/624-5472, which offers four-, six-, and 10-day trips aboard a 13-meter live-aboard motor cruiser. Departing from Prince Rupert and taking half a day to reach the sanctuary, the trips emphasize bear viewing, but time is also spent exploring other aspects of the area's natural and human history. **Harbour Air,** 250/627-1341, has a one-hour flightseeing trip that takes in the Khutzeymateen. These tours depart Prince Rupert's Seal Cove floatplane base on demand and cost $209 per person.

The 2.5-hour tour starts with a slide show in the museum and then boards a small, enclosed ferry. The first stop is the historic fishing village of **Dodge Cove** on Digby Island, which has been inhabited for over 5,000 years. Then the ferry takes you to the native village of **Metlakatla,** allowing time for a stroll through the village or along the beach. Throughout the tour, guides point out historical sites along the shoreline and pass around archaeological artifacts for your examination. Tours depart the museum in summer daily at 1 P.M.; adult $22, child $13.

All sorts of shuttle services run around the harbor to communities with no road connections. Times vary. Head down to the small docks at the bottom of McBride Street for route and schedule information, or call 250/624-3337. The shortest trip is a 15-minute run to **Dodge Cove** on Digby Island. There's not much to do on the island, but it's a nice cruise there and back, and it costs just $8 round-trip.

A ferry also cruises along the Portland Inlet to **Kincolith** (pop. 400), one of four traditional Nisga'a villages in the remote Nass Valley, and the only one accessible by boat. The village was founded by Anglican missionaries in the 1860s, with the aim of helping natives escape the influence of European traders. The *Centurion IV* departs Prince Rupert Monday and Friday at 8:30 A.M. and makes a short stop before returning midafternoon; $15 one-way. For details call **B.C. Ferries** at 250/624-5411. Also ask down at the docks about ferries to **Lax Kw'alaams** (Port Simpson), where a small native village occupies the former site of a Hudson's Bay Company fort, and to Metlakatla.

Seashore Charters, 250/624-5645 or 800/667-4393, keeps a list of all the local charter operators, their vessels, tours, and rates, and can provide more information on fishing tours, harbor tours, and adventure tours. Some of the options available include yacht trips; day-long cruises looking for eagles, waterfowl, seals, otters, porpoises, and killer whales; and fishing trips for salmon, halibut, or cod, with gear and bait supplied. Expect to pay from $90 per person for a fishing trip.

Industrial Tours

Prince Rupert's main industrial terminals—a **grain terminal** and a **coal terminal**—are on Ridley Island, a small island south of Kaien Island. Access is off Highway 16 via Ridley Island Industrial Road. Ninety-minute tours of both fully automated terminals are offered in summer. Make arrangements through the Prince Rupert Visitor Info Centre, 250/624-5637.

RECREATION

Hiking

Hiking opportunities abound around the city. The museum offers a **Heritage Walking Tour** daily at 1:30 P.M. to see the town's historical buildings and sites. Other trails lead from town to Cow Bay, Hays Creek, Morse Creek, the ferry terminals, and the low summit of Mt. Oldfield.

KING PACIFIC LODGE

King Pacific Lodge provides an unforgettable wilderness experience, far removed from the casual highway traveler. The floating lodge is on remote Princess Royal Island, best known for its population of Kermode, the albino-like "Spirit Bear." Its three-story timber structure is built over the waters of a protected cove, the perfect base for searching out the abundant marine mammals, kayaking, and fishing. It is the latter that attracts most guests, with chinooks (kings) biting best May through July and peak season for other salmon Aug.–September.

The minimum stay is three nights, with all packages including floatplane transportation from Prince Rupert, all meals and drinks, and all activities. The lodge itself holds 17 spacious guest rooms, each with ample amenities and luxurious furnishings. The Great Room is a sea level lounge centered on a huge stone fireplace; a wraparound veranda faces the ocean out front. Meals are served in an elegant setting overlooking the water, with fresh seafood the order of the day. For dates and pricing contact the lodge at 604/987-5452 or 888/592-5464, website www.kingpacificlodge.com.

Pick up a map and descriptions for all the local trails at the information center.

For views of Prince Rupert, the sound, southeastern Alaska, and plenty of bald eagles soaring through updrafts, ascend 732-meter-high **Mount Hays.** To get to the base of this local landmark take Wantage Road south off the Yellowhead Highway at the civic center. A gondola used to operate up to the mountain, opening up alpine hiking in summer and skiing in winter, but it hasn't operated for almost a decade. Today you can reach the summit by hiking up a gravel road that provides panoramic views of Digby Island and the town.

Sea Kayaking

The calm waters of Prince Rupert Harbour are perfect for kayaking. Even if you have had no experience in a kayak, **Eco-treks,** based at Cow Bay, 250/624-8311, will take you on an easy paddle along the shoreline for $40 per person. The company also rents kayaks; $40 per day for a single and $70 per day for a double, with cheaper rates for multiple days. Another rental agency is **Kaien Sports,** downtown at 344 2nd Ave., 250/624-3633.

Indoor Recreation

Prince Rupert has several sports venues at the corner of McBride St. and Wantage Road. In the **Civic Centre** building you can have a game of squash, or watch badminton, basketball, or volleyball in action. In the **Arena** you'll find a roller-skating rink in summer and an ice-skating rink in winter; skate rental is available. Next door is the **Earl Mah Aquatic Centre,** 250/627-7946, which has two pools, a sizzling whirlpool, two saunas, a diving board, and a fitness area; admission is adult $4, senior or child $2.

Arts and Entertainment

In the same complex as the recreation facilities listed above is the **Prince Rupert Performing Arts Centre,** corner McBride St. and Wantage Rd., 250/627-7529, where just about anything could be happening. Symphony concerts, plays, lectures, and operas are among the events scheduled here.

The most popular spot in town for a beer is **Breakers Pub,** 117 George Hills Way, Cow Bay, 250/624-5990. This popular local pub boasts plenty of atmosphere, an outdoor deck with harbor views, and a bistro-style restaurant; open daily noon–midnight. Many rowdy bars can be found downtown—just follow your nose and ears. For the dancing into the wee hours, try **Bogey's Cabaret** in the Coast Prince Rupert Hotel on 2nd Ave. between 6th and 7th Streets, or the **Surf Club** at 200 5th St., 250/624-3050. Most of the hotels also have licensed lounges with some form of entertainment, particularly on weekends. The **Moby Dick Inn,** 935 2nd Ave. W, 250/624-6961, and **Raffles Inn,** 1080 3rd Ave. W, 250/624-9161, have nightclubs.

Shoot pool with the local kids at the **Fuzzy Monkey,** 316 3rd St. W, 250/622-7665. It costs about $12 per table per hour, and hours are 11:30 A.M.–midnight.

Festivals and Events

The major annual celebration here is **Seafest,** on the second weekend of June. All sorts of wacky events involving the sea are scheduled—a canoe-dunking contest (the water's icy so no one wants to lose), bathtub races, and fish-filleting competitions. There's also a more serious side to the weekend—a memorial barbecue for those lost at sea followed by a ceremony to dedicate new bricks at the mariner's statue. Another event held in June is **First Nations Cultural Night,** featuring a salmon feast and plenty of authentic native dancing and singing.

ACCOMMODATIONS AND CAMPING

Prince Rupert has a great campground within easy walking distance of the ferry terminals. On the other hand, motel accommodations are generally overpriced and need to be booked well in advance during the busy summer months.

Under $50

The distinctive blue and green **Pioneer Hostel,** 167 3rd Ave. E, 250/624-2334 or 888/794-9998, has had the reputation of being a bit rough around the edges, but new owners and a new name are slowly turning things around. It's still mostly full of "steadies" in winter, but in summer daily and weekly accommodations are offered. Facilities include small rooms with shared bathrooms, an outside yard with a barbecue, a living room with TV, and a microwave and fridge for guest use; $28 per person. Rooms rapidly fill with ferry arrivals and departures. Reservations can be made over the phone a day or two ahead.

One of the best-value accommodations is the **Ocean View Hotel,** a 10-minute walk from downtown at 950 1st Ave. W., 250/624-6259. It is an old hotel that has been completely renovated, and although the rooms are small they are comfortably furnished and have water views. Rates are $45 s or d for a shared bath and $68 s or d for a room with a private bath. Downstairs is a bar and restaurant.

$50–100

My favorite Rupert accommodation is the **Eagle Bluff Bed and Breakfast,** 201 Cow Bay Rd., 250/627-4955 or 800/833-1550. The house is built out over the water, overlooking the marina and harbor, and lies within easy walking distance of cafés and restaurants. Rates are $45 s, $55 d for a shared bath; $60 s, $70 d for a private bath; and $90 for a large suite sleeping five. A cooked breakfast—complete with freshly baked muffins—is included.

A reasonably priced motel is the **Aleeda Motel,** on the west side of downtown at 900 3rd Ave. W, 250/627-1367. The small, basic rooms go for $58 s, $70 d. On the same block, and with a better standard of rooms and a restaurant, is **Moby Dick Inn,** 935 2nd Ave. W, 250/624-6961 or 800/663-0822, website www.moby dickinn.com; $79 s, $89 d. Also in the area are **Raffles Inn,** 1080 3rd Ave. W, 250/624-9161 or 800/663-3207, with basic rooms for $70 s, $75 d, and the **Pacific Inn,** 909 3rd Ave. W, 250/627-1711 or 888/663-1999, which charges $79 s, $84 d. A few blocks from downtown is **Inn on the Harbour,** 720 1st Ave. W, 250/624-9107 or 800/663-8155, where you'll pay $74 s, $85 d, most of that for the view.

NORTHERN B.C.

© ANDREW HEMPSTEAD

Eagle Bluff B&B

Close to the ferry terminal is **Anchor Inn,** 1600 Park Ave., 250/627-8522 or 888/627-8522, website www.anchor-inn.com, an ugly three-story place with a restaurant and lounge; $80 s, $85 d includes a light breakfast.

$100–150
The massive building right downtown is the 15-story **Highliner Inn,** 815 1st Ave. W, 250/624-9060 or 800/668-3115, website www.high linerinn.com, which has a downstairs restaurant and many rooms with balconies and harbor views. Rates are from $120 s or d.

In a prime harborside location, the full-service **Crest Hotel,** 222 1st Ave. W, 250/624-6771 or 800/663-8150, website www.cresthotel.bc.ca, holds a glass-enclosed waterfront café, a dining room, and a lounge with nightly entertainment. Rates for the stylishly decorated rooms—most with water views—start at $155 s or d. Rooms in the older wing are $115 s or d.

The **Coast Prince Rupert Hotel,** 118 6th St., 250/624-6711 or 800/663-1144, website www.coasthotels.com, offers 92 comfortable rooms, some with water views, and a downstairs restaurant and pub. Advertised rates are $165 s or d, but show your AAA card, for example, and you'll get a room for under $100.

Camping
Like the rest of Rupert's accommodations, **Park Avenue Campground,** 1750 Park Ave., 250/624-5861 or 800/667-1994, fills and empties on a daily basis with the arrival and departure of the ferries. If you know when you're arriving in the city, phone ahead to avoid any hassles. The campground is a one-km hike from both the city center and ferry terminals. Facilities include

NORTHERN B.C.

hot showers, cooking shelters, a grassy tenting area, pay phones, a mail drop, and visitor information. Unserviced sites are $14, full hookups $19. The other alternative is **Prudhomme Lake Provincial Park,** along the Yellowhead Highway 16 km east of downtown; $12 per night.

FOOD
Breakfast
Most of Rupert's larger motels have restaurants, but the place to head for substantial and inexpensive breakfasts is the **Moby Dick Inn,** 935 2nd Ave. W, 250/624-6961. You can order anything from a bowl of fruit and a muffin ($4) to eggs, bacon, and toast ($5) or steak and eggs ($8). It's always crowded, and service can be slow. Just around the corner, the **Raffles Inn,** 1080 3rd Ave. W, 250/624-9161, offers similar fare.

Cow Bay Cafés
East of downtown is Cow Bay, originally a fishy-smelling, rough-and-tumble part of town home to a large fishing fleet. The boats are still there, moored in a marina, and a few old buildings still stand. But for the most part, the bay is a changed place. Rowdy dives have been replaced by trendy art and crafts shops, restaurants, and two of the city's best cafés.

    Cowpuccino's, 25 Cow Bay Rd., 250/627-1395, is a great little coffeehouse with freshly brewed coffee, delicious desserts, newspapers and magazines to read, and a laid-back atmosphere. It's open daily from 7:30 A.M. to 10 or 11 P.M. each night. On the waterfront is the popular **Cow Bay Cafe,** 205 Cow Bay Rd., 250/627-1212, where you can sit at an outside table and take in the smells of the ocean, or stay inside and enjoy the greenery. Good home-cooked meals, including vegetarian dishes, and daily specials start at $6. It's open Tues.–Sun. 11 A.M.–8 P.M.; around lunchtime the tables fill up fast.

Seafood
Ask a local where to go for good seafood and the answer is invariably **Smile's Seafood Cafe,** 113 Cow Bay Rd., 250/624-3072. This diner-style café, decorated with black-and-white fishing

photos and colored-glass floats, has been serving seafood since 1934. It's always busy, mobbed by local fishermen, residents, and visitors no matter what time of day. The extensive menu includes seafood salads and sandwiches, burgers, fish and chips, shellfish, and seafood specialties. Prices range $6–25 per plate. Smile's is open daily 9 A.M.–10 P.M. in July and August, 11 A.M.–8 P.M. the rest of the year.

    Another notable place for fresh seafood is the casual **Boulet's Seafood & Chowder House,** in the Pacific Inn, 909 3rd Ave. W, 250/624-9309. Especially good is the lunchtime clam chowder, served with a small loaf of bread, dessert, and tea or coffee for $9. Boulet's is open Mon.–Sat. 11 A.M.–9 P.M.

Other Restaurants
Galaxy Gardens, 844 3rd Ave. W, 250/624-3122, boasts a flashy decor with lots of wicker and bamboo. On the menu are tasty chow meins, prawn and chicken dishes, and special combos. **Rhodos Pizza,** 716 2nd Ave., 250/624-9797, serves up pizza, steak, and delicious Greek specialties from $9. On the walls are Greek plates and artifacts, and the background music is, naturally, Greek. The **Waterfront Restaurant,** in the Crest Hotel, 222 1st Ave. W, 250/624-6771, offers panoramic views across the water and is one of the city's best restaurants, with a varied menu ranging from local seafood to Italian-style meat dishes. It also offers Rupert's best wine list.

TRANSPORTATION
Air
Prince Rupert Airport is west of town on Digby Island, linked to the city by a ferry that takes buses and foot passengers only—no vehicles. Airlines provide free bus transportation between the airport and downtown, via the ferry, but bus passengers must pay the ferry fare of $12 per person each way. **Air B.C.,** 888/247-2262, provides daily flights between Vancouver and Prince Rupert via Terrace.

    Developed by the Royal Canadian Air Force in 1941, **Seal Cove Air Base** lies at the east end of town and serves as the seaplane base for Prince Rupert. To get there, take 5th Avenue east from McBride Street and follow the signs to Seal Cove. The largest operator is **Harbour Air,** 250/627-1341 or 800/689-4234, which makes scheduled flights to Lax Kw'alaams ($43 each way), Kitkatla ($77), Kincolith ($85), Klemtu ($125), Masset ($144), and Sandspit ($205). The company also offers flightseeing excursions, including a 20-minute flight over the city for $76 per person, an hour-long trip to the Khutzeymateen Valley grizzly bear sanctuary for $209 per person, and a three-hour trip to Ketchikan for $410 per person. **Vancouver Island Helicopters,** also at the seaplane base, 250/624-2792, offers chopper charters, which are more expensive than the floatplane variety. Call for rates.

Rail

Prince Rupert is the western terminus of Canada's transcontinental rail system, which runs east from here to Prince George and Edmonton, across the prairies to Toronto, and on to the Atlantic provinces. The route through British Columbia is the highlight of the trip, especially the couple of hundred kilometers just outside Prince Rupert, where the line follows the Skeena River. To get to the **VIA Rail** station take 2nd Street north over the rail line, 250/627-7589 or 800/561-8630. Trains arrive in Prince Rupert on Monday, Thursday, and Saturday at 8 P.M. and depart on Wednesday, Friday, and Sunday at 8 A.M. The station, which could do with a coat of paint, is only open a couple of hours either side of arrivals and departures.

Bus

The **Greyhound** bus depot is at 822 3rd Ave. W (opposite Overwaitea), 250/624-5090 or 800/661-8747. Reservations are not taken—just turn up and buy your ticket on the day you want to go. From Prince Rupert, buses travel east along the Yellowhead Highway to Terrace and Prince George, then either north to the Alaska Highway, east to Jasper National Park and Edmonton, or south through Cariboo Country to Kamloops and on to Vancouver. The run between Prince George and Prince Rupert leaves twice daily.

B.C. Ferries

Prince Rupert is the northern terminus of the B.C. Ferries network, which offers regular services south to Port Hardy on Vancouver Island and west to the Queen Charlotte Islands. The terminal is two km from downtown, right alongside the Alaska Marine Highway terminal. Ferries serving Prince Rupert have both day rooms and sleeping cabins, shower facilities, food service, and plenty of room to sit back and relax. During the busy summer months it's imperative that you book well in advance, especially if you plan to transport a vehicle. For reservations call B.C. Ferries, 250/386-3431 or, toll-free in B.C., 888/223-3779, website www.bcferries.com.

The 15-hour, 440-km ferry trip from Prince Rupert to Port Hardy is a beautiful ride on the well-equipped *Queen of the North,* which departs in summer every second day at 7:30 A.M., arriving in Port Hardy that same night at 10:30 P.M. The rest of the year sailings are less frequent. The summer one-way fares are: adult $106, child 5–11 $53, vehicle $218. Discounts are available outside of summer and for B.C. seniors, and cabins ($43–52) are available by reservation.

Through summer the *Queen of Prince Rupert* cruises to Skidegate on the Queen Charlotte Islands five or six times a week, less frequently the rest of the year. Departure times vary, but most often it's 11 A.M. from Prince Rupert (arriving Skidegate at 5:30 P.M.) and 11 P.M. from Skidegate (arriving Prince Rupert at 6 A.M.). Peak one-way fares: adult $25, child 5–11 $12.50, vehicle $93, kayak or canoe $7, bicycles $6. Discounts are offered to B.C. seniors. Cabins are available for $32–46.

Alaska Marine Highway

The Alaska Marine Highway operates an extensive network of ferries through southeastern Alaska and down to Prince Rupert. The first stop north from Prince Rupert is Ketchikan, six hours away. Walk-on passengers need not make reservations, but if you require a cabin or have a vehicle, make reservations as far in advance as possible (up to one year), especially for sailings between May and September.

Alaska Marine Highway ferries serving Prince Rupert include the *Taku, Matanuska,* and

Malaspina, which together offer sailings five to six times weekly. Each of the comfortable boats offers cabins, a cafeteria, restaurant, bar, lounge areas, and showers. If you don't want to pay the extra for a cabin, sleep in one of the many lounge areas or out on the back of the boat. You can even pitch a tent in the solarium if you want.

Sample one-way fares (in US$) from Prince Rupert are as follows: to Ketchikan—adult $42, child 2–11 $20, vehicle up to 15 feet $79, cabin from $42; to Juneau—adult $117, child 2–11 $59, vehicle up to 15 feet $254, cabin from $92; to Haines—adult $138, child 2–11 $68, vehicle up to 15 feet $298, cabin from $116.

Check-in time is three hours ahead of sailing time—it takes up to two hours to go through Customs and one hour to load up. Foot passengers must be there one hour ahead of sailing.

For reservations or schedule information, contact Alaska Marine Highway, P.O. Box 25535, Juneau, AK 99802-5535, 907/465-3940 or 800/642-0066, website www.dot.state.ak.us/external/amhs. You can also call the Prince Rupert terminal direct at 250/627-1744. This terminal and ticket office is open daily 9 A.M.–4 P.M. and for up to two hours before and after arrival and departure of vessels.

Getting Around

Local bus service along four routes is provided by **Prince Rupert Transit System,** 2nd Ave. W, 250/624-3343. Adult fare starts at $2. All-day passes cost $3 and are available from the driver. Have exact fare ready—drivers don't carry change. The only car-rental agencies in town are **Budget,** 250/627-7400, and **National,** 250/624-5318. For a cab call **Skeena Taxis,** 250/624-2185.

SERVICES AND INFORMATION

Prince Rupert Regional Hospital is south of downtown at 1305 Summit Ave., 250/624-2171. The **post office** is on 2nd Ave. at 3rd Street. **Laundromats** are at 226 7th St. and 745 2nd Ave. W.

The **library** is just off McBride Ave. at 101 6th Ave., 250/627-1345; an adjacent room provides public Internet access for a minimal charge. If you're looking for books, especially on B.C. native art or history, spend some time at **Star of the West Books and Gallery,** 518 3rd Ave. W, 250/624-9053. A gallery in the back of the store features local wildlife, native art, and photography. Hours are Mon.–Fri. 9 A.M.–9 P.M., Saturday 9 A.M.–6 P.M.

Prince Rupert Visitor Info Centre is in the museum complex at the corner of 1st Ave. and McBride St., 250/624-5637 or 800/667-1994, website www.tourismprincerupert.com. It's one of the best information centers around, with a knowledgeable staff and lots of printed material on Prince Rupert sights, walking tours, restaurants, services, and ferry schedules. Hours are Mon.–Sat. 9 A.M.–8 P.M. and Sunday 9 A.M.–5 P.M. from early June to early September, Mon.–Sat. 9 A.M.–5 P.M. the rest of the year. To search out local history, head to **Prince Rupert City & Regional Archives,** 100 1st Ave. E, 250/624-3326, which holds 20,000 historical photographs, charts, and books; open Mon.–Fri. 10 A.M.–3 P.M.

NORTHERN B.C.

Queen Charlotte Islands

Wild. Quiet. Mysterious. Primordial. The Queen Charlotte Islands spread like a large upside-down triangle approximately 100 km off the northwest coast of mainland British Columbia, 48 km south of Alaska. Of the chain's 150 mountainous and densely forested islands and islets, the main ones are **Graham Island** to the north and **Moresby Island** to the south, separated by narrow **Skidegate Channel.** The islands stretch 290 km from north to south and up to 85 km across at the widest spot. Running down the west side of the islands are the rugged **Queen Charlotte** and **San Christoval** ranges, which effectively protect the east side from Pacific battering. Nevertheless, the east coast, where most of the population lives, still receives over 1,000 mm of rain annually.

Life on the islands is very different from elsewhere in the province. Isolated from the mainland by stormy Hecate Strait, the 4,500 residents share an island camaraderie and laid-back, away-from-it-all temperament. Visitors can expect a friendly reception and adequate services. Motel-style accommodations are available in each town, but bed and breakfasts provide a closer glimpse of the island lifestyle. Groceries are also available, though choices can be limited. Gasoline is slightly more expensive than on the mainland, and raging nightlife is nonexistent.

Island Fauna

The only land mammal indigenous to the islands is the Queen Charlotte otter, a subspecies of the mainland otter. The world's largest black bears, estimated to number almost 10,000, call the Queen Charlottes home. Though they're a lot heftier than their mainland cousins, they're not a distinct subspecies. Their size comes from a short hibernation and a summer-long salmon feast. No grizzlies live on the islands, but black-tailed deer are common. They were introduced as a meat source and have multiplied many times over. Other mammals include elk (also introduced), squirrels, beavers, and muskrats.

Stare out to sea to spot killer whales, dolphins, seals, sea lions, otters, and tufted puffins. If you visit between late April and June, you might spot gray whales feeding in Hecate Strait on their way from Mexico to Alaska. The best place to whale-watch is along Skidegate Inlet near the museum or at the northernmost tip of Rose Spit.

The Haida

The Haida people have lived on the Queen Charlottes since time immemorial. Fearless warriors, expert hunters and fishermen, and skilled woodcarvers, they owned slaves and threw lavish potlatches. They had no written language, but they carved records of their tribal history, legends, and important events on totem poles ranging from three to 104 meters high. Living in villages scattered throughout the islands, they hunted sea otters for their luxuriant furs, fished for halibut and Pacific salmon, and collected chitons, clams, and seaweed from tidepools.

The first contact the Haida had with Europeans occurred in 1774, when Spanish explorer Juan Perez discovered the Charlottes. The islands weren't given a European name until 1787, when British captain George Dixon arrived and began trading with the Haida. He named the islands after his queen, the wife of George III. The whites gave the Haida goods, liquor, tools, blankets, and firearms in exchange for sea otter furs; over a 40-year period the otters were hunted

The Haida people have lived on the Queen Charlottes since time immemorial. Fearless warriors, expert hunters and fishermen, and skilled woodcarvers, they had no written language, but they carved records of their tribal history, legends, and important events on totem poles ranging from three to 104 meters high.

NORTHERN B.C.

Dixon Entrance

Langara Island

Cape Knox

To Prince Rupert

Rose Spit

Naden Harbour

McIntyre Bay

Old Massett

Masset

Tow Hill

Cape Fife

Graham Island

Naikoon Provincial Park

16

Eden Lake

Ian Lake

East Beach

Masset Inlet

Port Clements

HAIDA CANOE

Awun Lake

Juskatla

Tlell

CHARLOTTE MAIN

16

Rennell Sound

Skidegate Village

P A C I F I C

HAIDA GWAII MUSEUM
Queen Charlotte City

Skidegate

Sandspit

Skidegate Channel

Alliford Bay

Copper Bay

Gray Bay

Mosquito Lake

Skidegate Lake

Moresby Camp

Moresby

Louise Island

SKEDANS

Island

H e c a t e   S t r a i t

Tasu Sound

Tanu Island

TANU

Lyell Island

WINDY BAY

Hotspring Island

QUEEN CHARLOTTE ISLANDS

Gwaii Haanas

Burnaby Island

National Park

O C E A N

Reserve

NINSTINTS

Anthony Island

Kunghit Island

0   25 mi

0   25 km

© AVALON TRAVEL PUBLISHING, INC.

almost to extinction. In addition, the white traders brought European diseases that ravaged the Haida population.

At the turn of the 19th century, white settlers from the mainland began moving over to the Charlottes to live along the low-lying east coast and the protected shores of Masset Inlet. By the 1830s the traditional lifestyle of the Haida was coming to an end. The governments on the mainland prohibited the Haida from owning slaves and throwing potlatches—an important social and economic part of their culture—and forced all Haida children to attend missionary schools. The Haida abandoned their village sites and moved onto reserves at Skidegate and Masset on Graham Island.

Today totem poles are rising once again on the Queen Charlottes, as a renewed interest in Haida art and culture is compelling skilled elders to pass their knowledge on to younger generations. The first totem pole to be erected in 90 years was put up in 1969 in Masset, followed by one in 1978 at Skidegate. In 1986 a 50-foot dugout canoe, created out of a single huge cedar log, was commissioned for Vancouver's Expo86, and a second canoe was launched in Old Massett.

For many years the Haida struggled alongside the Island Protection Society to preserve their heritage. Their longtime efforts paid off in two major events: in 1981 the best-known of the abandoned Haida villages, **Ninstints,** was declared a UNESCO World Heritage Site, and in 1988 the southern section of the archipelago was proclaimed **Gwaii Haanas National Park Reserve.**

TRANSPORTATION

Air

The main gateway is Sandspit, where the small air terminal holds car rental agencies (book ahead) and an information center, and across the road is the Sandspit Inn. **Air B.C.,** 888/247-2262, flies daily between Vancouver and Sandspit. **Harbour Air,** 250/627-1341, offers daily service between Prince Rupert and Sandspit for around $200 each way. The Airporter bus meets all Sandspit flights and transports passengers to Queen Charlotte City for $14.

Ferry

In summer, **B.C. Ferries** operates the *Queen of Prince Rupert* between Prince Rupert and Skidegate five or six times a week, less frequently the rest of the year. Departure times vary, but most often it's 11 A.M. from Prince Rupert (arriving Skidegate at 5:30 P.M.) and 11 P.M. from Skidegate (arriving Prince Rupert at 6 A.M.). Peak oneway fares: adult $25, child $12.50, vehicle $93, kayak or canoe $7, bicycle $6. B.C. seniors get a discount, as do all travelers outside the peak summer season. Cabins are available for $32–46. For more information call B.C. Ferries, 250/386-3431 or, toll-free in B.C., 888/223-3779, website www.bcferries.com.

The ferry terminal is five km east of Queen Charlotte City at Skidegate. Taxis usually wait at the terminal when the ferry arrives; expect to pay around $12 to get into town.

Getting Around

A ferry connects Graham and Moresby Islands, departing hourly in each direction 7 A.M.–10 P.M.; peak round-trip fare is adult $4.75, child $2.50, vehicle $12. Apart from that, the islands have no public transportation. The least expensive car rentals are available at **Rustic Car Rentals** in Queen Charlotte City, 250/559-4641, which charges from $55 a day plus 20 cents a kilometer for the smallest vehicles. Both **Budget,** 250/637-5688, and **Thrifty,** 250/637-2299, have offices in Sandspit. Book well ahead.

To get around by floatplane, including to Gwaii Haanas National Park Reserve, call **South Moresby Air Charters,** 250/559-4222.

QUEEN CHARLOTTE CITY

Perched along the shores of Bearskin Bay, five km west of the dock for the mainland ferry, picturesque Queen Charlotte City is not really a city at all but a small laid-back fishing village of 1,100 people. Several heritage buildings in town date back to 1909; most of them are along the main road. For good photographic possibilities,

© ANDREW HEMPSTEAD

Many island homes and businesses are decorated with colorful buoys, driftwood, and just about anything that floats.

wander out onto the marina and look back at the village.

The town is also home to the Queen Charlotte division of **Weyerhaueser,** the logging giant that leases much of the land on Graham Island. In summer, the company runs a five-hour bus tour detailing all stages of logging. If you don't have your own transportation and don't mind a bit of pro-logging propaganda, the tour is a good way to see some of Moresby Island. Free tours (take your own food and drinks) depart from Port Clements Museum in summer only on Tuesday and Thursday at 9 A.M. Book at 250/557-4212.

Accommodations and Camping

Queen Charlotte City is a good base for exploring the islands and has a wide variety of accommodations. Built in 1910, the old Premier Hotel has been totally renovated and now operates as **Premier Creek Lodging,** along the main drag at

3101 3rd Ave., 250/559-8415 or 888/322-3388, offering beds to suit all budgets. In the main lodge, single "sleeping rooms" with shared facilities cost $30 per person, but definitely worth the extra money are the rooms with private bathrooms, balconies, and harbor views (some with kitchens) for $65 s, $75 d. Behind the main lodge is the simple **Premier Creek Hostel** (same telephone numbers as the lodge). It has two four-bed dorms and one double room, a kitchen, living room, laundry, gas barbecue, and bike rentals ($30 per day); rates are $18 per person per night.

A few doors east of Premier Creek Lodging is rustic **Gracie's Place,** 3113 3rd Ave., 250/559-4262, website www.gracies-place.com, a delightful islands-style accommodation. Decorated with sea treasures and flowering plants, the five cozy guest rooms each have their own toilet, shower, and entrance. Rates are $50 s, $60 d for the two standard rooms, $80 s or d for one of the two kitchen-equipped units, and $125 for the two-bedroom suite.

Dorothy and Mike's Guest House, 3125 2nd Ave., 250/559-8439, features gardens and water views, use of a kitchen, and a cooked breakfast— all for $45 s, $55–75 d. **Spruce Point Lodging,** 609 6th Ave., 250/559-8234, has a great downtown location with superb water views and offers bed-and-breakfast lodging for $60 s, $70 d.

The motels in town may lack the atmosphere of the above accommodations, but they offer higher-standard rooms and more amenities. Try **Sea Raven Motel,** 3301 3rd Ave., 250/559-4423 or 800/665-9606, website www.searaven.com, overlooking the water and a seafood restaurant downstairs. Summer rates are from $65 s, $85 d.

Haydn Turner Park, through town to the west, has toilets, picnic tables, and fire rings for campers, but no showers or hookups; $8 per night.

Food

The place to go for breakfast is **Margaret's Cafe,** 3223 Wharf St., 250/559-4204. All the locals congregate here. In addition to water views, this place has plenty of atmosphere, and the food is good and plentiful for the price (cooked breakfasts from $6.50), but be prepared to wait for a table. It's open Mon.–Sat. 6:30 A.M.–3 P.M., Sunday 8 A.M.–3 P.M. For something more substantial, head to **Hummingbird Cafe,** in the Sea Raven Motel at 3301 3rd Ave., 250/559-8583. Specializing in local seafood, the Hummingbird is open nightly from 6 P.M. Another local favorite for seafood is **Claudette's Place,** corner 3rd Ave. and 2nd St., 250/559-8861. It's on the pricey side—most entrées run $17–22. Open daily 9 A.M.–10 P.M. The **Oceana Restaurant,** 3119 3rd Ave., 250/559-8633, specializes in Chinese dishes, and the service is fast and friendly.

Services and Information

Emergency services in Queen Charlotte City include **Queen Charlotte Islands General Hospital,** 3209 3rd Ave., 250/559-4300, and the **RCMP,** 250/559-4421. The **post office** and a **laundromat** are in the City Centre Building off 2nd Avenue. For island and North Coast litera-ture, head to **Bill Ellis Books,** 720 Hwy. 33, 250/559-4681. **Rainbows Gallery,** 3201 3rd Ave., 250/559-8420, also sells books, along with a good selection of locally crafted souvenirs.

Queen Charlotte Visitor Info Centre, down on the waterfront at 3220 Wharf St., 250/559-8316, offers natural history displays, a wide variety of brochures and information on everything that's going on around the islands, and current weather forecasts. Don't leave without buying a copy of the latest edition of the *Guide to the Queen Charlotte Islands,* which includes maps, details on all the villages, and more—all for $4.95. The center is open June–Aug. daily 10 A.M.–7 P.M., and in May and September daily 10 A.M.–2 P.M. The information center website, www.qcinfo.com, is updated infrequently; instead, search out the islands' Internet service provider, website www.qcislands.net, and click through the links to most local businesses.

NORTH TO PORT CLEMENTS

From Queen Charlotte City, Graham Island's main road follows the eastern coastline past the ferry terminal and Haida Gwaii Museum to the Haida community of Skidegate Village, from where it's a pleasant 65 km coastal drive to Port Clements.

Haida Gwaii Museum

While totem poles and other ancient Haida art can be seen in various places around the islands, this museum on the north side of the Skidegate Landing ferry terminal allows visitors the opportunity to see a variety of such art under one roof. Inside are striking Haida wood and argillite carvings, pioneer artifacts, a beautiful woven blanket, jewelry, historic black-and-white photos, stunning prints by Haida artist Robert Davidson, ancient totems from Tanu and Skedans dating to 1878, the skull of a humpback whale, shells galore, and a collection of stuffed birds. The museum is open in summer Mon.–Fri. 10 A.M.–5 P.M., Sat.–Sun. 1–5 P.M.; closed Sunday and Tuesday the rest of the year. Admission is $4. For further information call 250/559-4643.

NORTHERN B.C.

When you leave the museum, be sure to wander up the road and visit the longhouse-style **cedar carving shed,** where the fantastic 15-meter-long canoe *Loo Taas* (which means "Wave Eater") is housed. The striking red-and-black vessel was commissioned for Expo86 in Vancouver, after which it was paddled to the Queen Charlottes.

Between late April and early June, migrating **gray whales** rest and feed on shallow gravel bars of Skidegate Inlet in front of the museum on their annual 15,000-km odyssey between Mexico and Alaska. Behind the museum a wooden deck overlooking the water is a great vantage point for watching these magnificent creatures, or continue a few hundred yards farther around the bay and search them out from the roadside.

Skidegate Village and Vicinity

Continuing north from the museum you'll soon come to Skidegate Village, a Haida reserve of 700 residents. A weathered totem pole, over 100 years old, still stands here, and a new totem—this one carved by Haida artist Bill Reid—stands in front of the longhouse facing the beach. The longhouse is the Skidegate Haida Band Council House, where local artisans fashion miniature totem poles, argillite ornaments, and jewelry in traditional designs. Cross the road from the local rec center to the trailhead of a hiking trail to **Spirit Lake.** The trail passes through an old-growth forest of hemlock, Sitka spruce, and red cedar and passes two picturesque bodies of water, one with picnic tables. The round-trip is three km, an easy hour's walk.

From Skidegate, the road follows the shoreline of Hecate Strait, past driftwood-strewn beaches, an attractive old graveyard, and **Balance Rock,** one km north of Skidegate Village. A highway sign and turnout mark the start of a short trail down to the rock. Continuing north, the scenery becomes rural, as the road skirts land cleared by early settlers for cattle-grazing; watch for black-tailed deer in this area. Near **Lawn Hill** look for tree stumps that have been carved into the shapes of animals and birds.

Tlell

This small ranching community is the northernmost settlement on the east coast before the road swings inland toward Port Clements and Masset. Sandwiched between the Tlell River and the beach, Tlell has recently become a haven for artisans; look for signs pointing the way to their outlets, which are concentrated on Richardson Road off Wiggins Road. The Tlell River is favored by local anglers for its huge runs of coho salmon and steelhead.

Tlell River House, on Beitush Rd., 250/557-4211 or 800/667-8906, overlooks the river and is a short walk from the beach. Basic rooms go for $75 s, $80 d; downstairs is a good restaurant.

Naikoon Provincial Park (Southern End)

Just north of Tlell is the southern tip of Naikoon Provincial Park. While the park's main entrance is farther north out of Masset (see the full listing below), visitors exploring the Tlell area will find interesting things to see and do here in the park's south end as well. The main attraction down here is the wreck of the *Pezuta,* a wooden log barge that ran aground in 1928. To get there, park at the picnic area on the north side of the Tlell River and follow the river to its mouth, then walk north along the beach. It's about nine km (2.5 hours) each way. Keen hikers may want to attempt the **East Beach Hike,** a 94-km trail that leads all the way north from the Tlell River to Tow Hill via Rose Spit. For trail and other park details, stop in at **park headquarters** beside the highway in Tlell, 250/557-4390. **Misty Meadows Campground,** immediately north of park headquarters, is uncrowded and costs only $12 per site for one of 40 scenic campsites. Facilities include a picnic area and pit toilets.

Port Clements

Weatherbeaten houses decorated with driftwood, shells, fishing floats, and other seawashed treasures line the streets of this logging and fishing village on the northeast shore of Masset Inlet. **Port Clements Museum,** on Bayview Dr., 250/557-4443, houses an intriguing selection of pioneer artifacts and relics from the village, as well as

NORTHERN B.C.

black-and-white photos of logging camps and early village life. It's open through summer daily 1–5 P.M., weekends only the rest of the year.

Charlotte Main

This rough logging road links Port Clements to Queen Charlotte City via an inland route, a good alternative to returning via Tlell. To get to it, take Bayview Drive southwest out of Port Clements. Twelve km from town, a short trail leads through the forest to a **Haida canoe.** Many unfinished cedar canoes lie in the bush, but this is the only one that can be easily reached. The road soon passes through **Juskatla,** an old logging camp established in the 1940s to supply Queen Charlottes spruce for World War II airplanes. Here you'll find the start of the Charlotte Main logging road, as well as the main office for the MacMillan Bloedel logging company. The company actively logs off Charlotte Main, so travel along the road is safest outside of operating hours (Mon.–Fri. 6:30 A.M.–5:30 P.M.).

From Juskatla, the logging road continues south to Queen Charlotte City. A turnoff to the west (signposted) leads to **Rennell Sound,** the only point on the remote west coast accessible by road. At the end of the road await great beachcombing opportunities and free primitive campsites. The final descent to the shore is a

BEACHCOMBING ON THE CHARLOTTES

Beachcombing on the Queen Charlotte Islands is popular year-round, but it's especially good after heavy winter storms. You may find fishing floats from countries around the Pacific (glass balls from Japan are especially prized), bottles, rope, driftwood, shells, whale bones, semiprecious agate, or just about anything that floats. A few years back, a container of Nike runners broke apart somewhere in the Pacific; they were found scattered on beaches throughout the Charlottes and as far south as the Oregon coast. Before that, an abandoned fishing boat from Japan washed ashore and caused excitement; it's now on display in Prince Rupert.

hair-raising 24 percent gradient, one of the steepest public roads in North America.

MASSET AND VICINITY

Originally named Graham City, Masset (pop. 900) is the oldest town on the Queen Charlottes. The Graham Steamship, Coal, and Lumber Company founded the settlement in 1909, a few km east of a Haida community named Massett. Over time, Massett became known as Old Massett or Haida, and Graham City was incorporated as Masset (with one "t"). The population has decreased since downsizing began on the local Canadian Armed Forces Station, where at one time half the local population lived. Today, Masset's economy revolves around the ocean, with most workers involved in the fishing industry—either as fishermen or as workers in the local crab cannery or fish-freezing plant.

As you enter town from the south, passing the information center and seaplane base, continue straight ahead to reach Naikoon Provincial Park, or cross Delkatla Inlet for downtown Masset and Old Massett.

Town Sights

Masset makes a good base from which to explore the beautiful surrounding area and Naikoon Provincial Park, but there's not much to do in town. You might want to stroll around to see the **heritage buildings,** including the old schoolhouse and hospital, both on Collison Avenue, or head down to **government wharf,** where some interesting activity is almost always going on: boats coming and going, fishermen loading supplies or unloading their catch.

Delkatla Wildlife Sanctuary

Bordering Masset to the east is Delkatla Wildlife Sanctuary, where you can observe Canada geese, sandhill cranes, trumpeter swans, great blue herons, many varieties of ducks, and other waterfowl resting during migration. Several short walking trails wind through the preserve near town; follow Hodges Avenue west onto Trumpeter Drive and continue alongside the inlet to the trailhead. For better views, drive along Tow

Hill Road toward Naikoon Provincial Park, turning left at the sanctuary sign onto Masset Cemetery Road. Along this road, more signs mark trails or other points of interest. You first pass a turnout for the **Bird Walk Trail,** which winds along the edge of a marshy area for 500 meters. Then farther down the road, you come to **Simpson Viewing Tower.** The trail to the tower leads through a wide open meadow and marshes dotted with wildflowers, and the top of the lofty perch makes an excellent spot to watch the preserve's abundant waterfowl. You might also spy bald eagles, peregrine falcons, and other birds of prey, as well as four-legged marsh animals such as muskrats.

Back on Tow Hill Road, continue east to a parking lot and a trail to the beach. Just across from the parking lot is beautiful **Masset Cemetery,** where the graves are marked by large aboveground mounds of moss planted with flowering bulbs and surrounded by bushes and trees. It's a peaceful place to ponder the beauty of the Charlottes.

Old Massett

If you're in search of Haida treasures, head for the village of Old Massett, also known as Haida. It's just a five-minute drive from Masset, west down the coastal road. Go as far as the road takes you and you'll end up at the old blue schoolhouse, now **Ed Jones Haida Museum.** Inside, exhibits include a large collection of fascinating old photographs showing how the villages used to look, Haida art and prints, and some of the original totem poles from around the Queen Charlottes. Outside you'll find a partly completed canoe and a field sprinkled with more totems, these from a more recent era. The museum is open in summer Sat.–Sun. 9 A.M.–5 P.M.; admission by donation. Across from the museum is a carving shed where artists can be seen working throughout summer.

Continue up behind the museum to **Adams Family House of Silver,** 250/626-3215, to view or buy carved-wood items and silver jewelry directly from the artist (who also has a fantastic Haida print collection). It's open daily 10 A.M.–noon and 1–6 P.M. Next door, the impressive weathered building with the tall totem pole

out front is **Haida Arts and Jewellery,** 250/626-5560, open Mon.–Sat. 11 A.M.–5 P.M., Sunday noon–5 P.M. Here you can buy custom argillite carvings, silk-screen prints, handcrafted silver and abalone jewelry, books on native culture, printed sweatshirts, and greeting cards.

Langara Island

Langara Island, at the northwestern tip of the archipelago, is a rugged and remote place with wooded slopes ending at a rocky shoreline. A couple of small native villages, two lodges, and a beautifully restored 1913 lighthouse are the only human intrusions. The main attraction here is the salmon and halibut fishing; the provincial record-setting halibut, a 320-pounder, was pulled from local waters. Fishing is best April–Sept., when anglers book up the island's **Langara Fishing Lodge** and the newer **Langara Island Lodge.** The same company operates both, flying clients in on charter flights from Vancouver; from $3,195 and $3,675, respectively, for four days. For details call 604/232-5532 or 800/668-7544, website www.langara.com.

On the mainland, across a narrow strait from the island, are the abandoned Haida villages of Kiusta and Yaku, where some of the earliest contacts occurred between native Haida and whites. Access is difficult by boat because of often-rough seas.

Accommodations and Camping

Several B&Bs in Masset provide lodgings and local flavor. **Harbourview Lodging,** 1608 Delkatla St., 250/626-5109 or 800/661-3314, provides pleasant rooms (one with a view of the fishing pier) and a sauna, communal kitchen, and laundry. Rooms with shared bathrooms are $50 s or d, ensuites $75, including a light breakfast. Rustic **Copper Beech House,** next to the pier at 1590 Delkatla Rd., 250/626-5441, is decorated with sea treasures and has a beautiful flower garden. Rates of $60–80 per room include a delicious breakfast prepared by the enthusiastic host. **Alaska View Lodge,** east from Masset on Tow Hill Rd., 250/626-3333 or 800/661-0019, website www.alaskaviewlodge.com, is right on the beach and backed by dense temperate rainforest. Accommodations in the main building share bath-

NORTHERN B.C.

rooms and range $50–60 s, $70–80 d, depending on the view. Closer to the beach, two rooms in the "Guesthouse" feature practical beach furniture and a joined deck; $70 s, $90 d.

The only motel right in Masset is the 30-room **Singing Surf Inn,** 1504 Old Beach Rd., 250/626-3318, with large rooms and a restaurant and bar downstairs; $82 s, $92 d.

Village of Masset RV Site and Campground is on Tow Hill Rd. two km north of Masset, opposite the Delkatla Wildlife Sanctuary. The campground features large, fairly private campsites with tables among the trees, and washrooms with coin-operated hot showers. Unserviced sites are $11, powered sites $17. Another option for campers is to continue 20 km along the road into Naikoon Provincial Park (see below).

Food
Even though Masset has a large fishing fleet, most of the catch ends up in mainland canneries. Your best choice for seafood is **Cafe Gallery,** on the corner of Collison Ave. and Orr St., 250/626-3672, where the daily lunch specials are around $9 and dinner entrées range $14–20. The menu also includes steak, chateaubriand, and pasta dishes. Open Mon.–Sat. 8:30 A.M.–9 P.M.

Pearl's, on the corner of Main St. and Collison Ave., 250/626-3223, features Chinese cuisine in an almost hospital-like atmosphere. For around $12 you can get an enormous helping of chicken and vegetables in black bean sauce, along with a large bowl of steamed rice, tea, and the mandatory fortune cookie. Open Mon.–Sat. for lunch and daily for dinner. Head to **High Tide Cappuccino Bar,** Delkatla Rd., for coffee and cakes along with water views and a casual atmosphere.

Information
Masset Visitor Info Centre is beside the main road as you come into town from the south, 250/626-3982 or 888/352-9292. It's open mid-May through mid-September daily 9 A.M.–4 P.M.

NAIKOON PROVINCIAL PARK

This spectacular park encompasses some 72,640 hectares along the northeast tip of Graham Island. Tlell marks the park's southern boundary, while access to the northern reaches is via the road out to Tow Hill, 26 km east of Masset. The park's dominant features are its beaches, 97 kilometers of them, bordering Hecate Strait on the east and the turbulent Dixon Entrance on the north. Most of the rest of the park is lowlands, surrounded by stunted lodgepole pine, red and yellow cedar, western hemlock, and Sitka spruce. Wildlife is abundant; black-tailed deer, black bear, marten, river otter, raccoons, red squirrels, beaver, muskrat, small herds of wild cattle, and many species of birds inhabit the park. Dolphins, orcas, harbor porpoises, and hair seals swim offshore year-round, and northern fur seals and California gray whales migrate north past the park in May and June.

Sights
The drive out to the park from Masset is superb, passing through kilometer after kilometer of moss-draped trees. Along the way you pass **Tow Hill Ecological Reserve,** a beautiful spruce forest where birds tweet from the treetops and the ground and most of the trees are completely cushioned by spongy yellow moss.

The road passes the base of Tow Hill and ends at the southern end of long, sandy **North Beach.** This strip of sand is a beachcomber's delight, as it is strewn with shells, driftwood, and shiny, sea-worn pebbles of every color under the sun (the beach is best known for semiprecious agate, which is found among piles of pebbles that become exposed at low tide starting about three km along the beach. Continue along North Beach to **Rose Spit.** Known to the Haida as Naikoon, meaning "Long Nose," this narrow five-km-long point of land separates the waters of Hecate Strait and Dixon Entrance. It's about 10 km (three hours) one-way to the spit. Head in the other direction, along the shores of McIntyre Bay, and scramble over the rocks at the base of 130-meter-high **Tow Hill** to find more treasures and small sea creatures in the tidepools. Here you might see bald eagles soaring on the updrafts caused by the near-vertical cliffs.

© ANDREW HEMPSTEAD

a victim of the sea, Naikoon Provincial Park

Cape Fife Trail

From near the end of the park access road, the Cape Fife Trail (three hours each way) heads in a southeasterly direction, passing boglands and stunted pine trees on its 10-km route to **Fife Point,** overlooking Hecate Strait. The shore above the high-tide line is blanketed by a mass of driftwood logs, crushed together during the fierce storms that regularly lash this coast. A rough shelter at the end of the trail provides some protection from the elements. Backcountry camping is permitted; hide among the trees on especially windy days. From this point you can hike north along the beach to Rose Spit, at the northeastern tip of the Charlottes, then continue back along North Beach to the parking lot at Hiellen River—a total of 34 km and an easy two-day trip. Well-equipped adventurers can continue south from Fife Point along **East Beach** to finish at Tlell, a total distance of 72 km. This has become a popular hike—take your

time (allow 4–5 days) and bring adequate food and water.

Practicalities

Agate Beach Campground is near Tow Hill, about 26 km from Masset. The campsites lie along the back of the beach and offer outstanding views. A shelter and pit toilets are provided, but no showers. In summer you need to nab a spot early in the day—by late afternoon they're all taken. The campground is open year-round. Sites cost $12 per night May–Sept.; the rest of the year they're free. The **park headquarters,** 250/847-7320, and another campground are to the south at Tlell (see North to Port Clements, above).

SANDSPIT AND VICINITY

Across Skidegate Channel from Queen Charlotte City, Sandspit (pop. 450) is the only com-

NORTHERN B.C.

munity on Moresby Island. It occupies a low-lying, windswept spit overlooking Shingle Bay, 15 km east of the ferry dock. The rest of the island is wilderness. The northern half is largely given over to logging and holds remote logging camps. The southern half and over 100 outlying islands fall within Gwaii Haanas National Park Reserve (see below), which protects a high concentration of abandoned Haida villages.

Through town is **Willows Golf Course,** a windswept, nine-hole course on a coastal strip of land originally cleared for farming; greens fees are $15 and club rentals are available.

Into the Bush

Those determined to tour the forests in their own vehicle can make an enjoyable loop trip south out of Sandspit. Logging roads lace the forest, leading to beaches strewn with driftwood, streams alive with salmon and steelhead, and beautiful Skidegate and Mosquito Lakes (good trout fishing). Free campgrounds are available at Gray Bay and Mosquito Lake. Pick up a local map from any island information center.

Accommodations and Camping

Sandspit lacks the appeal of communities on Graham Island, but services are available. **Seaport B&B,** 371 Alliford Bay Rd., 250/637-5698, features three basic rooms in a waterfront home. Rates of $30 s, $40 d include a self-serve breakfast and use of kitchen facilities. Friendly **Moresby Island Guest House,** 385 Alliford Bay Rd., 250/637-5300, is a popular kayakers' hangout offering rooms with shared baths and kitchens; $30 s, $65–70 d, including a light breakfast and use of a laundry. **Sandspit Inn,** across from the airport, 250/637-5334, charges from $80 s, $90 d, and has Sandspit's only restaurant and bar.

Campgrounds are at **Gray Bay** and **Mosquito Lake** (named after the Mosquito airplane,

Ancient brooding totems and remnants of mighty Haida longhouses stand against a backdrop of lush wilderness—dense trees, thick spongy moss, and rock-strewn beaches with incredibly clear water. Colonies of nesting seabirds and an abundance of marinelife add to the atmosphere.

not the pesky insects), both on the logging roads detailed above.

Services and Information

Sandspit Airport, the main airport for the Queen Charlotte Islands, is on the east side of town beside Hecate Strait. It's served by **Air B.C.,** 888/247-2262, and **Harbour Air,** 250/637-5350. The **Airporter** bus meets all flights, transporting passengers to Queen Charlotte City for $14 per person. **Budget,** 250/637-5688, and **Thrifty,** 250/637-2299, have car rental agencies in Sandspit.

Sandspit Visitor Info Centre is a small desk inside the airport terminal, 250/637-5362. It's open in summer daily 9 A.M.–6 P.M. and for all flight arrivals.

GWAII HAANAS NATIONAL PARK RESERVE

Renowned around the world for its ancient Haida villages dotted with totem poles, this park encompasses the southern half of Moresby Island as well as 137 smaller islands in the south of the archipelago—a total of 1,480 hectares of land and 1,600 km of coastline. It's a remarkable place. Ancient brooding totems and remnants of mighty Haida longhouses stand against a backdrop of lush wilderness—dense trees, thick spongy moss, and rock-strewn beaches with incredibly clear water. Colonies of nesting seabirds and an abundance of marinelife—killer and minke whales, sea lions, tufted puffins—all add to the atmosphere.

Jointly managed by Parks Canada and the Haida nation, the park was established in 1988 after a long, bitter struggle between the Haida and forestry companies. The area now protected was home to seafaring Haida for almost 10,000 years, but by the early 1900s, less than 100 years after their first contact with whites, their communities were abandoned, the inhabitants having been

NORTHERN B.C.

wiped out by disease or having moved to Old Massett and Skidegate. More than 500 historic sites were left behind—from burial grounds to entire villages.

Ninstints, on tiny Anthony Island near the south end of the park, is the world's best-preserved totem village. Anthony Island was declared a UNESCO World Heritage Site in 1981, just 97 years after the last Haida families had abandoned their remote home. **Hotspring Island,** site of another village, holds hot springs and unique flora. Other well-known villages include **Skedans** (closest to Sandspit), **Tanu,** and **Windy Bay.**

Park Practicalities

The only access to the park is by air or sea. Before heading in you need to reserve a permit through Tourism BC, 250/387-1642 or 800/435-5622 ($15 per booking). A limited number of permits are issued for each day, and a few spots are left open on a standby basis. These can be claimed at the Queen Charlotte Visitor Info Centre (in Queen Charlotte City) at 8 A.M. on the day of departure. Either way, you must also purchase the permit itself ($10 pp per day) and participate in an orientation session; these are held at the Queen Charlotte Visitor Info Centre daily at 8 A.M. and 7:30 P.M.

All of the above is irrelevant if, like most visitors, you travel as part of a guided tour (although the operator will charge you the permit fee). **Moresby Explorers,** 250/637-2215 or 800/806-7633, website www.moresbyexplorers.com, and **Queen Charlotte Adventures,** 250/559-8990 or 800/668-4288, both offer guided kayak trips and can also provide drop-offs and pick-ups for those heading into the park unguided. Costs range $130 per person for a day trip to Skedans to $650 for a four-day trip to Ninstints.

Oceanlight II Adventures, 604/328-5339, website www.oceanlight2.bc.ca, has been conducting sailing trips through the south end of the archipelago since well before the proclamation of a park. Board the company's 71-foot *Ocean Light II* for eight days of sailing, visiting all the best-known abandoned Haida villages, exploring the waterways, and searching out land and sea mammals. All meals and accommodations aboard the boat are included in the rate of $2,650 per person.

South Moresby Air Charters, at the wharf in Queen Charlotte City, 250/559-4222, offers flightseeing trips to the park, including visits to Ninstints and the hot springs. Rates start at $350 per hour of flying time plus $50 for each hour of waiting time.

The Stewart-Cassiar Highway

An alternative to the Alaska Highway, this route turns off the Yellowhead Highway 45 km west of New Hazelton and leads north to the Yukon, joining the Alaska Highway just west of Watson Lake. The route opens up a magnificent area of northern wilderness that in many ways rivals that along the more famous Alaska Highway.

The highlight of the Stewart-Cassiar Highway is definitely the side trip west to the twin coastal villages of **Stewart** and **Hyder.** But the route also passes the remote river town of **Telegraph Creek** and jumping-off points for various wilderness adventures.

From the Yellowhead Highway it's 155 km north to Meziadin Junction, then 65 km west to Stewart, official beginning of the Stewart-Cassiar Highway. Total length of the trip between the Yellowhead and Alaska Highways is 733 km. Add another 130 km round-trip for the jaunt out to Stewart.

Be Prepared

The highway is mainly paved, but improved gravel sections are found on the 80-km stretch north of Meziadin Junction, the 40-km stretch south of Kinaskan Lake, and for around 30 km each side of Dease Lake. Be prepared for washboard conditions on these sections, especially after heavy rain. Dust and mud can also be problematic, and many narrow, one-lane bridges call for extra caution.

Gas stations and services can be found along the highway, but it's not a bad idea to fill up

© ANDREW HEMPSTEAD

lakeside camping along the Stewart-Cassiar Highway

NORTHERN B.C.

with gas wherever and whenever you get the opportunity. And to be on the safe side, take spare tires, belts, hoses, bailing wire, a strong adhesive, and spare parts. In summer, lots of RVs and logging trucks take this route, so if you do get stranded it shouldn't be too long before someone comes along.

FROM YELLOWHEAD HIGHWAY TO MEZIADIN JUNCTION

Tree-covered hills, dense patches of snow-white daisies, banks of pink-and-white clover and purple lupine, craggy mountains and distant peaks, beautiful lakes covered in yellow water lilies, and lots of logging trucks flying along the road—these are images of the 155 km between the Yellowhead Highway and Meziadin Junction, the turnoff to Stewart.

Kitwanga

This small village just north of the Yellowhead Highway is home to **Kitwanga Fort National Historic Site,** the first national historic site commemorating native culture in western Canada. The site protects 13-meter-high Battle Hill, where 200 years ago a native warrior named Nekt fought off attacks from hostile neighbors. A trail leads from the parking lot down to the flat area around the bottom of the hill, where you can read display panels describing the hill's history. The site is on Kitwanga Valley Road, overlooking the Kitwanga River, and is open year-round; admission free.

Kitwancool Totem Poles

Continuing north, you're paralleling what was commonly called the Grease Trail, the route coastal natives took to the interior to trade their greasy oolichans (minuscule fish) with other tribes. At the native village of Kitwancool, 25 km from Kitwanga, is an outstanding group of totem poles, most more than 100 years old. The oldest, "Hole in the Ice," is approximately 140 years old; some say it's the oldest standing totem pole in the world. It tells the story of a man preventing his people from starving by chopping a hole in the ice and doing a spot of ice fishing.

Meziadin Junction toward Stewart

At the junction is a gas station and a small information center, open July–Aug. only. Just south of the junction is 335-hectare **Meziadin Lake Provincial Park,** along the northeast shore of Meziadin Lake, two km from the highway. It's open June–Oct. and has a boat launch, pit toilets, and mostly gravel campsites, some on the lake's edge; $12 per night May–September.

From Meziadin Junction, Stewart is 65 km west along a spectacular stretch of highway that crosses the glaciated Coast Mountains. The first 40 km is all uphill, through thick subalpine forests and past lakes, waterfalls, and a string of glaciers sitting like thick icy slabs atop almost-vertical mountains. Suddenly, and quite unexpectedly, the highway rounds a corner and there in front of you is magnificent, eggshell-blue **Bear Glacier.** The glacier tumbles down into deep blue **Strohn Lake,** where large icebergs float across the surface in the breeze. From Bear Glacier it's downhill all the way to Stewart. Keep an eye out for three mighty waterfalls on the north side of the highway, one after another. One plummets down into a large buildup of ice, complete with blue ice cave. This stretch of road is good for wildlife-viewing; numerous mountain goats wander the hillsides, and black bears nose around the avalanche slopes in search of their next meal.

STEWART

The twin towns of Stewart, British Columbia, and Hyder, Alaska, straddle the international boundary at the headwaters of **Portland Inlet,** the world's fourth-longest fjord. Canada's most northerly ice-free port, Stewart (pop. 800) enjoys a stunning setting; snowcapped peaks rise over 2,000 meters from the surrounding fjord.

Two brothers, Robert and John Stewart, were the first permanent settlers at the head of Portland Canal, arriving shortly after the turn of the 20th century. Prospecting through the surrounding mountains, they came across incredible wealth. Word got out, and by 1910 Stewart's population had boomed to 10,000. The main street was lined with busy shops, the city had four daily newspapers, and at least

NORTHERN B.C.

every second day a steamer loaded with new arrivals and supplies would dock at one of two long wharves. But the boom was short-lived, especially after the Grand Trunk Pacific Railway decided to build its western terminus at Prince Rupert. By the end of World War I the population had dwindled to 20.

Stewart has seen its fortunes decline since the closure of the Granduc copper mine. The mine, northwest of town (through Hyder, but back within British Columbia; see The Road to Salmon Glacier, below), began operations in 1964, drilling a record 16-km-long tunnel into the Coast Mountains. The mining operation was not without its problems. During the initial year of operations, an avalanche killed 27 workers. And financial difficulties forced the mine's closure in the mid-1980s. Today, what's left of the local economy revolves around the timber industry, which uses the local port facilities to transport logs to southern markets.

To get the lowdown on the town's interesting past, head to **Stewart Historical Society Museum,** in the original city hall on Columbia St. between 6th and 7th Streets, 250/636-2568. Displays include a tool collection and exhibits on the town's boom-and-bust mining industry. It's open in summer daily 9:30 A.M.–4:30 P.M.

Practicalities

King Edward Hotel, on 5th Ave., 250/636-2244 or 800/663-3126, offers basic rooms for $65 s, $75 d. Across the road is the affiliated **King Edward Motel** (register at the hotel), where rooms are of a similar standard but are slightly larger and have kitchenettes; $75 s, $85 d.

Nestled below the towering peaks of the Coast Mountains at the back of town is **Rainey Creek Campground,** on 8th Ave., 250/636-2537. Facilities are basic, and you need quarters for the showers; $13–18 a night. If this place is full, continue through town to Hyder, where you'll find two more campgrounds.

The small but ever-busy **Brothers Bakery,** on 5th Ave., serves delicious cakes and breads at reasonable prices. Next door in an old three-story building is **Bitter Creek Cafe,** 250/636-2166, serving light meals at lunchtime. The only place open for dinner is the restaurant in the **King Edward Hotel,** 250/636-2244, but it's nothing special. Also in the hotel is a coffee shop, which is where the locals head for breakfast.

Stewart Visitor Info Centre overlooks the mudflats at the north end of 5th Ave., 250/636-9224 or 888/366-5999. The staff offers a wealth of local information, including directions out to Salmon Glacier, hiking-trail brochures, and history sheets. It's open mid-May through mid-September daily 8:30 A.M.–7 P.M. The main street (5th Ave.) also holds a grocery store, drugstore, post office, bank, and laundromat.

STEWART AND HYDER: SOME QUICK FACTS

The twin towns of Stewart (Canada) and Hyder (United States) are separated by an international border, but you'd hardly know it. Crossing into Hyder comes without any of the formalities or checkpoints you'd expect at a border, and upon re-entering Canada, an ATCO trailer serves as the port of entry (until the mid-1990s there were no border checks at all), mostly in place to check for cheap U.S. booze purchased at the Hyder liquor store.

Residents of Both Towns:
• send their kids to school in Canada;
• are supplied power by B.C. Hydro;
• use the Canadian phone system (area code 250);
• are policed by the RCMP;
• never have to wait for a drink—Hyder has one bar for every 30 residents.

Notes for the Traveler:
• buy your booze in Hyder—it's cheaper (but is only tax-free if you have been in town for more than 48 hours);
• use Canadian currency in both towns;
• post your mail on whichever side of the border saves the cost of international postage;
• bring your passport—border checks are made when re-entering Canada and when arriving or departing by ferry;
• don't miss the drive to Salmon Glacier.

HYDER AND VICINITY

Continue through Stewart along the Portland Canal and, next thing you know, you're in Hyder, Alaska, U.S.A. (pop. 90)—without all the formalities and checkpoints you'd expect at an international border. The "Friendliest little ghost town in Alaska" is a classic end-of-the-road town, its main drag lined with a motley assortment of buildings, some boarded up.

Settled by prospectors in the late 1890s, Hyder was called Portland City until the U.S. Postal Authority told residents there were too many cities already named Portland. The town thrived for many years, but today few of the original structures remain. Fires destroyed much of the old town, and no one ever bothered to rebuild. The most recent fire was the night before the 1995 Fourth of July celebrations. Fireworks stored for the occasion in the back of the fire hall exploded, burning that building to the ground and preventing locals from getting to the fire truck to stop the library and post office from suffering a similar fate.

Glacier Inn

At one time Hyder boasted over 20 bars; today, amazingly, three remain, each licensed to be open 23 hours a day. They serve a population of 90 residents, as well as Stewart locals and travelers keen to reach the end of the road. Oldest and best known is the **Glacier Inn,** an almost windowless two-story wooden structure on the main drag. Join the tradition and tack a bill to the wall to ensure that you won't return broke, then toss back a shot of 190-proof, pure grain alcohol ($2.50) in one swallow to qualify for your "I've been Hyderized" card.

Behind the inn are the mudflats that once held the bulk of Hyder's early buildings. Wander along the dike and onto the long wharf for views back across town and to the snowcapped mountains beyond.

Fish Creek

Turn right at the end of Hyder's main street and follow the gravel road through town and along the Salmon River. Several kilometers beyond, at

Fish Creek Viewing Platform, you can watch bears fishing and feasting at the all-you-can-eat salmon buffet. Generally, black bears arrive earliest, usually around the end of July. During August brown bears (called grizzlies in the interior) move down from higher elevations to feed. This is a unique opportunity to watch a number of bears at once—one that costs many hundreds of dollars in southwestern Alaska—but keep your distance. Forest service staff are on hand to keep the crowds away from the bears, but they also love talking about "their" bears.

The Road to Salmon Glacier

From Fish Creek, the road continues to follow the Salmon River, passing an abandoned mining operation and then the ruins of a covered bridge that provided access to a remote mine up the Texas Creek watershed. From this point the road narrows considerably and becomes increasingly steep (travel is not recommended for RVs), crossing back into Canada and winding through former living quarters for the abandoned gold and

Salmon Glacier

mineral ore Premier Mine. The road makes a loop around tailing ponds and continues climbing steeply, with **Salmon Glacier** first coming into view 25 km from Hyder. The road parallels the glacier and climbs to a high point after another 10 km, where the best lookout point is. This glacier, one of Canada's largest and most accessible, is one of British Columbia's most awesome sights, snaking for many kilometers through the highest peaks of the Coast Mountains.

Practicalities

Most services are back in Stewart, but Hyder does have accommodations and a couple of places to eat. Canadian money is used in all Hyder businesses except the post office, where only U.S. currency is accepted.

The **Sealaska Inn,** on Premier Ave., 250/636-2486, is an old two-story hotel with a row of basic rooms on the top floor. Rooms with shared bathroom facilities are $32 s, $38 d, while those with private facilities are $44 s, $54 d. Campers can set up their rigs behind the Glacier Inn (no services; free) or across the road at **Camp-run-a-muck,** 250/636-2486; $16 a night. The campground has showers and a laundry, and an overflow area on the road out to Fish Creek has water and electricity hookups (same rates). Also head to the Sealaska Inn if you're hungry; the kitchen serves Mexican food, pizza, and hamburgers. For local information, try any of the gift shops.

NORTH OF MEZIADIN JUNCTION

For the first 200 km north from Meziadin Junction, the highway follows a valley bordered by the Coast Mountains to the west and the Skeena Mountains to the east.

Around 100 km from the junction, **Bell II Lodge,** 250/558-7980 or 888/655-5566, website www.bell2lodge.com, comes into view. It's the winter base for Last Frontier Heli-skiing but is a lot more than a spot to spend the night before heading north through the rest of the year. Fishing is the biggest attraction, especially through summer for chinook salmon and in early fall for

steelhead. The lodge sells all the tackle you'll need and offers a variety of guiding services, including by helicopter to remote lakes. The lodge itself holds comfortable rooms for $109 s or d, a restaurant (open daily 7 A.M.–10 P.M.), and a bar. Tent camping is $10 while RVs and trailers pay $16–22.

Kinaskan Lake Provincial Park

At the 200-km mark is 1,800-hectare Kinaskan Lake Provincial Park, known for its hungry rainbow trout. It's also the gateway for hikers heading west into much larger Mount Edziza Provincial Park. (The 24-km Mowdade Lake Trail connects the two parks.) In the south of the park, a trail leads one kilometer to great fishing at **Natadesleen Lake,** then a further kilometer along an overgrown trail to beautiful, tiered **Cascade Falls.** Camping at the park is $12 a night.

Red Goat Lodge

Continuing north you'll come to Red Goat Lodge, a bed and breakfast, hostel, and campground overlooking Eddontenajon Lake. The tenting area is up the hill secluded among trees. Campsites, most overlooking the lake, cost $20. The hostel is an associate of Hostelling International. It offers 10 dorm beds, a kitchen, and a lounge area that comes alive at night with stories past and present, slide shows, and impromptu musical performances from guests gathered around the log fire. Beds are $15 per night for HI members, $18 for nonmembers. Showers ($1 for five minutes) and laundry facilities (take lots of quarters) are available to campers and hostellers alike. Also in the lodge are four tastefully decorated B&B rooms, each with private bath; rates of $65 s, $85 d include a delicious home-cooked breakfast served in the "Breakfast Room," which boasts beautiful lake and mountain views. For reservations or more information, call 250/234-3261 or 888/733-4628.

Iskut and Vicinity

The small Tahltan town of Iskut has a post office, gas station, and grocery store (open daily 8 A.M.–9 P.M.). North of Iskut is **Bear Paw Ranch Resort,** where cabins are $65 s or d and rooms in the adjacent Alpine Hotel (same owners) are $95 s or d. The ranch offers horseback riding, fishing, canoe trips, and amenities including a restaurant, lounge, hot tub, and sauna. For information and reservations call 250/234-3005, or call the operator and ask to be connected to Meehaus Channel 2M-3858.

Spatsizi Plateau Wilderness Provincial Park

This wilderness park is just that—656,785 hectares of total wilderness. Access is by foot or floatplane only. The park's varied topography includes broad plateaus, stunning peaks, glaciers, rivers, and lakes. Wildlife abounds; watch for grizzly bears, moose, wolves, wolverines, mountain goats, woodland caribou, and more than 100 species of birds.

Backcountry canoeing draws many, if not most, visitors to the park. The most popular trip begins with a floatplane flight to Tuaton Lake, at the headwaters of the Stikine River in the heart of the park. After putting in at the lake, you paddle the Stikine down to a pullout where the river crosses the Stewart-Cassiar Highway, a 250-km journey with two short portages. Another popular trip begins with a five-km portage from an old (and in some places rough) BC Rail grade that follows the park's southwestern boundary for 80 km. Reach the signposted trailhead via Eulue Lake Road, which spurs east from the Stewart-Cassiar Highway one km north of Tatogga Lake. The portage takes you to the upper reaches of the Spatsizi River, a tributary of the Stikine. This route passes Cold Fish Lake, where you'll find eight cabins, a rustic sauna, and a cookhouse; $10 per person per night. At least seven days should be allowed for either trip.

For more information on canoe routes, as well as general park information, contact the BC Parks office in Dease Lake, 250/771-4591, or check the website www.elp.gov.bc.ca/bcparks.

Between Iskut and Dease Lake

On this stretch, the highway runs through the **Stikine River Provincial Park,** a long and narrow 217,000-hectare park straddling the Stikine River and linking Spatsizi Plateau Wilderness Park and Mount Edziza Provincial Park. The bridge over the Stikine River is used as a pull-out point for canoe trips that start in Spatsizi Plateau Wilderness Provincial Park. Downstream from the bridge, the river flows in a torrent of white water through the **Grand Canyon of the Stikine,** an 85-km-long canyon with vertical rock walls towering more than 300 meters. Only a few teams have successfully kayaked the canyon. In early September 1992, an unassuming 37-year-old man from Montana quietly slipped his kayak into the water at the Highway 37 bridge and became the first person to successfully descend the canyon solo.

Dease Lake

The small community of Dease Lake, on the shores of its namesake lake 65 km north of Iskut, provides basic tourist services and a bit more.

Dease Lake's only accommodation is the **Northway Motor Inn,** 250/771-5341, charging $68 s, $72 d for a basic room, plus $5 for a kitchen. The town has no campgrounds, but 10 km south, where the highway crosses the **Tanzilla River,** is a rest area with picnic tables and pit toilets. The individual pull-through spots are large enough for most RVs.

The best place to eat is the **Boulder Cafe,** where an always-busy waitress will serve you breakfast ($4–8), lunch, or dinner (burgers $7, main dishes from $9) while you admire the old photographs lining the walls; open daily 8 A.M.–9 P.M. For takeout pizza and delicious soft-serve ice cream, head for the small ATCO trailer beside the gas station. Dease Lake also has a laundromat and an intriguing gift shop.

Telegraph Creek

From Dease Lake an unsealed road leads 119 km west along the Tanzilla River to Telegraph Creek (pop. 300), which lies on a terraced hill overlooking the Stikine River. The road passes through the Stikine River Recreation Area, where it drops over one incredibly steep and scary section.

Telegraph Creek, originally home of the Tahltan people, was on the first leg of the "Trail to the Interior" used during the Klondike Gold

Rush. Gold-seekers started in Wrangell, Alaska, continued up the Stikine River by steamer as far as was navigable, then continued overland through Telegraph Creek to Dease Lake and on to the Liard River. Later, Telegraph Creek grew as an important stopover point along the Yukon Telegraph Line, the main overland route between the Yukon and all points south before the construction of the Alaska Highway.

The town boasts friendly people, gorgeous scenery, and heritage buildings dating back to the 1860s. Riverboat charters are popular—by the hour or day, or right through to Wrangell or Petersburg, Alaska (book through Stikine Riversong Lodge, 250/235-3196). A 20-km road leads west from town to **Glenora,** which had 10,000 residents in its gold-rush heyday. Nowadays, only one or two of the original buildings remain.

Originally a Hudson's Bay Company store, the **Stikine Riversong Lodge,** 250/235-3196, website www.stikineriversong.com, has a café, general store, gas station, and rooms from $55–60 s or d. The owners can arrange transportation to Mount Edziza Provincial Park. Alternatively, two Forest Service campgrounds are along the road out to Glenora.

> *Telegraph Creek was on the "Trail to the Interior" used during the Klondike Gold Rush. Gold-seekers started in Wrangell, Alaska, continued up the Stikine River by steamer as far as was navigable, then continued overland through Telegraph Creek to Dease Lake and on to the Liard River.*

Mount Edziza Provincial Park

This 232,702-hectare wilderness west of the Stewart-Cassiar Highway is one of the province's most inaccessible parks, but it's also one of the most magnificent and intriguing. The long and narrow park is bordered to the north by the road out to Telegraph Creek, to the west by Mess Creek, and to the east by Little Iskut River and a string of four lakes. Within these boundaries lies a moonlike volcanic landscape, above the treeline and dominated by 2,787-meter **Mount Edziza,** an extinct volcano whose glaciated crater is over two km wide. Rather than blowing out in one massive and spectacular eruption, this volcano oozed periodically over the course of four million years, eventually covering 1,600 square kilometers with lava. Small eruptions in the vicinity of the central cone have created dozens of cinder cones, some perfectly symmetrical.

Access to the park is on foot, on horseback, or via a charter floatplane from Dease Lake or Telegraph Creek. The easiest overland access is from Kinaskan Lake Provincial Park, 55 km south of Iskut; from the west bank of the lake (accessed by boat), it's 24 km by trail to Mowdade Lake, then another 25 km to the first of the cinder cones, directly south of the main peak. This trail continues northward around Mt. Edziza to Buckley Lake, ending across the Stikine River from Telegraph Creek. Charter-flight operators can drop hikers at any of the main lakes, but Mowdade is most popular for its vicinity to the park's most spectacular volcanic features.

Continuing to the Alaska Highway

As you continue north from the turnoff to Telegraph Creek, the road parallels the east shore of Dease Lake. Good campsites are found by the lake, along with the occasional chunk of jade on the lakeshore—the area has been called the jade capital of the world. From Dease Lake to the Alaska Highway it's clear sailing for 235 km along the northern slopes of the Cassiar Mountains.

Cassiar, 115 km north of Dease Lake, was once a company town for Cassiar Asbestos Mine. The booming little burg held a thousand residents, a grocery store, liquor store, bank, supermarket, and a multimillion-dollar school. But in March 1992, the company pulled out and the residents followed suit. The following year the town was auctioned off right down to the last fence post. To get there head 16 km along the Cassiar Spur road, passing a few old cabins and the back of a monstrous pile of green tailings. Don't expect any services.

The next worthwhile stop is 4,597-hectare **Boya Lake Provincial Park,** 150 km north of Dease Lake and 85 km from the Alaska Highway. The lake is clear, icy cold, well stocked with fish, and ringed by white claylike beaches. Campsites are $12 per night.

From Boya Lake, the highway continues north, paralleling the Dease River for around 20 km and traversing the Liard Plain across the border and into the Yukon. From the border it's another four km to the junction of the Alaska Highway, then 21 km east to Watson Lake or 423 km west to Whitehorse.

North from Prince George

The landscapes and lifestyles in the area northeast of Prince George are closely aligned with neighboring northwest Alberta. The region's dominant natural feature, the **Peace River,** flows east from B.C.'s northern Rockies across the border into Alberta, lacing the two provinces together both topographically and economically. Rich farmland flanks the river on both sides of the border, creating a common agricultural zone whose hub is Grande Prairie, Alberta. This region of B.C. also shares Alberta's mountain time zone.

Most travelers use the route north from Prince George to access Mile Zero of the Alaska Highway at Dawson Creek. But this direct route, a distance of 405 km, bypasses the region's highlight at **Hudson's Hope,** halfway between Chetwynd and Fort St. John. Whichever route you take, there's plenty to see and do, with interesting provincial parks and towns offering northern hospitality.

ALONG THE CROOKED RIVER

Heading north out of Prince George, Highway 97 climbs through low rolling hills to the Nechako Plateau before descending alongside the Crooked River to massive Williston Lake. Pastoral farmland lines much of the route, and in summer the roadside is ablaze with red-orange Indian paintbrush and purple lupine.

The first worthwhile stop is 873-hectare **Crooked River Provincial Park,** 80 km north of Prince George. It's only a small park, but adjacent Bear Lake is good for rainbow trout fishing, swimming, and canoeing, and the large campground ($12 a night) usually has sites available.

Carp Lake Provincial Park

This 38,612-hectare park lies 140 km north of Prince George on Highway 97, then 32 km west (turn off at McLeod Lake) along a sometimes rough unsealed road. Over 6,000 hectares of the park is taken up by Carp Lake, a picturesque body of water dotted with islands and filled with fish, although you won't catch carp; the lake was named by explorer Simon Fraser, who noted Carrier Indians journeyed to the lake for fish "of the carp kind."

You really need a watercraft of some kind to truly appreciate the many coves and islands and to take advantage of the rainbow trout fishing opportunities. Boatless visitors can still find plenty to do. A three-km interpretive trail (allow 50 minutes round-trip) follows part of a route taken by early explorers and trappers, while from the main campground a A one-km trail (20 minutes each way) leads to Rainbow Lake. Another equally short trail, along the access road in the park's northeast corner, leads past 12-meter-high **War Falls** to **War Lake,** where you can drop a line for rainbow trout.

At the main facility area, **Carp Lake Campground** holds 90 lakeshore sites, each with a fire ring and picnic table. Back toward the park entrance is **War Lake Campground,** offering similar facilities. Both campgrounds charge $12 per site per night.

Mackenzie

The forestry town of Mackenzie (pop. 6,200) lies 180 km north of Prince George on the southern arm of massive Williston Lake, a reservoir created by the W.A.C. Bennett Dam. The town was founded in the 1960s as a base for the massive logging operation that cleared the way for construction of the dam. At the town's entrance is the world's largest tree crusher, used during that logging operation. Nearby **Morfee Lake** is a great swimming and boating spot, while the logging road to the summit of Morfee Hill offers lake views.

Tourist facilities in town are limited. The nicest place to stay, catering mostly to business travelers, is the **Alexander Mackenzie Hotel,** on Mackenzie Blvd., 250/997-3266 or 800/663-2964. All rooms are air-conditioned, and the complex includes a pub and restaurant. Rates are $75 s or d. Less expensive is **Timberman Inn,** also on Mackenzie Blvd., 250/997-6464 or 800/663-2964; $51 s or d. On the town's southern outskirts, **Mackenzie Municipal RV Park** is little more than a gravel parking lot, but it holds a few grassy tent sites. Picnic tables, firewood, hot showers, and hookups are all supplied for $12–16 a night.

Out at the junction of Highways 97 and 39 is **Mackenzie Visitor Info Centre,** open summers only daily 9 A.M.–6 P.M. For local information the rest of the year, head to the **Mackenzie Chamber of Commerce,** 86 Centennial Dr., 250/997-5459 or 877/622-5360; open Mon.–Fri. 8:30 A.M.–4:30 P.M.

To Powder King Mountain Resort

Continuing east toward Chetwynd, the landscape becomes more dramatic as the highway climbs steadily up the western slopes of the Rocky Mountains. Look for signs to the west for 40-hectare **Bijoux Falls Provincial Park,** a small day-use area where the Misinchinka River plummets over a rocky outcrop.

Near **Pine Pass,** Powder King is a legendary destination, among the northernmost of any North American resort, but best known for its incredible snowfall—over 12 meters annually. One triple chair and two surface lifts serve a vertical rise of 640 meters and 600 hectares. The season lasts from mid-November to late April. At the base area is a self-contained village, with a medium-sized lodge that sleeps around 100, a café and restaurant, a modern ski and board shop, rentals, and lessons. Lift tickets are adult $35, senior $28, child $15. Call for a snow re-

port at 250/964-0645 or check the website www.powderking.com.

From the resort, the highway meanders over one of its most scenic stretches—935-meter Pine Pass, atop the Continental Divide. From the pass, it's downhill all the way, following the Pine River to Chetwynd.

CHETWYND AND VICINITY

Chetwynd (pop. 3,200) lies at the relatively busy junction of Highways 97 and 29. The community was first established in 1912, when it was known as "Little Prairie." With the arrival of the railway in 1958 its name was changed to Chetwynd to honor a director of the P.G.E. Railway—a pioneer who had great faith in the future of the Peace River Country. Today Chetwynd is a forestry town and a center for artistic log-carving. The town promotes itself as the "Chainsaw Sculpture Capital of the World."

The one main road through town is lined with services. **Pinecone Motor Inn,** 5224 53rd Ave., 250/788-3311 or 800/663-8082, charges $60 s, $65 d for large rooms with comfortable beds. The best option for campers is to head 29 km north of town to **Moberly Lake Provincial Park,** with over 100 sites for $12 a night.

Chetwynd Visitor Info Centre is in a railway caboose beside the highway through town to the south, 250/788-1943, website www .gochetwynd.com. It's open in summer daily 8:30 A.M.–6 P.M.

Tumbler Ridge

Tumbler Ridge, 94 km south of Chetwynd, is a modern boomtown that sprang up much the same way gold-rush towns did a hundred years ago. Back in the early 1980s the provincial government struck a deal with several Japanese coal companies. The government agreed to improve regional infrastructure, including constructing a new railhead and coal-loading dock at Prince Rupert, if the companies would construct mines and a township at the site of the rich Northeast Coal Deposits. Tumbler Ridge (pop. 4,300) was created virtually overnight to allow the employees of the Northeast Coal Project to settle in quickly and comfortably. From the start it held all the creature comforts, services, and recreational facilities you'd expect in a long-established town.

The mining operation here is massive. The **Quintette Mine** moves 120 million tons of earth annually, from which 4.3 million tons of coal are extracted. From the mine, a 13-km-long conveyor belt transports raw coal to a processing plant and railhead from where it's shipped to the port city of Prince Rupert. Tours of the mine are offered in July and August. Book through the Visitor Info Centre, 250/242-4702.

The town's only motel is **Tumbler Ridge Inn,** right downtown, 250/242-4277 or 800/663-3898. Basic rooms are $56 s, $62 d, and the complex includes a coffee shop, pub, and restaurant. **Lions Flatbed Creek Campground** enjoys a pleasant riverside setting three km south of town toward Chetwynd. Facilities include hot showers and a cooking shelter; sites are $10. The other option for campers is **Gwillim Lake Provincial Park,** halfway between Tumbler Ridge and Chetwynd; $12.

Tumbler Ridge Visitor Info Centre, on Southgate Rd., 250/242-4702, is open year-round, Mon.–Fri. 8:30 A.M.–4:30 P.M.

Monkman Provincial Park

One of the most inspiring sights in the northern interior is **Kinuseo Falls,** where the Murray River cascades 60 meters in a spectacular fan-shaped arc to the valley floor below. The falls are at the north end of 54,185-hectare Monkman Provincial Park. From Tumbler Ridge a rough gravel road leads 60 km (90 minutes each way) southwest, ending at the northern entrance to this wild and mountainous wilderness. From the picnic area a short trail leads to the falls viewpoint. **Kinuseo Falls Campground** offers 42 sites alongside the Murray River; $12 a night. The park has no other facilities.

Moberly Lake Provincial Park

North of Chetwynd, the 65-km-long stretch of Highway 29 to Hudson's Hope passes Moberly Lake, a long and narrow body of water encircled by a typical boreal forest. Moberly Lake

Provincial Park, at the lake's eastern end, has a day-use area and a primitive campground where sites are $12 a night.

HUDSON'S HOPE

Human habitation of the Peace River Valley predated Alexander Mackenzie's 1793 journey along the river by many thousands of years. But Mackenzie's detailed reports encouraged an influx of white settlers to the valley. In 1805, fur traders founded Hudson's Hope at a picturesque riverside site. Today the town's population is just over 1,000.

W.A.C. Bennett and Peace Canyon Dams

These two dams are the area's main attractions, their sheer size an awe-inspiring sight. Together the two facilities generate almost 40 percent of the hydroelectricity used in the province.

Larger of the two, the W.A.C. Bennett Dam, seven km west of town, is one of the world's largest earth-filled structures. The 183-meter-high structure backs up 164,600-hectare **Williston Lake,** British Columbia's largest lake, which extends more than 300 km along three flooded valleys. At the top of the dam's control building is **Bennett Dam Visitor Centre,** 888/333-6667, where displays catalog the construction tasks, a film celebrates the dam's opening, and the uses of electricity are detailed. Free guided bus tours of the dam are scheduled on weekends in summer 9:30 A.M.–4:30 P.M. and are available the rest of the year by appointment. The visitor center is open in summer daily 9 A.M.–6 P.M.

The much smaller Peace Canyon Dam is downstream from Bennett Dam, five km south of Hudson's Hope on Highway 29. **Peace Canyon Dam Visitor Centre,** 250/783-9943, adjacent to the powerhouse, focuses on the fascinating natural history, exploration, and pioneers of the area, and the building of the Peace Canyon Project. You can also see the central control system, powerhouse, and switchgear station. Don't miss a trip up to the outside observation deck. This center is open in summer daily 8 A.M.–4 P.M.

DINOSAURS IN THE PEACE RIVER VALLEY

During construction of Peace Canyon Dam, fossilized remains of the **plesiosaur,** a marine reptile, were discovered. This wasn't the first time evidence of prehistoric life had been discovered in the Peace River Valley. As early as 1922, dinosaur footprints over 100 million years old were found in the area where Hudson's Hope now lies. The footprints belonged to several species of dinosaurs, most common among them the **hadrosaur.** This plant-eater was around 10 meters long and weighed about four tons. It was amphibious but preferred the land, walking around on its hind legs ever-alert for the ancestors of the dreaded tyrannosaurus.

Footprints are as important as skeletons in unraveling the mysteries of dinosaurs. They provide clues about the ratios of various dinosaurs in a particular area, and information on herds and how they traveled.

Most dinosaur footprints discovered in the valley have been excavated and transported to museums throughout Canada (a couple are on display in the Hudson's Hope Museum). Plant and shell fossils can still be found. The best time for searching them out is after heavy rain—try looking downstream from the dam (a few short trails lead from the highway into the canyon, but it's a bit of a scramble). The best opportunity to learn more about local dinosaurs is in the **Peace Canyon Dam Visitor Centre,** 250/783-9943, open in summer daily 8 A.M.–4 P.M.

Edmontosaurus

BOB RACE

Heritage Park

Across from Hudson's Hope Visitor Info Centre, this small chunk of parkland is dotted with historic buildings moved to the site from throughout the Peace River Valley. The site itself is of some historical significance—Simon Fraser spent the winter of 1805–06 here. The main displays are housed in **Hudson's Hope Museum,** 250/783-7535, which is crammed with geological specimens; dinosaur bones and casts of footprints discovered during dam construction; and historical artifacts that belonged to trappers, miners, and early homesteaders. The park also holds a trapper's cabin and fur cache, a log replica of a 1900 Hudson's Bay Company trading post, a furnished home from 1935, and the tiny log-walled St. Peter's Church. The grounds are open year-round; the museum (admission $3.50) is open in summer daily 9:30 A.M.–5:30 P.M.

Practicalities

Neither of the town's two accommodations is outstanding. The choices are **Peace Glen Hotel,** at the south end of town on Dudley Dr., 250/783-9966 or 877/783-5520, and **Sportsman Inn,** downtown at 10501 Carter Ave., 250/783-5523. Both have an in-house pub and restaurant and charge from $60 s or d a night.

The town's three municipal campgrounds each charge $7 per night. Closest to civilization is **King Gething Campground,** on the south end of town, which has flush toilets, coin-operated showers, and plenty of firewood. **Alwin Holland Park,** west of town, is more primitive (pit toilets) but is off the main highway and has some nice hiking trails. The third, **Dinosaur Lake Campground,** has pit toilets, firewood, and good fishing and swimming.

Hudson's Hope Visitor Info Centre is at 10507 105th Ave., 250/783-9154; open in summer daily 9 A.M.–6 P.M. The staff provides information on local attractions and offers brochures on nearby hiking opportunities. (The trails are enjoyable but not well marked.)

The Alaska Highway

When the Japanese threatened invasion of Canada and the United States during World War II, the Alaska Highway was quickly built to link Alaska with the Lower 48. It was the longest military road ever constructed in North America—an unsurpassed road-construction feat stretching 2,288 km between Dawson Creek, B.C., and Delta Junction, Alaska.

Construction began 9 March 1942 and was completed, incredibly, on 20 November that same year. In less than nine months troops had bulldozed a rough trail snaking like a crooked finger through almost impenetrable muskeg and forest, making literally hundreds of detours around obstacles and constructing 133 bridges.

At a cost of more than $140 million, the highway was the major contributing factor to the growth of northern British Columbia in the 1940s. At the height of construction, the region's population boomed. Dawson Creek's population alone rose from 600 to over 10,000, and Whitehorse replaced Dawson City as a more convenient capital of the Yukon.

Driving the highway was notoriously difficult in its earliest days. Highway travelers returned with tales of endless mud holes and dust, washed-out bridges, flat tires, broken windshields and smashed headlights, wildlife in the road, mosquitoes the size of hummingbirds, and sparse facilities. But they also sported "I drove the Alaska Highway" bumper stickers as though they'd won a prize. Nowadays the route doesn't merit quite the bravado—it's paved most of the way, has roadside lodges fairly frequently, and can easily be driven in three days, or two at a pinch. What hasn't changed is the scenery. You'll still see kilometer after kilometer of unspoiled wilderness, including boreal forests of spruce and aspen, the majestic, snow-dusted peaks of the northern Canadian Rockies, and gorgeous rivers and streams (and you can still buy the stickers).

Although official signage along the Alaska Highway is in kilometers, many services are marked in miles, a legacy of imperial measurement. This only becomes confusing when you consider that highway improvements have shortened the original route. For example, Liard River Hot Springs is still marked as Mile 496, though it's now only 754 km (462 miles) from Dawson Creek.

DAWSON CREEK

Although Dawson Creek (pop. 11,700) marks the southern end of the Alaska Highway, it's still a long way north—over 400 km northeast of Prince George and 1,200 km north of Vancouver. While the city thrives on its historic location at Mile Zero, it's also an important service center whose economy is more closely tied to neighboring Alberta, a few km to the east, than to British Columbia.

Dawson Creek was named after Dr. George Mercer Dawson, a Canadian geologist who surveyed the prairie here in 1879. His report noted the area's fertility—thereby encouraging settlement—and led to the subsequent discovery of gas and oil fields.

The first wave of settlers came to the area in 1912, but the arrival of the Northern Alberta Railway (N.A.R.) in 1931 put Dawson Creek on the map, establishing the city as an agricultural service center. Agriculture is still the basis of Dawson Creek's economy; local products include wheat, oats, barley, canola, vegetables, specialty crops, cattle, dairy, hogs, sheep, poultry, and honey. Oil and gas rigs stand in the Elmsworth Basin south of the city, while pipelines and processing plants lie to the east.

Northern Alberta Railway (N.A.R.) Park

This park, on the corner of Highway 2 and the Alaska Highway, makes a good first stop in town. Here you'll find Dawson Creek Visitor Info Centre, an art gallery, and the **Station Museum,** 250/782-9595. This marvelous and curious museum, housed in the original 1931 Northern Alberta Railway station, offers exhibits on a wide variety of topics, including construction of the

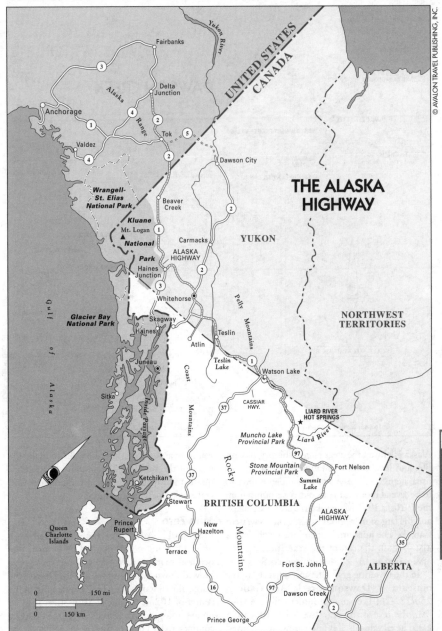

© AVALON TRAVEL PUBLISHING, INC.

Fairbanks

3

Delta
Junction

Anchorage

Alaska

4

1

2

Valdez

Range

Tok

5

4

2

UNITED STATES
CANADA

Dawson City

2

**THE ALASKA
HIGHWAY**

Wrangell-
St. Elias
National Park

Beaver
Creek

2

Kluane
Mt. Logan

1

YUKON

Carmacks

National

ALASKA
HIGHWAY

Park

Haines
Junction

2

Glacier Bay
National Park

3

Whitehorse

Skagway

**NORTHWEST
TERRITORIES**

Haines

Gulf

Atlin

Teslin

Pelly

Mountains

Juneau

Teslin
Lake

1

Watson Lake

of

Coast

Sitka

Mountains

37

CASSIAR
HWY.

**LIARD RIVER
HOT SPRINGS**

Alaska

Muncho Lake
Provincial Park

Liard River

Inside

Stone Mountain
Provincial Park

97

Ketchikan

37

Rocky

Passage

Summit
Lake

Fort Nelson

Queen
Charlotte
Islands

Stewart

BRITISH COLUMBIA

Mountains

ALASKA
HIGHWAY

Prince
Rupert

New
Hazelton

35

Terrace

Fort St. John

ALBERTA

0   150 mi

16

97

0   150 km

Prince George

Dawson Creek

2

Yukon River

NORTHERN B.C.

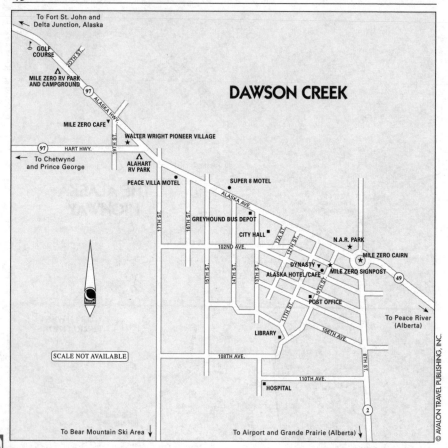

To Fort St. John and
Delta Junction, Alaska

GOLF
COURSE

MILE ZERO RV PARK
AND CAMPGROUND

97

ALASKA HWY.

DAWSON CREEK

MILE ZERO CAFE

WALTER WRIGHT PIONEER VILLAGE

97   HART HWY.

To Chetwynd
and Prince George

ALAHART
RV PARK

PEACE VILLA MOTEL

SUPER 8 MOTEL

ALASKA AVE.

17TH ST.

16TH ST.

GREYHOUND BUS DEPOT

CITY HALL

102ND AVE.

12A ST.

12TH ST.

N.A.R. PARK

MILE ZERO CAIRN

DYNASTY

MILE ZERO SIGNPOST

ALASKA HOTEL/CAFE

15TH ST.

14TH ST.

13TH ST.

10TH ST.

49

POST OFFICE

11TH ST.

To Peace River
(Alberta)

LIBRARY

106TH AVE.

SCALE NOT AVAILABLE

108TH AVE.

8TH ST.

110TH AVE.

HOSPITAL

2

To Bear Mountain Ski Area

To Airport and Grande Prairie (Alberta)

© AVALON TRAVEL PUBLISHING, INC.

NORTHERN B.C.

Alaska Highway, the area's railroad history, pioneer life, and local flora and fauna. Among the unusual items on display: a rack of antlers estimated to be several thousand years old, a gas pump from the 1920s, a 1941 Massey-Harris cream separator, and the largest mammoth tusks found in western Canada. The museum is open June–Sept. daily 8 A.M.–7 P.M., the rest of the year Tues.–Sat. 10 A.M.–noon and 1–4 P.M. Admission is $3.

In the towering grain elevator adjacent to the museum is **Dawson Creek Art Gallery,** 250/782-2601, open in summer daily 9 A.M.–5 P.M., the rest of the year Tues.–Sat. 10 A.M.–5 P.M. The elevator itself is fascinating. It was saved from demolition and redesigned with a spiral

walkway around the interior walls to make the most of the building's height. Inside are high-quality paintings and locally made arts and crafts—for viewing and buying.

Mile Zero

In front of N.A.R. Park is the Alaska Highway's official starting point, marked by a cairn. The original marker, a one-meter-high post, was mowed down by a car in the 1940s. Despite the cairn's official status, the Mile Zero signpost in the center of 102nd Avenue at 10th Street is more often photographed. It reads "May the highway continue to be a road to friendship" and notes the following distances: Fort St. John, 48 miles; Fort

Nelson, 300 miles; Whitehorse, 918 miles; and Fairbanks, 1,523 miles.

Walter Wright Pioneer Village

One km west of N.A.R. Park at the Highway 97 split, this village of historical buildings holds two pioneer churches, a furnished log house, a general store, the Napoleon Loiselle Blacksmith Shop (containing many of his inventions), a trapper's cabin with handmade furniture, and two old schoolhouses. Scattered around are pieces of old farm machinery, tools, and equipment used by the area's first homesteaders. The village is named for the man responsible for finding and bringing all the buildings together. It's open June–Sept. daily 10 A.M.–6 P.M.; admission is adult $5, senior or child $3.

Recreation

Dawson Creek Golf Course and Country Club offers 18 challenging holes next to the Mile Zero City Campground, on the Alaska Highway west of town, 250/782-7882. Wintertime recreation centers around **Bear Mountain,** south of downtown along 17th St., 250/782-4988. The small ski hill's one T-bar serves a 132-meter vertical rise. Rentals and lessons are available.

Festivals and Events

In May, **Mile Zero Celebrations** features a fiddlers' contest, dart tournament, craft show, horse show, pig races, pancake breakfasts, cookouts, and a parade at Walter Wright Pioneer Village. In June, July, and August, the **Muskeg North Musical Revue** brings old-time dancing and music to Walter Wright Pioneer Village. On the second weekend of August, the city hosts the **Dawson Creek Exhibition and Stampede,** one of British Columbia's premier rodeos. In addition to afternoon rodeo competitions, chuckwagon races are held, along with fun events like a children's rodeo and fireworks.

Accommodations and Camping

Dawson Creek's oldest and most colorful accommodation is the **Alaska Hotel,** right downtown at 10209 10th St., 250/782-7998, website www.alaskahotel.com. Known as the Dew Drop Inn when it first opened in 1928, the hotel has been renovated in a colorful heritage style. Rooms remain basic, with no televisions or phones and shared bathroom facilities; $50–65 s, $55–75 d. A popular café and a pub are downstairs. Along the road up to Alaska is **Peace Villa Motel,** 1641 Alaska Ave., 250/782-8175 or 888/782-8175, which charges $62 s, $68 d. Two blocks back toward town is **Super 8 Motel,** 1440 Alaska Ave., 250/782-8899 or 800/800-8000, website www.super8.com, featuring 48 smallish but modern rooms; a light breakfast is included in the rates of $72 s or d.

Mile Zero RV Park and Campground, 250/782-2590, isn't at Mile Zero of the famous highway—it's about one km north from downtown—but it's the pick of Dawson Creek's numerous campgrounds. Sites sit around a large shaded grassy area, and each one has a picnic table. Facilities include hot showers and a laundry. Rates are $10–17 a night. Another campground in town is **Alahart RV Park,** at the junction of the Alaska Hwy. and Hwy. 97, 250/782-4702.

Food

The best-known eatery in town is the **Alaska Cafe,** in the Alaska Hotel at 10209 10th St., 250/782-7040. What originally opened as a candy store in the 1930s is today colorfully decorated in an old-fashioned style and serves tasty burgers, sandwiches, and croissants at lunch, and steak, chicken, seafood, and pork dishes ($12–18) at dinner. The desserts are delicious. Equally popular is **Mile Zero Cafe,** 1901 Alaska Ave., 250/782-1456, with similar fare served in a casual setting. One of Dawson Creek's several Chinese restaurants, **Dynasty,** 1009 102nd Ave., 250/782-3138, also offers steak and seafood, a salad bar, and a buffet lunch.

Transportation

Dawson Creek Municipal Airport is south of town on Highway 2. It's served by **Air B.C.,** 888/247-2262, which operates daily scheduled flights between Dawson Creek and southern B.C. cities. The **Greyhound** bus depot is at 1201 Alaska Ave. between 12th and 14th Streets, 250/782-3131; scheduled services run between

NORTHERN B.C.

Dawson Creek and Prince George, Grande Prairie (Alberta), and north along the Alaska Highway to Whitehorse (Yukon).

Information

An almost obligatory stop for travelers heading north on the famous highway is **Dawson Creek Visitor Info Centre,** in N.A.R. Park on Alaska Ave., 250/782-9595. It's open in summer daily 8 A.M.–7 P.M., the rest of the year Tues.–Sat. 10 A.M.–4 P.M.

North toward Fort St. John

The initial 72 km of the Alaska Highway between Dawson Creek and Fort St. John skirts nearly flat croplands and fields of wildflowers brilliantly abloom in summer. **Kiskatinaw Provincial Park,** 28 km from Dawson Creek then four km off the highway, is only 58 hectares but offers a small campground ($12 a night) and fishing in the Kiskatinaw River. North of the park, the highway descends through a steep ravine to the Peace River and the small township of **Taylor,** site of a huge Petro-Canada Oil Refinery. Apart from this dominant man-made feature, Taylor is best known as home of the annual World Invitational Gold Panning Championships every August.

FORT ST. JOHN

As the second-largest community along the Alaska Highway (only Whitehorse, Yukon, is larger), Fort St. John (pop.15,100) is an important service center for local industries, including oil, gas, and coal extraction; forestry; and agriculture. It's one of the province's oldest nonnative settlements—the Beaver and Sekani tribes both occupied the area when white traders arrived in the 1790s—and served as a fur-trading post until 1823. But it wasn't until construction of the Alaska Highway began that Fort St. John really boomed.

Fort St. John–North Peace Museum

You can't miss this museum complex at 9323 100th St., 250/787-0430. Just look for the unique exhibits outside, including a skyscrap-

ing 40-meter-high **oil derrick** that came from Mile 143 of the Alaska Highway. In the museum local history springs to life with reconstructed historical interiors. A trapper's cabin recalls the original Rocky Mountain fort and fur-trading days, while the pioneer days are commemorated in fully furnished rooms, including a kitchen, bedroom, schoolroom, dentist's office, post office, outpost hospital, and blacksmith's shop. Don't miss the fur press, the birchbark canoe, and the grizzly bear with claws big enough to send shivers up your spine. Other exhibits detail the geological and mining ventures that the town thrives on today.

The museum also houses more than 6,000 restored and carefully cataloged artifacts; one display details the discovery in nearby Charlie Lake Cave of a bead and tools dating back some 10,500 years. Videos about the local area can be screened on request. The museum is open in summer daily 8 A.M.–8 P.M., the rest of the year Mon.–Sat. 11 A.M.–4 P.M. Admission is adult $4, senior $3, child $2.

Peace River Canyon Lookout

This lookout provides splendid panoramic views taking in the wide, deep-green Peace River, its rocky canyon walls, and the lush fields along the canyon rim. From the museum/information center head south along 100th Street, crossing the Alaska Highway and continuing along the gravel road, which ends at the edge of the canyon. It's well worth the short drive.

Charlie Lake

This picturesque lake is just north of Fort St. John; follow signs off the Alaska Highway. It's a remnant of an enormous ice-dammed lake that covered this area and northern Alberta more than 10,500 years ago. At Charlie Lake Cave, animal bones and artifacts such as stone tools, a fluted spear point, and a handmade stone bead—the oldest found in North America—were discovered, leading archaeologists to postulate that this area was one of the earliest North American sites occupied by humans.

Today the lake is a popular recreation area known for its good fishing—for trout, arctic grayling, walleye, and northern pike. Swimming isn't quite so delightful, as the lake can clog with algae at times.

Two small provincial parks occupy sections of the lake's shoreline. **Charlie Lake Provincial Park,** at the junction of the Alaska Hwy. and Hwy. 29, is mainly a campground ($12 per site), while 312-hectare **Beatton Provincial Park,** on the lake's east shoreline, features beautiful aspen-lined hiking trails, a beach, boating, fishing, swimming, cross-country skiing, snowmobiling, ice fishing (with warm-up huts), and a campground ($12 per site).

Accommodations and Camping

Most motels in town are strung out along the Alaska Highway. One of the least expensive is **Blue Belle Motel,** 9705 Alaska Hwy., 250/785-2613, which charges $49 s, $54 d. Of a similar standard, but with a coffee shop, restaurant, and pub, is **Northwoods Inn,** 10627 Alaska Hwy., 250/787-1616; $50 s, $55 d. The six-story **Northern Grand Hotel,** 9830 100th Ave., 250/787-0521 or 800/663-8313, is a full-service hotel with dining rooms, an indoor pool, a whirlpool and sauna, and an exercise room. Rates start at $100 s, $110 d.

Fort St. John Centennial RV Park, 9323 100th St., 250/785-3033, is close to the museum and information center, but it's small and doesn't offer much shade. Facilities include showers, a laundry, and hookups. Sites are $12–19 per night. A more pleasant option would be either one of the two provincial parks north of town on Charlie Lake (see above).

Food

Willson's Pizza, 10503 100th Ave., 250/785-8969, has the best pizza in town and good lasagna at reasonable prices. If you're in the mood for some tasty Chinese food, try **Jade's Garden,** 10108 101st Ave., 250/787-2585; the buffet is good value at around $13 per person, but all the dishes on the menu are reasonably priced. Open daily from 11 A.M. A few of the motels have dining rooms, including Northwoods Inn, where a cooked breakfast is $6–9.

Nightlife

For country music, locals flock to **Trappers Pub** in the Pioneer Inn. It's open till 2 A.M.; free admission. For rock 'n' roll try the cabaret **Northwoods,** on the Alaska Hwy. north of town; at "The Woods," as locals call it, you can expect to pay a couple of bucks cover charge on Friday and Saturday nights.

Services and Information

The airport is about nine km south of town and is serviced by **Air B.C.,** 888/247-2262, and **Central Mountain Air,** 250/785-6100. The **Greyhound** bus depot is at 10355 101st Ave., 250/785-6695.

The **hospital** is on 100th Ave., between 96th and 98th Streets; the **post office** is on the corner of 101st Ave. and 102nd St.; and the **library** is on 100th St. between 106th and 107th Avenues.

Fort St. John Visitor Info Centre is off the main highway at 9923 96th Ave., 250/785-3033. It's open May through mid-June daily 8 A.M.–6 P.M., mid-June through mid-September daily 8 A.M.–8 P.M., the rest of the year Mon.–Fri. 8 A.M.–5 P.M.

WONOWON TO PROPHET RIVER

Wonowon

The 374-km stretch of the Alaska Highway between Fort St. John and Fort Nelson passes through boreal forest and a landscape that becomes more and more mountainous. The first services are at Wonowon, 83 km north of Fort St. John at Mile 102. The Husky gas station, 250/772-3288, offers rooms from $50 and a few campsites for $15, as well as gas and a restaurant.

Pink Mountain

From Wonowon, the highway climbs steadily to Pink Mountain, at Mile 147. Numerous services perch on the low summit, where snow can fall year-round. On the west side of the highway, **Pink Mountain Campsite,** 250/772-3234, provides tent and RV sites for $16 (no hookups) and rustic cabins for $30 s, $40 d (showers are an extra $2.50).

A few kilometers beyond the summit is **Mae's Kitchen,** 250/772-3215, where breakfasts are

NORTHERN B.C.

huge and the pancakes ($5.50) and blueberry muffins ($2.80) are especially good. For lunch, try the house special Buffalo Burger, complete with fries and salad for $8.50. The restaurant is open daily 7 A.M.–10 P.M. Mae's Kitchen also offers a few inexpensive motel units.

Continuing northward, look for the "maintained" airstrip to the west—how would you like to land on that one? Not far north of Pink Mountain the highway passes into Pacific time—set your clock back one hour.

Sikanni Chief to Prophet River

The next services are 30 km north of Pink Mountain at Sikanni Chief, where the highway passes through a low-lying area frequented by moose. The modern **Sikanni River RV Park,** 250/774-1028, offers sites with hookups for $14–19 and small cabins with basic cooking facilities for $38 s, $50 d.

Twenty km north from Sikanni Chief you'll pass the small 55-hectare **Buckinghorse River Provincial Park,** which offers camping ($12 a night) and good river fishing. From here north, a new and scenic stretch of the highway runs through **Minaker River Valley** then parallels the **Prophet River,** passing a rustic campground (open May–Sept.; campsites $8) where a hiking trail leads down to the river. Farther along, at Mile 217, is the tiny community of **Prophet River,** with all visitor services.

North toward Fort Nelson

The highway north to Fort Nelson was rerouted during 1991–92, eliminating 132 bends and curves. The next place worth a detour, about 30 km south of Fort Nelson and 12 km south of the highway along a dirt road, is 174-hectare **Andy Bailey Provincial Recreation Area.** Adjacent to Jackfish Creek (which reportedly offers good pike fishing), the area has a sandy beach with good swimming and a boat launch. Camping is $9.

FORT NELSON

At Mile 300 of the Alaska Highway, Fort Nelson (pop. 4,100) is the largest town between Fort St. John and the Yukon. The **Muskwa, Prophet,** and **Sikanni Chief Rivers** all flow together here

to create the large **Fort Nelson River,** which in turn flows into the even larger **Liard River** at Nelson Forks to the northwest. Starting around 1800, many different trading posts were built on the site, but each was destroyed by natives, fire, or flood.

Fort Nelson's economy is based on forestry, oil, and gas. The town holds North America's second-largest gas-processing plant, as well as the world's largest chopstick-manufacturing company.

Sights

Fort Nelson Historical Museum, on the west side of the highway at the north end of town, 250/774-3536, contains a great collection of Alaska Highway construction items and native and pioneer artifacts. An interesting 30-minute movie, shown throughout the day, uses footage taken during the construction of the highway to effectively convey what a mammoth task the project was. The building is surrounded by machinery and vehicles used during the early days. Around back is a trapper's cabin crammed with antiques. The museum is open in summer daily 8:30 A.M.–7:30 P.M. Admission is adult $4.50, senior or child $3.

At the end of Mountain View Drive is the **Native Trail,** a four-km self-guided interpretive trail that passes two native-style shelters and holds signs describing native foods, local wildlife, and trapping methods. Allow at least one hour round-trip.

Accommodations and Camping

Fort Nelson has many hotels and motels spread out along the Alaska Highway. The nicest is **Blue Bell Inn,** 4103 50th Ave. (next to the Petro-Canada gas station), 250/774-6961 or 800/663-5267. The modern two-story lodging has nice rooms, a laundry, and an adjacent 24-hour restaurant. Rates are $60 s, $70 d, kitchens an extra $10.

Beside the museum is **Westend Campground,** 250/774-2340, where you can choose from tent sites in an open area or individual sites surrounded by trees. The tent sites are $13; hookups are $18. Facilities include coin-operated showers, a laundromat, grocery store, and free firewood. It's open April–October. On either side of town along the Alaska Highway, the closest camping is 20 km south at **Andy Bailey Provincial Recreation Area** or 77 km west at **Tetsa River Provincial Park.**

Food

As you enter town from the south, modern **Dan's Neighbourhood Pub,** 4204 50th Ave. N, 250/774-3929, wouldn't look out of place in Vancouver—and it's always busy. All the usual fare is offered, with burgers $6–9, salads $4–8.50, and steak, chicken, and Mexican dishes from $10. Open daily 11 A.M.–midnight.

Services and Information

The **Greyhound** bus depot is at 5031 51st Ave., 250/774-6322. Daily scheduled service runs south to Dawson Creek and north to Whitehorse. The **post office** is also on 51st Avenue. **Fort Nelson General Hospital** is at 5315 Liard St., 250/774-6916. The town also has plenty of gas stations, two banks, and a laundromat.

At Mile 300.5 of the Alaska Highway is **Fort Nelson Visitor Info Centre,** 250/774-6868. Here you can get information on road conditions and find out the current topics for the Visitor Welcome Program—a series of entertaining talks on local subjects, offered each summer's evening. The center is open daily 8 A.M.–8 P.M. in summer.

CONTINUING TO WATSON LAKE

Awaiting the traveler on this 525-km portion of the Alaska Highway are Rocky Mountain peaks, glacial lakes, mountain streams, provincial parks with some great scenery, and the mighty Liard River.

Soon after leaving Fort Nelson you'll come to a junction with the gravel **Liard Highway,** which runs north 175 km to Fort Liard in the Northwest Territories. From this junction, the Alaska Highway climbs the lower slopes of **Steamboat Mountain,** which, with a certain amount of

imagination, resembles an upturned boat. Here you'll have tremendous views of the Rocky Mountains and the valley below. **Tetsa River Provincial Park,** 85 km west of Fort Nelson and one km from the highway, offers grayling fishing in the river and short riverside hiking trails. A campground within the park has sites for $12 a night.

Summit Lake and Vicinity

This lake, 140 km west of Fort Nelson, is a popular stopping point for travelers. It lies at the north end of 25,691-hectare **Stone Mountain Provincial Park,** a vast wilderness of jagged peaks, lakes, and rivers named for the predominantly stony nature of the mountains. The best way to appreciate the surrounding panorama is by hiking the 2.6-km **Summit Peak Trail,** which ends in a treeless alpine area 1,000 vertical meters above the trailhead. The massive elevation gain means only the fittest of hikers should attempt the trail; allow at least two hours each way. The trailhead is on the north side of the highway, across from the campground. Much less strenuous is the 2.5-km trail to **Flower Springs Lake,** nestled in alpine peaks south of the highway. Allow one hour each way. The trailhead is three km along Microwave Tower Road, which spurs south at the café.

Wokkpash Recreation Area, 37,800 hectares of wilderness suitable only for experienced backcountry users, adjoins the southern boundary of Stone Mountain Provincial Park. Known for its hoodoos, deep gorges, and alpine meadows, the area is accessible on foot or by horseback along a 25-km route through the Wokkpash Valley to Wokkpash Lake.

At Summit Lake's eastern end is an exposed campground (expect snow at any time of the year) with pit toilets and picnic tables; $12 a night. The **Summit Cafe,** open daily 7 A.M.–10 P.M., is a popular truck stop; hearty breakfasts are $4.50–10, and sandwiches and burgers start at $6.

Just beyond the lake, the highway crosses 1,295-meter **Summit Pass,** highest point along the Alaska Highway. From this lofty summit, the highway continues to **One-fifteen Creek Provincial Park,** where a 300-meter trail leads to huge beaver dams. Camping in the park is $12. **Toad River,** 55 km from Summit Lake and at Mile 426 of the Alaska Highway, is the next small service center. Here you'll find **Poplars Campground,** 250/232-5465, which has gas, a restaurant, cabins from $55 s or d, and campsites with hookups for $18.

Muncho Lake Provincial Park

Lying among mountains and forested valleys at the north end of the Canadian Rockies, this 88,420-hectare park surrounds stunning **Muncho Lake,** one of the highlights of the Alaska Highway.

Upon entering the park from the east, **Folded Mountain** comes into view to the north. This easy-to-recognize peak is representative of the area's geology; it was created by extensive folding and faulting of limestone bedrock. But it's the park's namesake lake that will grab your attention. The magnificent, 12-km-long body of water is encircled by a dense spruce forest, which gives way to barren rocky slopes at higher elevations. North of the lake, natural mineral licks attract Stone sheep and woodland caribou to the roadside.

The small community of Muncho Lake spreads out along the eastern banks of the lake, providing services for park visitors. If you plan to overnight here, try to book ahead; motel rooms and campgrounds all fill up well in advance in July and August. **J & H Wilderness Motel & RV Resort,** 250/776-3453, offers motel rooms for $62 s or d as well as campsites with clean and modern facilities, including free hot showers, for $16–25. The resort's restaurant is particularly good, and portions are served with the trucker's appetite in mind; breakfasts from $4.50, dinners from $9, a burger with a huge portion of fries for $6.50. It's open daily 7 A.M.–10 P.M. The most pleasant camping is found at the two campgrounds in the provincial park itself, north of the town. Sites at these two campgrounds are all $12 a night, but with only 15 sites in each one, they fill up fast.

Liard River Hot Springs Provincial Park

One of the most wonderful places to stop on the whole highway is this 1,082-hectare park, 40 km north of Muncho Lake. Most travelers understandably rush to soak their tired, dusty limbs in the hot pools. But the rest of the park is also worth exploring. The hot springs have created a microclimate around the overflow area. Over 80 plant species here are found nowhere else in northern British Columbia. Also inhabiting the area are many species of small fish plus mammals such as moose, woodland caribou, and black bear.

Early indigenous people no doubt discovered the springs, but workers on the Alaska Highway constructed the boardwalk and pools that exist today. The 500-meter-long boardwalk leads from the main parking lot over warm-water swamps to **Alpha Pool,** where water bubbles up into a long, shallow concrete pool. The pool area, surrounded by decking, has pit toilets and changing rooms. A rough trail leads 200 meters farther to undeveloped **Beta Pool,** which is cooler, much deeper, and not as busy.

At the entrance to the hot springs is a campground providing toilets and showers. Firewood is available. Sites are $15 May–Aug. and $9 the rest of the year. The sites are often full by noon. Gates to the hot springs and campground are locked between 11 P.M. and 6 A.M.

Opposite the park entrance, at Mile 497, is **Trapper Ray's Liard Hot Springs Lodge,** 250/776-7349, which has rooms for $65 s or $70 d, campsites for $12–15, a small café, some grocery supplies, and gas. At Mile 496, **Lower Liard River Lodge,** 250/776-7341, offers rooms with shared facilities for $50 s, $55 d. This lodge has a great little café/restaurant and serves as the Greyhound bus stop.

To Watson Lake and Beyond

Anglers will find good fishing for grayling in the Liard River below **Smith River Falls,** 30 km or so northwest of the hot springs. Canyon and river views dot the highway heading north and west, and visitor services are available at **Coal River** and **Fireside.** The highway crosses the 60th parallel and enters the Yukon just before Contact

© ANDREW HEMPSTEAD

signpost forest at Watson Lake

Creek Lodge (all services). It then meanders back and forth across the border six times before reaching the final crossing, 57 km farther west.

Watson Lake (pop. 1,800), a major service center along the highway, lies just north of the British Columbia–Yukon border. The town is best known for the famous **Signpost Forest** started by Carl K. Lindley, a GI who was working on the Alaska Highway. Instructed to repair a directional sign, he added a mileage sign to his hometown of Danville, Illinois. Over the years others followed his lead, and today over 20,000 signs have been added. Behind the "forest" is the excellent **Visitor Reception Centre,** 403/536-7469, open in summer daily 8 A.M.–8 P.M. This facility provides visitors with historic information on the highway through extensive displays and an audiovisual presentation.

Twenty-one km west of Watson Lake, the Alaska Highway meets the Stewart-Cassiar High-

way (see above), which leads south to the Yellowhead Highway between Prince George and Prince Rupert. The distance between Prince George and Watson Lake is almost identical via either the Alaska Highway or the Stewart-Cassiar Highway. The loop trip up one and back the other is around 2,450 km.

Continuing north on the Alaska Highway, it's 444 km to Whitehorse, capital of the Yukon; 524 km to Skagway, northernmost point of the Alaska Marine Highway; and 1,990 km to Delta Junction, Alaska, the official end of the Alaska Highway. The best source of information for those continuing north is Don Pitcher's *Moon Handbooks: Alaska-Yukon.*

ATLIN

The small community of Atlin lies in the extreme northwest corner of British Columbia,

370 km west of Watson Lake along the Alaska Highway, then 100 km south along a mostly unpaved road. Isolated a long way from the rest of the province, it's one of British Columbia's most picturesque and intriguing communities. The glaciated peaks of the Coast Mountains form a stunning backdrop for the town, which is on a gently sloping hill overlooking beautiful **Atlin Lake,** one of British Columbia's largest natural lakes. The lake's southern end and a massive chunk of the Coast Range are encompassed in 301,140-hectare **Atlin Provincial Park.**

Atlin was a boomtown with more than 8,000 people during the 1898 Klondike gold rush, when gold was discovered in nearby Pine Creek. Today they're still finding some color hereabouts, but the town's population has dwindled to about 500.

The highlight of Atlin is the surrounding scenery. The film adaptation of Farley Mowat's *Never Cry Wolf* was shot here, and it's easy to understand why. Wandering along the lakeshore you'll have outrageous views of sparkling peaks, glaciers, waterfalls, and mountain streams. Tied up on the lake in front of town is the **SS Tarahne,** a steamer built in 1916. The vessel plied the lake for 20 years, providing freight and transportation services. If you want to get out on the lake yourself, contact **Norseman Adventures,** 250/651-7535, which rents small motorboats (from $80 for eight hours) and houseboats (from $1,095 for seven days).

Atlin Historical Museum, housed in a 1902 schoolhouse at the corner of 3rd and Trainor Streets, 250/651-7522, lets you relive the excitement of the gold rush and Atlin's early days and view a display of Tlingit artifacts. It's open in summer daily 9 A.M.–5:50 P.M.; admission is $3. Scattered through town are many historic buildings and artifacts pretty much untouched from the gold-rush era. The **Pioneer Cemetery,** two km east of town, reveals Atlin's pioneer history through stories and tales on weathered grave markers.

South of Atlin along Warm Springs Road are various lakes, camping areas, and, at the end of the road, **warm springs.** The springs bubble out of the ground at a pleasant 29° C (84° F) into shallow pools surrounded by flower-filled meadows.

Practicalities

The main accommodation in town is the **Atlin Inn,** on 1st St., 250/651-7546. It's right in the center of town and has a café downstairs (open daily 7 A.M.–9 P.M.). The rooms are luxurious, and at $105 s, $115 d they're still reasonable value. The inn also offers similarly priced kitchen-equipped cottages.

South of town, along the road to the warm springs, are several **campgrounds.** The first of these, Pine Creek, has pit toilets and firewood, and it's the only one with a fee; tents $7, RVs $9. The others at Palmer Lake, Atlin Lake, and the warm springs are free. **Atlin Visitor Info Centre** is in the museum at the corner of 3rd and Trainor Streets, 250/651-7522. It's open July–August daily 9 A.M.–5:30 P.M., weekends only in June and September.

Resources

Suggested Reading

Natural History

Baldwin, John. *Mountain Madness: Exploring British Columbia's Ultimate Wilderness.* Vancouver: Harbour Publishing, 1999. Filled with stunning photography, this coffee table book is a worthwhile purchase for climbers or anyone interested in the natural landscapes of the Coast Mountains.

Cannings, Richard. *British Columbia: A Natural History.* Vancouver, Douglas & McIntyre, 1996. The natural history of the province divided into 10 chapters, from the earliest origins of the land to problems faced in the new millennium. It includes lots of color photos, diagrams, and maps.

Folkens, Peter. *Marine Mammals of British Columbia and the Pacific Northwest.* Vancouver: Harbour Publishing, 2001. In a waterproof, fold-away format, this booklet provides vital identification tips and habitat maps for 50 marine mammals, including all species of whales present in local waters.

Gadd, Ben. *Handbook of the Canadian Rockies.* Jasper, Alberta: Corax Press, 1995. The latest edition of this classic guide is in color, and although bulky for backpackers it's a must-read for anyone interested in the natural history of the Canadian Rockies.

Gill, Ian. *Haida Gwaii: Journeys through the Queen Charlotte Islands.* Vancouver: Raincoast Books, 1997. A personal and touching view of the Queen Charlottes complemented by the stunning color photography of David Nunuk.

Haig Brown, Roderick. *Return to the River.* Vancouver: Douglas & McIntyre, 1997. Although fictional, this story of the life of one salmon and its struggle through life is based on fact,

and is a classic read for both anglers and naturalists. It was originally published in 1946 but has recently been reprinted and is available at most bookstores.

Hare, F. K., and M. K. Thomas. *Climate Canada.* Toronto: John Wiley & Sons, 1974. One of the most extensive works on Canada's climate ever written. Includes a chapter on how the climate is changing. Look for it in Vancouver's secondhand bookstores.

Herrero, Stephen. *Bear Attacks: Their Causes and Avoidance.* Toronto: Mclelland & Stewart, 1999. Canadian bear expert Herrero has written one of the best books on the subject of bear attacks.

Lyons, C. P. *Trees, Shrubs, and Flowers to Know in British Columbia.* Edmonton, Alberta: Lone Pine Publishing, 1995. This popular field guide makes the province's flora easy to identify through detailed descriptions and illustrations.

Osborne, Graham (photographer). *British Columbia: A Wild and Fragile Beauty.* Vancouver: Douglas & McIntyre, 1993. In my opinion this coffee table book depicts the natural beauty of British Columbia better than any other edition currently in print. A short section of moving text accompanies each photograph.

Sandford, R. W. *The Canadian Alps: The History of Mountaineering in Canada.* Canmore, Alberta: Altitude Publishing, 1990. Complete human history of the Canadian Rockies from the earliest explorers to first ascents of major peaks.

Whitaker, John. *National Audubon Society Field Guide to North American Mammals.* New York: Random House, 1997. One of a series of field guides produced by the National Audubon Society, this one details mammals through color plates and descriptions of characteristics, habitat, and range.

Human History

Coull, Cheryl. *A Traveller's Guide to Aboriginal B.C.* Vancouver: Whitecap Books, 1996. Although this book covers native sites throughout the province, the Lower Mainland (Vancouver) chapter is very comprehensive. Also included are details of annual festivals and events and hiking opportunities with a cultural slant.

Duff, Wilson. *The Indian History of British Columbia: The Impact of the White Man.* Victoria: University of British Columbia Press, 1997. In this book Duff deals with the issues faced by natives in the last 150 years but also gives a good overview of their general history.

Jenness, Diamond. *The Indians of Canada.* Toronto: University of Toronto Press, 1977. Originally published in 1932, this is the classic study of natives in Canada, although Jenness's conclusion, that they were facing certain extinction by "the end of this century," is obviously outdated.

Johnson, Pauline. *Legends of Vancouver.* Vancouver: Douglas & McIntyre, 1998. This recently reprinted book, first published in 1911, contains the writings of Pauline Johnson, a well-known writer and poet in the early part of the 1900s. She spent much of her time with native peoples, and this is her version of myths related to her by Joe Capilano, chief of the Squamish.

Lavallee, Omer. *Van Horne's Road.* Montreal: Railfare Enterprises, 1974. William C. Van Horne was instrumental in the construction of Canada's first transcontinental railway. This is the story of his dream and the boomtowns that sprung up along the route. Lavallee de-

votes the final chapter to Vancouver and how the arrival of the railway affected the young city and created a Canadian gateway to the Orient.

McMillan, Alan D. *Native Peoples and Cultures of Canada.* Vancouver: Douglas & McIntyre, 1995. A comprehensive look at the archaeology, anthropology, and ethnography of the native peoples of Canada. The last chapters delve into the problems facing these people today. The author is a professor at Vancouver's Simon Fraser University, so the chapters on the Pacific Northwest are particularly strong.

Nicol, Eric. *Vancouver.* Toronto: Doubleday Canada, 1970. An often-humorous look at Vancouver and its colorful past through the eyes of Eric Nicol, one of Vancouver's favorite columnists of the 1960s. It's been reprinted a few times, and although it has been out of print for many years, Vancouver's secondhand bookstores usually have multiple copies in stock.

Reksten, Terry. *Rattenbury.* Victoria: Sono Nis Press, 1998. The biography of Francis Rattenbury, British Columbia's preeminent architect at the turn of the 20th century. The histories of his most famous Victoria and Vancouver buildings are given, and the final chapter looks at his infamous murder at the hands of his wife's young lover.

Suttles, Wayne. *Northwest Coast.* Vol. 7, *Handbook of North American Indians.* Washington, D.C.: Smithsonian Institution, 1990. This volume is probably the most comprehensive piece ever written dedicated entirely to the natives of the Pacific Northwest.

Recreation Guides

Hudson, Rick. *Gold, Gemstones, and Mineral Sites of British Columbia.* Victoria: Orca Books, 1999. This still-evolving series currently has two volumes in print. Volume 1 details sites on Vancouver Island. Volume 2 covers sites around Vancouver and within a day's drive of the city. The history of each location, along with a map, what the site holds today, and interesting related facts make this a must-read for keen rockhounds.

Kariel, Herbert G. *Alpine Huts in the Canadian Rockies, Selkirks, and Purcells.* Canmore, Alberta: Alpine Club of Canada, 1986. Covers the history of all huts in the above ranges, with current access routes and status and descriptions of nearby peaks to climb.

Lebrecht, Sue, and Judi Lees. *52 Weekend Activities around Vancouver.* Vancouver: Douglas & McIntyre, 1995. There's something for everyone in this popular book, whether it be nude beaches or skiing at Whistler.

Macaree, Mary, and David Macaree. *109 Walks in British Columbia's Lower Mainland.* Vancouver: Douglas & McIntyre, 1997. The fourth edition of this guide details over 100 easy walks throughout Vancouver, the Fraser River Valley, and as far north as Whistler. Two pages are devoted to each walk, including detailed text, a hand-drawn map, and a black-and-white photo.

Patton, Brian, and Bart Robinson. *Canadian Rockies Trail Guide.* Banff, Alberta: Summerthought, 2000. This regularly updated guide, first published in 1971, covers all hiking trails in the mountain national parks.

Pratt-Johnson, Betty. *101 Dives from the Mainland of Washington and British Columbia.* Surrey, British Columbia: Heritage House Publishing, 1999. This book and its companion volume, *99 Dives from the San Juan Islands in Washington to the Gulf Islands,* are the best sources of detailed information on diving in British Columbia.

Woodsworth, Glenn. *Hot Springs of Western Canada.* West Vancouver: Gordon Soules Book Publishers, 1997. Details every known hot springs in western Canada, including both commercial and undeveloped sites. A short history, directions, and practicalities are given for each one.

Arts and Crafts

Allen, D. *Totem Poles of the Northwest.* Surrey, British Columbia: Hancock House Publishers Ltd., 1977. Describes the importance of totem poles to native culture and totem pole sites and their history.

Kew, Della, and P. E. Goddard. *Indian Art and Culture of the Northwest Coast.* Surrey, British Columbia: Hancock House Publishers Ltd., 1997.

Twigg, Alan. *Vancouver and its Writers.* Vancouver: Harbour Publishing, 1986. Vancouver has produced many fine writers, while other writers have moved to the city from elsewhere. This book gives short biographies on them all.

Encyclopedia

Francis, Daniel. *The Encyclopedia of British Columbia.* Vancouver: Harbour Publishing, 2000. This extraordinary compilation reputedly took 10 years of Francis's life to put together. It contains 4,000 entries over 824 pages in a coffee table–style format. The $99 book comes with an interactive CD-ROM, complete with hyperlinks. The book's website is www.knowbc.com.

Other Guidebooks

Canadian Automobile Association. *Tour Book: Western Canada and Alaska.* Another booklet available free to members.

Christie, Jack. *Inside Out British Columbia.* Vancouver: Raincoast Books, 1998. Although the organization of this book is sometimes difficult to follow, it is the most comprehensive guide available to all recreational opportunities the province has to offer, especially the provincial parks. Jack Christie is a prolific author who also writes *Day Trips from Vancouver* and *One-day Getaways from Vancouver* (both published by Douglas & McIntyre, Vancouver).

Hempstead, Andrew. *Moon Handbooks: Vancouver.* Emeryville, California: Avalon Travel Publishing, 2002. Comprehensive coverage of Vancouver in the same format as this book.

Hill, Kathleen, and Gerald Hill. *Victoria and Vancouver Island.* Connecticut: Globe Pequot Press, 1999. This emphasizes dining and shopping on Vancouver Island, with the final chapter detailing the island's history.

The Milepost. Bellevue, Washington: Vernon Publications. This annual publication is a must-have for those traveling through western Canada and Alaska. The maps and logged highway descriptions are incredibly detailed. Most northern bookstores stock *The Milepost,* or order by calling 800/726-4707 or online at www.milepost.com.

Pantel, Gerda. *The Canadian Bed and Breakfast Guide.* Toronto: Penguin Books Canada, 2002. Lists all bed and breakfasts prepared to pay a fee, so the reviews aren't very objective. Also lists prices.

Tourism British Columbia. *Accommodations.* Updated annually, this free booklet is available at information centers throughout British Columbia or by calling 250/387-1642 or 800/435-5622, or online at www.hellobc.com.

Western Canadian Bed and Breakfast Innkeepers Association. Contact this association for a copy of its annual accommodations guide, 604/255-9199, website www.wcbbia.com. It contains descriptions and prices of more than 120 properties.

Magazines

Beautiful British Columbia. Victoria. This quarterly magazine depicts the beauty of the province through stunning color photography and informative prose. It's available by subscription; 250/384-5456 or 800/663-7611, website www.beautifulbc.ca.

The Canadian Alpine Journal. Canmore, Alberta. Annual magazine of the Alpine Club of Canada with articles from its members and climbers from around the world. Website www.alpineclubofcanada.ca.

Canadian Geographic. Ottawa: Royal Canadian Geographical Society. Bimonthly publication pertaining to Canada's natural and human histories and resources. Website www.canadiangeographic.ca.

Equinox. Markham, Ontario. This bimonthly publication looks at Canada's natural world and humanity's relationship with it.

Explore. Calgary, Alberta. Bimonthly publication of adventure travel throughout Canada. Website www.explore-mag.com.

Nature Canada. Ottawa, Ontario. Quarterly magazine of the Canadian Nature Federation. Website www.cnf.ca.

Internet Resources

Accommodations

Accent Inns (www.accentinns.com)
Bed and Breakfast Online
 (www.bbcanada.com)
Best Western (www.bestwestern.com)
Choice Hotels Canada
 (www.choicehotels.ca)
Coast Hotels and Resorts
 (www.coasthotels.com)
Country Inns and Suites
 (www.countryinns.com)
Days Inn (www.daysinn.com)
Delta Hotels and Resorts
 (www.deltahotels.com)
Fairmont Hotels and Resorts
 (www.fairmont.com)
Hilton Worldwide (www.hilton.com)
Holiday Inns (www.holiday-inn.com)
Hostelling International Canada
 (www.hihostels.ca)
Howard Johnson (www.hojo.com)
Radisson (www.radisson.com)
Ramada (www.ramada.com)
Samesun (www.samesun.com)
Traveller's Inn (www.travellersinn.com)
Western Canadian Bed and Breakfast
 Innkeepers Association
 (www.wcbbia.com)

Airlines

Air BC (www.aircanada.ca)
Air Canada (www.aircanada.ca)
Air China (www.airchina.com)
Air New Zealand (www.nzair.com)
Air Pacific (www.airpacific.com)
Alaska Airlines (www.alaskaair.com)
All Nippon Airways website
 (www.ana.co.jp)
American Airlines (www.aa.com)
Baxter Aviation (www.baxterair.com)
British Airlines (www.britishairlines.com)

Canada 3000 (www.canada3000.com)
Continental Airlines
 (www.continental.com)
Eva Air (www.evaair.com.tw)
Harbour Air website
 (www.harbour-air.com)
Hawk Air (www.hawkair.net)
Horizon Air (www.horizonair.com)
Japan Airlines (www.jal.co.jp)
KD Air (www.kdair.com)
KLM (www.klm.nl)
Korean Air (www.koreanair.com)
Lufthansa (www.lufthansa.de)
North Vancouver Air
 (www.northvanair.com)
Northwest Airlines (www.nwa.com)
Pacific Coastal (www.pacific-coastal.com)
Philippine Airlines
 (www.philippineair.com)
Qantas (www.qantas.com.au)
Singapore Airlines (www.singaporeair.com)
Skywest (www.skywest.com)
United Airlines (www.ual.com)
West Coast Air (www.westcoastair.com)
WestJet (www.westjet.com)

Car and RV Rental

Alamo (www.alamo.com)
Avis (www.avis.com)
Budget (www.budget.com)
C.C. Canada Camper RV Rentals
 (www.canada-camper.com)
Cruise America (www.cruiseamerica.com)
Discount (www.discountcar.com)
Dollar (www.dollar.com)
Enterprise (www.enterprise.com)
Go West (www.go-west.com)
Hertz (hertz.com)
Lo Cost (www.locost.com)
National (www.nationalcar.com)
Rent-a-wreck (www.rentawreck.ca)
Thrifty (www.thrifty.com)

Government

Government of British Columbia
(www.gov.bc.ca)
Government of Canada (www.gc.ca)
Citizenship and Immigration Canada
(www.cic.gc.ca)
Canada Customs and Revenue Agency
(Visitor Rebate Program)
(www.ccra-adrc.gc.ca/visitors)
Parks Canada (www.parkscanada.gc.ca)

Bus, Ferry, and Rail

B.C. Ferries (www.bcferries.com)
BC Rail (www.bcrail.com)
Bigfoot Adventure Tours
(www.backpackertours.com)
Greyhound (www.greyhound.ca)
Laidlaw (www.victoriatours.com)
Moose Travel Network
(www.mooserun.com)
MV *Coho* (www.northolympic.com/coho)

Rocky Mountaineer Railtours
(www.rockymountaineer.com)
VIA Rail (www.viarail.ca)
Victoria Clipper (www.victoriaclipper.com)
Victoria Express (www.victoriaexpress.com)
Washington State Ferries
(www.wsdot.wa.gov/ferries)

Tourism Offices

Canadian Tourism Commission
(www.canadatourism.com)
Cariboo Tourism Association
(www.landwithoutlimits.com)
Northern BC Tourism Association
(www.northernbctravel.com)
Thompson/Okanagan Tourism Association
(www.thompsonokanagan.com)
Tourism Association of Vancouver Island
(www.islands.bc.ca)
Tourism British Columbia
(www.hellobc.com)
Tourism Rockies (www.bcrockies.com)
Tourism Victoria

Index

A

Abandoned Rails Interpretive Trail: 351
Abbotsford: 51, 95, 238
Abbotsford International Airshow: 29, 84
Abbott Ridge: 351–352
accommodations: 30–33, 464; *see also specific place*
Adams Family House of Silver: 432
Adams River Sockeye Run: 361
agriculture: 18, 252, 259, 263
Ainsworth Hot Springs: 295
airlines: 35–37, 113, 464
air transportation: 35–37, 39–40, 43–44, 112–113; *see also specific place*
Akamina-Kishinena Provincial Park: 304–305
Alaska Highway: 391, 448–458
Alaska Marine Highway: 39, 423–424
Alberni Harbour Quay: 179
Alberni Valley Museum: 179
Alcan: 412
Alcan Dragon Boat Festival: 83
alcohol: 33–34; drunk driving 42
Alert Bay: 126, 203–204
Alexandra Bridge Provincial Park: 244
Alexis Creek: 382
Alhambra Hotel: 54
Alice Lake Provincial Park: 224–225
Alpine Blossom Festival: 364
Alpine Wine Festival: 232
Anahim Lake: 383
Andy Bailey Provincial Recreation Area: 454
Anglican Church: 204
Anne Hathaway's Thatched Cottage: 133
anthropology: 62–63
Antique and Classic Boat Show: 266
Apex-Busk Cross-country Ski Area: 292
Apex Mountain Resort: 254
Apple Blossom Festival: 29, 266
arbutus: 4
archaeology: 417–418
arctic grayling: 10
area: 2
area codes: 46
Argenta: 296
argillite carving: 28
Arrowsmith, Mt.: 178

Art Gallery of Greater Victoria: 132
Art Gallery of the South Okanagan: 253
arts and crafts: 28, 82, 138–139, 159, 393, 429–430
Arts Club: 78
Assiniboine, Mt.: 324
astronomy: 62
Asulkan Glacier: 349
Asulkan Valley: 351
Athabascan people: 12–13
Atlin: 457–458

Art Galleries, Centers, and Museums

Art Gallery of Greater Victoria: 132
Art Gallery of the South Okanagan: 253
Arts Club: 78
Brackendale Art Gallery: 223
Cariboo Friendship Society: 380
Chan Centre for the Performing Arts: 78
Dawson Creek Art Gallery: 450
Eagle Aerie Gallery: 188
Emily Carr Institute of Art and Design: 57
Ford Centre for the Performing Arts: 78
Haida Gwaii Museum: 429–430
Kamloops Art Gallery: 362
Kelowna Art Gallery: 259
Kootenay Gallery: 284
Nanaimo Art Gallery: 172
Native Art Gallery: 393
Northern Light Studio: 411
Old Schoolhouse Gallery and Art Centre: 191
Pacific Institute of Culinary Arts: 106–107
Primal Song Gallery: 380
Prince Rupert Performing Arts Centre: 416, 419
Smithers Art Gallery: 405
Station House Gallery: 380
Studio 2880: 395
Terrace Public Library: 411
Two Rivers Art Gallery: 393
Vancouver Art Gallery: 53
Vernon Public Art Gallery: 271

Atlin Historical Museum: 458
Atlin Lake: 458
Atlin Provincial Park: 458
Avalanche Crest: 351
Azure Lake: 369

B
Babine Lake: 403
Babine Mountains Provincial Park: 405
backpacker accommodations: *see* hostels
backpacker buses: 40–41
backpacking: *see* hiking
Bailey's Chute: 369
Balance Rock: 430
bald eagles: 223
Balfour: 295
Ballet British Columbia: 78
Balu Pass: 352
Bamfield: 181
Banff-Windermere Road: 327, 330
banks: 47
Barclay Heritage Square: 60
Bard on the Beach: 78, 83
Barker, Billy: 387
Barkerville Historic Town: 348, 387–388
bars: Vancouver 78–79; Victoria 137–138; *see also specific place*
basketry: 28
Bastion, The: 168–170
Bastion Square: 130
Bavarian City Mining Railway: 308
Bavarian Platzl: 308
B.C. Firefighters Museum: 280
BC Forest Discovery Centre: 159
B.C. Golf Museum: 63
B.C. Lions: 76
B.C. Museum of Mining: 221–222
B.C. Orchard Industry Museum: 259
B.C. Place Stadium: 56
B.C. Sports Hall of Fame and Museum: 56
beachcombing: 431
Beacon Hill Park: 131
Beardale Castle Miniatureland: 359
Bear Glacier: 438
bears: 5, 6, 320, 410
Beatrice Lake Trail: 286
Beatton Provincial Park: 453
Beaumont Provincial Park: 401
Beaver Lake: 71
Beaver Pond Trail: 246

beavers: 8
bed and breakfasts: 31; Vancouver 95–96; Victoria 144–146; *see also specific place*
Bedwell Lake: 201
beer: 34, 298
Belcarra Regional Park: 69
Belfry Theatre: 138
Bella Coola: 384
Bella Coola Museum: 384
Benvoulin Heritage Park: 259
Berg Lake Trail: 373–374
bicycling: *see* cycling
Big Bar Lake Provincial Park: 378–379
bighorn sheep: 319
Big Sky Golf and Country Club: 230
Big White Ski Resort: 265
Bijoux Falls Provincial Park: 445
Billy Barker Days: 29, 385–386
Bird Walk Trail: 432
birds/bird-watching: 8, 65, 302, 320, 321, 380, 399, 431–432
Birkenhead Lake Provincial Park: 237
black bears: 5, 320
Blackjack: 281
Blanshard, Richard: 14
Bloedel Floral Conservatory: 64
Blood Alley: 54
Blue Grouse Interpretive Trail: 67
Blue River: 369–370
blues music: 80, 232
boating: 23–24; *see also specific place*
Bodega y Quadra, Don Juan Francisco de la: 13, 202
Boer Mountain Forestry Lookout: 402
bookstores: Vancouver 120; Victoria 154
Boston Bar: 244
Botanical Beach: 156
Boundary Museum: 279–280
Bowen Island: 68
Bowen Park: 170
Bowron Lake Provincial Park: 22, 388
Boya Lake Provincial Park: 444
Boyle Point Provincial Park: 192
Brackendale: 223
Brackendale Art Gallery: 223
Bralorne: 237
Brandywine Falls Provincial Park: 225, 234
Brentwood Bay: 134
Brisco: 324
Britannia Beach: 221–222

Britannia Heritage Shipyards: 64
British Columbia Wine Information Centre: 256
Brockton Point: 61
Broken Group Islands: 185
brown bears: *see* grizzlies
Bruce, Mt.: 164
Bruce, Randolph: 327
Bucket of Blood: 402
Buckinghorse River Provincial Park: 454
Bugaboo Glacier Provincial Park: 324
Bulkley Valley Museum: 405
Bull Canyon Provincial Park: 382
Bull Mountain: 381
bungee jumping: 172
Burgess Shale: 335
Burnaby: 51, 69, 94–95
Burnaby Mountain Park: 69
Burnaby Village Museum: 69
Burns Lake: 389, 401–402
buses: 38, 40–41, 465; *see also specific place*
business hours: 47
Butchart Gardens: 134–135
Buttle Lake: 201
Butze Rapids: 416
Byrnes Block: 54

C
Cache Creek: 376–377
Cactus Cup Mountain Bike Festival: 232
Calcheak Trail: 225
Calona Vineyards: 260
Cameron Lake: 178
Campbell River: 197–199
camping: 32–33; *see also specific place*
Canada Day: 29, 30, 83
Canada Place: 52, 53
Canadian Craft Museum: 53
Canadian Mountain Bike Festival: 364
Canadian Museum of Rail Travel: 300–302
Canadian Pacific Railway: 327, 335–336, 350–351
Canadian Rockies: *see* Rocky Mountains
Canal Flats: 312
Canfor: 393
Canim Beach Provincial Park: 379
Canim River Falls: 379
canoeing: 22–23; Powell River 217–218; Vancouver 74; Whistler 229
Cape Fife Trail: 434

Cape Mudge Lighthouse: 200
Cape Scott Lighthouse: 208
Cape Scott Provincial Park: 208
Capilano River Regional Park: 67
Capilano Salmon Hatchery and Regional Park: 66–67
Capilano Suspension Bridge: 66
Cariboo Country: 348, 376–388
Cariboo Friendship Society: 380
Cariboo gold rush: 14–15
Cariboo Mountains: 376
Cariboo Wagon Road: 15, 376
Carmanah Valley: 160
Carmanah Walbran Provincial Park: 155, 160–161
Carol Ships Parade of Lights: 85
Carp Lake Provincial Park: 444
Carr, Emily: 53, 57, 131
carriage tours: 136
car rentals: 42–43, 464; Vancouver 116; Victoria 153; *see also specific place*
Carrot Park: 204–205
car travel: 41–43
Cascade Falls: 441
Cascade Lookout: 245
Cassiar: 443
Castlegar: 283–285
Castle Park: 247
Cathedral Basin: 339
Cathedral Grove: 178
Cathedral Place: 53
Cathedral Provincial Park: 248
caves: 192, 295
Cedar Creek Estate Winery: 263
Celebration of Light: 84
Centennial Museum: 413
Centennial Square: 131
CFB Esquimalt Naval & Military Museum: 133
Chamber of Mines Museum: 290–291
Champion Lakes Provincial Park: 282
Chan Centre for the Performing Arts: 78
Charlie Lake: 452–453
Charlie Lake Provincial Park: 453
Chasm Provincial Park: 377–378
Chateau Whistler Golf Club: 229
Chemainus: 161
Cherryville: 288
Cheslatta Falls: 399
Chesterman Beach: 186
Chetwynd: 445

Chilcotin Coast: 382
Chilcotin Plateau: 382
Chilko Lake: 382–383
Chilliwack: 51
China Beach: 156
Chinatown (Vancouver): 53, 54–55, 106
Chinatown (Victoria): 131
Chinese Cultural Centre: 55
Chinese Mountain: 200
chinook salmon: 9
Christ Church Cathedral (Vancouver): 53
Christ Church Cathedral (Victoria): 132
Christina Lake: 280
Christina Lake Golf Club: 280
chum salmon: 9
Circlepac: 211
City Hall (Victoria): 131
City Park (Kelowna): 258
Clachnacudiann Range: 355
Clark's nutcracker: 320
Clayburn Village: 238
Clayoquot Sound: 186
Clearwater: 368
Clearwater Lake: 369
Clearwater Lakes Trail: 411
Cleveland Dam: 67
climate: 3–4, 183
Clinton: 377–378
Clinton Ball: 377
Cloverdale Rodeo and Exhibition: 83
Clover Point: 132
Coalmont: 247
Coal River: 456
Coast Mountains: 2, 221, 376
Coast Salish people: 11
Cody Caves Provincial Park: 295
coho salmon: 9
Coldstream Valley: 288
Columbia Brewery: 298
Columbia Mountains: 2
Columbia River: 3
Columbia River Wetland: 321
comedy clubs: Vancouver 80
Cominco Gardens: 308
Cominco Interpretive Centre: 282
commercial fishing: 18–19
Comox: 193
Comox Air Force Museum and Airpark: 193
Comox Valley: 191, 192–195
confederation: 15–16

Connaught Hill Park: 391
Connor Lake: 312
Continental Divide: 2, 318, 331
Cook, James: 13
Coombs: 178
Copperstain: 352–353
Coquihalla Canyon: 241
Coquihalla Canyon Provincial Park: 241–242
Coquihalla Highway: 244–245
Coquitlam: 51, 69–70
Cormorant Island: 203–204
Cortes Island: 200–201
costs: 45; accommodations 30; departure taxes
    35; flight 36
Cottonwood House Provincial Historic Park:
    387
Cottonwood Island Nature Park: 393, 395
cougars: 7, 320
Coursier, Mt.: 355
Courtenay: 193
Courtenay and District Museum: 193
Cowichan, Lake: 155, 157, 160
Cowichan River: 160
Cowichan River Provincial Park: 160
Cowichan sweaters: 28
Coyote Creek Trail: 408
coyotes: 7, 320
Craigdarroch Castle: 132–133
Craigellachie: 359
Craig Heritage Museum: 191
Cranberry: see Powell River
Cranbrook: 277, 299, 300–303
Crawford Bay: 297
Crescent Beach: 66
Creston: 297–298
Creston & District Museum: 298
Creston Valley Wildlife Management Area:
    297–298
Crooked River Provincial Park: 444
cross-country skiing: 231, 254, 281, 292, 381,
    395, 406; see also skiing
cruises: Nanaimo 172; Nootka Sound 202;
    Thompson River 364; Vancouver 117
Crystal Garden: 130
Crystal Mountain: 265
Crystal Pool: 137
cuisine: 33
Cultus Lake: 99
Cultus Lake Provincial Park: 239
Cumberland: 193

currency: 44–45
customs: 44
cycling: 22; Kamloops 364; Kelowna 264; Mount Revelstoke N.P. 356; Nelson 291; Rossland 281; Stanley Park 61; Vancouver 72, 116–117; Victoria 137, 154; Whistler 228–229, 232
Cypress Mountain: 75
Cypress Provincial Park: 52, 68

D

Dall's sheep: 7–8
dance: 78
D'Arcy: 237
Davison Orchards: 273
Dawson Creek: 391, 448–452
Dawson Creek Art Gallery: 450
Dawson Creek Exhibition and Stampede: 451
Dawson Creek Golf Course and Country Club: 451
Dawson Creek Rodeo: 29–30
Dawson Falls: 368
Dawson, Mt.: 349
Deadman's Island (Burns Lake): 402
Deadman's Island (Vancouver): 61
Dease Lake: 442
Deep Cove: 68
deer: 6–7, 319
Deighton, Jack: 54
Delkatla Wildlife Sanctuary: 431–432
Della Falls: 180
Delta: 51, 65, 94
Denman Island: 192
departure taxes: 35
Desert Centre: 252
Desolation Sound Marine Park: 23, 221
Deville Icefield: 349
dinosaurs: 447
disabled travelers, services for: 46, 118
Discovery Coast Passage: 384–385
diseases: 45–46
diving: 24–25, 74, 137, 172, 215, 218
Dodge Cove: 418
Dog Lake: 331
Dominion Hotel: 54
Douglas Border Crossing: 66
Douglas fir: 4
Douglas, James: 14
Doukhobor Bridge: 284

Doukhobor Heritage Centre: 279
Doukhobors: 279, 283–284
Doukhobor Village Museum: 283–284
Driftwood Canyon Provincial Park: 405
drinking age: 34
driving: 41–43; winter safety 46
Dr. Sun Yat-Sen Classical Chinese Garden: 55
Drumbeg Provincial Park: 177
Duffey Lake: 237
Duncan: 159–160
Dutch Creek Hoodoos: 312

E

Eagle Aerie Gallery: 188
Eagle Creek Agate Opal Site: 402
eagles: 223
Earls Cove: 211, 215
East Beach: 430, 434
Echo Valley Ranch Resort: 378
economy: 17–19
Edgewater: 324
Ed Jones Haida Museum: 432
Edziza, Mt.: 443
electricity: 47
Elgin Heritage Park: 66
Elizabeth Lake Bird Sanctuary: 302
elk: 7, 319
Elk Falls Provincial Park: 199
Elkford: 305–306
Elk Lake: 137
Elk Lakes Provincial Park: 306
Ellison Provincial Park: 273
Elphinstone Pioneer Museum: 212
Emerald Basin: 340
Emerald Lake: 337–338, 339–340
emergencies: 118
Emily Carr House: 131
Emily Carr Institute of Art and Design: 57
Emory Creek Provincial Park: 243
employment: 43
Empress Hotel: 128, 142, 148
Enchanted Forest: 359
English Bay Beach: 52, 57, 73
Englishman River Provincial Park: 178
entertainment: 27–28; *see also specific entertainment; specific place*
Eskers Provincial Park: 393
Esquimalt Lagoon: 133, 134
Ethel F. Wilson Provincial Park: 402
events: *see* festivals

Exchamsiks River Provincial Park: 412, 413
exchange rates: 44
exploration, European: 13–14

F
Fair, The (Pacific National Exhibition): 84
Fairmont Hot Springs: 312–313
Fairmont Hot Springs Ski Area: 313
Fairweather, Mt.: 2
Fairy Lake: 157
Fall Wine Festival: 266
False Creek: 55–57, 71–72
False Creek Ferries: 57
Fantasy North Waterslide: 395
Faquier: 288
fauna: 4–10, 183, 319, 326, 334, 350, 425; *see
    also specific animal*
Fernie: 299, 303–304
Fernie Alpine Resort: 279, 303–304
ferries: 38–39, 41, 465; Comox 195; Discovery
    Coast Passage 384–385; Nanaimo 176–177;
    Port Hardy 207; Prince Rupert 423; Queen
    Charlotte Islands 427; Southern Gulf Islands
    162; Sunshine Coast 211–212; Vancouver 57,
    68, 114–115, 116; Victoria 136, 151–152; *see
    also specific place*
Ferry Island: 410, 411
Festival of Banners: 173
Festival of Lights: 29, 85
festivals: 28–30; *see also specific festival; specific
    place*
Fete d'hiver: 396
Field: 334
Fife Point: 434
Filberg Festival: 29, 193
Filberg Heritage Lodge and Park: 193
Fillongley Provincial Park: 192
film processing: 118–119, 154
films/film industry: 19, 84–85, 241
Finlayson, Mt.: 134
Firehall Museum: 416
Fireside: 456
Fireweed Trail: 331
First Nations Cultural Night: 420
Fisgard Lighthouse: 133
Fish Creek: 440
fish/fishing: 8–10, 25–26; Campbell River 198;
    commercial 18–19; Nelson 291; northern
    B.C. 393–394, 399, 401, 402, 403, 404, 411;
    Port Alberni 179–180; Queen Charlottes

432;Sunshine Coast 214, 218; Vancouver 74
Fish Lake: 311
Fisherman's Wharf Park: 130
Fisherville: 299
fishing licenses: 25–26
Fitzwilliam Basin Trail: 374
flightseeing: Mount Robson Provincial Park 374;
    Vancouver 52, 67, 68, 117; Whistler 230
Floe Lake: 331–332
flora: 4, 183, 318, 326, 334, 350
Flower Springs Lake: 455
Fly Hills Scenic Drive: 360
Folded Mountain: 456
FolkFest: 29
food: 33–34; Pacific Institute of Culinary Arts
    106–107
football: 76
Forbidden Plateau: 193, 194
Forbidden Plateau Ski Area: 194
Ford Centre for the Performing Arts: 78
Forest Alliance Visitors Centre: 54
Forest Expo: 29, 396
Forest for the World: 393
Forestry Visitor Centre: 179
forestry: 17, 54, 159, 179, 392–393, 396, 428
Forest Service campgrounds: 33
forests: 4, 25
Fort Fraser: 401
Fort George Canyon Trail: 394
Fort George Park: 391, 395
Fort George Railway Station: 391
Fort Langley National Historic Site: 238
Fort Nelson: 454–455
Fort Nelson Historical Museum: 454
Fort Nelson River: 454
Fort Rodd Hill National Historic Site: 133
Fort St. James: 399–401
Fort St. James National Historic Site: 400
Fort St. John: 452–453
Fort St. John–North Peace Museum: 452
Fort Steele: 277, 306–307
Fort Steele Heritage Town: 306
Fort Victoria: 127
49th parallel: 161
fossils: 335, 405, 447
Fox, Terry: 370
Francois Lake: 401
Frank Island: 186
Fraser–Fort George Regional Museum: 391–392
Fraser Lake: 401

Fraser River: 3, 211, 243–244, 376
Fraser River Canyon: 243–244
Fraser, Simon: 13, 50, 240–241, 391, 400
Fraser Valley: 238–240
Fraserview Golf Course: 73
French Beach Provincial Park: 155
Friendly Cove: 202
Fringe Festival (Prince George): 396
Fringe Festival (Vancouver): 84
frostbite: 46
Furry Creek Golf and Country Club: 221
fur-trading: 13–14

G

Gabriola Island: 177–178
Gabriola Sands Provincial Park: 177
Galbraith's Ferry: 299
Galena Bay: 296
Galiano Island: 166–167
Gallagher's Canyon Golf & Country Club: 264
Ganges: 162
Gang Ranch: 379
Gaolers Mews: 54

Gardens

Bloedel Floral Conservatory: 64
Butchart Gardens: 134–135
Cominco Gardens: 308
Crystal Garden: 130
Dr. Sun Yat-Sen Classical Chinese Garden: 55
Gator Gardens: 204
Kasugai Gardens: 259
Nitobe Memorial Garden: 63
Pacific Undersea Gardens: 130
Point Ellice House and Garden: 133
UBC Botanical Garden: 63
VanDusen Botanical Garden: 63–64
Victoria Butterfly Gardens: 135

Garibaldi, Mt.: 224
Garibaldi Provincial Park: 224–225
Gastown: 50, 53, 54, 81–82, 105–106
Gator Gardens: 204
geography: 2–4
George C. Reifel Bird Sanctuary: 65
Gibson Lake: 294
Gibsons: 212–213
ginseng: 55

Gitksan people: 11, 408
Glacier Gulch: 406
Glacier Inn: 440
Glacier National Park: 24, 347–354
Gladstone Provincial Park: 280
Gleneagles Golf Course: 73
Glenora: 443
Goat Range Provincial Park: 296
goats: 8, 319
Godey Creek Hiking Trail: 245
Gold Bridge: 237
Golden: 315, 343–346
Golden Ears Provincial Park: 70, 99
Golden Golf and Country Club: 345
Golden Hinde, Mt: 3, 201
Goldmine Trail: 134
Gold Nugget Route: 237
Gold River: 201–202
gold rush: 14–15, 299, 376
Gold Rush Trail: 15, 376
Goldstream Provincial Park: 134, 147
golf: 26; Kelowna 264; Kootenays 280, 297, 309,
    313; northern B.C. 451; Queen Charlottes
    435; Rockies 321, 345; Vancouver 63, 72–73;
    Vernon 274; Whistler 229–230
goods and services tax: 45
Goodsir, Mt.: 334
Gordon Bay Provincial Park: 160
Gordon MacMillan Southam Observatory: 62
government: 19–20
Government House: 132
Graham Island: 425
Granby Provincial Park: 280
Grand Canyon of the Stikine: 442
Grand Forks: 279–280
Grand Okanagan: 258
Granisle: 403
Granite City: 247–248
Granite Creek Recreation Site: 248
Granville: 50
Granville Island: 57, 82, 106–107
Granville Island Museums: 57
Granville Island Public Market: 57
Granville Street: 51
Gray Monk Estate Winery: 263
gray whales: 9
Greater Vernon Museum and Archives: 271
Great Glacier: 351
Greene, Nancy: 281
Green Lake: 379

Golf Courses

B.C. Golf Museum: 63
Big Sky Golf and Country Club: 230
Chateau Whistler Golf Club: 229
Christina Lake Golf Club: 280
Dawson Creek Golf Course and Country Club: 451
Fraserview Golf Course: 73
Furry Creek Golf and Country Club: 221
Gallagher's Canyon Golf & Country Club: 264
Gleneagles Golf Course: 73
Golden Golf and Country Club: 345
Greywolf Golf Course: 313
Harvest Golf Club: 264
Kimberley Golf Course: 309
Kokanee Springs Golf Resort: 297
Langara Golf Course: 73
Mayfair Lakes & Country Club: 73
McCleery Golf Course: 73
Meadow Gardens Golf Course: 73
Michaelbrook Ranch Golf Club: 265
Mountainside golf course: 313
Nakusp Golf Course: 287
Nicklaus North: 229–230, 231
Okanagan Golf Club: 264–265
Predator Ridge Golf Course: 274
Radium Resort golf course: 321
Riverside golf course: 313
Sheep Pasture Golf Course: 377
Trickle Creek Golf Resort: 309
University Golf Course: 73
Whistler Golf Club: 229
Willows Golf Course: 435

Greywolf Golf Course: 313
Grice Bay: 183
Grist Mill: 249
grizzly bears: 5, 320
grouse: 320
Grouse Mountain: 67, 75
Grouse Mountain Skyride: 52, 67
Gulf of Georgia Cannery National Historic Site: 64
Gull Creek Trail: 408
Gwaii Haanas National Park Reserve: 24, 427, 435–436
Gyro Beach: 264

H
hadrosaurs: 447
Hague Lake: 200
Hagwilget Suspension Bridge: 408
Haida Gwaii Museum: 429–430
Haida people: 11, 425–427, 435–436
Hainle Vineyards Estate Winery: 260–263
Hamilton Beach: 165
Hamilton Falls: 340
handicapped travelers, services for: 118
handicrafts: see arts and crafts
Haney House: 360
Harper Mountain: 364–365
Harrisand World Championship Sand Sculpture Competition: 29
Harrison Hot Springs: 238, 239–240
Harrison Lake: 239
Harvest Golf Club: 264
Hastings Park Racecourse: 76
Hat Creek Ranch: 376
Haynes Point Provincial Park: 252
Hays, Charles M.: 414
Hays, Mt.: 419
Haywire Bay Regional Park: 219
Hazelton: 407–408
health: 45–46
Heather Trail: 245
Heckman Pass: 383
Height of the Rockies Provincial Park: 311–312
helicopter rides: see flightseeing; heli-skiing
heli-skiing: 27, 231; see also skiing
Helliwell Provincial Park: 192
Hell's Gate: 244
Helmcken Falls: 368
Helmcken House: 129
Heriot Bay: 200
Heritage Centre (Burns Lake): 402
Heritage Corner (Quesnel): 385
Heritage Days (Nanaimo): 173
Heritage Park (Hudson's Hope): 447
Heritage Park (Terrace): 410
Heritage River Trail (Prince George): 394
Heritage Village (Vanderhoof): 399
Hermit: 352
He-tin-kis Park: 181
Hillside Estate: 256
history: 11–16; see also specific place
hockey: 76
holidays: 30
holiday work visas: 43

Hiking

21–22
Brandywine Falls: 225
Bugaboo Glacier Provincial Park: 324
Glacier National Park: 351–353
Golden Ears Provincial Park: 70
Goldstream Provincial Park: 134
Kelowna: 264
Kokanee Glacier Provincial Park: 294–295
Kootenay National Park: 330–333
Manning Provincial Park: 245–246
Mount Assiniboine Provincial Park: 325
Mount Revelstoke National Park: 356
Mount Robson Provincial Park: 373–374
Nelson: 291
Pacific Rim National Park: 184
Powell River: 216–217
Prince Rupert: 419
Queen Charlottes: 434
Terrace: 410–411
Valhalla Provincial Park: 286
Vancouver: 71–72
West Coast Trail: 157–159
Whistler: 228
Yoho National Park: 338–341 *see also specific trail*

Hoodoo Trail: 340
Hope: 211, 240–243
Hope Museum: 241
Hope Slide: 242
Hornby Island: 192
Horne Lake Caves Provincial Park: 192
horseback riding: 246, 321, 338, 380–381
horse-drawn carriage tours: 136
Horsefly Lake Provincial Park: 379
horse racing: 76
Horseshoe Bay: 51, 69, 221
Horstman Glacier: 231
hospitals: Vancouver 118; Victoria 154; *see also specific place*
hostels: 32; Fernie 304; Kamloops 365–366; Kelowna 266; Nanaimo 173; Nelson 292; Penticton 255; Prince Rupert 420; Queen Charlottes 428; Revelstoke 357; Rossland 282; Salt Spring Island 164; Southern Gulf Islands 164; Squilax 361; Tofino 188; Vancouver 97–98; Victoria 146; Whistler 233; Yoho National Park 341
Hotel Europe: 54
hotels: 30–31; *see also specific place*
Hotel Vancouver: 53–54
Hotspring Island: 436
hot springs: 187, 239–240, 287, 295, 312–313, 327–330, 436; 456
houseboats: 360
Houston: 403
Howe Sound: 209, 221
H.R. MacMillan Space Centre: 62
Hudson Bay Mountain Lookout: 405
Hudson's Bay Company: 13–14, 391
Hudson's Hope: 444, 446–447
Hudson's Hope Museum: 447
Hugh Keenleyside Dam: 284
Hunlen Falls: 383
Hyack Festival: 83
Hyder: 391, 439, 440–441; *see also* Stewart
hypothermia: 46

I

ice hockey: 76
Iceline Trail: 339
ice wine: 33, 260–263
Idaho Peak: 287
Illecillewaet Glacier: 349
Indian Arm: 74
Indian Bighouse: 204
information: 47–48; Vancouver 121–122; Victoria 154; *see also specific place*
Inland Lake: 216
Inner Harbour: 128
International Folk Festival: 309
International Old Time Accordian Championship: 29, 309
Internet access: 47; Vancouver 118
Invermere: 313
Inverness, Mt.: 355
Ironman Canada: 255
Irving House Historic Centre: 70
Iskut: 441–442

J

jazz: 29, 80, 83, 138, 232, 255
Jeldness, Olaus: 281
Jimsmith Lake Provincial Park: 303
Joffre Lakes Provincial Park: 237
Joker Lakes: 295

Joker Millsite: 294
Jordan River: 156
Juan de Fuca Provincial Park: 156
Julyfest: 309
Junction Sheep Range Provincial Park: 382
Juniper Trail: 331
Juskatla: 431

K

Kaatza Station Museum: 160
Kalamalka Lake: 274
Kalamalka Lake Provincial Park: 274
Kal Beach: 274
Kamloops: 347, 361–367
Kamloops Art Gallery: 362
Kamloops Museum: 362
Kamloops Symphony Society: 364, 365
Kamloops Wildlife Park: 364
K&S Historic Trail: 287
Karst Creek Trail: 201
Kaslo: 295–296
Kasugai Gardens: 259
Kathlyn Glacier: 405–406
Kathlyn, Lake: 406
Kaufmann Lake: 332
Kawkawa Lake: 242
kayaking: 22–23; Broken Group Islands 185;
   Comox Valley 194; Desolation Sound 221;
   Nahatlatch River 244; Powell River 217–218;
   Prince Rupert 419; Southern Gulf Islands
   164, 166; Tofino 187–188; Vancouver 74;
   Victoria 136; Whistler 229
Kekuli Bay Provincial Park: 275
Kelowna: 250, 258–270; accommodations
   266–268; food 268–269; history 258;
   recreation 264–266; services and information
   270; sights 258–263; transportation 270
Kelowna Art Gallery: 259
Kelowna Comedy Festival: 266
Kelowna Fringe Festival: 266
Kelowna Land and Orchard Co.: 263
Kelowna Museum: 259
Kenney Dam: 399
Keremeos: 248–249
Keremeos Columns Provincial Park: 249
Kermode bear: 410
Kettle River Railway: 257
Kettle Valley Railway: 264
Khutzeymateen: 418
Kicking Horse Mountain Resort: 343–345

Kicking Horse River: 334
Kilby Historic Store and Farm: 239
killer whales: 9
Kimberley: 277, 299, 307–310
Kimberley Alpine Resort: 309
Kimberley Golf Course: 309
Kimberley Heritage Museum: 308
Kinaskan Lake Provincial Park: 441
Kinbasket Lake: 355
Kincolith: 418
Kindersley Summit: 331
King George, Mt.: 311
King Pacific Lodge: 419
Kinney Lake: 373
Kinuseo Falls: 446
Kiskatinaw Provincial Park: 452
Kispiox: 408
Kispiox Salmon Hatchery: 408
Kitimat: 412–413
Kitimat River Fish Hatchery: 413
Kitimat Works: 412–413
Kitsilano: 51, 52, 62, 110–111
Kitsilano Beach: 62, 74
Kitsilano Showboat: 83
Kitwancool: 438
Kitwanga: 438
Kleanza Creek Provincial Park: 412
Knox Mountain: 264
Knox Mountain Hill Climb: 264, 266
Kobau, Mt.: 252
Kokanee Creek: 291
Kokanee Creek Provincial Park: 292, 294
Kokanee Glacier Provincial Park: 279, 291,
   294–295
Kokanee Lake: 294
kokanee salmon: 10, 25
Kokanee Springs Golf Resort: 297
Kootenay Bay: 297
Kootenay Candles: 298
Kootenay Crossing: 330
Kootenay Forge: 297
Kootenay Gallery: 284
Kootenay Lake: 294–297
Kootenay Mountains: 277–314
Kootenay National Park: 24, 315, 326–333
Kootenay Pass: 283
Kootenay people: 11–12, 299, 327, 334–335
Kootenay River: 326, 330
'Ksan Historical Village and Museum: 408
Kwagiulth Museum: 200

Kwagiulth people: 11
Kwinitsa Station Railway Museum: 416
Kyuquot: 202

L

Lac La Hache: 379
Ladysmith: 161
Lake Cowichan: 160
Lakelse Lake Provincial Park: 410, 412
Lakes District: 401
land: 2–4
Landing, The: 54
Langara Golf Course: 73
Langara Island: 432
Langdale: 211
Langley: 51
language: 16
Lang Vineyards: 253
Laurel Point: 129–130
Law Courts: 53
Lawn Hill: 430
Lax Kw'alaams: 418
Le Roi Gold Mine: 281
Lewis Park: 193
Liard Highway: 455
Liard River: 3, 454
Liard River Hot Springs Provincial Park: 456
libraries: 119–120
licenses: fishing: 25–26; driver's 41–42
Lighthouse Park: 52, 69
Lightning Lake: 246
Lillooet: 377
Lillooet Museum: 377
Little Mountain: 52, 64
Little Qualicum Falls Provincial Park: 178
Lizard Lake: 157
Lockhart Beach Provincial Park: 297
logging: *see* forestry
Lois Lake: 217
London Mountain: 225
Long Beach: 183–184
Lonsdale Quay: 52, 66
Lookout!, The: 52
Lost Lagoon: 61
Lost Lake: 216–217, 228, 229
Loveland Bay Provincial Park: 199
Lower Falls Trail: 70
Lulu Island: 64
Lumby: 288
Lund: 220

Lupin Falls: 201
Lyall Harbour: 167
Lynn Canyon Park: 67
Lynn Headwaters Regional Park: 67
lynxes: 7, 320
Lytton: 243, 244

M

Mabel Lake Provincial Park: 288
Mackenzie: 444–445
Mackenzie, Alexander: 13, 384
Mackenzie Rock: 384
MacMillan Provincial Park: 178
magazines: 120–121
Magog, Lake: 325
mail: 46
Malkin Bowl: 60
mammals: 4–8, 9
Manning Park Resort: 246
Manning Provincial Park: 245–246
Manson's Landing Provincial Park: 200
Maple Tree Square: 54
maps: 47–48, 120
Marathon of Hope: 370
Marble Canyon: 330–331
Mariner's Reef Waterpark & Slides: 265
maritime commerce: 19, 62, 131
Maritime Museum of British Columbia: 131
marmots: 8
Marsh Trail: 134
Marysville: 308
Marysville Falls: 308–309
Masset: 431–433
Masset Cemetery: 432
Maxwell, Mt.: 164
Mayfair Lakes & Country Club: 73
Mayne Island: 167
McArthur, Lake: 338–339
McCabe Trail: 405
McCleery Golf Course: 73
McCulloch Forest Tour: 263
McDonald Provincial Park: camping 147
McPherson Playhouse: 138
Meadow Gardens Golf Course: 73
Meadows in the Sky Parkway: 356
measurements: 47
medication: 46
Meeting of the Waters Trail: 351
Merritt: 245
Merritt Mountain Music Festival: 245

Museums

27–28
Alberni Valley Museum: 179
Atlin Historical Museum: 458
B.C. Firefighters Museum: 280
B.C. Golf Museum: 63
B.C. Museum of Mining: 221–222
B.C. Orchard Industry Museum: 259
B.C. Sports Hall of Fame and Museum: 56
Bella Coola Museum: 384
Boundary Museum: 279–280
Bulkley Valley Museum: 405
Burnaby Village Museum: 69
Canadian Craft Museum: 53
Canadian Museum of Rail Travel: 300–302
Centennial Museum: 413
CFB Esquimalt Naval & Military Museum: 133
Chamber of Mines Museum: 290–291
Comox Air Force Museum and Airpark: 193
Courtenay and District Museum: 193
Craig Heritage Museum: 191
Creston & District Museum: 298
Doukhobor Village Museum: 283–284
Ed Jones Haida Museum: 432
Elphinstone Pioneer Museum: 212
Firehall Museum: 416
Fort Nelson Historical Museum: 454
Fort St. John–North Peace Museum: 452
Fraser–Fort George Regional Museum: 391–392
Granville Island Museums: 57
Greater Vernon Museum and Archives: 271
Haida Gwaii Museum: 429–430
Heritage Park: 410
Hope Museum: 241
Hudson's Hope Museum: 447
Kaatza Station Museum: 160
Kamloops Museum: 362
Kelowna Museum: 259
Kimberley Heritage Museum: 308
'Ksan Historical Village and Museum: 408
Kwagiulth Museum: 200
Kwinitsa Station Railway Museum: 416
Lillooet Museum: 377
Maritime Museum of British Columbia: 131
Model Ships Museum: 57
Model Trains Museum: 57

Mountain View Doukhobor Museum: 279
Museum at Campbell River: 198
Museum of Anthropology: 62–63
Museum of Northern British Columbia: 416
Museum of the Cariboo Chilcotin: 380
Nakusp Museum: 287
Nanaimo District Museum: 170
Nelson Museum: 290
New Westminster Museum: 70
North Pacific Cannery Village Museum:
    416–417
Pacific Mineral Museum: 54
Penticton Museum: 253
Port Clements Museum: 430–431
Port Hardy Museum: 205
Powell River Historical Museum: 215–216
Prince George Railway and Forestry Museum:
    392–393
Princeton and District Pioneer Museum: 247
Quesnel and District Museum: 385–386
Revelstoke Museum: 354
Revelstoke Railway Museum: 354
Roedde House Museum: 60
Rossland Museum: 280–281
Royal British Columbia Museum: 128–129
Royal London Wax Museum: 130
Salmon Arm Museum: 360
Sandon Museum: 287
Secwepemc Museum and Heritage Park:
    362–363
Sidney Museum: 135
Silvery Slocan Museum: 285
South Cariboo Historical Museum: 377
Sport Fishing Museum: 57
Squamish Valley Museum: 222
Station Museum: 448–450
Steveston Museum: 64
Stewart Historical Society Museum: 439
Vancouver Centennial Police Museum: 55
Vancouver Maritime Museum: 62
Vancouver Museum: 61–62
Vanderhoof Community Museum: 399
Windermere Valley Museum: 313
Wine Museum: 259
Yale Museum: 244

Metlakatla: 418
metric system: 47
Meziadin Junction: 438
Meziadin Lake Provincial Park: 438
Mica Dam: 354–355
Michaelbrook Ranch Golf Club: 265
Mid-Winter Break-Out: 255
Mile Zero: 450–451
Mile Zero Celebrations: 29, 451
Mill Bay: 134
Miners Bay: 167
Miniature World: 130
mining: 18, 54, 221–222, 281, 290–291, 308
Miracle Beach Provincial Park: 196
Mission: 238
Mission Hill Family Estate: 260
Moberly Lake Provincial Park: 446
Model Ships Museum: 57
Model Trains Museum: 57
Monashee Mountains: 277
Monashee Provincial Park: 288
Monashee Woolen Mill: 288
money: 44–45, 118
Monkman Provincial Park: 446
Montague Harbor Provincial Park: 166
moose: 6–7, 319, 394
Moose Lake: 371
Moose Marsh: 371
Moresby Island: 425
Morfee Lake: 445
Moricetown Canyon: 407
Moricetown Indian Reserve: 407
Morning Mountain Ski Area: 291–292
motels: 30–31; *see also specific place*
mountain biking: *see* cycling
mountain goats: 8, 319
Mountain View Doukhobor Museum: 279
mountains: 2–3; *see also specific mountain*
Mountainside golf course: 313
Mount Arrowsmith Regional Park: 178
Mount Assiniboine Provincial Park: 324–326
Mount Edziza Provincial Park: 443
Mount Fernie Provincial Park: 303
Mount Maxwell Provincial Park: 164
Mt. Pope Trail: 401
Mount Revelstoke National Park: 24, 355–356
Mount Robson Provincial Park: 348, 368, 370–375
Mount Seymour Provincial Park: 67–68
Mt. Timothy Ski Area: 381

Mt. Washington Alpine Resort: 193–194
Moyie: 299
Moyie Lake Provincial Park: 299
Mozart Festival: 266
mule deer: 6
Muncho Lake Provincial Park: 456
Murray Ridge Ski Hill: 401
Murrin Provincial Park: 222
Murtle Lake: 369
Murtle River: 368
Museum at Campbell River: 198
Museum of Anthropology: 62–63
Museum of Northern British Columbia: 416
Museum of the Cariboo Chilcotin: 380
museums: 27–28
Mush Bowl: 368
music: 29, 78, 80, 83, 138, 232, 245, 266, 364, 451
Muskeg North Musical Revue: 451
MV *Fintry Queen:* 264
MV *Lady Rose:* 179, 181, 185
MV *Uchuck III:* 202
Myra Falls: 201

N
Nahatlatch River: 244
Naikoon Provincial Park: 430, 433–434
Nairn Falls Provincial Park: 234, 237
Nakusp: 287–288
Nakusp Golf Course: 287
Nakusp Hot Springs: 287
Nakusp Museum: 287
Nanaimo Art Gallery: 172
Nanaimo: 168–178; accommodations 173–175; food 175–176; history 168; recreation 172–173; sights 168–172; services and information 177; transportation 176–177
Nanaimo District Museum: 170

National Parks

24–25, 33
Glacier: 24, 347–354
Gwaii Haanas: 24, 427, 435–436
Kootenay: 24, 315, 326–333
Mount Revelstoke: 24, 355–356
Pacific Rim: 24, 126, 157–159, 182–185
Yoho: 24, 315, 334–342

Nanaimo Marine Festival: 173
Nanaimo Theatre Group: 172
Naramata: 253
Natadesleen Lake: 441
National Geographic Theatre: 129
national park passes: 23, 318
Native Art Gallery: 393
native peoples: 11–13; arts and crafts 28; *see also specific group*
Natural Bridge: 337
Nechako Bird Sanctuary: 399
Nechako Plateau: 403
Neck Point Park: 172
Needles: 288
Nelson: 277, 289–294
Nelson Artwalk: 29, 291
Nelson Museum: 290
Netherlands Centennial Carillon: 129
Newcastle Island Provincial Marine Park: 170, 174
New Denver: 285–286
New Denver Glacier: 286, 287
New Hazelton: 407–409
newspapers: 120–121
Newton Lake: 200
New Westminster: 51, 70
New Westminster Museum: 70
Niagara Falls: 134
Nickel Plate Nordic Centre: 254
Nicklaus North: 229–230, 231
nightclubs: Vancouver 79–80; Victoria 138
Nimpkish Burial Ground: 204
Nimpkish Valley: 202
Nimpo Lake: 383
Ninstints: 425, 436
Nisga'a Memorial Lava Bed Provincial Park: 410
Nisga'a people: 11
Nitobe Memorial Garden: 63
Nootka Sound: 202
Nordic skiing: *see* cross-country skiing
North Beach: 433
Northern Alberta Railway Park: 448–450
Northern Light Studio: 411
North Pacific Cannery Village Museum: 416–417
North Pender Island: 165–166
North Shore: 66–69, 92, 95, 111–112
North Vancouver: 51, 66
North West Company: 13–14, 391
North Woven Broom: 297

O
Oak Bay: 132–133
observatories: 62
Ocean Falls: 385
Oesa, Lake: 338
Ogopogo: 263
O'Hara, Lake: 338–339, 342
Okanagan Game Farm: 253
Okanagan Golf Club: 264–265
Okanagan Lake: 250, 253
Okanagan Lake Bridge: 258
Okanagan Lake Dam: 253
Okanagan Lake Provincial Park: 257
Okanagan Mountain Provincial Park: 253, 264
Okanagan Valley: 250–276
Okanagan Valley Wine Train: 265
O'Keefe, Cornelius: 271
O'Keefe Ranch: 271–273
Okeover Arm: 220–221
Okeover Arm Provincial Park: 220
Oktoberfest: 232
Oldfield Creek Hatchery: 416
Old MacDonald's Farm: 265
Old Massett: 432
Old Schoolhouse Gallery and Art Centre: 191
Old Time Fair: 274
Old Town (Duncan): 159
Old Town (Victoria): 130–131
One-fifteen Creek Provincial Park: 456
150 Mile House: 379
100 Mile House: 376, 378
Only in Lillooet Days: 377
Ootsa Lake: 403
Opabin Plateau Circuit: 338
opera: 78, 138
orcas: 9
Orpheum Theatre: 78
Osoyoos Lake: 252
Othello-Quintette Tunnels: 241–242
otters: 425
outdoor equipment: 82–83
Overlanders: 15

P
Paarens Beach Provincial Park: 401
Pacifica Papers: 215
Pacific Crest Trail: 246
Pacific dogwood: 4
Pacific Institute of Culinary Arts: 106–107
Pacific Mariner's Memorial Park: 416

M

Index

Index

Provincial Parks

25, 33
Akamina-Kishinena: 304–305
Alexandra Bridge: 244
Alice Lake: 224–225
Atlin: 458
Babine Mountains: 405
Beatton: 453
Beaumont: 401
Big Bar Lake: 378–379
Bijoux Falls: 445
Birkenhead Lake: 237
Bowron Lake: 22, 388
Boya Lake: 444
Boyle Point: 192
Brandywine Falls: 225, 234
Buckinghorse River: 454
Bugaboo Glacier: 324
Bull Canyon: 382
Canim Beach: 379
Cape Scott: 208
Carmanah Walbran: 155, 160–161
Carp Lake: 444
Cathedral: 248
Champion Lakes: 282
Charlie Lake: 453
Chasm: 377–378
Cody Caves: 295
Coquihalla Canyon: 241–242
Cottonwood House Historic: 387
Cowichan River: 160
Crooked River: 444
Cultus Lake: 239
Cypress: 52, 68
Driftwood Canyon: 405
Drumbeg: 177
Elk Falls: 199
Elk Lakes: 306
Ellison: 273

Emory Creek: 243
Englishman River: 178
Eskers: 393
Ethel F. Wilson: 402
Exchamsiks River: 412, 413
Fillongley: 192
French Beach: 155
Gabriola Sands: 177
Garibaldi: 224–225
Gladstone: 280
Goat Range: 296
Golden Ears: 70, 99
Goldstream: 134, 147
Gordon Bay: 160
Granby: 280
Haynes Point: 252
Height of the Rockies: 311–312
Helliwell: 192
Horne Lake Caves: 192
Horsefly Lake: 379
Jimsmith Lake: 303
Joffre Lakes: 237
Juan de Fuca: 156
Junction Sheep Range: 382
Kalamalka Lake: 274
Kekuli Bay: 275
Keremeos Columns: 249
Kinaskan Lake: 441
Kiskatinaw: 452
Kleanza Creek: 412
Kokanee Creek: 292, 294
Kokanee Glacier: 279, 291, 294–295
Lakelse Lake: 410, 412
Liard River Hot Springs: 456
Little Qualicum Falls: 178
Lockhart Beach: 297
Loveland Bay: 199
Mabel Lake: 288

Pacific Mineral Museum: 54
Pacific Opera Victoria: 138
Pacific Rim National Park: 24, 126, 157–159, 182–185
Pacific Rim Whale Festival: 29, 188
Pacific Spirit Regional Park: 72
Pacific Undersea Gardens: 130

Pacific Wilderness Railway: 135–136
Paget Lookout: 340
painting: 28
Paint Pots: 330
Palliser Expedition: 335
Pandosy Mission Provincial Heritage Site: 259–260

Provincial Parks (cont'd)

MacMillan: 178
Manning: 245–246
Manson's Landing: 200
McDonald: 147
Meziadin Lake: 438
Miracle Beach: 196
Moberly Lake: 446
Monashee: 288
Monkman: 446
Montague Harbor: 166
Mount Assiniboine: 324–326
Mount Edziza: 443
Mount Fernie: 303
Mount Maxwell: 164
Mount Robson: 348, 368, 370–375
Mount Seymour: 67–68
Moyie Lake: 299
Muncho Lake: 456
Murrin: 222
Naikoon: 430, 433–434
Nairn Falls: 234, 237
Newcastle Island Marine: 170, 174
Nisga'a Memorial Lava Bed: 410
Okanagan Lake: 257
Okanagan Mountain: 253, 264
Okeover Arm: 220
One-fifteen Creek: 456
Paarens Beach: 401
Paul Lake: 364, 366
Petroglyph: 170–171
Pinecone Burke: 69–70
Pinnacle: 385
Porpoise Bay: 213
Porteau Cove: 99, 221
Prior Centennial: 165
Prudhomme Lake: 413, 422
Purcell Wilderness Conservancy: 279, 314
Purden Lake: 397

Rathtrevor Beach: 191
Red Bluff: 403
Roberts Creek: 213
Roderick Haig-Brown: 361
Rosebery: 286
Ross Lake: 407
Ruckle: 162–164, 165
Saltery Bay: 215
Sasquatch: 239, 240
Seymour: 52
Shannon Falls: 222
Silver Star: 275
Skagit Valley: 242
Smelt Bay: 200
Sowchea Bay: 401
Spatsizi Plateau Wilderness: 442
Sproat Lake: 181
Stagleap: 283
Stamp River: 180
Stikine River: 442
Stone Mountain: 455
Strathcona: 180, 193–194, 201
Sumas Mountain: 238–239
Sun-Oka Beach: 257
Syringa: 284–285
Ten Mile Lake: 385, 386
Tetsa River: 455
Thunder Hill: 312
Top of the World: 279, 311
Tribune Bay: 192
Ts'yl-os: 383
Tweedsmuir: 383–384, 402–403
Tyhee Lake: 405
Valhalla: 279, 286
Wasa: 311
Wells Gray: 348, 368–369
Whiteswan Lake: 311
Yahk: 299

Panorama Resort: 313–314
parasailing: 263
Parks Alive: 266
Parksville: 191
parliament buildings: 129
Paul Lake Provincial Park: 364, 366
Pavilion Theatre: 365

Peace Canyon Dam: 446
Peace River: 3, 444
Peace River Canyon: 452
Peach Festival: 255
Peachland: 257
Pemberton: 237
Pender Harbour: 214

Index

Pentastic Hot Jazz Festival: 255
Penticton: 250, 253–257
Penticton Highland Games: 255
Penticton Museum: 253
people: 16; native groups 11–13
Perez, Juan: 13
performing arts: 28; see also specific place
petrochemical plant: 413
Petroglyph Provincial Park: 170–171
Pinecone Burke Provincial Park: 69–70
Pine Creek Loop: 406
Pine Pass: 445
Pink Mountain: 453–454
pinks (salmon): 9–10
Pinnacle Provincial Park: 385
Pioneer Cemetery: 458
Piper's Lagoon Park: 171–172
Playhouse Theatre Company: 78
plesiosaurs: 447
Point Ellice House and Garden: 133
Point Grey: 51
Point Roberts: 65
Polar Bear Swim: 85
politics: 19–20
Polson Park: 271
population: 16
porcupines: 8
Porpoise Bay Provincial Park: 213
Port Alberni: 179–181
Port Alberni Salmon Festival: 180
Portal Lake: 373
Port Clements: 430–431
Port Clements Museum: 430–431
Porteau Cove Provincial Park: 99, 221
Port Essington: 414
Port Hardy: 126, 197, 204–208
Port Hardy Museum: 205
Portland Inlet: 438
Port McNeill: 203
Port Renfrew: 155, 156
Port Theatre: 172
postal services: 46
Powder King Mountain Resort: 395, 445
Powder Springs: 357
Powell Forest Canoe Route: 22, 217
Powell River: 209, 215–220
Powell River Historical Museum: 215–216
precipitation: 3
Predator Ridge Golf Course: 274
prescriptions: 46

Primal Song Gallery: 380
Prince George: 389, 391–398
Prince George Playhouse: 395
Prince George Railway and Forestry Museum: 392–393
Prince George Symphony Orchestra: 395
Prince Rupert: 389, 414–424; accommodations 420–422; food 422; history 414–416; recreation 419–420; services and information 424; sights 416–419; transportation 422–424
Prince Rupert Performing Arts Centre: 416, 419
Princeton: 247
Princeton and District Pioneer Museum: 247
Prior Centennial Provincial Park: 165
Prophet River: 454
Provincial Legislative Building: 129
Prudhomme Lake Provincial Park: 413, 422
Puntzi Lake: 382
Purcell Mountains: 277
Purcell Wilderness Conservancy Provincial Park: 279, 314
Purden Lake Provincial Park: 397
Purden Lake Ski Area: 395

Q
Quadra Island: 199–200
Quail's Gate Estate Winery: 260
Qualicum Beach: 191–192
Quanchus Mountains: 403
Quatse River Hatchery: 205–206
Queen Charlotte City: 427–429
Queen Charlotte Islands: 3, 389, 425–436
Queen Elizabeth Park: 64
Queen Elizabeth Theatre: 78
Queen Mary Lake: 312
Quesnel: 376, 385–387
Quesnel and District Museum: 385–386
Quesnel Lake: 379
Quesnel Rodeo: 386
Quintette Mine: 446
Quw'utsun' Cultural Centre: 159

R
Radium Hot Springs (hot springs): 327–330
Radium Hot Springs (town): 315, 321–324
Radium Resort golf course: 321
Radley Park: 413
Raft Cove: 208
rafting: 23, 229, 243, 244, 321, 343, 381
rail travel: 37, 40, 113, 115, 135–136, 153, 236,

257, 265, 300–302, 308, 354, 392–393, 416, 423, 448–450, 465
Rainbow Lake: 228
rainfall: 3
Rainforest Trail: 184
Rathtrevor Beach Provincial Park: 191
Rattenbury, Francis: 128, 130
rattlesnakes: 8
Raven Lake: 395
Ray Farm: 368–369
Rearguard Falls: 370
Rebecca Spit Marine Park: 200
recreation: 21–30; *see also specific recreation; specific place*
Red Bluff Provincial Park: 403
Redfish Creek: 291
Red Mountain: 279, 281
Reflection Lake: 343
Rennell Sound: 431
rental cars: 42–43, 464–465
reptiles: 8
reservations: 30–31
restaurants: 33; *see also specific place;*
Revelstoke: 347, 354–359
Revelstoke Dam: 354
Revelstoke Museum: 354
Revelstoke Railway Museum: 354
Richmond: 51, 64–65, 93–94
Riverfront Trail: 385
rivers: 3; *see also* rafting
Riverside golf course: 313
R.J. Haney Heritage Park: 360
Roberts Creek Provincial Park: 213
Robson Bight: 203
Robson Public Market: 60
Robson, Mt.: 2, 371
Robsonstrasse: *see* Robson Street
Robson Street: 53, 60, 91, 107–108
rock climbing: 222–223
Rockland: 132–133
rock music: 80, 138
Rockwall, The: 332
Rocky Mountains: 2, 315–346
rodeos: 83, 381, 386, 451
Roderick Haig-Brown Provincial Park: 361
Roedde House Museum: 60
Rogers, A.B.: 335–336, 350
Rogers Pass: 348, 349
Rootsfest: 29
Rosebery Provincial Park: 286

Rose Spit: 433
Ross Bay Cemetery: 132
Ross Lake: 340
Ross Lake Provincial Park: 407
Ross Lake Reservoir: 242
Rossland: 277, 280–282
Rossland Museum: 280–281
Rotary Beach: 264
Royal British Columbia Museum: 128–129
Royal Hudson: 115
Royal London Wax Museum: 130
Royal Theatre: 138
Ruckle Provincial Park: 162–164, 165
Russ Baker Memorial: 400
Russet Lake: 228
Ruth Lake: 379
RV rental: 43

S
Saanich Peninsula: 134–135
safety: 45–46; wildlife-watching 6
Sagebrush Theatre: 365
Salish people: 11, 258
Salmo: 282–283
Salmon Arm: 360–361
Salmon Arm Museum: 360
Salmon Glacier: 440–441
salmon: 8–10, 25–26, 66–67, 179–180, 205–206, 361, 408, 413, 416
Saltery Bay: 211, 215
Saltery Bay Provincial Park: 215
Salt Spring Island: 162–165
Saltwater Fishing Pier: 198
Sam Kee Building: 55
Sam Steele Days: 29, 302
Sandon Museum: 287
Sandon: 277, 286–287
Sandspit: 435
San Josef Bay: 208
San Juan Valley: 156–157
Sasquatch Provincial Park: 239, 240
Saturna Island: 167–168
Sayward: 202
Science World: 56–57
Scotiabank Dance Centre: 78
Scout Island Nature Centre: 380
scuba diving: *see* diving
SeaBus: 115
Sea Cavalcade: 212
Seafest: 29, 420

sea kayaking: *see* kayaking
Seal Bay Nature Park: 193
Sea Lion Festival: 172–173
Sea to Sky Highway: 209, 221–225
Seawall Promenade: 52, 60, 71
Sechart Whaling Station: 185
Sechelt: 213–214
Second Beach: 73
Secwepemc Museum and Heritage Park: 362–363
Selkirk Mountains: 277
Semiahoo Park: 66
Seven Sisters: 408
Seymour, Mt.: 67–68, 75
Seymour Provincial Park: 52
Shames Mountain: 411
Shannon Falls Provincial Park: 222
Shearwater: 385
Sheep Pasture Golf Course: 377
sheep: 7–8, 319
Shelter Point Regional Park: 220
Sherbrooke Lake: 340
shipping: 19
shopping: 28; Vancouver 81–83; Victoria 138–139; *see also specific place*
Shuswap Lake: 347, 360
Shuswap people: 334–335, 362–363
Sicamous: 359–360
Sidney: 135
Sidney Museum: 135
Signpost Forest: 457
Sikanni Chief: 454
Silver King Basin Trail: 405
Silversmith Mine Powerhouse: 287
Silver Star Cross-country Centre: 276
Silver Star Mountain Resort: 275–276
Silver Star Provincial Park: 275
Silvery Slocan Museum: 285
Similkameen Falls: 247
Similkameen River Valley: 248
Simon Fraser University: 69, 98
Singing Pass Trail: 228
Sitka deer: 6
Sitka spruce: 183
Skagit Valley Provincial Park: 242
Skeena River: 3
Skidegate Channel: 425
Skidegate Village: 430
Ski Mt. Cain: 202
Ski Smithers: 406

skiing: 26–27, 29; Cariboo Country 381; Kamloops 364–365; Kelowna 265; Kootenays 281, 303–304, 309, 313–314; Nelson 291–292; northern B.C. 394–395, 401, 406, 411, 445; Okanagan Valley 254, 276; Revelstoke 357; Rockies 343–345;
southwestern B.C. 246; Vancouver 74–75; Vancouver Island 193–194, 202; Whistler/Blackcomb 225–226, 230–231, 232
Skookumchuck Narrows Provincial Park: 214–215; *see also specific resort*
SkyTrain: 115
Slocan Valley: 285–287
Slush Cup: 232
Smelt Bay Provincial Park: 200
Smithers: 389, 405–407
Smithers Art Gallery: 405
Smith River Falls: 456
snakes: 8
snowboarding: *see* skiing
Sno-Cat skiing: 27; *see also* skiing
Snow Daze: 396
Snug Cove: 68
soccer: 76
sockeye salmon: 9
Sooke: 155
South Cariboo Historical Museum: 377
South Hazelton: 407
South Pender Island: 165
Southern Gulf Islands: 126, 162–168
Sowchea Bay Provincial Park: 401
space center: 62
Spahats Creek Falls: 368
Sparwood: 305
spas: 231
Spatsizi Plateau Wilderness Provincial Park: 442
Spillimacheen: 324
Spiral Tunnel Viewpoint: 336
Spirit Lake: 430
sportfishing: *see* fish/fishing
Sport Fishing Museum: 57
sports: 75–76; *see also specific sport*
Spotted Lake: 252
Spring Wine Festival: 29, 255, 266
Sproat Lake Provincial Park: 181
Spruce Fringe Loop: 184
Squamish: 222–224
Squamish Adventure Festival: 223–224
Squamish Days Logger Sports: 223
Squamish Valley Museum: 222

Squilax: 361
squirrels: 8
SS *Moyie*: 296
SS *Sicamous*: 253
Stagleap Provincial Park: 283
Stamp River Provincial Park: 180
stamps: 46
Stanley Glacier: 332–333
Stanley Park: 52, 53, 58–59, 60–61, 71, 72, 109
Stanley Theatre: 78
Station House Gallery: 380
Station Museum: 448–450
Stawamus Chief: 222–223
Steamboat Mountain: 455
steelhead: 25, 404
St. Elias Range: 2
St. Eugene's Mission Church: 302
Stellako River: 401
Steller's jay: 8
Steveston: 64–65
Steveston Landing: 64–65
Steveston Museum: 64
Steveston Salmon Festival: 83
Stewart: 391, 438–439; *see also* Hyder
Stewart-Cassiar Highway: , 437–444
Stewart Historical Society Museum: 439
St. John's Church: 244
Stikine River Provincial Park: 442
Stone Mountain Provincial Park: 455
Strathcona Provincial Park: 180, 193–194, 201
Strohn Lake: 438
Stuart Lake: 400
Studio 2880: 395
studying in Canada: 43
sturgeon: 10
Sullivan Mine: 308
Sumac Ridge Estate: 257
Sumas Mountain Provincial Park: 238–239
Summerland: 257
Summerland Sweets: 257
Summit Lake: 455
Summit Pass: 455
Summit Peak Trail: 455
Sun-Oka Beach Provincial Park: 257
Sun Peaks Resort: 364
Sun-Rype Products: 263
Sunset Beach: 73
Sunshine Coast Trail: 217
Sunshine Coast: 209, 211–221
surfing: 186

Surrey: 51, 66
Svoboda Bike Trail: 291
Swartz Bay: 134
Swim Lake: 225
swimming: 73–74, 137, 239, 395
Swiss Glacier: 349
Swy-A-Lana Lagoon: 168
Symphony of Fire: *see* Celebration of Light
Symphony Splash: 138
Syringa Provincial Park: 284–285

T
Tabor Mountain: 395
Takakkaw Falls: 336–337, 342
Takla-Nation Lakes: 400
taxes: 45, 35
taxis: 116, 152–153
Taylor: 452
Telegraph Cove: 126, 197, 202–203
Telegraph Creek: 437, 442–443
telephone services: 46–47; Vancouver 118
Telkwa: 404–405
temperatures: 3–4
Ten Mile Lake Provincial Park: 385, 386
Ten Ren Tea and Ginseng Co.: 55
Terrace: 389, 409–412
Terrace Mountain Nature Trail: 410–411
Terrace Public Library: 411
TerrifVic Jazz Party: 29
Terry Fox, Mt.: 370
Terry Fox Plaza: 370
Terry Fox Run: 370
Tetsa River Provincial Park: 455
Texada Island: 220
theater: Kamloops 365; Nanaimo 172; Prince
    George 395; Vancouver 78; Victoria 138
Theatre under the Stars: 78
Thetis Lake: 137
Third Beach: 61, 73
Thompson, David: 13, 299
Thompson River: 243
Three Valley Gap: 359
Thunderbird Park: 129
Thunder Hill Provincial Park: 312
time zones: 47, 353
tipping: 45
Tlell: 430
Tlingit: 11
Toad River: 456
Tofino: 126, 186–190

Topley Landing: 403
Top of the World Provincial Park: 279, 311
totem poles: 12, 159, 408, 438
tourism: 17
Tourism British Columbia: 48
tourism offices: 47, 48, 121–122, 154, 465
Townsite: see Powell River
Trail: 282–283
train travel: see rail travel
TransCanada Highway: 351
transcontinental railroad: 15, 359
Translink: 115
transportation: 35–43; air 35–37, 39–40,
    112–113; bus 38, 40–41, 113–114; car
    41–43; ferry 38–39, 41, 114–115; rail 37, 40,
    113, 115; see also specific place
travel seasons: 3–4
Tribune Bay Provincial Park: 192
Trickle Creek Golf Resort: 309
trolleys: 115–116
trout: 10, 25
Trout Lake: 296
Tsawwassen: 51
Tsimshian people: 11
Tsulquate Park: 204
Ts'yl-os Provincial Park: 383
Tumbler Ridge: 445–446
Tweedsmuir Provincial Park: 383–384, 402–403
Twin Falls (Babine Mountains P.P.): 406
Twin Falls (Yoho N.P.): 339
Two Hill Ecological Reserve: 433
Two River Junction: 29
Two Rivers Art Gallery: 393
Tyee Club: 198
Tyhee Lake Provincial Park: 405

U
UBC Botanical Garden: 63
Ucluelet: 181–182
U'Mista Cultural Centre: 204
ungulates: 319
University Golf Course: 73
University of Victoria: 132, 146
Upper Myra Falls Trail: 201

V
Valemount: 370
Valentine, Mt.: 216
Valhalla Provincial Park: 279, 286
Valhalla Wilderness Society: 286

Valley Trail: 228, 229, 231
Van Anda: 220
Vancouver: 49–122; accommodations 85–99;
    food 100–112; history 49–51; recreation 85;
    services and information 118–122; sights
    51–70; transportation 112–117
Vancouver Aquarium: 60–62
Vancouver Aquatic Centre: 74
Vancouver Art Gallery: 53
Vancouver Bach Choir: 78
Vancouver Breakers: 76
Vancouver Canucks: 76
Vancouver Centennial Police Museum: 55
Vancouver Chamber Choir: 78
Vancouver Chamber Music Festival: 83
Vancouver Folk Music Festival: 29, 83
Vancouver, George: 13, 50, 127, 202
Vancouver International Airport: 35, 93–94,
    112, 121
Vancouver International Children's Festival: 29, 83
Vancouver International Film Festival: 84–85
Vancouver International Jazz Festival: 29, 83
Vancouver International Marathon: 83
Vancouver International Writers Festival: 85
Vancouver Island: 3, 14, 123–208; see also specific
    place
Vancouver Little Theatre: 78
Vancouver Maritime Museum: 62
Vancouver Museum: 61–62
Vancouver Opera: 78
Vancouver Playhouse International Wine
    Festival: 29, 83
Vancouver Public Library: 119–120
Vancouver Sun Run: 83
Vancouver Symphony: 78
Vancouver Whitecaps: 76
Vanderhoof: 389, 399
Vanderhoof Community Museum: 399
VanDusen Botanical Garden: 63–64
Vanier Hall: 395
Vanier Park: 62
Verigin's Tomb: 284
Vermilion Pass Burn: 331
Vermilion River: 326
Vernon: 250, 271–278
Vernon, Forbes George: 271
Vernon Public Art Gallery: 271
Vernon Winter Carnival: 274
Victoria: 123, 127–154; accommodations
    139–147; food 147–151; history 127–128;

recreation 135–139; services and information 154–155; sights 128–135; transportation 151–154
Victoria Butterfly Gardens: 135
Victoria International Airport: 151
Victoria Operatic Society: 138
Victoria Symphony Orchestra: 138
vineyards: *see* wine/wineries
visas: 43
visitor information: *see* information; tourism offices

W

W.A.C. Bennett Dam: 446
Waddington, Mt.: 2, 376
walking: 71–72; *see also hiking*
walleye: 10
Walter Wright Pioneer Village: 451
Wapta Falls: 340–341
War Falls: 444
War Lake: 444
Wasa Provincial Park: 311
Watchman's Bay: 204
water parks: 253, 265, 395
Water Street: 54
water taxis: 152–153
Watson Lake: 457
weather: 3–4
Wells: 387
Wells Gray Provincial Park: 348, 368–369
West Canyon Trail: 70
West Coast Railway Heritage Park: 222
West Coast Trail: 22, 123, 155, 157–159
West End: 53, 57–60, 91–92, 95, 108–110
Western Canada Theatre: 365
western rattlesnakes: 8
Westminster Quay Market: 70
West Vancouver: 51, 66
Westview: *see* Powell River
Westwood Lake Park: 171
Weyerhaueser: 428
whales/whale-watching: 9, 136, 186–187, 188, 203, 214, 430
Whistler: 209–211, 225–236; accommodations 232–234; food 234–236; history 225–228; recreation 228–232; services and information 236; transportation 236
Whistler/Blackcomb ski resort: 225–226, 228, 230–231
Whistler/Blackcomb Ski and Snowboard

School: 230
Whistler Classical Music Festival: 232
Whistler Golf Club: 229
Whistler Jazz and Blues Festival: 232
Whistler Nordic Cross-country Ski Club: 231
Whistler Roots Festival: 232
whitefish: 10
White Grizzly Wilderness: 296
White Rock: 66
Whitesail Lake: 403
Whiteswan Lake Provincial Park: 311
white-tailed deer: 6
Whitewater Glacier Trail: 296
white-water rafting: *see* rafting
Whitewater Ski & Winter Resort: 279, 291
Wickaninnish Centre: 183–184
Wickaninnish Trail: 184
wildflowers: 4
Wild Horse Creek: 306–307
Wild Pacific Trail: 181
Wildwood: *see* Powell River
Williams Lake Stampede: 29, 381
Williams Lake: 376, 379–382
Willingdon Beach Trail: 216
Williston Lake: 446
Willows Beach: 137
Willows Golf Course: 435
Windermere Lake: 313
Windermere Valley Museum: 313
windsurfing: 229
Wine Museum: 259
wine/wineries: 29, 33–34, 83, 232, 253, 255, 256, 257, 259, 260–263, 266
Wings over the Rockies Bird Festival: 321
Winterfest: 309
Wokkpash Recreation Area: 455
wolves: 7, 320
Wonderful Waterworld: 253
Wonowon: 453
woodcarving: 28
woodland caribou: 7
woodpeckers: 320
World Championship Bathtub Race: 29, 173
World Championship Sand Sculpture Competition: 239
World Ski & Snowboard Festival: 29, 232

Y
yachting: 74
Yahk: 299

Yahk Provincial Park: 299
Yale: 243–244
Yale Museum: 244
Yaletown: 51–53
Yellowhead Mountain: 373, 374
Yellowhead Pass: 373
Yoho National Park: 24, 315, 334–342; hiking
  338–341; history 334–336; land 334;
  practicalities 341–342; sights 336–338

Yoho Pass: 339
Yoho River: 336
Yoho Valley: 336–337, 339
youth hostels: *see* hostels

Z
Zeballos: 202
Zuckerberg Island: 284

Index

Acknowledgments

A heartfelt thank you goes out to all the people who helped with the sixth edition of *Moon Handbooks: British Columbia;* to the British Columbians who shared their knowledge of B.C. and their insight; to all the well-trained staff of Visitor Info Centres and national and provincial parks throughout British Columbia; and to all the travelers/readers who took the time to write to us offering suggestions to make each updated edition more comprehensive.

Acknowledgements

The author thanks ... for ... the ... University of Northern British Columbia ...

AVALON TRAVEL

p u b l i s h i n g

How far will our travel guides take you? As far as you want.

Discover a rhumba-fueled nightspot in Old Havana, explore prehistoric tombs in Ireland, hike beneath California's centuries-old redwoods, or embark on a classic road trip along Route 66. Our guidebooks deliver solidly researched, trip-tested information—minus any generic froth—to help globetrotters or weekend warriors create an adventure uniquely their own.

And we're not just about the printed page. Public television viewers are tuning in to Rick Steves' new travel series, *Rick Steves' Europe*. On the Web, readers can cruise the virtual black top with *Road Trip USA* author Jamie Jensen and learn travel industry secrets from Edward Hasbrouck of *The Practical Nomad*.

In print. On TV. On the Internet.

We supply the information. The rest is up to you.

Avalon Travel Publishing

Something for everyone

www.travelmatters.com

Avalon Travel Publishing guides are available at your favorite book or travel store.

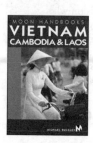

MOON HANDBOOKS provide comprehensive

coverage of a region's arts, history, land, people, and social
issues in addition to detailed practical listings for
accommodations, food, outdoor recreation, and
entertainment. Moon Handbooks allow complete immersion
in a region's culture—ideal for travelers who want to combine
sightseeing with insight for an extraordinary travel experience
in destinations throughout North America, Hawaii, Latin
America, the Caribbean, Asia, and the Pacific.

WWW.MOON.COM

Rick Steves shows you where to travel and how to travel—
all while getting the most value for your dollar. His Back
Door travel philosophy is about making friends, having fun,
and avoiding tourist rip-offs.

Rick has been traveling to Europe for more than 25
years and is the author of 22 guidebooks, which have sold
more than a million copies. He also hosts the award-winning
public television series *Rick Steves' Europe*.

WWW.RICKSTEVES.COM

ROAD TRIP USA

Getting there is half the fun, and Road Trip USA guides are your ticket to driving
adventure. Taking you off the interstates and onto
less-traveled, two-lane highways, each guide is filled with
fascinating trivia, historical information, photographs, facts
about regional writers, and details on where to sleep and
eat—all contributing to your exploration of the American
road.

"[Books] so full of the pleasures of the American road,
you can smell the upholstery."
~BBC radio

WWW.ROADTRIPUSA.COM

FOGHORN OUTDOORS guides are for campers, hikers, boaters, anglers, bikers, and golfers of all levels of daring and skill. Each guide focuses on a specific U.S. region and contains site descriptions and ratings, driving directions, facilities and fees information, and easy-to-read maps that leave only the task of deciding where to go.

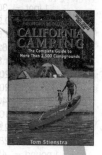

"Foghorn Outdoors has established an ecological conservation standard unmatched by any other publisher."
~Sierra Club

WWW.FOGHORN.COM

TRAVEL SMART guidebooks are accessible, route-based driving guides focusing on regions throughout the United States and Canada. Special interest tours provide the most practical routes for family fun, outdoor activities, or regional history for a trip of anywhere from two to 22 days. Travel Smarts take the guesswork out of planning a trip by recommending only the most interesting places to eat, stay, and visit.

"One of the few travel series that rates sightseeing attractions. That's a handy feature. It helps to have some guidance so that every minute counts."
~San Diego Union-Tribune

CiTY·SMaRT™ guides are written by local authors with hometown perspectives who have personally selected the best places to eat, shop, sightsee, and simply hang out. The honest, lively, and opinionated advice is perfect for business travelers looking to relax with the locals or for longtime residents looking for something new to do Saturday night.

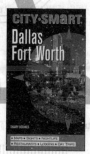